A History of English Literature

A History of English Literature

History of English Literature

by EDWARD ALBERT

Revised by J. A. STONE

FIFTH EDITION

HARRAP LONDON

First published in Great Britain 1923
by GEORGE G. HARRAP & CO. LTD
182 High Holborn, London WC1V 7AX

Reprinted: 1924; 1926; 1928; 1931

Second Edition, revised 1932

Reprinted: 1935; 1937; 1938; 1939; 1940; 1941;
1942; 1944; 1946; 1949; 1952

Third Edition, revised 1955

Reprinted: 1956; 1958; 1960; 1962; 1963; 1965; 1967

Fourth Edition, revised and enlarged 1971
Reprinted: 1973

Fifth Edition, revised and enlarged 1979
Reprinted, 1979

© *This edition George G. Harrap & Co. Ltd,* 1979

ISBN 0 245 53247 1 (*Limp*)
ISBN 0 245 53438 5 (*Boards, with jacket*)

Published in the U. S. A. 1979 by
HARPER & ROW, PUBLISHERS, INC.
BARNES & NOBLE IMPORT DIVISION
ISBN 0-06-490145-9
ISBN 0-06-490146-7 Pbk
LC 79-54165

*Composed in Times New Roman type and printed by
Western Printing Services Ltd, Bristol
Made in Great Britain*

PREFACE TO THE THIRD EDITION

Albert's *History of English Literature* has won for itself a secure place as a study of literary history and criticism. Its continued popularity suggests that the value of its judgments remains for the most part unimpaired. In places, however, the last twenty years have inevitably seen changes of perspective and revaluations; these the present edition seeks to incorporate, while yet preserving of its predecessor all that is in line with modern thought. The chapter on post-Victorian writers, which has felt most strongly the impact of fresh evaluations, has been completely rewritten, and, difficult though it is to view things so close at hand in any true perspective, the attempt has been made to bring the story of our literature up to date.

The entirely new bibliography will, it is hoped, enable those who wish to pursue their studies further to acquaint themselves not only with the standard authorities, but with more recent research, and thus gain some impression of the changing trends of critical opinion.

The method and layout of the original work have been preserved as far as possible, except that considerations of length have necessitated the omission of the exercises at the end of each chapter and at the end of the book as a whole.

For the revision of the first two chapters I am indebted to Dr Kenneth Cameron, Lecturer in English in Nottingham University.

J. A. S.

PREFACE TO THE FOURTH EDITION

It is a truism to say that in literary history, as in all else, nothing stands still; and it is therefore not surprising that in our time of vigorous literary activity further material on current trends should again be required. In view of this, considerable amendments have been made to statements in Chapter XIII, while Chapter XIV, on the contemporary literary scene, has been completely rewritten. The Bibliography for Chapter XIII has been updated, and a bibliographical section supplied for Chapter XIV. For this work of revision I am indebted to Dr G. G. Urwin.

J. A. S.

PREFACE TO THE FIFTH EDITION

Once again, the whirligig of time brings in his revenges, and in a relatively short time new notes and evaluations are once again called for. These are in fact more extensive than were undertaken for the fourth edition, and have resulted in some increase in length. Chapter XII, The Birth of Modern Literature, has suffered a few changes; Chapter XIII has again been extensively overhauled; Chapter XIV is once more rewritten. But the main point to emphasize is that the Bibliography has been entirely re-compiled to take into account more recent scholarship. This considerable task has produced a book-list that cannot but add immeasurably to the value of the work. For all these labours I am indebted once more to Dr G. G. Urwin.

J.A.S.

ACKNOWLEDGMENTS

For permission to use copyright extracts the publishers offer their grateful thanks to the following:

The Clarendon Press, Oxford, for *Cheddar Pinks*, from *New Verse*, and an extract from *The Testament of Beauty*, by Robert Bridges.

Messrs Faber and Faber, Ltd, for an extract from *The Waste Land*, by T. S. Eliot.

The Oxford University Press, for *Carrion Comfort*, from *Poems of Gerard Manley Hopkins*.

Messrs George Allen and Unwin, Ltd, for extracts from *Riders to the Sea* and *The Well of the Saints*, by John Millington Synge.

Mrs W. B. Yeats and Messrs Macmillan and Co., Ltd, for *The Lake Isle of Innisfree*, from *Collected Poems of W. B. Yeats*.

CONTENTS

Let us now praise famous men, . . .
Such as found out musical tunes,
And recited verses in writing, . . .
Their bodies are buried in peace;
But their name liveth for evermore.

The Wisdom of Jesus the Son of
Sirach or Ecclesiasticus

CHAPTER I

THE OLD ENGLISH PERIOD

THE BEGINNINGS

Little indeed is known of the origin of English Literature, though it is reasonable to assume that verse of an extemporary kind was composed long before the period of the earliest written records and that we can be certain that poetry made its appearance long before the first prose was written down. It is important from the outset to remember that the extant remains of Old English Literature have come down to us (for the most part) in late copies, some of which were made three hundred years after the composition of the poems themselves. So far as poets are concerned, again little or nothing is known beyond the names of two of them, but this has not prevented some scholars from writing their 'lives,' from hints in the texts themselves, fortified by scanty contemporary references (in the case of Cædmon) but mainly from a mass of conjecture, most of which cannot be described as intelligent. Indeed, the lengths to which critics will at times go is clearly indicated by the fact that one Old English poet has been provided with a wife on no valid evidence whatsoever. Notwithstanding the mists which shroud the beginnings and our lack of knowledge of the poets themselves Old English Literature has a richness which amazes the reader who overcomes the initial difficulty of the language, and it is hoped that this richness will be seen even in the meagre summary which appears in the following pages.

THE HISTORICAL BACKGROUND

The period is a long one, for it opens in the fifth century and does not conclude, as is often supposed, with the Norman Conquest in 1066, but rather continues in prose at least till *c.* 1150. The events, however, must be dismissed briefly. The departure of the Romans in 410 left the British population open to the inroads of the invaders from the north. According to British traditions the English from the

Continent came first as mercenaries to help in the defence against the Picts and Scots; but soon they began to settle in the country, and archæological evidence shows that certainly permanent settlements had been made in the last quarter of the fifth century if not before. In the course of time they gained possession of all the land from the English Channel to the Firth of Forth to a greater or lesser degree. Then followed the Christianization of the pagan English tribes, beginning in Northumbria with the work of Irish missionaries, though the influence from Rome begins in Kent (597). In succession followed the inroads of the Danes in the ninth century; the rise of Wessex among the early English kingdoms with the important contribution of Alfred the Great; the establishment of the Danelaw in England with the permanent settlement of Danes in the country; the accession of a Danish king (1017); and the Norman influence on the English court which began before the Conquest in 1066. All these events had their effect on the literature of the period.

LITERARY FEATURES OF THE PERIOD

1. Pagan Origins. Many of the poems of the period appear to have in them features which are associated with the pagan past, in particular *Widsith* and *Beowulf*, though the Christian elements in the latter are no longer looked upon, as was the case among the earlier scholars, as 'clumsy additions.' It appears likely, therefore, that the earliest poems or themes have their origin in the Continental home of the English peoples. Such themes were the common property of the gleemen or 'scops,' who sang them at the feasts of the nobles. As time went on Christian ideas influenced the earlier pagan, and, though the phraseology remains, it is impossible to refer to any of the extant poetry as 'pagan.' Indeed this is only what is to be expected when it is remembered that the manuscripts themselves were written down in the monasteries.

2. Anonymous Origins. Of all the Old English poets we have direct mention of only one Cædmon, though not one of the extant poems can definitely be ascribed to him. The name of another poet, Cynewulf, is known because of the fact that he signed his poems in runic letters at the end of four poems. Of the rest we do not even know their names. Prose, as we have noticed, came later, and as it was used for practical purposes its authorship in many cases is established.

3. The Imitative Quality. Much of the prose and some of the poetry is translated or adapted from the Latin, though the debt to the original varies greatly. The favourite works for translation were the books of the Bible, the lives of the saints, and various works of a practical nature. In some cases the translations are close and without much individuality, but in others the material is reshaped with expansions and comments and has considerable literary importance.

4. The Manuscripts. It is certain that only a portion of Old English poetry has survived, though it would appear likely that the surviving portion is representative. The manuscripts in which the poetry is preserved are late in date, are unique, and are four in number. They are (a) the *Beowulf* MS. (Cotton Vitellius A. XV in the British Museum), containing *Beowulf* and *Judith* and is to be dated c. 1000; (b) the Junius MS. (MS. Junius XI in the Bodleian Library, Oxford), so called since it belonged to Junius, librarian to Lord Arundel, and was first printed by him in 1655. It contains the so-called Cædmonian poems; (c) the Exeter Book (in the Chapter Library of Exeter Cathedral), known to have been donated to that Cathedral by Bishop Leofric c. 1050, containing two of the signed poems of Cynewulf; and (d) the Vercelli Book (in the Cathedral Library at Vercelli near Milan), containing also two of the signed poems of Cynewulf (including *Elene*) and *Andreas* and *The Dream of the Rood.*

THE LANGUAGE

The difficulty encountered in reading Old English Literature lies in the fact that the language is very different from that of to-day. Its vocabulary is for the most part native, though already there has been some borrowing from Latin. Its grammar shows declinable nouns, pronouns, and adjectives and a more elaborate verbal system than that of to-day. There were four main dialects: Northumbrian, which was the first to produce a literature; Mercian, the language of the Midlands; Kentish, the language of the south-east spoken in an area larger than that of the modern county of Kent; and West Saxon, the language of Alfred, which—due to the political supremacy of Wessex—became a 'standard' and in which almost all the extant texts are preserved.

OLD ENGLISH POETRY

BEOWULF

1. Origin of the Poem. The theme of the poem is Continental Germanic, and it is likely that it was the subject of lays long before its present version was composed. There is, it may be noted, no mention of England, and Beowulf himself is king of the 'Geatas.' Though there is much in the poem which can be considered 'pagan' and which suggests that the poem in origin may be considered as such, the extant version was clearly written by a Christian for the 'christianization' is no mere veneer. Of its actual authorship there is no evidence. Modern scholars in the main now look upon it as a reworking of older material by a Christian and not simply as a collection of tales strung together by one hand. The dialect of the text is West Saxon though there is clear evidence that it was written in some Anglian dialect, but whether Mercian or Northumbrian is uncertain.

2. The Story. There are so many episodes and digressions in the story of *Beowulf* that it is almost impossible briefly to give an adequate synopsis of the narrative. In outline it may be said that Beowulf, son of Ecgtheow, sails to Denmark with a band of warriors and rids the Danish King Hrothgar of a terrible mere-monster called Grendel. The mother of Grendel, seeking vengeance for the death of her son, meets the same fate, and Beowulf, fittingly feasted and rewarded, returns to his native land. He becomes king of the Geatas and after a prosperous reign of some forty years slays a dragon which had ravaged his land, but in the fight he himself receives a mortal wound. The poem concludes with the funeral ceremonies in honour of the dead hero.

3. Style. A short extract is printed below, with a literal translation, to illustrate the style. The extract describes the funeral rites of the hero, and occurs near the end of the poem (lines 3137–49).

Him ðā gegiredan   Gēata lēode
For him then the people of the Geats made ready
ād on eorðan   unwāclicne,
a splendid funeral pyre on the earth,
helmum behongen,   hildebordum,
hung around with helmets, with battle-shields,
beorhtum byrnum,   swā hē bēna wæs;
with shining corslets, as he requested;
ālegdon ðā tōmiddes   mærne þēoden
then they laid in the midst of it the illustrious prince,
hæleð hīofende,   hlāford lēofne.
the weeping warriors, the beloved lord.
Ongunnon þa on beorge   bælfȳra mæst
Then the warriors began to kindle on the cliff
wīgend weccan: wudurec āstāh
the greatest of funeral fires: the wood-smoke rose up
sweart ofer swioðole,   swōgende lēg,

dark above the fire, the roaring flames,
wōpe bewunden —windblond gelæg—
surrounded by lamentation—the tumult of the winds subsided—
oðþæt hē ðā bānhūs   gebrocen hæfde,
till it had completely crushed the body,
hāt on hreðre.   Higum unrōte
hot in his breast. Sad in mind
mōdceare mændon,   mondryhtnes cwealm.
they complained of the sorrow of their hearts, the death of their

liege-lord

It will be observed that the language is forceful and expressive, conveying with an economy of words the picture of the funeral pyre on the cliff top and the lamentation of the warriors for their dead king. The use of compound words should be noted especially, together with that of the *kenning*, which skilfully handled "took on the form of a compressed vivid statement of a highly original image." The best example in this passage is *bānhūs*—literally 'bone house,' *i.e.*, 'body.' A further stylistic characteristic which should be noted is the use of repetition and variation. The same idea is expressed more than once by the use of different words which were more or less synonymous. Such parallel phrasing can be seen in lines 5 and 6 above: *mærne þēoden* and *hlāford lēofne* ('illustrious prince' and 'beloved lord') and elsewhere as the translation will suggest. The verse is strongly rhythmical, based on a stress system with four stresses to the full line, two in each of the half-lines; it is also allitera- tive, there being two alliterating syllables in the first half-line and one (usually the first) in the second. The stressed syllables are the ones which bear the alliteration.

OTHER POETRY

1. The Pagan Poems. Most Old English poetry can be said to be 'Christian,' but a few pieces are distinctly secular. It would be better in many respects to refer to them as 'national' rather than pagan, for some included for convenience in this group are of tenth- century composition.

(a) *Widsith* (*i.e.*, 'the far traveller'), usually considered to be the oldest poem in the language. It consists of nearly 150 lines of verse, in which a traveller, more imaginary than real, recounts the places and illustrious people he has visited. The poem is of especial impor- tance from a historical point of view, but poetically it is of little merit.

(b) *Waldere* consists of two fragments, some sixty-three lines in all, telling of some of the exploits of Walter of Aquitaine. The work has vigour and power, and it is to be greatly regretted that so little is preserved. It might well have been one of the finest of narrative pieces.

(c) *The Fight at Finnsburh* is a fragment of some forty-eight lines with a finely told description of the fighting at Finnsburh, allusion to which is made in the Finn Episode in *Beowulf*.

(d) *The Battle of Brunanburh* is a spirited piece on the famous battle which took place in 937.

(e) *The Battle of Maldon* describes the battle which took place in 993, with emphasis on individual deeds of valour and on the feelings of the warriors. It is particularly outstanding for the sentiments expressed by the warriors, especially those of the aged Byrhtwold.

2. The Elegies. These poems, among which are *The Wanderer*, *The Seafarer*, *Wife's Lament*, and *Husband's Message*, appear in the Exeter Book. There is no connexion between the individual pieces, but they each display similar qualities, being meditative in character, and can perhaps be called monologues. The first two named are the finer artistic compositions, reaching real heights of personal feeling. In Old English literature they come nearest to the lyric, a type which is not represented among the extant corpus.

3. The so-called Cædmon Group. In his *Ecclesiastical History* Bede tells the story of the lay brother Cædmon, who by divine inspiration was transformed from a state of tongue-tied ineffectiveness into that of poetical ecstasy. He was summoned into the presence of the abbess Hilda of Whitby (658–80), became a monk, and afterwards sang of many Biblical events. Bede quotes in his story the *Hymn* said to have been composed by Cædmon, nine lines in length, displaying to a remarkable degree the qualities of repetition and parallel phrasing noted above.

This is all that is actually known of the life and work of Cædmon, but the four poems of the Junius MS. correspond in subject matter so closely to Bede's statement of the themes on which Cædmon wrote that they were long associated with his name. The *Genesis*, *Exodus*, *Daniel*, and three shorter poems often considered as one under the title *Christ and Satan* are of unequal merit. At best they are strong and spirited with some gift for descriptive writing and choice of incident; at worst they are tedious paraphrases of Biblical stories. They are certainly not all by one hand, and little if any is early enough to be ascribed to Cædmon himself. In all probability in spite of their long ascription to his name they have nothing to do with the Northumbrian poet himself.

4. The Cynewulf Group. Four poems contain the signature of Cynewulf in runic characters, *Juliana, Elene, Christ,* and *The Fates of the Apostles* (in the two last named spelt Cynwulf). This is all that is known of the poet, though unfortunately it has not prevented critics from 'deducing' additional facts about his life. Likewise other poems have on little or no authority been ascribed to him, the most important being *The Dream of the Rood*—undoubtedly the finest of all Old English religious poems in its intensity of feeling, brilliance of conception, and certainty of execution. It is the work of a real artist and poet.

The signed poems are much more scholarly compositions than the Cædmon poems. There is a greater power of expression, surer technique, and real descriptive powers. The ideas are broader and deeper, and a certain lyrical quality is found at times. Their date is probably ninth century.

PROSE

1. Alfred. Though there were some prose writings of an official nature (such as laws) before the time of Alfred, there can be little objection to the claim frequently made for him, that he is 'the father of English prose.' As he himself tells us in the preface to the *Pastoral Care* he began his series of translations due to the lamentable state of English learning, largely the result of the depredations of the Danes. Even the knowledge of Latin was declining, so the king, in order to encourage learning among the clergy, translated some popular books into his own tongue. These works are his contribution to our literature. Sometimes he translated word for word, at others more freely, but those passages which have greatest value both for an understanding of the character of the king and also for their literary qualities are originals freely introduced by way of explanation or expansion. The five important translations are the *Pastoral Care* of Pope Gregory, the *History of the World* of Orosius, Bede's *Ecclesiastical History*, Boethius' *Consolation of Philosophy*, and the *Soliloquies* of St Augustine, though it should be noted that Alfred's claim to the translation of Bede is disputed. There is in addition a *Handbook* or commonplace-book, the existence of which we know from Asser, the king's biographer, but which is no longer extant. The chronological order of the translations cannot be determined with any certainty, though it is clear that the *Pastoral Care* was the first and the *Soliloquies* the last of the series.

A brief extract is given below to illustrate his prose style, but it should be remembered that this is from his earliest work and comparison should be made with the Preface of the *Soliloquies* to see the development. It is not a polished style, but that cannot be expected in view of the stage of development of prose as a literary form. For the most part it is a simple, straightforward style, and though Alfred never completely masters it, there is always the feeling that he was an artist of considerable natural ability—though it is idle to speculate what he would have produced had he lived at a later period when a more highly developed prose-style had been evolved.

> Swa clæne hio wæs oðfeallen on Angelcynne ðætte swiðe feawe wæron behionan Humbre þe hiora ðenunga cuðen understandan on Englisc oððe furðum an ærendgewrit of Lædene on Englisc areccan, ond ic wene ðætte noht monige begeondan Humbre næren; swa feawe hiora wæron ðætte ic anne anlepne ne mæg geðencean besuðan Temese ðaða ic to rice feng. Gode ælmihtegum sie ðonc ðætte we nu ænigne onstal habbað lareowa. Forðam ic ðe bebeode ðæt ðu do swa ic gelife ðæt ðu wille. . . .

> *So completely has it [learning] decayed in England that there were very few on this side of the Humber who could understand their mass-books in English and could even translate a letter from Latin into English, and I believe there were not many beyond the Humber either; so few of them were there that I cannot remember a single one south of the Thames when I became king. To God Almighty be the thanks that we have now any supply of teachers. Therefore I command you that you do as I believe you will. . . .*

(Preface to *Pastoral Care*)

2. Ælfric, probably best known for his *Grammar*, was a churchman who became abbot of Eynsham in 1005. Several of his works are extant: the *Catholic Homilies*, two series of sermons suitable for delivery by priests, a third series—the *Lives of the Saints* (written before 998), and translations from the Scriptures. Ælfric's flowing and vigorous style shows remarkable skill in the art of putting complicated thought into narrative form. It is natural and easy and is often alliterative. His *Colloquy* is of great interest as a dialogue between master and pupils not only from the literary but also from the historical point of view.

3. Wulfstan was Bishop of Worcester and Archbishop of York. Several of his signed homilies survive, and there are many more which are believed on good evidence to be by him. His most famous piece is the *Sermo Lupi ad Anglos*, which is typical for its sheer force and vigour, its repetition of ideas, and the alliterative nature of its style. It is fluent and powerful; indeed Wulfstan must have been a most brilliant preacher.

4. The **Anglo-Saxon Chronicle** was in all probability inspired by Alfred, who himself may well have dictated some of the entries, more particularly those dealing with his own campaigns. It is extant in several manuscripts, the most important being the A or Parker and the E or Laud MSS. To the year 915 much of the material is common to most of the manuscripts, though the relations of each individual one to the others present serious difficulties. Local events and miscellaneous items are introduced into the various versions and they also show clearly varying points of view in their attitude to events. They all end at different dates, the latest being 1154 (E).

As is to be expected the style varies greatly from simple notices to long passages of narrative and description. Most interesting are certain character studies, particularly that of the Conqueror himself, while the well-known descriptions of the horrors of Stephen's reign are worthy of note. A brief extract from the description of William the Conqueror written in the annal for 1086 indicates fairly clearly certain of the stylistic features of the later part of the Chronicle:

> Se cyng Willelm þe we embe sprecað wæs swiðe wis man and swiðe rice and wurðfulre and strengere þonne ænig his foregenga wære. He wæs milde þam godum mannum þe God lufedon and ofer eall gemett stearc þam mannum þe wiðcwædon his willan. On ðam ilcan steode þe God him geuðe þæt he moste Engleland gegan he arerde mære mynster and munecas þær gesætte and hit wæll gegodade. On his dagan wæs þæt mære mynster on Cantwarbyrig getymbrad and eac swiðe manig oðer ofer eall Engleland.

> *King William, of whom we have spoken, was a very wise man and very powerful and more glorious and stronger than were any of his predecessors. He was mild to the good men who loved God and beyond measure stern to those men who opposed his will. At the same place where God granted him that he should conquer England, he established a glorious monastery and there established monks and endowed it well. In his days the illustrious monastery was built in Canterbury and also very many others over all England.*

THE DEVELOPMENT OF LITERARY FORMS

During the period Old English Literature undergoes a noticeable development, though it is well to remember that it is the result of hundreds of years of slow growth, and it is impossible to divide the types of verse, for example, into definite water-tight compartments.

1. Poetry. Poetry appears earlier than prose, and the heroic type of *Beowulf, Waldere,* and *The Fight at Finnsburh* persists throughout the period, for similar qualities are found in a poem as late as *The Battle of Maldon*.

(*a*) The *epic* exists in one of its forms in *Beowulf*, which lacks the 'finer' qualities of the classical epic, the strict unity, the high dignity, and the broad motive, though it possesses a vigour and a majesty which have obvious appeal. The so-called Christian epics have little claim to the title and should not be considered here.

(*b*) The *lyric* has no real example in Old English, though there are certain poems which have some of the expressive melancholy and personal emotion associated with the lyric, *e.g.*, *The Wanderer* and *The Seafarer*.

2. Prose. Although much of Old English prose consists of translation from Latin and is clearly influenced by the originals, it is by no means correct to consider the prose of the period as lacking in originality or personal qualities. The homilies of Ælfric and Wulfstan are at the beginning of the true line of development to the prose of the Authorized Version. The beginnings of historical writings are to be seen in the *Anglo-Saxon Chronicle*, and the development is clear by a comparison between the Cynewulf and Cyneheard episode in the annal for 755 and the later annals in the E MS.

THE DEVELOPMENT OF LITERARY STYLE

1. Poetry. A comparison between the so-called Cædmonian and Cynewulfian poems shows clearly a development in technique. There is an easier flow to the later poetry in general, a greater sureness in handling material, greater individuality of approach and feeling, less reliance on stock phrases, more subtle use of alliteration, and a greater desire for stylistic effect. This is the natural development of a literature, and though the alliterative type of poetry was apparently to receive the death-knoll with the Conquest, the flowering of a similar type in the fourteenth century shows that this is more apparent than real.

2. Prose. In spite of its limited scope as the vehicle in the main of the homily and historical writing a great advance in style is readily seen. From the earlier simple, halting prose of the Chronicle and Alfred, where the writers tend to become obscure and elliptical when presented with more abstruse thoughts, from the period where sentence structure is fairly loose and lacking the finer touches of rhythm and cadence, the later prose is noteworthy for its fluency, its animation, and indeed, as is to be expected, its confidence. There is in some, especially in the prose of Ælfric and Wulfstan, an excellent use of alliteration and of rhetorical figures. The personality of the author becomes truly apparent.

The effects of the Conquest on both poetry and prose have doubtlessly in the past been exaggerated. Rhyme was to take the place of alliteration, but already before the end of the period there are signs that this would have been a natural development due to the influence of Latin. The Conquest certainly removed from power the audience for which the older type was composed, and the impetus was lost; but, as will be noted, the later flowering of the alliterative type, with a looser structure it is true, shows clearly that the composition of the older type was never completely lost. The inflexional system was already becoming looser before the effects of the Conquest could make themselves felt, and while this process was undoubtedly hastened by the events following 1066, it cannot be maintained that there was in any real sense a decay of the prose style of, say, Wulfstan. The development in the Middle English period of the homiletic prose style has clearly been demonstrated to be in the true line from that of the Old English period. In other words, in spite of the Conquest the continuity is clear.

CHAPTER II

THE MIDDLE ENGLISH PERIOD

THE HISTORICAL BACKGROUND

The extensive period covered by this chapter saw many developments in the history of England: the establishment of Norman and Angevin dynasties; the internal struggles between king, nobles, clergy, and people; and the numerous wars both at home and abroad. From the literary point of view, however, more important than definite events were the general movements of the times: the rise of the religious orders, their early enthusiasm, and their subsequent decline; the blossoming of chivalry and the spirit of romance, bringing new sympathy for women and the poor; the Crusades and the widening of the European outlook which was gradually to expand into the rebirth of the intellect known as the Renaissance. All these were symptoms of a growing intelligence that was strongly reflected in the literature of the period.

STATE OF THE ENGLISH LANGUAGE

The period sees the development of Middle English with the gradual weakening of the inflexional system of the older period. The texts written down at the end of the Old English period are in the West Saxon dialect, but when texts reappear in the twelfth century they are written in the particular dialect of the author or scribe. Scandinavian and French loan-words are found, the latter in increasing numbers. The dialects which were noted in the Old English period continue to develop, and it is usual to distinguish five main dialect areas: Northern, which can be sub-divided into Lowland Scots and Northern English, corresponding to the old Northumbrian dialect; East Midlands and West Midlands, corresponding to Mercian; South-eastern, corresponding to Kentish; and South-western, corresponding to West Saxon. Gradually a standard is developed, which was to become the Received Standard English of to-day, from the East Midland dialect; this was due in part to the importance of that area in the period and to the importance of the capital, London.

LITERARY FEATURES OF THE AGE

The period under review provides a large amount of interesting, important, and often delightful works. The general features are somewhat difficult to give in brief outline, and emphasis will be placed later on individual works of outstanding importance.

1. The Transition. In many ways the period is one of transition and of experiment. The poets, for example, appear in part to be feeling for new media. The influence of French and Latin works is undoubtedly great, but at the same time there are some poets who are following in the line of development from the Old English period. The contrast is obvious and in the fourteenth century is clear with the work of the alliterative poets of the west, but in the earlier part too there are outstanding examples of this tendency, particularly Laʒamon's *Brut*. It is clear that oral tradition preserved the poetic models of the past, though apart from obvious examples it is not till the fourteenth century that they appear in extant texts.

2. The **anonymous** nature of the writing is still strongly evidenced. A large proportion of the works are entirely without known authors, and most of the authors whose names appear are, indeed, names only.

3. The Domination of Poetry. Much of the surviving work of the period is poetry, which is used for such fields as history, divinity, and science. Many of the authors are clerics, but at the same time some of the romances must be of a popular kind.

Because of the use of poetry for subjects which one would expect to be written in prose, the amount of the latter seems small by comparison. But it must be remembered that Latin was the language of official documents and, indeed, of learning. Much of the extant prose is homiletic in character, though none the less important for that. The *Katherine Group* and *Ancrene Riwle* are quite outstanding in their own way, though for most modern readers they lack interest and are mainly known to the general reader from certain 'purple patches.' Yet they are individual in style and, though many are translations, they are by no means slavish.

POETRY

For the sake of convenience this may be classified into three main groups, according to the nature of the subject:

1. Chronicles. During this period there is an unusual number of verse chronicles. They are distinguished by their use of stories which appear incredible, by their inventiveness, and in many cases by their vivacity of style. It should be remembered that in spite of the use of incredible adventures and the like the individual poets looked upon their work as history, though to the present day they appear rather to fit into the category of romance.

(a) Laȝamon's *Brut*. This was written about 1205 by Laȝamon, a monk of Arley Kings, in Worcestershire, and tells in some 16,000 long alliterative lines the history of Britain from the landing of Brutus to the death of Cadwallader. The chief source is the *Roman de Brut* of Wace, itself a translation into Norman-French of the *Historia Regum Britanniæ* of Geoffrey of Monmouth. The vocabulary is archaic and tends to preserve the poetic traditions of Old English poetry. Characteristic of Laȝamon's style is his use of epic formulæ, often in summing up a situation, and his use of similes. The alliterative metre is used, though with a good deal of licence and with the added presence of assonance and rhyme. Sometimes, indeed, alliteration and rhyme appear together. The following passage will serve as an example of the poem:

> þenne siȝeþ to segges under beorȝen,
> mid hornen, mid hunden mid hæȝere stefnen:
> hunten þer talieþ, hundes þer galieþ,
> þane fox driueþ ȝeond dales and ȝeond dunes.
> He flihþ to þan holme and his hol isecheþ,
> i þan firste ende, i þan hole wendeþ.
> þenne is þe balde fox blissen al bidæled;
> and mon him to delueþ on ælchere haluen.
> þenne biþ þer forcuþest deoren alre pruttest.

> *Then men come towards him at the foot of the hills*
> *with horns, with hounds, and with loud voices:*
> *huntsmen shout there, hounds, yelp there,*
> *they drive the fox over hill and dale.*
> *He flees to the hill and seeks his hole,*
> *in the nearest place he goes to earth.*
> *Then the bold fox is deprived of all joy;*
> *and men dig to him on each side.*
> *Then there is, there, most unhappy the proudest of all animals.*

(b) *Robert of Gloucester* is known from his rhyming chronicle. From internal evidence it is possible that there is more than one author to this work, but certainly one was Robert, a monk of Gloucester, who wrote some time towards the end of the thirteenth century. He drew largely on the work of Geoffrey of Monmouth, William of Malmesbury, and other chroniclers. He is no poet, and not particularly learned, though he attempts always to show impartiality in his approach to history. Above all, he shows a true love of his country and, as has been often pointed out, for him Arthur is the hero of his work. It is often lively enough, thoroughly sincere, but by no means outstanding in any way.

(c) *Robert Manning of Brunne* came from Bourne in Lincolnshire and though not himself in full orders was connected with the priory at Sempringham and later with Sixhill. His rhymed *Story of England* was completed, as he himself tells us, between three and four o'clock on the afternoon of Friday, May 25, 1338. It begins with Noah and the Deluge and ends with the death of Edward I. The first part translates closely Wace's *Brut*, while the second is based upon the Chronicle of Pierre de Langtoft, an Anglo-Norman work. There is little originality, and the work is designed for the unlearned, but is none the less entertaining. Written in alexandrine couplets, the metre, unfortunately, at times is marred by both internal and tail rhyme.

His other work *Handlyng Synne* was commenced in 1303, based upon the *Manuel des Péchiez* of William of Wadington and intended for the common people. It is written in four-stress lines in couplets. It is a series of stories, "an epitome of the various sins," with tales and anecdotes as illustrations. The work is enlivened by these anecdotes and undoubtedly shows a keen sense of observation, being in many ways more impartial in attitude than *Piers Plowman* and many of the political verse pieces.

2. Religious and Didactic Poetry. (a) The *Ormulum*, written by a certain Orm, is dated *c.* 1200. Of enormous length (some 10,000 lines and even then incomplete), it is preserved in what is probably the author's own autograph copy. The dialect is north-east Midlands. It consists of a large number of religious homilies addressed to a fellow canon-regular Walter. The work claims no literary quality and has none. The metre is based on the Latin *septenarius*, with fifteen syllables, and there is little to vary the sheer monotony of the rhythm. It has been neatly said "he is a merciless syllable-counter." The work is unique for its complicated system of spelling, with its frequent doubling of consonants, but scholars are not all satisfied as to the exact interpretation of this feature. No extract is necessary to illustrate the monotony of the metre; it is clearly indicated in the single line which tells us simply, "this book is called Ormulum because Orm wrote it."

þiss boc iss nemmnedd Orrmulum, forþi þatt Orrm *itt* wrohhte.

(b) *The Owl and the Nightingale*, the authorship of which is still doubtful, was probably written in the early part of the thirteenth century. It consists of a long argument between the nightingale, representing the lighter joys of life, and the owl, standing for wisdom and sobriety. The poem is among the most lively of its kind, and the argument at times is, to say the least, heated. In metre it is in short rhyming couplets handled with considerable skill. "Scholars have united in praise of the narrative skill of the author, his characterization and sense of form."

(c) The *Orison to Our Lady*, *Genesis* and *Exodus*, the *Bestiary*, the *Moral Ode*, the *Proverbs of Alfred*, and the *Proverbs of Hendyng* are to be dated in the first half of the thirteenth century, with the exception of the *Moral Ode* and the *Proverbs of Alfred*, which may be as early as 1150. They are all important from a metrical point of view, and the *Moral Ode* is one of the most important of the early poems. There may be little originality, but it is simple and dignified, remarkable for the steadiness and maturity of its lines.

(d) The *Cursor Mundi* was composed in the north in the first quarter of the fourteenth century. It is a religious work of an encyclopædic nature, treating almost all the Old and New Testament stories and much from later religious history also. It displays considerable ability in the handling of so much material and was immensely popular in its age and later, having influenced to some extent some of the plays in the miracle cycles. The metre, which is in the main the short couplet, shows considerable variety, and the author, who displays a 'wide humanity,' handles his form well.

(e) *Richard Rolle of Hampole*, who died in 1349, is one of the few literary figures about whom definite personal facts are recorded. He was born near Pickering in Yorkshire about 1300, educated at Oxford, and left home to become a hermit. Later he went to Hampole near Doncaster, where he is assumed to have written his *Pricke of Conscience* and where he died in 1349. He wrote various prose pieces, and while some are accepted as being definitely by him there are others which from time to time have been ascribed to him. His most important work was the long poem mentioned above, though it should be noted that its traditional ascription to him depends on a statement by Lydgate and that there are serious doubts as to whether it is indeed the work of Rolle. The work, which is based on the writings of the early Fathers, describes the joys and sorrows of a man's life as he is affected in turn by good and evil. The matter is abstract but is handled in a simple way, with several striking passages, and in spite of its lack of appeal to-day must have been tremendously popular judging from the number of manuscripts which are still preserved. The metre is four-stressed but by no means regular, for there are irregular numbers of unstressed syllables. The popularity of Rolle's work is clearly indicated by the fact that so many pieces have been attributed to him and also because due to his popularity his influence is traced to a whole 'school' of writers.

(f) **The Alliterative Poems.** In a unique manuscript, preserved in the British Museum, there are four remarkably fine poems written in a West Midland dialect: *Pearl*, *Purity*, *Patience*, and *Sir Gawain and the Green Knight*. There is no indication of authorship, but on various grounds it is considered likely that they are by the same poet. The date of the poems is uncertain, but it is possible they should be dated in the third quarter of the fourteenth century. The first three poems are religious in theme, and of them *Pearl* is undoubtedly the finest. This poem is allegorical and tells of a vision in which the poet seeks his precious pearl which he let slip into the grass. In his vision he sees his pearl which appears perhaps to be the vision of a dead maiden, and he obtains a glimpse of the New Jerusalem. The poem, which contains a long discussion between the poet and the pearl, has passages of real, moving beauty, of deep sincerity, and of passion. It is artistically a finished production, and its complicated metre is exceptionally well handled. *Purity* and *Patience*, more didactic in theme, are of less interest and beauty, but they are spirited and realistic and their exaltation makes them conspicuous among the poems of the period. Each is written in the long alliterative line showing a similar mastery of handling. *Sir Gawain and the Green Knight* is without doubt the finest of all the Middle English romances, for its mastery of plot handling, its realism, characterization, descriptive powers, and use of the alliterative long line. At times the poet achieves real heights in his poetry which can stand comparison with that of any period.

3. **The Romances.** The very great number of romances in this period can be classified according to subject, though it should be noted that they are both alliterative and rhyming in metre:

(a) The romances dealing with English history and its heroes are numerous. Of these the lively *King Horn* and *Havelock the Dane* and the popular *Guy of Warwick* and *Bevis of Hampton* are among the best. Sometimes contemporary history was drawn upon as in the well-known *Richard Cœur de Lion*. This group is often known as "The Matter of England."

(b) There are numerous romances connected closely or loosely with King Arthur. Some are of high merit, others worthless. *Sir Tristrem*, in spite of its shortcomings, is by no means one of the worst, while *Arthur and Merlin*, *Ywain and Gawain*, and the *Morte d'Arthure* have each various claims for consideration. As noted above, *Sir Gawain and the Green Knight* is the finest example of all Middle English romance. This group is often called "The Matter of Britain."

(c) Among the romances of "The Matter of Rome the Great" is a large number with classical themes, such as the exploits of Alexander the Great and the Siege of Troy. *King Alisaunder*, though long, is of more than average merit, as is also *The Destruction of Troy*.

(d) The group dealing with the Charlemagne legends is smaller and in general the quality is lower, though the late alliterative *Rauf Coilӡear*, a popular romance, had considerable merit. Also noteworthy is *Sir Ferumbras*. This group is sometimes called "The Matter of France."

(f) There is also a class of miscellaneous romances on various themes and of equally varying quality. *Amis* and *Amiloun* is a touching love story; *William of Palerne* has the familiar 'missing heir' theme; while *Floris and Blauchefleur*, telling of the love of a king's son for a captive maid, is one of the most charming of all romances.

It would take a volume to comment in detail upon the romances. The variety of their metre and style is very great; but in general terms we may say that the prevailing subject is of a martial and amatory nature; there is the additional interest of the supernatural, which enters freely into the story; and one of the most attractive features to the modern reader of this type of literature is the frequent glimpses obtained into the habits of the times.

PROSE

1. The **Ancrene Riwle** is the most important of the early prose texts of this period and, as has been frequently pointed out, the most influential. Its date is difficult to decide but is to be ascribed to the twelfth century. It was written for three noble ladies who had become anchoresses, and was revised soon after for a larger community. It is a manual designed to guide them in the life they had chosen. The guiding principle in this 'rule' is doubtlessly 'moderation in everything,' and the most characteristic feature of the author as it appears in the work is his broad humanity. The homely elements in the work are such as attract the modern reader. The

continuity of English prose style is now a commonplace in literary criticism, and here in the *Ancrene Riwle* the connection with the prose of Wulfstan and with that of the Authorized Version is clear. The following description of backbiters is given as an example of the text:

Bacbitares, þe biteð o þre men bihinden, beoð of two maneres; auh þe latere beoð wurse. Þe uorme cumeð al openliche, and seið vuel bi anoðer, and speouweð ut his atter, so muchel so him euer to muðe cumeð, and gulcheð al ut somed þet þe attri heorte sent up to þe tunge. Ac þe latere cumeð forð al an oþer wise, and is wurse ueond þen þe oðer, auh under ureondes huckel, weorpeð adun þet heaued, and foð on uor te siken er he owiht sigge, and make drupie chere; bisaumpleð longe abuten uor te beon betere ileued. And hwon hit alles cumeð forð þeonne is hit ȝeoluh atter.

Backbiters, who bite other men behind their backs, are of two kinds; but the latter are the worse. The first comes all openly, and speaks evilly about another, and spews up his poison, as much as ever comes to his mouth, and vomits all out together that the poisonous heart sent up to the tongue. But the latter kind comes forth in a completely different way, and is a worse fiend than the other, and in the guise of a friend casts down the head and begins to sigh before he says anything and puts on a dismal appearance; moralizes for a long time to be the better believed. But when it all comes forth then it is yellow poison.

What was true in the twelfth century is still apparently true to-day!

2. The **Aȝenbite of Inwyt** was written by Dan Michel of Northgate in 1340 and comes from Canterbury. It is a translation of a French work and a bad one at that. From the literary point of view it is of little importance and is well summed up by the word 'dull.' From the linguistic point of view, however, it has considerable importance, since the author's own autograph copy is preserved, and it is the most important text in the South-eastern and more particularly the Kentish dialect.

THE DEVELOPMENT OF LITERARY FORMS

1. **Poetry.** (a) *Metre.* One of the main features in this period is the development of rhymed metres, which in general displaced the alliterative line of Old English poetry, though the poems of the so-called alliterative revival in the fourteenth century are a clear warning (if any were needed) that it is foolish to dogmatize. It is clear, in fact, though written records do not show it, that the two types develop side by side, even though from the literary history point of view the alliterative is confined to the west and more particularly to the north-west. In extant texts the gap between the end of the Old

English and the Middle English period proper is covered by so few pieces that no clear indication can be seen of what was actually taking place. Certainly from the twelfth century, if not earlier, is the song supposed to have composed by King Canute about the monks of Ely:

> Merie sungen ðe Munekes binnen Ely
> ða Cnut ching reu ðer by.
> Roweð cnites noer the land
> and here we þæs Muneches sæng.

Merrily sang the monks in Ely when king Canute rowed by there.
"*Row men near the land and let us hear the song of the monks.*"

In this example there are two couplets. The first rhymes and the second is a fair example of assonance.

A definite advance is to be seen in the fragments of Godric, a hermit who died at Finchal *c.* 1170, the metre of which is based on that of St Anselm's hymns. Noticeable is a strict syllabic pattern with a consistent attempt at end-rhyme. The following four-line stanza is in honour of his patron, St Nicholas:

> Sainte Nicholaes godes druð
> tymbre us fairs scone hus.
> At þi burth at þi bare
> Sainte nicholaes, bring vs wel þare.

Laȝamon, writing in an alliterative metre, shows clearly how false it is simply to look at the period from the point of view of metre as a steady development towards rhymed verse, while Orm, using neither rhyme nor alliteration, is remarkable for the regularity of his metre. Some of the verse in the thirteenth century (for example *King Horn*, the earliest of the romances) is in couplet form—the result, as has been shown, of the short French couplet on the long alliterative line. A further example is the popular *Havelock the Dane*, and while the poet often uses tags, he nevertheless handles his metre competently enough.

> It was a king bi aredawes,
> þat in his time were gode lawes,
> He dede maken an ful wel holden;
> Hym loved yung, him lovede holde,
> Erl and barun, dreng and tayn,
> Knict, bondeman and swain,
> Wydues, maydnes, prestes and clerkes,
> And al for hise gode werkes.

Experiments with metre are often to be found in the period and perhaps more especially in the fourteenth century, when under

French influence the stanza form was used. There is, for example, among the romances the twelve-line tail-rhyme stanzas of *Amis* and *Amiloun* and *The King of Tars*, the intricate eleven-line stanzas with the *bob* or short line, as the tenth, of *Sir Tristrem*, the sixteen-line tail-rhyme stanza form of *Sir Percyvelle of Galles*, the thirteen-line rhyming stanzas with nine long alliterative lines and four short lines of *The Awntyers of Arthure*, and the six-line tail-rhyme stanzas of *The Turke and Gowen*. These examples will suffice to show the variety of the stanzaic forms attempted, though the excellent metre of *Sir Gawain and the Green Knight*, with its stanzas of varying length each concluding with five short lines rhyming *ababa* (the first with one stress, the others with three), should be noted as an example of the use of the alliterative long line at the same time as other poets are composing in the rhymed form. It is impossible to do justice briefly to the varying metrical forms of the period, but the examples quoted will serve as an indication of what was happening in this field in the Middle English period.

(*b*) *The Lyric*. Probably the form which has greatest appeal in this period for the modern reader is the lyric. It has been noted that there is no example of the true lyric from the Old English period, and it is impossible to say when they were first written in this country. Only a very few fragments have been preserved from the twelfth century, and it is not till the next that we have any in large numbers. No doubt they have been influenced considerably by French and Latin lyrics, but it is impossible to say whether they were inspired by these or had a native origin. Many of the early lyrics were devoutly religious in theme and tone, especially noteworthy being those addressed to the Virgin Mary. On the other hand the secular lyric is well represented too, both by what we should look upon as love-lyrics and those which have subjects from nature. However, it is difficult to separate the religious and the secular lyric, for it is clear that there is much mutual influence between them. Of the earlier examples perhaps the *Cuckoo Song* is as well known as any:

Sumer is icumen in,	*Summer is coming in*
Lhude sing cuccu!	*Sing loud, cuckoo!*
Groweþ sed and bloweþ med	*Seed grows, meadow bursts into flower*
And springþ þe wude nu.	*And the wood now sprouts.*
Sing cuccu!	*Sing cuckoo!*
Awe bleteþ after lomb,	*The ewe bleats for the lamb,*
Lhouþ after calue cu,	*The cow lows for its calf,*
Bulluc sterteþ, bucke uerteþ.	*Bullock leaps, buck breaks wind.*
Murie sing cuccu!	*Merry sing cuckoo!*

Cuccu, cuccu,	*Cuckoo, cuckoo,*
Wel singes þu cuccu.	*Well do you sing, cuckoo.*
Ne swik þu nauer nu!	*Never cease now!*

The regularity is particularly noteworthy.

(*c*) *The Romances.* It is important to note that the modern use of the word 'romance' can lead the reader astray when approaching medieval Romance, for, as has been pointed out by several scholars, it is highly doubtful that the contemporary audience would consider romance to be romantic: its virtue seems to have been its 'modernity,' for its setting was always medieval, even if it was an idealized setting. The influence was French, but romance was thoroughly acclimatized, and, as the period progresses, examples appear in greater numbers. Attention has already been drawn to the varied metre of this type, and something must be said of the other chief features. The story is usually long, with many intricacies of plot; above all the emphasis is on incident; martial exploits play a large part and are often made ridiculous (for the modern reader) by heaping battle on battle, exploit on exploit, so that the hero becomes a superman; the element of the supernatural is often introduced, again sometimes with ridiculous effect; characters are often of a type, though in the best examples characterization is excellent; the style is often simple and direct but with a lack of artistic finish, though again the best examples must be absolved from such strictures. The spirited approach makes the best good adventure stories. In spite of the exaggerations, extravagances, and ridiculous elements of the worst, the best of the romances provide a rich treasure-house of wonderful tales.

2. Prose. The prose for the main part is strictly practical in purpose, but the thread of a definite development has so often been demonstrated that the doctrine of the 'Continuity of English Prose' has become firmly rooted in English literary criticism to-day. The prose of the *Ancrene Riwle* and of the *Katherine Group* has at last been accepted for its true value.

THE DEVELOPMENT OF STYLE IN POETRY

That the poetry of the period under review has developed greatly from the stylistic point of view is clear from a comparison between, say, Laȝamon's *Brut* and *Sir Gawain and the Green Knight*, but it is difficult to describe in a few words, precisely, this development.

It is not too much of an exaggeration to say that from being 'artless' the poet becomes the conscious artist. Often enough the poets when faced with more difficult material tend to become obscure, and again in handling some of the difficult metres which they attempted the same result is achieved. Though humour is often enough lacking, there are touches here and there, sometimes of a grim kind. Pathos, too, of a solemn and elevated kind is to be found as well as that of a more simple *genre*. In the best the style is lucid, firm, controlled, and superb; in the worst it has every possible fault.

NOTE. For the quotations, some general conclusions, and for further reading, see R. M. Wilson, *Early Middle English Literature* (Methuen, 1935).

CHAPTER III

THE AGE OF CHAUCER

THE HISTORICAL BACKGROUND (1350–1450)

Compared with the periods covered by the last two chapters, the period now under review is quite short. It includes the greater part of the reign of Edward III and the long French wars associated with his name; the accession of his grandson Richard II (1377); and the revolution of 1399, the deposition of Richard, and the foundation of the Lancastrian dynasty. From the literary point of view, of greater importance are the social and intellectual movements of the period: the terrible plague called the Black Death, bringing poverty, unrest, and revolt among the peasants, and the growth of the spirit of inquiry, which was strongly critical of the ways of the Church, and found expression in the teachings of Wyclif and the Lollards, and in the stern denunciations of Langland.

LITERARY FEATURES OF THE AGE

1. The Standardizing of English. The period of transition is now nearly over. The English language has shaken down to a kind of average—to the standard of the East Midland speech, the language of the capital city and of the universities. The other dialects, with the exception of the Scottish branch, rapidly melt away from literature, till they become quite exiguous. French and English have amalgamated to form the standard English tongue, which attains to its first full expression in the works of Chaucer.

2. A curious 'modern' note begins to be apparent at this period. There is a sharper spirit of criticism, a more searching interest in man's affairs, and a less childlike faith in, and a less complacent acceptance of, the established order. The vogue of the romance, though it has by no means gone, is passing, and in Chaucer it is derided. The freshness of the romantic ideal is being superseded by the more acute spirit of the drama, which even at this early time is faintly foreshadowed. Another more modern feature that at once strikes the observer is that the age of anonymity is passing away. Though many of the texts still lack named authors, the greater number of the books can be definitely ascribed. Moreover, we have for the first time a figure of outstanding literary importance, who gives to the age the form and pressure of his genius.

3. Prose. This era sees the foundation of an English prose style. Earlier specimens have been experimental or purely imitative; now, in the works of Mandeville and Malory, we have prose that is both original and individual. The English tongue is now ripe for a prose style. The language is settling to a standard; Latin and French are losing grip as popular prose mediums; and the growing desire for an English Bible exercises a steady pressure in favour of a standard English prose.

4. Scottish Literature. For the first time in our literature, in the person of Barbour (1316 (?)–95), Scotland supplies a writer worthy of note. This is only the beginning; for the tradition is handed on to the powerful group of poets who are mentioned in the next chapter.

GEOFFREY CHAUCER (c. 1340–c. 1400)

1. His Life. In many of the documents of the time Chaucer's name is mentioned with some frequency; and these references, in addition to some remarks he makes regarding himself in the course of his poems, are the sum of what we know about his life. The date of his birth is uncertain, but it is now generally accepted as being 1340. He was born in London, entered the household of the wife of the Duke of Clarence (1357), and saw military service abroad, where he was captured. Next he seems to have entered the royal household, for he is frequently mentioned as the recipient of royal pensions and bounties. When Richard II succeeded to the crown (1377) Chaucer was confirmed in his offices and pensions, and shortly afterwards (1378) he was sent to Italy on one of his several diplomatic missions. More pecuniary blessings followed; then ensued a period of depression, due probably to the departure to Spain (1386) of his patron John of Gaunt; but his life closed with a revival of his prosperity. He was the first poet to be buried in what is now known as Poets' Corner in Westminster Abbey.

2. His Poems. The order of Chaucer's poems cannot be ascertained with certitude, but from internal evidence they can as a rule be approximately dated.

It is now customary to divide the Chaucerian poems into three stages: the French, the Italian, and the English, of which the last is a development of the first two. In none of these divisions, of course, is the one influence felt to the exclusion of the others. It is merely that one predominates.

(a) The poems of the earliest or French group are closely modelled upon French originals, and the style is clumsy and immature. Of such poems the longest is *The Romaunt of the Rose*, a lengthy allegorical poem, written in octosyllabic couplets and based upon *Le Romaunt de la Rose* of Guillaume de Lorris and Jean de Meung. This poem, only a fragment, though of 8000 lines, was once entirely ascribed to Chaucer, but recent research, based upon a scrutiny of Chaucerian style, has suggested that only the first part is his work. Other poems of this period include *The Book of the Duchesse*, probably his earliest and written in 1369, the year when John of Gaunt's wife died, *The Compleynt unto Pité*, *An A.B.C.*, and *The Compleynt of Mars*.

(b) The second or Italian stage shows a decided advance upon the first. In the handling of the metres the technical ability is greater, and there is a growing keenness of perception and a greater stretch of originality. To this period belong *Anelida and Arcite* and *The Parlement of Foules*. The latter has a fine opening, and, in the characterization of the birds, shows Chaucer's true comic spirit. *Troilus and Criseyde* is a long poem adapted from Boccaccio, but in its emphasis on character it is original, and indicative of the line of Chaucer's development. Reality and a passionate intensity underlie its conventions of courtly love and the tedious descriptions which this code demanded. The complex characters of Criseyde and Pandarus reveal a new subtlety of psychological development, and indicate Chaucer's growing insight into human motives. *Troilus and Criseyde* is held to be Chaucer's best narrative work. The rhyme royal stanzas are of much dexterity and beauty, and the pathos of the story is touched upon with deep feeling.

> If no love is, O God, what fele I so?
> And if love is, what thing and which is he?
> If love be good, from whennes com'th my wo?
> If it be wikke, a wonder thinketh me,
> When every torment and adversite
> That com'th of him, may to me savory thinke;
> For ay thurste I the more that ich it drinke.

The Hous of Fame, a poem in octosyllabic couplets, is of the dream-allegory type. In his dream Chaucer is carried by an eagle to the House of Fame and watches candidates for fame approach the throne, some being granted their requests and others refused. Though the story is rather drawn-out, and the allegorical significance obscure, it is of special interest because, in the verve and raciness of the Eagle, it shows gleams of the genuine Chaucerian humour. In this group is also included *The Legend of Good Women*, in which Chaucer, starting with the intention of telling nineteen affecting tales of virtuous women of antiquity, finishes with eight accomplished and the ninth only begun. After a charming introduction on the daisy, there is some masterly narrative, particularly in the portion dealing with Cleopatra. The poem is the first known attempt in English to use the heroic couplet, which is, none the less, handled with great skill and freedom.

(*c*) The third or English group contains work of the greatest individual accomplishment. The achievement of this period is *The Canterbury Tales*, though one or two of the separate tales may be of slightly earlier composition. For the general idea of the tales Chaucer may be indebted to Boccaccio, but in nearly every important feature the work is essentially English. For the purposes of his poem Chaucer draws together twenty-nine pilgrims, including himself. They meet at the Tabard Inn, in Southwark, in order to go on a pilgrimage to the tomb of Thomas à Becket at Canterbury. The twenty-nine are carefully chosen types, of both sexes, and of all ranks, from a knight to a humble ploughman; their occupations and personal peculiarities are many and diverse; and, as they are depicted in the masterly *Prologue* to the main work, they are interesting, alive, and thoroughly human. At the suggestion of the host of the Tabard, and to relieve the tedium of the journey, each of the pilgrims is to tell two tales on the outward journey, and two on the return. In its entirety the scheme would have resulted in an immense collection of over a hundred tales. But as it happens Chaucer finished only twenty, and left four partly complete. The separate tales are linked with their individual prologues, and with dialogues and scraps of narrative. Even in its incomplete state the work is a small literature in itself, an almost unmeasured abundance and variety of humour and pathos, of narrative and description, and of dialogue and digression. There are two prose tales, Chaucer's own *Tale of Melibeus* and *The Parson's Tale*; and nearly all the others are composed in a powerful and versatile species of the decasyllabic or heroic couplet.

To this last stage of Chaucer's work several short poems are ascribed, including *The Lak of Stedfastnesse* and the serio-comic *Compleynte of Chaucer to his Empty Purse*.

There is also mention of a few short early poems, such as *Origines upon the Maudeleyne*, which have been lost.

During his lifetime Chaucer built up such a reputation as a poet that many works were at a later date ascribed to him without sufficient evidence. Of this group the best examples are *The Flower and the Leaf*, quite an excellent example of the dream-allegory type, and *The Court of Love*. It has now been settled that these poems are not truly his.

3. His prose. The two prose tales may be apposite, but are not among Chaucer's successful efforts. Both—that is, *The Tale of Melibeus* and *The Parson's Tale* on penitence—are lifeless in style and full of tedious moralizings. Compared with earlier prose works they nevertheless mark an advance. They have a stronger grasp of sentence-construction, and in vocabulary they are copious and accurate. The other prose works of Chaucer are an early translation of Boëthius, and a treatise, composed for the instruction of his little son Lewis, on the astrolabe, then a popular astronomical instrument.

The following extract is a fair example of his prose:

> "Now, sirs," saith dame Prudence, "sith ye vouche saufe to be gouerned by my counceyll, I will enforme yow how ye shal gouerne yow in chesing of your counceyll. First tofore alle workes ye shall beseche the hyghe God, that he be your counceyll; and shape yow to suche entente that he yeue you counceyll and comforte as Thobye taught his sone. 'At alle tymes thou shall plese and praye him to dresse thy weyes; and loke that alle thy counceylls be in hym for euermore.' Saynt James eke saith: 'Yf ony of yow haue nede of sapience, axe it of God.' And after that than shall ye take counceyll in yourself, and examyne well your thoughtys of suche thynges as ye thynke that ben beste for your profyt. And than shall ye dryue away from your hertes the thynges that ben contraryous to good counceyl: this is to saye—ire, couetyse, and hastynes."
>
> *The Tale of Melibeus*

4. Features of his Poetry. (*a*) The first thing that strikes the eye is the *unique position* that Chaucer's work occupies in the literature of the age. He is first, with no competitor for hundreds of years to challenge his position. He is, moreover, the forerunner in the race of great literary figures that henceforth, in fairly regular succession, dominate the ages they live in.

(*b*) *His Observation.* Among Chaucer's literary virtues his acute faculty of observation is very prominent. He was a man of the world, mixing freely with all types of mankind; and he used his opportunities to observe the little peculiarities of human nature. He had the seeing eye, the retentive memory, the judgment to select, and the capacity to expound; hence the brilliance of his descriptions, which we shall note in the next paragraph.

(c) *His Descriptions.* Success in descriptive passages depends on vivacity and skill in presentation, as well as on the judgment shown in the selection of details. Chaucer's best descriptions, of men, manners, and places, are of the first rank in their beauty, impressiveness, and humour. Even when he follows the common example of the time, as when giving details of conventional spring mornings and flowery gardens, he has a vivacity that makes his poetry unique. Many poets before him had described the break of day, but never with the real inspiration that appears in the following lines:

> The bisy larke, messager of day,
> Salueth in her song the morwe gay,
> And firy Phœbus riseth up so brighte
> That all the orient laugheth with the lighte.
>
> *The Knight's Tale*

The *Prologue* contains ample material to illustrate Chaucer's power in describing his fellow-men. We shall add an extract to show him in another vein. Observe the selection of detail, the terseness and adequacy of epithet, and the masterly handling of the couplet.

> First on the wal was peynted a forest,
> In which ther dwelleth neither man nor best,
> With knotty, knarry, barreyne trees olde
> Of stubbes sharpe and hidouse to biholde,
> In which ther ran a rumbel and a swough,
> As though a storm sholde bresten every bough;
> And dounward from an hille, under a bente,
> Ther stood the temple of Mars armypotente,
> Wroght al of burned steel, of which the entree
> Was long and streit, and gastly for to see.
> The northern light in at the dores shoon,
> For wyndowe on the wal ne was ther noon
> Thurgh which men myghten any light discern,
> The dores were al of adament eterne,
> Y-clenched overthwart and endelong
> With iren tough, and for to make it strong,
> Every pyler, the temple to sustene,
> Was tonne greet, of iren bright and shene.
>
> *The Knight's Tale*

(d) *His Humour and Pathos.* In the literature of his time, when so few poets seem to have any perception of the fun in life, the humour of Chaucer is invigorating and delightful. The humour, which steeps nearly all his poetry, has great variety: kindly and patronizing, as in the case of the Clerk of Oxenford; broad and semi-farcical, as in the Wife of Bath; pointedly satirical, as in the Pardoner and the Summoner; or coarse, as happens in the tales of the Miller, the Reeve, and the Cook. It is seldom that the satirical intent is wholly lacking, as it is in the case of the Good Parson, but, except in rare cases, the satire is good-humoured and well-meant. The prevailing feature of Chaucer's humour is its urbanity: the man of the world's kindly tolerance of the weaknesses of his erring fellow-mortals.

Chaucer lays less emphasis on pathos, but it is not overlooked. In the poetry of Chaucer the sentiment is humane and unforced. We have excellent examples of pathos in the tale of the Prioress and in *The Legend of Good Women*.

We give a short extract from the long conversation between Chaucer and the eagle ("with fethres all of gold") which carried him off to the House of Fame. The bird, with its cool acceptance of things, is an appropriate symbol of Chaucer himself in his attitude toward the world.

> Thus I longe in his clawes lay,
> Til at the laste he to me spak
> In mannes vois, and seyde, "Awak!
> And be not so agast, for shame!"
> And called me tho by my name.
> And, for I sholde the bet abreyde—
> Me mette—"Awak," to me he seyde,
> Right in the same vois and stevene
> That useth oon I coude nevene;
> And with that vois, soth for to sayn,
> My minde cam to me agayn;
> For hit was goodly seyd to me,
> So nas hit never wont to be. . . .
> And sayde twyes "Seynte Marie!
> Thou art noyous for to carie." . . .
> "O god," thoughte I, "that madest kinde,
> Shal I non other weyes dye?
> Wher Ioves wol me stellifye,
> Or what thing may this signifye?
> I neither am Enok, nor Elye,
> Ne Romulus, ne Ganymede
> That was y-bore up, as men rede,
> To hevene with dan Iupiter,
> And maad the goddes boteler."

(e) *His Narrative Power*. As a story-teller Chaucer employs somewhat tortuous methods, but his narrative possesses a curious stealthy speed. His stories, viewed strictly as stories, have most of the weakness of his generation: a fondness for long speeches, for pedantic digressions on such subjects as dreams and ethical problems, and for long explanations when none are necessary. *Troilus and Criseyde*, heavy with long speeches, is an example of his prolixity, and *The Knight's Tale*, of baffling complexity and over-abundant in detail, reveals his haphazard and dawdling methods; yet both contain many admirable narrative passages. But when he rises above the weaknesses common to the time he is terse, direct, and vivacious. The extract given below will illustrate the briskness with which his story can move.

> This sely widwe, and eek hir doghtres two,
> Herden thise hennes crie and maken wo,
> And out at dores stirten they anon,
> And syen the fox toward the grove gon,
> And bar upon his bak the cok away,
> And cryden, "Out! Harrow! And weylaway!
> Ha! Ha! The fox!" And after hym they ran,
> And eek with staves many another man;
> Ran Colle, oure dogge, and Talbot, and Gerland
> And Malkyn, with a dystaf in hir hand;
> Ran cow and calf, and eek the verray hogges,
> So were they fered for berkynge of the dogges,
> And shoutyng of the men and wommen eek;
> They ronne so hem thoughte hir herte breek.
> They yolleden, as feendes doon in helle;
> The dokes cryden, as men wolde hem quelle;
> The gees, for feere, flowen over the trees;
> Out of the hyve cam the swarm of bees;
> So hidous was the noys, *a benedicitee!*
> Certes, he Jakke Straw, and his meynee,
> Ne made never shoutes half so shrille,
> Whan that they wolden any Flemyng kille,
> As thilke day was maade upon the fox.
>
> *The Nun's Priest's Tale*

(*f*) *His Metrical Skill.* In the matter of poetical technique English literature owes much to Chaucer. He virtually imported the decasyllabic line from France—it had been employed hardly at all in England previously—and he used it in both stanzaic and couplet forms. The seven-lined stanza *a b a b b c c* has become known as the Chaucerian or *rime royale*. Chaucer is no great lyrical poet but in some of his shorter poems—roundels and ballades—he shows a skill that is as good as the very best apparent in the contemporary poems.

(*g*) *Summary.* We may summarize Chaucer's achievement by saying that he is the earliest of the great moderns. In comparison with the poets of his own time, and with those of the succeeding century, the advance he makes is almost startling. For example, Manning, Hampole, and the romancers are of another age and of another way of thinking from ours; but, apart from the superficial archaisms of spelling, the modern reader finds in Chaucer something closely akin. All the Chaucerian features help to create this modern atmosphere: the shrewd and placidly humorous observation, the wide humanity, the quick aptness of phrase, the dexterous touch upon the metre, and, above all, the fresh and formative *spirit*—the genius turning dross into gold. Chaucer is indeed a genius; he stands alone, and for nearly two hundred years none dare claim equality with him.

OTHER POETS

1. William Langland, or **Langley (1332 (?)–1400 (?))**, is one of the early writers with whom modern research has dealt adversely. All we know about him appears on the manuscripts of his poem, or is based upon the remarks he makes regarding himself in the course of the poem. This poem, the full title of which is *The Vision of William concerning Piers the Plowman*, appears in its many manuscripts in three forms, called respectively the A, B, and C texts. The A text is the shortest, being about 2500 lines long; the B is more than 7200 lines; and the C, which is clearly based upon B, is more than 7300 lines. Until quite recently it has always been assumed that the three forms were all the work of Langland; but the latest theory is that the A form is the genuine composition of Langland, whereas both B and C have been composed by a later and inferior poet.

From the personal passages in the poem it appears that the author was born in Shropshire about 1332. The vision in which he saw Piers the Plowman probably took place in 1362.

The poem itself tells of the poet's vision on the Malvern Hills. In this trance he beholds a fair "feld ful of folk." The first vision, by subtle and baffling changes, merges into a series of dissolving scenes which deal with the adventures of allegorical beings, human like Do-wel, Do-bet, and Do-betst, or of abstract significance like the Lady Meed, Wit, Study, and Faith. During the many incidents of the poem the virtuous powers generally suffer most, till the advent of Piers the Plowman—the Messianic deliverer—restores the balance to the right side. The underlying motive of the work is to expose the sloth and vice of the Church, and to set on record the struggles and virtues of common folks. Langland's frequent sketches of homely life are done with sympathy and knowledge, and, unlike Chaucer, he portrays vividly the terrible hardships of the poor peasant.

The style has a sombre energy, an intense but crabbed seriousness, and an austere simplicity of treatment. The form of the poem is curious. It is a revival of the Old English rhymeless measure, having alliteration as the basis of the line. The lines themselves are fairly uniform in length, and there is the middle pause, with (as a rule) two alliterations in the first half-line and one in the second. Yet in spite of the Old English metre the vocabulary draws freely upon the French, to an extent equal to that of Chaucer himself.

The following lines illustrate the predominant tone of the poem. The fiery and direct denunciation of the vices of the times makes an interesting comparison with Chaucer's portrayal of the ecclesiastics in the Prologue to *The Canterbury Tales*. The reader should note the strong rhythm, and the regular system of alliteration.

> Heremites on an heep . With hoked staves,
> Wenten to Walsyngham . and here wenches after;
> Grete lobyes[1] and longe . that loth were to swynke,
> Clotheden hem in copis . to ben knowen fram othere,
> And shopen hem heremites . here ese to have.
>   I fonde there Freris . alle the foure ordres,
> Preched the peple . for profit to hem-selven,
> Preched the gospel . as hem good lyked,
> For coveitise of copis . construed it as thei wolde.

2. John Gower, the date of whose birth is uncertain, died in 1408. He was a man of means, and a member of a good Kentish family; he took a fairly active part in the politics and literary activity of the time, and was buried in London.

The three chief works of Gower are noteworthy, for they illustrate the unstable state of contemporary English literature. His first poem, *Speculum Meditantis*, is written in French, and for a long time was lost, being discovered as late as 1895; the second, *Vox Clamantis*, is composed in Latin; and the third, *Confessio Amantis*, is written in English, at the King's command according to Gower himself. In this last poem we have the conventional allegorical setting, with a disquisition on the seven deadly sins, illustrated by many anecdotes. These anecdotes reveal Gower's capacity as a story-teller. He has a diffuse and watery style of narrative, but occasionally he is brisk and competent. The metre is the octosyllabic couplet, of great smoothness and fluency.

---

[1] Lubbers.

3. John Barbour (1316 (?)–95) is the first of the Scottish poets to claim our attention. He was born in Aberdeenshire, and studied both at Oxford and Paris. His great work is his *Bruce* (1375), a lengthy poem of twenty books and thirteen thousand lines. The work is really a history of Scotland's struggle for freedom from the year 1286 till the death of Bruce and the burial of his heart (1332). The heroic theme is the rise of Bruce, and the central incident of the poem is the battle of Bannockburn. The poem, often rudely but pithily expressed, contains much absurd legend and a good deal of inaccuracy, but it is no mean beginning to the long series of Scottish heroic poems. This spirited passage from the first book is often quoted:

> A! fredome is a nobill thing!
> Fredome mayss[1] man to haiff liking!
> Fredome all solace to man giffis;
> He levys at ess that frely levys!
> A noble hart may haiff nane ess,
> Na ellys nocht that may him pless,
> Gyffe fredome failzhe: for fre liking
> Is zharnyt[2] our all othir thing.
> Na he, that ay hass levyt fre,
> May nocht knaw weill the propyrte,
> The angyr, na the wrechyt dome,
> That is couplyt to foule thyrldome.

PROSE-WRITERS

1. Sir John Mandeville is the English form of the name of **Jehan de Mandeville,** who compiled and published a French book of travels between 1357 and 1371. This French work was very popular, and it was translated into several languages, including English. The English version has a preface, in which it is stated that the author was a Sir John Mandeville, a knight, born at St Albans, who crossed the sea in 1322 and travelled in many strange regions. Much of the personal narrative is invention; nowadays the very existence of Sir John is denied. The real author of the book is said to be **Jehan de Bourgogne,** who died at Liége in 1372.

It has now been demonstrated that the so-called '*Travels*' is a compilation from several popular books of voyages, including those of a Friar Odoric, of an Armenian called Hetoum, and (to a very small extent) of the famous traveller Marco Polo. These, with a few grains of original matter, are ingeniously welded into one of the most charming books of its kind. The travels are full of incredible

[1] makes.   [2] yearned for.

descriptions and anecdotes, which are set down with delightful faith and eagerness. The style is sweet and clear, with some colloquial touches; and the short narrations freely dispersed through the text, tersely phrased and accurately gauged in length, are rendered with great skill.

We add an example to illustrate this admirable prose style. Observe the brief sentences, many of which begin with 'and,' the simple but effective diction, and the straightforward style of narrative.

> And zee schull undirstonde that whan men comen to Jerusalem her first pilgrymage is to the chirche of the Holy Sepulcr wher oure Lord was buryed, that is withoute the cytee on the north syde. But it is now enclosed in with the ton wall. And there is a full fair chirche all rownd, and open above, and covered with leed. And on the west syde is a fair tour and an high for belles strongly made. And in the myddes of the chirche is a tabernacle as it wer a lytyll hows, made with a low lityll dore; and that tabernacle is made in maner of a half a compas right curiousely and richely made of gold and azure and othere riche coloures, full nobelyche made. And in the ryght side of that tabernacle is the sepulcre of oure Lord. And the tabernacle is viij fote long and v fote wide, and xj fote in heghte. And it is not longe sithe the sepulcre was all open, that men myghte kisse it and touche it. But for pilgrymes that comen thider peyned hem to breke the ston in peces, or in poudr; therefore the Soudan[1] hath do make a wall aboute the sepulcr that no man may towche it. But in the left syde of the wall of the tabernacle is well the heighte of a man, is a gret ston, to the quantytee of a mannes hed, that was of the holy sepulcr, and that ston kissen the pilgrymes that comen thider. In that tabernacle ben no wyndowes, but it is all made light with lampes that hangen befor the sepulcr.

2. John Wyclif, or Wycliffe (1320–84), was born in Yorkshire about the year 1320. He was educated at Oxford, took holy orders, received the living of Lutterworth in Leicestershire (1374), and took a prominent part in the ecclesiastical feuds of the day. He was strong in his denunciation of the abuses then rampant, and only the influence of his powerful friends saved him from the fate of a heretic. He died peacefully in 1384.

An active controversialist, he wrote many Latin books in support of his revolutionary opinions. In addition, he issued a large number of tracts and pamphlets in English. An English translation of the Bible made at the end of his life has been popularly attributed to him, but, while it undoubtedly reflects his influence, its authorship remains uncertain. His English style is not polished, but it is

[1] Sultan.

vigorous and pointed, with a homely simplicity that makes its appeal both wide and powerful.

3. Sir Thomas Malory (died 1471 (?)) is included here, though his famous work, the *Morte d'Arthur*, was composed as late as the "ix yere of the reygne of Kyng Edward the furth" (1469). Nearly all we know about Malory is contained in the preface of Caxton, the first printer of the book. Caxton says that the book was written by Sir Thomas Malory "oute of certeyn bookes of frensshe."

The *Morte d'Arthur*, like the travels of Mandeville, is a compilation. The French Arthurian romances are drawn upon to create a prose romance of great length and detail. However diverse its sources, the book is written with a uniform dignity and fervour that express the very essence of romance and chivalry. It is a skilful blend of dialogue and narrative and is full of colour and life, while the style has a transparent clarity and a poetic sensitivity which make Malory our first great, individual, prose stylist. Remote in spirit from the everyday concerns of its age, the *Morte d'Arthur* stands outside the main stream of the development of English prose.

> And on the morn the damsel and he took their leave and thanked the knight, and so departed, and rode on their way until they came to a great forest. And there was a great river and but one passage, and there were ready two knights on the further side to let them the passage. "What sayest thou," said the damsel, "wilt thou match yonder knights, or turn again?" "Nay," said Sir Beaumains, "I will not turn again and they were six more." And therewithal he rushed into the water, and in the midst of the water, either brake their spears upon other to their hands, and then they drew their swords and smote eagerly at other. And at the last Sir Beaumains smote the other upon the helm that his head stonied, and therewithal he fell down in the water, and there was he drowned. And then he spurred his horse upon the land, where the other knight fell upon him and brake his spear, and so they drew their swords and fought long together. At the last Sir Beaumains clave his helm and his head down to the shoulders: and so he rode unto the damsel, and bade her ride forth on her way.

THE DEVELOPMENT OF LITERARY FORMS

The Chaucerian age saw a great and significant advance in poetical forms of literature, and noteworthy ones in the domain of prose.

1. Poetry. With regard to poetry, we can observe the various forms separating themselves and straightening out into form and coherence.

(*a*) The *lyric*, chiefly the religious and love-lyric, continues to be written and developed. Chaucer himself contributes very little toward it, but a number of anonymous bards add to the common stock. It is seldom that we can give precise dates to the lyrics of this period; but about this time were composed such exquisite pieces as *The Nut-brown Maid*, a curious hybrid between the lyric and the ballad, and the lovely carols of the Church.

(*b*) *The Rise of the Ballad.* By the late fourteenth century, the traditional ballad, of the type of *Chevy Chace, Sir Patrick Spens*, and the Robin Hood poems, had become an important source of popular entertainment, especially in the North. The origins of this form are much disputed, but, whether the ballad was composed by minstrels, or was the result of communal activity, it is essentially simple and popular. Mainly about love, local legends, the feats of local heroes, supernatural happenings, or religious stories, the ballad deals with man's elemental passions in frank and uninhibited terms, while its situations are such as affect the individual or family rather than the larger social unit of clan or nation. Its tone is impersonal and detached, and there is little or none of the composer's personality to be felt. The verse form (most commonly *abcb*, with alternating lines of four and three iambic feet) was subject to considerable variation, but was always simple and easily memorized. Frequent use of a refrain and of repetition are, similarly, products of this necessity to memorize the ballad, which also led to a concentration of emphasis (usually on a single incident), a complete lack of ornamental detail, and a rapidity of movement which made each stanza a definite step in the development of the story. It will be seen that the ballad is completely different from the romance, which is aristocratic in tone and theme, and cumulative in form, so that it could deal with any number of adventures. Collections of ballads were not made until the eighteenth century, so that we find many varying forms of the same ballad, and it seems likely that the versions we now possess differ considerably from the original.

(*c*) *The Rise of the Allegory.* This is perhaps the suitable place to note the rise of allegory, which in the age of Chaucer began to affect all the branches of poetry. Even at its best the allegorical method is crude and artificial, but it is a concrete and effective literary device for expounding moral and religious lessons. It appeals with the greatest force to minds which are still unused to abstract thinking; and about the period now under discussion it exactly suited the lay and ecclesiastical mind. Hence we have a flood of poems dealing with Courts of Love, Houses of Fame, Dances of the Seven Deadly

Sins, and other symbolical subjects. Especially in the earlier stages of his career, Chaucer himself did not escape the prevailing habit. We shall see that the craze for the allegory was to increase during the next century and later, till it reached its climax in *The Faerie Queene*.

(*d*) *Descriptive and Narrative Poems*. In this form of poetry *The Canterbury Tales* is the outstanding example, but in many passages of Langland and Gower we have specimens of the same class. We have already mentioned some of the weaknesses that are common to the narrative poetry of the day, and which were due partly to lack of practice and partly to reliance upon inferior models: the tantalizing rigmaroles of long speeches and irrelevant episodes, the habit of dragging into the story scientific and religious discussions, and an imperfect sense of proportion in the arrangement of the plot. In the best examples, such as those of Chaucer, there is powerful grip upon the central interest, a shrewd observation and humour, and quite often a brilliant rapidity of narration.

(*e*) The *metrical romance* is still a popular form, but the great vogue of the last century is on the wane. Among the lower classes it is being supplanted by the ballad; and the growing favour that is being shown to the *fabliau*—that is, the short French tale, realistic in subject and humorous-satirical in style—is leading to tales of the coarser Chaucer type.

2. Prose. The field for English prose is rapidly extending. The *Travels* of Mandeville presents an interesting departure as a prose work written for amusement rather than instruction. We have the translation of the Bible usually associated with Wyclif, and a prose version of Higden's *Polychronicon* by **John of Trevisa (1326–1412)**. But the most significant development is to be found in the clarity and vigour of the homely English used in civic records, and by letter-writers such as the Pastons, Celys, and Stonors. Simple, straightforward, and free from the stylistic ornamentation of the consciously literary prose, these everyday writings illustrate vividly the growing command of the native idiom in many sections of the community.

THE DEVELOPMENT OF LITERARY STYLE

1. Poetry. We have already stated that the time of transition and experiment is nearly over. English poetical style has established itself, and the main lines of development have been laid down. For this we are indebted almost entirely to Chaucer.

(*a*) With regard to *metre*, it is curious to observe that with increasing practice the tendency is toward simplicity. The extremely complicated stanzas are becoming less common, and rhyme royal and other shorter verses are coming into favour. Along with simplification is a greater suppleness and dexterity. There is less rigidity in the position of the pause, and a greater freedom in the substitution of three-syllabled feet for two-syllabled feet. These features are most strongly developed in the couplet forms. It is this union of simplicity and freedom that is to remain the dominating characteristic of English verse, thus contrasting with the quantitative system of the classical measures and the syllabic nature of the French.

(*b*) There is an interesting *revival in alliteration*. In the true alliterative poem the basis of the line is a system of repeating sounds, such as was the custom in Old English verse. One of the earliest examples of this type which occurs after the Norman Conquest is *Wynnere and Wastour* (1352), an anonymous poem of no great merit. The tradition is continued in the alliterative romances of the type of *Cleannesse*; and it attains its climax in *Piers Plowman*. Though this last poem gained a great popularity it left no important literary descendants. Hence the revival of the ancient system of alliteration remains as an interesting curiosity. In a very short time after Langland alliteration becomes simply an ornament to metre —sometimes a device of great beauty, but not vital to the metrical scheme.

As regards the actual *poetic diction* of the period, there is a considerable liking shown for ornate French and classical terms. This can be observed in the earlier poems of Chaucer and in the *Confessio Amantis* of Gower. We have not yet attained to the aureate diction of the succeeding generation, but the temptation to use French terms was too strong to be resisted. Langland, though he draws upon the French element, writes with much greater simplicity; and the ballads also are composed in a manner quite plain and unadorned.

2. Prose. The state of prose is still immature, but the everyday writings of the age show a vigour and clarity which are a great advance on the mingled French and English writing of the beginning of the period, when English was still struggling to shake off the dominance of French. Wyclif's prose is unpolished, though it can be pointed and vigorous. Mandeville's prose style, though it is devoid of artifices, attains to a certain distinction by reason of its straightforward methods, its short and workmanlike sentences, and a brevity rare in his day. In the case of Malory, who comes some time after the others, we have quite an individual style. It is still unadorned; but it has a distinction of phrase and a decided romantic flavour that make Malory a prose stylist of a high class. His prose is, indeed, quite distinct from that of his predecessors, and exerts little influence on the writers who follow.

CHAPTER IV

FROM CHAUCER TO SPENSER

THE HISTORICAL BACKGROUND (1450–1550)

The dates that appear at the head of this section are only approximate, but the general features of the time are well defined. In England the period begins with wars, unrest, and almost chaos; it concludes with a settled dynasty, a reformed religion, and a people united and progressive. Abroad, as well as in England, there is apparent the broad intellectual flood known as the Renaissance, running deep and strong: the renewed desire for knowledge, changes in religious ideals, the discovery of new worlds, both geographical and literary, and the enormous quickening of heart and mind. In England the scene is being prepared for the great age to follow.

LITERARY FEATURES OF THE AGE

1. Poverty of Material. Considering the length of the period, the poverty of the output is hard to explain. There is no English poet of any consequence; the prose writing is thin in quality and quantity; and if it were not for the activities of the Scottish poets the age would be poor indeed.

2. Scottish Poetry. Scottish poetry comes late into notice, but it comes with a bound. The poverty and disunion of Scotland, its severance from the intellectual stimulus of English thought, and the dearth of educational facilities all combine to retard its literary development. But these disadvantages are rapidly passing away, with the beneficial results apparent in this chapter.

3. The Development of the Drama. The popularity of the romance is almost gone; the drama, more suited to the growing intelligence of the time, is rapidly taking on a new importance. The professional actor and the playwright, owing to real demand for their services, are making their appearance. The development of the drama is sketched in this chapter.

4. The Importance of the Period. The importance of the time is belied by its apparent barrenness. In reality it is a season of healthy fallow, of germination, of rest and recuperation. The literary impulse, slowly awakening, is waiting for the right moment. When that moment comes the long period of rest gives the new movement swift and enduring force.

POETRY

1. The Scottish Poets. (a) **James I (1394–1437)** was captured by the English in 1406, and remained in England till 1424, when he married Joan Beaufort, the cousin of Henry V, and returned to Scotland. The chief poem associated with his name is *The Kingis Quair* (*quire* or *book*). The attempts to disprove his authorship have not been successful. It seems to have been written during his captivity, and it records his first sight of the lady destined to be his wife. It follows the Chaucerian model of the dream, the garden, and the introduction of allegorical figures. The stanza is the rhyme royal, which is said to have derived its name from his use of it. The diction, which is the common artificial blend of Scottish and Chaucerian forms, is highly ornamented; but there are some passages of really brilliant description, and a few stanzas of passionate declamation quite equal to the best of Chaucer's *Troilus and Criseyde*. It is certainly among the best of the poems that appear between the periods of Chaucer and Spenser. Other poems, in particular the more plebeian *Peblis to the Play* and *Christis Kirk on the Grene*, have been ascribed to James, but his authorship is extremely doubtful.

The two following stanzas are fair examples of James's poetry. The man who wrote them was no mean poet.

> Off hir array the form gif I sall write,
>   Toward hir goldin haire and rich atyre
> In fret-wise couchit[1] was with perllis quhite
>   And grete balas[2] lemyng[3] as the fyre,
>   With mony ane emeraut and faire saphire;
> And on hir hede a chaplet fresch of hewe,
> Off plumys partit rede, and quhite, and blewe;
>
> Full of quaking spangis[4] bryght as gold,
>   Forgit of schap like to the amorettis,[5]
> So new, so fresch, so plesant to behold,
>   The plumys eke like to the floure-Ionettis,[6]
>   And othir of schap like to the round crokettis,[7]
> And, aboue all this, there was, wele I wote,
> Beautee eneuch to mak a world to dote.
>
> *The Kingis Quair*

[1] inlaid. [2] rubies. [3] gleaming. [4] spangles.
[5] love-knots. [6] St John's wort. [7] curls.

(b) **Sir David Lyndsay (1490–1555)** was born in Fifeshire about the year 1490. He entered the royal service, and rose to fill the important position of Lyon King-of-Arms.

His longer works, which were written during his service at Court, include *The Dreme*, in rhyme royal stanzas, with the usual allegorical setting; *The Testament of Squyer Meldrum*, in octosyllabic couplets, a romantic biography with a strongly Chaucerian flavour; *The Testament and Compleynt of the Papyngo*, which has some gleams of his characteristic humour; and *Ane Pleasant Satyre of the Thrie Estaitis*, a morality-play, coarse and vulgar, but containing much of his best work. It is full of telling satire directed against the Church, and it shows acute observation of the frailties of his fellows. Lyndsay represents the ruder type of the Scottish Chaucerian. He has a coarseness beyond the standard even of his day; but he cannot be denied a bluff good-humour, a sound honesty of opinion, and an abundant and vital energy.

(c) **Robert Henryson (1429 (?)–c. 1508)** has left us few details regarding his life. In one of his books he is described as a "scholemaister of Dunfermeling"; he may have studied at Glasgow University; and he was dead when Dunbar (see below) wrote his *Lament for the Makaris* in 1508. Hence the dates given for his birth and death are only approximations.

The order of his poems has not been determined. His longest is a version of the *Morall Fabillis of Esope*, composed in rhyme royal stanzas and showing much dexterity and vivacity; *The Testament of Cresseid* is a continuation of Chaucer's *Troilus and Criseyde*, and it has a finely tragic conclusion; *Orpheus and Eurydice*, an adaptation from Boëthius, has, along with much commonplace moralizing, some passages of real pathos; and among his thirteen shorter poems *Robene and Makyne*, a little pastoral incident, is executed with a lightness, a brevity, and a precision that make it quite a gem among its fellows. His *Garmond of Gude Ladies*, though often quoted, is pedantically allegorical, and of no high quality as poetry.

We quote two stanzas from *The Testament of Cresseid*. The diction is an artificial blend of that of Chaucer and of colloquial Scots, and it is heavily loaded with descriptive epithet; but it is picturesque and dramatic, in some respects suggesting the later work of Spenser.

His face frosnit,[1] his lyre was lyke the leid,
  His teith chatterit, and cheverit[2] with the chin,
His ene[3] droupit, how,[4] sonkin in his heid,
  Out of his nois the meldrop[5] fast can rin,
  With lippis bla,[6] and cheikis leine and thin,
The iceschoklis that fra his hair doun hang,
Was wonder greit, and as ane speir als lang.

Atouir[7] his belt his lyart[8] lokkis lay
  Felterit[9] unfair, ouirfret with froistis hoir,
His garmound and his gyis[10] full gay of gray,
  His widderit weid[11] fra him the wind out woir;
  Ane busteous bow within his hand he boir,
Under his girdill ane flasche[12] of felloun flanis,[13]
Fedderit[14] with ice, and heidit with hailstanis.

The Testament of Cresseid

(d) **William Dunbar (1460 (?)–1530 (?))** is generally considered to
be the chief of the Scottish Chaucerian poets. He was born in East
Lothian, studied at St Andrews University (1477), and went to
France and became a wandering friar. Returning to Scotland, he
became attached to the household of James IV, and in course of
time was appointed official Rhymer. He died about 1530.

Dunbar wrote freely, often on subjects of passing interest; and
though his work runs mainly on Chaucerian lines it has an energy
and pictorial quality that are quite individual. Of the more than
ninety poems associated with his name the most important are the
Goldyn Targe, of the common allegorical-rhetorical type; *The
Thrissil and the Rois*, celebrating the marriage of James IV and the
English Margaret (1503); the *Dance of the Sevin Deidlie Synnis*,
with its strong *macabre* effects and its masterly grip of metre; the
Tua Mariit Wemen and the Wedo, a revival of the ancient allitera-
tive measure, and outrageously frank in expression; and *The
Lament for the Makaris*, in short stanzas with the refrain *Timor
Mortis conturbat me*, quite striking in its effect.

The following short extract reveals Dunbar's strong pictorial
quality and his command of metre.

"Lat se," quod he, "Now quha begynnis;
  With that the fowll Sevin Deidly Synnis

[1] frosted.	[2] shivered.	[3] eyes.	[4] hollow.
[5] moisture.	[6] blue.	[7] out over.	[8] gray.
[9] tangled.	[10] attire.	[11] tattered clothes.	
[12] sheaf.	[13] arrows.	[14] feathered.	

Begowth[1] to leip at anis.[2]
And first of all in dance wes Pryd,
With hair wyld[3] bak and bonet on syd,
Lyk to mak vaistie wanis;[4]
And round abowt him, as a quheill,[5]
Hang all in rumpillis[6] to the heill
His kethat[7] for the nanis:
Mony prowd trumpour[8] with him trippit
Throw skaldand[9] fyre, ay as thay skippit
Thay gyrnd[10] with hiddouss granis.[11]

. . . . .

Than Yre come in with sturt[12] and stryfe;
His hand wes ay vpon his knyfe,
He brandeist[13] lyk a beir.[14]

Dance of the Sevin Deidlie Synnis

(*e*) **Gawin Douglas (1474 (?)–1522)** was a member of the famous Douglas family, his father being the fifth Earl of Angus, Archibald 'Bell the Cat.' He studied at St Andrews University (1489) and probably at Paris, became a priest, and rose to be Bishop of Dunkeld. He took a great share in the high politics of those dangerous times, and in the end lost his bishopric, was expelled to England, and died in London.

His four works belong to the period 1501–13: *The Palice of Honour*, of elaborate and careful workmanship, and typical of the fifteenth-century manner; *King Hart*, a laboriously allegorical treatment of life, the Hart being the heart of life, which is attended by the five senses and other personifications of abstractions; *Conscience*, a short poem, a mere quibble on the word 'conscience,' of no great poetical merit; and the *Æneid*, his most considerable effort, a careful translation of Virgil, with some incongruous touches, but done with competence and some poetical ability. It is the earliest of its kind, and so is worthy of some consideration. Douglas is the most scholarly and painstaking of his group; but he lacks the native vigour of his fellows. His style is often overloaded and listless, and in the selection of theme he shows little originality.

2. John Skelton (1460 (?)–1529) comes late in this period, but he is perhaps the most considerable of the poets. His place of birth is disputed; he may have studied at Oxford, and he probably graduated at Cambridge. He took orders (1498), entered the household of the Countess of Richmond, the mother of Henry VII, and became a

[1] Began.	[2] once.	[3] combed.	[4] desolate houses.
[5] wheel.	[6] creases.	[7] long coat.	[8] deceiver.
[9] scalding.	[10] grimaced.	[11] groans.	[12] trouble.
[13] swaggered.	[14] bear.		

tutor to Prince Henry. In 1500 he obtained the living of Diss in Norfolk, but his sharp tongue ruined him as a rector. He fell foul of Wolsey, and is said to have escaped imprisonment by seeking sanctuary in Westminster Abbey, where he died in 1529.

In his *Garlande of Laurell* Skelton gives a list of his own works, most of which have perished. This poem itself is a dreary effort, stilted in style and diffuse in treatment. It is in satire that Skelton appears at his best. His satirical poems, in spite of their shuffling and scrambling metres, are usually sharp, often witty, and nearly always alive. *Why come ye nat to Court?* is addressed to Wolsey, and for jeering impertinence it is hard to find its equal, at that time at least; *The Tunnynge of Elynour Rummynge* is realism indeed, for it faithfully portrays the drunken orgies of a pack of women at an ale-house. His more serious poems include a *Dirge on Edward IV*, *The Bowge of Court*, and a quite excellent morality-play, *Magnificence*.

We quote an example of Skelton's peculiar metre, which came to be called 'Skeltonics.' It is a species of jingling octosyllabic couplet, but crumbling and unstable, often descending to doggerel. It is, however, lively, witty in a shallow fashion, and attractive. His own description of it is quite just:

> For though my rhyme be ragged,
> Tattered and jagged,
> Rudely rayne beaten,
> Rusty and moughte eaten,
> If ye take well therwith,
> It hath in it some pyth.

The following extract shows his powers of invective:

> But this mad Amelek
> Like to a Mamelek,
> He regardeth lordès
> Not more than potshordès;
> He is in such elation
> Of his exaltation,
> And the supportation
> Of our sovereign lordè,
> That, God to recordè,
> He ruleth all at will,
> Without reason or skill;
> Howbeit the primordial
> Of his wretched original,
> And his base progeny,
> And his greasy genealogy,
> He came of the sank[1] royal
> That was cast out of a butcher's stall.

Why come ye nat to Court?

[1] blood.

3. John Lydgate (1370–1451) had a great reputation in his day, but little of it has survived. He was born at Lydgate, near New-market, and became a monk at Bury St Edmunds, where he rose to be priest in 1397. He studied and wrote much, gaining a wide reputation both as a scholar and a poet. The dates of his birth and death are only approximately fixed.

Lydgate was a friend of Chaucer, upon whom he models much of his poetry. But as a poet he is no Chaucer. He has none of the latter's metrical skill and lively imagination, and the enormous mass of his poems only enhances their futility. *The Falls of Princes*, full of platitudes and wordy digressions, is no less than 7000 verses long; *The Temple of Glass*, of the common allegorical type, is mercifully shorter; and so is the *Story of Thebes*, a supposed addition to *The Canterbury Tales*. On rare occasions, as in *London Lickpenny*, he is livelier; but he has no ear for metre, and the common vices of his time—prolixity, lack of humour, and pedantic allegory—lie heavy upon him.

4. Thomas Occleve, or **Hoccleve (1368 (?)–1450 (?)),** may have been born in Bedfordshire; but we know next to nothing about him, and that he tells us himself. He was a clerk in the Privy Seal Office, from which in 1424 he retired on a pension to Hampshire.

His principal works are *The Regement of Princes*, written for the edification of Henry V, and consisting of a string of tedious sermons; *La Male Règle*, partly autobiographical, in a snivelling fashion; *The Complaint of Our Lady*; and *Occleve's Complaint*.

The style of Occleve's poetry shows the rapid degeneration that set in immediately after the death of Chaucer. His metre, usually rhyme royal or couplets, is loose and sprawling, the style is uninspired, and the interest of the reader soon ebbs very low. He himself, in his characteristic whining way, admits it with much truth:

> Fader Chaucer fayne wold han me taught,
> But I was dul, and learned lite or nought.

5. Stephen Hawes (1474 (?)–1530 (?)) was a Court poet during the first twenty years of the sixteenth century. Very little is known of him, even the dates of his birth and death being largely matters of surmise.

His chief works include *The Passetyme of Pleasure*, a kind of romantic-homiletic poem, composed both in rhyme royal stanzas and in couplets, and dealing with man's life in this world in a fashion reminiscent of Bunyan's; *The Example of Virtue; The Con-*

version of Swerers; and *A Joyfull Medytacyon.* Of all the poets now under discussion Hawes is the most uninspired; his allegorical methods are of the crudest; but he is not entirely without his poetical moments. His *Passetyme of Pleasure* probably influenced the allegory of Spenser.

6. **Alexander Barclay (1475 (?)–1552)** might have been either a Scotsman or an Englishman for all that is known on the subject. He was a priest in Devonshire, and later withdrew to a monastery in Ely. His important poem, the *Ship of Fools,* a translation of a German work by Sebastian Brant, represents a newer type of allegory. The figures in the poem are not the usual wooden creatures representing the common vices and virtues, but they are sharply satirical portraits of the various kinds of foolish men. Sometimes Barclay adds personal touches to make the general satire more telling. *Certayne Ecloges,* another of Barclay's works, is the earliest English collection of pastorals. It contains, among much grumbling over the times, quite attractive pictures of the country life of the day.

PROSE-WRITERS

1. **Reginald Pecock (1390 (?)–1461 (?))** may have been born in Wales, and perhaps in 1390. He was educated at Oxford, and took orders, when he became prominent through his attacks upon the Lollards. In his arguments he went so far that he was convicted of heresy (1457), forced to make a public recantation, and had to resign his bishopric of Chichester. He died in obscurity about 1460.

His two works were *The Repressor of Over-much Blaming of the Clergy* (*c.* 1445) and *The Book of Faith.* In his dogma he strongly supported the ancient usages of the Church; and in the style of his argument he is downright and opinionative. His prose, often rugged and obscure, is marked by his preference for English words in place of those of Latin origin. His books are among the earliest of English controversial works, and thus they mark a victory over the once all-important Latin.

2. **William Caxton (1422 (?)–91),** the first English printer, was born in Kent about the year 1422. He was apprenticed to a London mercer, and in his capacity of mercer went to Bruges to assist in the revival of English trade with the Continent. In Bruges, where he lived for thirty-three years, he started his translations from the French, and in that city he may have learned the infant art of printing. In 1476 he established himself in London as a printer. There he began to issue a series of books that laid the foundation of

English printing. The first book printed in England was *The Dictes and Sayengis of the Philosophers* (1477). The main part of the volume was the work of Lord Rivers, but Caxton, as was his habit, revised it for the press.

It would be difficult to overestimate the debt of English literature to Caxton. He printed almost every English work of real quality known in his day, including Chaucer and Malory. In addition, he made and printed twenty-four translations from French, Dutch, and Latin texts, of which the most remarkable were the two earliest, the *Recuyell of the Histories of Troye* (1471) and the *Game and Playe of the Chesse* (1475). The introductions of many of his books are of great personal and general interest, and show him to have been very conscious of his limitations as a literary artist. Anxious to use the elegant, ornate, 'literary' style, he found himself unqualified to do so, and decided to write in "Englysshe not ouer rude, ne curyous, but in suche termes as shall be vnderstanden by goddys grace." Even so, his style is marred by a very involved and confused sentence structure, which he never mastered, and a tendency to introduce foreign words and phrases which he neglected to translate.

We give a brief extract from his preface to the *Recuyell*. Observe the rather clumsy sentences and the plain language.

> When I remember that every man is bounden by the commandment and counsel of the wise man to eschew sloth and idleness, which is mother and nourisher of vices, and ought to put myself unto virtuous occupation and business, then I, having no great charge of occupation, following the said counsel, took a French book and read therein many strange and marvellous histories wherein I had great pleasure and delight, as well for the novelty of the same as for the fair language of French, which was in prose so well and compendiously set and written, which methought I understood the sentence and substance of every matter. And forsomuch as this book was new and late made and drawn into French, and never had seen it in our English tongue, I thought in myself it should be a good business to translate it into our English, to the end that it might be had as well in the realm of England as in other lands, and also for to pass therewith the time, and thus concluded in myself to begin this said work. And forthwith took pen and ink and began boldly to run forth as blind Bayard, in this present work which is named the *Recuyell* of the Trojan histories.

3. John Fisher (*c.* **1459–1535**) was born in Yorkshire about 1459, was educated at Cambridge, and entered the Church. In due course he became Bishop of Rochester. During the time of the

Reformation he opposed Henry VIII's desire to be acknowledged as the head of the English Church, and was imprisoned in the Tower (1534). While there he was made a cardinal by the Pope; and he was beheaded by the orders of Henry.

Fisher wrote much in Latin, and in English he is represented by a small collection of tracts and sermons and a longer treatise on the Psalms. Though they are of no great quantity, his prose works are in their nature of much importance. They are the first of the rhetorical-religious books that for several centuries were to be an outstanding feature of English prose. In addition, they show a decided advance in the direction of style. They are written in the style of the orator and are the result of the conscious effort of the stylist: the searching after the appropriate word (often apparent by the use of two or three words of like meaning), the frequent use of rhetorical figures of speech, and a rapid and flowing rhythm. In brief, in the style of Fisher we can observe the beginnings of an ornate style. It is still in the making, but it is the direct ancestor of the prose style of Jeremy Taylor and other divines of the same class.

In the following passage observe the use of such doublets as 'painful and laborious,' 'rest and ease,' and 'desire and love.' The rhythm is supple, there is a quick procession of phrases, and the vocabulary is copious and Latinized to a considerable extent.

> What life is more painful and laborious of itself than is the life of hunters which, most early in the morning, break their sleep and rise when others do take their rest and ease, and in his labour he may use no plain highways and the soft grass, but he must tread upon the fallows, run over the hedges, and creep through the thick bushes, and cry all the long day upon his dogs, and so continue without meat or drink until the very night drive him home; these labours be unto him pleasant and joyous, for the desire and love that he hath to see the poor hare chased with dogs. Verily, verily, if he were compelled to take upon him such labours, and not for this cause, he would soon be weary of them, thinking them full tedious unto him; neither would he rise out of his bed so soon, nor fast so long, nor endure these other labours unless he had a very love therein.

The Ways to Perfect Religion

4. Hugh Latimer (1485 (?)–1555) was born in Leicestershire, educated at Cambridge, and rose to be chaplain to Henry VIII and Bishop of Worcester. He resisted some of the reforms of Henry, was imprisoned in the Tower, and was released on the death of the King. At the accession of Mary he was once again thrown into jail, and was burnt at Oxford.

Latimer's English prose works consist of two volumes of sermons published in 1549. They are remarkable for their plain and dogmatic exposition, their graphical power, and their homely appeal. He is the first of the writers of plain style.

5. Sir Thomas More (1478–1535) was born in London, and was the son of a judge. He was educated in London, attached to the household of the Archbishop of Canterbury, and became a lawyer. A man of eager and aspiring mind, he fell under the influence of Erasmus, Colet, and other humanists of the period. For a time he sat in Parliament and saw State service. His refusal to accept the Act of Supremacy led to his imprisonment (1534), and he was beheaded in the following year.

Owing to their elegance and wit, his Latin works are of unusual importance. They include his *Utopia*, the description of his imaginary ideal state. This book was not translated into English until 1551, and so does not count as an English work of More's. His English prose works include *The Lyfe of John Picus*, *The Historie of Richard III*, and a number of tracts and letters. He writes ably and clearly, but with no great distinction of manner. He is the first writer of the middle style.

THE DEVELOPMENT OF LITERARY FORMS

1. Poetry. In this period we have to chronicle the appearance of the *eclogue* or *pastoral* in the work of Barclay (*Ecloges*) and in some shorter poems like Henryson's *Robene and Makyne*. The pastoral, which in classical times had been practised by Virgil and Theocritus, became a common form of poetical exercise in Italy, France, and Spain before in the sixteenth century it appeared in England. It was marked by a set of conventional shepherds and shepherdesses, possessing such names as Colin, Phyllis, and Phœbe; by stock scenes introducing sheep, meadows, and flowers; and it was often made the medium for philosophical and political theories. As yet the golden age of the pastoral had not made its appearance in England, but the beginning of the vogue was apparent.

A glance at the poems mentioned in this chapter will reveal the importance of the *allegory*. In this period it grew and hardened into a mechanical and soulless device, for the poets lacked sufficient poetical fire to give it life. The allegory, as we can see in Dunbar's *Goldyn Targe* and Lydgate's *Temple of Glass*, usually opened with a garden and a dream, conventionalized to an absurd degree, and it continued with the introduction of the Goddess of Love, the

Virtues and Vices, and similar stock personations. The allegory, however, in spite of its enormous elaborations, was not at the end of its popularity, and, as we shall see in the next chapter, it was to add another great poet to its list of devotees.

The development of the *ballad* and *carol* continued, with highly satisfactory results. These poems began to acquire polish and expertness, for the early rudeness was becoming a thing of the past. To this period probably belong the lovely carol to the Virgin Mary beginning "I sing of a maiden," and the ballads connected with Robin Hood, Fair Rosamund, and many others.

2. Prose. There were no outstanding achievements in prose, but facts all helped to reveal the waning influence of Latin and the increasing importance given to English. English prose appeared in theological works, as in those of Fisher; and **Cranmer (1489–1556)** gave it a new field in his notable English Prayer Book. Historical prose was represented by *The Chronicle of England* of **Capgrave (1393–1464)**, who wrote in a businesslike fashion; a species of philosophical prose appeared in *The Governance of England* of **Fortescue** (*c.* **1394–***c.* **1476)**, and in *The Boke named the Governour* of **Elyot** (*c.* **1490–***c.* **1546)**, a kind of educational work; *The Castle of Health*, also by the last author, was a medical work. The great race of Elizabethan translators is well begun by **Lord Berners (1467–1533)**, who translated Froissart with freedom and no mean skill; and, lastly, the English Bible was taking shape.

The Development of the English Bible

The work on the English Bible began as early as the eighth century, when Bede translated a portion of the Gospel of St John into Old English prose. The work was ardently continued during the Old English period—for example, in the Lindisfarne Gospels (about 100) and the prose of Ælfric (about 1000). During the Anglo-Norman period, owing to the influence of French and Latin, English translation did not flourish; but efforts were made, especially in the Psalms and the Pauline epistles. Translation was strongly stimulated by **Wyclif (1320–84)**, under whose influence two complete versions were carried through about 1384 and 1388. How much actual translation Wyclif accomplished will never be known, but his was the leading spirit, and to him falls the glory of being the leader in the great work. To the second of the Wycliffian versions is sometimes given the name of **John Purvey**, the Lollard leader who succeeded Wyclif. The two versions are simple and unpretentious renderings, the second being much more finished than the first.

After Wyclif translation flagged till the Reformation bent men's minds anew to the task. The greatest of all the translators was **William Tyndale** ((?)–**1536**), who did much to give the Bible its modern shape. Tyndale suffered a good deal of persecution owing to his hardihood, and was driven abroad, where much of his translation was accomplished, and where it was first printed. At Cologne (1525) a fragment of his English New Testament was printed. A feature of Tyndale's translation was its direct reliance upon the Hebrew and Greek originals, and not upon the Latin renderings of them. Of these Latin texts the stock version was the Vulgate, upon which Wyclif to a large extent relied.

Miles Coverdale (1488–1568) carried on the work of Tyndale. Though he lacked the latter's scholarship, he had an exquisite taste for phrase and rhythm, and many of the most beautiful Biblical expressions are of his workmanship. An edition of his translation (1535) was the first complete English Bible to be printed.

Translations now came apace. None of them, however, was much improvement upon Tyndale's. In 1537 appeared the finely printed version of 'Thomas Matthew,' who was said to be **John Rogers**, a friend of Coverdale, though it may be a pseudonym for Tyndale himself. The *Great Bible* (1539), the first of the authorized versions, was executed by a commission of translators, working under the command of Henry VIII. It was based on Matthew's Bible. Another notable translation was the Calvinistic *Geneva Bible* (1560). This book received the popular name of '*Breeches Bible*,' owing to its rendering of Genesis iii, 7: "They sewed fig leaves together, and made themselves breeches." In the reign of Elizabeth was issued the *Bishops' Bible* (1568), a magnificent folio, which was translated by a committee of bishops and learned men. It was intended to be a counterblast to the growing popularity of the Breeches Bible.

With these we are close upon the great *Authorized Version* (1611), which we shall mention in the next chapter, where also we shall briefly discuss the influence and the literary qualities of this translation.

3. The Drama. The later Middle Ages bring a rapid growth in the native drama, a preparation for the great age of Elizabeth; and we give now a brief sketch of its development.

The ancient classical drama had long ceased to be a vital force, and the only trace of it was in the *mimes* or professional strolling players to be found throughout the Middle Ages in all parts of Europe. To them medieval drama owes little or nothing. Popular mummings at great festivals, a crude survival of ancient pagan ritual, developed into more elaborate amusements, with morris dancing and simple dramatizations of the feats of such heroes as Robin Hood and St George. These festivities were the occasion of much popular fun and licence, particularly at the election of the 'Abbot of Unreason,' with his attendants, the hobby horse and the clown.

(a) THE MIRACLE-PLAY. It is in the Church and its liturgy that we find the stimulus which leads to the rebirth of drama. The commonly used antiphonal singing had in it the elements of dialogue, while the obvious dramatic possibilities in the Roman Catholic ritual, especially in the Mass, were gradually developed as part of the elaborate ceremonial of the great religious feasts like Easter. As early as the tenth century we hear of Easter representations of the empty tomb of Christ, with dialogue between one figure sitting outside and three others who come in as if seeking something. The authorities were quick to appreciate the instructional value of such presentations as an addition to the Latin liturgy, and to this dramatization of the *quem quæritis* (whom seek ye?) rapid additions seem to have been made, both at Easter and at other feasts.

The writers seem to have turned next to other New Testament stories, such as the Annunciation and the Nativity, and then to the Old Testament, where the Fall and the stories of Noah and Daniel were among the most popular. By the fourteenth century we have the evolution of complete cycles of plays, covering the history of the world from the Creation to the Day of Judgment, and there is a common tendency to incorporate into them material from legend and the saints' lives. It has long been the fashion to call the Biblical plays 'mysteries' and those dealing with saints' lives 'miracles,' but there is no evidence to justify this distinction in England, though it seems to have been used in France. We hear of no play being called a 'mystery' in England before the eighteenth century, and it seems probable that all out-of-door liturgical dramas in this country were known as 'miracles.'

From the eleventh century onward monastic and cathedral records frequently mention properties used in such dramatic representations. The performances were still part of the liturgy, spoken in Latin by clerics, and their rôle was a subordinate one. Slowly, however, the vernacular crept in to usurp the place of the Latin, minor clerics and then laymen were introduced as actors, and numerous episodes began to be found in single performances. This growth necessitated the moving of the presentation from the choir (its original place) to the nave of the church, and rapidly the liturgical drama grew to overshadow the ritual of which it had been a very small part. By the twelfth century the dramas, in quest of still more space, seem to have moved into the open, and the organization had begun to pass from ecclesiastical to lay hands. The vernacular was by now the usual medium, and the growing secularization of the drama is reflected in an edict of 1210 forbidding clergy to take part in the plays.

From the clergy, control passed first to the religious and social guilds, and then to the trade guilds, under the general control of the council of the town. The guilds, which were wealthy, and keen rivals in public show, became responsible for the productions. Each guild took on a separate episode from a cycle—often an episode suited to its own interests. Thus at Chester the water-leaders and drawers of the Dee performed Noah's Deluge. The growing elaboration of presentation, stimulated by guild rivalry, and the extension of the cycles led to the evolution of the ambulatory cycle, in which each episode was performed on a two-decked cart, or pageant. This pageant consisted of one enclosed room, which served both as Hell and as a tiring room, and a second storey open to the sky, on which the action was performed. It was towed round the town so that the play could be performed at fixed points, and at York we read of twelve places at which each play was given in a sequence which began at 4.30 A.M. and went on until the light failed. In London, about 1500, the plays, which were presented very elaborately, lasted from four to seven days.

For such elaborate cycles presented out of doors only summer festivals were really suitable, and after the creation, in 1311, of the feast of Corpus Christi, which fell in May or June, when weather was likely to be good and the hours of daylight were long, most of the play cycles began to attach themselves to that feast. Here and there, however, and notably at Chester, the plays were associated with Whitsuntide. The cycles, some of which were performed annually, and some only at intervals of several years, made Corpus Christi a great public holiday. Soon the licence and revelry of the crowds congregated in the great religious centres on this occasion were arousing strong ecclesiastical opposition and leading to a deterioration in the religious significance and spirit of the plays. Though their composition probably remained in clerical hands, a growing secularization of tone is clearly discernible. A realistic note, often coarse, but always vigorous, was creeping in, while Herod, Pilate, and Pharaoh, among others, were developed as popular comic rôles, on which the dramatist gave his imagination free rein.

In the fourteenth and fifteenth centuries traces can be found of miracle plays in about forty different districts in England, most frequently in the North and East. Many texts, most of them very corrupt, are still preserved, among them three complete cycles—those of Chester, York, and Wakefield. The Chester cycle (probably the earliest of the three) is of uncertain date, but was composed between 1350 and 1450. A complete cycle from the Fall of Satan to the Day of Judgment, it is more truly religious than the other two. The York cycle contains forty-eight plays, examination of which suggests that they may be the result of three separate periods of production at some time between 1350 and 1400, while the Wakefield plays (often known as the Towneley plays, from the name of the family which owned the manuscripts for many years) date from about 1430, and are notable for a very strong vein of realism which runs through many of them.

Stylistically the plays of these cycles are widely differing. All are in predominantly iambic verse, much of which is in elaborate metrical patterns. In the Chester cycle all are in one or other of the following patterns $aaa_4b_3ccc_4b_3$ or $aaa_4b_3aaa_4b_3$, the uniformity of the metrical pattern being a distinguishing feature of the series. At York there are many metrical forms, some of them much more elaborate than those at Chester, e.g. $ababcc_4dd_2e_2ff_3$, while many of the plays make much use of alliteration. In the Wakefield plays, the best that we have from a literary point of view, there is a considerable variety of stanza combined with a more artistic use of alliteration than is seen in the York cycle.

Of the following examples the first, from the Cornish play, *The Three Maries*, shows something of the true religious note, while the second, from the Wakefield second *Shepherds' Play*, illustrates clearly the more secular, and more truly dramatic development to be seen in many of the plays.

(1)   *Mary Magdalene.* Oh! let us hasten at once
                    For the stone is raised
                        From the tomb.
                    Lord, how will it be this night,
                    If I know not where goes
                        The head of royalty?

Mary, Mother of James. And too long we have stayed,
  My Lord is gone his way
    Out of the tomb, surely.
  Alas! my heart is sick;
  I know not indeed if I shall see him,
    Who is very God.

Mary Salome. I know truly, and I believe it,
  That he is risen up
    In this day.
  How will it be to us now,
  That we find not our Lord?
    Alas! woe! woe!

               [They sing.
            (*The Dirge*)

    Alas! mourning I sing, mourning I call,
    Our Lord is dead that bought us all.
                    The Three Maries

(2) *2nd Shepherd.* Mac, the devil in your ee, a stroke would I lend you.
   3rd Shepherd. Mac, know ye not me? By God, I could tell you.
   Mac. God look you all three, methought I had seen you.
     Ye are a fair company.
   1st Shepherd.   Can ye now moan you?
   2nd Shepherd.   Shrew, jape[1]!
     Thus late as thou goes,
     What will men suppose?
     And thou hast an ill noise[2]
      Of stealing of sheep.
   Mac. And I am true as steel all men wait,
     But a sickness I feel, that holds me full haytt,[3]
     My belly fares not well, it is out of its state.
   3rd Shepherd. Seldom lies the devil dead by the gate.
   Mac.   Therefore
     Full sore am I and ill,
     If I stand stock still;
     I eat not a nedyll[4]
      This month and more.
   1st Shepherd. How fares thy wife? By my hood, how fares she?
   Mac. Lies weltering! by the rood! by the fire, lo!
     And a house full of brood,[5] she drinks well too,
     Ill speed other good that she will do;
      But so
     Eats as fast as she can,
     And each year that comes to man,
     She brings forth a lakan,[6]
      And some years two.
     But were I not more gracious, and richer by far,
     I were eaten out of house, and of harbour,

[1] jest.   [2] repute.   [3] hot.   [4] literally 'needle'—hence 'scrap.'
[5] children.   [6] plaything.

Yet is she a foul dowse,[1] if ye come near.
There is none that trows, nor knows, a war[2]
Than ken I.

The Shepherds' Play

(*b*) THE MORALITY-PLAY registered a further advance. In such plays virtues and vices were presented on the stage as allegorical creations, often of much liveliness. Abstractions such as Justice, Mercy, Gluttony, and Vice were among the commonest characters. An important feature of this class of play is the development of characterization. It is almost crude; but it is often strongly marked and strongly contrasted, with broad farcical elements. The favourite comic character was Vice, whose chief duty was to tease the Devil.

Everyman (about 1490), perhaps the best of the morality-plays, is represented by the brief extract here given. The characters are simply but effectively drawn, and the play does not lack a noble pathos.

Everyman. O all thing faileth, save God alone;
        Beauty, Strength, and Discretion;
        For when Death bloweth his blast,
        They all run from me full fast.
Five-Wits. Everyman, my leave now of thee I take;
        I will follow the other, for here I thee forsake.
Everyman. Alas! then may I wail and weep,
        For I took you for my best friend.
Five-Wits. I will no longer thee keep;
        Now farewell, and there an end.
Everyman. O Jesu help, all hath forsaken me!
Good-Deeds. Nay, Everyman, I will bide with thee,
        I will not forsake thee indeed;
        Thou shalt find me a good friend at need.
Everyman. Gramercy, Good-Deeds; now may I true friends see;
        They have forsaken me every one;
        I loved them better than my Good-Deeds alone.
        Knowledge, will ye forsake me also?
Knowledge. Yea, Everyman, when ye to death do go:
        But not yet for no manner of danger.
Everyman. Gramercy, Knowledge, with all my heart.

(*c*) THE INTERLUDE. The last predecessor of the drama proper was the *interlude*, which flourished about the middle of the sixteenth century. It had several distinguishing points: it was a short play that introduced real characters, usually of humble rank, such as citizens and friars; there was an absence of allegorical figures;

---

[1] jade.   [2] worse.

there was much broad farcical humour, often coarse; and there were set scenes, a new feature in the English drama. It will be observed that the interlude was a great advance upon the morality-play. **John Heywood,** who lived throughout much of the sixteenth century, was the most gifted writer of the interlude. *The Four P's* is one of his best. It is composed in doggerel verse, and describes a lying-match between a Pedlar, a Palmer, a Pardoner, and a Potycary. His *Johan Johan* has much sharp wit and many clever sayings.

(*d*) THE EARLIEST DRAMAS. Our earliest dramas began to appear about 1550. Their immediate cause was the renewed study of the classical drama, especially the plays of Seneca (3 B.C.–A.D. 65), whose mannerisms were easily imitated by dramatic apprentices. The classical drama gave English drama its five acts, its set scenes, and many other features.

(1) *Tragedies.* The first tragedies had the Senecan stiffness of style, the conventional characters and plot, though in some cases they adopted the 'dumb show,' an English feature. *Gorboduc* (1562), afterwards called *Ferrex and Porrex*, written by Sackville and Norton, was most probably the earliest, and was acted at the Christmas revels of the Inner Temple. The metre was a wooden type of regular blank verse. Other plays of a similar character were *Appius and Virginia* (1563), of anonymous authorship; the *Historie of Horestes* (1567), also anonymous; *Jocasta* (1566); and Preston's *Cambyses, King of Percia* (1570). Hughes's *Misfortunes of Arthur* (1588) broke away from the classical theme, but, like the others, it was a servile imitation of classical models. Many of the plays, however, preserved a peculiarly English feature in the retention of the comic Vice.

(2) *Histories.* Along with the alien classical tragedy arose a healthier native breed of historical plays. These plays, the predecessors of the historical plays of Shakespeare, were dramatized forms of the early chronicles, and combined both tragic and comic elements. This union of tragedy and comedy was alien to the classical drama, and was the chief glory of the Elizabethan stage. Early historical plays were *The Famous Victories of Henry the Fifth* (before 1588), a mixture of crude verse and prose; *The Troublesome Raigne of King John* (before 1591); and *The Chronicle History of King Leir* (1594).

(3) *Comedies.* Though the comedies drew much upon Latin comic authors, like Plautus, and on Italian models also, they were to a great extent the growth of the English mumming element. They were composed usually in mixed verse and prose, the humour

was of a primitive character, but the best of them had verve and high good-humour, and they were distinguished by some worthy songs and ditties. *Ralph Roister Doister* (1551), by Nicholas Udall, is the earliest extant comedy. Its author was the headmaster of Eton, and the play seems to have been composed as a variant upon the Latin dramas that were the stock-in-trade of the schoolboy actors then common. Another comedy was *Gammer Gurton's Needle* (1575), the authorship of which is in dispute. The plot is slight, but the humour, though the reverse of delicate, is abundant, and the play gives interesting glimpses of contemporary English life.

We add a short scene from an early comedy. It shows the doggerel verse and the uninspired style—the homely natural speech of the time.

CHRISTIAN CUSTANCE   MARGERIE MUMBLECRUST

C. Custance. Who took thee this letter, Margerie Mumblecrust?
M. Mumble. A lusty gay bachelor took it me of trust,
    And if ye seek to him he will 'low[1] your doing.
C. Custance. Yea, but where learned he that manner of wooing?
M. Mumble. If to sue to him, you will any pains take,
    He will have you to his wife (he saith) for my sake.
C. Custance. Some wise gentleman, belike. I am bespoken:
    And I thought verily this had been some token
    From my dear spouse Gawin Goodluck, whom when him please,
    God luckily send home to both our hearts' ease.
M. Mumble. A joyly man it is, I wot well by report,
    And would have you to him for marriage resort;
    Best open the writing, and see what it does speak.
C. Custance. At this time, nurse, I will neither read ne break.
M. Mumble. He promised to give you a whole peck of gold.
C. Custance. Perchance, lack of a pint when it shall be all told.
M. Mumble. I would take a gay rich husband, an I were you.
C. Custance. In good sooth, Madge, e'en so would I, if I were thou.
    But no more of this fond talk now, let us go in,
    And see thou no more move me folly to begin.
    Nor bring me no more letters for no man's pleasure,
    But thou know from whom.
M. Mumble. I warrant ye shall be sure.

Ralph Roister Doister

Summary. We can thus see the material that lay to the hand of Shakespeare and his fellows. It was almost of uniform development and of ancient and diverse origin; it was frequently coarse and childish, but its material was abundant and vital. The time was at

---

[1] allow, approve.

hand, and so was the genius of the master to give this vast body a shape and impulse. Almost in a day, after centuries of slow ripening, the harvest came, with a wealth and excellence of fruition that is one of the marvels of our literature.

THE DEVELOPMENT OF LITERARY STYLE

1. Poetry. In English poetry there was a marked decadence in style. In the works of Lydgate, Skelton, and Hawes the metres often became mere doggerel; there was little trace of real poetical imagination and phrasing; and the actual vocabulary is not striking. Compared with that of Chaucer, their work seems childish and inept. Many reasons have been advanced to explain this rapid collapse. The most obvious one is the sheer lack of talent: there is nobody to carry on the Chaucerian tradition with any great credit. Another cause is probably the rapid decay of the use of the final *e*, which in the metre of Chaucer was an item of much moment. Pronunciation of English was rapidly changing, and the new race of poets had not the requisite skill to modify the old metre to suit the new age. In Scottish poetry there is much activity. To a large extent the Scottish poets were content to imitate the mannerisms of Chaucer. In one respect, indeed, they carried his descriptive-allegorical method too far, and made their poems lifeless. Such were the less successful poems of Dunbar (the *Goldyn Targe*), and of Gawin Douglas (*The Palice of Honour*). On the other hand, peculiar Scottish features were not lacking: a breezy and sometimes vulgar humour, bred, perhaps, of the ruder folk and the bleaker air; a robust independence and common sense; a note of passion and pathos; and a sense of the picturesque both in nature and in man. We find such features illustrated, wholly or in part, in such poems as Lyndsay's *Satyre of the Thrie Estaitis*, in Dunbar's *Lament for the Makaris*, and at the close of Henryson's *Testament of Cresseid*.

2. Prose. The development of prose style was marked by a number of small improvements which in the aggregate represented no small advance. Unlike the poetry of the time, prose suffered from no retrogression. There was a perceptible increase in skill, due to increased practice; there was a growing perception of the beauties of rhythm and cadence; and, in the purely formal sense, there was the appearance of the prose paragraph. Above all, the chief prose styles—the ornate, the middle, and the plain—are appearing faintly but perceptibly. With their arrival the rapid development of English prose is assured.

CHAPTER V

THE AGE OF ELIZABETH

TIME-CHART OF THE CHIEF AUTHORS

The thick line indicates the period of active literary production.

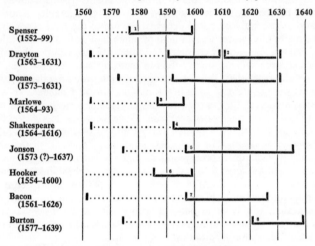

	1560	1570	1580	1590	1600	1610	1620	1630	1640

Spenser (1552–99)

Drayton (1563–1631)

Donne (1573–1631)

Marlowe (1564–93)

Shakespeare (1564–1616)

Jonson (1573 (?)–1637)

Hooker (1554–1600)

Bacon (1561–1626)

Burton (1577–1639)

[1] *The Shepheards Calender* (1579).
[3] *Tamburlaine* (1587).
[5] *Every Man in his Humour* (1598).
[7] *Essays* (1597).
[2] *Poly-Olbion* (1612).
[4] *Love's Labour's Lost* (1590–94).
[6] *Of the Laws of Ecclesiastical Polity* (1594).
[8] *Anatomy of Melancholy* (1621).

THE HISTORICAL BACKGROUND (1550–1630)

This chapter introduces the reign of Elizabeth, sees it reach its climax and conclusion, and then witnesses the literary decline under the first of the Stuarts. The dominating features of the period can be conveniently summarized under two heads.

1. Settlement. In politics the English nation was attaining to a state of stability. Dynastic problems, though still nerve-racking, did not cause open warfare, and the union of the Crowns finally set at rest the ancient quarrel between Scotland and England. This settlement was all for the good of literature.

2. Expansion. In our history this is perhaps the most remarkable epoch for the expansion of both mental and geographical horizons. New knowledge was pouring in from the East, and new worlds were opening in the West. The great voyagers, whose exploits were chronicled in the immortal pages of **Hakluyt (1552 (?)–1616)**, brought home both material and intellectual treasures from beyond the "still-vexed Bermoothes," as Shakespeare called them. It is unnecessary to enlarge upon the important effects which these revolutionary discoveries produced in literature.

LITERARY FEATURES OF THE AGE

1. The New Classicism. By the time of Elizabeth the Renaissance, as it was called, had made itself strongly felt in England. In particular, there was an ardent revival in the study of Greek, which brought a dazzling light into many dark places of the intellect. The new passion for classical learning, in itself a rich and worthy enthusiasm, became quite a danger to the language. In all branches of literature Greek and Latin usages began to force themselves upon English, with results not wholly beneficial. It said much for the native sturdiness of English that, after a brief and vexed period of transition, it threw off the worst effects of this deadening pressure. English did not emerge unscathed from the contest. But, applied to this slight extent, the new classical influences were a great benefit: they tempered and polished the earlier rudeness of English literature.

2. Abundance of Output. After the lean years of the preceding epoch the prodigal issue of the Elizabethan age is almost embarrassing. As we have pointed out, the historical situation encouraged a healthy production. The interest shown in literary subjects is quite amazing to a more chastened generation. Pamphlets and treatises were freely written; much abuse, often of a personal and scurrilous character, was indulged in; and literary questions became almost of national importance. To a great extent the controversies of the day were puerile enough, but at least they indicated a lively interest in the literature of the period.

3. The New Romanticism. The romantic quest is for the remote, the wonderful, and the beautiful. All these desires were abundantly fed during the Elizabethan age, which is our first and greatest romantic epoch. On the one hand, there was the revolt against the past, whose grasp was too feeble to hold in restraint the lusty youth of the Elizabethan age; on the other, there was a daring and resolute spirit of adventure in literary as well as in other regions; and, most important of all, there was an unmistakable buoyancy and freshness in the strong wind of the spirit. It was the ardent youth of English literature, and the achievement was worthy of it.

4. The Drama. The bold and critical attitude of the time was in keeping with the dramatic instinct, which is analytic and observant. Hence, after the long period of incubation detailed in the last chapter, the drama made a swift and wonderful leap into maturity.

Yet it had still many early difficulties to overcome. The actors themselves were at variance, so much so that outrageous brawls were frequent. On more than one occasion between 1590 and 1593 the theatres were closed owing to disturbances caused by the actors. In 1594 the problem was solved by the licensing of two troupes of players, the Lord Chamberlain's (among whom was Shakespeare) and the Lord Admiral's. Another early difficulty the drama had to face was its fondness for taking part in the quarrels of the time—for example, in the burning 'Marprelate' controversy. Owing to this meddling the theatres were closed in 1589. Already, also, a considerable amount of Puritanical opposition was declaring itself. The most important anti-dramatic book of the day was Gosson's virulent *Schoole of Abuse* (1579), to which Sidney replied with his *Apologie for Poetrie* (about 1580).

In spite of such early difficulties, the drama reached the splendid consummation of Shakespeare's art; but before the period closed decline was apparent.

5. Poetry. Though the poetical production was not quite equal to the dramatic, it was nevertheless of great and original beauty. As can be observed from the disputes of the time, the passion for poetry was absorbing, and the outcome of it was equal to expectation.

6. Prose. For the first time prose rises to a position of first-rate importance. The dead weight of the Latin tradition was passing away; English prose was acquiring a tradition and a universal application; and so the rapid development was almost inevitable.

7. Scottish Literature. A curious minor feature of the age was the disappearance of Scottish literature after its brief but remarkable appearance in the previous age. At this point it took to ground, and did not reappear till late in the eighteenth century.

POETRY

I. EDMUND SPENSER (1552–99)

1. His Life. From a passage in one of his sonnets it seems clear that Spenser was born in 1552; and from another passage, in his *Prothalamion*, we can deduce that he was born in London. His parentage is unknown; but, though Spenser claimed kinship with the noble branch of the Spenser family, it is fairly certain that he was a member of some northern plebeian branch. He was educated at the Merchant Taylors' School (just founded in 1560) and at Cambridge. He left Cambridge in 1576, and for a few years his movements are unknown, though he probably spent the time in the North of England. He comes into view in London during the year 1579 as a member of the famous literary circle surrounding Sir Philip Sidney and his uncle the Earl of Leicester. Sidney patronized Spenser, introducing him to the Queen and encouraging him in his imitation of the classical metres. In 1580 Sidney's patronage bore fruit, for Spenser was appointed secretary to Lord Grey de Wilton, who had just been appointed Lord-Deputy of Ireland.

In Ireland Spenser remained for eighteen years, serving the English Government in more than one capacity, and seeing his share of the rebellion, outrage, and misery that afflicted the unhappy land. In the end his services were requited by the grant of Kilcolman Castle, near Limerick, and an estate of three thousand acres. In 1589 he visited London to publish the first three books of *The Faerie Queene*. After remaining in London for nearly two years he returned to Ireland; married an Irishwoman (1594); revisited London in 1595, bringing a second instalment of his great work; and once more returned to Kilcolman, which was ultimately burnt down (1598) during one of the sporadic rebellions that tormented the country. One of his children perished in the fire. A ruined and disappointed man, he repaired to London, where in the next year he died, "for lack of bread," according to the statement of Ben Jonson.

2. His Minor Poems. The first of the poems that have descended to us is *The Shepheards Calender* (1579). The title, adopted from a popular compilation of the day, suggests the contents: a series of twelve eclogues, one for each month of the year. Each eclogue, as is common with the species, is in dialogue form, in which the stock pastoral characters, such as Cuddie, Colin Clout, and Perigot, take part. Skilful literary exercises on classical pastoral models, the pieces show great metrical dexterity. Their style is deliberately archaic, in keeping with the rustic characters, Spenser adopting the dialect and alliteration of the Midlands and North.

A volume of miscellaneous poems, including *The Ruins of Time*, *The Tears of the Muses*, *Mother Hubberd's Tale*, and *The Ruins of Rome*, appeared in 1591; in 1595 he published his *Amoretti*, eighty-eight Petrarchan sonnets celebrating the progress of his love; *Epithalamion*, a magnificent ode, rapturously jubilant, written in honour of his marriage; and *Colin Clout's come home Again*, somewhat wordy, but containing some interesting personal details. In 1596 appeared his *Four Hymns* and *Prothalamion*, the latter not so fine as the great ode of the previous year.

Spenser's shorter poems illustrate his lyrical ability, which is moderate in quality. His style is too diffuse and ornate to be intensely passionate; but, especially in the odes, he can build up sonorous and commanding measures which by their weight and splendour delight both mind and ear. To a lesser extent, as in *Mother Hubberd's Tale*, the shorter poems afford him scope for his satirical bent, which can be sharp and censorious.

We quote from the *Epithalamion*, which stands at the summit of English odes:

> Open the temple gates unto my love,
> Open them wide that she may enter in,
> And all the posts adorn as doth behove,
> And all the pillars deck with girlands trim,
> For to receive this Saint with honour due,
> That cometh into you.
> With trembling steps, and humble reverence,
> She cometh in, before the Almighty's view;
> Of her, ye virgins, learn obedience,
> When so ye come into those holy places,
> To humble your proud faces.
> Bring her up to the high altar, that she may
> The sacred ceremonies there partake,
> The which do endless matrimony make;
> And let the roaring organs loudly play
> The praises of the Lord in lively notes;
> The whiles, with hollow throats,
> The choristers the joyous anthem sing,
> That all the woods may answer, and their echo ring.

3. Prose. In addition to his letters, which are often interesting and informative, Spenser left one longish prose work, a kind of State paper done in the form of a dialogue. Called *A View of the Present State of Ireland* (1594), it gives Spenser's views on the settlement of the Irish question. His opinions are exceedingly hostile to the Irish, and his methods, if put in force, would amount to pure terrorism. The style of the pamphlet is quite undistinguished.

4. The Faerie Queene. In spite of the variety and beauty of his shorter poems, *The Faerie Queene* is by far the most important of Spenser's works.

(a) *Dates of Composition.* The work appeared in instalments. In 1589 Spenser crossed to London and published the first three books; in 1596 the second three followed; and after his death two cantos and two odd stanzas of Book VII appeared. It was reported that more of the work perished in manuscript during the fire at Kilcolman, but this is not certain.

(b) *The Plot.* The construction of the plot is so obscure ("clowdily enwrapped in Allegorical devises," as Spenser himself says) that he was compelled to write a preface, in the form of a letter to his friend Sir Walter Ralegh, explaining the scheme underlying the whole. There were to be twelve books, each book to deal with the adventures of a particular knight, who was to represent some virtue. As we have the poem, the first book deals with the Knight of the Red Cross, representing Holiness; the second with Temperance; the third with Chastity; the fourth with Friendship; and so on. The chief of all the twelve is Prince Arthur, who is to appear at critical moments in the poem, and who in the end is to marry Gloriana, the Queen of 'Faerie-londe.' The plot is exceedingly leisurely and elaborate; it is crammed with incident and digression; and by the fifth book it is palpably weakening. It is therefore no misfortune (as far as the plot is concerned) that only half of the story is finished.

(c) *The Allegory.* With its twelve divisions, each of which bears many smaller branches, the allegory is the most complex in the language. Through the story three strands keep running, twisting and untwisting in a manner both baffling and delightful. (1) There are the usual characters, poorly developed, of the Arthurian and classical romance, such as Arthur, Merlin, Saracens, fauns, and satyrs. (2) There are the allegorized moral and religious virtues, with their counterparts in the vices: Una (Truth), Guyon (Temperance), Duessa (Deceit), Orgoglio (Pride). (3) Lastly, there is the strongly Elizabethan political-historical-religious element, also strongly allegorized. For example, Gloriana is Elizabeth, Duessa may be Mary, Queen of Scots, Archimago may be the Pope, and Artegal (Justice) is said to be Lord Grey. Sometimes the allegory winds and multiplies in a bewildering fashion. Elizabeth, who is grossly and shamelessly flattered in the poem, is sometimes Gloriana, sometimes Belphœbe, or Britomart, or Mercilla. It is very ingenious, but it retards the story.

(*d*) *The Style.* No one, however, goes to Spenser for a story; one goes to steep the senses in the rich and voluptuous style. The style has its weaknesses: it is diffuse, and lacks judgment; it is weak in 'bite' and in sharpness of attack; and it is misty and unsubstantial. But for beauty long and richly wrought, for subtle and sustained melody, for graphic word-pictures, and for depth and magical colour of atmosphere the poem stands supreme in English. Its imitators, good and bad, are legion. Milton, Keats, and Tennyson are among the best of them, and its influence is still powerful.

(*e*) *The Technique.* To the formal part of the poem Spenser devoted the intelligence and care of the great artist. (1) First of all, he elaborated an archaic diction: "he writ no language," said Ben Jonson, who did not like the diction. When the occasion demanded it he invented words or word-forms; for example, he uses *blend* for *blind*, *kest* for *cast*, and *vilde* for *vile*. The result is not perhaps ideal, but on the whole it suits the old-world atmosphere of the poem. (2) He introduced the Spenserian stanza, which ever since has been one of the most important measures in the language. Longer than the usual stanza, but shorter than the sonnet, as a unit it is just long enough to give an easy pace to the slowly pacing narrative. The complicated rhymes of the stanza suit the interwoven harmonies of the style; and the long line at the end acts either as a dignified conclusion or as a longer and stronger link with the succeeding stanza. (3) The alliteration, vowel-music, and cadence are cunningly fashioned, adroitly developed, and sumptuously appropriate. In these last respects Spenser is almost peerless.

We add two brief extracts to illustrate some features of the style. The reader should analyse the stanza and observe the graphical power and the melodic beauty.

(1)   And more to lulle him in his slumber soft,
    A trickling streame from high rock tumbling downe,
    And ever-drizling raine upon the loft,
    Mixt with a murmuring winde, much like the sowne
    Of swarming Bees, did cast him in a swowne.
    No other noyse, nor peoples troublous cryes,

As still are wont t'annoy the walled towne,
Might there be heard; but carelesse Quiet lyes
Wrapt in eternall silence farre from enimyes.

(2) At last he came unto a gloomy glade,
Covered with boughes and shrubs from heavens light,
Whereas he sitting found in secret shade
An uncouth, salvage, and uncivile wight,[1]
Of griesly hew and foule ill favour'd sight;
His face with smoke was tand, and eies were bleard,
His head and beard with sout were ill bedight,
His cole-blacke hands did seeme to have ben seard
In smythes fire-spitting forge, and nayles like clawes appeard.

His yron cote, all overgrowne with rust,
Was underneath enveloped with gold;
Whose glistring glosse, dark'ned with filthy dust,
Well yet appeared to have beene of old
A worke of rich entayle[2] and curious mould,
Woven with antickes and wyld ymagery;
And in his lap a masse of coyne he told,
And turned upside downe, to feede his eye
And covetous desire with his huge threasury.

And round about him lay on every side
Great heapes of gold that never could be spent;
Of which some were rude owre,[3] not purifide
Of Mulcibers devouring element;
Some others were new driven, and distent[4]
Into great Ingowes[5] and to wedges square;
Some in round plates withouten moniment;
But most were stampt, and in their metal bare
The antique shapes of kings and kesars straunge and rare.

II. JOHN DONNE (1573–1631)

1. His Life. Donne, the son of a wealthy merchant, was born in London. His parents were Roman Catholics, and he was educated in their faith before going on to Oxford and Cambridge. He entered the Inns of Court in 1592, where he mingled wide reading with the life of a dissolute man-about-town. In these years (1590–1601) he wrote his *Satires*, the *Songs and Sonets*, and the *Elegies*, but, though widely circulated in manuscript, they were not published until 1633, after his death. Donne seemed ambitious for a worldly career, but this was ruined by a runaway marriage with the niece of his patron, after which he spent several years in suitorship

[1] Mammon.   [2] carving.   [3] ore.   [4] hammered.   [5] ingots.

of the great. In 1615 he entered the Anglican Church, after a severe personal struggle, and in 1621 became Dean of St Paul's, which position he held until his death in 1631. He was the first great Anglican preacher.

2. His Poetry. Donne was the most independent of the Elizabethan poets, and revolted against the easy, fluent style, stock imagery, and pastoral conventions of the followers of Spenser. He aimed at reality of thought and vividness of expression. His poetry is forceful, vigorous, and, in spite of faults of rhythm, often strangely harmonious.

His cynical nature and keenly critical mind led him to write satires, such as *Of the Progres of the Soule* (1601). They were written in the couplet form, later to be adopted by Dryden and then by Pope, and show clearly, often coarsely and crudely, Donne's dissatisfaction with the world around him.

His love poems, the *Songs and Sonets*, were written in the same period, and are intense and subtle analyses of all the moods of a lover, expressed in vivid and startling language, which is colloquial rather than conventional. A vein of satire runs through these too. The rhythm is dramatic and gives the illusion of excited talk. He avoids the smooth, easy patterns of most of his contemporaries, preferring to arrest attention rather than to lull the senses. His great variety of pace, his fondness for echoing sounds, his deliberate use of shortened lines and unusual stress contribute also to this effect of vivid speech, swift thought, and delicate emotional responses. He is essentially a psychological poet whose primary concern is feeling. His poems are all intensely personal and reveal a powerful and complex being. Among the best known and most typical of the poems of this group are *Aire and Angels*, *A Nocturnall upon S. Lucies day*, *A Valediction: forbidding mourning*, and *The Extasie*. The following stanzas from *A Valediction: of weeping* give some idea of Donne's use of striking imagery, and of the excitement of his rhythms:

> Let me powre forth
> My teares before thy face, whil'st I stay here,
> For thy face coines them, and thy stampe they beare,
> And by this Mintage they are something worth,
>   For thus they bee
>   Pregnant of thee;
> Fruits of much griefe they are, emblemes of more,
> When a teare falls, that thou falst which it bore,
> So thou and I are nothing then, when on a divers shore

> On a round ball
> A workeman that hath copies by, can lay
> An Europe, Afrique, and an Asia,
> And quickly make that, which was nothing, *All*,
> > So doth each teare,
> > Which thee doth weare,
> A globe, yea world by that impression grow,
> Till thy teares mixt with mine doe overflow
> This world, by waters sent from thee, my heaven dissolved so.

His religious poetry was written after 1610, and the greatest, the
nineteen *Holy Sonets*, and the lyrics such as *A Hymn to GOD THE
FATHER*, after his wife's death in 1617. They too are intense and
personal, and have a force unique in this class of literature. They
reveal the struggle in his mind before taking orders in the Anglican
Church, his horror of death, and the fascination which it had for
him, his dread of the wrath of God, and his longing for God's love.
They are the expression of a deep and troubled soul. In them are
found the intellectual subtlety, the scholastic learning, and the
'wit' and 'conceits' of the love poems. We give here one of the
Holy Sonets. It has the intensely personal note and the concern
with death which are so typical of Donne's religious works.

> What if this present were the worlds last night?
> Marke in my heart, O Soule, where thou dost dwell,
> The picture of Christ crucified, and tell
> Whether that countenance can thee affright,
> Teares in his eyes quench the amasing light,
> Blood fills his frownes, which from his pierc'd head fell.
> And can that tongue adjudge thee unto hell,
> Which pray'd forgivenesse for his foes fierce spight?
> No, no; but as in my idolatrie
> I said to all my profane mistresses,
> Beauty, of pitty, foulnesse only is
> A signe of rigour: so I say to thee,
> To wicked spirits are horrid shapes assign'd,
> This beauteous forme assures a pitious minde.

"He affects the metaphysics," said Dryden of Donne, and the
term 'metaphysical' has come to be applied to Donne and the group
of poets who followed him. Strictly the word means "based on
abstract general reasoning," but the poetry of Donne shows more
than this. It reveals a depth of philosophy, a subtlety of reasoning,
a blend of thought and devotion, a mingling of the homely and the
sublime, the light and the serious, which make it full of variety and
surprise. It is to these many characteristics, so widely differing yet

often brought together in a startling fusion, that the general term 'wit' is applied.

Probably the most distinctive feature of the metaphysicals is their imagery, which, in Donne, is almost invariably unusual and striking, often breath-taking, but sometimes far-fetched and fantastic. From his wide range of knowledge he draws many remarkable comparisons; parted lovers are like the legs of a pair of compasses, love is a spider "which transubstantiates all," his sick body is a map, his physicians cosmographers, and Death his "South-west discoverie."

3. His Prose. Donne's prose work is considerable both in bulk and achievement. *The Pseudo-Martyr* (1610) was a defence of the oath of allegiance, while *Ignatius His Conclave* (1611) was a satire upon Ignatius Loyola and the Jesuits. The best introduction to Donne's prose is, however, through his *Devotions* (1614), which give an account of his spiritual struggles during a serious illness. They have many of the qualities of his poetry, are directly personal, reveal a keen psychological insight, and the preoccupation with death and his own sinfulness which is also to be seen in his *Holy Sonets*. The strong power of his imagination and the mask of learning, which are features of the work, cannot hide the basic underlying simplicity of Donne's faith and his longing for rest in God. His finest prose works are his *Sermons*, which number about 160. In seventeenth-century England the sermon was a most important influence, and the powerful preacher in London was a public figure capable of wielding great influence. We possess great numbers of these sermons, which show the form to have a highly developed literary technique based on a well-established oratorical tradition. Donne's sermons, of which the finest is probably *Death's Duell* (1630), contain many of the features of his poetry. Intensely personal, their appeal is primarily emotional, and Donne seems to have used a dramatic technique which had a great hold on his audiences. They reveal the same sort of imagery, the same unusual wit, the keen analytical mind, and the preoccupation with morbid themes which exist in his poetry, and they are full of the same out-of-the-way learning.

We quote below the ending of his last sermon, *Death's Duell* (1630), "called by his Majesties household the doctors owne funerall sermon." Note the power of the dramatic appeal to the emotions, and the final peace so often sought for by Donne—rest in God.

There now hangs that sacred Body upon the Crosse, rebaptized in his owne teares and sweat, and embalmed in his owne blood alive. There are those bowells of compassion, which are so conspicuous, so manifested, as that you may see them through his wounds. There those glorious eyes grew faint in their light: so as the Sun, ashamed to survive them, departed with his light too. And then that Sonne of God, who was never from us, and yet had now come a new way unto us in assuming our nature, delivers that soule (which was never out of his Fathers hands) by a new way, a voluntary emission of it into his Fathers hands; For though to this God our Lord, belong'd these issues of death, so that considered in his owne contract, he must necessarily die, yet at no breach or battery, which they had made upon his sacred Body, issued his soule, but emisit, he gave up the Ghost, and as God breathed a soule into the first Adam, so this second Adam breathed his soule into God, into the hands of God. There wee leave you in that blessed dependancy, to hang upon him that hangs upon the Crosse, there bath in his teares, there suck at his woundes, and lie down in peace in his grave, till hee vouchsafe you a resurrection, and an ascension into that Kingdome, which hee hath purchas'd for you, with the inestimable price of his incorruptible blood. Amen.

4. His Influence. Although Donne was far too much of an individual for any succeeding poet to resemble him very closely, his influence is strongly felt in both the courtly and religious poetry of the following generation, and the 'metaphysical' school embraces such names as **George Herbert (1593–1633)**, **Richard Crashaw (1612 (?)–49)**, **Henry Vaughan (1621 (?)–95)**, **Robert Herrick (1591–1674)**, **Thomas Carew (1594 (?)–1639 (?))** and, in some respects the finest of all of them, **Andrew Marvell (1621–78)**. Yet all of these, while reflecting directly or indirectly the influence of Donne, differ in many important respects from their great predecessor.

OTHER POETS

1. Sir Thomas Wyatt (1503 (?)–42) was descended from an ancient Yorkshire family which adopted the Lancastrian side in the Wars of the Roses. He was educated at Cambridge, and, entering the King's service, was entrusted with many important diplomatic missions. In public life his principal patron was Thomas Cromwell, after whose death he was recalled from abroad and imprisoned (1541). Though subsequently acquitted and released, he died shortly afterward.

Wyatt's poems are short but fairly numerous. His ninety-six love poems appeared posthumously (1557) in a compendium called *Tottel's Miscellany*. The most noteworthy are thirty-one sonnets, the first in English. Ten of them were translations from Petrarch, while all were written in the Petrarchan form, apart from the couplet ending, which Wyatt introduced. Serious and reflective in tone, the sonnets show some stiffness of construction and a metrical uncertainty indicative of the difficulty Wyatt found in the new form. Yet their conciseness represents a great advance on the prolixity and uncouthness of much earlier poetry. Wyatt was also responsible for the most important introduction of the personal note into English poetry, for, though following his models closely, he wrote of his own experiences. His epigrams, songs, and rondeaux are lighter than the sonnets, and they also reveal a care and elegance that were typical of the new romanticism. His *Satires* are composed in the Italian *terza rima*, once again showing the direction of the innovating tendencies.

2. **Henry Howard, Earl of Surrey (1516 (?)–47)**, whose name is usually associated in literature with that of Wyatt, was the younger poet of the two. He was the son of Thomas Howard, Earl of Surrey, and when his father became Duke of Norfolk (1524) the son adopted the courtesy title of Earl of Surrey. Owing largely to the powerful position of his father, Surrey took a prominent part in the Court life of the time, and served as a soldier both in France and Scotland. He was a man of reckless temper, which involved him in many quarrels, and finally brought upon him the wrath of the ageing and embittered Henry VIII. He was arrested, tried for treason, and beheaded on Tower Hill.

About 1542 Surrey began his literary relations with Wyatt, who was his elder by fifteen years. His poems, which were the recreations of his few leisure moments, and which were not published till after his death, appeared (1557) along with Wyatt's in *Tottel's Miscellany*. They are chiefly lyrical, and include a few sonnets, the first of their kind, composed in the English or Shakespearian mode—an arrangement of three quatrains followed by a couplet. There are in addition a large number of love-poems. A greater metrical accuracy and a skilful variation of the cæsura make them smoother and more polished than Wyatt's poems. His most important poem was published separately: *Certain Bokes of Virgiles Æneis turned into English Meter* (1557). Though the actual translation is of no outstanding merit, the form is of great significance; it is blank verse, rather rough and frigid, and showing a fondness for the end-stopped line, but the earliest forerunner of the great achievements of Shakespeare and Milton.

In the development of English verse Surrey represents a further stage: a higher poetical faculty, increased ease and refinement, and the introduction of two metrical forms of capital importance—the English form of the sonnet, and blank verse. We add a specimen of the earliest English blank verse. It is wooden and uninspired, but as a beginning it is worthy of attention.

> But now the wounded quene with heavie care
> Throwgh out the vaines doth nourishe ay the plage,
> Surprised with blind flame, and to her minde
> Gan to resort the prowes of the man
> And honor of his race, whiles in her brest
> Imprinted stake his wordes and forme of face,
> Ne to her lymmes care graunteth quiet rest.
> The next morowe with Phœbus lampe the erthe
> Alightned clere, and eke the dawninge daye
> The shadowe darke gan from the pole remove.

3. **Thomas Sackville, Earl of Dorset (1536–1608)**, was born at Buckhurst, in Sussex, and was educated both at Oxford and Cambridge. He was called to the Bar, entered Parliament, took part in many diplomatic and public missions, and was created Lord Buckhurst in 1566. His plain speaking did not recommend itself to Elizabeth, and for a time he was in disgrace. He was restored to favour, created Lord High Treasurer, and made Earl of Dorset in 1604.

In bulk Sackville's poetry does not amount to much, but in merit it is of much consequence. Two poems, *The Induction* and *The Complaynt of Henry, Duke of Buckingham*, appeared in a miscellany called the *Myrroure for Magistrates* (1563). Both are composed in the rhyme royal stanza, are melancholy and elegiac in spirit and archaic in language, but have a severe nobility of thought and a grandeur of conception and of language quite unknown since the days of Chaucer. The poems undoubtedly assisted Spenser in the composition of *The Faerie Queene*.

Sackville collaborated with Norton in the early tragedy of *Gorboduc* (see p. 88).

We add a few stanzas from *The Induction* to illustrate the sombre graphical power of the poem:

> And next in order sad, Old Age wee found:
> His beard all hoare, his eyes hollow and blind;
> With drouping chere still poring on the ground,
> As on the place where nature him assigned
> To rest, when that the Sisters had untwyned
> His vitall thred, and ended with their knyfe
> The fleting course of fast declyning lyfe:

There heard wee him with broke and hollow plaint
Rew with him selfe his end approching fast,
And all for nought his wretched mind torment
With sweete remembraunce of his pleasures past,
And fresh delytes of lusty youth forewast;[1]
Recounting which, how would hee sob and shriek,
And to be yong again of Jove beseeke!

.   .   .   .   .   .

Crookbackt he was, tooth-shaken, and blere-eyed;
Went on three feete, and sometyme crept on foure;
With olde lame bones, that rattled by his syde;
His scalp all pilled,[2] and hee with eld forlore,
His withred fist still knocking at Deaths dore;
Fumbling and driveling as hee drawes his breath;
For briefe, the shape and messenger of Death.

4. George Gascoigne (1525 (?)–77) is another of the founders of the great Elizabethan tradition. He was born in Bedfordshire, educated at Cambridge, and became a lawyer. Later in life he entered Parliament.

In addition to a large number of elegant lyrics, he composed one of the first regular satires in the language, *The Steele Glas* (1576). This poem has the additional importance of being written in blank verse. Among his other numerous works we can mention his tragedy *Jocasta* (1566), a landmark in the growth of the drama (see p. 88); his *Supposes* (1566), the first prose comedy, which was the basis of Shakespeare's *Taming of the Shrew*; and *Certayne notes of Instruction concerning the making of verse or ryme in English* (1575), our first treatise on poetry. In ease and versatility Gascoigne is typical of the best early Elizabethan miscellaneous writers.

5. Sir Philip Sidney (1554–86) was the chief of an elegant literary coterie, and exercised an influence which was almost supreme during his short life. He was the most commanding literary figure before the prime of Spenser and Shakespeare. Born in Kent of an aristocratic family, he was educated at Shrewsbury and Oxford, and then travelled widely. He took a brilliant part in the military-literary-courtly life common with the young nobles of the time, and at the early age of thirty-two was mortally wounded at Zutphen when assisting the Dutch against the Spaniards.

Like the best of the Elizabethans, Sidney was successful in more than one branch of literature, but none of his works was published until after his death. His finest achievement was his connected

---

[1] utterly wasted.   [2] peeled.

sequence of 108 love sonnets, the *Astrophel and Stella* (published 1591). These sonnets, which owe much to Petrarch and Ronsard in tone and style, place Sidney as the greatest Elizabethan sonneteer except Shakespeare. Written to his 'mistress,' Lady Penelope Rich, though dedicated to his wife, they reveal a true lyric emotion couched in a language delicately archaic. In form Sidney usually adopts the Petrarchan octave (*abbaabba*), with variations in the sestet which include the English final couplet.

His pastoral romance, the *Arcadia* (published incomplete 1590, and complete 1598), is an intricate love-story, embodying the ideals of medieval chivalry, so congenial to Sidney's own spirit. The story is diffuse and involved, and many secondary love-stories interwoven with the main one distract attention. The characters are vague and idealized. The style, in both its strength and its weaknesses, is that of a poet writing prose—melodious, picturesque, rather artificial, and ornamental. The story contains a number of fine lyrics.

The *Apologie for Poetrie* (published 1595) has taken its place among the great critical essays in English. It is an answer to Gosson's *Schoole of Abuse* (see p. 72), an abusive Puritan pamphlet, and, in clear, manly English, defends poetry as greater than history or philosophy, and as an art which instructs by pleasing. In assessing Sidney's condemnation of the attitude of contemporary England towards poetry and his attacks on the English drama, it is important to remember that he wrote before most of the great poets and all the great dramatists of the age of Elizabeth had published their work.

6. **Michael Drayton (1563–1631)** represents the later epoch of Elizabethan literature. He was born in Warwickshire, was attached to a noble family as tutor, came to London about 1590, and for the remainder of his long life was busy in the production of his many poems.

His first book, metrical translations from the scriptures, was called *The Harmonie of the Church* (1591); then followed a number of long historical poems which include *England's Heroicall Epistles* and *The Barons' Wars* (1603). His *Poly-Olbion* is the most important of his longer poems, and belongs to a later period of his career. It is a long, careful, and tedious description of the geographical features of England, interspersed with tales, and written in alexandrines. His shorter poems, such as his well-known poem on Agincourt, and his verse tales and pastorals, such as *The Man in the Moon* and *Nymphidia*, are skilful and attractive. Drayton is rarely an inspired poet—the wonderful sonnet beginning "Since there's no help" is perhaps his only poem in which we feel inspiration flowing freely—but he is painstaking, versatile, and sometimes (as in *Nymphidia*) delightful.

7. Thomas Campion (1567–1620) was born in London, educated at Cambridge, studied law in Gray's Inn, but ultimately became a physician (1606). He wrote some masques that had much popularity, but his chief claim to fame lies in his attractive lyrics, most of which have been set to music composed partly by the poet himself. His best-known collections of songs were *A Booke of Ayres* (1601), *Songs of Mourning* (1613), and *Two Bookes of Ayres* (1612). Campion had not the highest lyrical genius, but he had an ear skilful in adapting words to tunes, the knack of sweet phrasing, and a mastery of complicated metres. He is one of the best examples of the accomplished poet who, lacking the highest inspiration of poetry, excels in the lower technical features.

The lyric of Campion's that we add is typical not only of his own grace and melody, but also of the later Elizabethan lyrics as a whole. The ideas, in themselves somewhat forced and fantastic, are expressed with great felicity.

> There is a garden in her face,
>   Where roses and white lilies blow;
> A heavenly paradise is that place,
>   Wherein all pleasant fruits do flow;
> There cherries grow which none may buy,
> Till "Cherry-ripe" themselves do cry.
>
> Those cherries fairly do enclose
>   Of orient pearl a double row,
> Which when her lovely laughter shows,
>   They look like rose-buds fill'd with snow;
> Yet them nor peer nor prince can buy,
> Till "Cherry-ripe" themselves do cry.
>
> Her eyes like angels watch them still;
>   Her brows like bended bows do stand,
> Threat'ning with piercing frowns to kill
>   All that attempt with eye or hand
> Those sacred cherries to come nigh,
> Till "Cherry-ripe" themselves do cry.

8. Phineas Fletcher (1582–1650) and **Giles Fletcher (1588 (?)–1623)** are usually associated in the history of literature. They were brothers, were both educated at Cambridge, and both took holy orders. Both were poetical disciples of Spenser.

Phineas Fletcher's chief poem is *The Purple Island, or The Isle of Man* (1633), a curious work in twelve cantos describing the human body in an allegorical-descriptive fashion. There is much digression, which gives the poet some scope for real poetical passages. In its plan the poem is cumbrous and artificial, but it contains many descriptions in the Spenserian manner. The stanza is a further modification of the Spenserian, which it resembles except for its omission of the fifth and seventh lines.

Giles's best-known poem is *Christ's Victorie and Triumph* (1610), an epical poem in four cantos. The title of the poem sufficiently suggests its subject; in style it is glowingly descriptive, imaginative, and is markedly ornate and melodious in diction. It is said partly to have inspired Milton's *Paradise Regained*. The style is strongly suggestive of Spenser's, and the stanza conveys the same impression, for it is the Spenserian stanza lacking the seventh line.

The Fletchers are imitators, but imitators of high quality. They lack the positive genius of their model Spenser, but they have intensity, colour, melody, and great metrical artistry.

9. Samuel Daniel (1562–1619) was born near Taunton in Somerset, educated at Oxford, and became tutor to the son of the Countess of Pembroke. For a time (1599) he was Poet Laureate, and was made (1603) Master of the Queen's Revels by James I.

His poems include a sonnet-series called *Delia* (1592), a romance called *The Complaynt of Rosamond* (1592), some long historical poems, such as *The Civil Wars* (1595), and a large number of masques, of which *The Queenes Wake* (1610) and *Hymen's Triumph* (1615) are the most important. His best work appears in his sonnets, which, composed in the English manner, carry on the great tradition of Sidney, Spenser, and Shakespeare. His *Defence of Ryme* (1602 (?)), a fine piece of English criticism, argues with restraint and clarity the futility of the objections made to rhyme by such works as Campion's *Observations in the Art of English Poesy* (1602). In it Daniel claims that English poets need not be governed by the practice of the classics, and that each literature is entitled to its own ways. In his longer poems he is prosy and dull, though the masques have pleasing touches of imagination.

10. The **poetical miscellanies** which abound during this period are typical of the time. By the very extravagance of their titles they reveal the enthusiasm felt for the revival of English poetry. Each volume consists of a collection of short pieces by various poets, some well known and others unknown. Some of the best poems are anonymous. Among much that is almost worthless, there are happily preserved many poems, sometimes by unknown poets, of great and enduring beauty. We have already drawn attention (p. 81) to *Tottel's Miscellany* (1557), which contained, among other poems, the pieces of Wyatt and Surrey. Other volumes are *The Paradyse of Daynty Devises* (1576), *A Handefull of Pleasant Delites* (1584), *The Phœnix Nest* (1593), and *The Passionate Pilgrim* (1599). The last book contains poems by Shakespeare, Marlowe, and Ralegh. The most important of the miscellanies is *England's Helicon* (1600), which surpasses all others for fullness, variety, and excellence of contents.

PRE-SHAKESPEARIAN DRAMA

The Influence of Seneca. In the last chapter we gave a summary of the rise of the English drama from the liturgical plays to the earliest Tudor times. But English tragedy, at any rate, was not to develop from the miracle play, but from the classical models of Seneca. The Latin dramatist, of the first century A.D., writing for a sophisticated, aristocratic audience, had produced tragedies notable for the horrors which filled them, for their exaggerated character-drawing, their violently rhetorical language coupled with emotional hyperboles, and a wealth of epigram. His influence was first felt in the Latin plays of the universities, especially Cambridge, where, between 1550 and 1560, the records become very Senecan, and his appeal was so strong that, by 1581, he had become the first classical dramatist to have all his works translated into English. From the universities, by way of the Inns of Court, the Senecan influence reached the popular stage, while many of the coming dramatists, such as Marlowe, Peele, and Greene, studied at the universities when this influence was strong. *Gorboduc* (1562) was the first English play in Senecan form, and was followed by Gascoigne's *Jocasta* (1566) and Hughes's *Misfortunes of Arthur* (1588), both on the Senecan model. Most important of the Senecan plays was Kyd's *The Spanish Tragedie* (*c.* 1589), which was followed by Daniel's *Cleopatra* (*c.* 1593) and *Philotas* (1604). With Kyd began the tradition of the 'Revenge' play, many features of which are to be seen in Shakespeare's *Hamlet*, and in the work of late Elizabethan or Jacobean dramatists like Webster, Tourneur, and Marston. Other Shakespearian plays showing a strong Senecan influence are *Richard III* and *Macbeth*.

THE UNIVERSITY WITS

These young men, nearly all of whom were associated with Oxford and Cambridge, did much to found the Elizabethan school of drama. They were all more or less acquainted with each other, and most of them led irregular and stormy lives. Their plays had several features in common.

(a) There was a fondness for heroic themes, such as the lives of great figures like Mohammed and Tamburlaine.

(b) Heroic themes needed heroic treatment: great fullness and variety; splendid descriptions, long swelling speeches, the handling of violent incidents and emotions. These qualities, excellent when held in restraint, only too often led to loudness and disorder.

(c) The style also was 'heroic.' The chief aim was to achieve strong and sounding lines, magnificent epithets, and powerful declamation. This again led to abuse and to mere bombast, mouthing, and in the worst cases to nonsense. In the best examples, such as in Marlowe, the result is quite impressive. In this connexion it is to be noted that the best medium for such expression was blank verse, which was sufficiently elastic to bear the strong pressure of these expansive methods.

(d) The themes were usually tragic in nature, for the dramatists were as a rule too much in earnest to give heed to what was considered to be the lower species of comedy. The general lack of real humour in the early drama is one of its most prominent features. Humour, when it is brought in at all, is coarse and immature. Almost the only representative of the writers of real comedies is Lyly, who in such plays as *Campaspe* (1584), *Endymion* (1592), and *The Woman in the Moone* gives us the first examples of romantic comedy.

1. George Peele (*c.* **1558–98**) was born in London, educated at Christ's Hospital and at Oxford, and became a literary hack and free-lance in London. His plays include *The Araygnement of Paris* (*c.* 1584), a kind of romantic comedy; *The Famous Chronicle of King Edward the First* (1593), a rambling chronicle-play; *The Old Wives' Tale* (1591–94), a clever satire on the popular drama of the day; and *The Love of King David and Fair Bethsabe* (published 1599). Peele's style can be violent to the point of absurdity; but he has his moments of real poetry; he can handle his blank verse with more ease and variety than was common at the time; he is fluent; he has humour and a fair amount of pathos. In short, he represents a great advance upon the earliest drama, and is perhaps one of the most attractive among the playwrights of the time.

We give a short example to illustrate the poetical quality of his blank verse:

> *David.* Now comes my lover tripping like the roe,
> And brings my longings tangled in her hair.
> To 'joy her love I'll build a kingly bower,
> Seated in hearing of a hundred streams,
> That, for their homage to her sovereign joys,
> Shall, as the serpents fold into their nests,
> In oblique turnings wind the nimble waves
> About the circles of her curious walks,
> And with their murmur summon easeful sleep
> To lay his golden sceptre on her brows.
> *The Love of King David and Fair Bethsabe*

2. **Robert Greene (1558–92)** wrote much and recklessly, but his plays are of sufficient merit to find a place in the development of the drama. He was born at Norwich, educated at Cambridge (1575) and at Oxford (1588), and then took to a literary life in London. If all accounts, including his own, are true, his career in London must have taken place in a sink of debauchery. He is said to have died, after an orgy in a London ale-house, "of a surfeit of pickle herringe and Rennish wine."

Here we can refer only to his thirty-five prose tracts, which are probably the best of his literary work, for they reveal his intense though erratic energy, his quick, malicious wit, and his powerful imagination. His plays number four: *Alphonsus, King of Aragon* (1587), an imitation of Marlowe's *Tamburlaine*; *Frier Bacon and Frier Bongay* (1589), easily his best, and containing some fine representations of Elizabethan life; *Orlando Furioso* (*c.* 1591), adapted from an English translation of Ariosto; and *The Scottish Historie of James the Fourth* (acted in 1592), not a 'historical' play, but founded on an imaginary incident in the life of the King. Greene is weak in creating characters, and his style is not of outstanding merit; but his humour is somewhat genial in his plays, and his methods less austere than those of the other tragedians.

3. **Thomas Nash (1567–1601)** was born at Lowestoft, educated at Cambridge, and then (1586) went to London to make his living by literature. He was a born journalist, but in those days the only scope for his talents lay in pamphleteering. He took an active part in the political and personal questions of the day, and his truculent methods actually landed him in gaol (1600). He finished Marlowe's

Dido, but his only surviving play is *Summer's Last Will and Testament* (1592), a satirical masque. His *The Unfortunate Traveller, or the Life of Jacke Wilton* (1594), a prose tale, is important in the development of the novel (see p. 278).

4. **Thomas Lodge** (*c*. 1558–1625) was the son of a Lord Mayor of London, was educated in London and at Oxford, and studied law. He deserted his legal studies, took to a literary career, and is said to have been an actor at one time.

His dramatic work is small in quantity. He probably collaborated with Shakespeare in *Henry VI*, and with other dramatists, including Greene. The only surviving play entirely his own is *The Woundes of Civile War*, a kind of chronicle-play. His pamphleteering was voluminous and energetic. His prose romances constitute his greatest claim to fame. Though his prose is elaborate in the euphuistic style of Lyly, and the tales often tedious, they contain exquisite lyrics. The most famous of his romances is *Rosalynde: Euphues Golden Legacie* (1590), which Shakespeare followed very closely in the plot of *As You Like It*.

5. **Thomas Kyd** (1558–94) is one of the most important of the University Wits. Very little is known of his life. He was born in London, educated (probably) at Merchant Taylors' School, adopted a literary career, and became secretary to a nobleman. He became acquainted with Marlowe, and that brilliant but sinister spirit enticed him into composing "lewd libels" and "blasphemies." Marlowe's sudden death saved him from punishment for such offences; but Kyd was imprisoned and tortured. Though he was afterwards released, Kyd soon died under the weight of "bitter times and privy broken passions."

Much of this dramatist's work has been lost. Of the surviving plays *The Spanish Tragedie* (about 1585) is the most important. Its horrific plot, involving murder, frenzy, and sudden death, gave the play a great and lasting popularity. There is a largeness of tragical conception about the play that resembles the work of Marlowe, and there are touches of style that dimly foreshadow the great tragical lines of Shakespeare. The only other surviving play known to be Kyd's is *Cornelia* (1593), a translation from the French Senecan, Garnier, but his hand has been sought in many plays including *Soliman and Perseda* (1588), the *First Part of Jeronimo* (1592), an attempt, after the success of *The Spanish Tragedie*, to write an introductory play to it, and Shakespeare's *Titus Andronicus*.

6. **Christopher Marlowe** (1564–93) was the greatest of the pre-

Shakespearian dramatists. He was born at Canterbury and educated there and at Cambridge. He adopted literature as a profession and became attached to the Lord Admiral's players. His combination of inquiring mind and dissolute life led him to be charged with atheism and immorality, and only his sudden death in a tavern brawl enabled him to avoid arrest.

Marlowe's plays, all tragedies, were written within five years (1587–92). He had no bent for comedy, and the comic parts found in some of his plays are always inferior and may be by other writers. As a dramatist Marlowe had serious limitations, though it is possible to trace a growing sense of the theatre through his plays. Only in *Edward II* does he show any sense of plot construction, while his characterization is of the simplest, and lacks the warm humanity of Shakespeare's. All the plays, except *Edward II*, revolve around one figure drawn in bold outlines. This character shows no complexity or subtlety of development and is the embodiment of a single idea. Indeed, to appreciate Marlowe properly we must put aside conventional ideas of the drama and view his plays as the representation of a poetic vision, the typically Renaissance quest for power—*l'amour de l'impossible*—combined with the quest for beauty. In *Tamburlaine the Great* the shepherd seeks the "sweet fruition of an earthly crown," in *The Jew of Malta* Barabbas seeks "infinite riches in a little room," while the quest of *Doctor Faustus* is for more than human knowledge. Each of the plays has behind it the driving force of this vision, which gives it an artistic and poetic unity. It is, indeed, as a poet that Marlowe excels. Though not the first to use blank verse in English drama, he was the first to exploit its possibilities and make it supreme. His verse is notable for its burning energy, its splendour of diction, its sensuous richness, its variety of pace, and its responsiveness to the demands of varying emotions. Full of bold primary colours, his poetry is crammed with imagery from the classics, from astronomy and from geography, an imagery barbaric in its wealth and splendour. Its resonance and power led Ben Jonson to coin the phrase "Marlowe's mighty line," but its might has often obscured its technical precision and its admirable lucidity and finish. At times Marlowe degenerates into bombast, and there is little attempt before *Edward II* to suit the speech to the speaker, but his blank verse is unequalled by any of his contemporaries except Shakespeare.

Tamburlaine the Great (1587), centred on one inhuman figure, is on a theme essentially undramatic, in that the plot allows no possibility of complication. The play is episodic and lacking any cohesion save the poetic one already referred to. Yet it contains much of Marlowe's best blank verse. Its sequel, *The Second Part of Tamburlaine the Great* (1588), is inferior to its predecessor. It contains still less plot and far more bombast. *The Jew of Malta* (1589) has two fine, economically handled opening acts, but deteriorates later when the second villain, Ithamore, enters. The later sections may, however, be by another hand (possibly Heywood's). The play is also of interest as showing Marlowe's attention turning towards the conventional Machiavellian villain. *Edward II* (1591) shows the truest sense of the theatre of all his plays. Its plot is skilfully woven, and the material, neatly compressed from Holinshed's *Chronicles*, shows a sense of dramatic requirements new in his plays, and, indeed, in English historical drama. The play has less poetic fervour than some of the others, and its hero is not great enough to be truly tragic, but it works up to a fine climax of deep pathos. In its multiplicity of 'living' characters and lack of bombast it stands apart from the other plays. *Doctor Faustus* (probably 1592, and not, as was long supposed, 1588–89) has a good beginning, and an ending which is Marlowe's supreme achievement, but the comic scenes in the middle are poor and may be by another hand. The play contains some interesting survivals of the miracle plays in the conversations of the Good and Evil Angels. *The Tragedy of Dido, Queen of Carthage* (*c.* 1593) is an inferior piece, in which Nash shared, and *The Massacre at Paris* (1593) is unfinished.

We give below a typical example of Marlowe's 'mighty line' as Tamburlaine boasts of his doings to his prisoner, and then part of the superb ending of *Doctor Faustus*, when Faustus realizes the near approach of his departure to Hell.

> The god of war resigns his room to me,
> Meaning to make me general of the world:
> Jove, viewing me in arms, looks pale and wan,
> Fearing my power should pull him from his throne:
> Where'er I come the Fatal Sisters sweat,
> And grisly Death, by running to and fro,
> To do their ceaseless homage to my sword:
> And here in Afric, where it seldom rains,
> Since I arriv'd with my triumphant host,
> Have swelling clouds, drawn from wide-gaping wounds,
> Been oft resolv'd in bloody purple showers,
> A meteor that might terrify the earth,
> And make it quake at every drop it drinks:
> Millions of souls sit on the banks of Styx,

Waiting the back-return of Charon's boat;
Hell and Elysium swarm with ghosts of men
That I have sent from sundry foughten fields
To spread my fame through hell and up to heaven.
Tamburlaine the Great

Stand still, you ever-moving spheres of heaven,
That time may cease, and midnight never come;
Fair Nature's eye, rise, rise again, and make
Perpetual day; or let this hour be but
A year, a month, a week, a natural day,
That Faustus may repent and save his soul!
O lente, lente currite, noctis equi!
The stars move still, time runs, the clock will strike,
The devil will come, and Faustus must be damn'd.
O, I'll leap up to my God!—Who pulls me down?—
See, see, where Christ's blood streams in the firmament!
One drop would save my soul, half a drop: ah, my Christ!—
Ah, rend not my heart for naming of my Christ!
Yet will I call on him: O, spare me, Lucifer!—
Where is it now? 'tis gone: and see, where God
Stretcheth out his arm, and bends his ireful brows!
Mountains and hills, come, come, and fall on me,
And hide me from the heavy wrath of God!
Doctor Faustus

WILLIAM SHAKESPEARE (1564–1616)

1. His Life. In considering the life of Shakespeare we have at our disposal a fair number of facts; but on these facts the industry of commentators has constructed an additional mass of great magnitude and complexity. It is therefore the duty of the historian with only a limited space at his disposal to keep his eye steadily upon the established facts and, without being superior or disdainful, to turn toward speculation or surmise, however ingenious or laborious, a face of tempered but obdurate scepticism.

The future dramatist, as we learn from the church records, was baptized in the parish church at Stratford-on-Avon on April 26, 1564. He may have been born on April 23, St George's Day, which happens also to be the date of his death in 1616. His father, John Shakespeare, was a burgess of the town, and seems to have followed the occupations of a butcher, a glover, and a farmer. The boy may have attended the grammar school of the town, though Ben Jonson, himself a competent scholar, affirmed that Shakespeare knew "small Latin and less Greek." From various entries in the town records it is clear that John Shakespeare, after flourishing for a time, fell on evil days, and the son may have assisted in the paternal butcher's shop. A bond dated November 28, 1582, affords clear evidence of Shakespeare's marriage on that date to a certain "Anne Hatthwey of Stratford." As at this time Shakespeare was only eighteen, and (as appears from the inscription on her monument) the bride was eight years older, speculation has busied itself over the somewhat ill-assorted match.

In 1584 Shakespeare left his native town. Why he did so is not known. The most popular explanation, which appeared after his death, is that he was convicted of poaching on the estate of a local magnate, Sir Thomas Lucy, and that he fled to escape the consequences. Then, until 1592, when he reappears as a rising actor, Shakespeare disappears from view. During this period he is said to have wandered through the country, finally coming to London, where he performed various menial offices, including that of holding horses at the stage-door. On the face of them such tales are not improbable, but they grew up when the dramatist had become a half-mythical figure. The most recent attempt (1949) to bridge this gap in Shakespeare's life is a suggestion that he may have spent much of the time in the Low Countries on service with the armies of the Earl of Leicester.

In 1592 Robert Greene, in a carping book called *A Groatsworth of Wit*, mentions "an upstart crow . . . in his own conceit the only Shakescene in a country."[1] This reference, most probably a gibe at Shakespeare, shows that he is now important enough to merit abuse. In 1595 his name appears on the payroll of the Lord Chamberlain's company of actors, who performed at the Court. This company, one of the most important in the town, also played in the provinces, especially during the plague of 1603, in the Shoreditch Theatre till it was demolished in 1598, in the Globe Theatre, and finally (after 1608) in the Blackfriars. During this period, as can be inferred from his purchases of property both in London and Stratford, Shakespeare was prospering in worldly affairs. He was a competent but not a great actor; tradition asserts that his chief parts were of the type of Adam in *As You Like It* and the Ghost in *Hamlet*. His chief function was to write dramas for his company, and the fruit of such labour was his plays.

About 1610 Shakespeare left London for Stratford, where he stayed at New Place, a house that he had bought in 1597. He may have written his last plays there; but it is likely that his connexion with his company of actors ceased when the Globe Theatre was

[1] The passage containing this reference appears on pp. 123-124.

burned down during a performance of *Henry VIII* in 1613. His will, a hurriedly executed document, is dated March 25, 1616. His death occurred a month later, April 23.

2. His Poems. Shakespeare's two long narrative poems were among the earliest of his writings. *Venus and Adonis* (1593), composed in six-line stanzas, showed decided signs of immaturity. Its subject was in accordance with popular taste; its descriptions were heavily ornamented and conventional; but it contained individual lines and expressions of great beauty. Already the hand of Shakespeare was apparent. *The Rape of Lucrece* (1594), in rhyme royal stanzas, is of less merit. As was common in the poetry of that day, the action was retarded with long speeches, but there were Shakespearian touches all through. In 1599 a collection of verse called *The Passionate Pilgrim* appeared with Shakespeare's name on the title-page. Of the constituent poems only one, taking its name from the title of the book, has been decidedly fixed as Shakespeare's. It consists of some sonnets of unequal merit.

In 1609 a collection of Shakespeare's sonnets was printed by Thomas Thorpe, who dedicated the volume to a certain "Mr W. H." as being "the onlie begetter" of the sonnets. Speculation has exhausted itself regarding the identity of "Mr W. H." The most probable explanation is that he was William Herbert, Earl of Pembroke. The sonnets themselves consist of 154 numbers, which are all composed in the English form of the sonnet, that of three quatrains clenched with a couplet. The entire collection falls into two groups of unequal size, divided, at number cxxvi, by a poem of six couplets. The first group consists largely of a series of cryptic references, often passionately expressed, to his friendship with a youth, apparently of high rank, who may be, and probably is, the mysterious "Mr W. H." The second group, also obscurely phrased, is taken up with reproaches addressed to his mistress, "a black beauty," whose hair is like "black wires." The identity of this 'Dark Lady of the Sonnets' is one of the romances of our literature. She may be, as is often asserted, Mary Fitton, who happened to be fair; but she probably did not exist at all. Among the numerous sonneteers of the time it was a common trick to apostrophize a lovely and fickle mistress, as a rule quite imaginary, and it may be that Shakespeare was following the custom of the period.

Concerning the literary quality of the sonnets there can be no dispute. In the depth, breadth, and persistency of their passion, in their lordly but never overweening splendour of style, and, above all, in their mastery of a rich and sensuous phraseology, they are unique. Byron once remarked that the tissue of poetry cannot be all brilliance, any more than the midnight sky can be entirely stars; but several of the sonnets (for example, xxx, xxxiii, lv, lxxi, cxvi) are thick clusters of starlight; and all through the series the frequency of lovely phrasing is great indeed. We quote one sonnet that is nearly perfect; the second that we give, after a splendid opening, deteriorates toward the conclusion.

(1) Let me not to the marriage of true minds
  Admit impediments. Love is not love
  Which alters when it alteration finds,
  Or bends with the remover to remove:
  O, no! it is an ever-fixed mark,
  That looks on tempests and is never shaken;
  It is the star to every wandering bark,
  Whose worth's unknown, although his height be taken.
  Love's not Time's fool, though rosy lips and cheeks
  Within his bending sickle's compass come;
  Love alters not with his brief hours and weeks,
  But bears it out even to the edge of doom.
   If this be error, and upon me proved,
   I never writ, nor no man ever loved.

Sonnet cxv

(2) When in the chronicle of wasted time
  I see descriptions of the fairest wights,
  And beauty making beautiful old rime,
  In praise of ladies dead and lovely knights,
  Then, in the blazon of sweet beauty's best,
  Of hand, of foot, of lip, of eye, of brow,
  I see their antique pen would have expressed
  Even such a beauty as you master now.
  So all their praises are but prophecies
  Of this our time, all you prefiguring;
  And, for they looked but with divining eyes,
  They had not skill enough your worth to sing:
   For we, which now behold these present days,
   Have eyes to wonder, but lack tongues to praise.

Sonnet cv

Shakespeare's later poetical work is worthily represented in the numerous lyrics that are scattered through the plays. It is not quite certain how much of the songs is original; it is almost certain that Shakespeare, like Burns, used popular songs as the basis of many of his lyrics. As they stand, however, the lyrics show a great range of accomplishment, most of it of the highest quality. It varies from the nonsense-verses in *Hamlet* and *King Lear* to the graceful perfection of Ariel's "Full fathom five"; from the homely rusticity of

"It was a lover and his lass" to the scholarly ease and wry humour of "O mistress mine"; it includes such gems as the willow-song in *Othello*, "Take, O take those lips away," in *Measure for Measure*, and the noble dirge, "Fear no more the heat o' the sun," in *Cymbeline*. If Shakespeare had not been our greatest dramatist, he would still be numbered among our greatest lyrical poets.

3. His Plays. Concerning the plays that are usually accepted as being Shakespeare's, almost endless discussion has arisen. In the following pages we shall indicate the main lines of Shakespearian criticism.

(*a*) THE ORDER OF THE PLAYS. All the manuscripts of the plays have perished; Shakespeare himself printed none of the texts; and though sixteen of them appeared singly in quarto form during his lifetime, they were all unauthorized editions. It was not till 1623, seven years after his death, that the First Folio edition was printed. It contained thirty-six dramas (*Pericles* was omitted), and these are now universally accepted as Shakespeare's. In the Folio edition the plays are not arranged chronologically, nor are the dates of composition given. The dates of the separate Quartos are registered at Stationers' Hall, but these are the dates of the printing. With such scanty evidence to hand to assign the order of the plays, a task fundamental to all discussion of the dramas, much ingenious deductive work has been necessary. The evidence can be divided into three groups.

(1) *Contemporary References*. With one important exception such are of little value. The exception occurs in a book by Francis Meres (1565–1647), an Elizabethan schoolmaster. In *Palladis Tamia, Wit's Treasury* (1598), he gives a list of contemporary authors, among whom is Shakespeare. Meres mentions twelve of Shakespeare's plays, along with "his *Venus and Adonis*, his *Lucrece*, and his sugred sonnets among his private friends." This valuable reference supplies us with a list of plays which were written before 1598.

(2) *Internal References*. In the course of the plays there occur passages, more or less obscure, that can be traced to contemporary events. Such are the references to "the imperial votaress" (perhaps Elizabeth) in *A Midsummer Night's Dream*, to "the two-fold balls and treble sceptres" (perhaps the Union of 1603) in *Macbeth*, and to a famous eclipse of the moon in the *Sonnets*. Owing to the invariable obscurity of the passages, this class of evidence should be used cautiously, but unfortunately it has been made the basis of much wild theorizing.

(3) *The Literary Evidence.* Soberly examined, and taken strictly in conjunction with the statement of Meres and the dates of the Quartos (when these are available), this type of evidence is by far the most reliable. We can examine the workmanship of the plays in such matters as the construction of the plot, the force and originality of the characters, and, most significant of all, the style and metrical dexterity of the writing. Broadly speaking, in the earlier plays, such as *Love's Labour's Lost*, Shakespeare's style is carefully studied and relatively ornamental, while the thought content is often too slight for the elaboration with which it is dressed out. In the middle period of his writing, as in *Julius Cæsar*, he attains an almost perfect balance between thought and expression, while the later plays, such as *The Winter's Tale*, show a preponderance of ideas over words. The sentences are full of closely packed ideas elliptically compressed; there are abrupt changes of thought, and the style is rich in imagery. Generally there is a greater proportion of rhyme in the early plays (e.g., *A Midsummer Night's Dream*) and more prose in the middle plays, while alexandrines, feminine endings, and enjambment are more freely used in the later works. Shakespeare's use of pauses is also significant. Mid-line pauses become more frequent as his technique develops, while the cæsura after the first and fourth foot of a line is a relatively late feature of his style.

(*b*) THE DATES OF THE PLAYS. The following table, which to a large extent is the outcome of generations of discussion and contention, represents a moderate or average estimate of the dates of the plays. It can be only an approximate estimate, for no exact decision can ever be possible.

1591–92	1595
1 *Henry VI*	*A Midsummer Night's Dream*
2 *Henry VI*	*The Two Gentlemen of Verona*
3 *Henry VI*	*King John*
1593	**1596**
Richard III	*Richard II*
The Comedy of Errors	*The Merchant of Venice*
1594	**1597**
Titus Andronicus	1 *Henry IV*
The Taming of the Shrew	
Love's Labour's Lost	**1598**
Romeo and Juliet	2 *Henry IV*
	Much Ado about Nothing

1599	1605
Henry V	*Macbeth*
Julius Cæsar	*King Lear*

1600	1606
The Merry Wives of Windsor	*Antony and Cleopatra*
As You Like It	*Coriolanus*

1601	1607
Hamlet	*Timon of Athens* (unfinished)
Twelfth Night	1608
	Pericles (in part)

1602	1609
Troilus and Cressida	*Cymbeline*
All's Well that Ends Well	

1603	1610
(Theatres closed)	*The Winter's Tale*
	1611
	The Tempest

1604	1613
Measure for Measure	*Henry VIII* (in part)
Othello	

(c) CLASSIFICATION OF THE PLAYS. It is customary to group the plays into sets that to some extent traverse the order given above.

(1) *The Early Comedies.* In these immature plays the plots are less original, the characters less finished, and the style lacks the power of the mature Shakespeare. They are full of wit and word play, usually put into the mouths of young gallants, but often the humour is puerile and the wit degenerates into mere verbal quibbling. Of this type are *The Comedy of Errors*, *Love's Labour's Lost*, and *The Two Gentlemen of Verona*.

(2) *The English Histories.* These plays show a rapid maturing of Shakespeare's technique. He now begins to busy himself with the developing character, such as Richard II or Prince Hal. He shows clearly the importance attached in his day to the throne, and the contemporary desire for stable government. Figures like Falstaff illustrate his increasing depth of characterization, and the mingling

of low life with chronicle history is an important innovation. The plays in this group, to which belong *Richard II*, 1 *Henry IV*, 2 *Henry IV*, and *Henry V*, contain much more blank verse than those of the earlier group.

(3) *The Mature Comedies*. Here is the fine flower of Shakespeare's comic genius. The comic spirit manifests itself at many levels—the sophisticated wit of Beatrice and Benedick or the clowning of Dogberry and Verges in *Much Ado about Nothing*; the jovial good humour of Sir Toby Belch in *Twelfth Night*; the lighter clowning of Launcelot Gobbo in *The Merchant of Venice*; the urbane worldly-wise humour of Touchstone in *As You Like It*. The plays are full of vitality, contain many truly comic situations, and reveal great warmth and humanity. In this group there is much prose.

(4) *The Sombre Plays*. In this group are *All's Well that Ends Well*, *Measure for Measure*, and *Troilus and Cressida*. Though comedies in the sense that the chief characters do not die, their tone is sombre and tragic. They reflect a cynical, disillusioned attitude to life, and a fondness for objectionable characters and situations. In them Shakespeare displays a savage desire to expose the falsity of romance and to show the sordid reality of life.

(5) *The Great Tragedies*. *Hamlet*, *Othello*, *Macbeth*, and *King Lear* are the climax of Shakespeare's art. In intensity of emotion, depth of psychological insight, and power of style they stand supreme.

(6) *The Roman Plays*. These are based on North's translation of Plutarch's *Lives*, and, though written at fairly wide intervals, are usually considered as a group. *Julius Cæsar*, contemporary with the English histories, shows the same concern with political security, and in its depth of character study is approaching the great tragedies. *Antony and Cleopatra* and *Coriolanus* follow the great tragic period, and, while the former, in soaring imagination and tragic power, is truly great, both of them show some relaxation of tragic intensity.

(7) *The Last Plays*. A mellowed maturity is the chief feature of this group, which contains *Cymbeline*, *The Winter's Tale*, and *The Tempest*. The creative touch of the dramatist, making living men out of figment, is abundantly in view; the style is notable and serenely adequate; and with the ease of the master the author thoroughly subdues the metre to his will. No more fitting conclusion —rich, ample, and graciously dignified—could be found to round off the work of our greatest literary genius than these plays of reconciliation and forgiveness.

4. His Prose. Shakespeare's prose appears all through the plays, sometimes in passages of considerable length. In the aggregate the amount is quite large. In the comedies the amount is considerable, but the proportion is apt to diminish in the later plays. With regard to the prose, the following points should be observed: (*a*) it is the common vehicle for comic scenes, though used too in serious passages (one of which is given below); (*b*) it represents the common speech of the period, and some of it, as can be seen in *Hamlet*, is pithy and bracing. Even the rather stupid clowning that often takes place cannot altogether conceal its beauty.

We quote a passage from *Hamlet*. The style is quite modern in phrase, and the beauty and grace of it are far beyond the ordinary standard of Shakespeare's literary contemporaries.

> I have of late—but wherefore I know not—lost all my mirth, forgone all custom of exercises; and indeed it goes so heavily with my disposition that this goodly frame, the earth, seems to me a sterile promontory; this most excellent canopy, the air, look you, this brave o'erhanging firmament, this majestical roof fretted with golden fire, why, it appears no other thing to me than a foul and pestilent congregation of vapours. What a piece of work is man! How noble in reason! how infinite in faculty! in form and moving how express and admirable! in action how like an angel! in apprehension how like a god! the beauty of the world! the paragon of animals! And yet, to me, what is this quintessence of dust?
>
> *Hamlet*

5. Features of his Plays. The extent, variety, and richness of the plays are quite bewildering as one approaches them. All that can be done here is to set down in order some of the more obvious of their qualities.

(*a*) *Their Originality.* In the narrowest sense of the term, Shakespeare took no trouble to be original. Following the custom of the time, he borrowed freely from older plays (such as *King Leir*), chronicles (such as Holinshed's), and tales (such as *The Jew*, the part-origin of *The Merchant of Venice*). To these he is indebted chiefly for his plots; but in his more mature work the interest in the plot becomes subordinate to the development of character, the highest achievement of the dramatist's art. He can work his originals deftly: he can interweave plot within plot, as in *A Midsummer Night's Dream*; he can solidify years of history into five acts, as in *King John* and *Antony and Cleopatra*; and, as in *Macbeth*, he makes the dust of history glow with the spirit of his imagination.

(*b*) *Characters.* (1) In sheer *prodigality of output* Shakespeare is unrivalled in literature. From king to clown, from lunatic and demi-devil to saint and seer, from lover to misanthrope—all are revealed with the hand of the master. Surveying this multitude, one can only cry out, as Hamlet does, "What a piece of work is man!"

(2) Another feature of Shakespeare's characterization is his *objectivity*. He seems indifferent to good and evil; he has the eye of the creator, viewing bright and dismal things alike, provided they are apt and real. In his characters vice and virtue commingle, and the union is true to the common sense of humanity. Thus the villain Iago is a man of resolution, intelligence, and fortitude; the murderer Claudius (in *Hamlet*) shows affection, wisdom, and fortitude; the peerless Cleopatra is narrow, spiteful, and avaricious; and the beast Caliban has his moments of ecstatic vision. The list could be extended almost without limit, but these examples must serve.

(3) Hence follows the *vital force* that resides in the creations of Shakespeare. They live, move, and utter speech; they are rounded, entire, and capable. Very seldom, and that almost entirely in the earlier plays, he uses the wooden puppets that are the stock-in-trade of the inferior dramatist. Of such a kind are some of his 'heavy' fathers, like Egeus (in *A Midsummer Night's Dream*), and his sentimental lovers, like Orsino (in *Twelfth Night*). Yet, as a rule, in the hands of Shakespeare the heavy father can develop into such living beings as the meddlesome old bore Polonius (in *Hamlet*), and the tediously sentimental lover can become the moody and headstrong Romeo, or the virile and drolly humorous Orlando (in *As You Like It*).

(c) *Metre*. As in all the other features of his work, in metre Shakespeare shows abnormal range and power. Some features of his metrical development have already been discussed (see p. 99); we go on now to amplify these points. In the earlier plays the blank verse is regular in beat and pause; there is a fondness for the stopped and rhymed couplet; and in a few cases the couplet passes into definite stanza-formation in a manner suggestive of the early pre-Shakespearian comedies.

> *Lysander.* Why should you think that I should woo in scorn?
> Scorn and derision never come in tears:
> Look, when I vow, I weep; and vows so born,
> In their nativity all truth appears.
> How can these things in me seem scorn to you,
> Bearing the badge of faith to prove them true?
> *A Midsummer Night's Dream*

As Shakespeare becomes more sure of his instrument the verse increases in ease and dexterity; the cadence is varied; the pause is shifted to any position in the line. And before he finishes he has utterly subdued the metre to his will. In the last line of the extract now given every foot is abnormal:

> *Lear.* And my poor fool is hanged! No, no, no life!
> Why should a dog, a horse, a rat, have life,
> And thou no breath at all? Thou'lt come no more,
> Never, never, never, never, never!
>
> *King Lear*

(*d*) *Style.* For lack of a better name we call Shakespeare's style Shakespearian. One can instantly recognize it, even in other authors, where it is rarely visible. It is a difficult, almost an impossible, matter to define it. There is aptness and quotability in it: sheaves of Shakespeare's expressions have passed into common speech. To a very high degree it possesses sweetness, strength, and flexibility; and above all it has a certain inevitable and final felicity that is the true mark of genius.

The following specimen shows the average Shakespearian style, if such a thing exists at all. It is not extremely elevated or poetical, but it is strong, precise, and individual.

> If thou didst ever hold me in thy heart,
> Absent thee from felicity awhile,
> And in this harsh world draw thy breath in pain,
> To tell my story.
>
> *Hamlet*

Such a style moves easily into the highest flights of poetry:

> (1)   That strain again! it had a dying fall:
> O! it came o'er my ear like the sweet sound
> That breathes upon a bank of violets,
> Stealing and giving odour.
>
> *Twelfth Night*

> (2) *Cleopatra.*   Come, thou mortal wretch,
> [*To the asp, which she applies to her breast.*
> With thy sharp teeth this knot intrinsicate
> Of life at once untie; poor venomous fool,
> Be angry, and despatch. . . .
> *Charmian.*   O eastern star!
> *Cleopatra.*   Peace, peace!
> Dost thou not see my baby at my breast,
> That sucks the nurse asleep?
>
> *Antony and Cleopatra*

Or it can plumb the depths of terror and despair. The following are the words of a condemned wretch shivering on the brink of extinction:

> Ay, but to die, and go we know not where;
> To lie in cold obstruction and to rot;
> This sensible warm motion to become
> A kneaded clod; and the delighted spirit
> To bathe in fiery floods, or to reside
> In thrilling region of thick-ribbed ice;
> To be imprisoned in the viewless winds,
> And blown with restless violence round about
> The pendant world; or to be worse than worst
> Of those that lawless and incertain thoughts
> Imagine howling: 'tis too horrible!
>
> *Measure for Measure*

The style lends itself to the serenely ecstatic reverie of the sage:

> Our revels now are ended. These our actors,
> As I foretold you, were all spirits and
> Are melted into air, into thin air:
> And, like the baseless fabric of this vision,
> The cloud-capped towers, the gorgeous palaces,
> The solemn temples, the great globe itself,
> Yea, all which it inherit, shall dissolve,
> And, like this insubstantial pageant faded,
> Leave not a rack behind. We are such stuff
> As dreams are made on, and our little life
> Is rounded with a sleep.
>
> *The Tempest*

It can express, on the other hand, the bitterest cynicism:

> But, man, proud man,
> Drest in a little brief authority,
> Most ignorant of what he's most assured,
> His glassy essence, like an angry ape,
> Plays such fantastic tricks before high heaven
> As make the angels weep.
>
> *Measure for Measure*

Or, in prose, Shakespeare can put into words the artless pathos of the humble hostess of the inn:

> *Hostess.* Nay, sure, he's not in hell: he's in Arthur's bosom, if ever man went to Arthur's bosom. A' made a finer end and went away an it had been any christom child; a' parted even just between twelve and one, even at the turning o' the tide; for after I saw him fumble with the sheets and play with flowers and smile upon his

fingers' ends, I knew that there was but one way; for his nose was
as sharp as a pen, and a' babbled of green fields. "How now, Sir
John?" quoth I: "what, man! be of good cheer." So a' cried out
"God, God, God!" three or four times.

Henry V

Shakespeare can rant, and often rants badly; but at its best his
ranting glows with such imaginative splendour that it becomes a
thing of fire and majesty:

> His legs bestrid the ocean; his reared arm
> Crested the world; his voice was propertied
> As all the tuned spheres, and that to friends;
> But when he meant to quail and shake the orb,
> He was as rattling thunder. For his bounty,
> There was no winter in 't, an autumn 'twas
> That grew the more by reaping; his delights
> Were dolphin-like, they showed his back above
> The element they lived in; in his livery
> Walked crowns and crownets, realms and islands were
> As plates dropped from his pocket.

Antony and Cleopatra

With such a style as this Shakespeare can compass the world of
human emotion, and he does so.

6. Summary. "He was the man," said Dryden, "who of all
modern, and perhaps ancient poets, had the largest and most
comprehensive soul."

POST-SHAKESPEARIAN DRAMA

In the following section it will be found that, although much of
the work was composed during Shakespeare's lifetime, the most
typical of the plays appeared after his death. On the whole, moreover, the work marks a decline from the Shakespearian standard,
and so we are probably justified in calling this type of drama post-
Shakespearian.

1. Ben Jonson (1573 (?)–1637) was born at Westminster, and
educated at Westminster School. His father died before Jonson's
birth, and the boy adopted the trade of his stepfather, who was a
master bricklayer. Bricklaying did not satisfy him for long, and he
became a soldier, serving in the Low Countries. From this he
turned to acting and writing plays, engaging himself, both as actor
and playwright, with the Lord Admiral's company (1597). At first
he had little success, and the discouragement he encountered then
must have done much to sour a temper that was not at any time

very genial. In his combative fashion he took part freely in the squabbles of the time, and in 1598 he killed a fellow-actor in a duel, narrowly escaping the gallows. On the accession of James I in 1603 there arose at the Court a new fashion for picturesque pageants known as masques, and Jonson turned his energies to supplying this demand, with great success. After this period (1603–15) he commanded great good-fortune, and during this time his best work was produced. In 1617 he was created poet to the King, and the close of James's reign saw Jonson the undisputed ruler of English literature. His favourite haunt was the Mermaid Tavern, where he reigned as dictator over a younger literary generation. He was buried in Westminster Abbey, and over him was placed the epitaph "O rare Ben Jonson!"

Jonson's numerous works, comedies, tragedies, masques, and lyrics, are of widely varying merit, but all of them, as well as his *Timber*, a kind of commonplace-book, which is of considerable interest for its critical comments on literature, show the unity of aim underlying his writing. Jonson was the first great English neoclassic. Like Donne, he was in revolt against the artistic principles of his contemporaries, and he sought in the classics a cure for the uncontrolled, romantic exuberance of Elizabethan literature. In all branches of his writings he is the conscious artist and reformer, working on clearly defined principles. To him the chief function of literature was to instruct.

His plays divide conveniently into comedies and tragedies, for Jonson, true to his classical models, did not combine the two. In his comedies he aimed to return to the controlled, satirical, realistic comedy of the classical dramatists, and the inductions of his plays make it clear that he hoped to reform the drama on these lines. His main concern was with the drawing of character, and his creations are important because they introduce the "comedy of humours," which portrays the individual as dominated by one marked characteristic. Many of his characters are, in consequence, types, but the best, like Bobadill in *Every Man in his Humour*, rise above the type and live as truly great comic characters. In nearly all his comedies Jonson opened up a vein that was nearly new and was to be very freely worked by his successors—the comedy of London life and humours, reflecting the manners of the day.

His early comedies, *Every Man in his Humour* (1598), *Every Man out of his Humour* (1599), *Cynthia's Revels* (1600), and *The Poetaster* (1601), show his ingenuity of plot, his hearty humour, his wit, and they are full of vivacity and fun. *Every Man in his Humour* is, perhaps, his greatest work. The middle group of comedies, *Volpone, or the Fox* (1605), *Epicœne, or the Silent Woman* (1609), *The Alchemist* (1610), and *Bartholomew Fayre* (1614), represent, as a group, his best work. More mature than the early works, they are all satirical in tone (*Volpone* is one of the most relentless exposures of vice in English), realistic and natural in dialogue, and ingenious in plot. The characters are less angular and more convincing. *Epicœne* and *Bartholomew Fayre* are written entirely in prose, while *The Alchemist* is entirely in blank verse. His later comedies, *The Devil is an Ass* (1616) and *The Staple of News* (1625), show a distinct falling-off in dramatic power.

The two historical tragedies, *Sejanus his Fall* (1603) and *Catiline his Conspiracy* (1611), are composed on classical models. They are too laboured and mechanical to be reckoned as great tragedies, though their author would fain have had them so. They show immense learning, they have power, variety, and insight, but they lack the last creative touch necessary to stamp them with reality, and to give them a living appeal.

As for his masques, they are abundant, graceful, and humorously ingenious. Into them Jonson introduced the device of the anti-masque, which parodied the principal theme. The best of them are *The Masque of Beauty* (1608), *The Masque of Queens* (1609), and *Oberon, the Fairy Prince* (1611).

The lyrics, many of which appeared in *Underwoods*, reflect no deep surge of emotion, but are controlled, poised, and urbane. If some of them are stiff, and most do not rise above mediocrity, the best of them, such as the well-known "Drink to me only with thine eyes," have a delicacy of touch and a clarity of style which are as fine as anything achieved by the Elizabethan lyrists. We quote two brief but typical pieces:

> (1) Have you seen but a bright lillie grow,
>   Before rude hands have touch'd it?
> Have you mark'd but the fall of the snow
>   Before the soyle hath smutch'd it?
> Have you felt the wooll of the bever?
>   Or the swan's downe ever?
> Or have smelt of the bud of the brier?
>   Or the nard on the fire?
> Or have tasted the bag of the bee?
> O so white! O so soft! O so sweet is she!
>
> *The Triumph*

(2)   Underneath this sable hearse
Lies the subject of all verse,
Sidney's sister, Pembroke's mother:
Death, ere thou hast slain another,
Learned, and fair, and good as she,
Time shall throw a dart at thee!
Epitaph on the Countess of Pembroke[1]

In the estimation of his own age Jonson stood second to none; to a later generation he is overshadowed by the towering bulk of Shakespeare. But even the enormous prestige of Shakespeare cannot or ought not to belittle the merits of Jonson. Of Jonson we can justly say that he had all good literary gifts except one, and that the highest and most baffling of all—true genius. He had learning—perhaps too much of it; industry and constancy well beyond the ordinary; versatility; a crabbed and not unamiable humour, diversified with sweetness, grace, and nimbleness of wit; a style quite adequate to his needs; and an insight into contemporary life and manners greater than that of any writer of his day. But the summit of it all —the magical phrase that catches the breath, the immortal spirit that creates out of words and buckram "forms more real than living man"—these were lacking; and without these he cannot join the circle of the very great.

2. Francis Beaumont (*c.* **1584–1616**) and **John Fletcher (1579–1625**) combined to produce a great number of plays, said to be fifty-two in all. How much of the joint work is to be assigned to the respective hands is not accurately known.

The elder, Fletcher, was a cousin of Giles and Phineas Fletcher (see p. 86), and was born at Rye, Sussex. He may have been educated at Cambridge, and he lived the life of a London literary man. He died of the plague in 1625. His colleague Beaumont, who was probably the abler of the two, was the son of a judge, Sir Francis Beaumont, was educated at Oxford, and entered the Inner Temple (1600), but was captivated by the attractions of a literary life. He died almost within a month of Shakespeare, and was buried in Westminster Abbey.

Beaumont and Fletcher excelled in comedy, especially in the comedy of London life. They felt the influence of both Shakespeare and Jonson, but their plays are generally more superficial. They are mainly tragi-comedies, full of striking incident and stage effect. Their plots sustain interest and are often ingenious, lively, and

[1] This piece is sometimes ascribed to William Browne (1588–1643).

entertaining, though rather loosely knit. The characters are numerous and widely varied, but the concentration on incident often makes them shallow. Full of witty dialogue, the plays attain a high level of lucidity and simplicity in their style, but they lack the Shakespearian wealth of imagery. A study of the style enables us to distinguish fairly clearly between the regular and flexible blank verse of Beaumont and the irregular verse of Fletcher, with its fondness for the extra syllable at the end of a line which is frequently end-stopped. Typical comedies are *A King and No King* (1611), esteemed by Dryden as the best of them all, *The Knight of the Burning Pestle* (1607 (?)), a very agreeable farce, and *The Scornful Lady* (1613–16). Their tragedies, such as *The Maid's Tragedy* (1610 (?)), *Philaster* (1611), which is very reminiscent of *Twelfth Night*, and *The Faithful Shepherdess* (by Fletcher alone), are not too tragical, and they are diversified by attractive incidents and descriptions.

3. **George Chapman** (*c.* **1559–1634**) was born at Hitchin. Beyond this fact little is known of him. He took part in the literary life of his time, for his name appears in the squabbles of his tribe. He died in London.

His first play, *The Blind Beggar of Alexandria* (1596), was followed by many more, both comical and tragical. Among them are *Bussy d'Ambois* (1604 (?)), *Charles, Duke of Byron* (1608), and *The Tragedie of Chabot* (*c.* 1613). These are historical plays, dealing with events nearly contemporary with his own time. Chapman's comedies include *All Fools* (1605) and *Eastward Hoe!* (1605), in the latter of which he combined with Jonson and Marston. Chapman writes agreeably and well; he has firmness, competence, and variety, and his comic and tragic powers are considerable. His translation of Homer has something of the pace and music of the original.

4. **John Marston** (*c.* **1575–1634**) was born at Coventry, was educated there and at Oxford, became a literary figure in London, and later took orders. Latterly he resigned his living in Hampshire, and died in London.

Marston, a member of the Senecan school (see p. 88), specialized in violent and melodramatic tragedies, which do not lack a certain impressiveness, but which are easily parodied and no less easily lead to abuse. They impressed his own generation, who rated him with Jonson. For a later age they are spoiled to a great extent by exaggeration, rant, and excessive speeches. Typical of them are *Antonio and Mellida* (1599) and *Antonio's Revenge* (1602), which were ridiculed by Jonson in *The Poetaster*.

5. Thomas Dekker (*c.* 1572–*c.* 1632) was born in London, where his life was passed as a literary hack and playwright. His plays, chiefly comedies, have an attraction quite unusual for the time. They have a sweetness, an arch sentimentality, and an intimate knowledge of common men and things that have led to his being called the Dickens of the Elizabethan stage. His plots are chaotic, and his blank verse, which very frequently gives place to prose, is weak and sprawling. The best of his plays are *Old Fortunatus* (1599), *The Shoemaker's Holiday* (1599), and *Satiromastix* (1602). He collaborated with other playwrights, including Ford and Rowley, with whom he wrote *The Witch of Edmonton* (1621), and Massinger, in *The Virgin Martyr* (*c.* 1620).

6. Thomas Middleton (*c.* 1570–1627) was born in London, wrote much for the stage, and in 1620 was made City Chronologer.

He is one of the most equable and literary of the dramatists of the age; he has a decided fanciful turn; he is a close observer and critic of the life of the time, and a dramatist who on a few occasions can rise to the heights of greatness. His most powerful play, which has been much praised by Lamb and others, is *The Changeling* (1624); others are *Women beware Women* (1622), *The Witch*, which bears a strong resemblance to *Macbeth*, and *The Spanish Gipsy* (1623), a romantic comedy suggesting *As You Like It*. Along with Dekker he wrote *The Roaring Girle, or Moll Cutpurse* (1611), which is a close dramatic parallel to the earliest novels.

7. Thomas Heywood (*c.* 1575–*c.* 1650) was born in Lincolnshire about 1575, was educated at Cambridge, and became an author and dramatist in London. He himself asserts that he had a hand ("or at least a main finger") in two hundred and twenty plays, of which twenty-three survive.

Like so many more dramatists of the time, he excelled in his pictures of London life and manners. He was a rapid and light improviser, an expert contriver of stage situations, but otherwise content with passable results, and caring little about the higher flights of the dramatist. His best play is *A Woman Killed with Kindnesse* (1603), which contains some strongly pathetic scenes; *The English Traveller* (1633) is only slightly inferior. Other plays of his are *The Royall King and the Loyall Subject* (1602 (?)), *The Captives* (1624), and a series of clumsy historical dramas, including *King Edward the Fourth* (1594–97).

8. John Webster, who flourished during the first twenty years of the seventeenth century, is regarded as the greatest post-Shakespearian dramatist. Next to nothing is known regarding his life, and much of his work has been lost.

The most striking follower of the Senecan Revenge tradition, Webster turns from the mere horror of event to the deep and subtle analysis of character. His plots are not well constructed and there is still some crudeness of incident, but his horrors are usually controlled, and are subordinate to the total artistic purpose of the play in which they occur. He deals with gloomy, supernatural themes, great crimes, turbulent emotions, and in largeness of tragic conception he resembles Marlowe. He is a great dramatic poet, whose verse, though sometimes faulty, often reaches the highest levels and has great power. Tender and pitiful scenes add a touch of fine pathos to his greatest works.

His career falls into three parts. After an early apprenticeship as a collaborator, especially with Dekker, he produced his two great tragedies, *The White Devil* (1609–12) and *The Duchess of Malfi* (1613–14), which, in Vittoria and the Duchess, contain two of the finest women characters in the Elizabethan drama. His later plays, which include *The Devil's Law Case* (1623), do not approach the great tragedies in quality.

9. Cyril Tourneur (1575 (?)–1626) seems to have been a soldier and to have served in the Low Countries. He took part in Buckingham's disastrous expedition to Cadiz, and on his return died in Ireland.

In the work of Tourneur, another and cruder follower of the 'Revenge' tradition, we have horrors piled on horrors. His two plays *The Revenger's Tragedy* (1600) and *The Atheist's Tragedy* (1607–11) are melodramatic to the highest degree. He attempts much, but achieves little. He does not lack a certain poetic sensibility; but he lacks grip, method, and balance, and he is weakest where Webster is strongest.

PROSE

The English Bible: the Authorized Version

In the last chapter we indicated the growth of the Bible from the earliest to Reformation times. The task of translation was completed by the issue of *King James's Bible*, or the *Authorized Version* (1611).

The need for a standard text was urged during the conference between the dissentient sects held at Hampton Court in 1604. James I, who was present at some stages of the conference, approved

of the project. Forty-seven scholars, including the ablest profes-
sorial and episcopal talent, were appointed for the task; they were
divided into six companies, each receiving a certain portion of the
Biblical text for translation; each company revised the work of its
fellow-translators. The task, begun in 1607, was completed in 1611.
Since that date little of sufficient authority has been done to shake
the Authorized Version's dominating position as the greatest of
English translations.

It may be of use here to set down some of the more obvious
features of this great work.

1. With regard to the actual work of **translation**, it ought to be
regarded simply as the climax of a long series of earlier translations.
The new translators came to handle a large mass of work already
in existence. All the debatable ground in the texts had been fought
over again and again, and in a dim fashion a standard was
emerging. The translators themselves acknowledge this in the
preface to their work: their task, they say, is "to make a good one
better, or out of many good ones one principal good one." In
other words, their task was largely one of selection and amendment.
The reliance upon earlier work resulted in a certain old-fashioned
flavour that was felt even in Jacobean times. "It is not the English,"
says Hallam, "of Daniel or Ralegh or Bacon. . . . It abounds,
especially in the Old Testament, in obsolete phraseology." It is a
tribute to the compelling power and beauty of the Authorized
Version that its archaisms have long been accepted as permissible,
and even inevitable. Allowing, however, for all the reliance upon
earlier work, one cannot overpraise the sound judgment, the artistic
taste, and the sensitive ear of every member of the band who built
up such a stately monument to our tongue.

2. Diversity of the Work. One can best appreciate the vastness
and complexity of the Bible by recollecting that it is not a single
book, but an entire literature, or even two literatures, for both in
time and temper the New Testament is separated from the Old.
The different books of the Bible were composed at widely different
times, and many hands worked at them. Their efforts resulted in a
huge collection of all the main species of literature—expository,
narrative, and lyrical. These will be noticed in their order below.

3. Unity of the Work. If the Bible were a collection of discordant
elements it would not possess its peculiar literary attraction. In
spite of the diversity of its sources it has a remarkable uniformity
of treatment and spirit. The core and substance of the entire work

is the belief and delight in the Divine Spirit; and, added to this, especially in the Old Testament, a fiery faith in the pre-eminence of the Jewish race. With regard to the literary style, it owes most to the translations of Tyndale and Coverdale (see p. 61), for it combines the strength of the former with the beautiful rhythms of the latter. From cover to cover it is almost unvaried: firm, clear, simple, dignified, and thoroughly English. It represents the broad and stable average of the labours of generations of devout and ardent men; and it endures unshaken.

4. The Expository Portions. Considered from the purely literary point of view, the expository parts (that is, those that contain exhortation, information, or advice) are of least importance. In bulk they are considerable, and include the Book of Deuteronomy in the Old Testament and the Pauline Epistles in the New. They have all the distinction of the Biblical style, and they are expressed with clearness, dignity, and precision.

5. The narrative portions include the bulk of the Bible, and are of great literary interest and value. In the Old Testament they comprise the Pentateuch and many other books, and in the New Testament they include the Gospels and the Acts of the Apostles. The tone of the Old Testament differs somewhat from that of the New. As can be supposed, the former is often harsher in note, and is sometimes confused and contradictory (from the unsatisfactory condition of some of the texts); the New Testament narrative, which came under the influence of the Greek, is more scholarly and liberal in tone. Both, however, have a breadth, solidity, and noble austerity of style that make the Biblical narrative stand alone. It is perhaps unnecessary to quote, but one short specimen may not be out of place:

> Then they took him, and led him, and brought him into the high priest's house. And Peter followed afar off.
>
> And when they had kindled a fire in the midst of the hall, and were set down together, Peter sat down among them.
>
> But a certain maid beheld him as he sat by the fire, and earnestly looked upon him, and said, This man was also with him.
>
> And he denied him, saying, Woman, I know him not.
>
> And after a little while another saw him, and said, Thou art also of them. And Peter said, Man, I am not.
>
> And about the space of one hour after another confidently affirmed, saying, Of a truth this fellow also was with him: for he is a Galilean.
>
> And Peter said, Man, I know not what thou sayest. And immediately, while he yet spake, the cock crew.
>
> And the Lord turned, and looked upon Peter. And Peter

remembered the word of the Lord, how he had said unto him, Before the cock crow, thou shalt deny me thrice.

And Peter went out, and wept bitterly.

St Luke

6. The Lyrical Portions. These (which include the Psalms, the Song of Solomon, much of the Book of Job, and the frequent passages, such as the song of Sisera, which occur in the narrative books) are perhaps the most important as literature. In addition to their native shrewdness and persistence, the Jews had a strongly emotional strain, which finds wide expression in the Bible. Their poetry, like that of the Old English, was rhythmic; it went by irregularly distributed beats or accents. The English translators to a large extent preserved the Jewish rhythms, adding to them the music, the cadence, the soar and the swing of ecstatic English prose. In theme Jewish poetry is the primitive expression of simple people regarding the relations of man and God and the universe. Its similes and metaphors are based upon simple elemental things—the heavens, the running water, and the congregations of wild beasts. The emotions are mystically and rapturously expressed, and convey the impression of much earnestness. The following extract is fairly typical of its kind:

As the hart panteth after the water brooks, so panteth my soul after thee, O God.

My soul thirsteth for God, for the living God: when shall I come and appear before God?

My tears have been my meat day and night, while they continually say unto me, Where is thy God?

When I remember these things, I pour out my soul in me: for I had gone with the multitude, I went with them to the house of God, with the voice of joy and praise, with a multitude that kept holyday.

Why art thou cast down, O my soul? and why art thou disquieted in me? hope thou in God: for I shall yet praise him for the help of his countenance.

The Book of Psalms

7. The Influence of the Bible. The English Bible has been a potent influence in our literature. Owing largely to their poetical or proverbial nature, multitudes of Biblical expressions have become woven into the very tissue of the tongue: "a broken reed," "the eleventh hour," "a thorn in the flesh," "a good Samaritan," "sweat of the brow," and so on. More important, probably, is the way in which the style affects that of many of our greatest writers. The influence is nearly all for the good; for a slight strain of the

Biblical manner, when kept artistically within bounds, imparts simplicity, dignity, and elevation. Bunyan shows the style almost undiluted; but in the works of such widely diverse writers as Ruskin, Macaulay, Milton, and Tennyson the effects, though slighter, are quite apparent.

FRANCIS BACON, BARON VERULAM, VISCOUNT ST ALBANS (1561–1626)

1. His Life. Bacon was born in London, the son of Sir Nicholas Bacon, the Lord Keeper of the Great Seal. The family was connected with the Cecils and other political magnates of the time. Bacon was a delicate youth, and for a time he was educated privately; then he proceeded to Cambridge, and thence entered Gray's Inn (1576). To complete his education he spent three years in France. On his being called to the Bar his family influence helped him to acquire a fair practice, but Bacon was ambitious and longed for the highest rewards that his profession could bestow. He became a member of Parliament in 1584, but the recognition that he expected from the Queen did not come his way, hard though he fought for it. He assisted in the prosecution of the Earl of Essex, a nobleman who had befriended him earlier in his career. Essex, an injudicious man, had involved himself in a charge of treason, and the ingenuity of Bacon was largely instrumental in bringing him to the block. On the accession of James I Bacon, who was never remiss in urging his own claims to preferment, began to experience prosperity, for he was tireless in urging the royal claims before Parliament. He was made a knight in 1603, and Attorney-General in 1613. In the latter capacity he was James's chief agent in asserting and enforcing the King's theories of divine right, and he became thoroughly unpopular with the House of Commons. His reward came in 1618, when he was appointed Lord Chancellor and created Baron Verulam, and in 1621, when he became Viscount St Albans. Popular dissatisfaction was mounting against the King and his agents, and when Parliament met in 1621 it laid charges of bribery and corrupt dealings against the Lord Chancellor. Bacon quailed before the storm; made what amounted to a confession of guilt; and was subjected to the huge fine of £40,000 (which was partially remitted), imprisonment during the King's pleasure (which was restricted to four days in the Tower of London), and exile from Court and office. He spent the last five years of his life in the pursuit of literary and scientific works.

2. His Works. Bacon wrote both in Latin and English, and of the two he considered the Latin works to be the more important.

(*a*) His English works include his *Essays*, which first appeared in 1597. Then they numbered ten; but the second (1612) and third (1625) editions raised the number to thirty-eight and fifty-eight respectively. They are on familiar subjects, such as Learning, Studies, Vainglory, and Great Place; and in method they represent the meditations of a trained and learned mind. His other English works were *The Advancement of Learning* (1605), containing the substance of his philosophy; *The History of Henry VII* (1622); *Apophthegms* (1625), a kind of jest-book; and *The New Atlantis*, left unfinished at his death, a philosophical romance modelled upon More's *Utopia*.

(*b*) His Latin works were to be fashioned into a vast scheme, which he called *Instauratio Magna*, expounding his philosophical theories. It was laid out on the following plan, but it was scarcely half finished:

(1) *De Augmentis Scientiarum* (1623). This treatise, in which the English work on the *Advancement of Learning* is embodied, gives a general summary of human knowledge, taking special notice of gaps and imperfections in science.

(2) *Novum Organum* (1620). This work explains the new logic, or inductive method of reasoning, upon which his philosophy is founded. Out of the nine sections into which he divides the subject the first only is handled with any fullness, the other eight being merely named.

(3) *Sylva Sylvarum* (left incomplete). This part was designed to give a complete view of what we call Natural Philosophy and Natural History. The subjects he has touched on under this head are four—the History of Winds, Life and Death, Density and Rarity, Sound and Hearing.

(4) *Scala Intellectus*. Of this we have only a few of the opening pages.

(5) *Prodromi*. A few fragments only were written.

(6) *Philosophia Secunda*. Never executed.

3. His Style. Of Bacon as a philosopher we can only say that he is one of the founders of modern systematic thought. His most important literary work is his *Essays*, which might be described as an appendix to his longer works, especially *The Advancement of Learning*, in that it provides a practical everyday philosophy of the life of his own world. In its three versions this work shows the development of Bacon's English style. In the first edition the style is crisp, detached, and epigrammatic, conveying the impression that each essay has arisen from some happy thought or phrase, around which other pithy statements are agglomerated. In the later editions the ideas are expanded, the expression loses its spiky pointedness, and in the end we have an approach to a freer middle style. In choice of subject and approach, they reveal his breadth of intellect, his worldly wisdom, his concern with public life and material advancement. They are impersonal, objective, and orderly in thought, and reflect a cool, scientific detachment, which makes them, in spite of an occasional flash of poetic fire, as in *Of Death*, rather formal and cold. Yet they are written in the language of ordinary men, and the imagery is that of everyday life. The essays are brief and full of condensed, weighty, antithetical sentences, which have the qualities of proverbial expressions, and are notable for their precision and clarity of phrasing. Many have striking openings: "Revenge is a wild kind of justice, which the more man's nature runs to, the more ought law to weed it out" (*Of Revenge*); "God Almighty first planted a garden; and indeed it is the purest of human pleasures" (*Of Gardens*); "Men fear death, as children fear to go in the dark" (*Of Death*). All are full of allusions to, and extracts from, other writings.

For the sake of comparison we quote the same extract from the first and third editions of the *Essays*. The second extract, it will be noticed, is a studied expansion of the first.

(1) Crafty men contemn them, simple men admire them, wise men use them; for they teach not their own use, but that is a wisdom without them and above them won by observation. Read not to contradict nor to believe, but to weigh and consider. Some books are to be tasted, others to be swallowed, and some few to be chewed and digested; that is, some books are to be read only in parts, others to be read but cursorily, and some few to be read wholly and with diligence and attention. Reading maketh a full man, conference a ready man, and writing an exact man. And therefore, if a man write little, he had need have a great memory; if he confer little, he had need have a present wit; and if he read little, he had need have much cunning to seem to know that he doth not. Histories make men wise; poets witty; the mathematics subtle; natural philosophy deep; moral grave; logic and rhetoric able to contend.

(2) Crafty men contemn studies, simple men admire them, and wise men use them; for they teach not their own use; but that is a wisdom without them, and above them, won by observation. Read not to contradict and confute; nor to believe and take for granted; nor to find talk and discourse; but to weigh and consider. Some books are to be tasted, others to be swallowed, and some few to be chewed and digested; that is, some books are to be read only in parts; others to be read, but not curiously; and some few to be

read wholly, and with diligence and attention. Some books also may be read by deputy, and extracts made of them by others; but that would be only in the less important arguments, and the meaner sort of books; else distilled books are like common distilled waters, flashy things. Reading maketh a full man; conference a ready man; and writing an exact man. And therefore, if a man write little, he had need have a great memory; if he confer little, he had need have a present wit; and if he read little, he had need have much cunning, to seem to know that he doth not. Histories make men wise; poets witty; the mathematics subtle; natural philosophy deep; moral grave; logic and rhetoric able to contend.

Of Studies

OTHER PROSE-WRITERS

1. Roger Ascham (1515–68) is representative of the earliest school of Elizabethan prose. He was born in Yorkshire, and educated privately and at St John's College, Cambridge, where he became a Fellow (1535) and a teacher of Greek (1540). He took part in the literary and religious disputes of the time, but managed to keep his feet on the shifting grounds of politics. He was appointed tutor to Elizabeth (1548) and secretary to Queen Mary; he visited the Continent as secretary to an embassy; and ultimately was appointed a canon of York Minster.

His two chief works were *Toxophilus* (1545), a treatise, in the form of a dialogue, on archery; and *The Scholemaster* (1570), an educational work containing some ideas that were then fairly fresh and enlightening. Ascham was a man of moderate literary talent, of great industry, and of boundless enthusiasm for learning. Though he is strongly influenced by classical models, he has all the strong Elizabethan sense of nationality. In *Toxophilus* he declares his intention of "writing this English matter in the English speech for Englishmen." In style he is plain and strong, using only the more obvious graces of alliteration and antithesis.

2. John Lyly (1554 (?)–1606) marks another stage in the march of English prose. He was born in Kent, educated at Oxford, and, failing to obtain Court patronage, became a literary man in London. At first he had considerable success, and entered Parliament; but at a later stage his popularity declined, and he died poverty-stricken in London.

We have already mentioned his comedies (see p. 89), which at the time brought him fame and money. But his first prose work, *Euphues, the Anatomy of Wit* (1579), made him one of the foremost figures of the day. He repeated the success with a second part, *Euphues and his England* (1580). The work is a kind of travel-romance, recounting the adventures of Euphues, a young Athenian. The narrative is interspersed with numerous discussions upon many topics. It was, however, the style of its prose that gave the book its great vogue. It is the first consciously fabricated prose style in the language. It is mannered and affected almost to the point of being ridiculous. Its tricks are obvious and easily imitated, and they were freely applied by the next generation: balanced phrases, intricate alliteration, laboured comparisons drawn from classical and other sources, and ornate epithets. The effect is quaint and not displeasing, but the narrative labours under the weight of it. It certainly suited the growing literary consciousness of its day, and hence its pronounced, though temporary, success.

The following extract will illustrate the euphuistic manner:

> Philautus being a town-born child, both for his own continuance and the great countenance which his father had while he lived crept into credit with Don Ferardo one of the chief governors of the city, who although he had a courtly crew of gentlewomen sojourning in his palace, yet his daughter, heir to his whole revenues, stained the beauty of them all, whose modest bashfulness caused the other to look wan for envy, whose lily cheeks dyed with a vermilion red, made the rest to blush at her beauty. For as the finest ruby staineth the colour of the rest that be in place, or as the sun dimmeth the moon, that she cannot be discerned, so this gallant girl more fair than fortunate, and yet more fortunate than faithful, eclipsed the beauty of them all, and changed their colours. Unto her had Philautus access, who won her by right of love, and should have worn her by right of law, had not Euphues by strange destiny broken the bonds of marriage, and forbidden the banns of matrimony.

Euphues, the Anatomy of Wit

3. **Richard Hooker (1554–1600)** was born near Exeter, and educated at Corpus Christi College, Oxford, where he was elected a Fellow (1577). In 1582 he took orders, and later was appointed to a living in Kent, where he died.

His great work, at which he laboured during the greater part of his life, was *Of the Laws of Ecclesiastical Polity*. The first four of the proposed eight books were issued in 1594; he finished one more; and though the remaining three were published under his name when he was dead, it is very doubtful if he was entirely responsible for them. In the work he supports Episcopacy against Presbyterianism. In style he is strongly affected by classical writers; but he usually writes with homeliness and point; his sentences are carefully constructed; the rhythm moves easily; and there is both precision and melody in his choice of vocabulary. His style is an early example of scholarly and accomplished English prose.

4. Sir Thomas Overbury (1581–1613) may be taken as typical of a fairly large class of Elizabethan writers. He was born in Warwickshire, educated at Oxford, and became a figure at the Court of King James. His chief friend at Court was James's favourite Robert Carr, with whom he quarrelled over a love-affair. For this Overbury fell into disfavour, and was imprisoned in the Tower, where he was poisoned under mysterious and barbarous circumstances.

Overbury survives in literature as the author of a series of *Characters* (1614), though he is probably not the author of all of them. Based on the ancient Greek work of Theophrastus, the book consists of a number of concise character-sketches of well-known types, such as a Milkmaid, a Pedant, a Franklin, and "an Affectate Traveller." They are written from the point of view of the courtier and are epigrammatic and full of 'conceits' and wit. They show a close and penetrating observation and a fine sense of humour. But they are important for several reasons: they are a curious development of the pamphlet, which was so common at that time; they are another phase of the 'humours' craze, seen so strongly in the Jonsonian and other dramas; and they are an important element in the growth of the essay. In style the book is strongly euphuistic, thus illustrating another tendency of the time. They were added to and imitated by other writers, including **John Earle (1601–65)**.

5. Robert Burton (1577–1640) was the son of a country gentleman, and was born in Leicestershire. He was educated at Oxford, where, in holy orders, he passed most of his life.

His famous work, *The Anatomy of Melancholy*, was first issued in 1621, and then constantly revised and reissued. It is an elaborate and discursive study of melancholy, its species and kinds, its causes, results, and cure. The book, though laboured and saturnine in tone, shows an underlying common sense and a true sympathy with humanity. It has exercised a strong fascination over many scholarly minds, including those of Dr Johnson and Charles Lamb. Its learning is immense and unconventional, being drawn from many rare authors; its humour curiously crabbed, subdued, and ironical; and its 'melancholy,' though pervading, is not oppressive. The diction has a colloquial naturalness and is rarely obscure; the enormous sentences, packed with quotation and allusion, are loosely knit. Both as a stylist and as a personality Burton occupies his own niche in English literature.

6. The Sermon-writers. At the beginning of the seventeenth century the sermon rose to a level of literary importance not hitherto attained, and afterwards rarely equalled. We have already mentioned Donne (see p. 80), probably the most notable of his group, and we give space to two other writers.

(a) **James Ussher (1581–1656)** was born in Dublin, and was descended from an ancient Protestant family. He was educated at Trinity College, Dublin, and rose to be Bishop of Meath and Archbishop of Armagh (1625). In 1640 he visited England, where, owing to the disturbed state of Ireland, he had to remain for the rest of his life. His many sermons, discourses, and tracts show learning, adroit argument, and a plain and easy style. His *Chronologia Sacra* was for a long time the standard work on Biblical chronology.

(b) **Joseph Hall (1574–1656)** was educated at Cambridge, took orders, and became a prominent opponent of the Puritans, among whom was Milton. He was appointed Bishop of Exeter (1627) and of Norwich (1641). When the Puritans rose to power Hall's opinions brought him into disgrace. He was imprisoned, and, though liberated, forbidden to preach. He died in retirement.

Hall's earliest work was in verse, and consisted of a series of satires called *Virgidemiarum* (1597), which were condemned by the Church as being licentious. His theological and devotional works, the product of his later years, are very numerous, and include tracts, sermons, and treatises. Though he is often shallow and voluble, he writes with literary grace. He is without doubt the most literary of the theologians of the time.

7. The Translators. The zeal for learning and spirit of adventure, which were such a prominent feature of the early Elizabethan times, were strongly apparent in the frequent translations. This class of literature had several curious characteristics. The translators cared little for verbal accuracy, and sometimes were content to translate from a translation, say from a French version of a Latin text. The translators, moreover, borrowed from each other and repeated the errors of their fellows. These habits deprived their work of any great pretensions to scholarship; but they were eager adventurers into the new realms of learning, and to a great extent they reproduced the spirit, if not the letter, of their originals.

The translators worked in many varied fields. Of the classics, Virgil was translated by **Phaer** (1558) and **Stanyhurst** (1562); Plutarch's *Lives* (a work that had much influence on Shakespeare and other dramatists) by **North** (1579); Ovid by **Golding** (1565 and

1567), **Turberville** (1567), and **Chapman** (1595); Homer by **Chapman** (1598). All Seneca was in English by 1581, and Suetonius, Pliny, and Plutarch's *Morals* were translated by **Holland**. Among the translations of Italian works were Machiavelli's *Arte of Warre* (1560) —his more famous and influential *The Prince* was not translated until 1640—Castiglione's *The Courtyer*, translated by **Hoby** (1561); the *Palace of Pleasure* by **Painter** (1566), a work which was used by Shakespeare, Marston, Webster, and Massinger, and accounted for much of the horror of later Elizabethan tragedy; and Ariosto's *Orlando Furioso*, translated by **Harrington** (1591). From France were drawn **Florio's** translation of the *Essays* of Montaigne (1603) and **Dannett's** *Commines* (1596), while Spain provided **North** with *The Diall of Princes* (1557).

8. The Pamphleteers. All through this period there is a flood of short tracts on religion, politics, and literature. It was the work of a host of literary hacks who earned a precarious existence in London. These men represented a new class of writer. The Reformation had closed the Church to them; the growth of the universities and of learning continually increased their numbers. In later times journalism and its kindred careers supplied them with a livelihood; but at this time they eked out their existence by writing plays and squabbling among themselves in the pages of broadsheets.

In its buoyancy and vigour, its quaint mixture of truculence and petulance, Elizabethan pamphleteering is refreshingly boyish and alive. It is usually keenly satirical, and in style it is unformed and uncouth. The most notorious of the pamphleteers were **Thomas Nash** (or **Nashe**) (**1567–1601**), **Robert Greene** (**1560** (?)**–92**), and **Thomas Lodge** (**1558** (?)**–1625**). We quote a well-known passage from a pamphlet of Greene, in which he contrives to mingle praise of his friends with sly gibes at one who is probably Shakespeare. The style is typical of the pamphlets.

> And thou,[1] no less deserving than the other two,[2] in some things rarer, in nothing inferior; driven (as myself) to extreme shifts, a little have I to say to thee; and were it not an idolatrous oath, I would swear by sweet St George, thou art unworthy better hap, sith thou dependest on so mean a stay. Base-minded men all three of you, if by my misery ye be not warned; for unto none of you (like me) sought those burs to cleave,—those puppets, I mean,— that speak from our mouths,—those antics garnished in our colours. Is it not strange that I, to whom they all have been beholding,—is it not like that you, to whom they all have been beholding,—shall

---

[1] Peele. [2] Nash and Marlowe.

(were ye in that case that I am now) be both at once of them for-saken? Yes, trust them not: for there is an upstart crow, beautified with our feathers, that with his tiger's heart wrapt in a player's hide, supposes he is as well able to bombast out a blank-verse as the best of you: and being an absolute *Johannes factotum*, is in his own conceit the only Shakescene in a country. Oh, that I might entreat your rare wits to be employed in more profitable courses, and let those apes imitate your past excellence, and never more acquaint them with your admired inventions! I know the best husband of you all will never prove an usurer, and the kindest of them all will never prove a kind nurse: yet, whilst you may, seek you better masters; for it is pity men of such rare wits should be subject to the pleasures of such rude grooms.

A Groatsworth of Wit bought with a Million of Repentance

THE DEVELOPMENT OF LITERARY FORMS

At the beginning of the Elizabethan age English literary forms were still to a large extent in the making; at the end of the period there is a rich and varied store of most of the chief literary species. All that can be done here is to give the barest outline of this development.

1. Poetry. (*a*) *Dramatic Poetry*. The exuberant, adventurous spirit of the age was nowhere more clearly to be seen than in its dramatic poetry. Though the heroic couplet was used, as by Shakespeare in *A Midsummer Night's Dream*, the ascendancy of blank verse was firmly established, and the development from the stiff end-stopped verse of *Gorboduc* (1562) to the variety of pace and flexibility of Shakespeare was one of extraordinary rapidity. By 1590 Peele was already showing more variety, ease, and fluency, while Marlowe, by 1592, had made blank verse supreme in the drama. Its energy, barbaric splendour, resonance, lucidity, and sensitivity to the demands of varying emotion made his the first truly great dramatic blank verse. Shakespeare used the medium with abnormal range and power, and with a flexibility that subdued the demands of the metre completely to his will. Less than fifty years after *Gorboduc*, dramatic poetry had attained the highest level of which it was capable. After Shakespeare came a steady decline. Beaumont and Fletcher had a striking lucidity and simplicity of style, but lacked the true greatness that was Shakespeare's. Marston's rant and Dekker's sprawling verse carried the deterioration still further, and of the post-Shakespearian dramatists, only Webster ever touched the greatest heights, and though his verse could have great power it was often faulty. Symptomatic of the decline of blank verse was the growing proportion of prose to be found in the drama of the later part of the period.

(b) *Lyrical Poetry*. The temper of the age was suited to the lyrical mood, and so the abundance of the lyric is very great. It begins with the first efforts of Wyatt and Surrey (published 1557); it continues through the dramas in all their stages; and it appears in the numerous miscellanies of the period. Then the lyrical impulse is carried on without a break into the melodies of Campion and the darker moods of Donne. The forms of the lyric are many, and on the whole its notes are musical, wild, and natural.

An interesting sub-species of the lyric is the *sonnet*. We have seen how it took two forms—the Italian or Petrarchan form, and the English or Shakespearian type. During this period both kinds flourished, the English kind to a greater degree. Wyatt began with a group of the Italian type; Surrey introduced the English form. Then the sonnet, in one or other of its two forms, was continued by Sidney in *Astrophel and Stella* (published in 1591), by Spenser in the *Amoretti* (1595), by Shakespeare, and by Daniel in *Delia* (1592). Later in the period the sonnet was less popular, though Drayton wrote at least one of great power.

(c) *Descriptive and Narrative Poetry*. This is a convenient title for a large and important class of poems. In this period it begins with such works as Sackville's *Induction* to the *Myrroure for Magistrates* (1563), continuing with Marlowe's *Hero and Leander* (published 1598) and Shakespeare's *Venus and Adonis* (1593) and *The Rape of Lucrece* (1594). It culminates in the sumptuous allegorical poetry of Spenser; and it begins its decline with the Spenserians of the type of the Fletchers and with Drayton's *Endimion and Phoebe* ((?) 1595). The pastoral, which is a kind of descriptive poem, is seen in Spenser's *Shepheards Calendar* (1579), in Browne's *Britannia's Pastorals* (1613), and in Drayton. Almost purely descriptive poetry is represented in Drayton's *Poly-Olbion* (1612); and a more strongly narrative type is the same poet's *England's Heroicall Epistles* (1597). All these poems are distinguished by strong descriptive power, freshness of fancy, and sometimes by positive genius of style.

(d) *Religious*, satirical, and *didactic poetry* cannot take a position equal in importance to the rest. During the period the satirical intent is quite strong, but it does not produce great poetry. Gascoigne's *Steele Glas* (1576) is one of the earliest satires; and it is followed by Donne's *Satires* (1590–1600?) and Hall's *Satires* (1597). Drayton's *The Harmonie of the Church* (1591) is religious in motive;

so are several poems of Donne, and also many of those of the Jesuit **Robert Southwell (1561 (?)–95)**.

2. Drama. The opening of the Elizabethan period saw the drama struggling into maturity. The early type of the time was scholarly in tone and aristocratic in authorship. An example of the earliest type of playwright is **Fulke Greville, Lord Brooke (1554–1628)**, who distinguished himself both as a dramatic and lyrical poet.

Next came the work of the University Wits, Peele, Greene, Lodge, Kyd, and, greatest of all, Marlowe. In their hands drama first began to realize its latent potentialities, and the exuberance and vitality which typify Elizabethan drama first made themselves felt.

To this stage succeeded that of Shakespeare, which covered approximately the years 1595 to 1615. Of this drama all we can say here is that it is the crown and flower of the Elizabethan literary achievement, and embodies almost the entire spirit both of drama and poetry.

The decline begins with Jonson, and continues with Beaumont and Fletcher, Dekker, Heywood, and the other dramatists mentioned in this chapter. The decline is made clear in several ways: in the narrowing of the ample Shakespearian motive, which comprises all mankind, into themes of temporary, local, and fragmentary importance; in the lack of creative power in the characterization, resulting sometimes in mere types or 'humours,' or (as in Dekker and Fletcher) in superficial improvisation, or in ponderous tragical figures (as in Webster and Tourneur); and, lastly, in the degradation of the style, which will be noted below. Sometimes the decline is gilded with delicate fancy, as in Fletcher's *The Faithful Shepherdess*, or in the exquisite *The Parliament of Bees* (1641) by **John Day** (fl. **1606**); but the grace and charm of such plays cannot conceal the falling-off in power and imagination.

With regard to the development of the different dramatic types, we have already noted that tragedy developed first; in Shakespeare all kinds received attention, tragedy most of all. In post-Shakespearian drama light comedy was a very popular species, partly because the tragic note of exalted pity had degenerated into melodrama and horrors.

A special word is perhaps necessary on the *masque*, which during this time had a brief but brilliant career. The masque is a short dramatic performance composed for some particular festive occasion, such as the marriage or majority of a great man's son; it is distinguished by ornate stage-setting, by lyrics, music, and dancing, and by allegorical characters. It finds a place in Shakespeare's *Tempest* and other plays; it is strongly developed in the works of Jonson, Fletcher, and other poets of the time; and it attains its climax during the next age in the *Comus* (1637) of Milton.

3. Prose. In Elizabethan times the development of prose was slower and slighter than that of poetry.

(*a*) The *essay*, beginning in the pamphlet, character-sketch, and other miscellaneous writing, develops in the work of Bacon. Its rise will be sketched more fully in a future chapter (see p. 217).

(*b*) The *novel* has some meagre but significant beginnings in More's *Utopia* (1516), Sidney's *Arcadia* (published in 1590), Lyly's *Euphues* (1579), Bacon's *New Atlantis* (1626), and most of all in Nash's *The Unfortunate Traveller* (1594). The rise of the novel is also reserved for a later chapter (see p. 276).

(*c*) *Literary Criticism.* The birth of literary criticism indicates the growing stature of the national literature and the realization of the need to establish principles of writing. Lacking good poetry from the previous century, critics turned to the classics for their guides and models. They were chiefly concerned with three topics:

(i) *the status and value of poetry.* Gosson attacked poetry as immoral in his puritanical *The Schoole of Abuse* (1579), and Sidney replied in his famous *Apologie for Poetrie* (written before 1582)—see p. 85. William Webbe, in *A Discourse of English Poetrie* (1586), attempted the first historical survey of poets and poetry, and Puttenham's *The Arte of English Poesy* (1589) is the first systematic consideration of poetry as an art.

(ii) *the importance of classical models.* Before the Elizabethan period Ascham had advocated versifying on classical models, and he was later supported by Webbe, while Puttenham held the balance even between the native and classical traditions.

(iii) *the merits and demerits of rhyme.* Intermittent discussion on this topic culminated in the debate between Campion and Daniel. In reply to Campion's condemnation of rhyme in his *Observations in the Art of English Poesie* (1602), Daniel's famous *A Defence of Rhyme* (1602) asserted the right of every literature to its own customs and traditions. It was a momentous declaration, and it is of interest to note that it is vindicated in the best possible way—through the successful use of rhyme by almost all the Elizabethan poets.

(*d*) *Miscellaneous prose*, in the pamphlets, theological works, sermons, translations, travels, and such abnormalities as Burton's *Anatomy of Melancholy* (1621), is exceedingly voluminous and important. We have here a large, loose, and varied mass of English prose, the central exercising-ground of the average prose-writer, that is to be the foundation of many important groups of the future.

THE DEVELOPMENT OF LITERARY STYLE

1. Poetry. The period immediately preceding was that of the clumsy poetry of Hawes, Skelton, and their kind; succeeding it is the strength and beauty of Elizabethan poetry. Between these two extremes the different stages of development are fairly well marked.

(*a*) The earliest period (say from 1550-80) is that of Wyatt, Surrey, Sidney, and the University Wits. This is the formative and imitative period, during which the dependence upon classical originals is particularly strong. The style has the precision and the erratic character of the diligent pupil. There are few deliberate innovations, and lapses into barbarism are not unknown. In this period appear the sonnet, blank verse, and many of the beautiful lyrical metrical forms. The lyrical style is least restrained by the influence of classical models.

(*b*) The Spenserian and Shakespearian stage (from about 1580 to 1615) is the stage of highest development. The native English genius, having absorbed the lessons of foreign writers, adds to them the youth and ardour of its own spirit. The result is a fullness, freshness, and grandeur of style unequalled in any other period of our literature. There are the lyrics and allegories of Spenser; the poems, dramas, and lyrics of Shakespeare; and the innumerable miscellanies, poems, and plays of other writers. The style is as varied as the poems; but the universal note is the romantic one of power and ease.

(*c*) In the second decade of the seventeenth century the decline is apparent. The inspired phraseology, the wealth and flexibility of vocabulary, and the general bloom of the style pass into the lightness of fancy and the tinkling unsubstantial verse of the nature of Campion's. Or the high seriousness degenerates into the gloomy manner of the Websterian tragedy. The handling of blank verse is typical of the movement. The sinewy Shakespearian blank verse becomes nerveless; in drama prose is commoner in quantity and coarser in fibre. In the lyric much of the old technical dexterity survives, but the deeper qualities of passion and sincerity are less common and robust.

2. Prose. Unlike that of poetry, the style of prose enjoys a steady development, continued from the previous age, and maintained

TABLE TO ILLUSTRATE THE DEVELOPMENT OF LITERARY FORMS

DATE	POETRY			DRAMA		PROSE		
	Lyric	Narrative-Descriptive	Didactic	Comedy	Tragedy	Essay	Narrative	Didactic
1550	Wyatt Surrey	Surrey						Ascham
1560								
1570		Sackville[2]						
1580		Spenser[1]	Gascoigne[3]				North[8]	Lyly
1590		Marlowe		Lyly Greene	Peele Kyd Greene Marlowe			
1600	Daniel Donne	Donne Shakespeare[4]		Shakespeare Chapman Dekker Jonson	Chapman Marston	Bacon[5]	Nashe	Hooker[6] Spenser
1610	Campion	Drayton G. Fletcher	Drayton		Shakespeare Jonson Heywood Tourneur			
1620				Beaumont Fletcher }	Webster Beaumont Fletcher }	Overbury[7]		Donne
1630				Middleton	Middleton		Bacon	Bacon Ussher Burton Hall
1640		P. Fletcher						

[1] *The Shepheards Calender* (1579).
[2] *The Steele Glas* (1576).
[5] *Essays* (1597).
[7] *Characters* (1614).
[2] *The Induction* to the *Myrroure for Magistrates* (1563).
[4] *Venus and Adonis* (1593).
[6] *Of the Laws of Ecclesiastical Polity* (1593).
[8] Plutarch's *Lives* (1579).

through the Elizabethan age. Euphuism, which appeared early in this epoch, was a kind of literary measles incidental to early growth, and it quickly passed away, leaving the general body of English prose healthier than before. There is an increase in the raw material of prose in the shape of many foreign words that are imported; there is a growing expertness in sentence- and paragraph-construction and in the more delicate graces of style, such as rhythm and melody. The prose of Hooker and Bacon (in his later stages) represents the furthest development of the time. Prose style has yet a great deal to learn, but it is learning fast.

CHAPTER VI

THE AGE OF MILTON

TIME-CHART OF THE CHIEF AUTHORS

The thick line indicates approximately the period of active literary production.

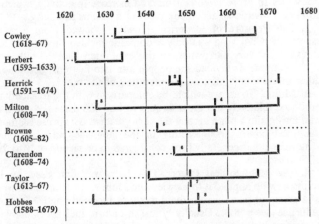

1 *Poetical Blossoms* (1633).
2 *Ode on the Morning of Christ's Nativity* (1629).
3 *Paradise Lost* (begun 1658).
4 *The History of the Rebellion and Civil Wars in England* (begun 1646).
5 *Holy Living* (1650).

2 *Noble Numbers* (1647).
5 *Religio Medici* (1642).
8 *Leviathan* (1651).

THE HISTORICAL BACKGROUND (1630–60)

The entire period covered by this chapter is dominated by the Civil War. The earlier years are marked by the quarrels and alarms which led up to actual hostilities in 1642; the middle of the period is occupied with the spasmodic fighting that lasted till the execution of Charles I in 1649; and the last portion covers the establishment of the Commonwealth, the rise and disappearance of Cromwell

(1653–58), the confusion following upon his death, and the final restoration of the monarchy in 1660.

LITERARY FEATURES OF THE AGE

1. The Reaction. During this period the decline from the high Elizabethan standard is apparent in several ways. (*a*) The output, especially of poetry, is much smaller, and the fashion is toward shorter poems, especially the lyric of a peculiar type. (*b*) There is a marked decay in the exalted poetical fervour of the previous age. In the new poetry there is more of the intellectual play of fancy than of passion and profundity. And, especially in prose, there is a matured melancholy that one is apt to associate with advancing years. (*c*) In prose there is a marked increase in activity, which is an almost invariable accompaniment of a decline in poetry.

2. The Pressure of Historical Events. Viewed from a broad aspect, the Civil War was only a domestic incident in English history; but the very narrowness of the issue intensified the bitterness of the contest. It divided the people into two factions, and among other things vitally affected the literature of the time.

3. Milton. In an age which, by comparison with the Elizabethan, produced relatively few great writers Milton stands as the one man who may claim a place among the very greatest. His prose is among the finest controversial writing in the language, and his poetic achievement has generally been considered to be second only to that of Shakespeare.

4. The Metaphysical Poets. This term was first used by Dr Johnson, who applied it to Cowley and Donne. It denotes the work of a group of poets who came directly or indirectly under Donne's influence (see p. 81). Usually lyrical in nature, their work shows a surprising blend of passion and thought; their poems are full of learned imagery and striking conceits, and, at their best, reveal great psychological insight and subtlety of thought development. In this category are included Crashaw, George Herbert, Vaughan, and Marvell. Their work will be considered in detail later in the chapter.

5. The Cavalier Poets. Where most of the metaphysical poets were of a religious and mystical cast, the Cavaliers, best represented by Herrick, Lovelace, and Suckling, dealt with themes of love. They followed Ben Jonson in their classical restraint and concise lucidity. Their work is simple and graceful in structure and finely polished in style.

6. The Expansion of Prose. The development of prose is carried on from the previous age. In spite of the hampering effects of the civil strife, the prose output was copious and excellent in kind. There was a notable advance in the sermon; pamphlets were abundant; and history, politics, philosophy, and miscellaneous kinds were well represented. In addition, there was a remarkable advance in prose style.

7. **The Collapse of the Drama.** Many things combined to oppress the drama at this time. Chief among these were the civil disturbances and the strong opposition of the Puritans. In temper the age was not dramatic. It is curious to note that Milton's greatest work, which in the Elizabethan age would probably have been dramatic in form, took on the shape of the epic. The actual dramatic work of the period was small and unimportant; and the unequal struggle was terminated by the closing of the theatres in 1642.

JOHN MILTON (1608–74)

1. **His Life.** Milton was born in Bread Street, Cheapside, London. His father was a money-scrivener, an occupation that combined the duties of the modern banker and lawyer. Milton was educated at St Paul's School, London, and at Cambridge. At the university his stubborn and irascible nature declared itself, and owing to insubordination he was 'sent down' for a term. On taking his final degree (1632) he abandoned his intention of entering the Church and retired to Horton, a small village in Buckinghamshire, some seventeen miles from London, whither his father had withdrawn from business.

Milton's next few years were those of a sequestered man of letters. Poetry, mathematics, and music were his main studies. In 1638 he left for a tour on the Continent, staying some months in Italy, where he met many scholars and literary men. He was recalled to England by the news that civil war was imminent. He settled down in London and set up a small private school, and when hostilities broke out a year or two later he took no part in the fighting. His pen, however, was active in support of the Parliamentary cause, to which he was passionately attached.

In 1643 he married a woman much younger than himself, and almost immediately his wife left him, and did not return for two years. This unfortunate circumstance led Milton to write two strong pamphlets on divorce, which caused a great scandal at the time. Then in 1649, after the execution of the King, he was appointed by the Commonwealth Government Secretary for Foreign

Tongues. In this capacity he became secretary to the Council of State, and drafted Latin documents for transmission to foreign Powers. In addition, he wrote numerous pamphlets in support of the republican cause. By this time his eyesight was failing; and when the Restoration came in 1660 to ruin his hopes, it found him blind, poor, and alone. He escaped, however, from the severe punishments that were inflicted upon many prominent Roundheads. He was slightly punished by a nominal imprisonment; retired to an obscure village in Buckinghamshire to write poetry; and died in London, where he was buried.

2. His Prose. Most of Milton's prose was written during the middle period of his life (1640–60), when he was busy with public affairs. The prose works have an unusual interest, because as a rule they have a direct bearing on either his personal business or public interests. In all they amount to twenty-five pamphlets, of which twenty-one are in English and the remaining four in Latin.

He began pamphleteering quite early (1641), when he engaged in a lively controversy with Bishop Hall over episcopacy. Then, while teaching, he wrote a rather poor tract, *Of Education* (1644). When his wife deserted him he composed two pamphlets on divorce (1643 and 1644), which scandalized the public by the freedom of their opinions and the slashing nature of their style. The critics of the pamphlets sought to confound Milton on a technical matter by pointing out that he had not licensed the books, as required by law. To this Milton retorted with the greatest of all his tracts, *Areopagitica* (1644), a noble and impassioned plea for the liberty of the Press. Later works include a defence (in Latin) of the execution of Charles I and of other actions of the Commonwealth Government. During the last years of his life Milton partly completed a *History of Britain* and other scholastic works.

When we consider the style of Milton's prose we must keep in mind how it was occasioned. His pamphlets were cast off at white heat and precipitated into print while some topic was in urgent debate either in Milton's or the public mind. Hence in method they are tempestuous and disordered; voluble, violent, and lax in style. They reveal intense zeal and pugnacity, a mind at once spacious in ideals and intolerant in application, a rich fancy, and a capacious scholarship. They lack humour, proportion, and restraint; but in spite of these defects they are among the greatest controversial compositions in the language. A short extract will illustrate some of the Miltonic features:

I deny not but that it is of greatest concernment in the Church and Commonwealth, to have a vigilant eye how books demean themselves as well as men; and thereafter to confine, imprison, and do sharpest justice on them as malefactors: for books are not absolutely dead things, but do contain a potency of life in them to be as active as that soul was whose progeny they are; nay, they do preserve as in a vial the purest efficacy and extraction of that living intellect that bred them. I know they are as lively, and as vigorously productive, as those fabulous dragon's teeth; and being sown up and down, may chance to spring up armed men. And yet on the other hand, unless wariness be used, as good almost kill a man as kill a good book; who kills a man kills a reasonable creature, God's image; but he who destroys a good book, kills reason itself, kills the image of God as it were in the eye. Many a man lives a burden to the earth; but a good book is the precious life-blood of a master spirit, embalmed and treasured up on purpose to a life beyond life.

Areopagitica

3. His Poetry. The great bulk of Milton's poetry was written during two periods separated from each other by twenty years: (a) the period of his university career and his stay at Horton, from 1629 to 1640; and (b) the last years of his life, from about 1660 to 1674. The years between were filled by a few sonnets.

(a) While still an undergraduate Milton began to compose poems of remarkable maturity and promise. They include the fine and stately *Ode on the Morning of Christ's Nativity* (1629), and the poems *On Shakespeare* (1630) and *On Arriving at the Age of Twenty-three* (1631). These poems show Milton's command of impressive diction and his high ideals, both literary and religious. While at Horton (probably in 1632) he composed *L'Allegro* and *Il Penseroso*, two longish poems in octosyllabic couplets dealing with the respective experiences of the gay and thoughtful man. The pieces are decorative rather than descriptive, artificial rather than natural, but they are full of scholarly fancy and adroit poetical phrasing. *Comus* (1634) belongs to this period, and is a masque containing some stiff but beautiful blank verse and some quite charming lyrical measures. *Lycidas* (1637) is an elegy on his friend Edward King, who was drowned on a voyage to Ireland. The real subject of the poem, however, is the uncertainty and torment occasioned in Milton's mind by his realization that death might forestall the achievement of the fame which was his ambition. In its varying moods we see the interplay of doubt, fear, anger, and, finally, a peaceful reliance on the belief that true fame rests on God and is only to be found in heaven. It is this underlying subject which gives the poem its passionate sincerity.

Lycidas, which is to be reckoned as among the highest of Milton's achievements, is something quite new in English poetry. In form it is pastoral, but this artificial medium serves only to show the power of Milton's grip, which can wring from intractable material the very essence of poetry. The elegy has the colour and music of the best Spenserian verse; but it has a climbing majesty of epithet and a dignified intensity of passion that Spenser does not possess. Its metre is an irregular stanza-sequence and rhyme-sequence of a peculiar haunting beauty.

> For, so to interpose a little ease,
> Let our frail thoughts dally with false surmise.
> Ay me! whilst thee the shores and sounding seas
> Wash far away,—where'er thy bones are hurled,
> Whether beyond the stormy Hebrides
> Where thou perhaps, under the whelming tide,
> Visit'st the bottom of the monstrous world;
> Or whether thou, to our moist vows denied,
> Sleep'st by the fable of Bellerus old,
> Where the great Vision of the guarded mount
> Looks towards Namancos and Bayona's hold. . . .

(*b*) This period (1660–74) gives us the poetry of the matured Milton. The work of the middle years is composed of a few sonnets. These, with some others written at different times, sufficiently show Milton's command of the Italian form, which he uses throughout. He gives it a sweep and sonorous impressiveness that set him alone beside Wordsworth, who in this respect is his poetical successor. The best of Milton's sonnets are *On his Blindness* and *On the Late Massacre in Piedmont*.

The great work of this time is *Paradise Lost*. It was begun as early as 1658, and issued in 1667. At first it was divided into ten books or parts, but in the second edition it was redivided into twelve. In form it follows the strict unity of the classical epic; in theme it deals with the fall of man; but by means of introduced narratives it covers the rebellion of Lucifer in heaven, the celestial warfare, and the expulsion of the rebels. In conception the poem is spacious and commanding; it is sumptuously adorned with all the detail that Milton's rich imagination, fed with classical and Biblical lore, can suggest; the characters, especially that of Lucifer, are drawn on a gigantic scale, and do not lack a certain tragic immensity; and the blank verse in which the work is composed is new and wonderful. This type of blank verse has founded a tradition in English; it has often been imitated and modified, but never paralleled. It lacks the suppleness of the Shakespearian measure, but it is instinct with beauty and scholarly care. It is almost infinite in modulation; varied cunningly in scansion, in pause, in cadence, and in sonorous dignity of music. It has its lapses into wordiness and bombast, but the lapses are few indeed.

In the following extract the construction of the blank verse should be carefully observed. The variation of foot, pause, and melody is worthy of the closest study.

> No sooner had the Almighty ceased, but all
> The multitude of angels, with a shout
> Loud as from numbers without number, sweet
> As from blest voices, uttering joy, Heaven rung
> With jubilee, and loud hosannas filled
> The eternal regions. Lowly reverent
> Towards either throne they bow, and to the ground,
> With solemn adoration, down they cast
> Their crowns inwove with amarant and gold—
> Immortal amarant, a flower which once
> In Paradise, fast by the tree of life,
> Began to bloom; but soon for man's offence
> To Heaven removed, where first it grew, there grows,
> And flowers aloft, shading the fount of life,
> And where the river of bliss, through midst of Heaven,
> Rolls o'er Elysian flowers her amber stream.

In 1671 Milton issued his last volume of poetry, which contained *Paradise Regained* and *Samson Agonistes*. The former poem, which tells of Christ's temptation and victory, is complementary to the earlier epic, and Milton hoped that it would surpass its predecessor. In this his hopes were dashed. It is briefer and poorer than *Paradise Lost*; it lacks the exalted imagination, the adornment, and the ornate rhythms of the earlier poem. There is little action, the characters are uninteresting, and the work approaches *Paradise Lost* only in a few outstanding passages.

Samson Agonistes, which tells of Samson's death while a prisoner of the Philistines, has a curious interest, for in the Biblical hero Milton saw more than one resemblance to himself. In form the work has the strict unity of time, place, and action universal in Greek tragedy. In style it is bleak and bare, in places harsh and forbidding; but in several places Milton's stubborn soul is wrung with pity and exalted by the hope that looks beyond. The speech of Samson's father over his dead son is no inappropriate epitaph for Milton himself:

> Come, come, no time for lamentation now,
> Nor much more cause; Samson hath quit himself
> Like Samson, and heroically hath finished
> A life heroic, on his enemies
> Fully revenged, hath left them years of mourning,
> And lamentation to the sons of Caphtor
> Through all Philistian bounds. To Israel
> Honour hath left, and freedom, let but them
> Find courage to lay hold on this occasion,
> To himself and father's house eternal fame;
> And, which is best and happiest yet, all this
> With God not parted from him, as was feared,
> But favouring and assisting to the end.
> Nothing is here for tears, nothing to wail
> Or knock the breast, no weakness, no contempt,
> Dispraise, or blame, nothing but well and fair,
> And what may quiet us in a death so noble.

4. Features of his Poetry. (*a*) *The Puritan Strain.* All through his life Milton's religious fervour was unshaken. Even his enemies did not deny his sincerity. It is seen even in one of his earliest sonnets:

> All is, if I have grace to use it so,
> As ever in my great Taskmaster's eye.

It persists even to the end, when it runs deeper and darker. In *Paradise Lost*, for example, his chief motive is to "justify the ways of God to men."

This religious tendency is apparent in (1) the choice of religious subjects, especially in the later poems; (2) the sense of responsibility and moral exaltation; (3) the fondness for preaching and lecturing, which in *Paradise Lost* is a positive weakness; (4) the narrowness of outlook, strongly Puritanical, seen in his outbursts against his opponents (as in *Lycidas*), in his belief regarding the inferiority of women, and in his scorn for the "miscellaneous rabble."

(*b*) *The Classical Strain.* Curiously interwrought with the severity of his religious nature is a strong bent for the classics, which is pagan and sensuous. His learning was wide and matured; he wrote Latin prose and verse as freely as he wrote English. His classical bent is apparent in (1) his choice of classical and semi-classical forms—such as the epic, the Greek tragedy, and the pastoral; (2) the elaborate descriptions and enormous similes in *Paradise Lost*; (3) the fondness for classical allusion, which runs riot through all his poetry; (4) the dignity of his style, and its precision and care. His very egoism takes a high classical turn. In his blindness he compares himself with

Blind Thamyris and blind Mæonides,
And Tiresias and Phineus, prophets old.

In his choice of diction we have the classical element abundantly apparent; and, lastly, the same element appears in the typical Miltonic grandeur and frigidity, the arrogant aloofness from men and mortals.

(c) *His Poetical Genius.* As a poet Milton is not a great innovator; his function is rather to refine and make perfect. Every form he touches acquires a finality of grace and dignity. The epic, the ode, the classical drama, the sonnet, the masque, and the elegy—his achievements in these have never been bettered and seldom approached. As a metrist he stands almost alone. In all his metres we observe the same ease, sureness, and success.

(d) *His Position in Literature.* In literature Milton occupies an important central or transitional position. He came immediately after the Elizabethan epoch, when the Elizabethan methods were crumbling into chaos. His hand and temper were firm enough to gather into one system the wavering tendencies of poetry, and to give them sureness, accuracy, and variety. The next generation, lacking the inspiration of the Elizabethans, found in him the necessary stimulus to order and accuracy; and from him, to a great extent, sprang the new 'classicism' that was to be the rule for more than a century.

OTHER POETS

1. **The Metaphysical Poets.** The works of this group of poets have several features in common: (i) the poetry is to a great extent lyrical; (ii) in subject it is chiefly religious or amatory; (iii) there is much metrical facility, even in complicated lyrical stanzas; (iv) the poetic style is sometimes almost startling in its sudden beauty of phrase and melody of diction, but there are unexpected turns of language and figures of speech (hence the name of the group).

(a) **George Herbert (1593–1633)** was born at Montgomery Castle, educated at Westminster School and at Trinity College, Cambridge, where he was appointed Fellow and reader, took holy orders, and, in 1630, became rector of Bemerton, near Salisbury.

None of his poems was published during his lifetime. *The Temple* (published 1633) shows his zeal for the Church of England and concern with practical theology. He himself described the work as "a picture of the many spiritual conflicts that have passed betwixt God and my soul, before I could subject mine to the will of Jesus

my Master; in whose service I have now found perfect freedom."
The poems are peculiarly honest, intimate, sincere, and modest.
They are homely, quiet, and colloquial, and touched with a quaint
humour. They are metaphysical in their unusual conceits (though
Herbert does not cultivate the learned scholastic imagery of Donne)
and in the blend of thought and feeling. Herbert was a careful
artist, precise and simple in expression, fond of unusual metrical
patterns (as in *Easter Wings*), and a lover of harmony. His poetry
is sensitive to the most delicate changes of feeling. We give here a
typical and well-known poem from *The Temple*:

THE COLLAR

I Struck the board, and cry'd, No more.
I will abroad.
What? shall I ever sigh and pine?
My lines and life are free; free as the rode,
Loose as the winde, as large as store.
Shall I be still in suit?
Have I no harvest but a thorn
To let me bloud, and not restore
What I have lost with cordiall fruit?
Sure there was wine
Before my sighs did drie it: there was corn
Before my tears did drown it.
Is the yeare onely lost to me?
Have I no bayes to crown it?
No flowers, no garlands gay? all blasted?
All wasted?
Not so, my heart: but there is fruit,
And thou hast hands.
Recover all thy sigh-blown age
On double pleasures: leave thy cold dispute
Of what is fit, and not; forsake thy cage,
Thy rope of sands,
Which pettie thoughts have made, and made to thee
Good cable, to enforce and draw,
And by thy law,
While thou didst wink and wouldst not see.
Away; take heed:
I will abroad.
Call in they deaths head there: tie up thy fears.
He that forbears
To suit and serve his need,
Deserves his load.
But as I rav'd and grew more fierce and wilde
At every word,
Me thoughts I heard one calling, *Childe*:
And I reply'd, *My Lord.*

(*b*) **Richard Crashaw (1613 (?)–49)**, the son of a Puritan clergyman, was born in London and educated at the Charterhouse and at Cambridge. During the Civil War his professed Royalist sympathies led to the loss (in 1644) of his fellowship at Peterhouse. He then went abroad and, in 1645, entered the Roman Church. He died at Loretto.

His best work is in *Steps to the Temple* (1646) and much of it was reprinted with valuable additions in *Carmen Deo Nostro* (1652).

In many ways Crashaw is not metaphysical: his poems reveal no complexity of mind, no conflict or tension: the manner is not colloquial, and the images are pictorial rather than intellectual, lacking the homeliness of Donne and Herbert. At the same time he has the metaphysical fondness for the striking conceit, which, in him, often becomes fantastic. His poetry is notable for its fire and fervour, and the impetus which it derives from his religious excitement and exaltation. It is emotional rather than thoughtful, and his long, irregular odes are full of gaudy extravagances and sensuous decoration, often showing an undisciplined rapture, though he is capable of simple beauty.

We quote an extract to show the exalted mood to which his poetry can ascend:

> Live in these conquering leaves; live all the same;
> And walk through all tongues one triumphant flame;
> Live here, great heart;[1] and love, and die, and kill;
> And bleed, and wound, and yield, and conquer still.
> Let this immortal life where'er it comes
> Walk in a crowd of loves and martyrdoms.
> Let mystic deaths wait on't; and wise souls be
> The love-slain witnesses of this life of thee.
> O sweet incendiary! show here thy art,
> Upon this carcase of a hard cold heart. . . .
> Oh thou undaunted daughter of desires!
> By all thy dower of lights and fires; . . .
> By all thy brim-filled bowls of fierce desire;
> By thy last morning's draught of liquid fire;
> By the full kingdom of that final kiss
> That seized thy parting soul, and sealed thee his; . . .
> Leave nothing of myself in me.

> *The Flaming Heart*

(*c*) **Henry Vaughan (1622 (?)–95)** was born in Wales, and was descended from an ancient family. After Oxford, he went to London to study law, then turned to medicine, and practised at Brecon.

[1] Of St Teresa.

His books include *Poems* (1646), *Olor Iscanus* (published 1651)
Silex Scintillans (1650), and *Thalia Rediviva* (1678).

Vaughan's love-poems, though they are often prettily and sometimes beautifully phrased, are inferior to his religious pieces,
especially those in *Silex Scintillans*. His religious fervour is nobly
imaginative, and strikes out lines and ideas of astonishing strength
and beauty. His regard for nature, moreover, has a closeness and
penetration that sometimes (for example, in *The Retreat*) suggest
Wordsworth.

(*d*) **Thomas Carew (1594 (?)–1639 (?))** was born in Kent, educated
at Oxford, and studied law in the Middle Temple. He attained to
some success as a courtier, but later died in obscurity.

His *Poems* (1640) show his undoubted lyrical ability. The pieces
are influenced by Donne and Jonson, but they have a character of
their own. The fancy is warmly coloured, though it is marred by
licence and bad taste. We quote a lyric which can be taken as
representative of the best of its kind. Its fancy is too rich and
beautiful to be called fantastic, and its golden felicity of diction is
rarely equalled.

> Ask me no more where Jove bestows,
> When June is past, the fading rose,
> For in your beauty's orient deep
> These flowers, as in their causes, sleep.
>
> Ask me no more whither do stray
> The golden atoms of the day,
> For, in pure love, heaven did prepare
> Those powders to enrich your hair.
>
> Ask me no more whither doth haste
> The nightingale when May is past,
> For in your sweet dividing throat
> She winters and keeps warm her note.
>
> Ask me no more where those stars light
> That downwards fall in dead of night,
> For in your eyes they sit, and there,
> Fixed, become as in their sphere.
>
> Ask me no more if east or west
> The phœnix builds her spicy nest,
> For unto you at last she flies,
> And in your fragrant bosom dies.

(*e*) **Abraham Cowley (1618–67)** was born in London, the son of a
wealthy citizen. He was educated at Westminster School and at
Cambridge, where he distinguished himself as a classical scholar.

In the Civil War he warmly supported the King; followed the royal family into exile, where he performed valuable services; returned to England at the Restoration; and for the remainder of his life composed books in retirement.

Cowley, even more than Pope and Macaulay, is the great example of the infant prodigy. When he was ten he wrote a long epical romance, *Pyramus and Thisbe* (1628), and two years later produced an even longer poem called *Constantia and Philetus* (1630). All through his life he was active in the production of many kinds of work—poems, plays, essays, and histories. His best-known poem was *The Davideis* (published 1656), a rather dreary epic on King David, in heroic couplets. Other poems were *The Mistress* (1647), a collection of love-poems, and the *Pindarique Odes*, which are a curious hybrid between the early freedom of the Elizabethans and the classicism of the later generation. His prose works included his *Essays* and *Discourse by way of Vision concerning the Government of Oliver Cromwell* (1661).

In Cowley the metaphysical strain had become feeble. He was learned and ingenious of fancy, but his work suffered from a lack of deep feeling, and in him the use of the metaphysical wit and conceit deteriorated into mere ingenuity and mannerism.

Both in prose and poetry he was a man of various methods, showing the wavering moods of the transitional poet. His heroic couplets and irregular odes foreshadow the vogue of the approaching 'correctness'; his essays, in their pleasant egoism and miscellaneous subject-matter, suggest Addison; and his prose style, plain and not inelegant, draws near to the mode of Dryden. His variety pleased many tastes; hence the popularity that was showered upon him during his day. But he excelled in no particular method; and hence the partial oblivion that has followed.

(*f*) **Andrew Marvell (1621–78)**, the son of a clergyman, was educated at Cambridge. After a period abroad he became tutor to the daughter of Lord Fairfax, and during this period (1650–52) he wrote most of his best poetry. From 1657 to 1659 he assisted Milton in his duties as Secretary for Foreign Tongues, and he helped to protect him from the royal wrath after 1660. He served as Member of Parliament for Hull from 1659 until his death.

His controversial prose writings were popular in his day, but, with the exception of his vindication of Milton in *The Rehearsal Transprosed* (1672–73), a work full of humour and charm, and his *News-letters*, which reported to his constituents the doings of Parliament during the period of his membership of the House, they are now of little interest.

His poems were circulated in manuscript during his life, but most were not published until 1681. They have been described as the finest flower of serious and secular metaphysical verse. Marvell's work has the subtlety of wit, the passionate argument and the learned imagery of the metaphysicals, combined with the clarity and control of the classical followers of Jonson and the gracefulness of the cavaliers. His rhythms are flexible, his melody delicate. He loved Nature and the freshness of gardens, and in all his work there is a high seriousness and absolute sincerity. We give below the well-known lines from *To his Coy Mistress*, which illustrate clearly the metaphysical blend of passion and fantastic conceit, handled by Marvell with his distinctive control and poise.

> But at my back I always hear
> Time's winged chariot hurrying near:
> And yonder all before us lie
> Deserts of vast Eternity.
> Thy beauty shall no more be found;
> Nor, in thy marble vault, shall sound
> My echoing song: then worms shall try
> That long preserved virginity:
> And your quaint honour turn to dust;
> And into ashes all my lust.
> The grave's a fine and private place,
> But none I think do there embrace.

2. The **Cavalier poets** are lyrical poets, and deal chiefly with love and war.

(*a*) **Robert Herrick (1591–1674)** was born in London, and educated at Cambridge. In 1629 he was appointed to a living in Devonshire, where he died.

His two volumes of poems are *Noble Numbers* (1647) and *Hesperides* (1648). Both are collections of short poems, sacred and profane. In them he reveals lyrical power of a high order: fresh, passionate, and felicitously exact, but at the same time meditative and observant. Herrick was strongly influenced by Jonson and the classics; he delighted in the good things of this world; but that did not prevent his having a keen enjoyment of Nature and a fresh outlook upon life. Among the best known of his shorter pieces are *To Anthea, To Julia,* and *Cherry Ripe.*

(*b*) **Richard Lovelace (1618–58)** was born at Woolwich, was educated at the Charterhouse and at Oxford. When the Civil War broke out he was imprisoned by the Roundheads; and, being liberated on parole, could do little actively to assist Charles. At a later stage he saw some soldiering in France, returned to England, and died in obscure circumstances.

His volume *Lucasta* (1649) contains the best of his shorter pieces, which had appeared at different times previously. His best-known lyrics, such as *To Althea, from Prison* and *To Lucasta, going to the Wars*, are simple and sincere, and free from the cynicism of his day, but most of his poems are careless in workmanship, full of affected wit and gallantry, and often rendered obscure by extravagant and grotesque conceits.

(c) **Sir John Suckling (1609–42)** was born in Middlesex, and at the age of eighteen fell heir to a large fortune. He was educated at Oxford, travelled on the Continent, served as a volunteer under Gustavus Adolphus, and became a favourite of Charles I. He was implicated in Royalist plots, and escaped abroad (1641), where he died under conditions that are somewhat mysterious.

To some extent (for he seems to have lacked physical courage) Suckling was the cavalier of the romances and the Restoration plays —gay, generous, and witty. His poems largely reflect these characteristics. As a poet he has great ability, but he is usually the elegant amateur, disdaining serious and sustained labour. Some of his poems, such as the *Ballad upon a Wedding* (given below) and *Why so Pale and Wan, Fond Lover?* show the tricksy elegance that is his chief attraction.

> Her finger was so small, the ring,
> Would not stay on, which they did bring,
>   It was too wide a peck:
> And to say truth (for out it must)
> It looked like the great collar (just)
>   About our young colt's neck.
>
> Her feet beneath her petticoat,
> Like little mice, stole in and out,
>   As if they feared the light:
> But O, she dances such a way!
> No sun upon an Easter-day
>   Is half so fine a sight.
>
> Her cheeks so rare a white was on,
> No daisy makes comparison,
>   (Who sees them is undone),
> For streaks of red were mingled there,
> Such as are on a Catherine pear
>   The side that's next the sun.

A Ballad upon a Wedding

DRAMA

1. Philip Massinger (1583–1640) was born at Salisbury, educated at Oxford, and became a literary man in London, writing plays for the King's Men, a company of actors. If we may judge from his begging letters that survive, he found in dramatic work little financial encouragement. He died and was buried in London.

Massinger began his career as a collaborator with older, better-known dramatists, and especially with Fletcher, whose influence over him was strong. Among his best-known plays are his comedies, *A New Way to Pay Old Debts* (published 1633) and *The City Madam* (published 1632), and his tragedies, *The Duke of Milaine* (published 1623) and *The Unnatural Combat* (published 1639). His finest qualities are the fluency and vitality of his blank verse, the clarity and strength of his plot construction, and his fine theatre sense. His characters (with one or two notable exceptions, like Sir Giles Overreach in *A New Way to Pay Old Debts*, and Luke Frugal in *The City Madam*) are usually types rather than individuals, and in situation, theatrical device, and characterization, he has a fondness for repetition which is a serious weakness. The shallow, boldly drawn characters often place too great a strain upon our credulity —his villains are villainous, and his women shameless, to an incredible degree. Predominantly serious in temper, Massinger often deals with the political issues of his day. He seems to lack real humour, and the comic garb can sit rather uneasily upon him.

2. John Ford (1586–1639?) was born in Devonshire, perhaps educated at Oxford, and studied, though he seems never to have practised, law. He became an active producer of plays, chiefly tragedies, both on his own account and in collaboration with other playwrights.

In his nature Ford had a morbid twist which gave him a strange liking for the horrible and the unnatural. His plays are unequal in quality; but the most powerful of them are prevented from being revolting by their real tragic force and their high literary aims. In *The Broken Heart* (published 1633) he harrows the reader's feelings almost beyond endurance, while *'Tis Pity She's a Whore* of the same year is a grim story of unhallowed passion; his *Perkin Warbeck* (1634), a historical tragedy, is reckoned to be among the best historical drama outside of Shakespeare; and in *The Witch of Edmonton* (soon after 1621) he collaborated with Dekker, Rowley, and others to produce a powerful domestic drama. Others of the sixteen plays attributed to him are *The Lover's Melancholy* (1628), *Love's Sacrifice* (1633), and *The Fancies, Chast and Noble* (1638).

PROSE

Sir Thomas Browne (1605–82) may be taken as representative of the best prose-writers of the period.

1. His Life. Browne was born in London, educated at Winchester and Oxford, and studied medicine. For a time he practised in Oxfordshire; then he travelled abroad, receiving his degree of M.D. at Leyden. Returning to England (*c.* 1634), he soon removed to Norwich (1637), where for the remainder of his life he successfully practised as a doctor,

2. His Works. Almost alone among his contemporaries, Browne seems to have been unaffected by the commotions of the time. His prose works, produced during some of the hottest years of civil contention, are tranquilly oblivious of unrest. His books are only five in number, are individually small in size, and are of great and almost uniform merit. *Religio Medici* (written *c.* 1635 and published 1642), his confession of faith, is a curious mixture of religious faith and scientific scepticism; *Pseudodoxia Epidemica*, or *Vulgar Errors* (1646), sharing the same mental inconsistency, resembles the work of Burton in its out-of-the-way learning; *Hydriotaphia: Urne Buriall* (1658), commonly considered to be his masterpiece, contains reflections on human mortality induced by the discovery of some ancient funeral urns; *The Garden of Cyrus* (1658) is a treatise on the quincunx. A last work, *Christian Morals*, was published after his death.

3. His Style. Browne's claim to fame is as a literary stylist rather than as a philosopher. He shows the ornate style of the time in its richest bloom. His diction is strongly Latinized, sometimes to the limit of obscurity; and he has the scholastic habit of introducing Latin tags and references. In this he resembles Burton; but in other respects he is far beyond the author of *The Anatomy of Melancholy*. His sentences are carefully wrought and artistically combined into paragraphs; and, most important from the purely literary point of view, the diction has a richness of effect unknown among other English prose-writers. The rhythm is harmonious, and finishes with carefully attuned cadences. The prose is sometimes obscure, rarely vivacious, and hardly ever diverting; but the solemnity and beauty of it have given it an enduring fascination. A brief extract will illustrate some of its qualities:

Pious spirits who passed their days in raptures of futurity, made little more of this world, than the world that was before it, while they lay obscure in the chaos of preordination, and night of their fore-beings. And if any have been so happy as truly to understand Christian annihilation, ecstasies, exolution, liquefaction, transformation, the kiss of the spouse, gustation of God, and ingression into the divine shadow, they have already had an handsome anticipation of heaven; the glory of the world is surely over, and the earth in ashes unto them.

To subsist in lasting monuments, to live in their productions, to exist in their names and predicament of chimeras, was large satisfaction unto old expectations, and made one part of their Elysiums. But all this is nothing in the metaphysics of true belief. To live, indeed, is to be again ourselves, which being not only an hope, but an evidence in noble believers, 'tis all one to lie in St Innocent's churchyard, as in the sands of Egypt. Ready to be anything, in the ecstasy of being ever, and as content with six foot as the *moles* of Adrianus.

Hydriotaphia

OTHER PROSE-WRITERS

1. Edward Hyde, Earl of Clarendon (1609–74), was born in Wiltshire, educated at Oxford, and studied law. A man of excellent address, he was a successful lawyer, and became a member of the House of Commons. At first he was attached to the Parliamentary side, but he separated from the party on account of their attitude to the Church. He changed over to the Royalists, and thenceforward became one of the foremost advocates of the King's cause. After the downfall of the Royalists he accompanied the young Charles into exile; and at the Restoration he was appointed Lord Chancellor and raised to the peerage as Earl of Clarendon. He was too severe for the frivolous Restoration times, was exiled (1667), and died in France. His body was buried in Westminster Abbey.

His great work, *The History of the Rebellion and Civil Wars in England*, was begun as early as 1646 and finished during the years of his last exile. It was not published till 1704. To some extent the work is based on his own knowledge of the struggle; it lacks proportion and complete accuracy; but the narrative is strong and attractive, and it contains masterly character-sketches of some of the chief figures in the struggle. It is composed in long, lumbering sentences, loaded with parentheses and digressions, but the style is readable. It is the most important English work of a historical nature up to the date of its issue.

2. Thomas Hobbes (1588–1679) was born at Malmesbury, and was the son of a clergyman. He finished his education at Oxford, and became tutor to the future Earl of Devonshire. He supported the Royalist cause, was exiled by the Roundheads, and at the Restoration was awarded a pension. The remainder of his long life was devoted to literature.

Hobbes took an active part in the intellectual broils of the period, and much of his work is violently contentious. His chief book was *Leviathan* (1651), which expounded his political theories. The ardour of his opinions embroiled him with both of the chief political parties, but the abuse that it occasioned gave the book an immense interest. The style in which it is written is hard, clear, and accurate —almost the ideal medium for sustained exposition and argument.

3. **Jeremy Taylor (1613–67)** is the most prominent literary divine of the period. The son of a barber, he was born and educated at Cambridge, though latterly he removed to Oxford. Taking holy orders, he distinguished himself as an ardent expounder of the Royalist cause, and for a time he was imprisoned by the Parliamentary party. At the Restoration he was rewarded by being appointed to the Irish bishoprics of Down and Dromore. He died in Ireland.

A learned, voluble, and impressive preacher, Taylor carried the same qualities into his prose works, which consisted of tracts, sermons, and theological books. His most popular works, in addition to his collections of sermons, were *The Liberty of Prophesying* (1647), *Holy Living* (1650), and *Holy Dying* (1651). In his writings he is fond of quotations and allusions and of florid, rhetorical figures, such as simile, exclamation, and apostrophe; and his language, built into long, stately, but comprehensible sentences, is abundant, melodious, and pleasing.

4. **Thomas Fuller (1608–61)** was born in Northamptonshire, his father being a clergyman. He was educated at Cambridge, and took holy orders. He received various appointments, and by his witty sermons attracted the notice of Charles I. During the Civil War he was a chaplain to the Royalist forces; but when his side was defeated he made his peace with the Parliamentary party and was permitted to carry on his literary labours. He died the year after the Restoration.

Fuller had an original and penetrating mind, a wit apt for caustic comment, and an industry that remained unimpaired till the end of his life. His literary works are therefore of great interest and value. His serious historical books include *The History of the Holy War* (1639), dealing with the Crusades, and *The Church History of Britain*

(1655). Among his pamphlets are *Good Thoughts in Bad Times* (1645), and *An Alarum to the Counties of England and Wales* (1660). The work that has given him his reputation is his *The Worthies of England*, published by his son in 1662. It shows his peculiar jocosity at its best.

THE DEVELOPMENT OF LITERARY FORMS

1. Poetry. (*a*) *The Lyric.* The period is rich in lyrical poetry of a peculiar kind. The theme is chiefly love or religion. With the exception of some of those of Marvell, most of the love-poems are dedicated to ladies of the usual literary convention, such as Althea, Celia, and Phyllis, who both in name and nature resemble the stock characters of the artificial pastoral poetry. The language addressed to such creations cannot be that of deep and genuine passion; it is rather that of polite compliment, verbal quibble, or courtly jest. This type of lyric is a charming literary exercise, but hardly the inspired searching of the lover's heart. We have already noticed the poems of Herrick, Lovelace, Suckling, and Carew as being representative of this class. To these names may be added those of **George Wither (1588–1667)**, who writes freshly and sweetly, and the numerous miscellaneous song-writers, mostly anonymous, who in inspired moments could produce such charming lyrics as "Phillida flouts me."

The religious lyric, on the other hand, as we can see in the case of Crashaw and Vaughan, is frequently passionately inspired; and we have commented upon the incongruity that frequently disfigures the style. In the case of Milton his lyrics are superbly phrased, but they too lack spontaneity. His sonnets, among the noblest of their class, have much more depth of feeling.

(*b*) *The Epic.* The true epic treats of a sublime subject in the grand manner. In some respects *Beowulf* is an epic, but strictly speaking the English epic does not appear till this age. Cowley's *Davideis* (1656) and Davenant's *Gondibert* (1650) aspire to be great epics; but though they subscribe to the rules governing the outward form of the species they lack the inner spirit and they are failures. Milton's *Paradise Lost* (begun in 1658) has the heat and inspiration, but the Puritan bias in his nature led him to the rather unsuitable subject of the fall of man. It is unsuitable because it is weak in heroic action. Much more appropriate would have been the story of King Arthur, which for a long time he thought of using. Otherwise Milton's treatment of the subject is strictly orthodox. Nominally at least he adheres to the epical unity of action; he draws his characters with the wide sweep; and the style is a triumph of English epical style. His *Paradise Regained* (1671) is worked out on the same lines, but it is shorter and weaker than the earlier epic.

(c) *The Ode.* In Spenser's *Epithalamion* and *Prothalamion* we have seen the irregular ode attain to a high degree of perfection. In this age we observe the appearance of the Pindaric ode, which was to be so popular in the succeeding generations. Though it appears to be irregular, the Pindaric ode is really bound by stringent rules; its language is ornately artificial; and its diction mannered and unreal. Therefore it is suited to the needs of a transitional period that desires artificiality with a show of freedom. Cowley's *Pindarique Odes* (1656) are the first of their class in English.

(d) *Descriptive and Narrative Poetry.* In this wide class we may include Milton's *L'Allegro* and *Il Penseroso*, Herrick's pastoral poems, and Crashaw's religious-descriptive pieces. To these may be added the *Cooper's Hill* (1642) of **Sir John Denham (1615–69)**, a descriptive poem much praised in its day, and the romantic poem *Pharonnida* (1659) by **William Chamberlayne (1619–89)**. In all these poems we may observe the growing tendency to avoid contact with actual wild nature, and to seek rather the conventional and bookish landscapes familiar in the more artificial classical authors. Already the new classicism is declaring itself.

2. Drama. Earlier in this chapter we have noticed the decline and temporary collapse of the drama (1642). The plays of Massinger sustain the expiring spirit of the great Elizabethans; those of Ford follow the tragical school of Webster and Tourneur. Other play-wrights are **James Shirley (1596–1666)**, who wrote some pleasing comedies of London life, such as *The Lady of Pleasure* (1635), and the feebler writers **Suckling** and **Davenant**.

3. Prose. While the period is almost devoid of narrative prose of the lighter sort, it is quite rich in prose of other kinds.

(a) *The Sermon.* This period has been called 'the Golden Age of the English pulpit.' No doubt the violent religious strife of the time has much to do with the great flow of sermon writing, which is marked with eloquence, learning, and strong argument. In addition to Jeremy Taylor and Fuller, already mentioned, we may notice **Robert South (1634–1716)**, who writes rather more briefly and simply than the rest, **Isaac Barrow (1630–77)**, learned and copious, and **Richard Baxter (1615–91)**, a Nonconformist, whose *The Saints' Everlasting Rest* (1649) has survived all his preachings.

(b) *Philosophical Works*. On the moral side there are the works of Sir Thomas Browne; on the political those of Hobbes; and on the religious side the books of **John Hales (1584–1656)**. Works of this type show a growing knowledge and advancing scholarship, joined sometimes to quaint conceits and artless credulity.

(c) *Historical Works*. In this class Clarendon's and Fuller's works stand pre-eminent. The development of the history will be noticed in a future chapter (see p. 280).

(d) *Miscellaneous Prose*. In this large and varied group may be included the pamphlets of Milton, Hobbes, Fuller, and many more; the attractive books of **Izaak Walton (1593–1683)**, whose *The Compleat Angler* (1653) is the classic of its kind; the interesting *Resolves*, short miscellaneous essays, of **Owen Felltham (1602 (?)–68)**; and the *Familiar Letters* (1645), an early type of essay-journalism, of **James Howell (1594 (?)–1666)**.

THE DEVELOPMENT OF LITERARY STYLE

1. Poetry. In surveying the poetical style of the age one is aware of conflicting tendencies, a state of affairs quite in keeping with the transitional nature of the time.

(a) The *lyrical style* shows a decline from the natural splendours of the Elizabethan age; but it shows an increase in care, in polish, and in actual metrical dexterity. Moreover, in the best examples of the time we find a melodious resonance and beauty that are quite peculiar to the period. The lyric of Carew quoted on p. 142 illustrates this felicity both of sound and expression. The startling 'metaphysical' quality of the works of many of the poets has been commented upon. It is revealed at its worst in the works of **John Cleveland (1613–58)**, whose more violent efforts came to be known as '*Clevelandisms*.' The following is a mild example of his manner:

> The flowers, called out of their beds,
> Start and raise up their drowsy heads;
> And he that for their colour seeks,
> May find it vaulting in her cheeks,
> Where roses mix; no civil war
> Between her York and Lancaster.
> The marigold, whose courtier's face
> Echoes the sun, and doth unlace
> Her at his rise, at his full stop
> Packs and shuts up her gaudy shop,
> Mistakes her cue, and doth display:
> Thus Phillis antedates the day.

> *Upon Phillis walking in a Morning before Sun-rising*

(b) In *blank verse* conflicting movements are also apparent. In Milton the style reaches a magnificent climax. But in the drama, especially in the drama of minor playwrights of the ability of Suckling and Davenant, it becomes a huddle of verse and prose, so bad that one hesitates to say where the verse ends and the prose begins. It is the last stage of poetical decrepitude.

(c) The *heroic couplet* begins to appear, ushering in its long reign. We have it appearing as early as Spenser's *Shepheards Calender* (1579) and Sandys' *Ovid's Metamorphoses* (1626) or (often with an eleventh unstressed syllable) as far back as Chaucer; but the true stopped couplet, as used by Dryden and developed by Pope, is usually set down to the credit of Cowley's *Davideis* (1656), or Denham's *Cooper's Hill* (1642), or the shorter poems of **Edmund Waller (1606–87)**, who wrote stopped couplets as early as 1623. The heroic couplet will receive further notice in the next chapter.

2. Prose. In prose also we see the opposing tendencies. The principal movement is toward ornate prose, in Browne, Jeremy Taylor, Clarendon, and in the Scottish writer **William Drummond of Hawthornden (1585–1649)**, whose *A Cypresse Grove* (1623) is in the fashionable funereal vein. In the middle style we have the precision of Hobbes in *Leviathan*. At the other extreme from the ornate, the miscellaneous writers adopt great simplicity. Of this class, which includes Howell and Felltham, the best example is Izaak Walton, whose artless prose is shown in the following specimen:

> *Piscator.* O sir, doubt not but that angling is an art. Is it not an art to deceive a trout with an artificial fly? a trout that is more sharp-sighted than any hawk you have named, and more watchful and timorous than your high-mettled merlin is bold! and yet I doubt not to catch a brace or two to-morrow for a friend's breakfast. Doubt not, therefore, sir, but that angling is an art, and an art worth your learning; the question is rather, whether you be capable of learning it? for angling is somewhat like poetry, men are to be born so—I mean with inclinations to it, though both may be heightened by discourse and practice; but he that hopes to be a good angler must not only bring an inquiring, searching, observing wit, but he must bring a large measure of hope and patience, and a love and propensity to the art itself; but having once got and practised it, then doubt not but angling will prove to be so pleasant that it will prove to be like virtue, a reward to itself.
>
> *The Compleat Angler*

TABLE TO ILLUSTRATE THE DEVELOPMENT OF LITERARY FORMS

DATE	POETRY			DRAMA		PROSE		
	Lyric	Epic	Descriptive	Comedy	Tragedy	Historical	Religious	Miscel-laneous
1630	Wither Milton[1]		Cowley	Massinger Davenant	Ford			
1640	Herbert Suckling Carew		Milton	Suckling		Fuller		
1650	Crashaw Vaughan Herrick Lovelace	Davenant	Denham			Clarendon[5]	Browne[4] Fuller Baxter Taylor[6]	Milton Howell Browne
1660	Marvell Cowley	Cowley Milton[2]	Chamber-layne				Barrow	Hobbes Walton Fuller
1670					Milton[2]			

[1] *Ode on the Morning of Christ's Nativity* (1629).
[2] *Samson Agonistes* (1671).
[3] *The History of the Rebellion and Civil Wars in England* (begun 1646).
[2] *Paradise Lost* (begun 1658).
[4] *Religio Medici* (1642).
[6] *Holy Living* (1650).

CHAPTER VII

THE AGE OF DRYDEN

TIME-CHART OF THE CHIEF AUTHORS

The thick line shows the period of active literary work.

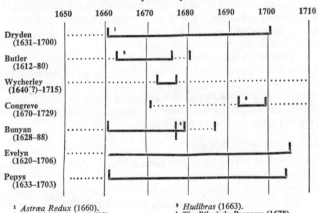

| | 1650 | 1660 | 1670 | 1680 | 1690 | 1700 | 1710 |

Dryden (1631–1700)
Butler (1612–80)
Wycherley (1640?)–1715)
Congreve (1670–1729)
Bunyan (1628–88)
Evelyn (1620–1706)
Pepys (1633–1703)

[1] *Astræa Redux* (1660).   [2] *Hudibras* (1663).
[3] *The Old Bachelor* (1693).   [4] *The Pilgrim's Progress* (1678).

THE HISTORICAL BACKGROUND (1660–1700)

Three historical events deeply influenced the literary movements of the time: the Restoration of the year 1660; the Roman Catholic controversy that raged during the latter half of Charles II's reign; and the Revolution of the year 1688.

1. The Restoration (1660). The Restoration of Charles II brought about a revolution in our literature. With the collapse of the Puritan Government there sprang up activities that had been so long suppressed that they flew to violent excesses. The Commonwealth had insisted on gravity and decorum in all things; the Restoration encouraged a levity that often became immoral and indecent. Along with much that is sane and powerful, this latter tendency is prominent in the writing of the time, especially in the comedies.

2. The Religious Question. The strength of the religious-political passions of the time is reflected in the current literature. The religion of the King was suspect; that of his brother James was avowedly Papist; and James was the heir-apparent to the crown. There was a prevalent suspicion of the Catholics, which, though it might have been groundless, was of such depth and intensity that it colours all the writings of the time. The lies of Titus Oates added to the popular frenzy, so that when the Earl of Shaftesbury sought to exclude James from the throne and supplant him by the Duke of Monmouth it needed all the efforts of Charles (himself secretly a Roman Catholic) to save his brother. The famous poem of Dryden, *Absalom and Achitophel*, is an outstanding example of a kind of poem that abounded during those troubled years.

3. The Revolution (1688). James succeeded to the throne in 1685; but so soon did he reveal his Roman Catholic prejudices that he was rejected in three years and was replaced by Protestant sovereigns. Henceforth religious passions diminish in intensity; and the literature of the succeeding years tends to emphasize the political rather than the religious side of public affairs.

THE NEW CLASSICISM

By the year 1660 Elizabethan romanticism had all but spent itself. Of the great figures of the earlier era only one survived, John Milton, and he had still to write *Paradise Lost*; but in everything Milton was of the past. At the Restoration he retired and worked in obscurity, and his great poem reveals no signs of the time in which his later years were cast.

At the Restoration the break with the past was almost absolute. It involved our literature in the deepest degree; subject and style took on a new spirit and outlook, a different attitude and aim. Hence the post-Restoration period is often set up as the converse and antithesis of the previous Elizabethan age. It is called *classical*, as opposed to the Elizabethan *romanticism*. Though the contrast between the two epochs need not be over-emphasized, yet the differences are very great. Let us see in what respects the new spirit is shown.

1. Imitation of the Ancients. Lacking the genius of the Elizabethans, the authors of the time turned to the great classical writers, in particular to the Latin writers, for guidance and inspiration. This habit, quite noticeable during the time of Dryden, deepened and hardened during the succeeding era of Pope—so much so that the latter laid down as a final test of excellence:

> Learn hence for ancient rules a just esteem;
> To copy Nature is to copy them.

2. Imitation of the French. Charles II had spent most of his years of exile in France, and when he returned to England he brought with him a new admiration for French literature. In particular the effects of this penetrated very deeply into the drama, especially into comedy, the most copious literary product of the Restoration. Of French comedy the great Molière was the outstanding exponent, and his influence was very great. In the more formal tragedy French and classical models were combined to produce a new type called the *heroic play*. The type is well represented by Dryden's *Tyrannic Love*.

3. The 'Correct' School. The Elizabethans too had drawn upon the ancients, but they used their gains freely and joyously, bending the work of the classical authors to their own wills. The imitative work of the new school was of a frigid and limited quality. The school of Dryden was loath to alter; the age of Pope abandoned freedom altogether. Pope puts it thus:

> Those Rules of old discovered, not devised,
> Are Nature still, but Nature methodised.

Thus they evolved a number of 'rules,' which can usefully be summarized in the injunction "Be correct." 'Correctness' means avoidance of enthusiasm; moderate opinions moderately expressed; strict care and accuracy in poetical technique; and humble imitation of the style of the Latin classics.

Dryden did not attain altogether to this ideal. Pope and his immediate successors called him "copious," thus hinting at a lack of care and an unrestrained vigour that were survivals of an earlier virility. Yet Dryden has the new tendency very clearly marked. To him Dr Johnson first applied the epithet "Augustan," saying that Dryden did to English literature what Augustus did to Rome, which he "found of brick and left of marble." Dryden is the first great exponent of the new ideas that were to dominate our literature till the end of the eighteenth century.

JOHN DRYDEN (1631–1700)

1. His Life. Dryden was born near Oundle in Northampton-shire, and may have begun his education at Oundle Grammar School. He later entered Westminster School and went on to Cambridge. In 1657 or 1658 he moved to London, where he remained for the rest of his life as a man of letters. His life was a long one. It was, in addition, an exceedingly fruitful one. For forty years he continued to produce an abundance of literary works of every kind—poems, plays, and prose works. The quality of it was almost unfailingly good, and at the end of his life his poetry was as fresh and vivacious as it had been in the prime of his manhood.

Of Dryden it can be said without qualification that he is representative of his age. Indeed, it has been urged as a fault against his character that he adapted himself with too facile a conscience to the changing fortunes of the times. His earliest work of any importance is pre-Restoration (1659), and consists of a laudation of the recently dead Oliver Cromwell. At the Restoration he changed his views, attaching himself to the fortunes of Charles II and to the Church of England. This loyalty brought its rewards in honours and pensions, so that for many years Dryden was easily the most considerable literary figure in the land. Yet his career was not without its thorns, for smaller men were busy with their slanders. On the accession of James II in 1685 Dryden changed his faith and political persuasion, becoming a Roman Catholic. To his new beliefs he adhered steadfastly, even when in 1688 the Revolution brought certain disaster to such public men as adhered to Catholicism. Thus Dryden lost his posts of Poet Laureate and Historiographer Royal. The Laureateship was conferred on Shadwell, his most rancorous foe; and Dryden retired with dignity to sustain his last years with his literary labours. To this last period of his career we owe some of his finest translations and narrative poems. When he died in 1700 he was accorded a splendid funeral in Westminster Abbey, though it was many years before his grave was marked by a tombstone.

2. His Poetry. Dryden began his life's work with poetry; he concluded it with poetry; and the years between are starred with the brightness of his greater poems. As early as February 1664 Pepys records in his diary that he met "Mr Dryden, the poet"; and he remained "Mr Dryden, the poet" till the day of his death. It is therefore as a poet that Dryden is chiefly to be judged.

His first published poem of any consequence was a series of heroic stanzas on the death of the Protector Oliver Cromwell (1659). It consists of thirty-seven quatrains of no particular merit. They move stiffly, and are quite uninspired by any political or personal enthusiasm, but they are a striking manifestation of Dryden's directness, and show a certain angular force and some metrical dexterity. Two stanzas will show the art of the earliest Dryden:

> His grandeur he derived from Heaven alone,
>   For he was great, ere Fortune made him so;
> And wars, like mists that rise against the sun,
>   Made him but greater seem, not greater grow.

> No borrowed bays his temples did adorn,
>   But to our crown he did fresh jewels bring;
> Nor was his virtue poisoned, soon as born,
>   With the too early thoughts of being king.

In 1660 he made a great step forward in poetical craftsmanship by publishing *Astræa Redux*, in celebration of Charles II's return. The poem represents a complete reversal of the poet's political opinions; but it is nevertheless a noteworthy literary advance. In its handling of the subject it shows a firmer grip and stronger common sense; in its style a new command of sonorous and dignified phrasing; and (as important a feature as any of the others) it is written in the heroic couplet.

> Methinks I see those crowds on Dover's strand,
> Who in their haste to welcome you to land
> Choked up the beach with their still growing store,
> And made a wilder torrent on the shore.

Here we see Dryden, though not yet at his best, coming to his own. The couplet marches with a steady but animated ring and swing. Its phrasing is apt and vivid; and it possesses a strength and music that are new. It marks the beginning of that adherence to the use of the couplet which was to be Dryden's lifelong habit, and which was to mark a new epoch in our literature.

Two other poems of this year, one on the coronation and one addressed to the Chancellor, Clarendon, resemble *Astræa Redux* in their main features, and are little inferior.

Dryden's early poetical work concludes with *Annus Mirabilis* (published 1667), which gives a spirited account of the Great Fire and the war with the Dutch in the previous year. The poem is in quatrains, and shows a great increase in ease and flexibility within the verse form. The two parts of the narrative are skilfully blended, and the description of the fire, in particular, is full of vigour and striking imagery. The poem abounds in fine images, though it sometimes reveals a lingering weakness for the fantastic conceit. It has a strong, dignified tone combined with the force and impetus which are characteristically Dryden's.

For more than fifteen years succeeding this Dryden devoted himself almost entirely to the writing of plays. Then, about 1680, events both political and personal drove him back to the poetical medium, with results both splendid and astonishing. Political passions over the Exclusion Bills were at their height, and Dryden appeared as the chief literary champion of the monarchy in the famous satirical allegory *Absalom and Achitophel* (1681). Absalom is the Duke of Monmouth, the unfortunate aspirant to the succession; and Achitophel is his daring but injudicious counsellor Shaftesbury. These two are surrounded by a cluster of lesser politicians, upon each of whom Dryden bestows a Biblical name of deadly aptness and transparency. The excellence of the work lies mainly in the numerous portraits, which show Dryden's keen insight. The satire is of amazing force and range, rarely stooping to scurrility, but punishing its victims with devastating scorn and aloofness; and it takes shape in the best quality of Dryden's couplet. Long practice in dramatic couplet-writing had now given Dryden a new metrical facility, tightening and strengthening the measure, and giving it crispness and energy without allowing it to become violent and obscure. We give a specimen of this measure, which in many ways represents the summit of Dryden's poetical achievement:

> Of these the false Achitophel was first;
> A name to all succeeding ages curst:
> For close designs and crooked counsels fit;
> Sagacious, bold, and turbulent of wit;
> Restless, unfixed in principles and place;
> In power unpleased, impatient of disgrace:
> A fiery soul, which, working out its way,
> Fretted the pigmy body to decay,
> And o'er-informed the tenement of clay.
> A daring pilot in extremity;
> Pleased with the danger when the waves went high,
> He sought the storms; but, for a calm unfit,
> Would steer too nigh the sands to boast his wit.
> Great wits are sure to madness near allied,
> And thin partitions do their bounds divide;
> Else why should he, with wealth and honour blest,

> Refuse his age the needful hours of rest?
> Punish a body which he could not please;
> Bankrupt of life, yet prodigal of ease?
> And all to leave what with his toil he won,
> To that unfeathered two-legged thing—a son.

Of such satire as this Dryden himself says not unfairly, "It is not bloody, but it is ridiculous enough. I avoided the mention of great crimes, and applied myself to the representing of blind sides and little extravagances." The hitting is hard, but not foul.

Next year he produced another political poem, *The Medal*, which called forth an answer from an old friend of Dryden's, Shadwell. Dryden retorted in *MacFlecknoe*, a stinging, destructive, personal lampoon degraded with much coarseness and personal spite. A similar poem is the second part of *Absalom and Achitophel* (1682), to which poem Dryden contributed a violent attack on Shadwell, giving him the name of Og. The main part of the work was composed by Nahum Tate, a satellite of Dryden's.

A new poetical development was manifest in *Religio Laici* (1682) and *The Hind and the Panther* (1687). The first poem is a thesis in support of the English Church; the second, written after the accession of James, is an allegorical defence of the Roman Catholic faith. Alterations like this in Dryden's opinions gave free play to the gibes of his enemies. In spite of their difference in opinion, these poems have much in common: a clear light of argument, a methodical arrangement of ideas, and a mastery of the couplet that often lifts the drabness of the expository theme into passages of noble feeling and splendour. The allegorical treatment of *The Hind and the Panther* allows of a livelier handling; but the poem is very long, consisting of more than one part, and much of it is dogmatic assertion and tedious argument.

After the Revolution, when he was driven from his public appointments, Dryden occupied himself chiefly with translations. He once more used the couplet medium, turning Virgil, Ovid, and Boccaccio into English, and adapting Chaucer to the taste of his time. The translation is so free that much of it is Dryden's own, and all of it teems with his own individuality. We give a passage to illustrate both the latest phase of his couplet and his power as a narrative poet:

> Scarce the third glass of measured hours was run,
> When like a fiery meteor sunk the sun,
> The promise of a storm; the shifting gales
> Forsake by fits and fill the flagging sails;

> Hoarse murmurs of the main from far were heard,
> And night came on, not by degrees prepared,
> But all at once; at once the winds arise,
> The thunders roll, the forky lightning flies.
> In vain the master issues out commands,
> In vain the trembling sailors ply their hands;
> The tempest unforeseen prevents their care,
> And from the first they labour in despair.
> The giddy ship betwixt the winds and tides,
> Forced back and forwards, in a circle rides,
> Stunned with the different blows; then shoots amain,
> Till counterbuffed she stops, and sleeps again.
>
> *Cymon and Iphigenia*

Though it is small in bulk, Dryden's lyrical poetry is of much importance. The longest and the best-known pieces of this class are his *Song for St Cecilia's Day* (1687) and *Alexander's Feast*, written for the same anniversary in 1697. Both show Dryden as a master of melodious verse and of a varied and powerful style. The numerous lyrics that appear in his plays are charming. One stanza will illustrate this sweetly facile phase of the poet's art:

> On a bank, beside a willow,
> Heaven her covering, earth her pillow
> Sad Amynta sighed alone;
> From the cheerless dawn of morning
> Till the dews of night returning,
> Singing thus she made her moan:
>   "Hope is banished,
>   Joys are vanished,
> Damon, my beloved, is gone!"

His numerous prologues and epilogues, written in couplets, show abundant wit and vivacity, yet they habitually appeal to the worst instincts of his audiences, being very often coarse and unmannerly.

3. His Drama. In his dramatic work, as elsewhere, Dryden is a faithful reflex of his time. His methods and objects vary as the public appreciation of them waxes and wanes, with the result that he gives us a historical summary of the popular fancy.

His first play was a comedy, *The Wild Gallant* (1663), which had but a very modest success. It has the complicated plot of the popular Spanish comedies and the 'humours' of Jonson's. After this unsuccessful attempt at public favour Dryden turned to tragedy, which henceforth nearly monopolizes his dramatic work.

His tragedies fall into two main groups:

(*a*) *The Heroic Play.* This is a new type of the tragedy that became prominent after the Restoration, and of which Dryden is one of the earliest and most skilful exponents. The chief features of the new growth are the choice of a great heroic figure for the central personage; a succession of stage incidents of an exalted character, which often, as Dryden himself realized, became ridiculous through their extravagance; a loud, declamatory style; and the rhymed couplet. Dryden's *The Rival Ladies* (1663) is a hybrid between the comic and heroic species of play; *The Indian Emperor* (1665), *Tyrannick Love* (1669), *The Conquest of Granada* (in two parts, 1669 and 1670), and *Aureng-zebe* (1675) show the heroic kind at its best and worst. Though Dryden is heavily weighted with the ponderous mechanism of the heroic play, his gigantic literary strength is often sufficient to give it an attraction and a kind of heavy-footed animation.

(b) *His Blank-verse Tragedies*. The heroic play was so easily parodied and made ridiculous that the wits of the Restoration were not slow to make a butt of it. Their onslaughts were not without their effect on Dryden, for already in *Aureng-zebe* a weakening of the heroic mannerisms is apparent. In the prologue to this play Dryden fairly admits it, saying that he

> Grows weary of his long-loved mistress, Rime.
> Passion's too fierce to be in fetters bound,
> And Nature flies him like enchanted ground.

His next play, *All for Love, or The World well Lost* (1678), is in blank verse, and is considered to be his dramatic masterpiece. For subject he chose that of Shakespeare's *Antony and Cleopatra*. It was a daring thing to attempt what Shakespeare had already done; but Dryden, while following the earlier play somewhat closely, never actually copies it. He produces a play of a distinctly different nature, and of a high merit. The characters are well drawn and animated, and the style, though lacking the demonic force of Shakespeare's at his best, is noble and restrained. We give Dryden's handling of the death of Cleopatra, a passage which should be compared with that of Shakespeare given on p. 104.

> (*Antony is lying dead on the stage; Charmion and Iras, the Queen's two handmaidens, are in attendance on her.*)
>
> *Charmion.*   To what end
>   These ensigns of your pomp and royalty?
> *Cleopatra.* Dull that thou art! Why, 'tis to meet my love;
>   As when I saw him first, on Cydnos' bank,
>   All sparkling, like a goddess. . . .

Haste, haste, both,
And dress the bride of Antony.
Charmion.   'Tis done.
Cleopatra. Now seat me by my lord; I claim this place. . .
Reach me the casket.
Iras.   Underneath the fruit
The aspic lies.
Cleopatra.   Welcome, thou kind deceiver!
                              [*Putting aside the leaves.*
Thou best of thieves, who with an easy key
Dost open life, and, unperceived by us,
Even steal us from ourselves. . . .
Haste, bare my arm, and rouse the serpent's fury.
                    [*Holds out her arm, and draws it back.*
Coward flesh,
Wouldst thou conspire with Cæsar to betray me,
As thou wert none of mine? I'll force thee to it,
And not be sent by him,
But bring, myself, my soul to Antony.
              [*Turns aside, and then shows her arm bloody.*
Take hence; the work is done. . . .
Charmion.   The next is ours.
Iras. Now, Charmion, to be worthy
Of our great queen and mistress.
                              [*They apply the aspics.*
Cleopatra. Already, death, I feel thee in my veins:
I go with such a will to find my lord,
That we shall quickly meet.
A heavy numbness creeps through every limb,
And now 'tis at my head: my eyelids fall,
And my dear love is vanquished in a mist.
Where shall I find him, where? O turn me to him,
And lay me on his breast! Cæsar, thy worst;
Now part us, if thou canst.
                                              [*Dies.*
              [*Iras sinks down at her feet, and dies; Charmion
              stands behind her chair, as dressing her head.*

After the Revolution he wrote *Don Sebastian* (1690), *Cleomenes* (1692), and *Love Triumphant* (1694). The last was a tragi-comedy and a failure. The other two, however, were quite up to the average of his plays. In addition, at various stages of his career he collaborated with Lee in two other tragedies, and attempted, with lamentable results, to improve upon Shakespeare's *The Tempest* and *Troilus and Cressida*.

4. His Prose. Dryden's versatility is apparent when we observe that in prose, as well as in poetry and drama, he attains to primacy in his generation. In the case of prose he has one rival, John Bunyan. No single item of Dryden's prose work is of very great length; but in his *Essay of Dramatick Poesie* (1668), in his numerous dedicatory epistles and prefaces, and in the scanty stock of his surviving letters we have a prose *corpus* of some magnitude. The general subject of his prose is literary criticism, and that of a sane and vigorous quality. The style is free, but not too free; there are slips of grammar, but they are not many. The *Essay of Dramatick Poesie* (1668) is his longest single prose work and a major piece of English literary criticism. It is in the form of a discussion between four characters, one of whom is Dryden himself, and treats, with an openness of mind and a lack of dogmatizing which are new in criticism, most of the major topics which interested contemporary dramatists. Among them were the question of rhyme or blank verse in drama; the comparison between French and English drama; and the possibility of making a judicious compromise between the strict observance of the classical unities and the greater freedom of the English dramatic tradition. Moreover, the essay is the first attempt to evaluate the work of the Elizabethan dramatists and especially of Shakespeare. The following passage illustrates, not only the directness and lucidity of his prose style, but his balanced critical judgment:

> To begin, then, with Shakespeare. He was the man who, of all modern and perhaps ancient poets, had the largest and most comprehensive soul. All the images of nature were still present to him, and he drew them not laboriously, but luckily; when he describes anything, you more than see it, you feel it too. Those who accuse him to have wanted learning, give him the greater commendation. He was naturally learned; he needed not the spectacles of books to read nature; he looked inwards and found her there. I cannot say he is everywhere alike; were he so, I should do him injury to compare him with the greatest of mankind. He is many times flat, insipid; his comic wit degenerating into clenches, his serious swelling into bombast. But he is always great when some great occasion is presented to him; no man can say he ever had a fit subject for his wit, and did not then raise himself as high above the rest of poets,
>
> *Quantum lenta solent inter viburna cupressi.*
> VIRG., *Ecl.*, i, 26

RESTORATION COMEDY

In comedy alone Dryden showed a certain incapacity; his mind seemed to be too rugged and unresilient to catch the sharper moods of the current wit. Fortunately this weakness of his was atoned for by the activities of a brilliant group of dramatists who made Restoration comedy a thing apart in English literature.

The new comedy was of slower growth than the heroic play (see p. 170), and, for some years after 1660, comedy was restricted to revivals of pre-Commonwealth plays, but the decadent, cynical spirit of the later age was alien to the romantic comedy of the Elizabethans. Even so, Restoration comedy drew its main inspiration from the native tradition which had flourished before the closing of the theatres in 1642. In particular it was indebted to Beaumont and Fletcher and to Ben Jonson. Like the heroic play, however, comedy was strongly influenced by Continental writers, and especially by Molière and the Spaniard, Calderon. It reflected closely the dissolute court life of the period, and, between that and the court life of France, there was a community of spirit which led naturally to an interest in French comedy. Molière provided English dramatists with ideas for plots and with an example of fine comic characterization; Spanish drama served to strengthen that love of intrigue and incident already firmly established in English comedy. But here it is important to stress that foreign influences, while important, were not the predominant factors in the evolution of Restoration comedy. They blended with a tradition already strongly established, and assisted the natural process of change demanded by the changing temper of the age, but they were transformed into something essentially English and contemporary. Thus the comedy of Molière was changed into a harder, more loosely knit form which lacked the warmth and depth of insight of the original.

The new drama is full of vitality, and moves with great pace, but the exuberance which led the Elizabethans to the poetic romance is supplanted by a polish and intellectual control which replaces emotion by wit, and poetry by a clear, concise prose which adds much point and gives a fine precision to the dialogue. Of this new style, the passage of Congreve given below is a good specimen. The pervading tone is one of cynicism, and the plays show a close, and often satirical, observation of life and manners which recalls the work of Ben Jonson. Plots and subplots are intricate and numerous, and centre mainly upon amorous intrigues, which reflect an open contempt for the ordinary standards of morality, that, in Wycherley and others, often takes the form of gross sensuality. In the hands of the best and most restrained of the dramatists, Etheredge and Congreve, the immorality still remains, but it is purged of much of its grossness and offensiveness by the fact that it is essentially intellectual, witty, and free from the cruder realism which mars Wycherley's work. The lack of passion and emotion in these plays gives them a polished, crystal hardness which saves them from the worst forms of licentiousness. The immorality of Restoration drama was the object of fierce Puritanical attacks, the most notorious of which was the *Short View of the Immorality and Profaneness of the English Stage* (1698) of **Jeremy Collier (1650– 1726)**. Though this work is notable only for its wrathful tone and its stupidity as dramatic criticism, it provoked many replies from the offending dramatists, but beyond this its objections seem to have had no effect.

The characters in Restoration comedies are largely types, whose dispositions are sufficiently indicated by a study of their names. We have Sir Fopling Flutter; Scrub (a servant); Colonel Bully; Sir John Brute; Squire Sullen; Gibbet (a highwayman); Lady Bountiful. They have thus many of the qualities of the Jonsonian character, with its predominant 'humour' (see p. 107). But by the last part of the period there has evolved something distinct from the comedy of humours—the comedy of manners. A 'manner' is difficult to define. It does not imply the portrayal of life so much as a genteel, sophisticated brilliant quality, what one critic has called "a grace or habit of refined culture."

William Congreve (1670–1729). Congreve was born at Bardsey, near Leeds, of a good family, and was educated in Ireland, finally at Trinity College, Dublin. In 1691 he came to London to enter the Middle Temple, but abandoned law for literature. He wrote all his plays before he was thirty, when he deserted the drama to spend the rest of his life as a very popular society gentleman, largely supported by generous government pensions.

His first comedy was *The Old Bachelor* (1693), and this was followed by *The Double Dealer* (1693), *Love for Love* (1695), and *The Way of the World* (1700). His one tragedy, *The Mourning Bride* (1697), was in the vein of the later Elizabethan tragedians.

Congreve is undoubtedly the greatest of the Restoration comedy-writers. In his work the comedy of manners reaches perfection. His plays are a faithful reflection of the upper-class life of his day, but their undoubted immorality is saved from being objectionable by artificial wit, a hard finish, and a total lack of realism. In the artificial society which he depicts moral judgments would be out of place. The tone is one of cynical vivacity, the characters are well drawn, and Congreve's prose is lucid, concise, and pointed and shows an excellent ear for rhythm and cadence. In all things he is the polished artist, whose distinctive quality is brilliance.

All Congreve's plays, except *The Way of the World*, had an immediate success, and it is ironical that this one should be singled out by posterity as his masterpiece. Free from the occasional sentimental touches which mar *The Double Dealer*, it is the best example of the comedy of manners, skilful in characterization, and completely free from the coarseness and realism which spoil the work of so many of his contemporaries. From it comes the following passage, in which two gentlemen are backbiting an acquaintance. It is a typical specimen of Congreve's prose.

> *Fainall.* He comes to town in order to equip himself for travel.
> *Mirabell.* For travel! Why the man that I mean is above forty.
> *Fainall.* No matter for that; 'tis for the honour of England, that all Europe should know we have blockheads of all ages.
> *Mirabell.* I wonder there is not an act of parliament to save the credit of the nation, and prohibit the exportation of fools.
> *Fainall.* By no means, 'tis better as 'tis; 'tis better to trade with a little loss, than to be quite eaten up with being overstocked.
> *Mirabell.* Pray, are the follies of this knight-errant, and those of the squire his brother, anything related?
> *Fainall.* Not at all; Witwoud grows by the knight, like a medlar grafted on a crab. One will melt in your mouth, and t'other set your teeth on edge; one is all pulp, and the other all core.
> *Mirabell.* So one will be rotten before he be ripe, and the other will be rotten without ever being ripe at all.

OTHER COMEDY-WRITERS

1. William Wycherley (1640–1715). The productive period of Wycherley's life was brief but fruitful. He produced four plays in five years: *Love in a Wood* (1671), *The Gentleman Dancing-Master* (1672), *The Country-Wife* (1674), and *The Plain Dealer* (1676). He was a man of good family, and he was at Court, where he seems to have been no better than the average courtier of his time.

His contemporaries call his plays "manly." By this they probably refer to a boisterous indecency that riots through his comedies, in which nearly every person is a fool, and every clever man a rogue and a rake. He is much coarser in the grain than Congreve, and cannot keep his work at such a high level. Yet he shows much wit in handling dialogue, and has a sharp, though distorted, vision for human weaknesses.

2. George Etheredge (1635 (?)–91). Not much is known regarding the life of Etheredge; but he appears to have been a courtier, and to have served abroad in the diplomatic service. His three plays are *The Comical Revenge, or Love in a Tub* (1664), *She Wou'd if she*

Cou'd (1668), and *The Man of Mode, or Sir Fopling Flutter* (1676). They are important in that they established the comedy of manners, which was later to be perfected by Congreve. They paint a true picture of the graceful, heartless, and licentious upper classes of the period. The prose dialogue is natural and brilliant, and its light, airy grace conceals some deficiency of plot and construction.

3. **Sir John Vanbrugh (1664–1726).** Vanbrugh's career, though much of it is obscure, seems to have been a varied one, for at different times he was a soldier, a herald, and an architect. His best three comedies are *The Relapse* (1696), *The Provok'd Wife* (1697), and *The Confederacy* (1705).

Vanbrugh's plays lack the art and elegance of Congreve's, but they are full of energy and genial humour. He is fond of farce and good at caricature, and his plots, if daring, are soundly constructed.

4. **George Farquhar (1678–1707).** He had an adventurous career, was in turn a clergyman, an actor, and a soldier, and died when he was twenty-nine years old. The pathos of his early death has given him a fame of its own. He wrote seven plays, the best of which are the last two, viz., *The Recruiting Officer* (1706) and *The Beaux' Stratagem* (1707).

Farquhar comes late among the Restoration dramatists, and by his time the cynical immorality of the age seems to have worn thin. His temper is certainly more genial, and his wit, though it has lapses, is more decorous. In *The Recruiting Officer* and the plays which followed Farquhar added something new to Restoration comedy, in taking his material from a wider life than the polite upper class depicted by Congreve, and his characters are more like ordinary people. His dialogue lacks the polish and sustained wit of Congreve, and is nearer the level of normal conversation. In his rapidly developing humanity, and his growing respect for moral standards, Farquhar looks forward to the drama of Steele and the succeeding age.

5. **Thomas Shadwell (1642 (?)–92).** Little is known of Shadwell's life, and he has been remembered chiefly on account of Dryden's portrait of him in *MacFlecknoe*. He deserves mention here, however, in his own right. He held the popular stage for over twenty years and wrote many plays, the best of which were *The Sullen Lovers* (1668), *The Squire of Alsatia* (1688), and *Bury Fair* (1689). Shadwell stood outside the development of the comedy of manners, and imitated closely Jonson's comedy of humours. His plays are generally coarse, but on occasion he shows real wit: his style lacks

literary grace, but his plots are usually well constructed and show a fertile invention. He reflects, more accurately than anyone else, the everyday life of his time, and he has a keen satirical sense. He frequently deserts the level of the artificial, intellectual world of Congreve and, like Wycherley, stoops to a coarseness of passion that is repulsive. His later plays show a growing fondness for farce, and look forward to the sentimental drama.

RESTORATION TRAGEDY

In this period tragic drama is represented by the heroic play, which has already been mentioned (see p. 162). During the first twenty years after the Restoration the rhymed heroic play reigned supreme. This form was introduced by Sir William Davenant and popularized by Dryden, who stated that "an heroick play ought to be an imitation (in little) of an heroic poem; and consequently that love and valour ought to be the subject of it." An impossibly idealistic love, in conflict with a strenuously proclaimed honour, led to exaggerated emotions and to stock characters, who were psychologically unconvincing and declaimed passages of bombastic rhetoric on all possible occasions. The form owed much to the contemporary interest in the French stage, in the work of Corneille and Racine, and in the French prose romances, from which many of its plots were taken. Even more important was the influence of the romantic drama of Beaumont and Fletcher, while the tradition of violent deeds, last seen in the work of Webster, Marston, and Ford, was here perpetuated in scenes of blood and crime. Stage settings were lavish in the extreme. From about 1680 onward we see the almost complete replacement of rhyme by blank verse, but the heroic motive remains, though this later period sees an increasingly frequent introduction of the pathetic note, which is seen at its strongest in Otway. It is also the period of numerous adaptations from the Elizabethan dramatists, and especially from Shakespeare. Perhaps the most notorious of them is the version of *King Lear* in which Nahum Tate provides the play with a happy ending. Though the Restoration period was less rich in tragedy than in comedy, there are a few tragedians who deserve a brief mention.

1. **Thomas Otway (1651–85).** As was so often the case with the dramatists of the time, Otway had a varied and troubled career, closed with a miserable death. His first play, *Alcibiades*, was produced in 1675; then followed *Don Carlos* (1676), *The Orphan* (1680), and his masterpiece, *Venice Preserv'd* (1682).

Otway began his career in the typical heroic strain of the age, and *Don Carlos* is a fair specimen of the type, though, in sentiment and language, it is less exaggerated than is usual. His reputation rests, however, on two plays. In *The Orphan*, which, allowing for its period, is lacking in heroics, Otway struck the note of deep pathos which is his distinguishing feature, while the play has a calmness of tone and absence of rant unusual in its day. *Venice Preserv'd* is his finest work. Here the tragedy is on a grander scale than in *The Orphan*, and the characters are skilfully handled—especially those of Jaffier and Pierre. The play has a rugged and sombre force, and reveals a considerable skill in working out a dramatic situation. One authority on the drama believes it to have been revived more often than any play outside Shakespeare—an undeniable proof of its dramatic possibilities.

2. Nathaniel Lee (1653 (?)–92). Lee's life is the usual tale of mishaps, miseries, and drunkenness, with a taint of madness as an additional calamity. He wrote many tragedies, some of which are *Nero* (1674), *Sophonisba* (1676), *The Rival Queens* (1677), and *Mithridates* (1678). He also collaborated with Dryden in the production of two plays.

During his own time Lee's name became a byword to distinguish a kind of wild, raving style, which in part at least seems to have been a product of his madness. But he can write well when the spirit is in him; he has a command of pathos, and all through his work he has touches of real poetic quality.

3. Elkanah Settle (1648–1724). Settle was in some ways the butt of his literary friends, and Dryden has given him prominence by attacking him in his satires. In his day he obtained some popularity with a heroic play, *The Empress of Morocco* (1673). It is a poor specimen of its kind, but his other dramas are worse.

4. John Crowne (c. 1640–1703 (?)). Crowne is another of the dramatists who attacked Dryden and who were in turn assailed by the bigger man. A voluminous playwright, Crowne's best-known works are the tragedies of *Caligula* (1698), a heroic play, and *Thyestes* (1681), in blank verse, and a comedy, *Sir Courtly Nice* (1685). Crowne is quite a good specimen of the average Restoration dramatist. The plays show some talent and a fair amount of skill in versification.

5. Nicholas Rowe (1674–1718). During his lifetime Rowe was a person of some importance, and was made Poet Laureate in 1715. His best-known plays are *Tamerlane* (1702), *The Fair Penitent*

(1703), and the popular *Jane Shore* (1714). Johnson says of him, "His reputation comes from the reasonableness of some of his scenes, the elegance of his diction, and the suavity of his verse."

POETRY

Samuel Butler (1612–80). Besides Dryden and the tragedy-writers the only considerable poet of the period is Samuel Butler, and his fame rests on one work, *Hudibras*.

Born in Worcestershire, the son of a farmer, Butler was educated at the cathedral school at Worcester. He held a number of clerical appointments in important households, and was, for a time, clerk to Sir Samuel Luke, one of Cromwell's officers for Bedfordshire, in whose service he probably obtained that experience of the Puritans which forms the basis of *Hudibras*. Although he was at one time the steward of Ludlow Castle, he spent the last years of his life in obscure penury in London. In 1663 he published *Hudibras*, which was at once a success. Two other parts followed in 1664 and 1678 respectively.

Hudibras was topical, for it was a biting satire on the Puritans, who were the reverse of popular when the King returned. In general outline it is modelled upon the adventures of Don Quixote and Sancho Panza, who find their respective parallels in Sir Hudibras and his squire Ralpho. Sir Hudibras is a Puritan knight who undergoes many absurd adventures with Ralpho, his Independent squire; but the poem lacks the real pathos and genuine insight of its great Spanish original. It is wholly satirical. The poem is composed artfully. The adventures are well chosen in order to throw the greatest amount of ridicule on the maladroit hero; the humour, though keen and caustic, is never absolutely brutal in expression; there is a freakish spattering of tropes and a mock-solemn parade of scholastic learning; and (a feature that added immeasurably to its success) it is cast in an odd jigging octosyllabic couplet. This metre of *Hudibras* is remarkable. It is varied and yet uniform, and it carries the tale with an easy relish. Though it is sometimes almost doggerel, it has always a kind of distinction, and each couplet is clenched with an ingenious rhyme that is the most amusing feature of all.

> He was in logic a great critic,
> Profoundly skilled in analytic;
> He could distinguish, and divide
> A hair 'twixt south and south-west side;

On either which he would dispute,
Confute, change hands, and still confute;
He'd undertake to prove by force
Of argument a man's no horse;
He'd prove a buzzard is no fowl,
And that a lord may be an owl—
A calf, an alderman—a goose, a justice—
And rooks, committee-men and trustees.
He'd run in debt by disputation,
And pay with ratiocination:
All this by syllogism, true
In mood and figure, he would do.
  For rhetoric, he could not ope
His mouth but out there flew a trope;
And when he happened to break off
I' th' middle of his speech, or cough,
H' had hard words, ready to show why
And tell what rules he did it by:
Else, when with greatest art he spoke,
You'd think he talked like other folk;
For all a rhetorician's rules
Teach nothing but to name his tools.

PROSE-WRITERS

1. John Bunyan (1628–88). In the domain of Restoration prose Bunyan alone contests the supremacy of Dryden. And Bunyan stands in a class by himself.

The main facts of his life are well known. He himself has given them an imperishable shape in his *Grace Abounding* (1666), a kind of religious autobiography. Though the statements of this book need not be taken too literally, he seems to have misspent his youth. He draws a horrible picture of his own depravity; but as religious converts are well known to delight in depicting their original wickedness in the darkest colours, this need not be taken too seriously. Bunyan, the son of a brazier, was born in Bedfordshire. He was educated at the village school, and at the age of sixteen was drafted into the Parliamentary army and saw service in the Civil War. In 1653 he joined a local Nonconformist sect in Bedford and shortly after began to preach there. His literary career began in 1656 with two pamphlets on the gospels, and in 1660 he was arrested as an unlicensed preacher. The next twelve years he spent in Bedford gaol, and on his release, in 1672, he obtained a licence and became pastor of a church in Bedford. This office he held until his death, although, in 1675, he spent six months in gaol when his licence was cancelled. In this second period of imprisonment he wrote the first part of *The*

Pilgrim's Progress (published 1678), and then came *The Life and Death of Mr Badman* (1680) and *The Holy War* (1682).

Except for *Grace Abounding*, all Bunyan's major works are allegorical. In each case the allegory is worked out with ease, force, and clearness. Readers of all ages enjoy the narrative, while they follow the double meaning without an effort. The allegorical personages—for example, Mr Worldly Wiseman, Mrs Diffidence, Giant Despair, Madame Wanton, My Lord Hategood, Mr Standfast —are fresh and apt, and are full of an intense interest and a raw dramatic energy. Their individual adventures combine and react with a variety that keeps the story from monotony, and yet the simple idea of a forward journey is never lost. The plot, working upon the fortunes of the different characters, gives us the nearest approach to the pure novel that had so far been effected. The numerous natural descriptions are simply done, but they are full of a great unspoilt ability. Lastly, Bunyan's style is unique in prose. Though it is undoubtedly based upon the great Biblical models, it is quite individual. It is homely, but not vulgar; strong, but not coarse; equable, but not monotonous; it is sometimes humorous, but it is never ribald; rarely pathetic, but never sentimental. It has remained the pattern of a plain style, and is one of the masterpieces of the English language.

The following extract gives us an idea of Bunyan's narrative and descriptive power, and is a fair specimen of his masculine prose:

> I saw then in my dream, so far as this valley reached, there was on the right hand a very deep ditch; that ditch is it into which the blind have led the blind in all ages, and have both there miserably perished. Again, behold, on the left hand, there was a very dangerous quag, into which, if even a good man falls, he can find no bottom for his foot to stand on. Into that quag King David once did fall, and had no doubt therein been smothered, had not HE that is able plucked him out.
>
> The pathway was here also exceeding narrow, and therefore good *Christian* was the more put to it; for when he sought, in the dark, to shun the ditch on the one hand, he was ready to tip over into the mire on the other; also when he sought to escape the mire, without great carefulness he would be ready to fall into the ditch. Thus he went on, and I heard him here sigh bitterly; for, besides the dangers mentioned above, the pathway was here so dark, and ofttimes, when he lift up his foot to set forward, he knew not where or upon what he should set it next.
>
>> Poor man! where art thou now? thy day is night.
>> Good man, be not cast down, thou yet art right,
>> Thy way to heaven lies by the gates of hell;
>> Cheer up, hold out, with thee it shall go well.

About the midst of this valley. I perceived the mouth of hell to be, and it stood also hard by the way-side. Now, thought *Christian*, what shall I do? And ever and anon the flame and smoke would come out in such abundance, with sparks and hideous noises, (things that cared not for *Christian's* sword, as did *Apollyon* before,) that he was forced to put up his sword, and betake himself to another weapon called *all-prayer*. So he cried, in my hearing, *O Lord, I beseech thee, deliver my soul!* Thus he went on a great while, yet still the flames would be reaching towards him. Also he heard doleful voices, and rushings to and fro, so that sometimes he thought he should be torn in pieces, or trodden down like mire in the streets.

The Pilgrim's Progress

2. Lord Halifax (1633–95). Halifax was an outstanding figure in the House of Lords during the exciting times of the Exclusion Bills, of which he was the chief opponent. He ranks high as an orator; as an author his fame rests on a small volume called *Miscellanies*. The book contains a number of political tracts, such as *The Character of a Trimmer*, and a piece of a more general character called *Advice to a Daughter*. In his writings Halifax adopts the manner and attitude of the typical man of the world: a moderation of statement, a cool and agreeably acid humour, and a style devoid of flourishes. In him we find a decided approach to the essay-manner of Addison.

3. Sir William Temple (1628–99). Temple also was a politician of some importance, filled diplomatic posts abroad, and was a moderate success in affairs at home. He is an example of the moneyed, leisured semi-amateur in literature. He wrote little and elegantly, as a gentleman should, and patronized authors of lesser fortune and greater genius. His chief works were his *Letters* (published by Swift in 1700 and 1703), his *Memoirs* (1691), and his *Miscellanea*, a series of essays on a variety of subjects, literary and general (published in three parts in 1680, 1690, and 1701). His style resembles that of Halifax in its mundane, cultured reticence; but at times he has higher flights, in which he shows some skill in the handling of melodious and rhythmic prose.

4. John Tillotson (1630–94). In Tillotson we have one of the popular preachers of the time, and his *Sermons* is mentioned by Addison as being a standard work of its class. He is a literary descendant of the great school of Jeremy Taylor and Thomas Fuller, but his style lacks their richness and melody, though it gains in clearness and crispness.

5. The Diarists. By a coincidence it happened that the two most famous diary-writers in English were working at the same time, and during this period. Not dissimilar in several respects, their works show both the drawbacks and the advantages of the diary manner. The books are private documents, and so have no formal pretensions to literary excellence in style, which is not an undiluted misfortune. Yet the style is often ragged and incoherent, and much reading at it produces a feeling of flatness and monotony. But, on the other hand, being private jottings, they are intimate, and so are interesting, full of information concerning public and personal affairs, and containing illuminating comments on people and incidents.

(a) **Samuel Pepys (1633–1703)** is the more lovable of the two, and is probably known more intimately to the world than any other writer. He was born in London, and educated at St Paul's and later at Cambridge. Through the influence of his kinsman, Sir Edward Montagu (later Earl of Sandwich), he became Clerk of the Acts of the Navy in 1660. From then on he prospered steadily, and eventually he became Secretary to the Admiralty and a Member of Parliament. The panic following the Popish Plot (1679) led to an unjustified charge of popery and a period in the Tower, followed by some years of unemployment. From 1684 to 1688 he was again Secretary to the Admiralty, and in these years he carried through an extensive reform of the administration of the Navy. With the arrival of the new government he lost his post, and he spent the remainder of his life in retirement.

Pepys' *Diary* opens on Jan. 1, 1660 and continues until May 31, 1669, when his failing eyesight led him to abandon writing at night. Written in cypher, which was not decoded until 1819, it was intended for no eyes but his own and is the most frank and intimate revelation of a human life which is known to us. It shows an amazing lack of reticence, and abounds in minute details of great personal and historical interest. It reveals Pepys as a man of the world, keenly interested in his material advancement; as a great lover of music and the theatre; above all it shows him as intensely human, with many endearing human qualities and many equally human failings—vanity, ill temper, a fondness for fine clothes, good food, and attractive women—a man constantly vowing to amend his way of life, and as constantly failing to do so. It does less than justice to Samuel Pepys, the industrious, clear-sighted enemy of corruption in the civil service, the administrator who rescued the Navy from graft and decrepitude, the honest official and the real patriot. Of this other Pepys something is seen in his *Memoires relating to the state of the Royal Navy* (1690). The *Diary* has no pretensions to literary style—its greatness and charm lie in the unaffected naturalness of the writing and its narrative skill. As a historical document it provides a fascinating view of the life of Restoration London and the impact upon it of the Great Plague and Great Fire.

> *May 1st*, 1669—Up betimes. Called up by my tailor, and there first put on a summer suit this year; but it was not my fine one of flowered tabby vest and coloured camelot tunic, because it was too fine with the gold lace at the bands, that I was afraid to be seen in it; but put on the stuff suit I made the last year, which is now repaired; and so did go to the office in it, and sat all the morning, the day looking as if it would be foul. At noon home to dinner, and there find my wife extraordinary fine, with her flowered tabby gown that she made two years ago, now laced exceeding pretty; and, indeed, was fine all over; and mighty earnest to go, though the day was very lowering; and she would have me put on my fine suit, which I did. And so anon we went alone through the town with our new liveries of serge, and the horses' manes and tails tied with red ribbons, and the standards there gilt with varnish, and all clean, and green reins, that people did mightily look upon us; and, the truth is, I did not see any coach more pretty, though more gay, than ours all the day.

(*b*) **John Evelyn (1620–1706)** is the other diarist, and is much more respectable and much less amusing than Pepys. His diary is a more finished production in the matter of style, and may have been produced with an eye on the public. The style is simple and lucid, but has little of the freshness that distinguishes Pepys'. The diary, however, is full of accurate information, and in some of the more moving incidents, such as that of the Great Fire, it warms into something like real eloquence.

THE DEVELOPMENT OF LITERARY FORMS

Viewed as a whole, this period is seen to be one of transition. The Elizabethan fervour had spent itself, and the new classicism was still in the making. Yet the time is important in the development of literary forms and style.

1. Poetry. (*a*) *The Lyric.* The form of the lyric shows little change. In bulk it is inconsiderable, for the lyrical spirit is largely in abeyance. Outside Dryden, who is the best of the lyrical poets, we have the slight work of the courtiers, the **Earl of Dorset (1638–1706)**, the **Earl of Rochester (1648–80)**, and **Sir Charles Sedley (1639 (?)–1701)**. These were fashionable men, taking their poetry with fashionable irresponsibility. Their poems, which nearly all deal with the love-theme in an artificial manner, have a decided charm and skill, being modelled on the Caroline poems that were the mode before the Civil War. Of real originality there is hardly a trace.

(b) *The Ode*. Once more Dryden towers pre-eminent in this class of poem. His two odes on the anniversary of St Cecilia's Day and his other ode on the death of Mrs Anne Killigrew are among the best of any period. Written in the irregular Pindaric metre, they are full of the high passion that gives the artificial medium some real fire and energy. We give the opening lines of the elegiac poem:

> Thou youngest Virgin-Daughter of the skies,
>   Made in the last promotion of the blest;
> Whose palms, new plucked from Paradise,
> In spreading branches more sublimely rise,
>   Rich with immortal green above the rest:
> Whether, adopted to some neighbouring star,
> Thou roll'st above us in thy wandering race,
>   Or in procession fixed and regular
> Moved with the heaven's majestic pace,
>   Or called to more superior bliss,
> Thou tread'st with seraphim the vast abyss.

(c) *The Satire*. Several circumstances combined to make this age abound in satirical writing. It was a period of bitter political and personal contention, of easy morals and subdued enthusiasms, of sharp wit and acute discrimination. For these reasons satire acquired a new importance and a sharper edge.

The older satire, such as is represented in the poems of Donne and of Andrew Marvell (1621–78), was of a more general kind, and seemed to have been written with deliberate clumsiness and obscurity. These habits were repugnant to the ideals of the new age, whose satire is more personal and more vindictive. Its effect is immensely more incisive, and it obtains a new freshness and point by the use of the heroic couplet, in which it is almost wholly written. Dryden's *Absalom and Achitophel* is an excellent example of the political satire, while his *MacFlecknoe* shows the personal type. Literary satire is also well represented in *The Rehearsal* (1670), which parodied the literary vices of the time, especially those of the heroic play. This work, which was reproduced year after year, with topical hits in every new edition, was the work of several hands, though the Duke of Buckingham receives the chief credit. Butler's

Hudibras is a satire on the Puritans. The miscellaneous satire of John Oldham (1653–83) had much of the earlier clumsiness.

(*d*) *Narrative Poetry.* Dryden's translations and adaptations of Chaucer, Virgil, Ovid, and Boccaccio are the chief examples of this form. Among others, he gives us Chaucer's *Wife of Bath's Tale*, *The Knight's Tale*, and several tales from Boccaccio. There is no fresh development to record. Butler's *Hudibras* is narrative of a kind, though the chief interest is satirical.

2. Drama. The development of the drama is considerable. We summarize briefly what has already been indicated.

(*a*) In *tragedy* the most novel in the matter of form is the *heroic play*, whose peculiarities have already been pointed out on pp. 162–163. There is little further development. The tragical faculty is weakening all through the period, even in comparison with the post-Shakespearian plays. The best plays of this type are Dryden's *All for Love* and Otway's *Venice Preserv'd*. The characters are becoming more stagy, and the situations are made as horrible as the ingenuity of the dramatist can devise.

(*b*) In *comedy* the advance is noteworthy. The comedy of 'humours' is dying out, though considerable traces of it are still visible, and is replaced by the comedy of manners. Comedy has acquired a new 'snap' and glitter, and the almost universal medium is prose. Congreve's *The Way of the World* (1700), Wycherley's *The Country-Wife* (1673), and Farquhar's *The Beaux' Stratagem* (1707) are good examples.

3. Prose. With the exception of the work of Dryden and Bunyan, the prose work of the time is of little moment. Dryden's prose is almost entirely devoted to literary criticism; Bunyan's contribution shows a remarkable development of the prose allegory. The remainder of the prose-writers deal with political and miscellaneous subjects, with, in addition, some theological and historical writing.

THE DEVELOPMENT OF LITERARY STYLE

The main tendency of the age, in all departments of literature, is toward a clear, plain, and forcible style.

1. Poetry. The new movement was seen most clearly in the development of the *heroic couplet*, which was soon to spread throughout poetry and through much of the drama. As we have seen (p. 153) in the previous age the couplet had become so loose that it resembled a cross between prose and verse. An exponent of such a measure is Chamberlayne (1619–89):

> Poor love must dwell
> Within no climate but what's parallel
> Unto our honoured births; the envied fate
> Of princes oft these burdens find from state,
> When lowly swains, knowing no parent's voice
> A negative, make a free and happy choice.

This is a curious liquid measure. The pause is irregularly distributed, and the rhythm is light and easy.

Cowley and Denham obtain much credit for the introduction of the new measure, but the chief innovator is Edmund Waller (1606–87). Dryden, in his dedication to *The Rival Ladies*, says, "Rime has all the advantages of prose besides its own. But the excellence and dignity of it were never fully known till Mr Waller taught it." An extract from Waller will suffice:

> While in this park I sing, the listening deer
> Attend my passion, and forget to fear;
> When to the beeches I report my flame,
> They bow their heads, as if they felt the same,
> To gods appealing, when I reach their bowers,
> With loud complaints, they answer me in showers.
>
> *At Penshurst*

The note here is quite different from that of the previous extract. The tread of the metre is steady and almost uniform, and the pauses cluster about the middle and the end of the lines. It must be noted, too, that a large proportion of Waller's poetry took this form.

Dryden adopted the heroic couplet, but he improved upon the wooden respectability of his predecessors' verse. While he retained all the couplet's steadiness and force, he gave it an additional vigour, a sinewy elegance, and a noble rhythm and beauty. It is worth while giving another example of his couplet:

> A milk-white hind, immortal and unchanged,
> Fed on the lawns and in the forest ranged;
> Without unspotted, innocent within,
> She feared no danger, for she knew no sin.
> Yet had she oft been chased with horns and hounds
> And Scythian shafts; and many winged wounds
> Aimed at her heart; was often forced to fly,
> And doomed to death, though fated not to die.
>
> *The Hind and the Panther*

In its own fashion this passage is as melodious and powerful as some of the noblest lines of Milton.

In other forms of poetry the style contains little to be commented upon. The *blank verse* continues the disintegration that (with the exception of the verse of Milton) began with the death of Shakespeare. We give a good example of this Restoration blank verse:

> Through a close lane as I pursued my journey,
> And meditated on the last night's vision,
> I spied a wrinkled hag, with age grown double,
> Picking dry sticks, and mumbling to herself;
> Her eyes with scalding rheum were galled and red,
> Cold palsy shook her head; her hands seemed withered;
> And on her crooked shoulders had she wrapped
> The tattered remnant of an old stript hanging.
>
> OTWAY, *The Orphan*

In this passage we can observe the absence of the high poetic fire of the Elizabethans and the lack of the thunderous depth of Milton. Observe the regularity of the beat, the uniformity of the pauses, and the frequency of the hypermetrical ending. There is, nevertheless, a certain sombre, dogged attraction about the style of the passage. The average blank verse of the time is much less regular, and much less attractive.

The *lyric* still shows a reflection of the Caroline manner, as can be seen in the following example:

> Love still has something of the sea,
>   From whence his mother rose;
> No time his slaves from doubt can free,
>   Nor give their thoughts repose.
>
> They are becalmed in clearest days,
>   And in rough weather tossed;
> They wither under cold delays,
>   Or are in tempests lost.
>
> SEDLEY, *Love like the Sea*

This lyric has an undoubted sweetness of expression, though it is artificial in thought.

2. Prose. Though the prose writing of the period is not great in bulk, it shows a profound change in style. Previous writers, such as Browne, Clarendon, and Hobbes, had done remarkable and beautiful work in prose, but their style had not yet found itself. It was wayward and erratic, often cumbrous and often obscure, and weighted with a Latinized construction and vocabulary. In Dryden's time prose begins definitely to find its feet. It acquires a general utility and a permanence; it is smoothed and straightened, simplified and harmonized. This is the age of average prose, and prepares the way for the work of Swift and Addison, who stand on the threshold of the modern prose style. Less than forty years intervene between Dryden and Sir Thomas Browne; yet Dryden and his school seem to be nearer the twentieth century than they are to Browne.

Not that Dryden's style is flawless. It is sometimes involved and obscure; there are little slips of grammar and many slips of expression; but on the average it is of high quality, and the impression that the reader receives is one of great freshness and abounding vitality. Further examples of this good average style will be found in the work of Temple and Halifax.

In the case of Bunyan the style becomes plainer still. But it is powerful and effective, and bears the narrative nobly. Pepys and Evelyn have no pretensions to style as such, but their work is admirably expressed, and Evelyn, particularly, has passages of more elevated diction.

In some authors of the period we find this desire for unornamented style degenerating into coarseness and ugliness. Such a one is **Jeremy Collier (1650–1726)**, whose *Short View of the Immorality and Profaneness of the English Stage* (1698) caused a great commotion in its day. It attacked the vices of the stage with great vigour, but the style of this famous book is so colloquial that it becomes in places ungrammatical. **Thomas Sprat (1635–1713)** was another disciple of the same school. He wrote on the newly formed Royal Society, which demanded from its members "a close, naked, natural way of speaking." This expresses the new development quite well. A greater man than Sprat, but a fellow-member of the Royal Society, was **John Locke (1632–1704)**, who in his famous *An Essay concerning Human Understanding* (1690) put the principle into practice. Locke's style is bare to baldness, but it is clear. We give an example:

> Some men are remarked for pleasantness in raillery; others, for apologues, and apposite, diverting stories. This is apt to be taken for the effect of pure nature, and that the rather, because it is not got by rules, and those who excel in either of them, never purposely set themselves to the study of it as an art to be learnt. But yet it is true, that at first some lucky hit, which took with somebody, and gained him commendation, encouraged him to try again, inclined his thoughts and endeavours that way, till at last he insensibly got a facility in it without perceiving how; and that is attributed wholly to nature, which was much more the effect of use and practice. I do not deny that natural disposition may often give the first rise to it; but that never carries a man far without use and exercise, and it is practice alone that brings the powers of the mind as well as

those of the body to their perfection. Many a good poetic vein is buried under a trade, and never produces anything for want of improvement. We see the ways of discourse and reasoning are very different, even concerning the same matter, at court and in the university. And he that will go but from Westminster Hall to the Exchange, will find a different genius and turn in their ways of talking; and one cannot think that all whose lot fell in the city were born with different parts from those who were bred at the university or inns of court.

TABLE TO ILLUSTRATE THE DEVELOPMENT OF LITERARY FORMS

Date	Poetry			Drama		Prose		
	Lyrical	Narrative	Satirical and Didactic	Tragedy	Comedy	Narrative	Essay	Miscellaneous
1660								Pepys
1670	Dryden Dorset Sedley Rochester	Dryden Butler		Dryden	Dryden Etheredge Shadwell	Bunyan	Dryden	Evelyn Dryden[1] Sprat Tillotson
1680			Oldham	Lee Otway	Wycherley			Halifax
1690			Shadwell Dryden[2] Dryden[3]	Dryden[4]			Temple	Temple
1700	Dryden[5]	Dryden[6]		Rowe	Congreve Vanbrugh Farquhar			

[1] His dedications, etc.   [2] *Religio Laici* (1682).   [3] *The Hind and the Panther* (1687).
Don Sebastian (1689).   [5] *Alexander's Feast* (1697).   [6] *Fables* (1700).

In one prominent case we have a survival of the more elaborate style of the past, and that is in the history of **Gilbert Burnet (1643–1715)**, Bishop of Salisbury, whose *The History of my own Time* was published after his death. The style of the book is modelled on that of Clarendon. Burnet's style is not of the same class as that of his predecessor: it has lapses into colloquialism; its sentences are snipped into small pieces by means of frequent colons and semicolons; and he has not Clarendon's command of vocabulary.

CHAPTER VIII

THE AGE OF POPE

TIME-CHART OF THE CHIEF AUTHORS

The thick line shows the period of active literary work.

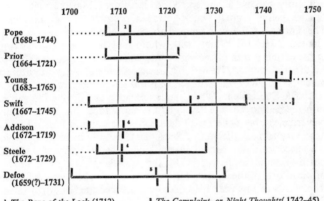

¹ *The Rape of the Lock* (1712).
³ *Gulliver's Travels* (1726).
⁵ *Robinson Crusoe* (1719).

² *The Complaint, or Night Thoughts* (1742–45)
⁴ *The Spectator* (1711).

THE HISTORICAL BACKGROUND (1700–50)

In the beginning of the eighteenth century the old quarrels take on new features.

1. The Rise of the Political Parties. In the reign of Charles II the terms 'Whig' and 'Tory' first became current; by the year 1700 they were in everybody's mouth. About that time domestic politicians became sharply cleft into two groups that were destined to become established as the basis of our political system. Domestic affairs, while they never approached the stage of bloodshed, took on a new acrimony that was to affect literature deeply. Actual points of political faith upon which the parties were divided are not of great importance to us here; but, generally speaking, we may say that the Whig party stood for the pre-eminence of personal freedom as opposed to the Tory view of royal divine right. Hence the Whigs supported the Hanoverian succession, whereas the Tories were Jacobites. The Tories, whose numbers were recruited chiefly from the landed classes, objected to the foreign war upon the score that they had to pay taxes to prolong it; and the Whigs, representing the trading classes generally, were alleged to be anxious to continue the war, as it brought them increased prosperity. In the matter of religion the Whigs were Low Churchmen and the Tories High Churchmen.

2. The Foreign War. This War of the Spanish Succession was brilliantly successful under the leadership of Marlborough, who, besides being a great general, was a prominent Tory politician. The Tories, as the war seemed to be indefinitely prolonged, supplanted (1710) the Whigs, with whom they had been co-operating in the earlier stages of the war, and in 1713 they concluded the war by the unfortunate Treaty of Utrecht. Contemporary literature is much concerned both with the war and the peace.

3. The Succession. When Anne ascended the throne the succession seemed to be safe enough, for she had a numerous family. Nevertheless, her children all died before her, and in 1701 it became necessary to pass the Act of Settlement, a Whig measure by which the succession was settled upon the House of Hanover. On the death of Anne, in the year 1714, the succession took effect, in spite of the efforts of the Tories, who were anxious to restore the Stuarts. The events of this year 1714 deeply influenced the lives of Addison, Steele, Swift, and many other writers of lesser degree.

4. The Spirit of the Age. After the succession of the House of Hanover the first half of the eighteenth century was a period of stabilization and steadily growing wealth and prosperity. The evils of the approaching Industrial Revolution had not yet been realized, and the country, still free from any suggestion of acrimonious class consciousness, underwent a period of comfortable aristocratic rule, in which local government rested on the squires, typified by Sir Roger de Coverley. It was an age of tolerance, moderation, and common sense, which, in cultured circles at least, sought to refine manners and introduce into life the rule of sweet reasonableness. The balance of political power, in spite of the fifty years' superiority of the Whig oligarchy, was so even as to preclude fanatical party policies, while the Established Church pursued a placid middle way, and all religion was free from strife over dogma and the fanaticism which it called 'enthusiasm' until Wesley and Whitefield began the Evangelical Revival. This middle way of control and reason, and the distrust of 'enthusiasm,' are faithfully reflected in the literature of the period.

THE PREDOMINANCE OF PROSE

The age of Pope intensified the movement that, as we have seen, began after the Restoration. The drift away from the poetry of passion was more pronounced than ever, the ideals of 'wit' and 'common sense' were more zealously pursued, and the lyrical note was almost unheard. In its place we find in poetry the overmastering desire for neatness and perspicuity, for edge and point in style, and for correctness in technique. These aims received expression in the devotion to the heroic couplet, the aptest medium for the purpose. In this type of poetry the supreme master is Pope; apart from him the age produced no great poet. On the other hand, the other great names of the period—Swift, Addison, Steele, Defoe—are those of prose-writers primarily, and prose-writers of a very high quality.

Some other outstanding conditions of the age remain to be considered. Most of them, it will be noticed, help to give prose its dominating position.

1. Political Writing. We have already noticed the rise of the two political parties, accompanied by an increased acerbity of political passion. This development gave a fresh importance to men of literary ability, for both parties competed for the assistance of their pens, bribed the authors with places and pensions (or promises of them), and admitted them more or less deeply into their counsels. In previous ages authors had had to depend on their patrons, often capricious beings, or upon the length of their subscription lists; they now acquired an independence and an importance that turned the heads of some of them. Hardly a writer of the time is free from the political bias. After being a Whig, Swift became a virulent Tory; Addison was a tepid Whig; Steele was Whig and Tory in turn. It was indeed the Golden Age of political pamphleteering, and the writers made the most of it.

2. The Clubs and Coffee-houses. Politicians are necessarily gregarious, and the increased activity in politics led to a great addition to the number of political clubs and coffee-houses, which became the *foci* of fashionable and public life. In the first number of *The Tatler* Steele announces as a matter of course that the activities of his new journal will be based upon the clubs. "All accounts of Gallantry, Pleasure, and Entertainment shall be under the article of White's Chocolate-House; Poetry under that of Will's Coffee-House; Learning under the title of Grecian; Foreign and Domestic News you will have from Saint James' Coffee-House." These coffee-houses became the 'clearing-houses' for literary business, and from them branched purely literary associations such as the famous Scriblerus and Kit-Cat clubs, those haunts of the fashionable writers which figure so prominently in the writings of the period.

3. Periodical Writing. The development of the periodical will be noticed elsewhere (see pp. 216–217). It is sufficient here to point out that the struggle for political mastery led both factions to issue a swarm of *Examiners, Guardians, Freeholders*, and similar publications. These journals were run by a band of vigorous and facile prose-writers, who in their differing degrees of excellence represent almost a new type in our literature.

4. The New Publishing Houses. The interest in politics, and probably the decline in the drama, caused a great increase in the size of the reading public. In its turn this aroused the activities of a number of men who became the forerunners of the modern publishing houses. Such were Edmund Curll (1675–1747), Jacob Tonson (1656 (?)–1736), and John Dunton (1659–1733). These men employed numbers of needy writers, who produced the translations, adaptations, and other popular works of the time. It is unwise to judge a publisher by what authors say of him, but the universal condemnation levelled against Curll and his kind compels the belief that they were a breed of scoundrels who preyed upon authors and public, and (what is more remarkable) upon one another. The miserable race of hack-writers—venomously attacked by Pope in *The Dunciad*—who existed on the scanty bounty of such men lived largely in a thoroughfare near Moorfields called Grub Street, the name of which has become synonymous with literary drudgery.

5. The New Morality. The immorality of the Restoration, which had been almost entirely a Court phenomenon and was largely the reaction against extreme Puritanism, soon spent itself. The natural process of time was hastened by opinion in high quarters. William III was a severe moralist, and Anne, his successor, was of the same character. Thus we soon see a new tone in the writing of the time and a new attitude to life and morals. Addison, in an early number of *The Spectator*, puts the new fashion in his own admirable way: "I shall endeavour to enliven morality with wit, and to temper wit with morality." Another development of the same spirit is seen in the revised opinion of women, who are treated with new respect and dignity. Much coarseness is still to be felt, especially in satirical writing, in which Swift, for instance, can be quite vile; but the general upward tendency is undoubtedly there.

PROSE-WRITERS

I. JONATHAN SWIFT (1667–1745)

1. His Life. Swift was born in Dublin, and, though both his parents were English, his connexion with Ireland was to be maintained more or less closely till the day he died. His father dying before Jonathan's birth, the boy was thrown upon the charity of an uncle, who paid for his education in Ireland. He seems to have been very wretched both at his school at Kilkenny and at Trinity College, Dublin, where his experiences went to confirm in him that savage melancholia that was to endure all his life. Much of this distemper was due to purely physical causes, for he suffered from an affection of the ear that ultimately touched his brain and caused insanity. In 1686, at the age of nineteen, he left Trinity College (it is said in disgrace), and in 1689 entered the household of his famous kinsman Sir William Temple, under whose encouragement he took holy orders, and on the death of Temple in 1699 obtained other secretarial and ecclesiastical appointments. His real chance came in 1710, when the Tories overthrew the Marlborough faction and came into office. To them Swift devoted the gigantic powers of his pen, became a political star of some magnitude, and, after the manner of the time, hoped for substantial rewards. He might have become a bishop, but it is said that Queen Anne objected to *A Tale of a Tub* and had doubts about his orthodoxy and in the wreck of the Tory party in 1715 all he could save was the Deanery of St Patrick's, in Dublin, which he had received in 1713. An embittered man, he spent the last thirty years of his life in gloom, and largely in retirement. His last years were passed in silence and, at the very end, lunacy.

2. His Poetry. Swift would have been among the first to smile at any claim being advanced for him on the score of his being a great poet, though he always longed to excel in poetry, yet in bulk his verse is considerable. His poems were to a large extent recreations: odd verses (sometimes humorously doggerel) to his friends; squibs and lampoons on his political and private enemies, including the famous one on Partridge, the quack astrologer; and one longish one, *Cadenus and Vanessa* (1712–13), which deals with his affection for Esther Vanhomrigh. In his poems he is as a rule lighter of touch and more placable in humour than he is in his prose. His favourite metre is the octosyllabic couplet, which he handles with a dexterity that reminds the reader of Butler in *Hudibras*. He has lapses of taste, when he becomes coarse and vindictive; and sometimes the verse, through mere indifference, is badly strung and colloquially expressed.

The following is from some bitter verses he wrote (1731) on his own death just before the final night of madness descended. Note the fierce misery inadequately screened with savage scorn.

> Yet thus, methinks, I hear 'em speak:
> "See, how the Dean begins to break!
> Poor gentleman, he droops apace!
> You plainly find it in his face.
> That old vertigo in his head
> Will never leave him, till he's dead.
> Besides, his memory decays:
> He recollects not what he says;
> He cannot call his friends to mind;
> Forgets the place where last he dined;
> Plies you with stories o'er and o'er;
> He told them fifty times before.
> How does he fancy we can sit
> To hear his out-of-fashion'd wit?
> But he takes up with younger folks
> Who for his wine will bear his jokes.
> Faith, he must make his stories shorter
> Or change his comrades once a quarter:
> In half the time he talks them round,
> There must another set be found."

3. His Prose. Almost in one bound Swift attained to a mastery of English prose, and then maintained an astonishing level of excellence. His first noteworthy book was *The Battle of the Books*, published in 1704. The theme of this work is a well-worn one, being the dispute between ancient and modern authors. At the time Swift wrote it his patron, Sir William Temple, was engaged in the controversy on behalf of the ancients, and Swift's tract was in support of his kinsman's views. Swift gives the theme a half allegorical, mock-heroic setting, in which the books in a library at length literally contend with one another. The handling is vigorous and illuminating, and refreshed with many happy remarks and allusions. The famous passage where a bee, accidentally blundering into a spider's web, argues down the bitter remarks of the spider, is one of Swift's happiest efforts.

A Tale of a Tub, also published in 1704, though it was written as early as 1696, is regarded by many as Swift's best work. It certainly reveals his power at its highest. It is a religious allegory, perhaps suggested by the work of Bunyan, on three men: Peter, who stands for the Roman Catholic Church; Jack, who represents the Dissenters; and Martin, the personification of the Anglican and Lutheran Churches. Each of the three has a coat left to him by his father, and they have many experiences, beginning with the changes that they make on the coats that have been left to them. The book was intended as an attack on the 'enthusiasm' of Roman Catholics and Dissenters alike, and culminates in a fierce attack upon Jack. But, though Martin escapes comparatively lightly, Swift's contempt is poured on so many of the fundamental principles of religion that the book led many to suspect his own Christianity. Indeed, the scope of the work widens until it becomes a merciless dissection of human nature in general, and of intellectual pride and religious hypocrisy in particular. Within the narrative are digressions on such subjects as critics and the value of madness to the community, which reveal the deep irony of Swift's satire at its best.

A Tale of a Tub is full of wit, and brilliant in its imaginative power and the incisiveness of its thought. The style is terse, and has a sustained vigour, pace, and colourfulness which Swift did not equal in his later works. Many years after the writing of the book he was heard to mutter, while looking at a copy, "Good God! what a genius I had when I wrote that book!"

The following extract shows the suggestiveness of his allegory, the corrosive power of his satire, and his redoubtable style:

> Whenever it happened that any rogue of Newgate was condemned to be hanged, Peter would offer him a pardon for a certain sum of money; which when the poor caitiff had made all shifts to scrape up, and send, his lordship would return a piece of paper in this form:
>
> "To all mayors, sheriffs, jailors, constables, bailiffs, hangmen, etc. Whereas we are informed that A. B. remains in the hands of you, or any of you, under the sentence of death. We will and command you, upon sight hereof to let the said prisoner depart to his own habitation whether he stands condemned for murder, etc., etc., for which this shall be your sufficient warrant; and if you fail

hereof, God damn you and yours to all eternity; and so we bid you heartily farewell. Your most humble man's man, Emperor Peter."

The wretches, trusting to this, lost their lives and money too.

It will be no difficult part to persuade the reader that so many worthy discoveries met with great success in the world; though I may justly assure him that I have related much the smallest number, my design having been only to single out such as will be of most benefit for public imitation, or which best served to give some idea of the reach and wit of the inventor. And therefore it need not be wondered at if, by this time, Lord Peter was become exceeding rich. But, alas! he had kept his brain so long and so violently upon the rack, that at last it shook itself, and began to turn round for a little ease. In short, what with pride, projects, and knavery, poor Peter was grown distracted, and conceived the strangest imaginations in the world. In the height of his fits (as it is usual with those who run mad out of pride) he would call himself God Almighty, and sometimes monarch of the universe. I have seen him (says my author) take three old high-crowned hats and clap them on his head three-storey high, with a huge bunch of keys at his girdle, and an angling-rod in his hand. In which guise, whoever went to take him by the hand in the way of salutation, Peter, with much grace, like a well-educated spaniel, would present them all with his foot, and if they refused his civility, then would he raise it as high as their chops, and give them a damned kick on the mouth, which has ever since been called a salute.

A Tale of a Tub

From a literary point of view, the next important period of his life was from 1710, when he deserted the Whigs for the Tories, to 1714, when the latter party fell from power. For them he wrote political tracts of great power, which made him a leading political figure of the day. Several of them were written for *The Examiner*, a Tory journal of which he was given charge, and the best known are *The Conduct of the Allies* (1711), *Some Remarks on the Barrier Treaty* (1712), and *The Public Spirit of the Whigs* (1714). To this period also belongs the *Journal to Stella*, which is a kind of informal private log-book written by him and sent regularly to Esther Johnson. It has all Swift's shrewdness and vivacity, without much of the usual scorn and coarseness. It is not as intimate and revealing as the diary of Pepys, yet it gives us many glimpses of the inner man: vain and arrogant, ambitious and crafty, but none the less a generous and considerate friend and a loyal ally.

During the third period—that of his final stay in Ireland—the shadow deepens. The earlier years produce one of the most compelling efforts of his pen. He supported the Irish in their revolt against 'Wood's halfpence,' writing in their cause his *The Drapier's Letters* (1724). This gained for him an almost embarrassing popularity. Then followed some miscellaneous political work, aimed at the improvement of the lot of the oppressed and poverty-stricken Irish, and then his longest and most famous book, *Gulliver's Travels* (written between 1720 and 1725, and published 1726). The main idea of this book is an old one, being at least as old as the time of Lucian, a Greek writer of the second century: it deals with imaginary voyages, in Gulliver's case among the pigmies (Lilliputians), the giants (Brobdingnagians), the moonstruck philosophers (Laputans), and the race of horses (Houyhnhnms), with their human serfs the Yahoos.

Gulliver's Travels resembles its fellow-allegory *The Pilgrim's Progress* in its popularity and human interest; but in temper the two books are worlds apart. Bunyan views human failings with a discerning eye, but he accepts them with a benign quiescence, and with a tempered faith in man's ultimate redemption. Swift, on the other hand, said to Pope, "I heartily hate and detest that animal called man," and this book is an elaboration of that attitude. He magnifies man into a giant, and then he diminishes him into a mannikin, and he finds him wicked and insolent and mean; he regards man in his wisdom, and he finds him a fool; in despair, in the last book of the *Travels*, he turns from man altogether, and in the brute creation he discovers a charity and sagacity before which humanity grovels as a creature beastly beyond measure. The last stages of the book are morbid and often revolting, but always we are aware of the clarity of the author's mind.

The two earlier stages of the *Travels* have a charm and vivacity that delight old and young. The satire lurks in the allegory, but it is so delicately tinselled over that it does not repel. The crowded incidents are plausible and lively, and they are often spiced with a quaint and alluring humour; his comments upon mankind are shrewd and arresting, as well as satirical, and are yet not brutal nor obscene. The style is Swift's best: not mannered or laboured; clean, powerful, and tireless; easy without being slovenly, and as clear as summer noonday.

> The queen, who often used to hear me talk of my sea-voyages, and took all occasions to divert me when I was melancholy, asked me whether I understood how to handle a sail or an oar, and whether a little exercise of rowing might not be convenient for my health. I answered, that I understood both very well; for although my proper employment had been to be surgeon or doctor to the ship, yet often upon a pinch I was forced to work like a common mariner. But I could not see how this could be done in their

country, where the smallest wherry was equal to a first-rate man-of-war among us, and such a boat as I could manage would never live in any of their rivers. Her majesty said, if I would contrive a boat, her own joiner should make it, and she would provide a place for me to sail in. The fellow was an ingenious workman, and, by my instructions, in ten days finished a pleasure-boat, with all its tackling, able conveniently to hold eight Europeans. When it was finished, the queen was so delighted, that she ran with it in her lap to the king, who ordered it to be put in a cistern full of water with me in it by way of trial; where I could not manage my two sculls, or little oars, for want of room. But the queen had before contrived another project. She ordered the joiner to make a wooden trough of three hundred foot long, fifty broad, and eight deep, which being well pitched, to prevent leaking, was placed on the floor along the wall in an outer room of the palace. It had a cock near the bottom to let out the water, when it began to grow stale; and two servants could easily fill it in half an hour. Here I often used to row for my diversion, as well as that of the queen and her ladies, who thought themselves agreeably entertained with my skill and agility. Sometimes I would put up my sail, and then my business was only to steer, while the ladies gave me a gale with their fans; and when they were weary, some of the pages would blow my sail forward with their breath, while I showed my art by steering starboard or larboard, as I pleased. When I had done, Glumdalclitch always carried back my boat into her closet, and hung it on a nail to dry.

Swift is the greatest English satirist. Unlike Pope he restricts himself to general rather than personal attacks, and his work has a cosmic, elemental force, which is irresistible and, at times, almost frightening. His dissection of humanity shows a powerful mind relentlessly and fearlessly probing into follies and hypocrisy, but he is never merely destructive. Always underlying his work is the desire for the greater use of common sense and reason in the ordering of human affairs. Often the satire is cruel and violent, and sometimes it is coarse and repulsive—perhaps the result of his own physical disabilities, and his keen disappointment at his failure to gain the preferment which he felt himself to have merited. But the terrible savagery of *A Voyage to the Houyhnhnms*, and *A Modest Proposal for preventing the children of poor people from being a burden to their parents* (by selling them as food for the rich) should not blind us to the great range of his work. Between these two and the playfulness of *Predictions for the ensuing year*, 1708, *by Isaac Bickerstaff, Esq.*, or the almost boyish humour of his *Discourse to prove the Antiquity of the English Tongue*, there is a range of satirical force which indicates a fertility of imagination and an ingenuity of fancy unparalleled among his rivals in this field.

II. JOSEPH ADDISON (1672–1719)

1. His Life. Educated at the Charterhouse, Addison went to Oxford, where he became a Fellow of Magdalen College. He early made his mark as a serious and accomplished scholar, and seems to have attracted the notice of the Whig leaders, who marked him out as a future literary prop of their faction. He obtained a travelling scholarship of three hundred pounds a year, and saw much of Europe under favourable conditions. Then the misfortunes of the Whigs in 1703 reduced him to poverty. In 1704, it is said at the instigation of the leaders of the Whigs, he wrote the poem *The Campaign*, praising the war policy of the Whigs in general and the worthiness of Marlborough in particular. This poem brought him fame and fortune. He obtained many official appointments and pensions, married a dowager countess (1716), and became a Secretary of State (1717). Two years later he died, at the early age of forty-seven.

2. His Poetry. In his Latin verses Addison attained early distinction. These verses were highly praised at a time when praise for proficiency in such a medium was of some significance. Then his *The Campaign* in 1704 gave him a reputation as one of the major poets of the age. The poem is poor enough. It is written in the heroic couplet, and with some truth it has been called a "rhymed gazette." The story is little more than a pompous catalogue of places and persons; the style is but mediocre, and warms only when it is feebly stirred by the ignorant enthusiasm that a sedentary civilian feels for the glory of war. The hero is Marlborough, who is drawn on a scale of epic grandeur. The most famous passage of the work is that comparing the general to the angel that rides the storm. The poem literally made Addison's fortune; for after reading it the Whig Lord Treasurer Godolphin gave him the valuable appointment of Commissioner of Appeals.

> 'Twas then great Marlbro's mighty soul was prov'd,
> That, in the shock of charging hosts unmov'd,
> Amidst confusion, horror, and despair,
> Examin'd all the dreadful scenes of war;
> In peaceful thought the field of death survey'd,
> To fainting squadrons sent the timely aid,
> Inspir'd repuls'd battalions to engage,
> And taught the doubtful battle where to rage.
> So when an angel by divine command
> With rising tempests shakes a guilty land,

> Such as of late o'er pale Britannia past,
> Calm and serene he drives the furious blast;
> And, pleas'd th' Almighty's orders to perform,
> Rides in the whirlwind, and directs the storm.

His only other poetical works worthy of notice are his hymns, which are melodious, scholarly, and full of a cheerful piety. The one that begins "The spacious firmament on high" is among the best.

3. His Drama. Addison was lucky in his greatest dramatic effort, just as he was lucky in his longest poem. In 1713 he produced the tragedy of *Cato*, part of which had been in manuscript as early as 1703. It is of little merit, and shows that Addison, whatever his other qualities may be, is no dramatist. It is written in laborious blank verse, in which wooden characters declaim long, dull speeches. But it caught the ear of the political parties, both of which in the course of the play saw pithy references to the inflamed passions of the time. The play had the remarkable run of twenty nights, and was revived with much success. Addison also attempted an opera, *Rosamond* (1707), which was a failure; and the prose comedy of *The Drummer* (1715) is said, with some reason, to be his also. If it is, it adds nothing to his reputation.

4. His Prose. Several political pamphlets are ascribed to Addison, but as a pamphleteer he is not impressive. He lacked the directness of Swift, whose pen was a terror to his opponents. It is in fact almost entirely as an essayist that Addison is justly famed.

These essays began almost casually. On April 12, 1709, Steele published the first number of *The Tatler*, a periodical that was to appear thrice weekly. Addison, who was a school and college friend of Steele, saw and liked the new publication, and offered his services as a contributor. His offer was accepted, and his first contribution, a semi-political one, appeared in No. 18. Henceforward Addison wrote regularly for the paper, contributing about 42 numbers, which may be compared with Steele's share of about 188. *The Tatler* finished in January 1711; then in March of the same year Steele began *The Spectator*, which was issued daily. The paper had some variations of fortune, price, and time of issue, but eventually it ran until December 1712, obtained an unprecedented popularity (it was said that in its palmiest days it sold ten thousand copies of each issue), and exercised a great influence upon the reading public of the period. In *The Spectator* Addison rapidly became the dominating spirit, wrote 274 essays out of a complete total of 555, and wholly shaped its policy when Steele tired of the project. Steele wrote 236 essays. In March 1713 Addison assisted Steele with *The Guardian*, which Steele began. It was only a moderate success, and terminated after 175 numbers, Addison contributing 51.

In all, we thus have from Addison's pen nearly four hundred essays, which are of nearly uniform length, of almost unvarying excellence of style, and of a wide diversity of subject. They are a faithful reflection of the life of the time viewed with an aloof and dispassionate observation. He set out to be a mild censor of the morals of the age, and most of his compositions deal with topical subjects—fashions, head-dresses, practical jokes, polite conversation. His aim was to point out "those vices which are too trivial for the chastisement of the law, and too fantastical for the cognizance of the pulpit. . . . All agreed that I should be at liberty to carry the war into what quarters I pleased; provided I continued to combat with criminals in a body, and to assault the vice without hurting the person." Deeper themes were handled in a popular fashion—immorality, jealousy, prayer, death, and drunkenness. Politics were touched, but gingerly. In all things he advocated moderation and tolerance and was the enemy of 'enthusiasm.' Sometimes he adopted the allegory as a means of throwing his ideas vividly before his readers; and so we have the popular *The Vision of Mirza* and the political allegory of *Public Credit*. Literary criticism, of a mild and cautious kind, found a prominent place in the essays, as well as many half-personal, half-jocular editorial communications to the readers. And, lastly, there was the famous series dealing with the Spectator Club.

It is certain that Steele first hit on the idea of Sir Roger de Coverley, an imaginary eccentric old country knight who frequented the Spectator Club in London. Around the knight were grouped a number of contrasted characters, also members of the mythical club. Such were Will Honeycomb, a middle-aged beau; Sir Andrew Freeport, a city merchant; Captain Sentry, a soldier; and Mr Spectator, a shy, reticent person, who bears a resemblance to Addison himself. Addison seized upon the idea of the club; gave it life, interest, and adventure; cast over it the charm of his pleasant humour; and finished up by making the knight die with affecting deliberation and decorum. Sandwiched between essays on other topics, this series appeared at intervals in the pages of *The Spectator*, and added immensely to the popularity of the journal. In literature it has an added value. If Addison had pinned the Coverley papers together with a stronger plot; if, instead of only referring to the widow who had stolen the knight's affections, he had introduced a definite love-theme; if he had introduced some important female characters, we should have had the first regular novel in our tongue. As it is, this essay-series brings us within measurable distance of the genuine eighteenth-century novel.

We give an extract to illustrate both his humour and his style. His humour is of a rare order. It is delicately ironical, gentlemanly, tolerant, and urbane. To Swift, with his virile mind, such a temper seemed effeminate and priggish. "I will not meddle with *The Spectator*," he wrote to Stella; "let him *fair sex* it to the world's end."

His style has often been deservedly praised. It is the pattern of the middle style, never slipshod, or obscure, or unmelodious. He has an infallible instinct for the proper word, and an infallible ear for a subdued and graceful rhythm. In this fashion his prose moves with a demure and pleasing grace, in harmony with his subject, with his object, and with himself.

As I was yesterday morning walking with Sir Roger before his house, a country fellow brought him a huge fish, which, he told him, Mr William Wimble had caught that very morning; and that he presented it with his service to him, and intended to come and dine with him. At the same time he delivered a letter, which my friend read to me as soon as the messenger left him.

"SIR ROGER,

"I desire you to accept of a jack, which is the best I have caught this season. I intend to come and stay with you a week, and see how the perch bite in the Black river. I observed with some concern, the last time I saw you upon the bowling-green, that your whip wanted a lash to it; I will bring half a dozen with me that I twisted last week, which I hope will serve you all the time you are in the country. I have not been out of the saddle for six days last past, having been at Eton with Sir John's eldest son. He takes to his learning hugely.

"I am, Sir, your humble servant,
"WILL WIMBLE"

This extraordinary letter, and message that accompanied it, made me very curious to know the character and quality of the gentleman who sent them; which I found to be as follow:—Will Wimble is younger brother to a baronet, and descended of the ancient family of the Wimbles. He is now between forty and fifty; but being bred to no business and born to no estate, he generally lives with his elder brother as superintendent of his game. He hunts a pack of dogs better than any man in the country, and is very famous for finding out a hare. He is extremely well versed in all the little handicrafts of an idle man. He makes a May-fly to a miracle; and furnishes the whole country with angle-rods. As he is a good-natured, officious fellow, and very much esteemed upon account of his family, he is a welcome guest at every house, and keeps up a good correspondence among all the gentlemen about him. He carries a tulip root in his pocket from one to another, or exchanges a puppy between a couple of friends, that live perhaps in the opposite sides of the country. Will is a particular favourite of all the young heirs, whom he frequently obliges with a net that he has weaved, or a setting-dog that he has made himself. He now and then presents a pair of garters of his own knitting to their mothers and sisters; and raises a great deal of mirth among them, by inquiring as often as he meets them, how they wear? These gentleman-like manufactures and obliging little humours make Will the darling of the country.

The Spectator

III. SIR RICHARD STEELE (1672–1729)

1. His Life. Steele had a varied and rather an unfortunate career, due largely to his own ardent disposition. Like Addison, he was educated at the Charterhouse, and then proceeded to Oxford, leaving without taking a degree. His next exploit was to enter the army as a cadet; then he took to politics, became a Member of Parliament, and wrote for the Whigs. Steele, however, was too impetuous to be a successful politician, and he was expelled from the House of Commons. He became a Tory; quarrelled with Addison on private and public grounds; issued a number of periodicals; and died ten years after his fellow-essayist.

2. His Drama. Steele wrote some prose comedies, the best of which are *The Funeral* (1701), *The Lying Lover* (1703), *The Tender Husband* (1705), and *The Conscious Lovers* (1722). They follow in general scheme the Restoration comedies, but are without the grossness and impudence of their models. Indeed, Steele's one importance as a dramatist rests on his foundation of the sentimental comedy, avowedly moral and pious in aim and tone. In places his plays are lively, and reflect much of Steele's amiability of temper.

3. His Essays. It is as a miscellaneous essayist that Steele finds his place in literature. He was a man fertile in ideas, but he lacked the application that is always so necessary to carry those ideas to fruition. Thus he often sowed in order that other men might reap. He started *The Tatler* in 1709, *The Spectator* in 1711, and several other short-lived periodicals, such as *The Guardian* (1713), *The Englishman* (1713), *The Reader* (1714), and *The Plebeian* (1719). After the rupture with Addison the loss of the latter's steadying influence was acutely felt, and nothing that Steele attempted had any stability.

Steele's working alliance with Addison was so close and so constant that the comparison between them is almost inevitable. Of the two writers, some critics assert that Steele is the worthier. In versatility and in originality he is at least Addison's equal. His humour is broader and less restrained than Addison's, with a naïve, pathetic touch about it that is reminiscent of Goldsmith. His pathos is more attractive and more humane. But Steele's very virtues are only his weaknesses sublimed; they are emotional, not intellectual; of the heart, and not of the head. He is incapable of irony; he lacks penetration and power; and much of his moralizing is cheap and obvious. He lacks Addison's care and suave ironic insight; he is reckless in style and inconsequent in method. And so, in the final estimate, as the greater artist he fails.

The aim of Steele's essays was frankly didactic; he desired to bring about a reformation of contemporary society manners, and is notable for his consistent advocacy of womanly virtue and the ideal of the gentleman of courtesy, chivalry, and good taste. His essays on children are charming, and he is full of human sympathy.

The passage given illustrates Steele's easy style, the unconstrained sentences, the fresh and almost colloquial vocabulary, and the sentimentality to which he is prone.

[*Mr Bickerstaff, the 'Mr Spectator' of "The Tatler," visits an old friend.*]

As soon as we were alone, he took me by the hand. "Well, my good friend," says he, "I am heartily glad to see thee; I was afraid you would never have seen all the company that dined with you to-day again. Do not you think the good woman of the house a little altered since you followed her from the playhouse, to find out who she was, for me?" I perceived a tear fall down his cheek as he spoke, which moved me not a little. But, to turn the discourse, I said, "She is not indeed quite that creature she was, when she returned me the letter I carried from you; and told me she hoped, as I was a gentleman, I would be employed no more to trouble her, who had never offended me; but would be so much the gentleman's friend as to dissuade him from a pursuit which he could never succeed in. You may remember I thought her in earnest; and you were forced to employ your cousin Will, who made his sister get acquainted with her, for you. You cannot expect her to be for ever fifteen." "Fifteen!" replied my good friend: "Ah! you little understand, you that have lived a bachelor, how great, how exquisite a pleasure there is in being really beloved! It is impossible that the most beauteous face in nature should raise in me such pleasing ideas as when I look upon that excellent woman. That fading in her countenance is chiefly caused by her watching with me in my fever. This was followed by a fit of sickness, which had like to have carried her off last winter. I tell you sincerely, I have so many obligations to her that I cannot, with any sort of moderation, think of her present state of health. But as to what you say of fifteen, she gives me every day pleasures beyond what I ever knew in the possession of her beauty, when I was in the vigour of youth. Every moment of her life brings me fresh instances of her complacency to my inclinations, and her prudence in regard to my fortune. Her face is to me much more beautiful than when I first saw it; there is no decay in any feature which I cannot trace from the very instant it was occasioned by some anxious concern for my welfare and interests."

The Tatler

IV. DANIEL DEFOE (1659 (?)–1731)

1. His Life. Much of Defoe's life is still undetermined. He was born in London, became a soldier, and then took to journalism. He is one of the earliest, and in some ways the greatest, of the Grub Street hacks. He worked for both the Whigs and the Tories, by whom he was frequently employed in obscure and questionable work. He died in London.

2. His Prose. This is of amazing bulk and variety, and for convenience can be divided into two groups.

(a) *Political Writings.* Like most of the other writers of his time Defoe turned out a mass of political tracts and pamphlets. Many of them appeared in his own journal, *The Review*, which, issued in 1704, is in several ways the forerunner of *The Tatler* and *The Spectator*. His *The Shortest Way with the Dissenters* (1702) brought upon him official wrath, and caused him to be fined, imprisoned, and pilloried. He wrote one or two of his political tracts in rough verses which are more remarkable for their vigour than for their elegance. The best known of this class is *The True-born Englishman* (1701). In all his propaganda Defoe is vigorous and acute, and he has a fair command of irony and invective.

(b) *His Fiction.* His works in fiction were all produced in the latter part of his life, at almost incredible speed. First came *Robinson Crusoe* (1719); then *Duncan Campbell, Memoirs of a Cavalier*, and *Captain Singleton*, all three books in 1720; in 1722 appeared *Moll Flanders, A Journal of the Plague Year*, and *Colonel Jacque*; then *Roxana* (1724) and *A New Voyage round the World* (1725).

This great body of fiction has grave defects, largely due to the immense speed with which it was produced. The general plan of the novel in each case is loose and unequal; as, for example, in *Robinson Crusoe*, where the incomparable effect of the story of the island is marred by long and sometimes tedious narratives of other lands. Then the style is unpolished, but has a vigorous, homely raciness and a colloquial vocabulary which make it ideal for his purpose. At its best, as in the finest parts of *Robinson Crusoe*, his writing has a realism that is rarely approached by the most ardent of modern realists. This is achieved by Defoe's grasp of details and his unerring sense of their supreme literary value, a swift and resolute narrative method, and a plain and matter-of-fact style that inevitably lays incredulity asleep. To the development of the novel Defoe's contribution is priceless.

In the passage now given note Defoe's completely unadorned style, the loosely constructed sentences, and the attention to the minutest detail:

> I went to work upon this boat the most like a fool that ever man did who had any of his senses awake. I pleased myself with the design, without determining whether I was able to undertake it; not but that the difficulty of launching my boat came often into my head; but I put a stop to my own inquiries into it, by this foolish answer: Let us first make it: I warrant I will find some way or other to get it along when it is done.
>
> This was a most preposterous method; but the eagerness of my fancy prevailed, and to work I went. I felled a cedar-tree, and I question much, whether Solomon ever had such a one for the building of the Temple at Jerusalem; it was five feet ten inches diameter at the lower part next the stump, and four feet eleven inches diameter at the end of twenty-two feet, where it lessened, and then parted into branches. It was not without infinite labour that I felled this tree; I was twenty days hacking and hewing at the bottom, and fourteen more getting the branches and limbs and the vast spreading head of it cut off; after this it cost me a month to shape it and dub it to a proportion, and to something like the bottom of a boat, that it might swim upright as it ought to do. It cost me near three months more to clear the inside, and work it out so as to make an exact boat of it: this I did indeed without fire, by mere mallet and chisel, and by the dint of hard labour, till I had brought it to be a very handsome periagua, and big enough to have carried six-and-twenty men, and consequently big enough to have carried me and all my cargo.

Robinson Crusoe

OTHER PROSE-WRITERS

1. John Arbuthnot (1667–1735). Arbuthnot was born in Kincardineshire, Scotland, studied medicine at Oxford, and spent the latter part of his life in London, where he became acquainted with

Pope and Swift. His writings are chiefly political, and include the *Memoirs of Martinus Scriblerus* (1709), which, though published (1741) in the works of Pope, is thought to be his; *The History of John Bull* (1712 or 1713), ridiculing the war-policy of the Whigs; and *The Art of Political Lying* (1712).

Arbuthnot writes with wit and vivacity, and with many pointed allusions. At his best he somewhat resembles Swift, though he lacks the great devouring flame of the latter's personality.

2. Lord Bolingbroke (1678–1751). Henry St John, Viscount Bolingbroke, was one of the chief political figures of the period. At the age of twenty-six he was Secretary for War in the Tory Government; was thereafter implicated in Jacobite plots; was compelled to flee to France; was permitted to return to England in 1725; had once more to return to France in 1735; then, after seven years' exile, was finally restored to his native land.

Bolingbroke prided himself on being both a patron of letters and a man of letters. He influenced Pope, not always to the latter's advantage. In 1753 appeared his *Letter to Sir William Wyndham* (written in 1717); then in 1736 he produced *A Letter on the Spirit of Patriotism* and in 1738 *The Idea of a Patriot King*. These reflect the Tory sentiments of their author, are written with lucidity and a vigour that is often near to coarseness, and have all the tricks and vices of the rhetorician.

3. George Berkeley (1685–1753). Born in Ireland, Berkeley was educated at Dublin, where he distinguished himself in mathematics. Having taken holy orders, he went to London (1713), and became acquainted with Swift and other wits. He was a man of noble and charitable mind, and interested himself in many worthy schemes. He was appointed a dean, and then was made Bishop of Cloyne in 1734. He was a man of great and enterprising mind, and wrote with much charm on a diversity of scientific, philosophical, and metaphysical subjects.

Among his books are *The Principles of Human Knowledge*, a notable effort in the study of the human mind that appeared in 1710, *Three Dialogues between Hylas and Philonous* (1713), and *Alciphron, or The Minute Philosopher* (1732). He is among the first, both in time and in quality, of the English philosophers who have dressed their ideas in language of literary distinction. He writes with delightful ease, disdaining ornament or affectation, and his command of gentle irony is capable and sure.

4. Lady Mary Wortley Montagu (1689–1762). This lady, famous in her day for her masculine force of character, was the eldest daughter of the Duke of Kingston. In 1712 she married Edward Wortley Montagu, and moved in the highest literary and social circles. In 1716 her husband was appointed ambassador at Constantinople, and while she was in the East she corresponded regularly with many friends, both literary and personal. She is the precursor of the great letter-writers of the later portion of the century. Her *Letters* are written shrewdly and sensibly, often with a frankness that is a little staggering. She had a vivid interest in her world, and she can communicate her interest to her reader.

5. Earl of Shaftesbury (1671–1713). Anthony Ashley Cooper, third Earl of Shaftesbury, is another example of the aristocratic *dilettante* man of letters. He had little taste for the politics of the time, and aspired to be famous as a great writer. He travelled much, and died at Naples in 1713.

His books are written with great care and exactitude, and are pleasant and lucid without being particularly striking. His *Characteristics of Men, Manners, Opinions, and Times* (1711), though it contains nothing very original or profound, suited the taste of the time and was widely popular.

POETRY

ALEXANDER POPE (1688–1744)

1. His Life. Pope was born in London, the only son of a considerable city tradesman. From his birth two conditions were to influence very deeply the career of the future poet: first, he was puny and delicate, and, secondly, he was baptized into the Roman Catholic faith. His bodily infirmity, which amounted almost to deformity, caused him to be privately educated; and to the end of his life his knowledge had that extensive range, joined to the liability to make the grossest blunders, which is so often the mark of an eager and precocious intelligence imperfectly trained. Pope's religious faith, though he was never excessively devout as a Roman Catholic, closed to him all the careers, professional and political, in which a man of his keen intelligence might have been expected to succeed. He was thus forced into the pursuit of letters as his only road to fame. From his earliest youth we find him passionately desirous of making his name as an author.

His youth was passed at Binfield, his father's small estate near Windsor Forest. Before he was twenty years old he got into touch with Wycherley, now old and besotted. Through him Pope became acquainted with Addison, Swift, and Steele, whose friendship he eagerly cultivated. His early verses, admirably attuned to the ear of the age, brought him recognition and applause; his translation of Homer brought him wealth; and from that point he never looked back. He became the dominating poetical personality of the day. In 1719 he removed to his house at Twickenham, whose pinchbeck beauties became the wonder, envy, and derision of literary and social London. It remained his home till "that long disease, his life," was finished in 1744.

2. His Character. In this book it is fortunately seldom that we are called upon to analyse the character of an English writer in any detail, but in the case of Pope it is necessary. With no man more than Pope are such personal considerations relevant and cogent. The complexity of his character is reflected in the contradictory estimates of his biographers. One sees him as "a good and exceedingly lovable man," and others as the personification of all that is mean, spiteful, and aggressive. His character seems to be a mass of contradictions, and his own deliberate misrepresentation and concealment of facts about his life, and parentage, and his editing of his published letters have done nothing to help in the elucidation of the truth. It seems certain that his character was gravely affected by his physical weakness, and the mental agony occasioned by the taunts and sneers of his enemies. To this may be attributed much of his sensitiveness to insult, and his virulence in making and replying to attacks. His life was a series of skirmishes with rivals for poetic fame, many of whom, though beneath his contempt, he treated with a coarseness and violence which, though typical of their age, are none the less objectionable. He combined a sensitiveness to criticism, and a pride in his own artistic gifts, with an eye which saw clearly the weaknesses of his enemies and a cold calculation which mercilessly dissected them. His animosity was intensely personal and vindictive and gave to his satirical portraits a vigour and incisiveness which have made them immortal.

On the other hand, Pope suffered much at the hands of his enemies, who spared neither his works, his family, nor his personal deformities. He had, too, a fine feeling for beauty, an exquisite artistic taste, and a high sense of the poet's vocation, which underlay many of his attacks on the denizens of Grub Street. *The Dunciad* (see later) was the product of an offended artistic conscience as well as of personal malice. To his friends he was loyal and generous, as we may see from his treatment of Swift, Richard Savage, and Martha Blount, while his claim to have been a good son to his ageing parents seems to have been justified. By religion and physical deformity a social outcast, he saw literature as his one way to fame. For it, and for poetry in particular, he lived; everything he wrote was stamped with the joy of creation and his desire for perfection and permanency; and it is as an artist that he will finally be judged.

3. **His Poetry.** Pope's earliest important work was his *Pastorals*. These poems, almost certainly written before he was eighteen, were published in 1709. The characters and scenery, based as they are on classical models, lack vigour and reality, but the work is important as an experiment in verse technique. Pope has already chosen his medium, the heroic couplet, which is here handled with great metrical skill, variation of speed and tone, and delicacy of touch. The rich descriptions are, perhaps, overloaded with epithet, and the diction is often artificial. We give a specimen of his earliest numbers:

> And yet my numbers please the rural throng,
> Rough satyrs dance, and Pan applauds the song:
> The nymphs, forsaking ev'ry cave and spring,
> Their early fruit, and milk-white turtles bring;
> Each am'rous nymph prefers her gifts in vain,
> On you their gifts are all bestowed again.
> For you the swains the fairest flow'rs design,
> And in one garland all their beauties join;
> Accept the wreath which you deserve alone,
> In whom all beauties are compris'd in one.
>
> *Summer: The Second Pastoral*

In 1711 appeared *An Essay on Criticism*, also written in heroic couplets. The poem professes to set forth the gospel of 'wit' and 'nature' as it applies to the literature of the age. There is no attempt at originality of thought, Pope's aim being merely to restate the code of the ancients. This he does with a conciseness and epigrammatic neatness which have given his remarks the permanence of proverbs. We give below four well-known examples:

> A little learning is a dangerous thing!

> And snatch a grace beyond the reach of art

> To err is human: to forgive, divine

> True wit is nature to advantage dressed;
> What oft was thought, but ne'er so well express'd.

Windsor Forest (1713) is another pastoral in the familiar metre. Artificial still, it nevertheless shows a broader treatment and a still stronger grip of the stopped couplet.

In 1712 was published the first version of *The Rape of the Lock*, one of the most brilliant poems in the language. In it Pope tried to laugh back into good humour two families who had been estranged when Lord Petrie cut off a lock of hair from the head of Miss Arabella Fermor. It is in the mock-heroic strain, and its effectiveness was greatly increased when, in 1714, Pope added the machinery of the sylphs to the original version. The poem combines with its humorous, epic treatment of the trivial theme a delicate fancy and a good deal of satire on the weaknesses of the fair sex and on society manners in general. For the most part, this satire is gentle and goodhumoured, though occasionally the last half-line of a couplet gives us a foretaste of the more incisive tones of the later Pope.

The Rape of the Lock has a flawless, airy grace and a sustained lightness of touch which are unparalleled in our literature. An infinite variety of verbal music is included in its fine descriptions, usually of the sylphs, which, for sheer pictorial beauty, are the finest things Pope achieved. A close study of the workmanship of the poem reveals an almost incredible subtlety of control over the texture of his verse. The first of the passages quoted below is typical in its mock-heroic tone and gentle satire on the vanity of the fair sex, while the second is a fair example of the delicate beauty of description:

> And now, unveil'd, the toilet stands display'd,
> Each silver vase in mystic order laid.
> First, robed in white, the nymph intent adores,
> With head uncover'd, the cosmetic powers.
> A heav'nly image in the glass appears,
> To that she bends, to that her eye she rears;
> Th' inferior priestess, at her altar's side,
> Trembling, begins the sacred rites of pride.
> Unnumber'd treasures ope at once, and here
> The various offerings of the world appear;
> From each she nicely culls with curious toil,
> And decks the goddess with the glitt'ring spoil.
> This casket India's glowing gems unlocks,
> And all Arabia breathes from yonder box.
> The tortoise here and elephant unite,
> Transform'd to combs, the speckled and the white.
> Here files of pins extend their shining rows,
> Puffs, powders, patches, Bibles, billet-doux.
> Now awful beauty puts on all its arms;
> The fair each moment rises in her charms,

Repairs her smiles, awakens every grace,
And calls forth all the wonders of her face:
Sees by degrees a purer blush arise,
And keener lightnings quicken in her eyes.
The busy sylphs surround their darling care,
These set the head, and those divide the hair,
Some fold the sleeve, while others plait the gown;
And Betty's praised for labours not her own.

Some to the sun their insect-wings unfold,
Waft on the breeze, or sink in clouds of gold;
Transparent forms, too fine for mortal sight,
Their fluid bodies half dissolved in light.
Loose to the wind their airy garments flew,
Thin glittering textures of the filmy dew,
Dipp'd in the richest tincture of the skies,
Where light disports in ever-mingling dyes;
While ev'ry beam new transient colours flings,
Colours that change whene'er they wave their wings.

By this time Pope was well known, and he set about his ambitious scheme of translating the *Iliad*, which was completed in 1720. As a translation it is faulty, for Pope had no sound knowledge of Greek and was often led into errors by his reference to earlier translations. On the other hand, it is a brilliant poem, fast moving, and full of eloquent speeches, though it is far removed from the direct vigour of the original. The true epic strain was not really congenial to Pope. The *Iliad* was followed, in 1725 and 1726, by the *Odyssey*, translated with the aid of two classical scholars, Fenton and Broome. Both works were so successful as to make Pope a wealthy man, but brought upon him jealousy and criticism, and led to many quarrels, notably with Addison. The following passage will give some idea of the general tone of the work:

The troops exulting sat in order round,
And beaming fires illumined all the ground.
As when the moon, refulgent lamp of night,
O'er heaven's pure azure spreads her sacred light,
When not a breath disturbs the deep serene,
And not a cloud o'ercasts the solemn scene,
Around her throne the vivid planets roll,
And stars unnumber'd gild the glowing pole,
O'er the dark trees a yellower verdure shed,
And tip with silver every mountain's head:
Then shine the vales, the rocks in prospect rise,
A flood of glory bursts from all the skies;
The conscious swains, rejoicing in the sight,
Eye the blue vault, and bless the useful light.

Still more criticism was evoked by his edition of Shakespeare, published in 1725. This was a task for which he lacked the necessary Elizabethan scholarship, but he prefaced the work with a fine appreciation. His many mistakes and cavalier treatment of the text were quickly seized upon by his critics, particularly by the Shakespearian scholar, Theobald, in *Shakespeare Restored* (1726).

Theobald's criticism gained him the throne of dullness in *The Dunciad*, which appeared anonymously in 1728, and again in 1742, with the addition of a fourth book and the dethronement of Theobald in favour of Colley Cibber. In this poem, modelled on Dryden's *MacFlecknoe*, Pope turns to rend the host of minor writers whose attacks had been making his life a misery. But the poem is not merely a settlement of old scores; Pope is concerned for the integrity of the art for which he lived. It shows his satirical powers at their best and their worst. It is charged with a stinging wit, and has great vigour and variety of pace, but is spiteful, venomous, and often coarse, and is too monotonous in its method of attack. Too often Pope condemns the good with the bad. Yet here as elsewhere, he has many fine passages, among the best of which is the conclusion, which we here quote:

> In vain, in vain—the all-composing hour
> Resistless falls: the Muse obeys the Power.
> She comes! She comes! The sable throne behold
> Of Night primeval and of Chaos old!
> Before her, Fancy's gilded clouds decay,
> And all its varying rainbows die away.
> Wit shoots in vain its momentary fires,
> The meteor drops, and in a flash expires. . . .
> See skulking Truth to her old cavern fled,
> Mountains of casuistry heaped o'er her head! . . .
> See Mystery to Mathematics fly!
> In vain! They gaze, turn giddy, rave, and die.
> Religion blushing veils her sacred fires,
> And unawares Morality expires. . . .
> Lo! thy dread empire, CHAOS! is restored;
> Light dies before thy uncreating word;
> Thy hand, great Anarch! lets the curtain fall
> And universal darkness buries all.

Between 1731 and 1735 Pope published a series of philosophical poems, including *To Lord Bathurst*, *Of the Use of Riches*, *Of the Knowledge and Characters of Men*, *Of the Characters of Women*, and, most famous of all, *An Essay on Man*, in which he discussed man's place in the universe. These *Moral Essays* were written under the influence of Lord Bolingbroke, and their confused reasoning shows Pope's lack of philosophical training and background. They do, however, contain passages full of force and beauty, and the verse has Pope's usual care and lucidity.

The years 1733 and 1737 mark Pope's last important period of production. In them appeared his *Imitations of Horace*, in which, using the Latin satirist as his model, Pope launched his attacks in a series of poetical epistles on the greed and corruption of his day, and especially of the Whig party then in power. His famous *Prologue to the Satires*, better known by its other title, *An Epistle to Dr Arbuthnot* (1735), contains some of his most brilliant and finished work. The style shows the ultimate development of Pope's couplet in its ease, naturalness, and versatility. The poem contains the famous portraits of Lord Hervey and Addison, of which the latter is given below. They are masterpieces of satirical portraiture.

> Peace to all such! but were there one whose fires
> True genius kindles, and fair fame inspires;
> Blest with each talent and each art to please,
> And born to write, converse, and live with ease;
> Should such a man, too fond to rule alone,
> Bear, like the Turk, no brother near the throne
> View him with scornful, yet with jealous eyes,
> And hate for arts that caused himself to rise;
> Damn with faint praise, assent with civil leer,
> And without sneering, teach the rest to sneer;
> Willing to wound, and yet afraid to strike,
> Just hint a fault, and hesitate dislike;
> Alike reserved to blame, or to commend,
> A timorous foe, and a suspicious friend;
> Dreading even fools, by flatterers besieged,
> And so obliging, that he ne'er obliged;
> Like Cato, give his little senate laws,
> And sit attentive to his own applause;
> While wits and templars every sentence raise,
> And wonder with a foolish face of praise:—
> Who but must laugh, if such a man there be?
> Who would not weep, if Atticus were he?

4. Summary. It is now useful to draw together the various features of the work of this important poet.

(*a*) Both in subject and in style his poems are *limited*. They take people of his own social class, and they deal with their common experiences and their common interests and aspirations. Pope rarely dips below the surface, and when he does so he is not at his best. With regard to his style, we have seen that it is almost wholly restricted to the heroic couplet, used in a narrative and didactic subject. He is almost devoid of the lyrical faculty, and the higher artistic emotions—"passion and apathy, and glory and shame"—are beyond his artistic grasp.

(b) Within these limits his work is *powerful* and *effective*. The wit is keen; the satire burns like acid; and his zeal is unshakable. In serious topics, as in *An Essay on Man*, he can give imperishable shape to popular opinions.

(c) Above all, he was a great *artist*. A study of his technique shows a meticulous sense of the exact word in the exact place. One word, or the variation of the cæsura, is enough to crystallize a mood or an idea. His diction develops from the rather artificial pastoral or mock-heroic language of the years before 1717 to the natural, everyday, distinctive speech of his later satires. This naturalness, together with a great flexibility and a condensed precision, is seen at its best in *An Epistle to Dr Arbuthnot*. Pope's is the true art which conceals art. Well might he say:

> True ease in writing comes from art, not chance,
> As those move easiest who have learned to dance.
> *An Essay on Criticism*

(d) His *metre*. Pope's use of the heroic couplet marks a great change from that of Dryden. The couplet is tighter and more compressed, and there are few of the alexandrines or triplets which help to give Dryden's poetry its typical sweep. Instead we have 'correctness' and finish. But there is little monotony in Pope—the range of his couplet can be seen by a comparison of *The Rape of the Lock* with the *Epistle to Dr Arbuthnot*. The latter is typical of his later work. Its epigrammatic pungency, often the result of a skilful use of antithetical balance, shows us Pope's couplet in all its strength, clearness, and point. For this kind of poetry it has never been equalled.

OTHER POETS

1. Matthew Prior (1664–1721). Born in Dorsetshire, Prior studied at Cambridge, and was early engaged in writing on behalf of the Tories, from whom he received several valuable appointments. In 1701 he entered the House of Commons; and in 1715, becoming involved in Jacobite intrigues, he was imprisoned. He was liberated in 1717, and died in 1721.

His first long work is *The Hind and the Panther Transvers'd to the Story of the Country and the City Mouse* (1687), written in collaboration with Charles Montagu, and ridiculing *The Hind and the Panther*. Other longer works are *Alma: or the Progress of the Mind* (1718) and *Solomon on the Vanity of the World* (1718). The first imitates Butler in *Hudibras*, and with fair success; the second, written in the heroic couplet, aims at being a serious poem, but its seriousness is often marred with levity, and it shows no wisdom or insight.

Prior's chief distinction lies in his miscellaneous verse, which is varied, bulky, and of a high quality. In some respects it resembles the verses of Swift, for much of it is composed in the octosyllabic couplet, and it has a fair amount of Swift's force and dexterity. Prior lacks Swift's deadly power and passion, but he surpasses the Dean in versatility, in an easy wit and impudence, and in sentimentality. In this pleasant ease of verse and sentiment he is rarely approached. Some of the best of his shorter pieces are *The Chameleon, The Thief and the Cordelier*, and a number of poems, *To Chloe*.

2. John Gay (1685–1732). Gay was born in humble circumstances, and was apprenticed to a silk-mercer; but, being ambitious, he entered the service of the Duchess of Queensberry (1712). His poems having brought him some fame, he sought a public appointment. He was only moderately successful in this search, and his lazy and indifferent habits spoiled the chances that came in his way. He died in London, an amiable and shiftless idler.

His chief works are *The Rural Sports* (1713), written in the heroic couplet, and resembling Pope's *Pastorals*, *The Shepherd's Week* (1714), and *The What d' Ye Call It* (1715), a pastoral farce. *Trivia, or The Art of Walking the Streets of London* (1716) is a witty parody of the heroic style, and it contains bright descriptions of London streets. He is, however, best remembered for his *Fables* (1727), which are in colloquial, easy octosyllabics, though only a few of them are really of permanent interest, and *The Beggar's Opera* (1728). This last play had a great success, which has lasted to the present day. It became the rage, and ran for sixty-two performances. It deserved its success, for it contains some pretty songs and much genuine though boisterous humour. It is also of importance as the beginning of the tradition of comic opera which culminates in the work of Gilbert and Sullivan. Gay had the real lyrical gift, which was all the more valuable considering the age he lived in. His ballad *Black-eyed Susan* is still popular.

3. Edward Young (1683–1765). Young had a long life, and produced a large amount of literary work of variable quality. He was born in Hampshire, went to Oxford, and late in life (about 1730) entered the Church. He lived much in retirement, though in his later years he received a public appointment.

His major works are *The Last Day* (1714) and *The Force of Religion* (1714), which are moralizings written in the heroic couplet; *The Love of Fame* (1725–28), which shows an advance in the use of the couplet; and a poem in blank verse, *The Complaint, or Night Thoughts on Life, Death, and Immortality* (1742). This last poem, which was inspired by the death of his wife, had a great and long-enduring popularity, which has now vanished. Like Young's other poems, it shows some power of expression and a sombre satisfaction at his own misery. In the history of literature it is of some consequence, for the blank verse is of considerable strength, and as a reaction against the dominance of the couplet its value is undeniable.

4. Sir Samuel Garth (1661–1719). Garth was an older man than most of the other poets mentioned in this chapter. He was a popular physician, assisted Pope in the young man's first efforts, and was knighted when George I ascended the throne.

The Dispensary, published in 1699, is the one work which gives him his place. It deals with a long-defunct squabble between physicians and apothecaries, and its importance is due to its being written in a kind of heroic couplet that is a link in style between Dryden and Pope.

5. Lady Winchilsea (1661–1720). Born in Hampshire, the daughter of Sir William Kingsmill, Anne, Countess of Winchilsea, passed most of her life in London, where she became acquainted with Pope and other literary notables. Some of her poems, which were of importance in their day, are *The Spleen* (1701), a Pindaric ode; *The Prodigy* (1706); and *Miscellany Poems* (1713), containing *A Nocturnal Reverie*.

Wordsworth says, "Now it is remarkable that, excepting the *Nocturnal Reverie* of Lady Winchilsea, and a passage or two in the *Windsor Forest* of Pope, the poetry intervening between the publication of the *Paradise Lost* and *The Seasons* does not contain a single new image of external nature." This statement is perhaps an exaggeration, but there is no doubt that Lady Winchilsea had the gift of producing smooth and melodious verse, and she had a discerning eye for the beauties of nature. They were, however, the beauties of a garden, rather than those of the wilds.

6. Ambrose Philips (1675–1749). Philips was a Shropshire man, was educated at Cambridge, and became a considerable figure in the literary world. He was a friend of Pope until his *Pastorals* appeared with Pope's in Tonson's *Miscellany* (1709). Stung by the praise lavished on Philips, the latter published a skilfully satirical 'eulogy' of his poems which mercilessly exposed their shortcomings. The quarrel which followed led Pope to immortalize Philips in *The Dunciad* and others of his works. Philips obtained several posts under the Government, and passed a happy and prosperous life.

He wrote three tragedies, the best of which is *The Distressed Mother* (1712). He produced a fair amount of prose for the periodicals, and his miscellaneous verse, of a light and agreeable kind, was popular in its day. His poetry was called 'namby-pamby,' from his Christian name; and the word has survived in its general application.

7. Thomas Parnell (1679–1718). Parnell was born in Ireland, entered the Church, became an archdeacon, and prospered in his post. His poems consist of miscellaneous work, and were extremely popular in their day. The best of his work is contained in *The Hermit* (1710), which is written in heroic couplets, and in places reminds the reader of *The Deserted Village*. He shows skill as a versifier, and he has a genuine regard for nature.

8. Allan Ramsay (1686–1758). Born in Lanarkshire, Ramsay came to Edinburgh at the age of fourteen, and became a wig-maker. He soon took to writing verses, which admitted him into the society of the Edinburgh wits. He started a bookseller's shop in the city, and became a kind of local unofficial Poet Laureate. His ballads became very popular, and he brought upon himself the notice of the leaders of the literary world in London.

Ramsay published much miscellaneous writing, of which a large amount was issued to satisfy a passing demand. The quality can be poor enough; but some of it is more meritorious. A piece like *Lochaber No More* is quite noteworthy, and others reveal his freakish and pleasing sense of humour. His *The Gentle Shepherd* (1725), a pastoral drama, has many of the vices of its species; but on the other hand it contains pleasing natural descriptions, some delightful though sentimental characters, and a few charming lyrics. As a literary ancestor of Burns Ramsay is important. He influenced the poetry of the Ayrshire man, who freely acknowledged the aid he obtained. Equally important was his publication of many of the works of the old Scots "makaris" in *The Evergreen* (1724). This collection led to a renewed appreciation of early vernacular poetry, and was largely responsible for a rebirth of interest in popular song. Ramsay also shows how the natural genius of Scotland, while bowing to the supremacy of the school of Pope, nevertheless diverged on lines natural to itself.

THE DEVELOPMENT OF LITERARY FORMS

The period under review marks a hardening of the process discernible in the last chapter. The secession from romanticism is complete; the ideals of classicism reign supreme. Yet even at the lowest ebb of the romantic spirit, a return to nature is feebly beginning. In the next chapter we shall notice this new movement, for in the next period we shall see it becoming full and strong.

1. Poetry. In no department of literature is the triumph of classicism seen more fully than in poetry.

(a) The *lyric* almost disappears. What remains is of a light and artificial nature. The best lyrics are found in some of Prior's shorter pieces, in Gay's *The Beggar's Opera*, and in Ramsay's *The Gentle Shepherd*.

(b) The *ode* still feebly survives in the Pindaric form. Pope wrote a few with poor success, one of them being *On St Cecilia's Day*, in imitation of Dryden's ode. Lady Winchilsea was another mediocre exponent of the same form.

(c) The *satiric* type is common, and of high quality. The best example is Pope's *Dunciad*, a personal satire. Of political satire in poetry we have nothing to compare with Dryden's. Satire tends to be lighter, brighter, and more cynical. It is spreading to other forms of verse besides the heroic couplet, and we can observe it in the octosyllabic couplet in the poems of Swift, Prior, and Gay. A slight development is the epistolary form of the satire, of which Pope became fond in his latter years. Such is his *Epistles of Horace Imitated*.

(d) *Narrative Poetry.* This is of considerable bulk, and contains some of the best productions of the period. Pope's translation of Homer is a good example, and of the poorer sort are Blackmore's abundant epics. We have also to notice a slight revival of the ballad, which was imitated by Gay and Prior. Their imitations are bloodless things, but they are worth noticing because they show that the interest is there.

(e) *The Pastoral.* The artificial type of the pastoral was highly popular, for several reasons. It gave an air of rusticity to the most formal of compositions; it was thought to be elegant; it was easily written; and it had the approval of the ancients, who made free use of the type. Pope and Philips have been mentioned as examples of the pastoral poets.

2. **Drama.** Here there is almost a blank. The brilliant and exotic flower of Restoration comedy has withered, and nothing of any merit takes its place. In tragedy Addison's *Cato* is almost the only passable example. In comedy Steele's plays are a survival of the Restoration type, but they have a sentimental, didactic piety quite alien from their models. The only advance in the drama is shown in *The Beggar's Opera*, whose robust vitality, sprightly music, and charming songs make it stand alone in its generation.

3. **Prose.** In prose we have to chronicle a distinct advance. For the first time we have periodical literature occupying a prominent place in the writing of the time. At this point, therefore, it is convenient to summarize the rise of periodical literature.

(*a*) *The Rise of the Periodical Press.* The first periodical published in Europe was the *Gazetta* (1536), in Venice. This was a manuscript newspaper which was read publicly in order to give the Venetians information regarding their war with the Turks. In England newssheets were published during the reign of Elizabeth, but they were irregular in their appearance, being issued only when some notable event, such as a great flood or fire, made their sale secure. The first regular English journal was a weekly publication begun in 1622 by **Thomas Archer** and **Nicholas Bourne**, who were authorized to print information on foreign wars. Such publications, concerned exclusively with foreign news, became known as *corantos*, and they continued to appear until they were banned in 1632. But, in 1638, they reappeared when **Nathaniel Butter** and Nicholas Bourne obtained a monopoly for the printing of foreign news. It is noticeable that during this period, when 'the Press' was coming into being, governments seemed to fear the power of the printed word, and prosecutions of journalists and publishers, as well as suppressions of all periodicals, were not infrequent. The political passions which led to the Civil War produced a spate of journalistic writing, during which the *corantos* were submerged beneath the newsbooks and *Diurnalls* which, for the first time, in 1641, began to print home news. These newsbooks had most of the features of the modern newspaper, including editorial comments. The Civil War proper gave rise to numerous ephemeral *Posts*, *Spies*, and *Scouts*, and to the *Mercuries* published by both sides. On the Royalist side appeared the *Mercurius Aulicus* (1643–45), the *Mercurius Academicus* (1645–

46), and the *Mercurius Pragmaticus* (1647–50), while the Round-heads replied with such journals as the *Mercurius Britannicus* (1643–46) and *Mercurius Politicus* (1650–52). In 1655 Cromwell suppressed the licensed press with the exception of the official organ, *The Publick Intelligencer*, which appeared weekly until 1660. The suppression continued, with a short break at the beginning of 1659, until the end of that year, at which time only three people were allowed to publish journals. Among them was the greatest of all seventeenth-century journalists, **Henry Muddiman**, who published *The Parliamentary Intelligencer* (1659), the *Mercurius Publicus* (1660–63), and his greatest journal, *The London Gazette* (1665). The office of Gazetteer became an official appointment, and Steele held it for a time.

In 1682 the freedom of the Press was restored, and large numbers of *Mercuries* and other periodicals appeared and flourished in their different fashions. Advertisements began to be a feature of the papers. In *The Jockey's Intelligencer* (1683) the charge is "a shilling for a horse or coach, for notification, and sixpence for renewing." In 1702 *The Daily Courant*, the first daily newspaper, was published, and it survived until 1735. Then in the early years of the eighteenth century the fierce contests between the Whigs and the Tories brought a rapid expansion of the Press. The most famous of the issues were Defoe's *Review* (1704), a Whig organ whose writings brought its editor into disrepute, and its opponent *The Examiner*, the Tory paper to which men like Swift and Prior contributed regularly. These newspapers are almost entirely political, but they contain satirical work of much merit.

Then in 1709 Steele published *The Tatler*. At first it was Steele's intention to make it partly a *news*-paper; but under the pressure of his own genius and of that of Addison its literary features were accentuated till the daily essay became the feature of leading interest. *The Spectator*, begun in March 1711, carried the tendency still farther. The literary journal has come to stay. Steele's *The Plebeian* (1719) is an early example of the political periodical.

(*b*) *The Rise of the Essay*. Johnson defines an essay as "a loose sally of the mind; an irregular indigested piece; not a regular or orderly composition." This definition is not quite complete, for it does not cover such an elaborate work as Locke's *An Essay concerning Human Understanding*. But for the miscellaneous prose essay, which it is our immediate business to consider here, the definition will do. An essay, therefore, must in other words be short, unmethodical, personal, and written in a style that is literary, easy, and elegant.

The English essay has its roots in the Elizabethan period, in the miscellaneous work of Lodge, Lyly, and Greene, and other literary free-lances (see p. 123). Sir Philip Sidney's *Apologie for Poetrie*, published in 1595, is a pamphlet that attains a rudimentary essay-form. But the first real essayist in English is Francis Bacon (1561–1626), who published a short series of essays in 1597, enlarged in two later editions (1612 and 1625). His work follows that of the French writer Montaigne, whose essays appeared about 1580 and in English in 1603. In Bacon we have the miscellany of theme and the brevity, but we lack the intimacy of treatment and of style. Bacon's essays are rather the musings of the philosopher than the personal opinions of the literary executant.

The defects of Bacon were remedied by Abraham Cowley (1618–67), who writes on such subjects as *Of Myself*, *The Garden*, and other familiar themes. His style is somewhat heavy, but he has a pleasant discursive manner, different from the dry and distant attitude of Bacon. He provides the link between Addison and Bacon. Another advance is marked by a group of character-writers who flourished in the first half of the seventeenth century. They gave short character-sketches, often very acute and humorous, of various types of people. The best known of such writers are Joseph Hall (1574–1656), John Earle (1601–65), and Sir Thomas Overbury (1581–1613). Overbury wrote short accounts of such types as the *Tinker*, the *Milkmaid*, and the *Franklin*. His sketches are short, are pithily expressed, and reveal considerable knowledge and insight.

During the Restoration period we have Dryden's *Essay of Dramatick Poesie* (1668), Locke's *An Essay concerning Human Understanding* (1690), and Temple's *Essay of Poetry* (1685). The two first works are too long to be called essays proper, and fall rather under the name of treatises. Temple's essay, one of many that he published, is rather long and formal, but it is nearer the type we are here considering.

With the development of the periodical press the short essay takes a great stride forward. It becomes varied, and acquires character, suppleness, and strength. The work of Addison and Steele has already been noticed at some length. In *The Tatler* (1709) and *The Spectator* (1711) they laid down the lines along which the essay was to be developed by their great successors. Other essayists of the time were Swift and Pope, who contributed to the periodicals, and

Defoe, whose miscellaneous work is of wide range and of considerable importance.

(c) *Prose Narrative*. Much of the narrative is still disguised as allegory, as in Swift's *Gulliver's Travels* and Addison's *The Vision of Mirza*. In his method Swift shows some advance, for he subordinates the allegory and adds to the interest in the satire and the narrative. The prominence given to fiction is still more noticeable in the novels of Defoe, such as *Robinson Crusoe*. We are now in touch with the novel proper, which will be treated in the next chapter.

(d) *Miscellaneous Prose*. There is a large body of religious, political, and philosophical work. Much of it is satirical. In political prose Swift is the outstanding figure, with such books as *The Drapier's Letters*; and in religious writing his *Tale of a Tub* has a sinister importance. Other examples are Bolingbroke's *A Letter on the Spirit of Patriotism* (political), Berkeley's *Alciphron* (philosophical), and Steele's *The Christian Hero* (religious).

THE DEVELOPMENT OF LITERARY STYLE

1. Poetry. In poetry we have to chronicle the domination of the *heroic couplet*. This metre produced a close, clear, and pointed style, as we have noticed in the work of Pope. Blank verse is still found in Young's *Night Thoughts*. Another example of blank verse is found in the mock epic of **John Philips (1676–1709)** called *The Splendid Shilling* (1701). The use of blank verse at this time is important, for it marks both a resistance to the use of the couplet and a promise of the revival of the freer forms of verse. The following is a fair example of the blank verse of the period. In style it is quite uninspired, its philosophy is dull, but it is metrically accurate and has a certain dignity and force.

> Amidst my list of blessings infinite
> Stands this the foremost, "That my heart has bled."
> 'Tis Heaven's last effort of goodwill to man;
> When pain can't bless, Heaven quits us in despair.
> Who fails to grieve, when just occasion calls,
> Or grieves too much, deserves not to be blest
> Inhuman, or effeminate, his heart:
> Reason absolves the grief, which reason ends.
> May Heaven ne'er trust my friend with happiness,
> Till it has taught him how to bear it well,
> By previous pain; and made it safe to smile!
>
> YOUNG, *Night Thoughts*

The *lyric* still survives as a pale reflection of the Caroline species. A short specimen will suffice to show the facile versification and the lack of real passion that marks the treatment of the almost universal love-theme:

> Blessed as the immortal gods is he,
> The youth who fondly sits by thee,
> And hears and sees thee all the while
> Softly speak, and sweetly smile.
>
> 'Twas this deprived my soul of rest,
> And raised such tumults in my breast;
> For while I gazed, in transport tossed,
> My breath was gone, my voice was lost.
> <div align="right">Ambrose Philips, <i>A Fragment of Sappho</i></div>

The only other kind of metre of any consequence is the *octosyllabic couplet*, which is largely employed in occasional and satirical compositions. Its style is neat, sharp, and dexterous, as can be observed in Swift's and Prior's verses.

2. Prose. In prose the outstanding feature is the emergence of the middle style. Of this the chief exponent is Addison, of whom Johnson says, "His prose is the model of the middle style; . . . pure without scrupulosity, and exact without apparent elaboration; always equable, and always easy, without glowing words or pointed sentences." We now find established a prose suitable for miscellaneous purposes—for newspaper and political work, for the essay, for history and biography. The step is of immense importance, for we can say that with Addison the modern era of prose is begun.

Along with this went the temporary disappearance of ornate prose. Prose of this style, though it had its beauties, was yet liable to be full of flaws, and was unacceptable to the taste of the age of Pope. It was therefore avoided. When ornate prose re-emerged later in the work of Johnson and Gibbon it was purged of its technical weaknesses, a development largely due to the period of maturing that it had undergone in the time we are now considering.

While the school of Addison represents the middle style, the plainer style is represented in the work of Swift and Defoe. Swift reveals the style at its best—sure, clean, and strong. Defoe's writing is even plainer, and often descends to carelessness and inaccuracy. This is due almost entirely to the haste with which he wrote. We give an example of this colloquial style:

"Well," says I, "honest man, that is a great mercy, as things go now with the poor. But how do you live then, and how are you kept from the dreadful calamity that is now upon us all?" "Why, sir," says he, "I am a waterman, and there's my boat," says he, "and the boat serves me for a house; I work in it in the day, and I sleep in it in the night, and what I get I lay down upon that stone," says he, showing me a broad stone on the other side of the street, a good way from his house; "and then," says he, "I halloo and call to them till I make them hear, and they come and fetch it."

DEFOE, *A Journal of the Plague Year*

TABLE TO ILLUSTRATE THE DEVELOPMENT OF LITERARY FORMS

DATE	POETRY			DRAMA		PROSE		
	Lyrical	Narrative	Satirical and Didactic	Tragedy	Comedy	Narrative	Essay	Miscellaneous
1700		Addison[3]	Garth Lady Winchilsea		Steele[7]		Defoe	Defoe[8] Swift[1]
1710		Pope[10]					Steele[5]	Addison
	Gay Prior		Pope[11] Young	A. Philips Addison[4]		Steele[6] Addison[6] Defoe[9]	Addison[5] Swift	Steele Arbuthnot Bolingbroke Berkeley Lady M. W. Montagu
1720								
1730	A. Ramsay		Swift Pope[12]		A. Ramsay Gay	Swift[2]		
1740								

---

[1] *The Battle of the Books* (1704).   [2] *Gulliver's Travels* (1726).   [3] *The Campaign* (1704).
[4] *Cato* (1713).   [5] *The Tatler* (1709).   [6] The Coverley essays.
[7] *The Funeral* (1701).   [8] *The Review* (1704).   [9] *Robinson Crusoe* (1719).
[10] *Pastorals* 1709).   [11] *An Essay on Criticism* (1711).   [12] *The Dunciad* (1728).

CHAPTER IX

THE AGE OF TRANSITION

TIME-CHART OF THE CHIEF AUTHORS

The thick line shows the period of active literary work.

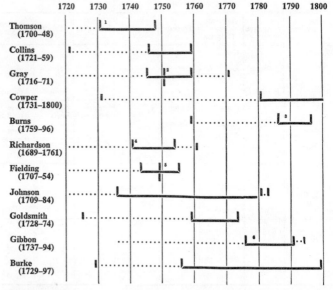

| | 1720 | 1730 | 1740 | 1750 | 1760 | 1770 | 1780 | 1790 | 1800 |

Thomson (1700–48)

Collins (1721–59)

Gray (1716–71)

Cowper (1731–1800)

Burns (1759–96)

Richardson (1689–1761)

Fielding (1707–54)

Johnson (1709–84)

Goldsmith (1728–74)

Gibbon (1737–94)

Burke (1729–97)

[1] *The Seasons* (1730).
[2] *Elegy written in a Country Churchyard* (1751).
[3] *Poems* (Kilmarnock edition, 1786).
[4] *Pamela* (1740).
[5] *Tom Jones* (1749).
[6] *The Decline and Fall of the Roman Empire* (1776).

THE TRANSITION IN POETRY

The following table is meant to convey a rough idea of the drift of poetry towards Romanticism. In the table the lateral position of the title of a work gives an approximate estimate of its approach to the Romantic ideal. Such an estimate, especially in the case of the transitional poems, cannot be determined absolutely, and need not be taken as final. The table, nevertheless, reveals not only the steady drift, but also the manner in which the different stages of development overlap.

DATE	CLASSICAL	TRANSITIONAL	ROMANTIC
1730	The Dunciad	The Seasons	
1740	Epistle to Arbuthnot London		
1750	Vanity of Human Wishes	Night Thoughts Collins's Odes	The Castle of Indolence
1760		Gray's Elegy	
1770		The Traveller	Ossian
1780		The Deserted Village	Chatterton's poems
1790		The Village	The Task Burns's poems Blake's poems

THE HISTORICAL BACKGROUND (1740–1800)

The period covered by the present chapter is that of the middle and later stages of the eighteenth century. During this time several relevant historical movements call for notice.

1. Decline of the Party Feud. The contest between the Whigs and the Tories still continues, but it is hardly of the previous bitterness. The chief reason for this change is found in the weakness of the Tory party, which by rash management and precipitate action made itself so unpopular that for nearly thirty years—those in the middle of the century—the Whigs had hardly any opposition. With the accession of George III in 1760 the Tories swiftly climbed into power, and, with the shadow of the French Revolution already looming up, party feeling soon acquired additional ferocity.

2. Commercial and Imperial Expansion. Under the pacific

management of the great Whig minister Walpole, and owing to the successful wars of his successors, the eighteenth century saw an immense growth in the wealth and importance of the British Empire. On literature this material welfare had its effect by endowing and stimulating research and original work. The possession of India and America in itself was an inspiration, and when the new territories brought new burdens, like that of the American revolt, the clash of ideals led to fresh literary effort, as can easily be seen in the work of Burke.

3. The French Revolution. Long before it burst, the storm of the Revolution was, in the words of Burke, blackening the horizon. During the century new ideas were germinating; new forces were gathering strength; and the Revolution, when it did come in 1789, was only the climax to a long and deeply diffused unrest. Revolutionary ideas stirred literature to the very depths; the present chapter, and the next as well, are a chronicle of their effects upon the literature of England.

THE AGE OF TRANSITION

Like all other periods of transition, the one under review is disturbed and confused. It is a matter of great difficulty to trace the different tendencies, but with care the task may be accomplished with some accuracy.

1. The Double Tendency. Two movements can be clearly observed in the writing of the time, namely:

(*a*) The allegiance to the old order of classicism. In this movement the chief and almost the only figure is that of Samuel Johnson. He is a host in himself, however.

(*b*) The search after the new order of Romanticism. In their different degrees, as can be seen from the second table at the beginning of this chapter, many writers were engaged in the search. It began as early as 1730, with the publication of Thomson's *Seasons*; and though it lapsed for a time, it was to continue with gathering force during the latter years of the century.

2. The New Romanticism. The general features of the Romantic movement were:

(*a*) A return to nature—to the real nature of earth and air, and not to the bookish nature of the artificial pastoral.

(*b*) A fresh interest in man's position in the world of nature. This led to great activity in religious and political speculation, as will be seen on the next page.

(c) An enlightened sympathy for the poor and oppressed. In English literature during this time one has but to think of the work of Cowper, Burns, and Crabbe, and even of the classically minded Gray, to perceive the revolution that is taking place in the minds of men.

(d) A revolt against the conventional literary technique, such as that of the heroic couplet. On the other hand, we have a desire for strength, simplicity, and sincerity in the expression of the new literary ideals.

(e) Fresh treatment of Romantic themes in such poems as *The Lay of the Last Minstrel*, *The Ancient Mariner*, *La Belle Dame sans Merci*. Writers turned to supernatural stories, legends, and the more colourful periods of history, especially the Middle Ages.

In the present chapter we shall perceive all the above features dimly taking shape. In the next chapter they will be the dominating features of the era.

3. The New Learning. The middle and later stages of the eighteenth century show a minor Renaissance that touched nearly all Europe. The increase in wealth and comfort coincided with a general uplifting of the standard of the human intellect. In France particularly it was well marked, and it took for its sign and seal the labours of the Encyclopædists and the social amenities of the older *salons*. Many of the leading English writers, including Gibbon, Hume, and Sterne, visited Paris, which was the hub of European culture.

In England the new learning took several channels. In literature we have the revival of the Romantic movement, leading to (a) research into archaic literary forms, such as the ballad, and (b) new editions of the older authors, such as Shakespeare and Chaucer. The publication of Bishop Percy's *Reliques* (1765), which contained some of the oldest and most beautiful specimens of ballad-literature, is a landmark in the history of the Romantic movement. Both Pope and Johnson were moved to edit Shakespeare, the former's ingenious guesses at meanings and cavalier treatment of his text contrasting strongly with the latter's shrewd, common-sense notes and attempt to restore the original readings. Other editions, by Theobald and Warburton, were examples of scholarly and enlightened research.

4. The New Philosophy. The spirit of the new thinking, which received its consummate expression in the works of Voltaire, was marked by keen scepticism and the zest for eager inquiry. Scotland very early took to it, the leading Scottish philosopher being Hume.

It would seem, perhaps, that this destructive spirit of disbelief would injure the Romantic ideal, which delights in illusion. But finally the new spirit actually assisted the Romantic ideal by demolishing and clearing away heaps of the ancient mental lumber, and so leaving the ground clear for new and fresher creations.

5. The Growth of Historical Research. History appears late in our literature, for it presupposes a long apprenticeship of research and meditation. The eighteenth century witnessed the swift rise of historical literature to a place of great importance. Like so many other things we have mentioned, it was fostered in France, and it touched Scotland first. The historical school had a glorious leader in Gibbon, who was nearly as much at home in the French language as he was in English.

6. The New Realism. At first, as might be expected, the spirit of inquiry led to the suppression of romance; but it drew within the circle of literary endeavour all the ranks of mankind. Thus we have the astonishing development of the novel, which at first concerned itself with domestic incidents. Fielding and his kind dealt very faithfully with human life, and often were immersed in masses of sordid detail. In the widest sense of the word, however, the novelists were Romanticists, for in sympathy and freshness of treatment they were followers of the new ideal.

7. The Decline of Political Writing. With the partial decay of the party spirit the activity in pamphleteering was over; poets and satirists were no longer the favourites of Prime Ministers. Walpole, the greatest of contemporary ministers, openly despised the literary breed, for he did not need them. Hence writers had to depend on their public, which was not entirely an evil. This caused the rise of the man of letters, such as Johnson and Goldsmith, who wrote to satisfy a public demand. Later in the century, when the political temperature once again approached boiling-point, pamphlets began again to acquire an importance, which rose to a climax in the works of Junius and Burke.

THE REACTIONARY SCHOOL

SAMUEL JOHNSON (1709–84)

1. His Life. Johnson has a faithful chronicler in Boswell, whose *Life of Samuel Johnson* makes us intimate with its subject to a degree rare in literature. But even the prying zeal of Boswell could not extort many facts regarding the great man's early life. Johnson was born at Lichfield, the son of a bookseller, whose pronounced Tory views he inherited and steadfastly maintained. From his birth he was afflicted with a malignant skin-disease (for which he was unsuccessfully 'touched' by Queen Anne) which all through his life affected his sight and hearing, and caused many of the physical peculiarities that astonished and amused the friends of his later years. After being privately educated, he proceeded to Oxford, where he experienced the miseries and indignities that are the lot of a poor scholar cursed with a powerful and aspiring mind. Leaving the university, he tried school-teaching, with no success; married a woman twenty years older than himself; and then in 1737 went to London and threw himself into the squalors and allurements of Grub Street.

In his *Essay on Boswell's Life of Johnson* Macaulay has given an arresting description of the miseries endured by the denizens of Grub Street; and in this case even the natural exaggeration of Macaulay is not quite misplaced. We know next to nothing regarding the life of Johnson during this early period. It is certain that it was wretched enough to cause the sturdy old fellow, in after years, to glance at this period of his life with a shudder of loathing, and to quench the curiosity of Boswell with ultra-Johnsonian vehemence. Very slowly he won his way out of the gutter, fighting every step with bitter tenacity; for, as he puts it in his poem of *London*,

> Slow rises worth by poverty depresseu.

From the obscure position of a publisher's hack he became a poet of some note by the publication of *London* (1738), which was noticed by Pope; his *Dictionary* (1747–55) advanced his fame; then somewhat incomprehensibly he appears in the limelight as one of the literary dictators of London, surrounded by a circle of brilliant men. In 1762 he received a pension from the State, and the last twenty years of his life were passed in the manner most acceptable to him: dawdling, visiting, conversing, yet *living* with a gigantic vitality that made his fellows wonder.

It is in these latter years that we find him imperishably figured in the pages of Boswell. All his tricks of humour—his bearishness, his gruff good-will, his silent and secret benevolences; his physical aberrations—his guzzlings, his grunts, his grimaces, his puffings and wallowings; his puerile superstitions; his deep and beautiful piety; his Tory prejudices, so often enormously vocal; his masterful and unsleeping common sense; the devouring immensity of his conversational powers: we find all these set out in *The Life of Samuel Johnson*.

2. His Poetry. He wrote little poetry, and none of it, though it has much merit, can be called first-class. His first poem, *London* (1738), written in the heroic couplet, is of great and sombre power. It depicts the vanities and the sins of city life viewed from the depressing standpoint of an embittered and penurious poet. His only other longish poem is *The Vanity of Human Wishes* (1749). The poem, in imitation of the Tenth Satire of Juvenal, transfers to the activities of mankind in general the gloomy convictions raised ten years earlier by the spectacle of London. The metre is the same as in *London*, and there is the same bleak pessimism, but the weight and power of the emotion, the tremendous conviction and the stern immobility of the author, give the work a great value. There are many individual lines of solemn grandeur. The following passage shows all he has to offer to the young aspirant to literary fame:

> When first the college rolls receive his name,
> The young enthusiast quits his ease for fame;
> Resistless burns the fever of renown,
> Caught from the strong contagion of the gown.
> O'er Bodley's dome his future labours spread,
> And Bacon's mansion trembles o'er his head.
> Are these thy views? Proceed, illustrious youth,
> And Virtue guard thee to the throne of Truth!
> Yet, should thy soul indulge the generous heat
> Till captive Science yields her last retreat;
> Should Reason guide thee with her brightest ray
> And pour on misty Doubt resistless day;
> Should no false kindness lure to loose delight,
> Nor praise relax, nor difficulty fright;
> Should tempting Novelty thy cell refrain,
> And Sloth effuse her opiate fumes in vain;
> Should Beauty blunt on fops her fatal dart,
> Nor claim the triumph of a letter'd heart;
> Should no disease thy torpid veins invade,
> Nor Melancholy's phantoms haunt thy shade;
> Yet hope not life from grief or danger free,
> Nor think the doom of man revers'd for thee:
> Deign on the passing world to turn thine eyes,
> And pause awhile from letters, to be wise;
> There mark what ills the scholar's life assail,
> Toil, envy, want, the patron, and the jail.
> See nations, slowly wise, and meanly just,
> To buried merit raise the tardy bust.
> If dreams yet flatter, once again attend,
> Hear Lydiat's life and Galileo's end.

3. His Drama. When he first came to London in 1737 he brought the manuscript, in part, of *Irene*, a solemn, ponderous, undramatic, blank verse tragedy. In 1749, through the heroic exertions of his old pupil David Garrick, who was then manager of Drury Lane Theatre, it was given a hearing, and had a run of nine nights. Even Johnson's best friends had to admit that it was no success, and it then utterly disappeared, taking with it Johnson's sole claim to dramatic merit.

4. His Prose. Johnson's claims to be called a first-rate writer must rest on his prose. His earliest work appeared in Cave's *The Gentleman's Magazine*, between the years 1738 and 1744. For this periodical he wrote (1741–44) imaginary Parliamentary debates, based on the mere skeletons of facts which he could obtain without attending the House, and elaborated by his own invention and embellished with his own vigorous style. In 1744 appeared *The Life of Savage*, his penurious poet friend, who had recently died in gaol. It was later incorporated in *The Lives of the Poets* and throws much light on Johnson's early hardships and struggles. Greater schemes were now contemplated, but his first move towards his edition of Shakespeare came to nothing owing to the impending appearance of Warburton's edition.

Then, in 1747, he began work on his *Dictionary of the English Language*. This was his greatest contribution to scholarship. It has its weaknesses: it was a poor guide to pronunciation; the etymology was sometimes inaccurate; some quotations lacked dates and references; some definitions were incorrect, some prejudiced, some verbose. But it was vastly superior to any previous dictionary; for the first time, authorities for the actual use of words were quoted; it showed Johnson's remarkable talent for definition based on common sense, though marred occasionally by humour; and it was introduced by a very fine Preface setting forth his lofty aims—to "preserve the purity and ascertain the meaning of our English idiom," and prevent the language from being overrun with 'cant' and Gallicized words.

While working on this project he also wrote periodical essays for *The Rambler* (1750–52). The papers, which appeared twice a week, are full of deep thought and observation, and are founded upon his own experience of life, but they lack the elegance of *The Spectator*, and they were too obviously didactic to be popular, though, when issued in volume form, they ran through several editions during his lifetime. Even so, *The Rambler* re-established the periodical essay at a time when it was in danger of being superseded by the newspaper. In these essays the mannerisms which came to be known as the distinguishing features of 'Johnsonese' (see p. 231) are more obvious than in his later work, but there is frequent evidence of his trenchant force and vigour.

He wrote *Rasselas, Prince of Abyssinia* (1759), in order to pay for his mother's funeral. It was meant to be a philosophical novel, but it is really a number of *Rambler* essays, strung together through the personality of an inquiring young prince called Rasselas. It is hardly a novel at all; the tale carries little interest, the characters are rudimentary, and there are many long, dull discussions. In the book, however, there are many shrewd comments and much of Johnson's sombre clarity of vision.

During this period (1758–60) he was contributing a series of papers, under the title of *The Idler*, to the *Universal Chronicle, or Weekly Gazette*. They were lighter in touch and shorter than those of *The Rambler*.

Then came Johnson's second truly great work—his fine edition of *Shakespeare*, published in 1765. Based on a wide reading in Elizabethan literature, the edition offered nothing new in the way of method, but aimed at the restoration of the original text wherever possible and the clearing away of the jungle of fanciful conjecture which had led to its corruption. He succeeded in producing a purer text than any then in existence, and the trenchant common sense which underlies his notes has given many of them a permanent place in modern editions. There can have been few saner attempts to elucidate the obscurities of the text, and the Preface is remarkable for its forthright honesty in recognizing Shakespeare's faults and in defending him against the charge of having ignored the classical unities, and for its analysis of the causes of corruption in the text. Johnson's preface to his *Shakespeare* is a landmark, not only in Shakespearian scholarship, but in English criticism as a whole. It established firmly his belief that "there is always an appeal open from criticism to nature."

His later years were almost unproductive of literary work. Yet he kept himself deeply interested in the events of the day. For instance, he started a violent quarrel with Macpherson, whose *Ossian* had startled the literary world. We give a letter that Johnson wrote to the Scotsman, which shows that he often wrote as he spoke—crisply, clearly, and scathingly:

MR JAMES MACPHERSON,

I received your foolish and impudent letter. Any violence offered me I shall do my best to repel; and what I cannot do for myself, the law shall do for me. I hope I shall never be deterred from detecting what I think a cheat by the menaces of a ruffian.

What would you have me retract? I thought your book an imposture: I think it an imposture still. For this opinion I have given my reasons to the public, which I here dare you to refute. Your rage I defy. Your abilities, since your Homer, are not so formidable; and what I hear of your morals inclines me to pay regard not to what you shall say, but to what you shall prove. You may print this if you will.

SAM. JOHNSON

His *A Journey to the Western Islands of Scotland* (1775), a travel book, shows the faculty of narrative, and contains passages of great skill. His last work of any consequence was *The Lives of the Poets* (1777–81), planned as a series of introductions to the works of fifty-two poets. In Johnson's hands the introductions, half biographical, half critical, grew beyond their proposed size, and they are now regarded as criticism of great and permanent value. The poets dealt with are those of the seventeenth and eighteenth centuries, the period which Johnson found most congenial. He is best when truly in sympathy with his subject, as in the lives of Dryden and Pope, and, though personal antipathies distort his judgments of Milton and Gray, there can be no doubt of his intention to try to be just. Indeed, the forthright honesty of his opinions, based on strong common sense, and phrased with a pithy, concise vigour, is the distinguishing feature of the work. Though he shows limitations as a critic, such as his uncertain ear for the delicacies of melody and rhythm, Johnson here stands revealed as a level-headed adherent of the classical standards, resting his judgment on a strong sense of reality, and anxious to destroy affectation and extravagance in literature, that it might once again recapture the power of speaking direct to the heart on themes of universal interest.

5. His Style. Johnson's prose style has been the object of much ridicule, epitomized in the popular conception of 'Johnsonese' as pompous, artificial, verbose prose. While this view undoubtedly contains some truth, it reflects but one aspect of his writing. In his early work, and notably in *The Rambler* and in *Rasselas, Prince of Abyssinia*, the prose is heavy, rhetorical in structure, full of affectation, and highly Latinized, and, at all periods of his life, when Johnson wrote on a trivial subject, he was in danger of becoming

pompous and over-elaborate. These early mannerisms steadily disappear as we follow the course of his writings, until, in *The Lives of the Poets*, his prose has the ease, lucidity, force, and vigorous directness of his conversation. Given a subject worthy of his mettle, Johnson writes in sentences packed full with meaning, and their dogmatic tone is but a challenge to the reader to give them the thought which they demand and deserve.

When we come to estimate the man and his work we shall probably arrive at the conclusion that the towering eminence which he held among really able men was due as much to the personality of the man as to the greatness of the writer, but to attempt to deny the latter would be pointless.

We give below two specimens of his prose. The first is typical of his early period and has earned for itself the title of 'Johnsonese'; the second is the mature Johnson.

In this work, when it shall be found that much is omitted, let it not be forgotten that much likewise is performed; and though no book was ever spared out of tenderness to the author, and the world is little solicitous to know whence proceeded the faults of that which it condemns, yet it may gratify curiosity to inform it, that the English Dictionary was written with little assistance of the learned, and without any patronage of the great; not in the soft obscurities of retirement, or under the shelter of academic bowers, but amid inconvenience and distraction, in sickness and in sorrow. It may repress the triumph of malignant criticism to observe, that if our language is not here fully displayed, I have only failed in an attempt which no human powers have hitherto completed. If the lexicons of ancient tongues, now immutably fixed, and comprised in a few volumes, be yet, after the toil of successive ages, inadequate and delusive; if the aggregated knowledge and co-operating diligence of the Italian academicians did not secure them from the censure of Beni; if the embodied critics of France, when fifty years had been spent upon their work, were obliged to change its economy, and give their second edition another form, I may surely be contented without the praise of perfection.

Preface to "Dictionary"

It is not to be inferred that of this poetical vigour Pope had only a little, because Dryden had more; for every other writer since Milton must give place to Pope; and even of Dryden it must be said, that if he has brighter paragraphs he has not better poems. Dryden's performances were always hasty, either excited by some external occasion, or extorted by domestic necessity; he composed without consideration, and published without correction. What his mind could supply at call, or gather in one excursion, was all that he sought, and all that he gave. The dilatory caution of Pope enabled him to condense his sentiments, to multiply his images, and to accumulate all that study might produce or chance might supply. If the flights of Dryden therefore are higher, Pope continues longer on the wing. If of Dryden's fire the blaze is brighter, of Pope's the heat is more regular and constant. Dryden often surpasses expectation, and Pope never falls below it. Dryden is read with frequent astonishment, and Pope with perpetual delight.

The Lives of the Poets

THE TRANSITIONAL POETS

I. JAMES THOMSON (1700–48)

Thomson can hardly be called a great poet, yet in the history of literature he is unusual enough to be regarded (chronologically) as a freak. As such he is important, and it is necessary to give him some prominence.

1. His Life. Born near Kelso, close to some of the loveliest valleys on the Scottish side of the Border, Thomson early came to London (1725) to seek a patron and fame. His *Winter* (1726), though its novelty embarrassed the critics, brought him recognition and afterward praise; he obtained the patronage of the great, and assiduously cultivated it; travelled as a tutor to a noble family; obtained Government places and emoluments; and passed a happy and prosperous life at his cottage near Richmond.

2. His Poetry. His *Winter* was afterward quadrupled in size by including the other three seasons, and became *The Seasons* (1730). It is a blank-verse poem, and consists of a long series of descriptive passages dealing with natural scenes, mainly those with which he was familiar during his youth on the Scottish Border. There is a great deal of padding, and the style is often marked by clumsy expressions; yet on the whole the treatment is exhilarating, full of concentrated observation and joy in the face of nature. Above all, it is real nature, obtained from the living sky and air, and not from books; and, coming when it did, the poem exerted a strong counter-influence against the artificial school of poetry.

Thomson also wrote *Liberty* (1735–36), a gigantic poem in blank verse, intolerably dull. It had no success. As Johnson says, "The praises of Liberty were condemned to harbour spiders, and to gather dust."

In the last year of his life he published *The Castle of Indolence*, which is even more remarkable than *The Seasons*. The poem is written in Spenserian stanzas, and in the true Spenserian fashion it gives a description of a lotus-land into which world-weary souls are invited to withdraw. The work is imitative, and so cannot claim to be of the highest class, but it is an imitation of the rarest merit. For languid suggestiveness, in dulcet and harmonious versification, and for subtly woven vowel-music it need not shirk comparison with the best of Spenser himself. Yet the likeness is confined to similarity of tone and technique; Thomson's sentiments are too commonplace to merit comparison with the more profound thought and philosophy which underlie Spenser's work. We give three verses of this remarkable poem. Coming at such a period, and expressing as they do the essence of romantic idealism, the verses are well worth quoting:

> Joined to the prattle of the purling rills,
> Were heard the lowing herds along the vale,
> And flocks loud-bleating from the distant hills,
> And vacant shepherds piping in the dale:
> And now and then sweet Philomel would wail,
> Or stock-doves 'plain amid the forest deep,
> That drowsy rustled to the sighing gale;
> And still a coil the grasshopper did keep:
> Yet all these sounds yblent inclined all to sleep.
>
> Full in the passage of the vale, above,
> A sable, silent, solemn forest stood;
> Where nought but shadowy forms was seen to move,
> As Idless fancied in her dreaming mood.
> And up the hills, on either side, a wood
> Of blackening pines, ay waving to and fro,
> Sent forth a sleepy horror through the blood;
> And where this valley winded out, below,
> The murmuring main was heard, and scarcely heard, to flow.
>
> A pleasing land of drowsyhed it was,
> Of dreams that wave before the half-shut eye;
> And of gay castles in the clouds that pass,
> For ever flushing round a summer sky:
> There eke the soft delights, that witchingly
> Instil a wanton sweetness through the breast,
> And the calm pleasures always hovered nigh;
> But whate'er smacked of noyance, or unrest,
> Was far far off expelled from this delicious nest.
>
> *The Castle of Indolence*

Thomson also wrote some dramas, including one bad tragedy, *Sophonisba* (1729); and in collaboration with Mallet he produced the masque *Alfred* (1740), which happens to contain the song *Rule, Britannia*. The song is usually said to be Thomson's.

II. OLIVER GOLDSMITH (1728–74)

As another typical example of the transition poet we take Goldsmith, whose work was produced a full generation after that of Thomson.

1. His Life. Much of Goldsmith's early life is obscure, and our knowledge of it rests upon his own unsupported and hardly reliable evidence. He was probably born at Pallas, a small village in County Longford, in Ireland, and he was the son of the poor but admirable curate of the village. His father, the village, and various local features are duly registered, and unduly idealized, in the poem *The Deserted Village*. In 1744 Goldsmith proceeded to Trinity College, Dublin; graduated, after some misadventures; and then tried various careers in turn—law, medicine, and playing the flute—at various places, including Dublin, Edinburgh, Leyden, Venice, and Padua. At the last-mentioned place he graduated, according to his own account, as a doctor, and claimed title as such. In truth, a settled career was beyond Goldsmith's capacity. He had all the amiable vices of the stage Irishman: he was shiftless and improvident, but generous and humane; unstable and pitifully puerile in mind, but with bright, piercing flashes of humour and insight. During his years of wandering he roved over Europe, playing the flute for a living; then in 1756 he returned to England, poor, unknown, but undaunted.

Then followed desperate attempts at making a living. In succession he was apothecary's assistant, printer's reader, usher in a school, and finally (the last refuge of the literary down-at-heels) publisher's hack and a denizen of Grub Street. In time, however, by their sheer merit, his writings drew upon him the regard of famous persons, including Dr Johnson and Charles James Fox, the eminent politician. Once recognition came, it came with a rush; money and praise poured in; but his feckless habits kept him poor, and he drifted about in mean London lodgings till his death in 1774. It was said that he brought his doom upon himself by over-use of a patent medicine. He left debts for two thousand pounds. During his latter years he was a member of Johnson's famous club, where his artless ways—his bickerings, witticisms, and infantile vanity— were the cause of the mingled amusement, admiration, and contempt of his fellow-members.

2. His Poetry. Though his poetical production is not large, it is notable. His first poem, *The Traveller* (1764), deals with his wanderings through Europe. The poem, about four hundred lines in length, is written in the heroic couplet, and is a series of descriptions and criticisms of the places and peoples of which he had experience.

It contains descriptive passages of considerable beauty phrased in simple language, and the couplet is melodious and polished. The poem has his characteristic charm and grace, and reveals a clear perception of the sufferings of the poor, where "laws grind the poor, and rich men make the laws." His only other poem of any length is *The Deserted Village* (1770). In this poem, as he deals with the memories of his youth, the pathetic note is more freely expressed. His natural descriptions have charm and genuine feeling; but his remedies for the agricultural depression of Ireland are innocently empty of the slightest practical value.

The peculiar humour and pathos of Goldsmith are hard to analyse. Both emotions arise from simple situations, and are natural and free from any deep guile, yet they have a certain agreeable tartness of flavour, and show that Goldsmith was no fool in his observation of mankind. Often the humour is so dashed with pathos that the combined effect is attractive to a very high degree. The passage given below illustrates his artless emotion naturally expressed:

> In all my wanderings round this world of care,
> In all my griefs—and God has given my share—
> I still had hopes my latest hours to crown,
> Amidst these humble bowers to lay me down;
> To husband out life's taper at the close,
> And keep the flame from wasting by repose:
> I still had hopes, for pride attends us still,
> Amidst the swains to show my book-learned skill
> Around my fire an evening group to draw,
> And tell of all I felt, and all I saw;
> And as a hare whom hounds and horns pursue,
> Pants to the place from whence at first he flew,
> I still had hopes, my long vexations past,
> Here to return—and die at home at last.
>
> *The Deserted Village*

Goldsmith's miscellaneous poems are important, for they include some of his characteristic humorous and pathetic writing. The ballad called *The Hermit* is done in the sentimental fashion, the witty *Elegy on the Death of a Mad Dog* is suggestive of Swift without Swift's savage barb, and the fine lines beginning "When lovely woman stoops to folly" are among the best he ever wrote.

3. His Drama. Goldsmith wrote two prose comedies, both of which rank high among their class. The first, called *The Good-natur'd Man* (1768), is not so good as the second, *She Stoops to Conquer* (1773). Each, but especially the latter, is endowed with an ingenious and lively plot, a cast of excellent characters, and a vivacious and delightful style. Based on the Restoration comedy, they lack the Restoration grossness. The second play had an immense popularity, and even yet it is sometimes staged.

4. His Prose. The prose is of astonishing range and volume. Among his works of fiction we find *The Citizen of the World* (1759), a series of imaginary letters from a Chinaman, whose comments on English society are both simple and shrewd. This series was contributed to *The Public Ledger*, a popular magazine. He wrote many other essays in the manner of Addison, almost as well done as those of Addison. His other important work of fiction is his novel *The Vicar of Wakefield* (1766), which is in the first rank of the eighteenth-century novels. The plot of the novel is simple, though sometimes inconsistent, the characters are human and attractive, and the book has all the Goldsmith qualities of humour and pathos.

We give an example of his style. The passage is taken from one of his essays, in which he sketches the character of a man who, while he pretends to be hard-hearted, is in reality of a generous disposition. The humour is typical; it is artless, but it is acute and pervading, and shows us quite plainly that the writer was by no means the zany that Boswell (who disliked Goldsmith) desired us to imagine in his *Life of Johnson*.

> He was proceeding in this strain, earnestly to dissuade me from an imprudence of which I am seldom guilty, when an old man, who still had about him the remnants of tattered finery, implored our compassion. He assured us that he was no common beggar, but forced into the shameful profession, to support a dying wife, and five hungry children. Being prepossessed against such falsehoods, his story had not the least influence upon me; but it was quite otherwise with the man in black; I could see it visibly operate upon his countenance, and effectually interrupt his harangue. I could easily perceive that his heart burned to relieve the five starving children, but he seemed ashamed to discover his weakness to me. While he thus hesitated between compassion and pride, I pretended to look another way, and he seized this opportunity of giving the poor petitioner a piece of silver, bidding him at the same time, in order that I should hear, go work for his bread, and not tease passengers with such impertinent falsehoods for the future.
>
> *The Citizen of the World*

In addition, Goldsmith produced a great mass of hack-work, most of which is worthless as historical and scientific fact, but all of which is enlightened with the grace of his style and personality. Some of these works are *An Inquiry into the Present State of Polite Learning in Europe* (1759), his first published book; *The History of*

England (1771); and *An History of Earth and Animated Nature*, a kind of text-book on natural history, which was published posthumously.

5. Summary. Goldsmith's work is so varied and important that it is necessary to summarize briefly. The following are its main features:

(*a*) *Variety.* In his projected Latin epitaph on Goldsmith Johnson gives prominence to the statement that Goldsmith touched on nearly every type of writing and adorned them all:

> Qui nullum fere scribendi genus
> Non tetigit,
> Nullum quod tetigit non ornavit.

(*b*) Its *high quality* is also apparent. In grace, charm, and amiable good-humour he is in the first flight of our writers.

(*c*) As a *transitional poet* he is worthy of careful observation. In the mechanics of poetry—such as metre, rhyme, and rhetorical devices—he follows the older tradition; but in his broad humanity of outlook, in his sympathetic treatment of natural scenes, and in the simplicity of his humour and pathos he is of the coming age.

OTHER TRANSITIONAL POETS

1. Thomas Gray (1716-71). Gray was born in London, the son of a money-scrivener, a kind of lawyer, who was in affluent circumstances. Gray, however, owed his education largely to the self-denial of his mother; he was educated at Eton and Cambridge, at the former of which places he met Horace Walpole. With Walpole he toured Italy and France; then, returning to the university, he took his degree, finally settling down to a life that was little more than an elegant futility. He was offered the Laureateship, but refused it (1757); he obtained a professorship at Cambridge, but he never lectured. He wrote a little, travelled a little; but he was a man of shrinking and fastidious tastes, unapt for the rough shocks of the world, and, fortunately for himself, able to withdraw beyond them.

His first poem was the *Ode on a Distant Prospect of Eton College* (1747), which contained gloomy moralizings on the approaching fate of those "little victims," the schoolboys. Then, after years of revision and excision, appeared the famous *Elegy written in a Country Churchyard* (1751). This poem was smooth and graceful; it contained familiar sentiments turned into admirable, quotable phrases; and so, while it was agreeably familiar, it was fresh enough to be attractive. Its popularity has been maintained to the present day. His *Pindaric Odes* (1757) were unsuccessful, being criticized for their obscurity. *The Bard* and *The Progress of Poesy*, the two Pindaric odes in the book, certainly require some elucidation, especially to readers not familiar with history and literature. At the first glance Gray's odes are seen to have all the odic splendour of diction; in fact, the adornment is so thickly applied that it can almost stand alone, like a robe stiff with gems and gold lace. Yet the poems have energy and dignity. Johnson, who had a distaste for both the character and the work of Gray, cavils at the work, saying that it has a strutting dignity. "He is tall by walking on tiptoe. His art and his struggle are too visible."

The prose work of Gray is notable. It consists partly of letters written during his travels, describing the scenes he visits. In them he shows vigour of style, and a sharp eye and a generous admiration for the real beauties of nature. His descriptions, such as those of the Lake District, are quite admirable, and well in advance of the general taste of his age.

In spite of its slender bulk, Gray's achievement both in prose and verse is of great importance. He explored the origins of romance in the early Norse and Celtic legends; his sympathies with the poor and oppressed were genuine and emphatically expressed; and his treatment of nature was a great improvement upon that of his predecessors.

Johnson's final estimate of Gray is not unfair, and we can leave the poet with it: "His mind had a large grasp; his curiosity was unlimited, and his judgment cultivated; he was a man likely to love much where he loved at all, but he was fastidious and hard to please."

2. **William Collins (1721–59).** Collins was born at Chichester, and was educated at Winchester and Oxford, where he graduated in 1743. He next tried to follow a literary career in London, but with scant success, being arrested for debt. He was released by the generosity of his publishers, and a fortunate legacy relieved him from the worst of his financial terrors. Recovering after several violent fits of insanity, he lapsed into a mild species of melancholia, finally dying in his native city at the early age of thirty-eight.

The work of Collins is very small in bulk, and even of this scanty stock a fair proportion shows only mediocre ability. His *Persian Eclogues* (1742) are in the conventional style of Pope, and though they profess to deal with Persian scenes and characters the Oriental setting shows no special information or inspiration. The book that gives him his place in literature is his *Odes* (1746), a small octavo volume of fifty-two pages. The work is a collection of odes to Pity, Fear, Simplicity, and kindred abstract subjects. Some of the odes are overweighted with the cumbrous, creaking machinery of the Pindaric; but the best of them, especially the *Ode to Evening* (done in unrhymed verse), are instinct with a sweet tenderness, a subdued and shadowy pathos, and a magical enchantment of phrase. In the same book two short elegies, one beginning "How sleep the brave" and the other on James Thomson ("In yonder grave a Druid lies"), are captivating, with their misty lights and murmuring echoes of melancholy. In the finest work of Collins, with his eager and wistful searching, with what Johnson morosely called his "flights of imagination which pass the bounds of nature," we are ushered over the threshold of romance.

3. **William Cowper** (1731–1800). Cowper was born at Great Berkhampstead, in Hertfordshire, where his father was rector. He was to have been a barrister, and was actually called to the Bar (1754), but a great and morbid timidity of disposition, which increased till it became religious and suicidal mania, hampered him cruelly through life. Family influence obtained for him the offer of a good post on the clerical staff of the House of Lords, but his extreme shyness made him quite unfit for this semi-public appointment. The consequent disappointment disordered his wits, and he attempted suicide, but was fortunately prevented. The latter part of his life was spent chiefly at Olney, in Buckinghamshire, where his good friends the Unwins treated him with great kindness and good sense. His feeling of gratitude for their care, expressed or implicit in many of his poems and letters, is one of the most touching features in the literature of the time. This comparatively happy state of affairs did not last till the end, for the years immediately preceding his death were much clouded with extreme mental and bodily affliction.

Cowper's poems were produced late in life, but in bulk the work is large. It is curiously mixed and attractive in its nature. His first published work was a number of hymns contributed to the *Olney Hymns* (1779). They are notable for their direct sincerity, and several of them are still among the best known of English hymns. Among them are: *Oh! for a closer walk with God*; *Hark, my soul! it is the Lord*; and *God moves in a mysterious way*. His *Poems* (1782) contains little that is noteworthy. The bulk of it is taken up with a collection of satirical set pieces in heroic couplets, quite in the usual manner, on such subjects as *The Progress of Error*, *Truth*, *Hope*, and *Charity*. At the very end of the volume a few miscellaneous short pieces are more encouraging as novelties. One of them is the well-known poem containing the reflections of Alexander Selkirk ("I am monarch of all I survey"). His next work is *The Task* (1785), a long poem in blank verse, dealing with simple and familiar themes and containing many fine descriptions of country scenes. In places the style is marked by the prevailing artificial tricks, and as a whole the poem is seldom inspired with any deep or passionate feeling; but his observation is acute and humane, it includes the homeliest detail within its kindly scope, and he gives us real nature, like Thomson in *The Seasons*. At the end of this volume the ballad of *John Gilpin* finds a place. It is an excellent example of Cowper's prim but sprightly humour, an extraordinary gift for a man of his morbid temperament. Other short poems were added to later editions of his first volume. These include the *Epitaph on a Hare*, curiously and touchingly pathetic; lines *On the Receipt of my Mother's Picture*, which reveal only too painfully the suppressed convulsions of grief and longing that were stirred within him by memories of the past; and *The Castaway*, written in a lucid interval just before the end, and sounding like the wail of a damned spirit. The poem gives a tragic finality to his life. It describes the doom of a poor wretch swept overboard in a storm, and concludes:

> No poet wept him; but the page
> Of narrative sincere,
> That tells his name, his worth, his age,
> Is wet with Anson's tear;
> And tears by bards or heroes shed
> Alike immortalize the dead.
>
> I therefore purpose not, or dream,
> Descanting on his fate,
> To give the melancholy theme
> A more enduring date:
> But misery still delights to trace
> Its semblance in another's case.
>
> No voice divine the storm allay'd,
> No light propitious shone,
> When, snatch'd from all effectual aid,
> We perished, each alone:
> But I beneath a rougher sea,
> And whelm'd in deeper gulfs than he.

Cowper's letters, private epistles addressed to various personal friends, are among the most delightful of their kind. They show the man at his best—almost jovial in a delicate fashion, keenly observant, and with a genuine gift for narrative. The style is so clear that the disposition of the writer shines through it with unruffled benignity.

Cowper's work is of considerable significance in the movement from the classical to the romantic tradition. The simple sincerity with which he expressed his love of the details of homely life, his accurate and realistic description of natural landscapes, and the warm, yet gentle, humanity which led him to support and love the underdog, all foreshadow Wordsworth, though he lacks the latter's burning faith and depth of vision. His lyric gift, all too rarely seen among the great quantities of his didactic and satirical verse, was another quality which linked him with the age that was to come, rather than with that which was passing away.

4. George Crabbe (1754–1832). Crabbe comes very late among the poets now under review, but in method he is largely of the eighteenth century. He was born in Suffolk, at Aldeburgh, where his father had been a schoolmaster and a collector of customs. He was apprenticed to a surgeon, but later left his native town to seek fame as an author in London (1780). He had little success at first, but gradually attracted attention. He fixed on a settled career by taking holy orders, and obtained the patronage of several influential men. Ultimately he obtained the valuable living of Trowbridge (1814), where he died as late as 1832, only a few months before Sir Walter Scott.

His chief poetical works are *The Library* (1781), *The Village* (1783), which made his name as a poet, *The Borough* (1810), and *Tales* (1812). The poems in their succession show little development, resembling each other closely both in subject and style. They are collections of tales, told in heroic couplets with much sympathy and a good deal of pathetic power, dealing with the lives of simple countryfolk such as Crabbe encountered in his own parish. There is a large amount of strong natural description, though it is subsidiary to the human interest in the stories themselves. The motivating power behind Crabbe's poetry was his desire to state the plain, unvarnished truth about the life of the peasant, and to destroy the idealized, artificial picture of it presented by the eighteenth-century pastoral. He has often been criticized for being too gloomy and pessimistic; he is pessimistic in the sense that he is stubbornly alive to the miseries of the poor, and he is at a loss how to relieve them. Though, in technique, he was a life-long follower of the school of Pope, his work was warmly recognized by Wordsworth and other thinkers who had the welfare of the poor at heart. Crabbe, however, cannot be classed as a great poet; he lacks the supreme poetic gift of transforming even squalor and affliction into things of splendour and appeal; but he is sympathetic, sincere, and an acute observer of human nature.

5. **Mark Akenside (1721–70).** Akenside was born at Newcastle, studied medicine at Edinburgh, and graduated at Leyden in 1744. He started practice at Northampton, but did not succeed. Later he had more success in London. He was a well-known character, and is said to have been caricatured by Smollett in *Peregrine Pickle*.

His best political poem is his *An Epistle to Curio* (1744), which contains some brilliant invective against Pulteney. His best-known book is *The Pleasures of the Imagination* (1744), a long and rambling blank-verse poem. The style is somewhat Miltonic in its energy and its turn of phrase, but it is deficient in the Miltonic genius. The poem has some loud but rather fine descriptive passages, especially those dealing with his native Tyne, for the beauties of which he shows a laudable enthusiasm.

6. **Christopher Smart (1722–71).** Smart was born in Kent, and was educated at Cambridge, where he graduated. He was a man of unbalanced mind, which, leading him into many extravagances, brought him finally to a madhouse and a miserable death in a debtor's prison.

The poem connected with his name is *A Song to David* (1763), which is said to have been partly written on the walls of the madhouse in which he was confined. The poem, consisting of nearly a hundred six-line stanzas, is a wild, rhapsodical effusion, full of extravagance and incoherence, but in places containing bursts of tremendous poetic power. The following stanzas, the last in the poem, give an idea of these poetical bomb-shells:

> Glorious the sun in mid career;
> Glorious th' assembled fires appear;
>   Glorious the comet's train:
> Glorious the trumpet and alarm;
> Glorious the Almighty's stretch'd-out arm;
>   Glorious th' enraptured main:
>
> Glorious the northern lights astream;
> Glorious the song, when God's the theme;
>   Glorious the thunder's roar:

> Glorious hosanna from the den;
> Glorious the catholic amen;
>   Glorious the martyr's gore:
>
> Glorious—more glorious—is the crown
> Of Him that brought salvation down,
>   By meekness call'd thy Son;
> Thou that stupendous truth believed,
> And now the matchless deed's achieved;—
>   Determined, dared, and done.

7. William Shenstone (1714–63). Born at the Leasowes, in Worcestershire, Shenstone was educated at Oxford. After leaving the university he retired to his estate, which he beautified in the fashion of the time. He was a man of an agreeable nature, but was shy and retiring, and spent nearly all his life in the country.

His published works consist chiefly of odes, elegies, and what he called *Levities, or Pieces of Humour* (often dreary enough), and *The Schoolmistress* (1742). His poems are largely pastoral, but they are by no means the artificial pastoral of Pope. He studies nature himself, and does not derive his notions from books. In this matter he resembles Cowper. *The Schoolmistress*, which by a notable advance is written in the Spenserian stanza, deals in rather a sentimental fashion with the teacher in his first school; it is sympathetic in treatment, and in style is an interesting example of the transition.

8. Charles Churchill (1731–64). Churchill was educated at Westminster School and at Cambridge, took orders (1756), and obtained a curacy. When he was about twenty-seven years old he suddenly started on a wild course of conduct, abandoned his curacy, took to politics and hack journalism, and to drinking and debauchery. He died at Boulogne at the age of thirty-three.

Churchill lives in literature as a satirist of trenchant force and sustained vigour. Though his work lacks constructional skill, his use of both the octosyllabic and decasyllabic couplet has a greater freedom and strength than were common in his day. He has something of the energy and verve of Dryden, his acknowledged master. His wit is amusing, and his satirical portraits are firmly, if not memorably, drawn. The work which established his reputation was *The Rosciad* (1761), a slashing attack on the leading figures of the contemporary stage, and it was followed by a series of political satires, of which the best is *The Prophecy of Famine* (1763), where he attacked the Scots, a race for whom he had an intense dislike.

9. Robert Blair (1699–1746). Blair was born at Edinburgh, and became a clergyman in East Lothian. The poem that brought him his transitory reputation was *The Grave* (1743). It is a long blank-verse poem of meditation on man's mortality. It does not make cheerful reading, and the sentiments are quite ordinary. It has, however, a certain strength and dignity, and the versification shows skill and some degree of freshness. The poem is reminiscent of Young's *Night Thoughts*.

THE NEW SCHOOL

1. ROBERT BURNS (1759–96)

In this section we shall deal with those poets who wrote in the middle and later years of the eighteenth century, and who abandoned the classical tradition. In their generation they came too early to be definitely included in the school of Wordsworth and Coleridge, but in their work they are often as romantically inclined as any of their great successors. We begin with Burns, one of the latest, and probably the greatest, of Wordsworth's poetical forebears. With the appearance of Burns we can say that the day of Romanticism is come. There had been false dawns and deceptive premonitions, but with him we have, in the words of Swinburne,

> A song too loud for the lark,
> A light too strong for a star.

1. His Life. He was born in a small clay-built cottage, the work of his father's hands, in the district of Kyle, in Ayrshire. His father, a small farmer, was a man of an unbending disposition, and the boy had to toil with the rest of the family to wring subsistence from the soil. He had not much formal education, and all his life he tried spasmodically to improve it; but it was mainly the force of his own natural ability that permitted him to absorb the moderate amount of learning he did acquire. As he grew older he showed himself to be the possessor of a powerful and lively mind, which was often afflicted with spasms of acute mental depression. The audacity of his temper soon brought him into extravagances of conduct which were visited by the censure and punishment of the rigid Scottish Church. For Burns's own sake it is unfortunate that his memory has been pursued with an infatuation of hero-worship that seeks to extenuate and even to deny facts that are grave and indisputable. One can only say that his chief weaknesses—drink and dissipation

—were largely the faults of his time. He was no worse than many other men of his age; but his poetic gifts proclaimed and perhaps exaggerated his vices, of which he repented when he was sober and unwisely boasted when he was otherwise.

His life was hard and bitter; his different attempts at farming and at other occupations met with no success, and he determined to seek his fortune in the West Indies (1786). In the nick of time he learned that the small volume of verse that he had recently issued at Kilmarnock was attracting much attention, and he was persuaded to remain in Scotland and discover what fame had in store for him. The reputation of his poems rose with prodigious rapidity, and within a year there was a demand for an Edinburgh edition. He was in Edinburgh in 1787, where he became a nine days' wonder to the lion-hunting society of the capital city. He then qualified for a small post in the Excise, and, taking a farm near Dumfries, married and essayed to lead a regular life. He found this impossible, for fame brought added temptation. His farming was a failure, and the income from his Excise post and his poems was insufficient to keep him decently. At the age of thirty-seven he died at Dumfries, of premature old age.

2. His Poetry. His sole poetical work of any magnitude is his volume of *Poems* (1786), which he edited five times during his lifetime, with numerous additions and corrections on each occasion. At different times he contributed to *The Scots Musical Museum* and to Thomson's *Select Collection of Original Scottish Airs*. After the poet's death his literary editor, Dr Currie, published (1800) a large number of additional pieces, along with a considerable amount of correspondence.

We have thus one tale, *Tam o' Shanter*, which was included in the third edition of the poems, that of 1793; one longish descriptive piece, *The Cotter's Saturday Night*; more than two hundred songs, ranging in quality from very good to middling; and a great number of short epistles, epigrams, elegies, and other types of miscellaneous verse.

3. Features of his Poetry. The poetry is of such a miscellaneous character, and its composition was often so haphazard in the matter of time, that it is almost impossible to give a detailed chronology of it. We shall therefore take it in the mass, and attempt the difficult task of giving an analysis of its various features.

(*a*) The best work of Burns was almost entirely *lyrical* in motive. He is one of the rare examples, like Shelley, of the born singer who can give to human emotion a precious and imperishable utterance. He was essentially the inspired egoist: what interested him was vivid and quickening; what lay outside his knowledge and experience was without life or flavour. He thought of reviving the Scottish drama, but, even if he had entered on the project, it is doubtful if he would have succeeded, for he lacked the faculty of putting himself completely in another man's place. His narrative gift, as it is revealed in *Tam o' Shanter*, becomes fused with the heat of some lyrical emotion (in this case that of drunken jollity), and then it shines with a clear flame. But with the departure of the lyrical emotion the narrative impulse ends as well.

(*b*) While keeping within the limits of the lyric he traverses an *immense range* of emotion and experience. The feelings he describes are those of the Scottish peasant, but the genius of the poet makes them germane to every member of the human race; he discovers the touch of nature that makes the whole world kin. Here we have the "passion and apathy, and glory and shame" that are the inspiration of the lyrical poet, and we have them in rich abundance.

(*c*) His *humour and pathos* are as copious and varied as his subject-matter. His wit can be rollicking to coarseness, as it is in *The Jolly Beggars*; and there are no poems richer in bacchanalian flavour than *Willie brewed a Peck o' Maut* and *Tam o' Shanter*. He can run to the other extreme of emotion, and be graceful and sentimental, as in *Afton Water* and *O My Luve's like a Red, Red Rose*. We have beautiful homely songs in *John Anderson, my Jo* and *Of a' the Airts*; and he can be bitter and scornful in such poems as *Address to the Unco Guid* and *The Holy Fair*. His pathos ranges from the piercing cry of *Ae Fond Kiss*, through the pensive pessimism of *Ye Banks and Braes*, to the tempered melancholy of *My Heart's in the Highlands*. The facility of this precious lyrical gift became a positive weakness, for he wrote too freely, and much of his song-writing is of mediocre quality.

We give brief extracts to illustrate these features of his poetry. The first shows him in his mood of vinous elation; in the second he is acutely depressed and almost maudlin; the third for pure loveliness is almost unexcelled.

(1)   O, Willie brewed a peck o' maut,
          And Rob and Allan cam' to see;
        Three blither hearts, that lee-lang night
          Ye wad na find in Christendie.

Chorus

We are na fou, we're nae that fou,
    But just a drappie in our ee;
The cock may craw, the day may daw,
    And aye we'll taste the barley bree.

Here are we met, three merry boys,
    Three merry boys, I trow, are we;
And mony a night we've merry been,
    And mony mae we hope to be.

It is the moon—I ken her horn,
    That's blinkin' in the lift sae hie;
She shines sae bright to wyle us hame,
    But, by my sooth, she'll wait a wee!

(2)   Thou ling'ring star, with less'ning ray,
        That lov'st to greet the early morn,
    Again thou usher'st in the day
        My Mary from my soul was torn.
    O Mary! dear departed shade!
        Where is thy place of blissful rest?
    Seëst thou thy lover lowly laid?
        Hear'st thou the groans that rend his breast?

        .   .   .

    Still o'er these scenes my mem'ry wakes,
        And fondly broods with miser care!
    Time but th' impression deeper makes,
        As streams their channels deeper wear.
    My Mary, dear departed shade!
        Where is thy place of blissful rest?
    Seëst thou thy lover lowly laid?
        Hear'st thou the groans that rend his breast?
                                    To Mary in Heaven

(3)   O, my luve's like a red, red rose,
        That's newly sprung in June;
    O, my luve's like the melodie
        That's sweetly played in tune.

    As fair art thou, my bonny lass,
        So deep in luve am I;
    And I will luve thee still, my dear,
        Till a' the seas gang dry.

    Till a' the seas gang dry, my dear,
        And the rocks melt wi' the sun:
    I will luve thee still, my dear,
        While the sands o' life shall run.

And fare thee well, my only luve!
  And fare thee well a while!
And I will come again, my luve,
  Though it were ten thousand mile.

(*d*) The poet's *political and religious views* have been given prominence by his admirers, but they scarcely deserve it. His politics, as
expressed in such poems as *A Man's a Man for a' That*, are merely
the natural utterances of a strong and sensitive mind deeply alive
to the degradation of his native people. His religious views, in so
far as they are coloured by his unhappy personal experiences with
the Scottish Church, are of value solely as the inspiration of capital
satirical verse, but in *The Cotter's Saturday Night* Burns pays a
spontaneous and beautiful tribute to the piety of the Scottish peasant.
The following extract from *Holy Willie's Prayer* sufficiently reveals
his personal bias:

Lord, bless Thy Chosen in this place,
For here Thou hast a chosen race:
But God confound their stubborn face,
    And blast their name,
Wha bring Thy rulers to disgrace,
    And open shame.

Lord, mind Gaw'n Hamilton's deserts,
He drinks, and swears, and plays at cartes,
Yet has sae mony takin' arts,
    Wi' great and sma',
Frae God's ain priests the people's hearts
    He steals awa'.

   .   .   .   .   .

But, Lord, remember me and mine,
Wi' mercies temp'ral and divine,
That I for grace and gear may shine,
    Excelled by nane,
And a' the glory shall be Thine,
    Amen, amen!

(*e*) His *style* is noteworthy for the curious double tendency that
is typical of the transition. When he writes in the 'correct' manner
he has all the petty vices of the early school. The opening lines of
his *Address to Edinburgh* are:

Edina! Scotia's darling seat!
  All hail thy palaces and tow'rs,
Where once beneath a monarch's feet
  Sat Legislation's sov'ran pow'rs!

Here we see a paltry classicism and a metrical scrupulousness (leading to the mutilation of words like 'pow'rs') that were far below Burns's notice. The latter vice will be seen even in such poems as *To Mary in Heaven*, quoted above. But when he shakes himself free from such trifling arts his style is full and strong, and as redolent of the soil as his own mountain daisy.

(*f*) As the *national poet* of Scotland his position is unique. He is first, and the rest nowhere. His rod, like Aaron's, has swallowed up the rods of the other Scottish poets; so that in the popular fancy he is the author of any striking Scottish song, such as *Annie Laurie* or *Auld Robin Gray*. His dominating position is due to three factors:

(1) The subject matter and tone of his work are the natural consummation of the Scottish vernacular tradition descending from the period of Dunbar and through Fergusson, to the latter of whom Burns was considerably indebted. In this traditional poetry are found the zest, pace, hilarity, and realism which are characteristic of his work.

(2) He has a matchless gift of catching traditional airs and wedding them to words of simple and searching beauty. It is almost impossible to think of *Auld Lang Syne* or *Scots wha hae* or *Green grow the Rashes, O!* without their respective melodies being inevitably associated with them. And these tunes were born in the blood of the Scottish peasant.

(3) He rejoices in descriptions of Scottish scenery and customs. *The Cotter's Saturday Night* is packed with such features, and all through his work are glimpses of typical Scottish scenes. The opening stanzas of *A Winter Night* are often quoted to show his descriptive power:

> When biting Boreas, fell and doure,
> Sharp shivers thro' the leafless bow'r;
> When Phœbus gies a short-liv'd glow'r,
>   Far south the lift,
> Dim-dark'ning thro' the flaky show'r,
>   Or whirling drift:

> Ae night the storm the steeples rocked,
> Poor Labour sweet in sleep was locked,
> While burns, wi' snawy wreeths up-choked,
>   Wild-eddying swirl,
> Or thro' the mining outlet bocked,[1]
>   Down headlong hurl.

(4) Lastly, he came just at the time when the Scottish tongue, as a

[1] vomited.

separate literary medium, was fast vanishing. The Edinburgh society that prided itself on being the equal of the literary society of London was soon to pass away with the greatest of Edinburgh writers. Burns captured the dialect of his fellows, and gave it permanence.

2. WILLIAM BLAKE (1757–1827)

No greater contrast could be found than that between Burns and Blake. Burns was realistic, humorous, close to the earth, and lacking entirely the visionary romanticism of Coleridge, Wordsworth, Shelley, or Keats. Though his democratic belief in the equality of man, his warm sympathy with humble folk, his use of "the real language of men in a state of vivid sensation," and the sincerity of his lyric impulse are all qualities of the new school of poetry, they derive from the traditional vernacular poetry of Scotland. Blake, on the other hand, was the embodiment of the romantic 'vision.' To him imagination and the sensations of the heart were the sole guides to truth; and the only possible means of restoring the unity of spirit which the predominance of reason had destroyed. He distrusted nothing more than scientific thought and cold, logical argument. He made continual war against the codes of convention, which, he declared, these processes had set up, and passionately preached the freedom, which for him was best exemplified in the innocence and spontaneous happiness of childhood. He was a romantic, not only in his passion for liberty, but in his love for children, his love of nature, and his interest in the medieval and gothic.

1. His Life. Blake was born in London, the son of a hosier. He received no formal education, though in his early years he seems to have made the acquaintance of the works of Shakespeare and Milton, and, perhaps most significant of all, to have been very familiar with the Bible. At the age of fourteen he was apprenticed to an engraver, and this trade he followed, mainly in London, throughout his life. He was, indeed, better known as an illustrator than as a writer during his own lifetime. All but two of his works were engraved by his own hand, and were not printed in the normal way, so that he was never widely known to the reading public of his day. When young, Blake seems to have seen visions which he declared to be the real things in life, while the things normally held to be real he declared to be illusory.

2. His Poetry. Blake's first publication was *Poetical Sketches* (1783), a series of imitative poems, in which he experimented with various verse forms in the manner of Shakespeare, Milton, and Spenser. He is obviously most at home in the lighter lyric measures, which have the direct spontaneity typical of his best lyrical work, and there is little of the later symbolism to be seen. These were followed by *Songs of Innocence* (1789), short lyrics embodying Blake's view of the original state of human society, symbolized in the joy and happiness of children. The poems are free from the imitation of the earlier volume, and their style betrays a sureness of touch which is all Blake's own. They betray a passionate sincerity and deep sympathy with the child. The joy of this world is well exemplified in the following:

> When the green woods laugh with the voice of joy
> And the dimpling stream runs laughing by,
> When the air does laugh with our merry wit,
> And the green hill laughs with the noise of it,
>
> When the meadows laugh with lively green,
> And the grasshopper laughs in the merry scene,
> When Mary and Susan and Emily
> With their sweet round mouths sing "Ha, Ha, He!"
>
> When the painted birds laugh in the shade
> Where our table with cherries and nuts is spread,
> Come live and be merry and join with me,
> To sing the sweet chorus of "Ha, Ha, He!"
>
> *Laughing Song*

The Book of Thel (1790), which embodies much the same spirit of love as his earlier works, was followed by the first series of revolutionary prophetic books, *The French Revolution* (1791), *The Visions of the Daughters of Albion* (1793), *America* (1793), and *Europe* (1794). In *The French Revolution* and *America* the contemporary political conflicts are seen as one step towards, not only political freedom, but freedom from the restrictions of convention and established morality, while *The Visions of the Daughters of Albion* is a vigorous defence of the satisfaction of physical appetite, and an exposure of the wrongs to which woman is subject.

The year 1794 saw the appearance of *Songs of Experience*, in which the mood of spontaneous love and happiness revealed in *Songs of Innocence* is replaced by a less joyful note. In these lyrics, which have an intensity not to be found in the earlier ones, we see Blake presenting the two conflicting aspects of a nature which is so beautiful yet so cruel. This two-sided picture of natural things is well shown in what is, perhaps, his finest lyric, *The Tyger*:

Tyger, Tyger, burning bright
In the forests of the night,
What immortal hand or eye
Could frame thy fearful symmetry?

In what distant deeps or skies
Burnt the fire of thine eyes?
On what wings dare he aspire?
What the hand dare seize the fire?

And what shoulder and what art,
Could twist the sinews of thy heart?
And when thy heart began to beat,
What dread hand? and what dread feet?

What the hammer? what the chain,
In what furnace was thy brain?
What the anvil? what dread grasp
Dare its deadly terrors clasp?

When the stars threw down their spears
And water'd heaven with their tears,
Did he smile his work to see?
Did he who made the Lamb make thee?

Tyger, Tyger, burning bright
In the forests of the night,
What immortal hand or eye
Dare frame thy fearful symmetry?

Songs of Experience was Blake's last considerable work as a lyric poet. A number of occasional lyrics from the Rossetti and Pickering manuscripts were posthumously published, but they do not attain to the level of the two major collections. In 1794–95 appeared the visionary works, *The First Book of Urizen* (1794), *The Book of Ahania* (1795), *The Book of Los* (1795), and *The Song of Los* (1795), in which he described the struggle of Urizen, the spirit of reaction, of restrictive convention, of cold intellect, against the spirit of the impassioned imagination, under the names, first of Orc, and then of Los.

Blake spent the years 1800–3 at Felpham in Sussex with his friend William Hayley. This period he felt to be the most important in his spiritual development, and it turned his philosophy into definitely Christian channels. The conflict between imagination and reason he now felt to have been resolved by the coming of Christ, and this new Christian ethic is seen in *Milton* and *Jerusalem*, both begun in 1804. The symbolism of these works is involved and obscure, yet many of Blake's typical ideas are clearly expressed. In their passionate declaration of the fundamental importance of the imagination, they are obviously of a piece with Blake's earlier work, and they contain excellent descriptive passages.

3. Features of his Poetry. Owing to the obscurity of Blake's later work, he has been known chiefly as a lyric poet. In this vein he is far removed from the classical restraint of the previous age. In simple yet beautifully apt language, his lyrics reveal a variety and spontaneity of feeling which place them on a par with the best in our literature. Blake has to the highest degree the faculty of un-reserved self-revelation, and his style has the quality of 'rightness' which is the mark of all truly great poetry. The prophetic books, in spite of their complex symbolism, have a vehement energy and a passionate sincerity which are unmistakable. They are full of vigorous, descriptive passages, of which the following is a representative specimen:

> Solemn heave the Atlantic waves between the gloomy nations,
> Swelling, belching from its deeps red clouds and raging fires.
> Albion is sick, America faints! enrag'd the Zenith grew.
> As human blood shooting its veins all round the orbed heaven,
> Red rose the clouds from the Atlantic in vast wheels of blood,
> And in the red clouds rose a Wonder o'er the Atlantic sea,
> Intense! naked! a Human fire, fierce glowing as the wedge
> Of iron heated in the furnace; his terrible limbs were fire,
> With myriads of cloudy terrors, banners dark, and towers
> Surrounded: heat but not light when thro' the murky atmosphere.
>
> *America*

OTHER POETS OF THE NEW SCHOOL

1. James Macpherson (1736–96). This writer was born at Kingussie, in the county of Inverness, and was educated for the Church. He never became a regular minister, for at the age of twenty he was producing bad poetry, and soon after he definitely adopted a literary career. He travelled in the Highlands of Scotland and abroad, settled in London (1766), and meddled in the politics of the time. Then he entered Parliament, realized a handsome fortune, and died in his native county.

After producing some worthless verse in the conventional fashion, in 1760 he issued something very different. It was called *Fragments of Ancient Poetry collected in the Highlands of Scotland, and translated from the Gaelic or Erse language*. The work received a large share of attention, and a subscription was raised to allow him to travel in the Highlands to glean further specimens of native poetry.

The fruits of this were seen in *Fingal* (1762) and *Temora* (1763) Macpherson declared that the books were his translations of the poems of an ancient Celtic bard called Ossian. Immediately a violent dispute broke out, many people (including Johnson) alleging that the books were the original compositions of Macpherson himself. The truth is that he gave substance to a large mass of misty Gaelic tradition, and cast the stories into his peculiar prose style.

The controversy hardly matters to us here. What matters is that the tales deal largely with the romantic adventures of a mythical hero called Fingal. They include striking descriptions of wild nature, and they are cast in a rhythmic and melodious prose that is meant to reproduce the original Gaelic poetical measure. As an essay in the Romantic method these works are of very high value. (See p. 287.)

2. Thomas Chatterton (1752–70). Chatterton was born at Bristol, and was apprenticed to an attorney. At the age of eighteen he went to London to seek his fortune as a poet. Almost at once he lapsed into penury, and, being too proud to beg, poisoned himself with arsenic. He was eighteen years old.

The brevity and pathos of Chatterton's career have invested it with a fame peculiar in our literature. He is held up as the martyr of genius, sacrificed by the callousness of the public. His fate, however, was largely due to his own vanity and recklessness, and his genius has perhaps been overrated. In 1768, while still at Bristol, he issued a collection of poems which seemed archaic in style and spelling. These, he said, he had found in an ancient chest lodged in a church in Bristol; and he further stated that most of them had been written by a monk of the fifteenth century, by name Thomas Rowley. The collection received the name of *The Rowley Poems*, and includes several ballads, one of which is *The Battle of Hastings*, and some descriptive and lyrical pieces, such as the *Song to Ælla*. A slight knowledge of Middle English reveals that they are forgeries thinly disguised with antique spelling and phraseology; but, especially after their author's death, they gained much currency, and had some influence on their time. There is much rubbish in the poems, but in detached passages there is real beauty, along with a marvellous precocity of thought.

3. Robert Fergusson (1750–74). Fergusson was born in Edinburgh, and received his education at the university of St Andrews, but soon fell into loose and disreputable habits. He contributed much to the local press, and acquired some reputation as a poet of the vernacular. His irregular habits led to the madhouse, in which he died at the early age of twenty-four.

Fergusson is chiefly notable as the forerunner of Burns, who was generous in his praise of the earlier poet. His best poems are short descriptive pieces dealing with Scottish life, such as *The King's Birthday in Edinburgh*, *To the Tron-Kirk Bell*, and *The Farmer's Ingle*. This last poem perhaps suggested Burns's *The Cotter's Saturday Night*. Fergusson gives clear and accurate descriptions, and his use of the vernacular Scots tongue is vigorous and natural, thus providing Burns with a model for his best style. (See p. 284.)

THE NOVELISTS

I. SAMUEL RICHARDSON (1689–1761)

1. His Life. Richardson was born in Derbyshire, the son of a joiner, by whom he was apprenticed to a London printer. Richardson was an industrious youth, and in the course of time rose high in the pursuit of his occupation. He became a master-printer, produced the journals of the House of Commons, and became printer to the King. He was a man of retiring and almost effeminate habits, but was generous and well liked.

2. His Novels. Richardson's first attempts at writing fiction began at the age of thirteen, when he was the confidant of three illiterate young women, for whom he wrote love-letters. This practice afterward stood him in good stead. He was over fifty years old before he printed a novel of his own, called *Pamela, or Virtue Rewarded* (1740). The book, which takes the form of a series of letters, deals with the fortunes of Pamela, a poor and virtuous maid, who resists, then finally marries and afterwards reforms her wicked master. The work was instantly successful, exhausting four editions during the first six months of its issue. The characters, especially the chief female character, slowly but accurately fabricated during the gradual evolution of the simple plot, were new to the readers of the time, and mark a great step forward in the history of the English novel. Richardson's next novel, which was also constructed in the form of letters, was *Clarissa Harlowe* (1747–48). This treats of the perfidy of men, as illustrated in the tragedy of the heroine, who is persecuted by the villainous Lovelace. Considered by many Richardson's masterpiece, *Clarissa Harlowe* shows his characterization at its best. Not only Clarissa herself, but many of the minor characters are well drawn, with Richardson's usual attention to minute psychological analysis. The story has a strong, if obvious, emotional appeal, and is remarkable for the way in which it achieves a sense of the inevitability of its tragic close. His third and last novel, also in letter-form, was *Sir Charles Grandison* (1753–54), dealing chiefly with persons still higher in the social world. Richardson contemplated calling the book *A Good Man*, for he intended the hero to be the perfection of the manly virtues. But Sir Charles is too good, and succeeds only in being tedious and unreal. The character of the social *milieu* in which the action is cast also weighs heavily upon Richardson, with the result that this book, which he intended to be his masterpiece, is the hollowest of the three.

3. **Features of his Novels.** Richardson's works are largely the reflection of the man himself, and, in spite of their faults and limitations, are of immense importance in the development of the novel.

(*a*) Their most striking feature is Richardson's *moral purpose*. A professed teacher, he is the embodiment of the religious earnestness of the rising Puritan middle class. The virtue he advocates is typically utilitarian rather than fanatical, and its reward is material prosperity. Thus Pamela marries her wicked master and prospers in the world as a direct reward for her virtue.

(*b*) The books are extremely *long*, partly because the adoption of the epistolary method necessitated numerous repetitions or slightly differing versions of the same incident. The plots have little complexity and are slow in development, and the novels tend to be shapeless, though his last work, *Sir Charles Grandison*, shows signs of more complexity and skill in this direction.

(*c*) Equally responsible for the length of Richardson's novels is his use of *minute detail*, both of character and incident. He is an adept in the intimate analysis of motive and emotion which gradually evolves a character that is entire and convincing, and he fills in his sketch with a multitude of tiny strokes. For such detailed analysis a lengthy book is essential, so that length is a vital part of Richardson's technique.

(*d*) Richardson's greatest ability lies in *characterization*. His psychological insight into human motives and feelings, and particularly his understanding of the feminine heart, has seldom been surpassed since his day. Clarissa is his finest portrait, but each successive novel shows a greater range and variety of character. Part of Richardson's importance in the history of the novel lies in his introduction of characters of the lower-middle classes, whom he portrays with great accuracy.

(e) The appeal of Richardson's novels is a frankly sentimental one to the *heart*, and on occasions, as in the protracted account of the approaching death of Clarissa, he is guilty of dwelling too long on the mental sufferings of his characters.

(f) His *style* lacks distinction. Adequate for his purpose, it is at times over-deliberate, or even elaborately precious, as in much of *Sir Charles Grandison*, and he never rises to the subtlety of differing styles for different writers in his series of letters.

II. HENRY FIELDING (1707–54)

1. His Life. A younger son of an ancient family, Fielding was born in Somersetshire, was educated at Eton, and studied law at Leyden. Lack of funds stopped his legal studies for a time; he took to writing plays for a living, but the plays were of little merit; then, having married, he resumed his studies and was called to the Bar. After some time in practice he was appointed (1748) Bow Street magistrate, a post which brought him a small income ("of the dirtiest money on earth," as he said) and much hard work. His magisterial duties, however, had their compensations, for they gave him a close view of many types of human criminality which was of much use to him in his novels. Fielding himself was no Puritan, and his own excesses helped to undermine his constitution. In the hope that it would improve his health, he took a voyage to Portugal (1754); but he died some months after landing, and was buried at Lisbon.

2. His Novels. In 1742 appeared *Joseph Andrews*, which begins in laughter at the namby-pamby Pamela of Richardson. In the story Joseph Andrews, the hero, is a footman, and the brother of Pamela. Along with a poor and simple curate called Abraham Adams he survives numerous ridiculous adventures. In a short time Fielding forgets about the burlesque, becomes interested in his own story, and we then see a novel of a new and powerful kind. From the very beginning we get the Fielding touch: the complete rejection of the letter-method; the bustle and sweep of the tale; the broad and vivacious humour; the genial and half-contemptuous insight into human nature; and the forcible and pithy prose style. His next works were *A Journey from this World to the Next* (1743) and *Jonathan Wild the Great* (1743). *Jonathan Wild* is the biography of the famous thief and 'thief-taker' who was hanged at Newgate. The story is one long ironical comment upon human action. In it Fielding deliberately turns morality inside out, calling good by the name of evil, and evil by the name of good. In the hands of a lesser writer such a method would at length become teasing and troublesome; but Fielding, through the intensity of his ironic insight, gives us new and piercing glimpses of the ruffian's mentality. We give an extract to illustrate Fielding's ironic power, which in several respects resembles that of Swift:

> In Wild everything was truly great, almost without alloy, as his imperfections (for surely some small ones he had) were only such as served to denominate him a human creature, of which kind none ever arrived at consummate excellence. But surely his whole behaviour to his friend Heartfree is a convincing proof that the true iron or steel greatness of his heart was not debased by any softer metal. Indeed, while greatness consists in power, pride, insolence, and doing mischief to mankind—to speak out—while a great man and a great rogue are synonymous terms, so long shall Wild stand unrivalled on the pinnacle of GREATNESS. Nor must we omit here, as the finishing of his character, what indeed ought to be remembered on his tomb or his statue, the conformity above mentioned of his death to his life; and that Jonathan Wild the Great, after all his mighty exploits, was, what so few GREAT men can accomplish—hanged by the neck till he was dead.
>
> *Jonathan Wild the Great*

His greatest novel, *Tom Jones* (1749), completes and perfects his achievement. In the book we have all his previous virtues (and some of his weaknesses), with the addition of greater symmetry of plot, clearer and steadier vision into human life and human frailty, and a broader and more thickly peopled stage. His last novel, *Amelia* (1751), had as the original of the heroine Fielding's first wife, and the character of the erring husband Booth is based upon that of Fielding himself. This novel, though possessing power and interest, lacks the spontaneity of its great predecessor. The last work he produced was his *Voyage to Lisbon*, a diary written during his last journey. It possesses a painful interest, for it reveals a strong and patient mind, heavy with bodily affliction, yet still lively in its perception of human affairs.

3. Features of his Novels. (*a*) Like Richardson, Fielding had a genius for sounding the emotions of the human heart, but his methods are different. Richardson pores over human weaknesses with puckered brow and with many a sigh; Fielding looks, laughs, and passes on. He does not seek to analyse or over-refine; and so his characters possess a breadth, humanity, and attraction denied to Richardson's. Even a sneaking rogue like Blifil in *Tom Jones* has a Shakespearian roundness of contour that keeps him from being quite revolting.

(*b*) *Realism* is the keynote of all his work. He had a fierce hatred of all that savoured of hypocrisy, which is seen at its most pungent in *Jonathan Wild the Great*. His lively, ironical pen has something of the power of Swift, but his mood is tempered by the warmth of his human sympathy. His prime interest is in the depicting of the everyday life of the ordinary man, and he is particularly striking in his descriptions of low life. Unlike Richardson, he has no heroes, and few out-and-out villains—his characters are men, with all men's weaknesses, and the range of his portrait gallery has not often been exceeded. His work has a masculinity of tone quite different from the relative bloodlessness of Richardson's.

(*c*) Fielding is breezy, bustling, and energetic in his *narrative*. He shows us life on the highway, in the cottage, and among the streets of London. Coleridge truly said that to take up Fielding after Richardson is like emerging from the sick-room on to the open lawn.

(*d*) Fielding's *humour* is boisterous and broad to the point of coarseness—a kind of over-fed jollity. But it is frank and open, with none of the stealthy suggestiveness of Richardson. In dealing with this aspect of Fielding's work (an aspect frequently repulsive to the more squeamish taste of the moderns) we must make allowance for the fashion of his time, which united a frankness of incident with a curious decorum of speech. He had also in him a freakishness of wit, the excess of his grosser mood, which led to fantastic interludes and digressions in his novels. For instance, in describing the numerous scuffles among his characters, he frequently adopts an elaborate mock-heroic style not quite in accordance with later taste. Fielding's comic characters, such as Partridge, the humble companion of Tom Jones, are numerous, diversified, and exceedingly likeable and lively.

(*e*) A word must be given to his *style*. He breaks away from the mannered, artificial style of the earlier novelists, and gives us the good 'hodden grey' of his own period. His style has a slight touch of archaism in the use of words like 'hath,' but otherwise it is fresh and clear. His use of dialogue and conversation is of a similar nature.

We add an extract to illustrate Fielding's easy style, his almost haphazard cast of sentence, and his use of natural dialogue:

> As soon as the play, which was *Hamlet, Prince of Denmark*, began, Partridge was all attention, nor did he break silence till the entrance of the ghost; upon which he asked Jones: "What man

that was in the strange dress; something," said he, "like what I have seen in a picture. Sure it is not armour, is it?" Jones answered: "That is the ghost." To which Partridge replied, with a smile: "Persuade me to that, sir, if you can. Though I can't say I ever actually saw a ghost in my life, yet I am certain that I should know one if I saw him better than that comes to. No, no, sir; ghosts don't appear in such dresses as that neither." In this mistake, which caused much laughter in the neighbourhood of Partridge, he was suffered to continue till the scene between the ghost and Hamlet, when Partridge gave that credit to Mr Garrick which he had denied to Jones, and fell into so violent a trembling that his knees knocked against each other. Jones asked him what was the matter, and whether he was afraid of the warrior upon the stage. "O la! sir," said he, "I perceive now it is what you told me. I am not afraid of anything, for I know it is but a play; and if it was really a ghost, it could do one no harm at such a distance, and in so much company; and yet if I was frightened, I am not the only person." "Why, who," cries Jones; "dost thou take to be such a coward here besides thyself?" "Nay, you may call me coward if you will; but if that little man there upon the stage is not frightened, I never saw any man frightened in my life. Ay, ay; go along with you! Ay, to be sure! Who's fool, then? Will you? Lud have mercy upon such foolhardiness!—Whatever happens, it is good enough for you.— Follow you? I'd follow the devil as soon. Nay, perhaps it is the devil—for they say he can put on what likeness he pleases.—Oh! here he is again! No farther! No, you've gone far enough already; further than I'd have gone for all the king's dominions!" Jones offered to speak, but Partridge cried: "Hush, hush! dear sir; don't you hear him?" And during the whole speech of the ghost, he sat with his eyes fixed partly on the ghost, and partly on Hamlet, and with his mouth open; the same passions, which succeeded each other in Hamlet, succeeding likewise in him.

Tom Jones

OTHER NOVELISTS

1. Tobias Smollett (1721–71). Smollett was a Scotsman, being born in Dumbartonshire. Though he came of a good family, from an early age he had to work for a living. He was apprenticed to a surgeon, and, becoming a surgeon's mate on board a man-of-war, saw some fighting and much of the world. He thus stored up abundant raw material for the novels that were to follow. When he published *The Adventures of Roderick Random* (1748) the book was so successful that he settled in London; and the remainder of his life is mainly the chronicle of his works.

Roderick Random is an example of the 'picaresque' novel: the hero is a roving dog, of little honesty and considerable roguery; he traverses many lands, undergoing many tricks of fortune, both good and bad. The story lacks symmetry, but it is nearly always lively, though frequently coarse, and the minor characters, such as the seaman Tom Bowling, are of considerable interest. His other novels are *The Adventures of Peregrine Pickle* (1751), *The Adventures of Ferdinand, Count Fathom* (1753), *The Adventures of Sir Launcelot Greaves* (1762), and *The Expedition of Humphry Clinker* (1771).

The later books follow the plan of the first with some fidelity. Most of the characters are disreputable; the plots are as a rule formless narratives of travel and adventure; and a coarse and brutal humour is present all through. Smollett, however, brings variety into his novels by the endless shifting of the scenes, which cover many portions of the globe, by his wide knowledge and acute perception of local manners and customs, and by his use of a plain and vigorous narrative style. His characters, especially his female characters, are crudely managed, but his naval men—comprising Commodore Trunnion, Lieutenant Hatchway, and Boatswain Pipes —form quite a considerable gallery of figures. Smollett is the first of our novelists to introduce the naval type.

2. Laurence Sterne (1713–68). Sterne was born at Clonmel, was educated at Cambridge, took orders, and obtained a living in Yorkshire (1738). His habits were decidedly unclerical, even though we judge them by the easy standard of the time. He temporarily left his living for London to publish the first two parts of *The Life and Opinions of Tristram Shandy, Gent* (1760), which was completed in 1767. Then he toured abroad, returned to England to write his second novel, and died in London while visiting the city on business connected with the production of his book.

His two novels are *The Life and Opinions of Tristram Shandy, Gent* (1760–67), which won him immediate recognition, and *A Sentimental Journey through France and Italy* (1768). Unique in English literature, they are the accurate reflection of the singular personality of their author. They are made up of Sterne's peculiar blend of pathos and humour, and, though the pathos is sometimes overdone to the point of becoming offensively sentimental, the humour is subtle and intellectual, and constantly surprises by the unusual forms in which it is found. Indeed, for many, Sterne is merely the eccentric who appealed to his own age by such unusual devices as a completely black page in the middle of his story. But his characters are his chief claim to greatness. Basically, they are 'humorous,' in the Jonsonian sense of the word, but they are built up with a subtle analysis of feeling that makes them lifelike and completely human. Perhaps the most famous of them are "my uncle Toby" and his

Corporal Trim, but all Sterne's characters are minutely delineated, with a striking appreciation of the value of gesture and expression as guides to personality. There is little story in these works, but they are written in a delicate, digressive style admirably suited to their subject matter.

The following is an exciting incident that occurred just after the birth of Tristram Shandy. Susannah, the serving-maid, rouses Mr Shandy with the news that the child is in a fit. Observe the staccato dialogue and the ingenious variation of the paragraph. The humour is typical of Sterne.

> "Bless me, sir," said Susannah, "the child's in a fit"—"And where's Mr Yorick?"—"Never where he should be," said Susannah, "but his curate's in the dressing-room, with the child upon his arm, waiting for the name—and my mistress bid me run as fast as I could to know, as Captain Shandy is the godfather, whether it should not be called after him."
>
> "Were one sure," said my father to himself, scratching his eyebrow, "that the child was expiring, one might as well compliment my brother Toby as not—and it would be a pity in such a case, to throw away so great a name as Trismegistus upon him—But he may recover."
>
> "No, no"—said my father to Susannah, "I'll get up"—"There is no time," cried Susannah, "the child's as black as my shoe." "Trismegistus," said my father—"But stay—thou art a leaky vessel, Susannah," added my father; "can'st thou carry Trismegistus in thy head the length of the gallery without scattering?"— "Can I?" cried Susannah, shutting the door in a huff—"If she can, I'll be shot," said my father, bouncing out of bed in the dark, and groping for his breeches.
>
> Susannah ran with all speed along the gallery.
>
> My father made all possible speed to find his breeches.

3. Horace Walpole (1717–97). Walpole was the son of Sir Robert Walpole, the famous Whig minister. He touched upon several kinds of literature, his letters being among the best of their kind. His one novel, *The Castle of Otranto* (1764), is of importance, for it was the first of the productions of a large school (sometimes called the 'terror school') of novelists who dealt with the grisly and supernatural as their subject. Walpole's novel, which he published almost furtively, saying that it was a translation of a sixteenth-century Italian work, described a ghostly castle, in which we have walking skeletons, pictures that move out of their frames, and other blood-curdling incidents. The ghostly machinery is often cumbrous, but the work is creditably done, and as a return to the romantic elements of mystery and fear the book is noteworthy.

4. Other Terror Novelists. (*a*) **William Beckford (1759–1844).** The one novel now associated with Beckford's name is *Vathek* (1786). Beckford, who was a man of immense wealth and crazy habits, drew largely upon *The Arabian Nights* for material for the book. The central figure of the novel is a colossal creature, something like a vampire in disposition, who preys upon mankind and finally meets his doom with suitable impressiveness. Beckford had a wild, almost staggering, magnificence of imagination, and his story has been described as the best oriental tale in English.

(*b*) **Mrs Ann Radcliffe (1764–1823).** This lady was the most popular of the terror novelists, and published quite a large number of books that followed a fairly regular plan. Among such were her *A Sicilian Romance* (1790), *The Romance of the Forest* (1791), and the most popular of them all, *The Mysteries of Udolpho* (1794). Her stories took on almost a uniform plot, involving mysterious manuscripts, haunted castles, clanking chains, and cloaked and saturnine strangers. At the end of all the horrors Mrs Radcliffe rather spoils the effect by giving away the secrets of them, and revealing the fact that the terrors were only illusions after all. Nowadays the novels appear tame, but they showed the way to a large number of other writers, for they were fresh to the public of their time.

(*c*) **Matthew Gregory Lewis (1775–1818).** Lewis is perhaps the crudest of the terror school, and only one book of his, *The Monk* (1795), is worth recording. Lewis, who is lavish with his horrors, does not try to explain them. His imagination is grimmer and fiercer than that of any of the other writers of the same class, and his book is probably the 'creepiest' of its kind.

5. Henry Mackenzie (1745–1831). This novelist is the most considerable of the sentimental school, who took Sterne for their master. His best-known work is *The Man of Feeling* (1771), in which maudlin sentiment has free play. To his contemporaries Mackenzie was known as 'the Man of Feeling.'

6. Frances Burney (1752–1840), whose married name was Madame D'Arblay, is an important figure in the history of the novel. The first of the women novelists, she departed from the preaching morality of Richardson and the extravagances of the horror school to create the novel of domestic life. Her four novels are *Evelina* (1778), *Cecilia* (1782), *Camilla* (1796), and *The Wanderer* (1814), but her fame rests on the first two. These are written with a fine simplicity of style, and show her to possess a considerable narrative faculty and a great zest for life. Johnson, whose friendship she enjoyed, called her a "character-monger," a tribute to her large gallery of striking portraits, the best of which are convincing and amusing caricatures of the Dickensian type. Her observation of life was keen and close, and her descriptions of society are in a delightfully satirical vein, in many ways like that of Jane Austen. *Evelina* is additionally interesting in that it reverts to the epistolary method of Richardson. Her last two novels lack the lightness of touch of the two best; the influence of Dr Johnson upon her style was not a happy one.

Fanny Burney's letters and *Diary* are cleverly satirical and informative pictures of the society life of her day, and the latter in particular exhibits clearly the keen observation of manners, and the eye for a character, which are to be seen in her best novels.

THE HISTORIANS

EDWARD GIBBON (1737–94)

1. His Life. Gibbon, who was born at Putney, was a sickly child, and, according to his own grateful acknowledgment, he owed his life to the exertions of his aunt, Catherine Porten. He had little regular schooling, but from his early years he was an eager reader of history. At the age of fifteen he entered Magdalen College, Oxford, an institution of which he always spoke afterwards with aversion and contempt. "To the University of Oxford," he writes, "I acknowledge no obligation, and she will as readily renounce me for a son, as I am willing to disclaim her for a mother." His private historical studies led him to become a Roman Catholic when he was sixteen years old, to the great horror of his father, and resulted in his expulsion from the university. His father packed him off to Lausanne, in Switzerland, in the hope that the Protestant atmosphere of the place would wean him from his new faith.

From his stay in Lausanne began Gibbon's long and affectionate acquaintance with French language and learning, two sources from which he was to draw the chief inspiration for his masterpiece. He returned to England in 1758, and had a brief and mixed experience in the Militia; afterward he toured the Continent, visiting the famous *salons* of Paris and seeing Rome. Returning to England after some years, he entered Parliament (1774), hoping for political preferment. In this he was only moderately successful, for he was a lukewarm and rather cynical politician. He returned to Lausanne, where he completed his great work in June 1787. He finally came back to England, and died in lodgings in London.

2. His Works. His first projected book, *A History of Switzerland* (1770), was never finished. Then appeared the first volume of *The Decline and Fall of the Roman Empire* (1776). At nearly regular intervals of two years each of the other five volumes was produced, the last appearing in 1788. His *Autobiography*, which contains valuable material concerning his life, is his only other work of any importance, and it is written with all his usual elegance and suave, ironic humour.

To most judges *The Decline and Fall* ranks as one of the greatest of historical works, and is a worthy example of what a history ought to be. In time it covers more than a thousand years, and in scope it includes all the nations of Europe. It sketches the events leading up to the dissolution of the Roman Empire, and traces the rise of the states and nations that previously formed the component parts of the Roman world, concluding with the fall of Constantinople in the fifteenth century. For this great task Gibbon's knowledge is adequate; recent specialized research has rarely been able to pick holes in his narrative. Moreover, he had also that infallible sense of proportion which is the mark of the born historian: he knows what and when to omit, to condense, or give in full. In consequence his gigantic narrative has the balance and the beauty that result from a single and indivisible *mind* directing it, and suggests in plan and workmanship a vast cathedral.

Exception has been taken to Gibbon's humour, and with some reason. His sceptical bias, the product of his studies in French, pervades the entire work. This mental attitude need be no disadvantage to the historian, for it leads him to scrutinize his evidence very severely. But in the case of Gibbon it is troublesome at times, especially when he deals with the rise of the Christian faith. In the chapters devoted to the early Christians he sets the facts down solemnly, but all the time he is subtly and sneeringly ironical, a characteristic that aroused the great indignation of Johnson. At many other points when recording disagreeable incidents Gibbon reveals a sniggering nastiness of humour unworthy of so great a writer.

His prose style, deliberately cultivated as being most suited to his subject, is peculiar to himself. It is lordly and commanding, with a full, free, and majestic rhythm. Admirably appropriate to its gigantic subject, the style has nevertheless some weaknesses.

Though it never flags, and rarely stumbles, the very perfection of it tends to monotony, for it lacks ease and variety. The extract shows the elaborate construction of the sentences and the rolling character of the rhythm:

> Three days Mahomet and his companion were concealed in the cave of Thor, at the distance of a league from Mecca; and in the close of each evening, they received from the son and daughter of Abubeker a secret supply of intelligence and food. The diligence of the Koreish explored every haunt in the neighbourhood of the city; they arrived at the entrance of the cavern; but the providential deceit of a spider's web and a pigeon's nest is supposed to convince them that the place was solitary and inviolate. "We are only two," said the trembling Abubeker. "There is a third," replied the prophet; "it is God himself." No sooner was the pursuit abated, than the two fugitives issued from the rock, and mounted their camels; on the road to Medina they were overtaken by the emissaries of the Koreish; they redeemed themselves with prayers and promises from their hands. In this eventful moment the lance of an Arab might have changed the history of the world. The flight of the prophet from Mecca to Medina has fixed the memorable era of the Hegira, which, at the end of twelve centuries, still discriminates the lunar years of the Mahometan nations.

OTHER HISTORIANS

1. David Hume (1711–76). Born and educated at Edinburgh, Hume first distinguished himself as a philosopher, publishing *A Treatise of Human Nature* (1739–40) and *Essays, Moral and Political* (1741 and 1742). Later he turned to historical work, writing *The History of England*, in six volumes, which appeared between the years 1754 and 1761. At first the work was coldly received, for it traversed the popular Whig notions, but in time the book raised Hume to the position of the leading historian of the day. He died in the same year that witnessed the issue of the first volume of *The Decline and Fall*.

As a historian Hume makes no pretence at profound research, so that his work has little permanent value as history. He possesses a clear and logical mind and a swift and brilliant narrative style. In the history of literature his work is of importance as being the first of the popular and literary histories of the country.

2. William Robertson (1721–93). Robertson also was a Scot, being born in the county of Midlothian. After leaving the university he entered the Scottish Church. He had an active and successful career as a historian, producing among other works *The History of Scotland during the Reigns of Queen Mary and of James VI until* *his Accession to the Crown of England* (1759), *The History of Charles V* (1769), and *The History of America* (1771).

The range of Robertson's subject-matter shows that he could have been no deep student of any particular epoch of history. He aimed at a plain and businesslike narrative of events, taking the average man's view of the facts he chronicled, and he is never conspicuously personal in his opinions.

3. **James Boswell (1740–95)** was born in Edinburgh of a good Scottish family. He studied law, but his chief delight was the pursuit of great men, whose acquaintance he greedily cultivated.

He lives in literature by his supreme effort, *The Life of Samuel Johnson* (1791), which ranks as one of the best biographies in existence. Boswell sought and obtained Johnson's friendship; endured any humiliation for the sake of improving it; and for twenty-one years, by means of an astonishing amount of patience, pertinacity, and sheer thick-skinned imperviousness to slight and insult, obtained an intimate personal knowledge of Johnson's life and habits. Boswell has suffered at the hands of Macaulay, who has pictured him as being a knavish buffoon. No doubt he had glaring faults; but on the other hand he had great native shrewdness, a vigorous memory, a methodical and tireless industry which made him note down and preserve many details of priceless value, and a natural genius for seizing upon points of supreme literary importance. All these gifts combine to make his book a masterpiece.

The following extract illustrates Boswell's acute perception, his eye for detail, and his limpid and vivacious style:

> That the most minute singularities which belonged to him, and made very observable parts of his appearance and manner, may not be omitted, it is requisite to mention, that while talking or even musing as he sat in his chair, he commonly held his head to one side towards his right shoulder, and shook it in a tremulous manner, moving his body backwards and forwards, and rubbing his left knee in the same direction, with the palm of his hand. In the intervals of articulating he made various sounds with his mouth, sometimes as if ruminating, or what is called chewing the cud, sometimes giving a half-whistle, sometimes making his tongue play backwards from the roof of his mouth, as if clucking like a hen, and sometimes protruding it against his upper gums in front, as if pronouncing quickly under his breath, *too, too, too*: all this accompanied sometimes with a thoughtful look, but more frequently with a smile. Generally when he had concluded a period, in the course of a dispute, by which time he was a good deal exhausted by violence and vociferation, he used to blow out his breath like a whale. This I suppose was a relief to his lungs; and seemed in him

to be a contemptuous mode of expression, as if he had made the arguments of his opponent fly like chaff before the wind.

The Life of Samuel Johnson

PROSE

EDMUND BURKE (1729–97)

Burke shares with Gibbon the place of the greatest prose stylist of the period now under review. He is, moreover, recognized as one of the masters of English prose.

1. His Life. Born in Dublin, Burke was educated at Trinity College, Dublin, and then removed to London to study law in the Middle Temple. He soon showed that his real bent lay toward politics and literature, and it was not long before he published some books that attracted a good deal of attention and admitted him into the famous Johnson Club. In politics he attached himself to the Whig party, obtained some small appointments, and became member for Wendover (1765). In 1774 the citizens of Bristol invited him to represent them as their Member of Parliament. Though his support of Catholic emancipation and of free trade with Ireland cost him his seat six years later, a statue which stands in Bristol records to this day the city's pride in the connexion. Both as an orator and as a pamphleteer he was a powerful advocate for his party, and very soon his splendid gifts won for him a leading place in the House of Commons. His style of oratory, often laboured, rhetorical, and theatrical, exposed him to much censure and ridicule, and his speeches were frequently prolonged to the point of dullness. But at its best his eloquence was powerful in attack and magnificent in appeal, rising to the very summit of the orator's art. When the Whigs attained to office in 1782 Burke was appointed Paymaster of the Forces. He was leader in the prosecution of Warren Hastings, making a speech of immense length and power (1788). On the outbreak of the French Revolution in 1789 he left his party and attacked the revolutionaries with all his great energy. In 1794, broken in health, he retired from Parliament, but continued to publish pamphlets till his death in 1797.

2. His Works. The considerable sum of Burke's achievement can for the sake of convenience be divided into two groups: his purely philosophical writings, and his political pamphlets and speeches.

(*a*) His philosophical writings, which comprise the smaller division of his product, were composed in the earlier portion of his career. *A Vindication of Natural Society* (1756) is a parody of the style and ideas of Bolingbroke, and, though it possesses much ingenuity, it has not much importance as an original work. *A Philosophical Inquiry into the Origin of our Ideas of the Sublime and Beautiful* (1756) is his most considerable attempt at philosophy. As philosophy the book is only middling, for its theory and many of its examples are questionable, but it has the sumptuous dressing of Burke's language and style.

(*b*) His political works are by far his most substantial claim to fame. In variety, breadth of view, and illuminating power of vision they are unsurpassed in the language. They fall, broadly, into two groups, the speeches and the pamphlets. It is in the former that Burke's artistry and power are at their best. The greatest of them, his speeches *On American Taxation* (1774) and on *Conciliation with the Colonies* (1775), are passionate in their pleading and conviction, rich in rhetorical effect, and brilliant in their marshalling of material and in the statesmanlike insight which underlies their arguments. Burke was always at his best when deeply moved, and the rights of the American colonists gave him a subject worthy of his mettle. His speeches during the trial of Warren Hastings (1788–94), though they lack the discerning judgment of his American speeches, are also of a high level. He certainly does less than justice to the motives of Hastings, but the speeches show all his usual power and élan. Of his best-known pamphlets, the first to be produced was *Thoughts on the Cause of the Present Discontents* (1770), a resounding attack on the Tory Government then in power, which, though it falls below his other pamphlets as political thinking, shows all his peculiar qualities of style and method. Then, between 1790 and 1797, appeared a number of pamphlets, of which *Reflections on the Revolution in France* (1790), *A Letter to a Noble Lord* (1795), and *Letters on a Regicide Peace* (1797) are the most noteworthy. All three show some falling away from the level reached in his great speeches, perhaps because, as pamphlets, they lacked the stimulus of an immediate audience. *Reflections on the Revolution in France*, a fierce challenge to the atheistical, revolutionary ideas of the Jacobins, is a fine exposition of his own principles, and, though it lacks something of the architectural skill of his American speeches, it has many fine passages of moving eloquence. *A Letter to a Noble Lord*, in which Burke defends his right to receive a state pension, is a masterpiece of irony, but *Letters on a Regicide Peace* is marred by an almost hysterical anger, which impairs much of the judgment and breadth of vision for which he is so renowned.

3. Features of his Work. Though the occasion of Burke's political writings has vanished, the books can still be read with profit and pleasure. Burke was the practical politician, applying to the problems of his day the light of a clear and forcible intelligence; yet, above this, he had an almost supreme faculty for discerning the eternal principles lying behind the shifting and troubled scenes of his time. He could distil from the muddy liquid of contemporary party strife the clear wine of wisdom, and so deduce ideas of unshakable permanence. Thus pages of his disquisition, scores of his dicta, can still be applied almost without qualification to the problems of any civilized state and time.

We have, in addition, the permanent attraction of Burke's style. Dignified rather than graceful, it is the most powerful prose of his day, and is marked by all the devices of the orator—much repetition, careful arrangement and balance of parts, copious use of rhetorical figures (such as metaphor, simile, epigram, and exclamation), variation of the sentence structure, homely illustrations, and a swift, vigorous rhythm. It is full of colour and splendour, and is fired by an impassioned imagination. The skilful ordering of his ideas indicates a mind of extraordinary powers, and he makes effective use of his wide knowledge. Significant reference and quotation, besides much unacknowledged verbal reminiscence, are a marked feature of his prose. Burke lacks the gentler, persuasive tones of pathos and genuine humour, but his sarcasm and irony can be formidable. At its best his prose is vigorous and sinewy, at its worst it becomes heavy, extravagant, and, on occasion, almost hysterical.

In the extract now given, note that the actual vocabulary does not abound in long Latinized words as in the case of Johnsonese. The ornate effect is produced rather by the elevation of the sentiment and the sweeping cadence of the style.

> On the scheme of this barbarous philosophy, which is the off-spring of cold hearts and muddy understandings, and which is as void of solid wisdom as it is destitute of all taste and elegance, laws are to be supported only by their own terrors, and by the concern which each individual may find in them from his own private speculations, or can spare to them from his own private interests. In the groves of *their* Academy, at the end of every vista, you see nothing but the gallows! Nothing is left which engages the affections on the part of the commonwealth. On the principles of this mechanic philosophy, our institutions can never be embodied, if I may use the expression, in persons, so as to create in us love, veneration, admiration, or attachment. But that sort of reason which banishes the affections is incapable of filling their place.

These public affections, combined with manners, are required sometimes as supplements, sometimes as correctives, always as aids, to law. The precept given by a wise man, as well as a great critic, for the construction of poems is equally true as to states: "Non satis est pulchra esse poemata, dulcia sunto." There ought to be a system of manners in every nation which a well-formed mind would be disposed to relish. To make us love our country, our country ought to be lovely.

Reflections on the Revolution in France

OTHER PROSE-WRITERS

1. Adam Smith (1723–90). This author was born at Kirkcaldy, in Fifeshire, and completed his education at Glasgow and Oxford. In 1751 he was appointed professor at Glasgow University. He issued his famous book *The Wealth of Nations* in 1776.

In the history of economics the work is epoch-making, for it lays the foundations of modern economic theory. In the history of literature it is noteworthy because it is another example of that spirit of research and inquiry that was abroad at this time, playing havoc with literary convention as well as with many other ideas. The book is also a worthy example of the use of a plain businesslike style in the development of theories of far-reaching importance.

2. William Paley (1743–1805) may be taken as the typical theological writer of the age. He was a brilliant Cambridge scholar, and obtained high offices in the Church, finally becoming an archdeacon. His chief books are *Principles of Moral and Political Philosophy* (1785), *Horæ Paulinæ* (1790), and *A View of the Evidences of Christianity* (1794). His style is lively and attractive, and he possessed much vigour of character and intellect.

3. The Earl of Chesterfield (1694–1773) was of the famous Stanhope family. In his day he was an illustrious wit and man of fashion, and held high political offices. He is an example of the aristocratic amateur in literature, and he wrote elegant articles for the fashionable journals, such as *The World*.

His *Letters to his Son*, which were published in 1774, shortly after his death, caused a great flutter. They appeared diabolically cynical and immoral, and as such they were denounced by Johnson. No doubt they affect the tired cynicism of the man of the world, but that does not prevent them from being keen and clever, and underneath their bored indifference to morality they reveal a shrewd judgment of men and manners. (See p. 281.)

4. William Godwin (1756–1836) is a prominent example of the revolutionary man of letters of the time. He was the son of a dissenting minister, and intended to follow the same profession, but very soon drifted away from it. He then devoted himself to the pursuit of letters, in which he developed his extreme views on religion, politics, sociology, and other important themes. His *Political Justice* (1793) was deeply tinged with revolutionary ideas, and had a great effect on many young and ardent spirits of the age, including Shelley. His novel *Caleb Williams* (1794) was a dressing of the same theories in the garb of fiction. Godwin is worth notice because he reveals the spread of the revolutionary doctrines that were so strongly opposed by Burke.

5. **Gilbert White** (1720–93) deserves mention as the first naturalist who cast his observations into genuine literary form. He was born at Selborne, Hampshire, studied at Oxford, and took holy orders. He settled at his native place, and published *The Natural History of Selborne* (1789). The book is a series of genuine letters written to correspondents who are interested in the natural history of the place. White reveals much closeness and sympathy of observation, and he can command a sweet and readable style. He shows the 'return to nature' in a practical and praiseworthy form.

DRAMA

In an age which is unaccountably poor in drama, only two playwrights achieve excellence. The comedies of Goldsmith have already been mentioned (see p. 236); the more brilliant, if less human, work of Sheridan must now be considered.

RICHARD BRINSLEY SHERIDAN (1751–1816)

1. **His Life.** Sheridan was born in Dublin, the son of an actor-manager, Thomas Sheridan, and was educated at Harrow. He was intended to read law, but eloped with a famous young beauty, and the necessity of providing for a wife made him turn to literature as a means of making money. At the age of twenty-three he wrote his first play, *The Rivals*, and by the time he was twenty-nine he had written his last, *The Critic*. After this he entered Parliament as M.P. for Stafford, and lived a busy social and political life. His plays were so successful that he was able to buy a third of Garrick's share in Drury Lane in 1776, and he became manager of this famous theatre company, a post he held until 1809.

2. **His Works.** His prose comedy, *The Rivals* (1774), had an enormous success. It was followed in 1775 by a farce called *St Patrick's Day: or, The Scheming Lieutenant*, and an operatic play,

The Duenna, for which his father-in-law, Thomas Linley, composed and arranged the music. *The Duenna* had a phenomenal success. *A Trip to Scarborough* appeared in 1776, and his best play, *The School for Scandal*, in 1777. This contains his best character, Lady Teazle, and in it his dialogue is at its most brilliant. His last play was *The Critic: or, a Tragedy Rehearsed* (1779). It is a very telling attack on the popular sentimental drama, and has been called the best burlesque of its age.

3. Features of his Plays. Sheridan's prose comedies all resemble the best of the Restoration comedies without the immorality of the Restoration plays. Again we see the polite world of fashion, but Sheridan makes its vices appear foolish by exaggerating them in humorous portraiture. The plots are ingenious and effective, though they depend largely on a stagy complexity of intrigue. The characters, among whom are the immortal figures of Mrs Malaprop, Bob Acres, and Sir Fretful Plagiary, are stage types, but they are struck off with daring skill, and we find them quite irresistible. The dialogue is brilliant in its picturesque, epigrammatic repartee—indeed, the wit sometimes obscures the characters, nearly all of whom speak with the same brilliance. The plays are remarkable for their vivacity and charm. We give below a typical specimen of Sheridan's dialogue.

> [*Lady Sneerwell, Mrs Candour, Lady Teazle, Crabtree, and Sir Benjamin Backbite are discussing their friends.*]
>
> *Lady Teazle.* What's the matter, Mrs Candour?
>
> *Mrs Can.* They will not allow our friend Miss Vermilion to be handsome.
>
> *Lady Sneer.* Oh, surely she is a pretty woman.
>
> *Crab.* I am very glad you think so, ma'am.
>
> *Mrs Can.* She has a charming fresh colour.
>
> *Lady Teazle.* Yes, when it is fresh put on.
>
> *Mrs Can.* Oh, fie! I'll swear her colour is natural: I have seen it come and go!
>
> *Lady Teazle.* I dare swear you have, ma'am: it goes off at night, and comes again in the morning.
>
> *Sir Ben.* True, ma'am, it not only comes and goes; but, what's more, egad, her maid can fetch and carry it!
>
> *Mrs Can.* Ha! ha! ha! how I hate to hear you talk so! But surely, now, her sister is, or was, very handsome.
>
> *Crab.* Who? Mrs Evergreen? O Lord! She's six-and-fifty if she's an hour!
>
> *Mrs Can.* Now positively you wrong her; fifty-two or fifty-three is the utmost—and I don't think she looks more.
>
> *Sir Ben.* Ah! there's no judging by her looks, unless one could see her face.

Lady Sneer. Well, well, if Mrs Evergreen does take some pains to repair the ravages of time, you must allow she effects it with great ingenuity; and surely that's better than the careless manner in which the widow Ochre caulks her wrinkles.

Sir Ben. Nay, now, Lady Sneerwell, you are severe upon the widow. Come, come, 'tis not that she paints so ill—but, when she has finished her face, she joins it on so badly to her neck, that she looks like a mended statue, in which the connoisseur may see at once that the head is modern, though the trunk's antique!

Crab. Ha! ha! ha! Well said, nephew!

Mrs Can. Ha! ha! ha! Well, you make me laugh; but I vow I hate you for it. What do you think of Miss Simper?

Sir Ben. Why, she has very pretty teeth.

Lady Teazle. Yes; and on that account, when she is neither speaking nor laughing (which very seldom happens), she never absolutely shuts her mouth, but leaves it always on ajar, as it were—thus.   *[Shows her teeth]*

The School for Scandal

THE DEVELOPMENT OF LITERARY FORMS

This, being an age of transition, is an age of unrest, of advance and retreat, of half-lights and dubious victories. But if we bring together the different types of literature, and mark how they have developed during the period, we can see that the trend of the age is quite clear.

1. Poetry. In 1740 we have Pope still alive and powerful, and Johnson an aspiring junior; in 1800, with Burns and Blake, Romanticism has unquestionably arrived. This great change came gradually, but its stages can be observed with some precision.

(*a*) The first symptom of the coming change was the *decline of the heroic couplet*, the dominance of which passed away with its greatest exponent, Pope. Toward the middle of the century a large number of other poetical forms can be observed creeping back into favour.

(*b*) The change was first seen in the free use of the *Pindaric ode* in the works of Gray and Collins, which appeared in the middle years of the century. The Pindaric ode is a useful medium for the transitional stage, for it has the double advantage of being 'classical' and of being free from the more formal rules of couplet and stanza. Gray's *The Bard* (1757) and Collins's ode *The Passions* (1747) are among the best of the type.

(*c*) Another omen was the revival of the *ballad*, which was due to renewed interest in the older kinds of literature. The revived species, as seen in Goldsmith's *The Hermit* and Cowper's *John Gilpin*, has not the grimness and crude narrative force of the genuine ballad, but it is lively and often humorous. Another ballad-writer was **Thomas Percy (1729–1811)**, who, in addition to collecting the *Reliques* (1765), composed ballads of his own, such as *The Friar of Orders Grey*. Chatterton's *Bristowe Tragedie* has much of the fire and sombreness of the old ballads.

(*d*) The *descriptive and narrative poems* begin with the old-fashioned *London* (1738) of Johnson; the development is seen in Goldsmith's *The Traveller* (1764) and *The Deserted Village* (1770), in which the heroic couplet is quickened and transformed by a real sympathy for nature and the poor; the advance is carried still further, by the blank-verse poems of Cowper (*The Task*), the heroic couplets of Crabbe (*The Village*) and the Spenserian stanzas of minor poets like Shenstone (*The Schoolmistress*).

(*e*) Finally there is the rise of the *lyric*. The Pindarics of Collins and Gray are lyrics in starch and buckram; the works of Chatterton, Smart, Macpherson, Cowper, and, lastly, of Burns and Blake show in order the lyrical spirit struggling with its bonds, shaking itself free, and finally soaring in triumph. Romanticism has arrived.

2. Drama. In this period nothing is more remarkable than the poverty of its dramatic literature. Of this no real explanation can be given. The age was simply not a dramatic one; for the plays that the age produced, with the exceptions of a few notable examples of comedy, are hardly worth noticing.

Tragedy comes off worst of all. The sole tragedy hitherto mentioned in this chapter is Johnson's *Irene* (1749), which only the reputation of its author has preserved from complete oblivion. A tragedy which had a great vogue was *Douglas* (1756), by **John Home (1722–1808)**. It is now almost forgotten. **Joanna Baillie (1762–1851)** produced some historical blank-verse tragedies, such as *Count Basil* (1798) and *De Monfort* (1798). Her plays make fairly interesting reading, and some of their admirers, including Scott, said that she was Shakespeare revived.

3. Prose. The prose product of the period is bulky, varied, and of great importance. The importance of it is clear enough when we recollect that it includes, among many other things, possibly the best novel in the language (*Tom Jones*), the best history (*The Decline and Fall*), and the best biography (*The Life of Samuel Johnson*).

(*a*) *The Rise of the Novel.* There are two main classes of fictional prose narratives, namely, the tale or romance and the novel. The distinction between the two need not be drawn too fine, for there is a large amount of prose narrative that can fall into either group; but, broadly speaking, we may say that the tale or romance depends for its chief interest on incident and adventure, whereas the novel depends more on the display of character and motive. In addition the story (or *plot*, or *fable*) of the novel tends to be more complicated than that of the tale, and it often leads to what were called by the older writers "revolutions and discoveries"—that is, unexpected developments in the narrative, finishing with an explanation that is called the *dénouement*. The tale, moreover, can be separated from the romance: the plot of the tale is commonly matter-of-fact, while that of the romance is often wonderful and fantastic.

There is little doubt that the modern novel has its roots in the medieval romances, such as *Sir Gawain and the Green Knight* and those dealing with the legends of King Arthur. Another source of the novel was the collections of ballads telling of the adventures of popular heroes of the type of Robin Hood. These romances were written in verse; they were supplied with stock characters, like the wandering knight, the distressed damsel, and the wicked wizard; they had stock incidents, connected with enchanted castles, fiery dragons, and perilous ambushes; and their story rambled on almost interminably. They were necessary to satisfy the human craving for fiction, and they were often fiction of a picturesque and lively kind.

The age of Elizabeth saw the rise of the prose romance. We have examples in the *Euphues* (1579) of Lyly and the *Arcadia* of Sidney. As fiction these tales are weighed down with their fantastic prose styles, and with their common desire to expound a moral lesson. Their characters are rudimentary, and there is little attempt at an integrated plot. Yet they represent an advance, for they are fiction.

They are interesting from another viewpoint. They show us that curious diffidence that was to be a drag on the production of the novel even as late as the time of Scott. Authors were shy of being novelists for two main reasons: first, there was thought to be something almost immoral in the writing of fiction, as it was but the glorification of a pack of lies; and, secondly, the liking for fiction was considered to be the craving of diseased or immature intellects, and so the production of it was unworthy of reasonable men. Thus if a man felt impelled to write fiction he had to conceal the narrative with some moral or allegorical dressing.

A new type of embryo novel began to appear at the end of the sixteenth century, and, becoming very popular during the seventeenth, retained its popularity till the days of Fielding and Smollett.

This class is known as the *picaresque* novel, a name derived from the Spanish word *picaro*, which means a wandering rogue. As the name implies, it is of Spanish origin. For hero it takes a rascal who leads a wandering life, and has many adventures, most of them of a scandalous kind. The hero is the sole link between the different incidents, and there is much digression and the interposing of other short narratives. In Spain the picaresque type originated in parodies of the old romances, and of such parodies the greatest is the *Don Quixote* (1605 and 1615) of Cervantes. In France the type became common, the most famous example of it being the *Gil Blas* (1715–35) of Le Sage.

In England the picaresque novel had an early start in *The Unfortunate Traveller, or the Life of Jacke Wilton* (1594), by Nash (1567–1601), whose work often suggests that of Defoe. Nash's work is crude, but it has vigour and some wit. A later effort in the same kind is *The English Rogue* (1665), by Richard Head (1637 (?)–86 (?)). The book is gross and scandalous to an extreme degree, but it has energy, and, as it takes the hero to many places on the globe, the reader obtains interesting glimpses of life in foreign parts.

Another type that came into favour was the heroic romance. This was based on the similar French romances of Mademoiselle de Scudéry (1607–1701) and others. This class of fiction was the elegant variety of the grosser picaresque novel, and it was much duller. The hero of a heroic romance was usually of high degree, and he underwent a long series of romantic adventures, many of them supernatural. There was much love-making, involving long speeches containing "noble sentiments, elegantly expressed." The length of these romances was enormous; the *Le Grand Cyrus* of Mademoiselle de Scudéry ran to ten large volumes. Popular English specimens were Ford's *Parismus, the Renowned Prince of Bohemia* (1598) and *Parthenissa* (1654), by Roger Boyle. It is worth noting that the artificial heroic romance collapsed about the end of the seventeenth century, whereas the picaresque class, which in spite of its grave faults was a human and interesting type of fiction, survived and influenced the novel in later centuries.

By the end of the seventeenth century the novel is dimly taking shape. **Aphra Behn (1640–89)** wrote stories that had some claims to plot, character-drawing, and dialogue. Her *Orinooko, or The Royal Slave* (1698) shows some power in describing the persecution of a noble negro, a kind of Othello, at the hands of brutal white men. The work of Bunyan (1628–88) was forced to be allegorical, for the

Puritans, of whom he was one, abhorred the idea of writing fiction, which they regarded as gilded lies. Yet *The Pilgrim's Progress* (1678) abounds in qualities that go to make a first-rate novel: a strong and smoothly working plot, troops of human and diverse characters, impressive descriptive passages, and simple dialogue dramatically sound. His other works, notably *The Life and Death of Mr Badman* (1680), are also very close to the novel proper.

In the eighteenth century we see another development in the Coverley papers (1711) of Steele and Addison. There is little plot in this essay-series, and only a rudimentary love-theme; but the allegorical fabric is gone, there is much entertaining character-sketching, and the spice of delicate humour. We should note also that we have here the beginnings of the society and domestic novel, for the papers deal with ordinary people and incidents.

The genuine novel is very near indeed in the works of Defoe (1659 (?)–1731). His novels are of the picaresque type in the case of *Captain Singleton* (1720), *Moll Flanders* (1722), and *Colonel Jacque* (1722). They have many of the faults of their kind: the characters are weakly drawn, the plots are shaky and sprawling, and much of the incident is indecorous; yet they have a virile and sustaining interest that is most apparent in the best parts of *Robinson Crusoe* (1719).

Then, toward the middle of the century, came the swift and abundant blossoming of the novel, raising the type to the rank of one of the major species of literature. The time was ripe for it. The drama, which had helped to satisfy the natural human desire for a story, was moribund, and something had to take its place. Here we can only summarize very shortly the work of the novelists already discussed in this chapter. Richardson's *Pamela* (1740) had the requisites of plot, characters, and dialogue, and these of high merit; but the diffidence of the early fiction-writer possessed him, and he had to conceal the novel-method under the clumsy disguise of a series of letters. Fielding's robust common sense had no such scruples, and his *Tom Jones* (1749) shows us the novel in its maturity. Later novelists could only modify and improve in detail; with Fielding the principles of the novel were established.

The modifications of Fielding's immediate successors can be briefly noticed. Smollett reverted to the picaresque manner, but he added the professional sailor to fiction, and gave it types of Scottish character that Scott was to improve upon; Sterne made the novel sentimental and fantastic, and founded a sentimental school; the Radcliffe novels, popular toward the end of the century, made fiction terrific; while in *The Vicar of Wakefield* (1766) Goldsmith showed us what the novel can do in respect of a simple yet effective plot, human and lovable personages, dialogue of a dramatic kind, and a tender and graceful humour. Johnson's *Rasselas* (1759), which reverted to the methods of *Euphues*, was pure reaction, but it possesses an interest as a reversion to a long-dead type.

(b) *The Rise of the Historical Work*. The development of history came late, but almost necessarily so. The two main requirements of the serious historian are knowledge of his subject and maturity of judgment. Before the year 1750 no great historical work had appeared in any modern language. Ralegh's *History of the World* (1614) is not a real history; it is only the fruit of the mental exertions of an imprisoned man who seeks relaxation. Clarendon's *History of the Rebellion and Civil Wars in England*, which was not published till 1704, is largely the record of his own personal experiences and opinions. He makes little attempt at an impartial and considered judgment or at placing the rebellion in its proper perspective.

The general advance in knowledge and the research into national affairs which were the features of eighteenth-century culture quickly brought the study of history into prominence. France led the way, and the Scots, traditionally allied to the French, were the first in Britain to feel the influence. Hence we have Hume's *History of England* (1754–62) and the works of Robertson. These books excelled in ease and sense, but the knowledge displayed in them was not yet sufficient to make them epoch-making. Gibbon's *Decline and Fall of the Roman Empire* (1776–88) in knowledge, in method, and in literary style is as near perfection as human frailty can attain. Thus within twenty or thirty years the art of writing history in English advanced from a state of tutelage to complete development.

(c) *Letter-writing*. The habit of writing letters became very popular during the eighteenth century, and flourished till well into the nineteenth, when the institution of the penny post made letter-writing a convenience and not an art. It was this popularity of the letter that helped Richardson's *Pamela* into public favour.

A favourite form of the letter was a long communication, sometimes written from abroad, discussing some topic of general interest. Such a letter was semi-public in nature, and was meant to be handed round a circle of acquaintances. Frequently a series of letters was bound into book-form. Collections of this kind were the letters of Lady Mary Wortley Montagu (1689–1762), written to Pope and others from Constantinople, and of Thomas Gray, from the Lake

District and the Continent. Sometimes the letters contain comments on political and social matters, as in the famous compositions of Lord Chesterfield to his son, which we have already noticed. We give an extract from one of Chesterfield's letters, for it is valuable as an example of witty and polished prose. A letter of the type of Chesterfield's is really an essay which is given a slightly epistolary form.

LONDON, *May* 27, 1753

. . . You are now but nineteen, an age at which most of your countrymen are illiberally getting drunk in Port at the University. You have greatly got the start of them in learning; and, if you can equally get the start of them in the knowledge and manners of the world, you may be very sure of outrunning them in Court and Parliament, as you set out so much earlier than they. They generally begin but to see the world at one-and-twenty; you will by that age have seen all Europe. They set out upon their travels unlicked cubs; and in their travels they only lick one another, for they seldom go into any other company. They know nothing but the English world, and the worst part of that too, and generally very little of any but the English language; and they come home, at three or four-and-twenty, refined and polished (as is said in one of Congreve's plays) like Dutch skippers from a whale-fishing. The care which has been taken of you, and (to do you justice) the care you have taken of yourself, has left you, at the age of nineteen only, nothing to acquire but the knowledge of the world, manners, address, and those exterior accomplishments. But they are great and necessary acquisitions, to those who have sense enough to know their true value; and your getting them before you are one-and-twenty, and before you enter upon the active and shining scene of life, will give you such an advantage over all your contemporaries, that they cannot overtake you: they must be distanced. You may probably be placed about a young prince, who will probably be a young king. There all the various arts of pleasing, the engaging address, the versatility of manners, the *brillant*, the Graces, will outweigh and yet outrun all solid knowledge and unpolished merit. Oil yourself therefore, and be both supple and shining, for that race, if you would be first, or early, at the goal.

A type of letter which is frankly a work written for publication is well represented by the famous *Letters of Junius*, which caused a great stir in their day. They are what are called 'open letters'— that is, they are for general perusal, while they gain additional point by being addressed to some well-known personage. The public, as it were, has the satisfaction of looking over the shoulder of the man to whom they are addressed. 'Junius' is now supposed to have been **Sir Philip Francis (1740–1818)**, though the identity of the writer was long concealed. They began to appear in *The Public Advertiser* in 1769, and by their immensely destructive power they shook the

Government to its base. In force and fury they resemble Swift's *The Drapier's Letters*, but they tend to become petty and spiteful.

The more intimate and private letters of this period, of which there is a large and interesting collection, are of a deeper significance to us now, for they contain a human interest by revealing the nature of the people who wrote them. In *The Life of Samuel Johnson* Boswell published many of Johnson's letters, the most famous of which contains the snub to Chesterfield. Horace Walpole, as we have already noted (p. 263), left a voluminous correspondence which for wit, vivacity, and urbane and shallow common sense is quite remarkable. The private letters of Cowper are attractive for their easy and unaffected grace and their gentle and pervasive humour. We add an extract from a letter by Cowper. The style of it should be compared with that of Chesterfield.

(*To William Hayley*)

WESTON, *February* 24, 1793

. . . Oh! you rogue! what would you give to have such a dream about Milton, as I had about a week since? I dreamed that being in a house in the city, and with much company, looking towards the lower end of the room from the upper end of it, I descried a figure which I immediately knew to be Milton's. He was very gravely, but very neatly attired in the fashion of his day, and had a countenance which filled me with those feelings that an affectionate child has for a beloved father, such, for instance, as Tom has for you. My first thought was wonder, where he could have been concealed so many years; my second, a transport of joy to find him still alive; my third, another transport to find myself in his company; and my fourth, a resolution to accost him. I did so, and he received me with a complacence, in which I saw equal sweetness and dignity. I spoke of his *Paradise Lost*, as every man must, who is worthy to speak of it at all, and told him a long story of the manner in which it affected me, when I first discovered it, being at that time a schoolboy. He answered me by a smile and a gentle inclination of his head. He then grasped my hand affectionately, and with a smile that charmed me, said, "Well, you for your part will do well also"; at last recollecting his great age (for I understood him to be two hundred years old), I feared that I might fatigue him by much talking; I took my leave, and he took his, with an air of the most perfect good breeding. His person, his features, his manner, were all so perfectly characteristic, that I am persuaded an apparition of him could not represent him more completely. This may be said to have been one of the dreams of Pindus,[1] may it not? . . . With Mary's kind love, I must now conclude myself, my dear brother, ever yours,   LIPPUS[2]

---

[1] Mount Pindus, sacred to the Muses. Hence, a poet's dream.
[2] That is, 'the blind one.' A reference to Milton's blindness.

(d) *The Periodical Essay*. Compared with the abundance of the earlier portion of the century, the amount produced later seems of little importance. The number of periodicals, however, was as great as ever. Johnson wrote *The Rambler* and *The Idler*, and contributed also to *The Adventurer* and others; Goldsmith assisted *The Bee* during its brief career. *The Connoisseur*, to which Cowper contributed for a space, *The Mirror*, and *The Lounger*, published in Edinburgh by Mackenzie, 'the Man of Feeling,' *The Observer* and *The Looker-On* all imitated *The Spectator* with moderate success, but show no important development in manner or matter.

(e) *Miscellaneous Prose*. The amount of miscellaneous prose is very great indeed, and a fair proportion of it is of high merit. We have already given space to the political and philosophical writings of Burke, whose work is of the highest class, as represented in *A Philosophical Inquiry into the Origin of our Ideas of the Sublime and Beautiful* and *Reflections on the Revolution in France*. Political writing of a different aim is seen in Godwin's *Political Justice*; and the religious writings of Paley, the critical writings of Percy, and the natural history of Gilbert White are all to be included in this class.

THE DEVELOPMENT OF LITERARY STYLE

1. Poetry. In poetical style the transitional features are well marked. The earlier authors reveal many artificial mannerisms—for example, extreme regularity of metre and the frequent employment of the more formal figures of speech, such as personification and apostrophe. The Pindaric odes of Gray and Collins are examples of the transitional style:

> Ye distant spires! ye antique towers!
>   That crown the wat'ry glade,
> Where grateful Science still adores
>   Her Henry's holy shade;
> And ye that from the stately brow
> Of Windsor's heights th' expanse below
>   Of grove, of lawn, of mead survey,
> Whose turf, whose shade, whose flowers among
> Wanders the hoary Thames along
>   His silver-winding way.
>   GRAY, *Ode on a Distant Prospect of Eton College*

In this verse there are the conventional personifications of Science and the Thames, and such stock phrases as "the wat'ry glade."

The whole poem, however, is infused with a new spirit of mingled energy and meditation.

As the century draws to a close we have many of the newer styles appearing: the more regular blank verse of Cowper; the lighter heroic couplet of Goldsmith; the archaic medley of Chatterton; and the intense simplicity of the lyrics of Burns and Blake. As a further example of the new manner we quote a few stanzas from a poem by Fergusson, who, dying in the year 1774 (ten years before the death of Johnson), wrote as naturally as Burns himself:

> As simmer rains bring simmer flowers,
> And leaves to cleed the birken bowers;
> Sae beauty gets by caller showers
>   Sae rich a bloom,
> As for estate, or heavy dowers
>   Aft stands in room.

> What makes auld Reekie's dames so fair?
> It canna be the halesome air;
> But caller burn, beyond compare,
>   The best o' ony,
> That gars them a' sic graces skair[1]
>   An' blink sae bonny.

> On Mayday, in a fairy ring,
> We've seen them roun' Saint Anthon's spring,
> Frae grass the caller dew-draps wring,
>   To weet their e'en,
> An' water, clear as crystal spring,
>   To synd[2] them clean.

Caller Water

2. Prose. As in poetry, we have in prose many men and many manners. The simplest prose of the period is found chiefly in the works of the novelists, of whom Fielding and Smollett are good examples. Smollett's prose, as in the following example, is almost colloquial in its native directness.

> After we had been all entered upon the ship's books, I inquired of one of my shipmates where the surgeon was, that I might have my wounds dressed, and had actually got as far as the middle deck (for our ship carried eighty guns) in my way to the cockpit, when I was met by the same midshipman, who had used me so barbarously in the tender: he, seeing me free from my chains, asked, with an insolent air, who had released me? To this question, I foolishly answered with a countenance that too plainly declared the state of my thoughts; "Whoever did it, I am persuaded

---

[1] share.   [2] rinse.

did not consult you in the affair." I had no sooner uttered these words, than he cried, "Damn you, you scurvy son of a bitch, I'll teach you to talk so to your officer." So saying, he bestowed on me several severe stripes, with a supple jack he had in his hand: and going to the commanding officer, made such a report of me, that I was immediately put in irons by the master-at-arms, and a sentinel placed over me.

The Adventures of Roderick Random

The excellent middle style of Addison, the prose-of-all-work, survives, and will continue to survive, for it is indispensable to all manner of miscellaneous work. Goldsmith's prose is one of the best examples of the middle style, and so is the later work of Johnson, as well as the writings of the authors of miscellaneous prose already mentioned in this chapter. The following passage from Goldsmith shows his graceful turn of sentence and his command of vocabulary. The style is clearness itself.

The next that presented for a place, was a most whimsical figure indeed. He was hung round with papers of his own composing, not unlike those who sing ballads in the streets, and came dancing up to the door with all the confidence of instant admittance. The volubility of his motion and address prevented my being able to read more of his cargo than the word *Inspector*, which was written in great letters at the top of some of the papers. He opened the coach-door himself without any ceremony, and was just slipping in, when the coachman, with as little ceremony, pulled him back. Our figure seemed perfectly angry at this repulse, and demanded gentleman's satisfaction. "Lord, sir!" replied the coachman, "instead of proper luggage, by your bulk you seem loaded for a West India voyage. You are big enough, with all your papers, to crack twenty stage-coaches. Excuse me, indeed, sir, for you must not enter."

The Bee

The more ornate class of prose is represented by the *Rambler* essays of Johnson and the writings of Gibbon and Burke. Of the three Johnson's style is the most cumbrous, being overloaded with long words and complicated sentences, though it has a massive strength of its own. Gibbon bears his mantle with ease and dignity, and Burke has so much natural vitality that his style hardly weighs upon him at all; he does stumble, but rarely, whereas it is sometimes urged as a fault of the prose of Gibbon that it is so uniformly good that the perfection of it becomes deadening.

A fresh and highly interesting style is the poetic prose of Macpherson's *Ossian*. Macpherson's style is not ornate, for it is drawn from the simplest elements; it possesses a solemnity of expression,

TABLE TO ILLUSTRATE THE DEVELOPMENT OF LITERARY FORMS

Date	POETRY			DRAMA		PROSE		
	Lyrical	Narrative-Descriptive	Satirical and Didactic	Comedy	Tragedy	Novel	Essay	Miscellaneous
1750	Collins	Shenstone Thomson[6]	Johnson[1] Johnson[2]		Johnson[3]	Richardson[13] Fielding[14] Smollett		Hume
1760		Gray[10]			Home	Johnson[5] Sterne	Johnson[4] Goldsmith	Burke Robertson
1770	Chatterton	Goldsmith[7] Chatterton Fergusson	Churchill[12]	Goldsmith[8] Sheridan		Walpole Goldsmith[9] Mackenzie Burney		
1780								Gibbon[15] Cowper
1790	Blake Burns	Crabbe Cowper[11]				Beckford		White
1800					Baillie	Radcliffe Godwin		

---

[1] *London* (1738).
[3] *Irene* (1749).
[6] *Rasselas* (1759).
[7] *The Traveller* (1764).
[9] *The Vicar of Wakefield* (1766).
[11] *The Task* (1785).
[13] *Pamela* (1740).
[15] *The Decline and Fall of the Roman Empire* (1776–88).

[2] *The Vanity of Human Wishes* (1749).
[4] *The Rambler* (1750).
[5] *The Castle of Indolence* (1748).
[8] *The Good-natur'd Man* (1768).
[10] *Elegy written in a Country Churchyard* (1751).
[12] *The Rosciad* (1761).
[14] *Joseph Andrews* (1742).

and so decided a rhythm and cadence, that the effect is almost lyrical. In the passage now given the reader should note that the sentences are nearly of uniform length, and that they could easily be written as separate lines of irregular verse:

Her voice came over the sea. Arindal my son descended from the hill; rough in the spoils of the chase. His arrows rattled by his side; his bow was in his hand; five dark grey dogs attend his steps. He saw fierce Erath on the shore; he seized and bound him to an oak. Thick wind the thongs of the hide around his limbs; he loads the wind with his groans. Arindal ascends the deep in his boat, to bring Daura to land. Armar came in his wrath, and let fly the grey-feathered shaft. It sung: it sunk in thy heart, O Arindal my son; for Erath the traitor thou diedst. The oar is stopped at once; he panted on the rock and expired. What is thy grief, O Daura, when round thy feet is poured thy brother's blood! The boat is broken in twain. Armar plunges into the sea, to rescue his Daura, or die. Sudden a blast from the hill came over the waves. He sank, and he rose no more.

CHAPTER X

THE RETURN TO NATURE

TIME-CHART OF THE CHIEF AUTHORS

The thick line shows the period of important literary work.

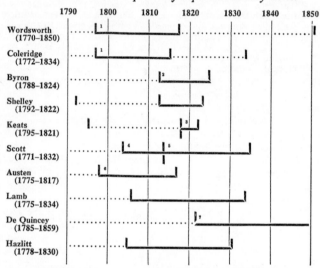

| | 1790 | 1800 | 1810 | 1820 | 1830 | 1840 | 1850 |

Wordsworth (1770–1850)
Coleridge (1772–1834)
Byron (1788–1824)
Shelley (1792–1822)
Keats (1795–1821)
Scott (1771–1832)
Austen (1775–1817)
Lamb (1775–1834)
De Quincey (1785–1859)
Hazlitt (1778–1830)

[1] *Lyrical Ballads* (1798).
[3] *Endymion* (1818).
[5] *Waverley* (1814).
[7] *The Confessions of an English Opium Eater* (1821).
[2] *Childe Harold's Pilgrimage* (1812).
[4] *The Lay of the Last Minstrel* (1805).
[6] *Northanger Abbey* (begun 1798, pub. 1818).

THE HISTORICAL BACKGROUND (1790–1830)

To an overwhelming extent the history of the time is the record of the effects of the French Revolution.

1. The European War. The close of the eighteenth century saw England and France engaged in open warfare (1793). Many causes contributed to set the war in motion, and many more kept it intractably in operation. Hostilities dragged on till 1815, in the end bringing about the extinction of the French Republic, the birth of which was greeted so joyfully by the English Liberals, the rise and destruction of the power of Napoleon, and the restoration of the Bourbon dynasty. These events had their effects in every corner of Europe, and in none more strongly than in England.

2. The Reaction. It has been well said: "At the beginning of every revolution men hope, for they think of all that mankind may gain in a new world; in its next phase they fear, for they think of what mankind may lose." This was the case with the French Revolution. The elder writers of the period, with Wordsworth and Coleridge as conspicuous examples, hailed the new era with joy. Then, as the Revolution proceeded to unexpected developments, there came in turn disappointment, disillusion, dejection, and despair, and, notably in the case of Wordsworth, the rejection of youthful ideals and the soured adoption of the older reactionary faith. The younger writers, such as Leigh Hunt, Shelley, and Keats, still adhered to the Revolutionary doctrines, but the warmth of the early days had already passed away.

3. Social Conditions. The conclusion of the long war brought inevitable misery; low wages, unemployment, and heavy taxation gave rise to fiery resentment and fierce demands on the part of the people. Men like Shelley and Ebenezer Elliott called aloud for social justice; in gentler mood Mrs Hemans and Tom Hood bewailed the social misery. We have the massacre of Peterloo and the wild rioting over the Reform Bill and the Corn Laws.

The Reform Bill (1832) was a grudging concession to the general discontent. To conservative minds, like those of Scott and the maturer Wordsworth, the Bill seemed to pronounce the dissolution of every social tie. But the Bill brought only disappointment to its friends. In the next chapter we shall see how the demand for social amelioration deepened and broadened, and coloured the literature of the time.

The interest in social conditions became intensified toward the end of the nineteenth century, until it has grown to be one of the chief features of modern literature.

THE RETURN TO NATURE

In the last chapter we noted the beginnings and development of the new feeling for nature. This chapter sees the full effects of the movement, and the subsequent reaction that followed.

1. Abundant Output. Even the lavishness of the Elizabethans cannot excel that of this age. The development of new ideas brings fresh inspiration for poetry, and the poetical sky is bright with luminaries of the first magnitude. In prose we may note especially the fruitful yield of the novel, the rejuvenation of the essay, and the unprecedented activity of critical and miscellaneous writers. This is the most fertile period of our literature.

2. Great Range of Subject. The new and buoyant race of writers, especially the poets, lays the knowledge and experience of all ages under a heavy toll. The classical writers are explored anew, and are drawn upon by the genius of Keats and Shelley; the Middle Ages inspire the novels of Scott and the poems of Coleridge, Southey, and many more; modern times are analysed and dissected in the work of the novelists, the satires of Byron, and the productions of the miscellaneous writers. This is indeed the return to nature, for all nature is scrutinized and summed up afresh.

3. Treatment of Nature. If for the moment we take the restricted meaning of the word, and understand by 'nature' the common phenomena of earth, air, and sea, we find the poetical attitude to nature altering profoundly. In the work of Cowper, Crabbe, and Gray the treatment is principally the simple chronicle and sympathetic observation of natural features. In the new race of poets the observation becomes more matured and intimate. Notably in the case of Wordsworth, the feeling for nature rises to a passionate veneration that is love and religion too. To Wordsworth nature is not only a procession of seasons and seasonal fruition: it is the eye of all things, natural and supernatural, into which the observant soul can peer and behold the spirit that inhabits all things. Nature is thus amplified and glorified; it is to be sought, not only in the flowers and the fields, but also in

> the light of setting suns,
> And the round ocean and the living air,
> And the blue sky, and in the mind of man.

4. Political and Periodical Writing. The age did not produce a pamphleteer of the first class like Swift or Burke, but the turbulence of the period was clearly marked in the immense productivity of its political writers. The number of periodicals was greatly augmented, and we notice the first of the great daily journals that are still a strong element in literature and politics. *The Morning Chronicle* (1769) was started by William Woodfall, *The Morning Post* (1772) by a syndicate of London tradesmen, and *The Times* (1785), under the name of *The Daily Universal Register*, by John Walter. Of a more irresponsible type were the Radical *Political Register* (1802) of Cobbett and *The Examiner* (1808) of Leigh Hunt. A race of powerful literary magazines sprang to life: *The Edinburgh Review* (1802), *The Quarterly Review* (1809), *Blackwood's Magazine* (1817), *The London Magazine* (1820), and *The Westminster Review* (1824). Such excellent publications reacted strongly upon authorship, and were responsible for much of the best work of Hazlitt, Lamb, Southey, and a host of other miscellaneous writers.

5. The Influence of Germany. The increasing bitterness of the long war with France almost extinguished the literary influence of the French language, which, as was indicated in the last chapter, had been affecting English literature deeply. In the place of French, the study of German literature and learning came rapidly into favour. The first poetical work of Scott is based on the German, and the effects of the new influence can be further observed in the works of Coleridge, Shelley, Byron, and many more. In the course of time German increased its hold upon English, until by the middle of the nineteenth century it was perhaps the dominating foreign tongue.

6. American Literature. Already the infant nation across the Atlantic was showing promise of a literary future. As might be expected, the first efforts were largely imitations of the more mature English products; but in Fenimore Cooper the novel had a good beginning, and Washington Irving is the first of the line of notable American men of letters.

POETS

I. WILLIAM WORDSWORTH (1770–1850)

1. His Life. Wordsworth was born at Cockermouth, a town which is actually outside the Lake District, but well within hail of it. His father, who was a lawyer, died when William was thirteen years old. The elder Wordsworth left very little money, and that was mainly in the form of a claim on Lord Lonsdale, who refused outright to pay his debt, so that William had to depend on the generosity of two uncles, who paid for his schooling at Hawkshead, near Lake Windermere. Subsequently Wordsworth went to Cambridge, entering St John's College in 1787. His work at the university was quite undistinguished, and having graduated in 1791 he left with no fixed career in view. After spending a few months in London he crossed over to France (1791), and stayed at Orléans and Blois for nearly a year. An enthusiasm for the Revolution was aroused in him; he himself has chronicled the mood in one of his happiest passages:

> Bliss was it in that dawn to be alive,
> But to be young was very heaven!

He returned to Paris in 1792, just after the September massacres, and the sights and stories that greeted him there shook his faith in the dominant political doctrine. Even yet, however, he thought of becoming a Girondin, or moderate Republican, but his allowance from home was stopped, and he returned to England. With his sister Dorothy (henceforward his lifelong companion) he settled in a little cottage in Dorset; then, having met Coleridge, they moved to Alfoxden, a house in Somersetshire, in order to live near him. It was there that the two poets took the series of walks the fruit of which was to be the *Lyrical Ballads*.

After a visit to Germany in 1798–99 the Wordsworths settled in the Lake District, which was to be their home for the future. In turn they occupied Dove Cottage, at Town End, Grasmere (1799), Allan Bank (1808), Grasmere Parsonage (1811), and lastly the well-known residence of Rydal Mount, which was Wordsworth's home from 1813 till his death. Shortly before he had moved to Rydal Mount he received the sinecure of Distributor of Stamps for Westmorland, and was put out of reach of poverty.

The remainder of his life was a model of domesticity. He was carefully tended by his wife and sister, who, with a zeal that was noteworthy, though it was injudicious, treasured every scrap of his poetry that they could lay their hands on. His great passion was for travelling. He explored most of the accessible parts of the Continent, and visited Scotland several times. On the last occasion (1831) he and his daughter renewed their acquaintance with Scott at Abbotsford, and saw the great novelist when he was fast crumbling into mental ruin. Wordsworth's poetry, which at first had been received with derision or indifference, was now winning its way, and recognition was general. In 1839 Oxford conferred upon him the degree of D.C.L.; in 1842 the Crown awarded him a pension of £300 a year; and on the death of Southey in 1843 he became Poet Laureate.

Long before this time he had discarded his early ideals and

become the upholder of conservatism. Perhaps he is not "the lost leader" whose recantation Browning bewails with rather theatrical woe; but he lived to deplore the Reform Bill and to oppose the causes to which his early genius had been dedicated. Throughout his life, however, he never wavered in his faith in himself and his immortality as a poet. He lived to see his own belief in his powers triumphantly justified. It is seldom indeed that such gigantic egoism is so amply and so justly repaid.

2. **His Poetry.** He records that his earliest verses were written at school, and that they were "a tame imitation of Pope's versification." This is an interesting admission of the still surviving domination of the earlier poet. At the university he composed some poetry, which appeared as *An Evening Walk* (1793) and *Descriptive Sketches* (1793). In style these poems have little originality, but they already show the Wordsworthian eye for nature. The first fruits of his genius were seen in the *Lyrical Ballads* (1798), a joint production by Coleridge and himself, which was published at Bristol.

Regarding the inception of this remarkable book both Wordsworth and Coleridge have left accounts, which vary to some extent, though not materially. Coleridge's may be taken as the more plausible. He says in his *Biographia Literaria*:

> it was agreed that my endeavours should be directed to persons and characters supernatural, or at least romantic, yet so as to transfer from our inward nature a human interest and a semblance of truth sufficient to procure for these shadows of imagination that willing suspension of disbelief for the moment which constitutes poetic faith. Mr Wordsworth, on the other hand, was to propose to himself as his object, to give the charm of novelty to things of every day, and to excite a feeling analogous to the supernatural, by awakening the mind's attention to the lethargy of custom, and directing it to the loveliness and the wonders of the world before us.

This volume is epoch-making, for it is the prelude to the Romantic movement proper. Wordsworth had the larger share in the book. Some of his poems in it, such as *The Thorn* and *The Idiot Boy*, are condemned as being trivial and childish in style; a few, such as *Simon Lee* and *Expostulation and Reply*, are more adequate in their expression; and the concluding piece, *Tintern Abbey*, is one of the triumphs of his genius.

During the years 1798-99 Wordsworth composed some of his finest poems, which appeared in 1800, together with his contributions to the *Lyrical Ballads*. Among the most noteworthy of the new works in this collection were *Michael, The Old Cumberland Beggar*,

She dwelt among the untrodden ways, Strange fits of passion have I known, and *Nutting.* Although some of them, such as *Michael* and *The Old Cumberland Beggar*, are uneven in quality, the new poems show Wordsworth less preoccupied with his theories of poetic diction, and the lyrics are striking in their moving restraint and delicacy of touch.

The Prelude, which was completed in 1805 but not published until 1850, after Wordsworth's death, is the record of his development as a poet. He describes his experiences with a fullness, closeness, and laborious anxiety that are unique in our literature. The poem, which runs to fourteen books, is often dull and prosy, but at times, particularly when he is describing the formative influence of nature, and his emotions when confronted by seemingly unreal natural objects, the blank verse is impassioned, and inspired by his exaltation, wonder, and awe. Such are the famous passages on skating and boating.

The Prelude was intended to form part of a vast philosophical work called *The Recluse* which was never completed. Another section of this same work was *The Excursion*, much of which was composed in the years now under review, though it was not published until 1814. It lacks the greatness of the finest parts of *The Prelude*, and its nine long books are, on the whole, rather monotonous and uninspired, and often prosaic. Even so, it does contain some good pictures and tales of country life.

Next to be published, in 1807, were two volumes of poems which represent the fine flower of his genius. It is impossible here to list even the very great poems in these volumes, but in every poetic form that he used, with the possible exception of the narrative, Wordsworth is here seen at the height of his powers. To mention but a few of the successes of this volume, we have, in the lyric vein, *The Solitary Reaper, The Green Linnet, I wandered lonely as a cloud*; in the philosophical, *Ode on the Intimations of Immortality, Resolution and Independence, Ode to Duty*; and the *Sonnets dedicated to National Independence and Liberty* are of a quality which has led many critics to hail them as the finest sonnets in the language.

After the publication of *The Excursion* Wordsworth's poetical power was clearly on the wane, but his productivity was unimpaired. His later volumes include *The White Doe of Rylstone* (1815), *The Waggoner* (1819), *Peter Bell* (1819), *Yarrow Revisited* (1835), and *The Borderers* (1842), a drama. The progress of the works marks the decline in an increasing degree. There are flashes of the old spirit, such as we see in his lines upon the death of "the Ettrick Shepherd"; but the fire and stately intonation become rarer, and mere garrulity becomes more and more apparent.

3. His Theory of Poetry. In the preface to the second edition of the *Lyrical Ballads* (1800) Wordsworth set out his theory of poetry. It reveals a lofty conception of the dignity of that art which is "the breath and finer spirit of all knowledge," and which is the product of "the spontaneous overflow of powerful feelings," taking its origin from "emotion recollected in tranquillity." The qualifications of the poet are on a level with the dignity of his art. To Wordsworth, he is a man "possessed of more than usual organic sensibility," and one who has also "thought long and deeply." How far this view differs from that of poetry as a graceful social accomplishment is quite obvious: it partly explains Wordsworth's sense of his own importance. Apart from these general views on the poet and his art, Wordsworthian dogma can be divided into two portions concerning (*a*) the subject and (*b*) the style of poetry.

(*a*) Regarding subject, Wordsworth declares his preference for "incidents and situations from common life": to obtain such situations, "humble and rustic life was generally chosen, because in that condition the essential passions of the heart find a better soil in which they can attain their maturity." Over these incidents Wordsworth proposes to throw "a certain colouring of the imagination whereby ordinary things should be presented to the mind in an unusual aspect."

(*b*) Wordsworth's views on poetical style are the most revolutionary of all the ideas in this preface. Discarding the "gaudiness and inane phraseology of many modern writers," he insists that his poems contain little poetic diction, and are written in "a selection of the real language of men in a state of vivid sensation." His views on poetic diction he summed up with these words: "there neither is nor can be any *essential* difference between the language of prose and metrical composition."

The extent to which Wordsworth's own practice as a poet justified his theories is a question which has long occupied the attention of critics. In the realm of subject matter he remained staunch to his declared opinions, for the majority of his poems deal with humble and rustic life. That he was aware of the dangers inherent in his theory he makes clear in these words: "in some instances, feelings, even of the ludicrous, may have been given to my readers by expressions which appeared to me tender and pathetic." It is in this way that he sometimes fails. Generally, though, when Wordsworth writes under a strong emotional stimulus, his style is free from banality and prosaisms. It is touchingly simple in some of his *Lucy* poems, gay and joyous in other lyrics, and vigorous, with something of a Miltonic sweep and resonance, in his greatest sonnets and blank verse. In truth, though in his best blank verse it is fired by the passion of his imaginative insight to a grandeur above ordinary speech, it does not stray very far from the *selection* of the real language of men which he advocated. At other times, however, when the emotional stimulus is small or entirely lacking, he writes with his theories in the forefront of his mind, and the result is the prosaic banality of some sections of *Simon Lee*.

4. Features of his Poetry. (*a*) *Its Inequality and its Limitations.* All the critics of Wordsworth are at pains to point out the mass of inferior work that came from his pen. Matthew Arnold, one of the acutest of the poet's admirers, closes the record of Wordsworth's best work with the year 1808, even before the completion of *The Excursion*. This poem is long, meditative, and often prosaic, and these tendencies become more marked as the years pass. Before the year 1808 he had produced poems as intensely and artistically beautiful as any in the language. It was hard, however, for Wordsworth to appreciate his limitations, which were many and serious. He had little sense of humour, a scanty dramatic power, and only a meagre narrative gift, but he strove to exploit all these qualities in his work. His one drama, *The Borderers*, was only a partial success, and his narrative poems, like *Ruth* and *The White Doe of Rylstone*, are not among the best of his work.

(*b*) *Its Egoism.* In a person of lesser calibre such a degree of self-esteem as Wordsworth's would have been ridiculous; in his case, with the undoubted genius that was in the man, it was something almost heroic. Domestic circumstances—the adoration of his wife and sister and the cloistral seclusion of the life he led—confirmed him in the habit of taking himself too seriously. The best of his shorter poems deal with his own experiences; and his longest works, *The Prelude* and *The Excursion*, describe his spiritual development in the most minute detail.

(*c*) In spite of this self-obsession he is curiously deficient in the purely *lyrical* gift. He cannot bare his bosom, as Burns does; he cannot leap into the ether like Shelley. Yet he excels, especially in the face of nature, in the expression of a reflective and analytic mood which is both personal and general. The following lyric illustrates this mood to perfection:

> My heart leaps up when I behold
> A rainbow in the sky:
> So was it when my life began;
> So is it now I am a man;
> So be it when I shall grow old,
> Or let me die!
> The Child is father of the Man;
> And I could wish my days to be
> Bound each to each by natural piety.

Sometimes he does touch on intimate emotions, but then he tends to be restrained, hinting at rather than proclaiming the passions that he feels. The series of *Lucy* poems are typical of their kind:

> She dwelt among the untrodden ways
> Beside the springs of Dove,
> A Maid whom there were none to praise,
> And very few to love.
>
> A violet by a mossy stone
> Half hidden from the eye!
> Fair as a star, when only one
> Is shining in the sky.
>
> She lived unknown, and few could know
> When Lucy ceased to be;
> But she is in her grave, and, oh,
> The difference to me!

Such a lyrical gift, reflective rather than passionate, finds a congenial mode of expression in the sonnet, the most complicated and expository of the lyrical forms. In his sonnets his lyrical mood burns clear and strong, and as a result they rank among the best in English poetry. Wordsworth's use of the Petrarchan form was so striking that he re-established its supremacy over the Shakespearian sonnet, which had eclipsed it in popularity during the last great age of sonneteering—the Elizabethan. The influence of Milton is clearly felt, and the sonnets have strength, flexibility, and, in many cases, a controlled intensity of feeling. Some of them are patriotic, others express his passion for liberty, and yet others, such as the famous one composed on Westminster Bridge, deal with nature. All show clearly the beneficial influence on Wordsworth of the restrictions of the sonnet form, whose fourteen lines curbed his tendency toward prolixity.

(*d*) *His Treatment of Nature.* His dealings with nature are his chief glory as a poet.

(1) His treatment is accurate and first-hand. As he explained, he wrote with his eye "steadily fixed on the object." Even the slightest of his poems have evidence of close observation:

> The cattle are grazing,
> Their heads never raising;
> There are forty feeding like one.

The most polished of his poems have the same stamp, as can be seen in *Resolution and Independence.* "The image of the hare," he says with reference to this poem, quoted below. "I then observed on the ridge of the Fell."

> There was a roaring in the wind all night;
> The rain came heavily and fell in floods;
> But now the sun is rising calm and bright;
> The birds are singing in the distant woods;
> Over his own sweet voice the Stock-dove broods;
> The Jay makes answer as the Magpie chatters;
> And all the air is filled with pleasant noise of waters.
>
> All things that love the sun are out of doors;
> The sky rejoices in the morning's birth;
> The grass is bright with rain-drops;—on the moors
> The hare is running races in her mirth;
> And with her feet she from the plashy earth
> Raises a mist, that, glittering in the sun,
> Runs with her all the way, wherever she doth run.

(2) This personal dealing with nature in all her moods produces a joy, a plenteousness of delight, that to most readers is Wordsworth's most appealing charm. Before the beauty of nature he is never paltry; he is nearly always adequate; and that is perhaps the highest achievement that he ever desired. The extracts just quoted are outstanding examples of this aspect of his poetry.

(3) In his treatment of nature, however, he is not content merely to rejoice: he tries to see more deeply and to find the secret springs of this joy and thanksgiving. He says:

> To me the meanest flower that blows can give
> Thoughts that do often lie too deep for tears.

He strives to capture and embody in words such deep-seated emotions, but, almost of necessity, from the very nature of the case, with little success. He gropes in the shadows, and comes away with empty hands. He cannot solve the riddle of

> those obstinate questionings
> Of sense and outward things,
> Fallings from us, vanishings.

Yet, with a remarkable fusion of sustained thought and of poetic imagination, he does convey the idea of "the Being that is in the clouds and air," the soul that penetrates all things, the spirit, the mystical essence, the divine knowledge that, as far as he was concerned, lies behind all nature. Lastly, in one of the most exalted poetical efforts in any language, he puts into words the idea of the continuity of life that runs through all existence:

> Our birth is but a sleep and a forgetting:
> The Soul that rises with us, our life's Star
>   Hath had elsewhere its setting,
>   And cometh from afar;
>   Not in entire forgetfulness,
>   And not in utter nakedness,
> But trailing clouds of glory do we come
>   From God, who is our home.
>   *Ode: Intimations of Immortality*

(4) This deeper insight underlying Wordsworth's treatment of nature distinguishes him from many lesser poets. Though he is no inconsiderable landscape painter, as the opening lines of *Tintern Abbey* will show, he is seldom content to draw beautiful scenes for their own sake. He looks on nature to hear "the still, sad music of humanity," and his portrayal of man seen against a background of nature gives rise to some of his best-known poems, such as *The Solitary Reaper*, *Resolution and Independence*, and *Michael*. These figures have something of the strength, dignity, and austerity of their settings. Even more striking are the poems such as *Tintern Abbey*, *Ode on the Intimations of Immortality*, and some parts of *The Prelude*, which trace the development of his own relations with nature, from his boyish days with their "glad animal movements," through his youth, when natural beauty

> had no need of a remoter charm
> By thought supplied, nor any interest
> Unborrowed from the eye. . . .

to his maturity, of which he wrote,

> For I have learned
> To look on nature, not as in the hour
> Of thoughtless youth; but hearing oftentimes
> The still, sad music of humanity,
> Nor harsh nor grating, though of ample power
> To chasten and subdue. And I have felt
> A presence that disturbs me with the joy
> Of elevated thoughts; a sense sublime
> Of something far more deeply interfused,
> Whose dwelling is the light of setting suns,
> And the round ocean and the living air,
> And the blue sky, and in the mind of man:
> A motion and a spirit, that impels
> All thinking things, all objects of all thought,
> And rolls through all things.

(e) In *style* Wordsworth presents a remarkable contrast, for he ranges from the sublime (as in the extract last quoted) to the ridiculous:

> In the sweet shire of Cardigan,
> Not far from pleasant Ivor-hall,
> An old Man dwells, a little man,—
> 'Tis said he once was tall.
> Full five-and-thirty years he lived
> A running huntsman merry;
> And still the centre of his cheek
> Is red as a ripe cherry.
>
> *Simon Lee*

This verse illustrates the lower ranges of his style, when he is hagridden with his theories of poetic diction. The first two lines are mediocre; the second pair are absurd; and the rest of the verse is middling. This is simplicity overdone; yet it is always to be remembered that at his best Wordsworth can unite simplicity with sublimity, as he does in the lyrics we have already quoted. He has a kind of middle style; at its best it has grace and dignity, a heart-searching simplicity, and a certain magical enlightenment of phrase that is all his own. Not Shakespeare himself can better Wordsworth when the latter is in a mood that produces a poem like the following:

> "She shall be sportive as the fawn
> That wild with glee across the lawn,
> Or up the mountain springs;
> And hers shall be the breathing balm,
> And hers the silence and the calm,
> Of mute insensate things.

"The floating clouds their state shall lend
To her; for her the willow bend;
Nor shall she fail to see
Even in the motions of the Storm
Grace that shall mould the Maiden's form
By silent sympathy.

"The stars of midnight shall be dear
To her; and she shall lean her ear
In many a secret place
Where rivulets dance their wayward round,
And beauty born of murmuring sound
Shall pass into her face."
Three Years she grew in Sun and Shower

II. SAMUEL TAYLOR COLERIDGE (1772–1834)

1. His Life. Coleridge was born in Devonshire, and was the youngest of the thirteen children of the vicar of Ottery St Mary. As a child he was unusually precocious: "I never thought as a child," he says, "never had the language of a child." When he was nine years old his father died; he then obtained a place in Christ's Hospital, where he astonished his schoolmates, one of whom was Charles Lamb, with his queer tastes in reading and speculation. He went to Cambridge (1791), where he was fired with the revolutionary doctrines. He abandoned the university and enlisted in the Light Dragoons, but a few months as a soldier ended his military career. In 1794 he returned to Cambridge, and later in the year became acquainted at Oxford with Southey, with whom he planned the founding of an ideal republic in America. With Southey he lived for a space at Bristol, and there he met Southey's wife's sister, whom he eventually married. At Bristol Coleridge lectured, wrote poetry, and issued a newspaper called *The Watchman* (1796), all with the idea of converting humanity; yet in spite of it all humanity remained unperturbed in its original sin. At this time (1797) he met Wordsworth, and, as has already been noticed, planned their joint production of the *Lyrical Ballads*, which was published at Bristol.

After a brief spell as a Unitarian minister, Coleridge, who was now dependent on a small annuity from two rich friends, studied German philosophy on the Continent; returned to England (1799), and for a time lived in the Lake District. There followed a serious attempt at political journalism, which failed because of his constitutional incapacity to provide regular contributions. In 1800 he was at Keswick, and, during what was to be his final period of great poetical inspiration, produced the second part of *Christabel* and his ode *Dejection*. By now he was in almost continual ill-health, and by 1803 he had become enslaved to the opium which was to have such disastrous effect upon him. Ill-health and an unhappy domestic life sent him abroad to Malta and Italy (1804–06), and on his return he began a period of restless wandering round the country, never staying very long anywhere. It was during these restless years that his lectures were given, starting with a very poor series at the Royal Institution in 1808. The year 1811 saw his finest series of lectures, those on Shakespeare and other poets, which were followed by a further series in 1812 and 1813. During this period he struggled with little success to break himself of the opium habit which was sapping his abilities, and then, in 1816, he entered the house of a Mr Gillman, in Highgate. This provided for him a kind of refined and sympathetic inebriates' home. Here he gradually shook himself free from opium-taking, and he spent the last years of his life in an atmosphere of subdued content, visited by his friends, and conversing interminably in that manner of wandering but luminous intelligence that marked his later years. From the house in Highgate he issued a few books that, with all their faults, are among the best of their class.

2. His Poetry. The real blossoming of Coleridge's poetical genius was brief indeed, but the fruit of it was rich and wonderful. With the exception of a very few pieces, the best of his poems were composed within two years, 1797–98.

His first book was *Poems on Various Subjects* (1796), issued at Bristol. The miscellaneous poems that the volume contains have only a very moderate merit. Then, in collaboration with Wordsworth, he produced the *Lyrical Ballads* (1798). This remarkable volume contains nineteen poems by Wordsworth and four by Coleridge; and of these four by far the most noteworthy is *The Rime of the Ancient Mariner*.

Wordsworth has set on record the origin of *The Ancient Mariner*. He and Coleridge discussed the poem during their walks on the Quantock Hills. The main idea of the voyage, founded on a dream of his own, was Coleridge's; Wordsworth suggested details, and they thought of working on it together. Very soon, however, Coleridge's imagination was fired with the story, and his friend very sensibly left him to write it all. Hence we have that marvellous series of dissolving pictures, so curiously distinct and yet so strangely fused into one: the voyage through the polar ice; the death of the albatross; the amazing scenes during the calm and the storm; and the return home. In style, in swift stealthiness of narrative speed, and in its weird and compelling strength of imagination the poem is without a parallel.

In 1797 Coleridge also wrote the first part of *Christabel*, but, though a second part was added in 1800, the poem remained unfinished, and lay unpublished till 1816. *Christabel* is the tale of a kind of witch, who, by taking the shape of a lovely lady, wins the confidence of the heroine Christabel. The tale is barely begun when it collapses. Already Coleridge's fatal indecision is declaring itself. Incomplete as it is, and with its second part somewhat inferior to its first, the poem is yet clear evidence of Coleridge's superlative power as a poet. The supernatural atmosphere is here less obviously created than in *The Ancient Mariner*; Coleridge relies on the most delicate and subtle suggestion, hidden in minute but highly significant details in the story. There are passages of wonderful beauty and of charming natural description, though they scarcely reach the heights of *The Ancient Mariner*. The metre, now known as the *Christabel* metre, is a loose but exceedingly melodious form of the octosyllabic couplet full of skilful rhythmic variations. It became exceedingly popular, and its influence is still unimpaired. We give a brief extract to show the metre, and also to give a slight idea of the poet's descriptive power:

> There is not wind enough to twirl
> The one red leaf, the last of its clan,
> That dances as often as dance it can,
> Hanging so light, and hanging so high,
> On the topmost twig that looks up at the sky.

Kubla Khan, written in 1798, was, like *Christabel*, unfinished, and it also remained unpublished until 1816. It is the echo of a dream—the shadow of a shadow. Coleridge avers that he dreamt the lines, awoke in a fever of inspiration, threw the words on paper, but before the fit was over was distracted from the composition, so that the glory of the dream never returned and *Kubla Khan* remained unfinished. The poem, beginning with a description of the stately pleasure-dome built by Kubla Khan in Xanadu, soon becomes a dreamlike series of dissolving views, each expressed in the most perfect imagery and most magical of verbal music, but it collapses in mid-career.

In the same year Coleridge composed several other poems,

including the fine *Frost at Midnight* and *France: An Ode.* In 1802 he wrote the great ode *Dejection*, in which he already bewails the suspension of his "shaping spirit of Imagination." Save for a few fragments, such as the beautiful epitaph *The Knight's Tomb*, the remainder of his poems are of poorer quality and slight in bulk. His play *Remorse* was, on the recommendation of Byron, accepted by the management of the Drury Lane Theatre and produced in 1813. It succeeded on the stage, but as literature it is of little importance.

3. Features of his Poetry. Within its peculiar limits his poetical work, slight though it is, is of the highest.

(*a*) The most conspicuous feature of the poems is their intense *imaginative power*, superbly controlled, in his finest poems, by his unerring artistic sense. It exploits the weird, the supernatural, and the obscure. Yet, such is the power of true imagination, it can produce what Coleridge calls "that willing suspension of disbelief," and for the moment he can compel us to believe it all. He sees nature with a penetrating and revealing glance, drawing from it inspiration for the stuff of his poetry. He is particularly fine in his descriptions of the sky and the sea and the wider and more remote aspects of things.

(*b*) No poet has ever excelled Coleridge in *witchery of language*. His is the song the sirens sang. *The Ancient Mariner* has more than one passage like the following:

> And now 'twas like all instruments,
> Now like a lonely flute;
> And now it is an angel's song,
> That makes the heavens be mute.
>
> It ceased; yet still the sails made on
> A pleasant noise till noon,
> A noise like of a hidden brook
> In the leafy month of June,
> That to the sleeping woods all night
> Singeth a quiet tune.

The epitaph we have mentioned is another fine example:

> Where is the grave of Sir Arthur O'Kellyn?
> Where may the grave of that good man be?
> By the side of a spring, on the breast of Helvellyn,
> Under the twigs of a young birch tree.
> The oak that in summer was sweet to hear,
> And rustled its leaves in the fall of the year,

And whistled and roared in the winter alone,
Is gone,—and the birch in its stead is grown.—
The knight's bones are dust,
And his good sword rust:—
His soul is with the saints, I trust.

The reader of such passages can discover something of the secret of their charm by observing the dexterous handling of the metre, the vowel-music, and other technical features, but in the last analysis their beauty defies explanation: it is there that genius lies.

(c) Along with his explosive fervour Coleridge preserves a fine *simplicity of diction*. He appeals directly to the reader's imagination by writing with great clearness. In this respect he often closely resembles Wordsworth. His meditative poem *Frost at Midnight* strongly shows this resemblance:

Therefore all seasons shall be sweet to thee,
Whether the summer clothe the general earth
With greenness, or the redbreast sit and sing
Betwixt the tufts of snow on the bare branch
Of mossy apple-tree, while the nigh thatch
Smokes in the sun-thaw; whether the eave-drops fall
Heard only in the trances of the blast,
Or if the secret ministry of frost
Shall hang them up in silent icicles,
Quietly shining to the quiet moon.

4. His Prose. The same blight that afflicted Coleridge's poetry lies upon his prose. It is scrappy, chaotic, and tentative. In bulk it is large and sprawling; in manner it is diffuse and involved; but in its happier moments it possesses a breadth, a depth, and a searching wisdom that are as rare as they are admirable.

Most of his prose was of journalistic origin. In theme it is chiefly philosophical or literary. In 1796 he started *The Watchman*, a periodical, ambitious in scope, which ran to ten numbers only. To this journal Coleridge contributed some typical essays, which, among much that is both obscure and formless, show considerable weight and acuteness of thought. He followed with much more miscellaneous prose, some of it being written for *The Morning Post*, to which he was for a time a contributor. In 1808 he began a series of lectures on poetry and allied subjects, but already the curse of opium was upon him, and the lectures were failures. While he resided in the Lake District he started *The Friend* (1809), which was published at Penrith, but like *The Watchman* it had a brief career.

Then in 1817, when he had shaken himself free from opium, he published *Biographia Literaria* and *Sibylline Leaves*.

Biographia Literaria is his most valuable prose work. It pretends to record his literary upbringing, but as a consecutive narrative it is quite worthless. After sixteen chapters of philosophizing, almost entirely irrelevant, he discusses the poetical theory of his friend Wordsworth, and then in the last seven chapters of the book he gives a remarkable demonstration of his critical powers. He analyses the Wordsworthian theory in masterly fashion, and, separating the good from the bad, upon the sounder elements bases a critical dogma of great and permanent value. These last chapters of the book, which are the most enduring exposition of the Romantic theory as it exists in English, place Coleridge in the first flight of critics.

Second only in importance to *Biographia Literaria* in establishing Coleridge as the greatest of English critics are his lectures on Shakespeare and other poets, delivered at intervals between 1808 and 1819. It is unfortunate that they were never prepared for publication by Coleridge himself, and that we have to rely on the imperfect records, prepared from notes and reports by his daughter in 1836, and by Payne Collier in 1856. As a result, the lectures, as we have them, lack the finish of works properly prepared for publication. None the less they show Coleridge as a giant in the ranks of English critics. His examination of Shakespeare's plays and of poems by other writers gives us something more than an acute, logical dissection according to certain predetermined canons; it is subtly suggestive, stimulating the reader to keener perceptions, and formulating for him his own vague, half-crystallized reactions. Every work of art he sees as an organic, developing whole, subject only to the laws of its own existence. A true romantic, Coleridge revolts against the Augustan conception of poetry as an art to instruct. For him the aim of poetry is to provide pleasure—pleasure "through the medium of beauty."

In addition, he wrote (1825) *Aids to Reflection*. But he seemed to be incapable of writing a work of any size. After his death his *Table Talk* was published (1835), giving fleeting glimpses of a brilliant and erratic mind.

We give a short extract from his prose. This shows not only his sincere and temperate admiration for the poems of Wordsworth, but also the nature of his prose style. As a style it is not wholly commendable. It is too involved, and clogged with qualifications and digressions; but, though he develops his ideas in a curious indirect fashion, he makes rapid progress. At its best Coleridge's prose has much of the evocative suggestiveness of his finest poetry, and is an admirable stimulus to keener perception in the reader, while his choice of language is discriminating, particularly in the fine distinctions he makes while describing the processes of artistic creation.

> Had Mr Wordsworth's poems been the silly, the childish things, which they were for a long time described as being; had they been really distinguished from the compositions of other poets merely by meanness of language and inanity of thought; had they indeed contained nothing more than what is found in the parodies and pretended imitations of them; they must have sunk at once, a dead weight, into the slough of oblivion, and have dragged the preface along with them. But year after year increased the number of Mr Wordsworth's admirers. They were found, too, not in the lower classes of the reading public, but chiefly among young men of strong sensibility and meditative minds; and their admiration (inflamed perhaps in some degree by opposition) was distinguished by its intensity, I might almost say, by its *religious* fervour. These facts, and the intellectual energy of the author, which was more or less consciously felt, where it was outwardly and even boisterously denied, meeting with sentiments of aversion to his opinions, and of alarm at their consequences, produced an eddy of criticism, which would of itself have borne up the poems by the violence with which it whirled them round and round. With many parts of this preface, in the sense attributed to them, and which the words undoubtedly seem to authorise, I never concurred; but on the contrary objected to them as erroneous in principle, and as contradictory (in appearance at least) both to other parts of the same preface, and to the author's own practice in the greater part of the poems themselves. Mr Wordsworth in his recent collection has, I find, degraded this prefatory disquisition to the end of his second volume, to be read or not at the reader's choice. But he has not, as far as I can discover, announced any change in his poetic creed.
>
> *Biographia Literaria*

III. LORD BYRON (1788–1824)

1. His Life. George Gordon Byron, sixth Lord Byron, was as proud of his ancestry as he was of his poetry, and his ancestors were as extraordinary as was his poetry. They stretched back to the Norman Conquest, and included among them a notorious admiral, Byron's grandfather. The poet's father was a rake and a scoundrel. He married a Scottish heiress, Miss Gordon of Gight, whose money he was not long in squandering. Though the poet was born in London, his early years were passed in Aberdeen, his mother's native place. At the age of ten he succeeded his grand-uncle in the title and in the possession of the ruinous Abbey of Newstead, and Scotland was left behind for ever. He was educated at Harrow and Cambridge, where he showed himself to be heir to the ancestral nature, dark and passionate, but relieved by humour and affection. All his life through Byron cultivated the sombre and theatrical side of his disposition, which latterly became a byword; but there can be little doubt that his 'Byronic' temperament was not entirely affected. His mother, a foolish, unbalanced woman, warped the boy's temper still more by her frequent follies and frenzies. The recollection of the tortures he underwent in the fruitless effort to cure him of a malformity of his foot remained with him till his death.

Leaving the university (1808), he remained for a while at Newstead, where with a few congenial youths he plunged into orgies of puerile dissipation. In the fashion of the time, he gloried in the reputation he was acquiring for being a dare-devil, but he lived to pay for it. Wearying of loose delights, he travelled for a couple of years upon the Continent (1809–11). He had previously taken his seat in the House of Lords, but made no mark in political affairs.

Then with a sudden bound he leaped into the limelight. *Childe Harold's Pilgrimage* (1812), his poem on his travels, became all the rage. He found himself the darling of society, in which his youth, his title, his physical beauty, his wit, and his picturesque and romantic melancholy made him a marvel and a delight. He married an heiress (1815), but after a year his wife left him. Regarding his conduct dark rumours grew apace; his popularity waned, and in the face of a storm of abuse he left England for good (1816). For the last eight years of his life he wandered about the Continent, visiting Switzerland, where he met Shelley, and, later, Italy. Finally the cause of Greek independence caught his fancy. He devoted his money, which was inconsiderable, and the weight of his name, which was gigantic, to the Greeks, who proved to be very ungrateful allies. He died of fever at Missolonghi, and his body was given a grand funeral in the England that had cast him out.

2. His Poetry. Byron's first volume was a juvenile effort, *Hours of Idleness* (1807), which was little more than the elegant trifling of a lord who condescends to be a minor poet. This frail production was roughly handled by *The Edinburgh Review*, and Byron, who never lacked spirit, retorted with some effect. He composed a satire in the style of Pope, calling it *English Bards and Scotch Reviewers* (1809). The poem is immature, being often crudely expressed, and it throws abuse recklessly upon good writers and bad; but in the handling of the couplet it already shows some of the Byronic force and pungency. The poem is also of interest in that it lets us see how much he is influenced by the preceding age.

> Next view in state, proud prancing on his roan,
> The golden-crested haughty Marmion,
> Now forging scrolls, now foremost in the fight,
> Not quite a felon, yet but half a knight,
> The gibbet or the field prepared to grace;
> A mighty mixture of the great and base.
> And think'st thou, Scott! by vain conceit perchance,
> On public taste to foist thy stale romance,
> Though Murray with his Miller may combine
> To yield thy muse just half-a-crown per line?

Then followed the two years of travel, which had their fruit in the first two cantos of *Childe Harold's Pilgrimage* (1812). The hero of the poem is a romantic youth, and is very clearly Byron himself. He is very grand and terrible, and sinister with the stain of a dark and awful past. He visits some of the popular beauty-spots of the Continent, which he describes in Spenserian stanzas of moderate skill and attractiveness. The poem is diffuse, but sometimes it can be terse and energetic; the style is half-heartedly old-fashioned, in deference to the stanza. Byron is to do much better things, but already he shows a real appreciation of nature, and considerable dexterity in the handling of his metre.

> On, on the vessel flies, the land is gone,
> And winds are rude in Biscay's sleepless bay.
> Four days are sped, but with the fifth, anon,
> New shores descried make every bosom gay;
> And Cintra's mountain greets them on their way
> And Tagus dashing onward to the deep,
> His fabled golden tribute bent to pay;
> And soon on board the Lusian pilots leap,
> And steer 'twixt fertile shores where yet few rustics reap.

Childe Harold brought its author a dower of fame, which in the next few years he was to squander to the uttermost. In the intervals of society functions he produced poetic tales in astonishing profusion: *The Giaour* and *The Bride of Abydos* in 1813, *The Corsair* and *Lara* in 1814, *The Siege of Corinth* and *Parisina* in 1815 (published 1816). These tales deal with the romantic scenes of the East; they almost uniformly reproduce the young Byronic hero of *Childe Harold*; and to a great extent they are mannered and stagy.

Written in the couplet form, the verse is founded on that of the metrical tales of Scott, whom Byron was not long in supplanting in popular favour, although the masculine action of Scott's poems is lacking from his work. Instead there are vehement passions, which give his stories an impetuosity and speed quite different from the easy lucidity of Scott's narrative poems. A vividness of description, based on Byron's own experience of Mediterranean countries, fills them with patches of striking colour, but, though *The Giaour*, *The Bride of Abydos*, and *Parisina* are written in a more natural style than *The Corsair* and *Lara*, all reveal the lack of melody, the unevenness, and, in varying degrees, the artificiality which are typical of Byron's work at this period.

In 1816 Byron was hounded out of England, and his wanderings are chronicled in the third (1816) and fourth (1818) cantos of *Childe Harold's Pilgrimage*. In metre and general scheme the poem is unaltered, but in spirit and style the new parts are very different from the first two cantos. The descriptions are firmer and terser, and are often graced with a fine simplicity; the old-fashioned mannerisms are entirely discarded; and the tone all through is deeper and more sincere. There is apparent an undercurrent of bitter pessimism that is only natural under the circumstances, though he dwells too lengthily upon his misfortunes. The following stanza is a fair specimen of this later and simpler style:

> They keep his dust in Arqua, where he died;
> The mountain village where his latter days
> Went down the vale of years, and 'tis their pride—
> An honest pride—and let it be their praise,
> To offer to the passing stranger's gaze
> His mansion and his sepulchre; both plain
> And venerably simple, such as raise
> A feeling more accordant with his strain
> Than if a pyramid formed his monumental fane.

During these years on the Continent he was not idle. Some of his longer poems are *The Prisoner of Chillon* (1816) and *Mazeppa* (1819), the last of his metrical tales. He also composed a large number of lyrics, most of them only mediocre in quality; and he added several great satirical poems, the most notable of which are *Beppo* (1818, published 1819), *The Vision of Judgment* (1822), directed mainly against Southey, and, the longest of all, *Don Juan*.

The Vision of Judgment is one of the finest of English political satires. Underlying the attack on Southey there is a bitter indignation, hidden beneath a mask of humorous burlesque and a sparkling, vivacious wit. The poem, which is written in *ottava rima*, shows a mastery of satirical portraiture only rivalled by that of Dryden and Pope.

In range, in vigour, and in effectiveness *Don Juan* ranks as one of the greatest of satirical poems. It was issued in portions during the years 1819–24, just as Byron composed it. It is a kind of picaresque novel cast into verse. The hero, as in the picaresque novel, has many wanderings and adventures, the narration of which might go on interminably. At the time of its publication it was denounced by a shocked world as vile and immoral, and to a great extent it deserves the censure. In it Byron expresses the wrath that consumes him, and all the human race comes under the lash. The strength and flexibility of the satire are beyond question, and are freely revealed in bitter mockery, in caustic comment, and in burning rage. However, the mood of anger is but one of the many widely differing moods in this work, which is the fullest revelation of Byron's complex personality. The stanzas, written in *ottava rima*, are as keen and supple as a tempered steel blade. The style is a kind of sublimated, half-colloquial prose, showing a disdainful abrogation of the finer poetical trappings; but in places it rises into passages of rare and lovely tenderness. When affliction came upon him, in the words of Lear he had vowed a vow:

> No, I'll not weep;
> I have full cause of weeping, but this heart
> Shall break into a hundred thousand flaws
> Or ere I'll weep.

But sometimes the poet prevails over the satirist, and the mocking laughter is stifled with the sound of bitter weeping.

The first extract given below shows Byron in his bitter and cynical mood; the tone of the second and third is far removed from such asperity:

(1) Ovid's a rake, as half his verses show him,
>   Anacreon's morals are a still worse sample,
> Catullus scarcely has a decent poem,
>   I don't think Sappho's Ode a good example,
> Although Longinus tells us there is no hymn
>   Where the sublime soars forth on wings more ample;
> But Virgil's songs are pure, except that horrid one
> Beginning with "Formosum Pastor Corydon."

Lucretius' irreligion is too strong
    For early stomachs to prove wholesome food;
I can't help thinking Juvenal was wrong,
    Although no doubt his real intent was good,
For speaking out so plainly in his song,
    So much indeed as to be downright rude;
And then what proper person can be partial
To all those nauseous epigrams of Martial?

(2) Round her she made an atmosphere of life;
        The very air seemed lighter from her eyes,
    They were so soft and beautiful, and rife
        With all we can imagine of the skies,
    As pure as Psyche ere she grew a wife—
        Too pure even for the purest human ties;
    Her overpowering presence made you feel
    It would not be idolatry to kneel.

    Her eyelashes, though dark as night, were tinged—
        It is the country's custom—but in vain;
    For those large black eyes were so blackly fringed,
        The glossy rebels mocked the jetty stain,
    And in their native beauty stood avenged:
        Her nails were touched with henna; but again
    The power of art was turned to nothing, for
    They could not look more rosy than before.

(3) Thus lived—thus died she; never more on her
        Shall sorrow light, or shame. She was not made
    Through years or moons the inner weight to bear,
        Which colder hearts endure till they are laid
    By age in earth: her days and pleasures were
        Brief, but delightful—such as had not stayed
    Long with her destiny; but she sleeps well
    By the sea-shore, whereon she loved to dwell.

    That isle is now all desolate and bare,
        Its dwellings down, its tenants passed away;
    None but her own and father's grave is there,
        And nothing outward tells of human clay;
    Ye could not know where lies a thing so fair;
        No stone is there to show, no tongue to say
    What was; no dirge except the hollow sea's
    Mourns o'er the beauty of the Cyclades.

3. His Drama. Byron's dramas are all blank-verse tragedies that were composed during the later stages of his career, when he was in Italy. The chief are *Manfred* (1817), *Marino Faliero* (1821), *The Two Foscari* and *Cain* (1821), and *The Deformed Transformed* (1824.) In nearly all we have a hero of the Byronic type. In *Cain*, for example, we have the outcast who defies the censure of the world; In *The Deformed Transformed* there are thinly screened references to Byron's own deformity. In this fashion he showed that he had little of the real dramatic faculty, for he could portray no character with any zeal unless it resembled himself. The blank verse has power and dignity, but it lacks the higher poetic inspiration.

4. Features of his Poetry. (a) For a man of his egotistical temper Byron's *lyrical gift* is disappointingly meagre. He wrote many tuneful and readable lyrics, such as *She walks in Beauty* and *To Thyrza*. His favourite theme draws on variations of the following mood:

> Do thou, amid the fair white walls,
> If Cadiz yet be free,
> At times, from out her latticed halls,
> Look o'er the dark blue sea;
>
> Then think upon Calypso's isles,
> Endeared by days gone by;
> To others give a thousand smiles,
> To me a single sigh.
> *Stanzas composed during a Thunder-storm*

In such lyrics he is merely sentimental, and the reader cannot avoid thinking that he is posturing before the world. When he attempts more elevated themes, as he does in *The Isles of Greece* (*Don Juan*, Canto III), he is little better than a poetical tub-thumper. Of the genuine passionate lyric there is little trace in his poems.

(b) His *satirical power* is gigantic. In the expression of his scorn, a kind of sublime and reckless arrogance, he has the touch of the master. Yet in spite of his genius he has several defects. In the first place, his motive is to a very large extent personal, and so his scorn becomes one-sided. It is, however, a sign of the essential bigness of his mind that he hardly ever becomes mean and spiteful. Secondly, he lacks the deep vision of the supreme satirist, like Cervantes, who behind the shadows of the crimes and follies of men can see the pity of it all. In the third place, he is often deliberately outrageous. When he found how easily and deeply he could shock a certain class of people he went out of his way to shock them, and succeeded only too well.

(c) His *style* is quite distinct from that of any other romantic poet. Always an admirer of Pope, though he lacked his finish and artistry, he never completely freed himself from the poetic diction, personification, and conventional epithets of the previous age. His faults as an artist are glaring: he had no ear for melody, his workmanship was careless, he had frequent lapses of taste, his dramatic blank verse was often rhetorical and declamatory in tone, and, especially when writing of himself, he was often guilty of repetition and over-emphasis. On the other hand, there is in much of his work a vehemence and passion which give it an impetuous vigour. In his best satires the tone approaches the conversational in its natural-ness, and he displays an epigrammatic wit and great vivacity. Sometimes he writes with simplicity and a tender beauty, as in the Juan-Haidée idyll in *Don Juan*.

(*d*) A word is necessary regarding the fluctuations of his *reputation*. In his earlier manhood he was reckoned among the great poets; he lived to hear himself denounced, and his poetry belittled. After his death Victorian morality held up hands in horror over his iniquity, and his real merits were steadily decried. Since those days his reputation has been climbing back to take a stable position high above the second-rate poets. In some European countries he still ranks second to none among English poets. He broke down the laboured insularity of the English, and he gave to non-English readers a clear and forcible example of what the English language can accomplish.

IV. Percy Bysshe Shelley (1792–1822)

1. His Life. Shelley was born in Sussex, the heir to a baronetcy and a great fortune. He was educated at Eton and Oxford, but from a very early age showed great eccentricity of character. He frequented graveyards, studied alchemy, and read books of dreadful import. While he was at the university he wrote several extra-ordinary pamphlets, one of which, *The Necessity of Atheism*, caused him to be expelled from Oxford. He had already developed extreme notions on religion, politics, and morality generally, a violence that was entirely theoretical, for by nature he was among the most unselfish and amiable of mankind. His opinions, as well as an early and unhappy marriage which he contracted, brought about a painful quarrel with his relatives. This was finally com-posed by the poet's father, Sir Timothy Shelley, who settled an annuity upon his son. The poet immediately took to the life that suited him best, ardently devoting himself to his writing, and wandering where the spirit led him. In 1816 his first wife com-mitted suicide; and Shelley, having married the daughter of William

Godwin, settled in Italy (1818), the land he loved the best. The intoxication of Rome's blue sky and the delicious unrestraint of his Italian existence set his genius blossoming into the rarest beauty. In the full flower of it he was drowned, when he was only thirty years old, in a sudden squall that overtook his yacht in the Gulf of Spezzia. His body—a fit consummation—was burned on the beach where it was found, and his ashes were laid beside those of Keats in the Roman cemetery that he had nobly hymned. It is impossible to estimate the loss to literature that was caused by his early extinction. The crudeness of his earlier opinions was passing away, and his vision was gaining immeasurably in clearness and intensity.

2. His Poetry. His earliest effort of any note is *Queen Mab* (1813). The poem is clearly immature; it is lengthy, and contains much of Shelley's cruder atheism. It is written in the irregular unrhymed metre that was made popular by Southey. The beginning is worth quoting, for already it reveals a touch of the airy music that was to distinguish his later work:

> How wonderful is Death,
> Death and his brother Sleep!
> One, pale as yonder waning moon
> With lips of lurid blue;
> The other, rosy as the morn
> When throned on ocean's wave
> It blushes o'er the world:
> Yet both so passing wonderful!

Alastor, or The Spirit of Solitude (1816) followed. It is a kind of spiritual autobiography, in which the chief character, a shadowy projection of Shelley's own moods, travels through a wilderness in quest of the ideal beauty. The poem is long, rather obscure, and formless, and is remembered chiefly for its lyrical passages and striking, typically Shelleyan imagery. It is written in blank verse that shows Shelley's growing skill as a poet. After this came *Laon and Cythna* (1817), afterward (1818) called *The Revolt of Islam*. It has the fault of its immediate predecessor—lack of grip and coherence; but it is richer in descriptive passages, and has many outbursts of rapturous energy.

Then Shelley left for Italy. The firstfruits of his new life were apparent in *Prometheus Unbound* (1818–19, published 1820). This wonderful production is a combination of the lyric and the drama. The story is that of Prometheus, who defied the gods and suffered for his presumption. There is a small proportion of narrative in blank verse, but the chief feature of the poem is the series of lyrics that both sustain and embellish the action. As a whole the poem has a sweep, a soar, and an unearthly vitality that sometimes stagger the imagination. It is peopled with spirits and demigods, and its scenes are cast in the inaccessible spaces of sky, mountain, and sea.

In *The Cenci* (1819) Shelley started to write formal drama. In this play he seems deliberately to have set upon himself the restraints that he defied in *Prometheus Unbound*. The plot is not of the sky and the sea; it is a grim and sordid family affair; in style it is neither fervent nor ornate, but bleak and austere. Yet behind this reticence of manner there is a deep and smouldering intensity of passion and enormous adequacy of tragic purpose. Many of the poet's admirers look upon it as his masterpiece; but it falls short of the highest tragic level in the lack of subtlety in its character drawing and the inadequacy of its dramatic action. Even so, it stands as one of the best tragedies since Webster. The last words of the play, when the heroine goes to her doom, are almost heart-breaking in their simplicity:

> *Beatrice.* Give yourself no unnecessary pain,
> My dear Lord Cardinal. Here, mother, tie
> My girdle for me, and bind up this hair
> In any simple knot; ay, that does well.
> And yours I see is coming down. How often
> Have we done this for one another! Now
> We shall not do it any more. My lord
> We are quite ready. Well, 'tis very well.

The poems of this period are extraordinary in their number and quality. Among the longer ones are *Julian and Maddalo* (1818) and *The Masque of Anarchy* (1819, published 1832). The latter, inspired by the news of the massacre of Peterloo, expresses Shelley's revolutionary political views, and is very severe on Lord Castlereagh. The second stanza of the poem is startling enough:

> I met Murder on the way,
> He had a mask like Castlereagh;
> Very smooth he looked, yet grim;
> Seven bloodhounds followed him.

In *The Witch of Atlas* (1820, published 1824) and *Epipsychidion* (1821) Shelley rises further and further into the ether of poetical imagination, until he becomes almost impossible of comprehension. The former, the lightest and most delicate of all Shelley's fantasies, is rich in music and imagery, while *Epipsychidion*, with the same wealth of imagery, contains some of his most fervent writing. *Adonais* (1821) is a lament for the death of Keats modelled on the classical elegy. Though there is a jarring note in the attack on the critics, whom Shelley held to be responsible for the poet's early death, the Spenserian stanza is here used with a splendid resonance and a force which increases as the poem progresses. It glows with some of the most splendid of Shelley's conceptions.

> He has outsoared the shadow of our night.
> Envy and calumny and hate and pain,
> And that unrest which men miscall delight,
> Can touch him not and torture not again.
> From the contagion of the world's slow stain
> He is secure; and now can never mourn
> A heart grown cold, a head grown grey, in vain—
> Nor, when the spirit's self has ceased to burn,
> With sparkless ashes load an unlamented urn.
>
> He lives, he wakes—'tis Death is dead, not he;
> Mourn not for Adonais—Thou, young Dawn,
> Turn all thy dew to splendour, for from thee
> The spirit thou lamentest is not gone!
> Ye caverns and ye forests, cease to moan!
> Cease, ye faint flowers and fountains! and, thou Air,
> Which like a mourning veil thy scarf hadst thrown
> O'er the abandoned Earth, now leave it bare
> Even to the joyous stars which smile on its despair!

With the longer poems went a brilliant cascade of shorter lyrical pieces. To name them is to mention some of the sweetest English lyrics. The constantly quoted *To a Skylark* and *The Cloud* are among them; so are some exquisite songs, such as *The Indian Serenade, Music, when soft voices die, On a Faded Violet, To Night,* and the longer occasional pieces—for example, *Lines written among the Euganean Hills,* and the *Letter to Maria Gisborne.* Of his many beautiful odes, the most remarkable is *Ode to the West Wind.* The stanzas have the elemental rush of the wind itself, and the conclusion, where Shelley sees a parallel to himself, is the most remarkable of all:

> Make me thy lyre, ev'n as the forest is:
> What if my leaves are falling like its own!
> The tumult of thy mighty harmonies
>
> Will take from both a deep autumnal tone,
> Sweet though in sadness. Be thou, Spirit fierce,
> My spirit! be thou me, impetuous one!

> Drive my dead thoughts over the universe
> Like wither'd leaves, to quicken a new birth;
> And, by the incantation of this verse,
>
> Scatter, as from an unextinguish'd hearth
> Ashes and sparks, my words among mankind!
> Be through my lips to unawaken'd earth
>
> The trumpet of a prophecy! O Wind,
> If Winter comes, can Spring be far behind?

3. His Prose. Shelley began his literary career with two boyish romances, *Zastrozzi* and *St Irvyne*. These books were written when he was still at school, and are almost laughably bad in style and story. The only other prose work that is worth mention is his short essay *The Defence of Poetry* (1821, published 1840). The work is soundly written, and is a strong exposition of the Romantic point of view. His published letters show him to have been a man of considerable common sense, and not merely the crazy theorist of popular imagination. His prose style is somewhat heavy, but always clear and readable.

4. Features of his Poetry. (*a*) His *lyrical power* is equal to the highest to be found in any language. It is now recognized to be one of the supreme gifts in literature, like the dramatic genius of Shakespeare. This gift is shown at its best when it expresses the highest emotional ecstasy, as in the lyrics of *Prometheus Unbound*. It is a sign of his great genius that, in spite of the passion that pervades his lyrics, he is seldom shrill and tuneless. He can also express a mood of blessed cheerfulness, a sane and delectable joy. To the Spirit of Delight he says:

> I love Love, though he has wings
>   And like light can flee,
> But above all other things,
>   Spirit, I love thee.
> Thou art love and life! O come,
> Make once more my heart thy home.

He can also express the keenest note of depression and despair, as in the lyric *O World! O Life! O Time!*

(*b*) Shelley's *choice of subject* makes it convenient to divide his work into two broad groups, the one consisting of his visionary, prophetic works such as *Alastor, or the Spirit of Solitude*, *The Revolt of Islam*, *Prometheus Unbound*, and similar poems, and the other of his shorter lyrics. In almost all of the visionary poems we see the Shelleyan hero, a rebel against tyranny and a leader in the struggle which is to bring about the ultimate happiness of humanity. Like the Byronic hero, these figures are, to a large extent, projections of the character of their creator. Often the symbolism of the poems is not sufficiently clear or sustained, and the result is some confusion in the mind of the reader. In the subjects of his shorter poems he differs from such a poet as Burns, who is almost the only other poet who challenges him as master of the lyric. Shelley lacks the homely appeal of Burns; he loves to roam through space and infinity. In his own words he

> feeds on the aerial kisses
> Of shapes that haunt thought's wildernesses.

He rejoices in nature, but nature of a spiritual kind, which he peoples with phantoms and airy beings:

> I love all that thou lovest,
>   Spirit of Delight!
> The fresh Earth in new leaves drest,
>   And the starry night;
> Autumn evening, and the morn
> When the golden mists are born.
>
> I love snow, and all the forms
>   Of the radiant frost:
> I love waves, and winds, and storms,
>   Everything almost
> Which is nature's, and may be
> Untainted by man's misery.

Frequently he is concerned with the thought of death or his own sense of despair or loneliness:

> O world! O life! O time!
> On whose last steps I climb,
>   Trembling at that where I had stood before;
> When will return the glory of your prime?
>   No more—Oh, never more!
>
> Out of the day and night
> A joy has taken flight;
>   Fresh spring, and summer, and winter hoar,
> Move my faint heart with grief, but with delight
>   No more—Oh, never more!

(c) His *descriptive power* at once strikes the imagination. The effect is instantaneous. His fancy played among wild and elemental things, but it gave them form and substance, as well as a radiant loveliness. His favourite device for this purpose is personification, of which the following is an excellent example:

> For Winter came; the wind was his whip;
> One choppy finger was on his lip;
> He had torn the cataracts from the hills,
> And they clanked at his girdle like manacles.
>
> *The Sensitive Plant*

We add another extract to show his almost unearthly skill in visualizing the wilder aspects of nature. Note the extreme simplicity and ease of the style:

> We paused amid the pines that stood
> The giants of the waste,
> Tortured by storms to shapes as rude
> With stems like serpents interlaced.
>
> *The Pine Forest of the Cascine near Pisa*

(*d*) His *style* is perfectly attuned to his purpose. Like all the finest lyrical styles, it is simple, flexible, and passionate. It has a direct clarity, an easy, yet striking, lucidity, and a purity of language which are peculiarly Shelley's own. Sometimes, as in *The Cenci*, it rises to a commanding simplicity. The extracts already given sufficiently show this.

(*e*) Shelley's *limitations* are almost as plain as his great abilities. His continual rhapsodizings tend to become tedious and baffling; in his narrative he is diffuse and argumentative; he lacks humour; and his political poetry is often violent and unreasonable.

(*f*) *His Reputation.* During his lifetime Shelley's opinions obscured his powers as a poet. Even to Scott, who with all his Tory prejudices was liberal enough in his views on literature, he was simply "that atheist Shelley." After his death his reputation rose rapidly, and by the middle of the nineteenth century his position was assured. By the curious alternation that seems to affect popular taste, his fame since that time has paled a little; but no fluctuations in taste can ever remove him from his place among the great.

V. JOHN KEATS (1795–1821)

1. His Life. Keats was born in London, the son of the well-to-do keeper of a livery stable. He was educated at a private school at Enfield, and at the age of fifteen was apprenticed to a surgeon. In 1814 he transferred his residence to London, and followed part of the regular course of instruction prescribed for medical students. Already, however, his poetical bent was becoming apparent. Surgery lost its slight attraction, and the career of a poet became a bright possibility when he made the acquaintance of Leigh Hunt (1816), the famous Radical journalist and poet, whose collisions with the Government had caused much commotion and his own imprisonment. Keats was soon intimate with the Radical brotherhood that surrounded Leigh Hunt, and thus he became known to Shelley and others. In 1817 he published his first volume of verse, but it attracted little notice, in spite of the championship of Hunt. By this time the family tendency to consumption became painfully manifest in him, and he spent his time in searching for places, including the Isle of Wight and the suburbs of London, where his affliction might be remedied. While he was staying in London he became acquainted with Fanny Brawne, and afterward was engaged to her for a time. His malady, however, became worse, and the mental and physical distress caused by his complaint, added to despair regarding the success of his love-affair, produced a frantic state of mind painfully reflected in his letters to the young lady. These letters were foolishly printed (1878), long after the poet's death.

His second volume of verse, published in 1818, was brutally assailed by *The Quarterly Review* and by *Blackwood's Magazine*. These Tory journals probably struck at him because of his friendship with the Radical Leigh Hunt. Keats bore the attack with apparent serenity, and always protested that he minded it little; but there can be little doubt that it affected his health to some degree. In 1820 he was compelled to seek warmer skies, and died in Rome early in the next year, at the age of twenty-five.

2. His Poetry. When he was about seventeen years old Keats became acquainted with the works of Spenser, and this proved to be the turning-point in his life. The mannerisms of the Elizabethan immediately captivated him, and he resolved to imitate him. His earliest attempt at verse is his *Imitation of Spenser* (1813), written when he was eighteen. This and some other short pieces were published together in his *Poems* (1817), his first volume of verse. This book contains little of any outstanding merit, except for some of its sonnets, which include the superb *On first looking into Chapman's Homer*. The poems, which include *Sleep and Poetry* and *I stood tip-toe upon a little hill*, show the influence of Spenser and, more immediately, of Leigh Hunt, to whom the volume was dedicated.

Of a different quality was his next volume, called *Endymion* (1818). Probably based partly on Drayton's *The Man in the Moon* and Fletcher's *The Faithful Shepherdess*, this remarkable poem of *Endymion* professes to tell the story of the lovely youth who was kissed by the moon-goddess on the summit of Mount Latmos. Keats develops this simple myth into an intricate and flowery and rather obscure allegory of over four thousand lines. The work is clearly immature, and flawed with many weaknesses both of taste and of construction, but many of the passages are most beautiful, and the poem shows the tender budding of the Keatsian style—a rich and suggestive beauty obtained by a richly ornamented diction. The first line is often quoted, and it contains the theory that Keats followed during the whole of his poetical career:

> A thing of beauty is a joy for ever.

The crudeness of the work laid it temptingly open to attack, and, as we have noticed, the hostile reviews found it an easy prey.

Keats's health was already failing, but the amount of poetry he wrote is marvellous both in magnitude and in quality. His third and last volume, published in 1820 just before he left England, contains a collection of poems of the first rank, which were written approximately in the order that follows.

Isabella, or The Pot of Basil (1818), is a version of a tale from Boccaccio, and deals with the murder of a lady's lover by her two wicked brothers. The poem, which is written in *ottava rima*, marks a decided advance in Keats's work. The slips of taste are fewer; the style deeper in tone; the tale is told with an economy and precision new in Keats; and the conclusion, though it is sentimentally treated, is not wanting in pathos.

In *Hyperion* (begun 1818, abandoned 1819) Keats took up the epic theme of the primeval struggle between the older race of gods, such as Saturn and Hyperion, and the younger divinities, such as Apollo. Both in style and structure the poem is modelled on *Paradise Lost*. The blank verse has not only many of the typically Miltonic tricks of style, but also much of the sonorous weight and dignity of its model. At the same time, it replaces the vigour and passion of Milton with a repose and charm of its own. As the poem progresses the Miltonic is gradually supplanted by a tone more truly Keats's own, and in the third book it ends abruptly, because, as Keats himself said, it was too Miltonic. It is doubtful whether it could ever have been completed as it lacks the gripping action which must be the basis of the epic poem. Yet, as far as it goes, *Hyperion* is a successful work, which has been claimed by some critics as Keats's greatest achievement. Book II provides us with the fullest exposition he was ever to give of his theory that "first in beauty shall be first in might," and the poem shows clearly his growing control over structure and style. It is full of striking passages, of which the following, the opening lines, is a good example:

> Deep in the shady sadness of a vale
> Far sunken from the healthy breath of morn,
> Far from the fiery noon, and eve's one star,
> Sat gray-hair'd Saturn, quiet as a stone,
> Still as the silence round about his lair;
> Forest on forest hung about his head
> Like cloud on cloud. No stir of air was there,
> Not so much life as on a summer's day
> Robs not one light seed from the feather'd grass,
> But where the dead leaf fell, there did it rest.
> A stream went voiceless by, still deaden'd more
> By reason of his fallen divinity
> Spreading a shade: the Naiad 'mid her reeds
> Press'd her cold finger closer to her lips.

The Eve of St Agnes (1819), regarded by others as his finest narrative poem, is a tale of the elopement of two lovers. The story is slight but moves quickly; the background of family feud is kept well in mind, and the love scenes are more controlled than those in *Isabella, or the Pot of Basil*. In the chivalric tone, the stanza form, and the occasional archaisms the influence of Spenser is seen; but the style is Keats's own, and the poem is full of beauties of description, imagery, and colour. It is sensuous and highly decorative without being cloying. Typical of its exquisite beauty is the following stanza:

> Full on this casement shone the wintry moon,
> And threw warm gules on Madeline's fair breast,
> As down she knelt for heaven's grace and boon;
> Rose-bloom fell on her hands, together prest,
> And on her silver cross soft amethyst,
> And on her hair a glory, like a saint:
> She seem'd a splendid angel, newly drest,
> Save wings, for heaven:—Porphyro grew faint:
> She knelt, so pure a thing, so free from mortal taint.

In the same year was written *The Eve of Saint Mark*, which remains unfinished. It has the fine pictorial work of *The Eve of St Agnes*, but the material is handled with more restraint. In style it is effortless, and free from Keats's fault of over-luxuriance.

The story of *Lamia* (1819) is taken from Burton's *The Anatomy of Melancholy* (see p. 121) and tells of a beautiful enchantress. The narrative is well handled, runs smoothly, and shows a truer sense of proportion than *Endymion*, though, here again, the story is rendered somewhat obscure by the introduction of a rather confused allegory. In style it is modelled on the fables of Dryden, and the heroic couplet is skilfully used. The poem is full of typically Keatsian pictorial richness, which, on occasion, becomes rather excessive. The following description of the snake-enchantress is one of the more gorgeous parts of the story:

> She was a gordian shape of dazzling hue,
> Vermilion-spotted, golden, green, and blue;
> Striped like a zebra, freckled like a pard,
> Eyed like a peacock, and all crimson barr'd;
> And full of silver moons, that, as she breathed,
> Dissolv'd, or brighter shone, or interwreathed
> Their lustres with the gloomier tapestries—
> So rainbow-sided, touch'd with miseries,
> She seem'd, at once, some penanced lady elf,
> Some demon's mistress, or the demon's self.
> Upon her crest she wore a wannish fire
> Sprinkled with stars, like Ariadne's tiar:
> Her head was serpent, but ah, bitter-sweet!
> She had a woman's mouth with all its pearls complete:
> And for her eyes: what could such eyes do there
> But weep, and weep, that they were born so fair?
> As Proserpine still weeps for her Sicilian air.
> He throat was serpent, but the words she spake
> Came, as through bubbling honey, for Love's sake.

At the end of 1819 Keats made an attempt to refashion his unfinished epic in *The Fall of Hyperion, a Dream*. Casting off the Miltonic style of the first version, Keats here creates a blank verse of his own, flexible, powerful, and sonorous, a blank verse which accords well with a severer and more thoughtful tone than is to be found in any other of his poems. It carries still further Keats's philosophy of beauty, which he now feels to be attainable only by those who have experienced pain. Over the merits of this revision, as compared with the original draft, controversy has raged. A comparison of parallel versions of the same passage will show that, in many cases, the splendour and magic of the first have gone. On the other hand, it may be argued that not only is the poem more truly Keats's own, but that it shows a deeper insight into human problems.

Together with the longer poems are many shorter pieces of supreme beauty. The great odes—*To a Nightingale, On a Grecian Urn, To Psyche, On Melancholy, To Autumn*—were nearly all written in 1819, and in their approach to flawless perfection the best of them are unequalled in Keats. Between the impassioned longing for escape of the first and the calm of fruition of the last there is a very great difference, but all, with the exception of *To Autumn*, show a concern with the poet's desire for true beauty, and they thus have a close link with *Endymion, Hyperion, Lamia,* and *The Fall of Hyperion.* The odes are experiments in verse form based on the sonnet. All, except *To Autumn*, which has an eleven-line stanza, are in stanzas of ten lines, made up of the Shakespearian quatrain and the Petrarchan sestet. We quote the first stanza of the well-known *Ode to Autumn*, probably the most perfect poem Keats ever wrote:

> Season of mists and mellow fruitfulness,
>   Close bosom-friend of the maturing sun;
> Conspiring with him how to load and bless
>   With fruit the vines that round the thatch-eaves run;
> To bend with apples the moss'd cottage-trees,
>   And fill all fruit with ripeness to the core;
>   To swell the gourd, and plump the hazel shells
> With a sweet kernel; to set budding more,
>   And still more, later flowers for the bees,
>   Until they think warm days will never cease,
>   For Summer has o'er-brimm'd their clammy cells.

As a sonneteer Keats ranks with the greatest English poets. Of his sixty-one sonnets some ten, including *On first looking into Chapman's Homer, When I have fears that I may cease to be,* and *Bright Star, would I were stedfast as thou art,* are worthy to be ranked with those of Shakespeare. After a strict adherence to the Petrarchan form in the 1817 volume, Keats turned to the Shakespearian form, which undoubtedly suited him better. The sonnet quoted below will show how effortless is his best work in this medium:

> When I have fears that I may cease to be
>   Before my pen has glean'd my teeming brain,
> Before high-piled books, in charactery,
>   Hold like rich garners the full ripen'd grain;
> When I behold, upon the night's starr'd face,
>   Huge cloudy symbols of a high romance,

And think that I may never live to trace
  Their shadows, with the magic hand of chance;
And when I feel, fair creature of an hour,
  That I shall never look upon thee more,
Never have relish in the faery power
  Of unreflecting love;—then on the shore
Of the wide world I stand alone, and think
Till love and fame to nothingness do sink.

Among the other shorter poems *La Belle Dame sans Merci*, a kind of lyrical ballad, is considered to be one of the choicest in the language.

In 1819 Keats collaborated in a drama, *Otho the Great*, and began another, *King Stephen*, which he did not complete. Neither effort is of much consequence. *The Cap and Bells*, a longish fairy-tale which also is unfinished, is much below the level of his usual work.

3. Features of his Poetry. (*a*) His *choice of subject* differs from that of most of the other major romantic poets. His love of nature is intense and is constantly to be seen in the imagery of his poems, but it involves none of the mystical worship of the "mighty being" which we have seen in Wordsworth. He has none of the satirical bent of Byron, and little of the prophetic vein of Shelley; rather is he the poet of legend and myth, of romance and chivalric tale. He had no knowledge of Greek and little of Greece, but none of his contemporaries was so moved by the spirit of Greece, and none so skilfully captured the charm of its seaboard as did Keats in this passage:

Who are these coming to the sacrifice?
  To what green altar, O mysterious priest,
Lead'st thou that heifer lowing at the skies,
  And all her silken flanks with garlands drest?
What little town by river or sea-shore,
  Or mountain-built with peaceful citadel,
    Is emptied of this folk, this pious morn?
And, little town, thy streets for evermore
  Will silent be; and not a soul to tell
    Why thou art desolate, can e'er return.

On a Grecian Urn

From the first, however, there was intermingled with his love of romantic story a concern for deeper spiritual issues, and in his last long work, *The Fall of Hyperion, a Dream*, we find his most mature exposition of his belief in the sovereign power of beauty. Previously it had found expression in *Endymion*, *Hyperion*, *Lamia*, and the ode *On a Grecian Urn*. In his sonnets and odes he had moments of lyrical self-revelation, and, though his lyric work is less in quantity than his narrative, its quality is such as to suggest that here, too, had he lived, Keats might have rivalled the greatest.

(b) *His style* is even more distinctively his own, and it has had a great effect on later English poets, most notably on Tennyson and the Pre-Raphaelites. The most striking feature of his work is the speed with which he learned his craft, and evolved from the imitator of Leigh Hunt, Spenser, Shakespeare, or Milton to the artist with a style of his own. His early verse was rich in melodic beauty and decorative effect, full of colour and the images of the senses (particularly of touch). In his own metaphor, every rift was loaded with ore. But often the result was an over-luxuriance and a lack of restraint which betray his, as yet, uncertain taste and the weakness of his artistic economy. Two years from the publication of *Endymion* sufficed for him to evolve the blank verse of *The Fall of Hyperion*, and to reach perfection in narrative and lyric forms in *The Eve of St Agnes* and the best of his odes. In the new Keats all the qualities of the old are controlled by a restraint and poise, a delicacy of touch and a purer taste, and the result is one of the most striking of all English poetic styles.

4. His Prose. Unlike Wordsworth, Keats made no attempt at a systematic formulation of his views on his art. His *Letters*, however, give a clearer insight into his mind and artistic development than any formal treatise could have done. Written with a spontaneous freshness and an easy intimacy, they are the most interesting letters of their day. They reveal his profound insight into his own spiritual growth, and show how passionate was his love for poetry. We give one or two typically significant passages:

> I find I cannot exist without poetry—without eternal poetry—half the day will not do—the whole of it—I began with a little but habit has made me a Leviathan. I had become all in a trouble from not having written anything of late—the sonnet overleaf did me good. I slept the better last night for it.

> I am certain of nothing but the holiness of the heart's affections, and the truth of imagination. What the imagination seizes as beauty must be truth.

> . . . with a great poet the sense of beauty overcomes every other consideration, or rather obliterates all consideration.

> . . . if poetry comes not as naturally as the leaves to a tree it had better not come at all.

Do you not see how necessary a world of pains and troubles is to school an intelligence and make it a soul?

OTHER POETS

1. Robert Southey (1774–1843). Southey was born at Bristol, educated at Westminster School and at Oxford, and settled down to lead the laborious life of a man of letters. He produced a great mass of work, much of which is of considerable merit, and he ranked as one of the leading writers of his age. Most of his work was written at Greta Hall, near Keswick, where he lived most of his life. He was made Poet Laureate in 1813. His reputation, especially as a poet, has not been maintained.

His poems, which are of great bulk, include *Joan of Arc* (1798), *Thalaba the Destroyer* (1801), *The Curse of Kehama* (1810), and *Roderick, the Last of the Goths* (1814). Typically romantic in theme, most of them were too ambitious for a poet of Southey's limitations. In style they are straightforward and unaffected, but they lack the transfiguring fire of true genius and are now almost forgotten. Some shorter pieces, such as *The Holly-tree*, *The Battle of Blenheim*, and *The Inchcape Rock*, are still in favour, and deservedly so.

His numerous prose works include *The History of Brazil* (1810–19) and *The History of the Peninsular War* (1823–32). The slightest of them all, *The Life of Nelson* (1813), is the only one now freely read. It shows Southey's easy 'middle' style at its best.

2. Thomas Moore (1779–1852). Moore was born in Dublin, took his degree at Trinity College, and studied law in London at the Inner Temple. He was imbued with revolutionary notions, and attempted to apply them to Ireland, but with no success. He obtained a valuable appointment in the Bermudas, the duties of which were discharged by a deputy, who in this case proved faithless and caused Moore financial loss. Moore was a friend of Byron and a prominent literary figure of the time. Most of his life was passed as a successful man of letters.

His poems were highly successful during his lifetime, but after his death there was a reaction against them. His *Irish Melodies* are set to the traditional musical airs of Ireland. They are graceful, and adapt themselves admirably to the tunes. Moore, however, lacked the depth and far-ranging strength of Burns, and so he failed to do for Ireland what the Ayrshire poet did for Scotland: he did not raise the national sentiment of Ireland into one of the precious things of literature. His *Lalla Rookh* (1817) is an Oriental romance, written in the Scott-Byron manner then so popular. The poem had an immense success, which has now almost totally faded. It contains an abundance of florid description, but as poetry it is hardly second-rate. Moore's political satires, such as *The Twopenny Postbag* (1813), *The Fudge Family in Paris* (1818), and *Fables for the Holy Alliance* (1823), are keen and lively, and show his Irish wit at its very best.

His prose works include his *Life of Byron* (1830), which has taken its place as the standard biography of that poet. It is an able and scholarly piece of work, and is written with much knowledge and sympathy, though it lacks the clear-cut vigour of the masterpieces of Boswell and Lockhart (see pp. 268 and 358).

3. Thomas Campbell (1777–1844). Campbell was born in Glasgow, of a poor but ancient family. After studying at Glasgow University he became tutor to a private family; but his *Pleasures of Hope* (1799) brought him fame, and he adopted the career of a poet. He visited the Continent, and saw much of the turmoil that there reigned. Returning, he settled in London, where he was editor of *The New Monthly Magazine* from 1820 to 1830.

His longer poems are quite numerous, and begin with the *Pleasures of Hope*, which consists of a series of descriptions of nature in heroic couplets, written in a style that suggests Goldsmith. Other longer poems include *Gertrude of Wyoming* (1809), a longish tale of Pennsylvania, written in Spenserian stanzas, and *The Pilgrim of Glencoe* (1842). Campbell, however, is chiefly remembered for his stirring songs, some of which were written during his early Continental tour and were published in newspapers. His most successful are *Ye Mariners of England* and *The Battle of the Baltic*, which are spirited without containing the bluster and boasting that so often disfigure the patriotic song.

4. Samuel Rogers (1763–1855). Rogers was born at Stoke Newington, the son of a rich banker. He soon became a partner in his father's firm, and for the rest of his life his financial success was assured. His chief interest lay in art and poetry, which he cultivated in an earnest fashion. He was a generous patron of the man of letters, and was acquainted with most of the literary people of the time. His breakfasts were famous.

His *The Pleasures of Memory* (1792) is a reversion to the typical eighteenth-century manner, and as such is interesting. He could compose polished verses, but he has little of the poet. Other works are *Columbus* (1812), *Jacqueline* (1814), a tale in the Byronic manner, and *Italy* (1822), of which a second part appeared in 1828.

Rogers was a careful and fastidious writer, but his excellence does not go much further. His name is a prominent one in the literary annals of the time, but his wealth rather than his merit accounts for this.

5. **Leigh Hunt (1784–1859)**, unlike Rogers, was not a wealthy amateur who could trifle for years with mediocre production; he was of the arena, taking and giving hard knocks in both political and literary scuffles. He was born in Middlesex, educated at Christ's Hospital, and while still in his teens became a journalist, and remained a journalist all his life. His Radical journal *The Examiner* (1808) was strongly critical of the Government, and Hunt's aptitude for abuse landed him in prison for two years. His captivity, as he gleefully records, made a hero of him; and most of the literary men who prided themselves upon their Liberalism— among them being Wordsworth, Byron, Moore, Keats, and Shelley —sought his friendship. Hunt had a powerful influence on Keats, and published some of the latter's shorter poems in *The Examiner*. He tried various other journalistic ventures, but none of them had the success of *The Examiner*, though *The Indicator* (1819) contained some of his finest essays; his attempted collaboration in journalism with Byron was a lamentable failure. He died, like Wordsworth and others, a respectable pensioner of the Government he had once so strongly condemned.

Hunt does not rank highly as a poet, though, in his own day, his work was very popular. Too often his poems are trivial, and most, if not all, are marred by lapses of taste or slipshod workmanship. His best long poem, *The Story of Rimini* (1816), is an Italian tale modelled on Dante's lines on Paolo and Francesca, and is quite well told in easy, facile couplets. It is somewhat spoilt by its maudlin sentimentality and the looseness of some of its verse, but it is of peculiar interest because its style was the model for Keats's *Endymion*. Hunt is seen at his best in his shorter pieces, such as his sonnet on *The Nile* and *Abou Ben Adhem*, where he retains all his usual ease and has less opportunity for his too frequent lapses. His chief importance as a poet is, however, historical. In his love of a good story free from didacticism, and in his unrestrained revelling in beauty and the riches of the imagination, he is a definite contributory force in the march away from the eighteenth century and toward the age of romance.

His prose includes an enormous amount of journalistic matter, which was occasionally collected and issued in book form. Such was his *Men, Women, and Books* (1847). His *Autobiography* (1850) contains much interesting biographical and literary gossip. He is an agreeable essayist, fluent and easygoing; his critical opinions are solid and sensible, though often half-informed. He wrote a novel, *Sir Ralph Esher* (1832), and a very readable book on London called *The Town* (1848). Hunt is not a genius, but he is a useful and amiable second-rate writer.

6. **James Hogg (1770–1835).** Hogg became known to the world as "the Ettrick Shepherd," for he was born of a shepherd's family in the valley of the Ettrick, in Selkirkshire. He was a man of much natural ability, and from his infancy was an eager listener to the songs and ballads of his district. He was introduced to Walter Scott (1802) while the latter was collecting the Border minstrelsy, and by Scott he was supported both as a literary man and as a farmer. Many of his admirers assisted him in the acquisition of a sheep-farm, but Hogg proved to be a poor farmer. He was known to most of the members of the Scottish literary circle, but his shiftless and unmanageable disposition alienated most of his friends. He died in his native district.

Hogg had little education and very little sense of discrimination, so that much of his poetry is very poor indeed. Sometimes, however, his native talent prevails, and he writes such poems as *Bonny Kilmeny* and *When the Kye comes Hame*. The latter is a lyric resembling those of Burns in its humour and simple appeal. The former was one of a series of songs and lays, modelled on the lays of Sir Walter Scott, which made up *The Queen's Wake* (1813), the work which established Hogg's poetic reputation. In it he achieves what is commonly held to be the true Celtic note: the eerie description of elves and the gloaming, and murmuring and musical echoes of things half seen and half understood. He has also to his credit a number of vigorous Jacobite war songs, of which the best known is *Lock the door, Lariston*. Some of his books are *The Forest Minstrel* (1810), a volume of songs, of which the majority were by him and the rest by his friends, and *The Brownie of Bodsbeck* (1818), a prose tale.

7. **Ebenezer Elliott (1781–1849).** Elliott was born at Masborough, in Yorkshire, and worked as an iron-founder. The struggles of the poor, oppressed by the Corn Laws, were early borne in upon him, and his poetical gift was used in a fierce challenge to

the existing system. Like Crabbe, he devoted himself to the cause of the poor; and it is a tribute to his merit as a poet that, in spite of his bristling assertiveness, he produced some work of real value. He became known as the 'Corn Law Rhymer,' and he lived to see the abolition of the laws that he had always attacked.

His best book is *Corn Law Rhymes* (1828), which includes the powerful and sombre *Battle-song*. This poem is a kind of anthem for the poor, and breathes a spirit of fierce unrest.

8. Felicia Hemans (1793–1835). Mrs Hemans's maiden name was Browne, and she was born at Liverpool. Later she removed to Wales, where a large part of her life was spent. Before she was fourteen she began to write poetry, and persisted in the habit all her life. She married somewhat unhappily, but she lived to be a highly popular poetess, and produced a large amount of work. She died in Dublin.

Nobody can call Mrs Hemans a great poetess, but her verses are facile and fairly melodious, and she can give simple themes a simple setting. One can respect the genuine quality of her emotions, and the zeal with which she expressed them. Some of her better lyrics —for example, *The Homes of England*, *The Graves of a Household*, and *The Landing of the Pilgrim Fathers in New England*—are in their limited fashion well done.

9. Thomas Hood (1799–1845). Hood was a native of London, the son of a partner in a book-selling firm. He took to a literary career, and contributed to many periodicals, including *The London Magazine*. For a time he edited *The New Monthly Magazine*, but he was much troubled by illness, and died prematurely.

Hood's earliest works were narrative poems in the vein of Spenser and Keats, and *Hero and Leander*, *The Two Swans*, and *The Plea of the Midsummer Fairies* (1827) have something of the sensuous richness of their models. It was, however, with a collection of humorous verse, published under the title of *Whims and Oddities* (1826 and 1827), that he first gained notoriety, and he did not afterwards return to the earlier experiments. To modern taste the humour is rather cheap, for it consists largely of verbal quibblings, such as the free use of the pun. It seemed to be acceptable to the public of the time, for the book had much success. Other volumes in the same vein were *The Comic Annual* (1830), *Up the Rhine* (1840), and *Whimsicalities* (1844). Hood, in spite of his cleverness, could not keep free of vulgarity, and his wit often jars. In direct contrast to his comic poems were those tragic works of a tearful intensity, such as *The*

Death-bed and *The Bridge of Sighs* (1846), and his horror poems, which dealt with subjects akin to those of the Radcliffian horror novel. The best known of this latter type are *The Haunted House* and *The Dream of Eugene Aram* (1829). In both kinds Hood's work suffers from a lack of restraint and a certain crudity of taste. He was also responsible for a number of pieces of social verse such as *The Song of the Shirt*, first published in *Punch* in 1843, in an attempt to help the sweated sempstress of his day, and for a few really good, serious lyrics, including the well-known *Ruth*, which rise above the less than mediocre level of so much of his work.

10. **John Clare (1793–1864)** was a true peasant poet, and in his day he had a great popularity. After his death his works fell into neglect, but a twentieth-century reissue of his poems, some of them new to the public, has recalled attention to the considerable value of much that he wrote. He was born near Peterborough, his father being a cripple and a pauper. At the age of thirteen he saved sufficient money to buy a copy of *The Seasons*, which fired his poetic ability. His first publication, *Poems Descriptive of Rural Life and Scenery* (1820), was much praised, but later collections, *The Village Minstrel* (1821), *The Shepherd's Calendar* (1827), and *The Rural Muse* (1835), had not the same success. The patronage of rich admirers put him above poverty, but a tendency to insanity developed, and, like Christopher Smart, he died in a madhouse.

Clare's poems are seen at their best when they deal with simple rustic themes, and then they are quite charming. He rejoices in the ways of animals and insects. He is not a great poet, but there are many poets with flaunting credentials who have less claims to consideration than he.

11. **James Smith (1775–1839)** and **Horace Smith (1779–1849)**, two brothers, collaborated in the production of a work that was one of the 'hits' of the period. This book was *Rejected Addresses* (1812). When the Drury Lane Theatre was burned down and rebuilt the management offered a prize for the best poem to be recited on the opening night. The Smiths hit on the idea of making parodies of the notable poets of the time and pretending that they were the rejected entries of the writers mentioned. The result is the classical collection of parodies in English. Scott, Wordsworth, and other well-known authors are imitated, usually with much cleverness. The Wordsworth poem is recited by Nancy Lake, a girl of eight, who is drawn upon the stage in a perambulator:

> My brother Jack was nine in May,
> And I was eight on New Year's Day;
>   So in Kate Wilson's shop
> Papa (he's my papa and Jack's)
> Bought me, last week, a doll of wax,
>   And brother Jack a top.

12. William Cullen Bryant (1794–1878) is the first American poet of more than passing fame. He was born in Massachusetts, became a lawyer, and took to literature. At an early age he wrote poetry, his first volume being *The Embargo* (1808). His most famous works are *Thanatopsis* (1817), a poetical meditation on death, and *The Ages* (1821). An English edition of his volume of 1832 was published by Washington Irving in the same year. Bryant models much of his poetry on that of Wordsworth, but he lacks the faculty of fervent self-revelation which distinguishes the latter's nature poetry. He is really in the classical tradition of the eighteenth century, restrained and always serious in outlook. His style is marked by its purity, dignity, precision, and evenness of flow. Bryant's verse has its own meditative beauty, and some of his shorter pieces—for example, *To a Waterfowl*—are of real distinction. His descriptive passages dealing with North America were highly appreciated by his English readers.

NOVELISTS

I. SIR WALTER SCOTT (1771–1832)

1. His Life. Scott was born in Edinburgh, of an ancient stock of Border freebooters. At the age of eighteen months he was crippled for life by a childish ailment; and though he grew up to be a man of great physical robustness he never lost his lameness. He was educated at the High School of Edinburgh and at the university; and there he developed that powerful memory which, though it rejected things of no interest to it, held in tenacious grasp a great store of miscellaneous knowledge. His father was a lawyer, and Scott himself was called to the Scottish Bar (1792). As a pleader he had little success, for he was much more interested in the lore and antiquities of the country. He was glad, therefore, to accept a small legal appointment as Sheriff of Selkirkshire (1799). Just before this, after an unsuccessful love-affair with a Perthshire lady, he had married the daughter of a French exile. In 1806 he obtained the valuable post of Clerk of Session, but for six years he received no salary, as the post was still held by an invalid nominally in charge.

In 1812, on receipt of his first salary as Clerk of Session, he removed from his pleasant home of Ashiestiel to Abbotsford, a small estate near Melrose. For the place he paid £4000, which he characteristically obtained half by borrowing and half on security of the poem *Rokeby*, still unwritten. During the next dozen years he played the laird at Abbotsford, keeping open house, sinking vast sums of money in enlarging his territory, and adorning the house in a manner that was frequently in the reverse of good taste. In 1826 came the crash. In 1802 he had assisted a Border printer, James Ballantyne, to establish a business at Edinburgh. In 1805 Scott became secretly a partner. As a printing firm the concern was a fair success; but in an evil moment, in 1809, Scott, with another brother, John Ballantyne, started a publishing business. The new firm was poorly managed from the beginning; in 1814 it was only the publication of *Waverley* that kept it on its legs, but the enormous success of the later Waverley Novels gave it abounding prosperity—for the time. Then John Ballantyne, a reckless fellow, plunged heavily into further commitments, which entailed great loss; Scott in his easy fashion also drew heavily upon the firm's funds; and in 1826 the whole erection tumbled into ruin. With great courage and sterling honesty Scott refused to take the course that the other principals accepted naturally, and compound with his creditors. Instead he attempted what turned out to be the impossible task of paying the debt and surviving it. His liabilities amounted to £117,000, and before he died he had cleared off £70,000. After his death the remainder was made good, chiefly from the proceeds of Lockhart's *Life*, and his creditors were paid in full.

The gigantic efforts he made brought about his death. He had a slight paralytic seizure in 1830. It passed, but it left him with a clouded brain. He refused to desist from novel-writing, or even to slacken the pace. Other illness followed, his early lameness becoming more marked. After an ineffectual journey to Italy, he returned to Abbotsford, and died within sound of the river he loved so well.

2. His Poetry. Scott's earliest poetical efforts were translations from the German. *Lenore* (1796), the most considerable of them, is crude enough, but it has much of his later vigour and clatter. In 1802 appeared the first two volumes of *The Minstrelsy of the Scottish Border*, to be followed by a third volume in the next year. In some respects the work is a compilation of old material; but Scott patched up the ancient pieces when it was necessary, and added some original poems of his own, which were done in the ancient manner. The best of his own contributions, such as *The Eve of St John*, have a strong infusion of the ancient force and fire, as well as a grimly supernatural element.

In *The Lay of the Last Minstrel* (1805) there is much more originality. The work is a poem of considerable length written in the *Christabel* metre, and professing to be the lay of an aged bard who seeks shelter in the castle of Newark. As a tale the poem is confused and difficult; as poetry it is mediocre; but the abounding vitality of the style, the fresh and intimate local knowledge, and the healthy love of nature made it a revelation to a public anxious to welcome the new Romantic methods. The poem was a great and instant success, and was quickly followed up with *Marmion* (1808).

In popular estimation *Marmion* is held to be Scott's masterpiece. The story deals with Flodden Field, and is intricate in detail, as Scott labours to obtain a *dénouement*. For several cantos the tale is cumbered with the masses of antiquarian and topical matter with which Scott's mind was fully charged. Once the narrative is within touch of Flodden it quickens considerably. The passage dealing with the close of the battle is one of the triumphs of martial verse:

> But as they left the dark'ning heath,
> More desperate grew the strife of death.
> The English shafts in volleys hail'd,
> In headlong charge their horse assail'd;
> Front, flank, and rear, the squadrons sweep
> To break the Scottish circle deep,
>   That fought around their King.
> But yet, though thick the shafts as snow,
> Though charging knights like whirlwinds go,
> Though bill-men ply the ghastly blow,
>   Unbroken was the ring;
> The stubborn spear-men still made good
> Their dark impenetrable wood,
> Each stepping where his comrade stood,
>   The instant that he fell.
> No thought was there of dastard flight;
> Link'd in the serried phalanx tight,
> Groom fought like noble, squire like knight
>   As fearlessly and well;
> Till utter darkness closed her wing
> O'er their thin host and wounded King. . . .

Next came *The Lady of the Lake* (1810), which was a still greater success. It has all Scott's usual picturesqueness, and makes particularly effective use of the wild scenery of the Trossachs. It is crammed with incident and free from the rather wearying digressions of the earlier lays. Without rising to the heights of great poetry, it has considerable vigour and spirit, and contains some of his best lyrics. In *Rokeby* (1813) the scene shifts to the North of England. As a whole this poem is inferior to its predecessors, but some of the lyrics have a seriousness and depth of tone that are quite uncommon in the spur-and-feather pageantry of Scott's verse. *The Bridal of Triermain* (1813) and *The Lord of the Isles* (1814) mark a decline in quality.

In addition to these longer poems Scott composed many lyrics, some of which are found in the lays, others in his novels, and some of which were contributed to magazines and similar publications. Though his lyrical note is on occasion uncertain, these poems are generally of a more sustained quality than his narrative work, and, to modern tastes, Scott is here seen at his best. One eminent critic has even gone so far as to describe him as the chief lyrical poet between Burns or Blake and Shelley. Though he is no love poet, he successfully handles a wide variety of subjects, from the hearty gaiety of *Waken, lords and ladies gay* or *Bonny Dundee* to the martial ardour of *Pibroch of Donuil Dhu* or the moving, elegiac sadness of *Proud Maisie*. It is in this last type that he touches on something deeper and finer which provides us with his best lyrics.

> He is gone on the mountain,
>   He is lost to the forest,
> Like a summer-dried fountain,
>   When our need was the sorest.
> The font re-appearing
>   From the rain-drops shall borrow;
> But to us comes no cheering,
>   To Duncan no morrow!
>
> The hand of the reaper
>   Takes ears that are hoary
> But the voice of the weeper
>   Wails manhood in glory.
> The Autumn winds rushing,
>   Waft the leaves that are searest,
> But our flower was in flushing,
>   When blighting was nearest.
>
> Fleet foot on the correi,
>   Sage counsel in cumber,
> Red hand in the foray,
>   How sound is thy slumber!

Like the dew on the mountain,
Like the foam on the river,
Like the bubble on the fountain,
Thou art gone, and for ever!

Coronach

As a narrative poet Scott's reputation has depreciated, though, as we have seen, his lyrical qualities have more recently been acclaimed. Of his narratives it may be said that his faults, like his merits, are all on the surface: he lacks the finer poetical virtues, such as reflection, melody, and delicate sympathy; he (in poetry) is deficient in humour; he records crude physical action simply portrayed. Even the vigour that is often ascribed to him exists fitfully, for he loads his narrative with over-abundant detail, often of a technical kind. When he does move freely he has the stamp, the rattle, and the swing of martial music. One must nevertheless do credit to the service he did to poetry by giving new zest to the Romantic methods that had already been adopted in poetry.

3. His Prose. About 1814 Scott largely gave up writing poetry, and save for short pieces, mainly in the novels, wrote no more in verse. As he confessed in the last year of his life, Byron had 'bet' him by producing verse tales that were fast swallowing up the popularity of his own. In 1814 Scott returned to a fragment of a Jacobite prose romance that he had started and left unfinished in 1805. He left the opening chapters as they stood, and on to them tacked a rapid and brilliant narrative dealing with the Forty-five. This made the novel *Waverley*, which was issued anonymously in 1814. Owing chiefly to its ponderous and lifeless beginning, the book hung fire for a space; but the remarkable remainder was almost bound to make it a success. After *Waverley* Scott went on from strength to strength: *Guy Mannering* (1815), *The Antiquary* (1816), *The Black Dwarf* (1816), *Old Mortality* (1816), *Rob Roy* (1818), *The Heart of Midlothian* (1818), *The Bride of Lammermoor* (1819), and *A Legend of Montrose* (1819). All these novels deal with scenes in Scotland, but not all with historical Scotland. They are not of equal merit, and the weakest is *The Black Dwarf*. Scott now turned his gaze abroad, producing *Ivanhoe* (1820), the scene of which is Plantagenet England; then turned again to Scotland and suffered failure with *The Monastery* (1820), though he triumphantly rehabilitated himself with *The Abbot* (1820), a sequel to the last. Henceforth he ranged abroad or stayed at home as he fancied in *Kenilworth* (1821), *The Pirate* (1822), *The Fortunes of Nigel* (1822),

Peveril of the Peak (1823), *Quentin Durward* (1823), *St Ronan's Well* (1824), *Redgauntlet* (1824), *The Betrothed* (1825), and *The Talisman* (1825). By this time such enormous productivity was telling even on his gigantic powers. In the latter books the narrative is often heavier, the humour more cumbrous, and the descriptions more laboured.

Then came the financial deluge, and Scott began a losing battle against misfortune and disease. But even yet the odds were not too great for him; for in succession appeared *Woodstock* (1826), *The Fair Maid of Perth* (1828), *Anne of Geierstein* (1829), *Count Robert of Paris* (1832), and *Castle Dangerous* (1832). The last works were dictated from the depths of mental and bodily anguish, and the furrows of mind and brow are all over them. Yet frequently the old spirit revives and the ancient glory is renewed.

It should never be forgotten that along with these literary labours Scott was filling the office of Clerk of Session, was laboriously performing the duties of a Border laird, and was compiling a mass of miscellaneous prose. Among this last are his editions of Dryden (1808) and Swift (1814), heavy tasks in themselves; the *Lives of the Novelists* (1821–24); the *Life of Napoleon* (1827), a gigantic work that cost him more labour than ten novels; and the admirable *Tales of a Grandfather* (1828–30). His miscellaneous articles, pamphlets, journals, and letters are a legion in themselves.

4. Features of his Novels. (*a*) *Rapidity of Production.* Scott's great success as a novelist led to some positive evils, the greatest of which was a too great haste in the composition of his stories. His haphazard financial methods, which often led to his drawing upon future profits, also tended to over-production. Haste is visible in the construction of his plots, which are frequently hurriedly improvised, developed carelessly, and finished anyhow. As for his style, it is spacious and ornate, but he has little ear for rhythm and melody, and his sentences are apt to be shapeless. The same haste is seen in the handling of his characters, which sometimes finish weakly after they have begun strongly. An outstanding case of this is Mike Lambourne in *Kenilworth*.

It is doubtful if Scott would have done any better if he had taken greater pains. He himself admitted, and to a certain extent gloried in, his slapdash methods. So he must stand the inevitable criticisms that arise when his methods are examined.

(*b*) His *contribution to the novel* is very great indeed. To the historical novel he brought a knowledge that was not pedantically exact, but manageable, wide, and bountiful. To the sum of this knowledge he added a life-giving force, a vitalizing energy, an insight, and a genial dexterity that made the historical novel an entirely new species. Earlier historical novels, such as Clara Reeve's *Old English Baron* (1777) and Miss Porter's *The Scottish Chiefs* (1810), had been lifeless productions; but in the hands of Scott the historical novel became of the first importance, so much so that for a generation after his time it was done almost to death. It should also be noted that he did much to develop the domestic novel, which had several representatives in the Waverley series, such as *Guy Mannering* and *The Antiquary*. To this type of fiction he added freshness, as well as his broad and sane handling of character and incident.

(c) His *Shakespearian Qualities*. Scott has often been called the prose Shakespeare, and in several respects the comparison is fairly just. He resembles Shakespeare in the free manner in which he ranges high and low, right and left, in his search for material. On the other hand, in his character-drawing he lacks much of the Elizabethan's deep penetration. His villains are often melodramatic and his heroes and heroines wooden and dull. His best figures are either Lowland Scots of the middle and lower classes or eccentrics, whose idiosyncrasies are skilfully kept within bounds. He has much of Shakespeare's genial, tolerant humour, in which he strongly resembles also his great predecessor Fielding. It is probably in this large urbanity that the resemblance to Shakespeare is observed most strongly.

(d) His *Style*. The following extract will give some idea of Scott's style at its best. It lacks suppleness, but it is powerful, solid, and sure. In his use of the Scottish vernacular he is exceedingly natural and vivacious. His characters who employ the Scottish dialect, such as Cuddie Headrigg or Jeanie Deans, owe much of their freshness and attraction to Scott's happy use of their native speech:

> Fergus, as the presiding judge was putting on the fatal cap of judgment, placed his own bonnet upon his head, regarded him with a steadfast and stern look, and replied in a firm voice: "I cannot let this numerous audience suppose that to such an appeal I have no answer to make. But what I have to say you would not bear to hear, for my defence would be your condemnation. Proceed, then, in the name of God, to do what is permitted to you. Yesterday and the day before you have condemned loyal and honourable blood to be poured forth like water. Spare not mine. Were that

of all my ancestors in my veins, I would have perilled it in this quarrel." He resumed his seat, and refused again to rise.

Evan Maccombich looked at him with great earnestness, and, rising up, seemed anxious to speak; but the confusion of the court and the perplexity arising from thinking in a language different from that in which he was to express himself, kept him silent. There was a murmur of compassion among the spectators, from the idea that the poor fellow intended to plead the influence of his superior as an excuse for his crime. The judge commanded silence, and encouraged Evan to proceed.

"I was only ganging to say, my lord," said Evan, in what he meant to be an insinuating manner, "that if your excellent Honour and the honourable court would let Vich Ian Vohr go free just this once, and let him gae back to France, and no to trouble King George's government again, that ony six o' the very best of his clan will be willing to be justified in his stead; and if you'll just let me gae down to Glennaquoich, I'll fetch them up to ye mysell, to head or hang, and you may begin wi' me the very first man."

Waverley

II. JANE AUSTEN (1775–1817)

1. Her Life. Jane Austen, the daughter of a Hampshire clergyman, was born at Steventon. She was educated at home; her father was a man of good taste in the choice of reading material, and Jane's education was conducted on sound lines. Her life was unexciting, being little more than a series of pilgrimages to different places of residence, including the fashionable resort of Bath (1801). On the death of the rector his wife and two daughters removed to the neighbourhood of Southampton, where the majority of Jane Austen's novels were written. Her first published works were issued anonymously, and she died in middle age, before her merits had received anything like adequate recognition.

2. Her Novels. The chronology of Jane Austen's novels is not easy to follow, for her works were not published in their order of composition.

Her first novel was *Pride and Prejudice* (1796–97), published 1813). In it, as in all her works, we have middle-class people pursuing the common round. The heroine is a girl of spirit, but she has no extraordinary qualities; her prejudice and the pride of rank and wealth are gently but pleasingly titillated, as if they are being subjected to an electric current of carefully selected intensity. The style is smooth and unobtrusive, but covers a delicate pricking of irony that is agreeable and masterly in its quiet way. Nothing quite like it had appeared before in the novel. In unobtrusive and dexterous art the book is considered to be her masterpiece.

Sense and Sensibility (1797–98, published 1811) was her second novel, and it followed the same general lines as its predecessor. It was followed by *Northanger Abbey* (1798, published posthumously 1818). The book begins as a burlesque of the Radcliffian horror novel, which was then all the rage. The heroine, after a visit to Bath, is invited to an abbey, where she imagines romantic possibilities, but is in the end ludicrously undeceived. The incidents of the novel are commonplace and the characters flatly average. Yet the treatment is deft and touched with the finest needle-point of satiric observation.

Between 1798 and 1811 there was a pause in her writing, but then followed in quick succession her other three great novels, *Mansfield Park* (1811–13, published 1814), *Emma* (1815, published 1816), and *Persuasion* (1815–16, published 1818). The novels of this latter group are of the same type as the earlier ones; if there is any development it is seen in the still more inflexible avoidance of anything that is unusual or startling. Jane Austen's novels are all much the same, yet subtly and artistically different.

3. Features of her Novels. (*a*) *Her Plots.* Her skilfully constructed plots are severely unromantic. Her first work, beginning as a burlesque of the horrible in fiction, finishes by being an excellent example of her ideal novel. As her art develops, even the slight casualties of common life—such as an incident, for example, as the elopement that appears in *Pride and Prejudice*—become rarer; with the result that the later novels, such as *Emma*, are the pictures of everyday existence. Life in her novels is governed by an easy decorum, and moments of fierce passion, or even deep emotion, never occur. Only the highest art can make such plots attractive, and Jane Austen's does so.

(*b*) Her *characters* are developed with minuteness and accuracy. They are ordinary people, but are convincingly alive. She is fond of introducing clergymen, all of whom strike the reader as being exactly like clergymen, though each has his own individual characteristics. She has many characters of the first class, like the servile Mr Collins in *Pride and Prejudice*, the garrulous Miss Bates in *Emma*, and the selfish and vulgar John Thorpe in *Northanger Abbey*. Her characters are not types, but individuals. Her method of portrayal is based upon acute observation and a quiet but incisive irony. Her male characters have a certain softness of thew and temper, but her female characters are almost unexceptionable in perfection of finish.

(c) Her *place in the history of fiction* is remarkable. Her qualities are of a kind that are slow to be recognized, for there is nothing loud or garish to catch the casual glance. The taste for this kind of fiction has to be acquired, but once it is acquired it remains strong. Jane Austen has won her way to a foremost place, and she will surely keep it.

We add a short extract to illustrate her clear and careful style, her skill in handling conversation, and the quiet irony of her method.

> (*Catherine Morland, the heroine of the novel, is introduced to the society of Bath, where she cuts rather a lonely figure till she meets a young man called Tilney—"not quite handsome, but very near it." The following is part of their conversation at a dance.*)

After chatting some time on such matters as naturally arose from the objects around them, he suddenly addressed her with—"I have hitherto been very remiss, madam, in the proper attentions of a partner here; I have not yet asked you how long you have been in Bath; whether you were ever here before; whether you have been at the Upper Rooms, the theatre, and the concert; and how you like the place altogether. I have been very negligent—but are you now at leisure to satisfy me in these particulars? If you are I will begin directly."

"You need not give yourself that trouble, sir."

"No trouble, I assure you, madam." Then forming his features into a set smile, and affectedly softening his voice, he added, with a simpering air, "Have you been long in Bath, madam?"

"About a week, sir," replied Catherine, trying not to laugh.

"Really!" with affected astonishment.

"Why should you be surprised, sir?"

"Why, indeed?" said he, in his natural tone; "but some emotion must appear to be raised by your reply, and surprise is more easily assumed, and not less reasonable, than any other.—Now let us go on. Were you never here before, madam?"

"Never, sir."

"Indeed! Have you yet honoured the Upper Rooms?"

"Yes, sir, I was there last Monday."

"Have you been to the theatre?"

"Yes, sir, I was at the play on Tuesday."

"To the concert?"

"Yes, sir, on Wednesday."

"And are you altogether pleased with Bath?"

"Yes—I like it very well."

"Now I must give one smirk, and then we may be rational again."

Northanger Abbey

OTHER NOVELISTS

1. Maria Edgeworth (1767–1849) was born in Oxfordshire, but, after her earliest years, spent most of an uneventful life in Ireland. Her books are numerous but are to-day little read, though they enjoyed great popularity in her own day. They fall into three classes, short stories for children, such as *Simple Susan*, which were collected in *The Parent's Assistant* (1795–1800) and *Early Lessons* (1801–15); Irish tales, which include her best works, *Castle Rackrent* (1800), *The Absentee* (1809), and *Ormond* (1817); and full-length novels, such as *Belinda* (1801), *Leonora* (1806), *Patronage* (1814), and *Harrington* (1817). With the solitary exception of her finest book, *Castle Rackrent*, in which she kept her moral purpose in the background, all her writings are marred by her overmastering didactic urge. This results in an over-simplification of life and of character in order to show clearly the inevitable triumph of virtue. Yet her children's stories show a fine understanding of, and sympathy with, the outlook of children, and her Irish tales are notable for a level-headed, accurate, and vivid portrayal of many levels of Irish life, and the creation of such fine characters as King Corny, in *Ormond*, or Thady, in *Castle Rackrent*. Her field is the limited domestic circle also explored by Jane Austen and, like the latter she writes in simple, unaffected style. Sir Walter Scott declared that her tales of Irish life inspired his attempt to do something similar for Scotland.

2. John Galt (1779–1839) was born in Ayrshire, and there he passed the early years of his life, afterward removing to Greenock. After spending some years as a clerk, he moved to London to read for the Bar, but he abandoned his studies to take up a business appointment abroad. After much travelling he settled in Scotland, and produced a large amount of literary work. He engaged unsuccessfully in business transactions, then took once more to writing novels and to journalism. He died at Greenock, where his career had commenced.

The best of his novels are *The Ayrshire Legatees; or, the Pringle Family* (1821), in the form of a letter-series, containing much amusing Scottish narrative; *The Annals of the Parish* (1821), his masterpiece, which is the record of a fictitious country minister, doing in prose very much what Crabbe had done in verse; *The Provost* (1822); and *The Entail; or, the Lairds of Grippy* (1823). Galt had a vigorous style and abundant imagination, with a great deal of humour and sympathetic observation. He is too haphazard and uneven to be a great novelist, though he has value as a painter of Scottish manners, and his portraits are masterly in their terseness and power of self-revelation.

3. **William Harrison Ainsworth (1805–82)**, the son of a solicitor, was born at Manchester, where he was educated at the grammar school. After some attempt to study law he took to literature as a career. He tried publishing without success, and then, in 1840, became editor of *Bentley's Miscellany*. In 1853 he acquired *The New Monthly Magazine*. He died at Reigate.

An early imitator of Scott, Ainsworth wrote a great number of novels, which cover many periods of English history. The first was *Sir John Chiverton* (1826), written in collaboration with John Aston, but his great success was scored with *Rookwood* (1834). A few of the many others were *Jack Sheppard* (1839), an immense success, *The Tower of London* (1840), *Old St Paul's* (1841), *Windsor Castle* (1843), *The Star Chamber* (1854), *The Constable of the Tower* (1861), and *Preston Fight, or the Insurrection of* 1715 (1875). Ainsworth possesses little of Scott's genius, for his handling of historical material is crude and cavalier in the extreme. His brutal realism and crude sensationalism give his work a melodramatic effect similar to that of the Radcliffian horror novel. His characterization is poor and his style unpolished, but when he is in the right vein he can give the reader a vigorous narrative, seen, perhaps, at its best in his account of Turpin's ride to York in *Rookwood*.

4. **George P. R. James (1801–60)** was another follower of the method of Scott, and he was responsible for a hundred and eighty-nine volumes, chiefly novels. He was born in London; travelled abroad; settled down to novel-writing; on the strength of some serious historical work was appointed Historiographer Royal; entered the Consular Service; and died at Venice.

Richelieu. A Tale of France (1829), which bears a strong resemblance to *Quentin Durward*, was his earliest, and is by many considered to be his best, novel. Others include *Darnley, or the Field of the Cloth of Gold* (1830), *De l'Orme* (1830), *The Gipsey* (1835), and *Lord Montagu's Page* (1858). As was almost inevitable with such mass-production, he makes his novels on a stock pattern. He is fond of florid pageantry, and can be rather ingeniously mysterious in his plots. He has little power in dealing with his characters, and no imaginative grasp of history. In style he is pompous and monotonous, and his dialogue is stilted and formal.

5. Charles Lever (1806–72). Lever was born in Dublin, was educated at Trinity College and Göttingen, and became a physician. The success of his novels caused him to desert his profession, and in the course of time (1842) he became editor of *The Dublin University Magazine*, which had published his first stories. In his latter years he lived abroad, was appointed consul in Spezia (1857), and after some other changes died when consul at Trieste.

The Confessions of Harry Lorrequer (1839), his first novel, made a great hit. It is a novel of the picaresque type, dealing with the adventures of the hare-brained but lovable hero. *Charles O'Malley, the Irish Dragoon* (1841), is of the same species, and others are *Jack Hinton* and *Tom Burke of 'Ours,'* which appeared together (1843–44) as *Our Mess*. All these novels are either set in Ireland or deal with Irish characters. There is little plot, what there is consisting of the scrapes of the heroes; the humour is rough-and-tumble, though agreeably lively; and the heroes, who are all much the same, are amiable fellows, with a propensity for falling into trouble and falling out of it. A later class of Lever's novels was more of the historical cast, and includes *The O'Donoghue* (1845) and *The Knight of Gwynne* (1847). Others dealt with the Continent, and include *The Dodd Family Abroad* (1852–54) and *The Fortunes of Glencore* (1857). These latter are more stable and serious, but, though they are more careful in structure and finished in style, Lever lacked the necessary depth of insight to deal adequately with serious social topics, and we miss the racy, spirited tone of his earlier and more typical picaresque novels.

6. Frederick Marryat (1792–1848) followed the Smollett tradition of writing sea-stories. He was born in London, entered the Navy at an early age (1806), and saw some fighting during the Napoleonic Wars. He saw further service in different parts of the world, rose to be a captain, and spent much of his later life writing the novels that have given him his place in literature.

His earliest novel was *The Naval Officer; or Scenes and Adventures in the Life of Frank Mildmay* (1829), a loose and disconnected narrative, which was followed by *The King's Own* (1830), a much more able piece of work. From this point he continued to produce fiction at a great rate. The best of his stories are *Jacob Faithful* (1834), *Peter Simple* (1834), *Japhet in Search of a Father* (1836), *Mr Midshipman Easy* (1836), and *Masterman Ready* (1841–42). All his best books deal with the sea, and have much of its breeziness. Marryat has a considerable gift for plain narrative, and his humour, though it is often coarse, is entertaining. His characters are of the stock types, but they are lively and suit his purpose, which is to produce a good yarn.

7. **Michael Scott (1789–1835)** was another novelist whose favourite theme was the sea. Scott was not a sailor like Marryat, but a merchant, first in Jamaica and then in his native city of Glasgow. His two tales, *Tom Cringle's Log* and *The Cruise of the Midge*, were published in *Blackwood's Magazine* (1829–33). As picaresque novels they are good, and notable for their narrative powers and the fine descriptions in which Scott captures the beauty and magic of the sea. But they cannot rank among the best, for most of the characters are grotesque, and the stories are full of violent sensation and horseplay.

8. **Thomas Love Peacock (1785–1866)**, the son of a London merchant, was born at Weymouth. He was privately educated, and unsuccessfully tried a number of clerical and business posts before joining the East India Company in 1819. A very efficient servant of this company, he was chief examiner between 1836 and 1856. In 1812 he had met Shelley, with whom he maintained a close friendship until the latter's death.

His fame rests upon his novels rather than upon his verse, though the songs which he scattered through his novels are extremely good. His early verses, such as *Palmyra, and Other Poems* (1806), *The Genius of the Thames* (1810), and *The Philosophy of Melancholy* (1812) lack the finish of his later lyrics, but *Rhododaphne; or the Thessalian Spell* (1818) shows some felicity and smoothness.

He wrote seven novels, *Headlong Hall* (1816), *Melincourt* (1817), *Nightmare Abbey* (1818), *Maid Marian* (1822), *The Misfortunes of Elphin* (1829), *Crotchet Castle* (1831), and *Gryll Grange* (1860). None of them has a plot really worthy of the name, though all contain well-recounted incidents. In varying degrees, they are the vehicle for his ironical and satirical attacks on the cranks and fads of his day. His favourite butt was the contemporary cult of romanticism and all who practised it. Wordsworth, as Mr Paperstamp of Mainchance Villa, Coleridge, as Mr Flosky, Shelley, as Mr Scythrop, Byron, as Mr Cypress, and many others were all caricatured with telling skill. No contemporary idea, from paper money to modern science, escaped his pen. The novels consist mainly of discussions phrased in a concise, polished, scholarly style, full of wit and pointed satire, in which characters embodying contemporary ideas dissect themselves with devastating effect. The books contain fine spirited lyrics, of which the best known is *The War Song of Dinas Vawr*.

Peacock's *The Four Ages of Poetry*, in which his own age is classed as the age of brass, "the second childhood of poetry," is in the familiar mocking, ironical style of the novels. Its only importance lies in the fact that it drew from Shelley his famous *The Defence of Poetry*.

9. Washington Irving (1783–1859) was the first American novelist to establish a European reputation. He was called to the Bar, but his real bent was literary. His life was that of a busy man of letters, varied with much travelling in Europe and America. His works were admired by Scott, who did much to popularize them on this side of the Atlantic.

His *History of New York* (1809) was the comic history of an imaginary Dutchman called Knickerbocker. The humour now appears strained and overdone, but the book is written with ease and grace. His *The Sketch-book* (1820) brought his name before the English public. The volume is a collection of short tales and sketches, the two favourites, those of Rip van Winkle and of Sleepy Hollow, being the best of his productions. It was followed by *Bracebridge Hall* (1822), a series of sketches of the life of the English squirearchy, done in the Addisonian manner. His later travels helped him in the writing of *Tales of a Traveller* (1824), *Legends of the Alhambra* (1832), and other works. As a story-teller Irving lacks animation and fire, but his humour in the later books is facile, though thin, and his descriptions are sometimes impressive. His style reminds the reader of that of Goldsmith, whose *Life* (1849) he wrote. He produced other historical works, such as *History of the Life and Voyages of Columbus* (1828), *The Conquest of Granada* (1829), and his *Life of Washington* (1859), more noteworthy for the ease of their narrative than for their deep learning or insight.

10. James Fenimore Cooper (1789–1851) was born in New Jersey, and educated at Yale College. He passed his boyhood on an ancestral estate near Lake Otsego, and so gained much material for his Indian works. He was in the Navy for six years, and then retired to write books. He travelled and wrote much. He was a man of acrimonious temper, and his extravagant estimation of his abilities drew him into many quarrels.

His first novel, *Precaution* (1820), was a conventional study of society and was of little merit. Then *The Spy* (1821) began a series of vigorous adventure stories, some of which, like *The Pilot* (1824) and *The Red Rover* (1828), deal with the sea. Cooper's technical knowledge and appreciation of the beauty of the sea are here used to advantage, though his characters are stiff. The best of his works, however, are the Leatherstocking novels, which deal with frontier life in Indian territory. They include *The Pioneers* (1823), *The Last of the Mohicans* (1826), *The Pathfinder* (1840), and *The Deerslayer* (1841). Their view of the Indian is romanticized, but they opened up a new field for American fiction, and have plenty of incident and suspense. Cooper set himself up as a rival of Scott, but he has little of Scott's ability. He lacks humour, his characters are, with rare exceptions such as Leatherstocking, lifeless and unconvincing, and his style is wordy and heavy. But at times he can make his story move rapidly, and he is skilful in his suggestion of the charm and dangers of the primeval forest.

Cooper attempted many other forms of literature, including highly controversial novels about Europe, bitter satire, a history of the American Navy, and propagandist attacks on cruelty and oppression. But he wrote too much and too carelessly. He affected to despise popular criticism, but, except for his Indian tales, his work has little permanent value.

WRITERS OF MISCELLANEOUS PROSE

I. CHARLES LAMB (1775–1834)

1. His Life. Lamb was born in London, his father being a kind of factotum to a Bencher of the Inner Temple. The boy, who was a timid and retiring youth, was educated at Christ's Hospital, where he was a fellow-pupil of Coleridge, whose early eccentricities he has touched upon with his usual felicity. He obtained a clerkship first in the South Sea House, then (1792) in the India House, where the remainder of his working life was spent. There was a strain of madness in the family which did not leave him untouched, for in 1795–96 he was under restraint for a time. In the case of his sister, Mary Lamb, the curse was a deadly one. In September 1796 she murdered her mother in a sudden frenzy, and thereafter she had intermittent attacks of insanity. Lamb devoted his life to the welfare of his afflicted sister, who frequently appears in his essays under the name of Cousin Bridget. After more than thirty years' service Lamb retired (1825) on a pension, and the last ten years of his life were passed in blessed release from his desk. He was a charming man, a delightful talker, and one of the least assuming of writers. His reputation, based upon his qualities of humour, pathos, and cheery good-will, is unsurpassed in our literature.

2. His Essays. Lamb started his literary career as a poet, producing short pieces of moderate ability, including the well-known *The Old Familiar Faces* and *To Hester*. He attempted a tragedy, *John Woodvil* (1802), in the style of his favourite Elizabethan playwrights, but it had no success on the stage. His *Tales from Shakespeare* (1807), written in collaboration with his sister, are skilfully done, and are agreeable to read. His critical work, the most substantial selection of which is to be found in his *Specimens of English Dramatic Poets, who lived about the Time of Shakespeare* (1808), is remarkable for its delicate insight and good literary taste. His work on the Elizabethan dramatists rescued them from the unmerited oblivion in which they had long rested, and led to a fresh appreciation of their fine qualities. All these writings, however, are of little importance compared with his essays.

The first of his essays appeared in *The London Magazine* in 1820, when Lamb was forty-five years old. It was signed "Elia," a name taken almost at random as that of a foreigner, a clerk in the old South Sea House. The original series was published as *The Essays of Elia* (1823), and a second under the title of *The Last Essays of Elia* (1833).

The essays are unequalled in English. In subject they are of the usual miscellaneous kind, ranging from chimney-sweeps to old china. They are, however, touched with personal opinions and recollections so oddly obtruded that interest in the subject is nearly swamped by the reader's delight in the author. No essayist is more egotistical than Lamb; but no egotist can be so artless and yet so artful, so tearful and yet so mirthful, so pedantic and yet so humane. It is this delicate clashing of humours, like the chiming of sweet bells, that affords the chief delight to Lamb's readers.

It is almost impossible to do justice to his style. It is old-fashioned, bearing echoes and odours from older writers like Sir Thomas Browne and Fuller; it is full of long and curious words; and it is dashed with frequent exclamations and parentheses. The humour that runs through it all is not strong, but airy, almost elfish, in note; it vibrates faintly, but in application never lacks precision. His pathos is of much the same character; and sometimes, as in *Dream-Children*, it deepens into a quivering sigh of regret. He is so sensitive and so strong, so cheerful and yet so unalterably doomed to sorrow.

The extract given below deals with the playhouse, which was one of his greatest passions. The reader can easily observe some of the above-mentioned features of his style.

> In those days were pit orders. Beshrew the uncomfortable manager who abolished them!—with one of these we went. I remember the waiting at the door—not that which is left—but between that and an inner door in shelter—O when shall I be such an expectant again!—with the cry of nonpareils, an indispensable play-house accompaniment in those days. As near as I can recollect, the fashionable pronunciation of the theatrical fruiteresses then was, "Chase some oranges, chase some numparels, chase a bill of the play";—chase *pro* chuse. But when we got in, and I beheld the green curtain that veiled a heaven to my imagination, which was soon to be disclosed—the breathless anticipations I endured! I had seen something like it in the plate prefixed to *Troilus and Cressida*, in Rowe's Shakespeare—the tent scene with Diomede—and a sight of that plate can always bring back in a measure the feeling of that evening.—The boxes at that time, full of well-dressed women of quality, projected over the pit; and the pilasters reaching down were adorned with a glistering substance (I know not what) under glass (as it seemed), resembling—a homely fancy—but I judged it to be sugar-candy—yet, to my raised imagination, divested of its homelier qualities, it appeared a glorified candy!—The orchestra lights at length arose, those "fair Auroras!" Once the bell sounded. It was to ring out yet once again—and, incapable of the anticipation, I reposed my shut eyes in a sort of resignation upon the maternal lap. It rang the second time. The curtain drew up—I was not past six years old—and the play was *Artaxerxes*!
>
> *My First Play*

Every aspect of Lamb's character and thought is to be found still more clearly revealed in the natural, intimate *Letters*, which cover the last thirty-eight years of his life. Among his many correspondents were Wordsworth, Coleridge, Southey, and Hazlitt.

II. THOMAS DE QUINCEY (1785–1859)

1. His Life. De Quincey was born at Manchester, where his father was a rich merchant. The elder De Quincey left considerable property, but De Quincey himself was improvident and unreliable in his financial affairs. He was educated at Manchester Grammar School and then at Oxford. There he studied for a long time (1803–08), distinguishing himself by his ability in Greek. While he was an undergraduate (1804) he first became acquainted with opium, soaking his tobacco in the drug and then smoking it in order to alleviate the pains of neuralgia. His money was always easily spent, and his early struggles were a painful effort to make both ends meet. He earned a precarious livelihood by journalism, and spent the years 1809-30, for the most part, in the Lake District, becoming intimate with the local literary celebrities. During this time his devotion to the drug was excessive, but he produced a large amount of work. Then, becoming loosely attached to the staff of *Blackwood's Magazine*, he removed to Edinburgh. In this neighbourhood he remained till the end of his long life, and was buried in the Scottish capital.

2. His Works. De Quincey is one of the authors whose work is to be rigorously sifted. He wrote a large amount of prose; most of it is hack-work, a fair proportion is of good quality, and a small amount is of the highest merit. He wrote no book of any great length, in this respect resembling another opium-eater, Coleridge.

The book that made his name was his *Confessions of an English Opium Eater* (1821), which appeared in *The London Magazine*. The work, which is chaotic in its general plan, is a series of visions that melt away in the manner of dreams. Much is tawdry and unreal, but the book contains passages of great power and beauty. The remainder of his work is a mass of miscellaneous production, the best of which is *The English Mail-coach* (1849), *Suspiria de Profundis* (1845), and *On Murder considered as One of the Fine Arts* (1827; second part, 1839).

A great part of his work is dreary and diffuse, and vitiated by a humour that is extremely flat and ineffective. He displays a wide range of knowledge, though it is often flawed with inaccuracy. In style he is apt to stumble into vulgarity and tawdriness; but when inspiration descends upon him he gives to the English tongue a wonderful strength and sweetness. In these rare moments he plunges into an elaborate style and imagery, but never loses grip, sweeping along with sureness and ease. In rhythm and melody he is almost supreme; he can "blow through bronze" and "breathe through silver," and be impressive in both.

The passage we now give is among his most impressive efforts. It has the unity and passion of the lyric, and its effect is both thrilling and profound. Observe the studied rhythm, often ejaculatory, the deep and solemn beauty, and the simplicity of diction. This is poetic prose at its best:

> As a final specimen, I cite one of a different character, from 1820. The dream commenced with a music which now I often heard in dreams—a music of preparation and of awakening suspense; a

music like the opening of the coronation anthem, and which, like *that*, gave the feeling of a vast march--of infinite cavalcades filing off—and the tread of innumerable armies. The morning was come of a mighty day—a day of crisis and of final hope for human nature, then suffering some mysterious eclipse, and labouring in some dread extremity. Somewhere, I knew not where—somehow, I knew not how—by some beings, I knew not whom—a battle, a strife, an agony was conducting—was evolving like a great drama, or piece of music; with which my sympathy was the more insupportable from my confusion as to its place, its cause, its nature, and its possible issue. I, as is usual in dreams (where, of necessity, we make ourselves central to every movement), had the power, and yet had not the power, to decide it. I had the power, if I could raise myself, to will it; and yet again had not the power, for the weight of twenty Atlantics was upon me, or the oppression of inexpiable guilt. "Deeper than ever plummet sounded," I lay inactive. Then, like a chorus, the passion deepened. Some greater interest was at stake; some mightier cause than ever yet the sword had pleaded, or trumpet had proclaimed. Then came sudden alarms: hurryings to and fro: trepidations of innumerable fugitives, I knew not whether from the good cause or the bad: darkness, and lights: tempest, and human faces; and at last, with the sense that all was lost, female forms, and the features that were worth all the world to me, and but a moment allowed,—and clasped hands, and heart-breaking partings, and then—everlasting farewells! and with a sigh, such as the caves of hell sighed when the incestuous mother uttered the abhorred name of Death, the sound was reverberated —everlasting farewells! and again, and yet again reverberated— everlasting farewells!

And I awoke in struggles, and cried aloud—"I will sleep no more!"

Confessions of an English Opium Eater (edition of 1821)

III. WILLIAM HAZLITT (1778–1830)

The period now under review is very rich in critical and miscellaneous work. Of the writers of literary criticism Hazlitt may be taken as representative.

1. His Life. The son of a Unitarian minister, Hazlitt was born at Maidstone, and, after a brief stay in America, spent most of his youth in Shropshire. His early studies for the Unitarian ministry were soon abandoned. Shortly after he met Coleridge (1798), whose zeal for the ideals of the French Revolution he shared. His next ambition was to become a painter, but this, too, he soon abandoned in favour of a literary career. The year 1812 saw him in London, where he was in turn lecturer, parliamentary reporter, and theatre critic. From 1814 until his death he contributed to *The Edinburgh Review*, while others of his articles appeared in *The Examiner*,

The Times, and *The London Magazine*. All through his life his unusual political views and headstrong temperament involved him in frequent quarrels.

2. His Works. Hazlitt's earliest writings consisted of miscellaneous philosophical and political works, which are of interest for the light they throw upon his mind, but are now little read. His reputation rests on the lectures and essays on literary and general subjects all published between 1817 and 1825. Of the former we have his lectures on *Characters of Shakespeare's Plays* (1817), *The English Poets* (1818), *The English Comic Writers* (1819), and *The Dramatic Literature of the Age of Elizabeth* (1820). His best essays were collected in *The Round Table* (1817), *Table Talk; or, Original Essays on Men and Manners* (1821–22), and *The Spirit of the Age; or, Contemporary Portraits* (1825). Between 1828 and 1830 he published an unsuccessful biography of Napoleon.

Modern opinion has endorsed the contemporary recognition of Hazlitt's eminence as a critic. His writing is remarkable for its fearless expression of an honest and individual opinion, and, while he lacks the learned critical apparatus of more modern critics, he is unsurpassed in his ability to communicate his own enjoyment, and in his gift for evoking unnoticed beauties. His judgments are based on his emotional reactions rather than on objectively applied principles. Consequently, they are sometimes marred by personal bias, as in some of the portraits in *The Spirit of the Age*. But, for the most part, they show his enthusiasm guided by a strong common sense. The catholicity of his taste embraces almost every major English author from Chaucer to his own day, most of them treated with a discrimination and sympathetic insight which are not blunted by his obvious enthusiasm.

In style Hazlitt contrasts strongly with the elaborate orchestration of the complex sentence and the magic of the delicate word tracery which we have seen in De Quincey. His brief, abrupt sentences have the vigour and directness which his views demand. His lectures have a manly simplicity, and something of the looseness of organization which is typical of good conversation. Essays and lectures alike show a fondness for the apt and skilfully blended quotation, and for the balanced sentence, often embodying a contrast. Always his diction is pure and his expression concise. The following extract is of interest as showing his courageous exposition of an opinion, diametrically opposed to that generally accepted, on the relative merits of Addison and Steele:

It will be said, that all this is to be found, in the same or a greater degree, in the *Spectator*. For myself, I do not think so; or, at least, there is in the last work a much greater proportion of commonplace matter. I have, on this account, always preferred the *Tatler* to the *Spectator*. Whether it is owing to my having been earlier or better acquainted with the one than the other, my pleasure in reading these two admirable works is not at all in proportion to their comparative reputation. The *Tatler* contains only half the number of volumes, and, I will venture to say, nearly an equal quantity of sterling wit and sense. "The first sprightly runnings" are there—it has more of the original spirit, more of the freshness and stamp of nature. The indications of character and strokes of humour are more true and frequent; the reflections that suggest themselves arise more from the occasion, and are less spun out into regular dissertations. They are more like the remarks which occur in sensible conversation, and less like a lecture. Something is left to the understanding of the reader. Steele seems to have gone into his closet chiefly to set down what he observed out of doors. Addison seems to have spent most of his time in his study, and to have spun out and wire-drawn the hints, which he borrowed from Steele, or took from nature, to the utmost. I am far from wishing to depreciate Addison's talents, but I am anxious to do justice to Steele, who was, I think, upon the whole, a less artificial and more original writer. The humorous descriptions of Steele resemble loose sketches, or fragments of a comedy; those of Addison are rather comments, or ingenious paraphrases, on the genuine text.

Lectures on the English Comic Writers

OTHER WRITERS OF MISCELLANEOUS PROSE

1. Walter Savage Landor (1775–1864). Landor had a long life, for he was born five years after Wordsworth, and lived to see the full yield of the Victorian era. Of an ancient family, he was born in Warwickshire, and was educated at Rugby and Oxford. Later he was fired with republican ideas and supported the revolutionaries in Spain. In temper he was impulsive to the point of mania; and his life is marked by a succession of violent quarrels with his friends and enemies. The middle years of his life were passed in Italy. He returned to England in 1835 and lived in Bath from 1838 to 1858. In this last year his pugnacity involved him in an action for libel, in which, as defendant, he cut a lamentable figure. Poor and dishonoured, he forsook England, and settled again in Florence, where he died.

Though Landor is remembered chiefly as a prose writer, by far the greater part of his life was devoted to poetry. His *Poems* (1795) was a collection of miscellaneous works modelled on the classics, in which the influence of the Miltonic style is clearly to be seen. It was followed by his epic poem, *Gebir* (1798), *Hellenics* (1846, augmented 1847 and 1859), *Last Fruits off an Old Tree* (1853), and *Heroic Idylls* (1863). In these collections Landor tries many kinds of verse, all of which are used with the greatest metrical accuracy. His longer poems, such as *Gebir*, are not without a certain stately dignity of tone and passages of descriptive beauty, but too often they are frigid and unappealing, by reason of their lack of animation and the excessive compression of their imagery. Landor is seen at his best in his shorter works. The *Hellenics*, brief narratives based on Greek mythology, are for the most part in blank verse. Many of them have a pleasing conciseness of style and lightness of touch, though some are marred by the weaknesses of *Gebir*. His lyrics have often a classical restraint and delicacy.

His dramas, of which the best is *Count Julian* (1812), are all lacking in true dramatic qualities, though Landor shows some power as a creator of individual scenes.

His literary fame rests, however, on his *Imaginary Conversations*, published at intervals between 1824 and 1846. These dialogues between actual persons of the past, or of Landor's own day deal with a wide variety of topics—from literary criticism to politics, and the method of exposition varies almost as much as the subjects discussed. The quality of their thought is not particularly high, but some of the characters, especially the women, are very effectively portrayed. *Imaginary Conversations* is, however, of greatest interest as a specimen of the new poetic prose, which we have also seen in De Quincey. It is full of rich imagery and ornate diction, while in rhythmical effect it differs little from Landor's verse. In it are passages which show the epigrammatic brilliance of his shorter poems.

2. **Francis Jeffrey (1773–1850)**, one of the founders of *The Edinburgh Review*, was born at Edinburgh, educated at the high school and university of his native city, and was called to the Scottish Bar. Though for many years an industrious writer for his journal, he maintained a considerable legal practice, and distinguished himself in politics as an ardent Whig. When his party came into office he was rewarded by being appointed Lord Advocate, and played a considerable part in the passage of the Reform Bill of 1832. This meant the abandonment of his position on the *Review*, though he always kept a paternal eye on its progress. He was finally appointed to the Bench, with the title of Lord Jeffrey.

The Edinburgh Review was at first a joint production of a group of young and zealous Whigs, including Sydney Smith and Henry Brougham. Within a year of its foundation Jeffrey was responsible editor, and he drew around him a band of distinguished contributors, including at one time Sir Walter Scott. The journal led the way among the larger reviews, and was noted for its briskness. It was not above prejudice, as was shown in its opposition to the Lake School, but it did much to raise the standard of criticism, and it succeeded in bringing much talent to light, including the early efforts of Macaulay.

3. Sydney Smith (1771–1845) was for a time a colleague of Jeffrey. He was born in Essex, was educated at Winchester and Oxford, and became a clergyman. He settled for a time at Edinburgh as a tutor, and assisted in the launching of *The Edinburgh Review* (1802). He took a large share in the political squabbles of the time, and wrote much on behalf of the Whig party.

His works consist of many miscellaneous pieces, most of them of a political character. The most noteworthy of them is a collection called *Letters on the Subject of the Catholics, to my Brother Abraham, who Lives in the Country, by Peter Plymley* (1807–08), which deals with Catholic Emancipation. A more general selection from his writings was published in 1855, and his *Wit and Wisdom* in 1860. Nowadays it is somewhat difficult to account for his great influence, for he has left so little of real merit; but to his own contemporaries he was a very important person. He was admired and feared as a wit, and some of his best witticisms have been preserved. He was always a gentlemanly opponent, always easy but deadly in the shafts he levelled against his political foes. He wrote the prose of an educated man, and is clear and forcible.

4. John Wilson (1784–1854), who appears in literature as **Christopher North,** was born at Paisley, the son of a wealthy manufacturer. He was educated at Glasgow and Oxford, wrote poetry, and for a time settled in the Lake District. He lost most of his money, tried practice as a barrister, and then joined the staff of *Blackwood's Magazine.* He was appointed in 1820 Professor of Moral Philosophy at Edinburgh University.

His early poems, *The Isle of Palms* (1812) and *The City of the Plague* (1816), are passable verse of the romantic type. His novels—for example, *The Trials of Margaret Lyndsay* (1823)—are sentimental pictures of Scottish life. Wilson's longest work, and the one that perpetuates his name, is his *Noctes Ambrosianæ* (beginning in 1822), which had a long and popular run in *Blackwood's* until 1835.

This is an immensely long series of dialogues on many kinds of subjects. The characters are the members of a small club who meet regularly, consume great quantities of meat and drink, and frequently indulge in immoderate clowning. The talk is endless, and is often tedious in the extreme. At times Wilson rises into striking descriptive passages, more florid and less impressive than De Quincey's, but beautiful in a sentimental fashion. His taste, however, cannot be trusted, and his humour is too often crude and boisterous. Here, as in his other writing for *Blackwood's Magazine*, we have the product of a boisterous, high-spirited critic, to whose temperament, restraint, whether in praise, blame, or humour, was alien.

5. **John G. Lockhart (1794–1854)** was born at Cambusnethan, educated at Glasgow and Oxford, and became a member of the Scottish Bar. He soon (1817) became a regular contributor to *Blackwood's Magazine*, sharing in its strong Tory views and its still stronger expression of them. He rather gloried in these literary and political fisticuffs, which in one case led to actual bloodshed, though he did not participate in it. In 1820 he married Scott's favourite daughter Sophia, and lived to be the biographer of his famous father-in-law. He was editor of *The Quarterly Review* from 1825 till 1853.

Lockhart wrote four novels, the best of which are *Valerius* (1821) and *Adam Blair* (1822). They are painstaking endeavours, but they lack the fire of genius, and are now almost forgotten. His poetry is quite lively and attractive, especially his *Ancient Spanish Ballads* (1823). *Peter's Letters to his Kinsfolk* (1819) is a collection of brilliant sketches of Edinburgh and Glasgow society. Lockhart's fame, however, rests on *Memoirs of the Life of Sir Walter Scott* (1837–38), which was first published in seven volumes. This book ranks as one of the great biographies in the language. Though it is full of intimate and loving detail, it possesses a fine sense of perspective and coherence; and while it is influenced by a natural partiality for its subject, the story is judiciously told. In this book Lockhart casts aside his aggressiveness of manner. His descriptions, as, for example, that of the death of Scott, have a masterly touch.

6. **William Cobbett (1762–1835)** was born at Farnham, Surrey, and was the son of a farm-labourer. He enlisted in the Army, rose to be sergeant-major, emigrated to America, where he took to journalism, and returned to England, to become actively engaged in politics. In 1831 he was elected to Parliament, but was not a success

as a public man. He was a man of violent opinions, boxed the political compass, and died an extreme Radical.

He was an assiduous journalist, beginning with *The Porcupine* (1800–01). His other journal was *Cobbett's Weekly Political Register*, which he began in 1802 and carried on almost unaided until 1835. His literary reputation rests, however, on one of his few full-length books, his *Rural Rides* (1830), which gives an account of the English counties through which he wandered. A true son of the soil, Cobbett writes with insight and understanding of the agricultural conditions of his day. His close and honest observation of life and manners finds expression in a plain, homely style, which has none of the graces of fine writing, but all the vigour and simple directness of a Defoe. Instinctively right in his choice of language, he speaks straight to the heart of the reader, and, though his work is realistic rather than imaginative, the beauty of the English scene is impressed on many a page of the *Rural Rides*. He is shamelessly partisan in his opinions, but his writings betray an expansive and cordial generosity of spirit.

7. The historians belonging to this period are both numerous and important, but we can mention only a few.

(a) **Henry Hart Milman (1791–1868)** was educated at Eton and Oxford, and afterward wrote some plays, including the tragedy *Fazio* (1815). His chief historical works are *The History of the Jews* (1829) and *The History of Latin Christianity* (1854–55). Milman is a solid and reliable historian, with a readable style.

(b) **George Grote (1794–1871)** was a London banker, and entered politics. His *A History of Greece* (1846–56) is based on German research, and is well informed and scholarly. The work, however, is sometimes considered to be too long and tedious in its detail.

(c) **Henry Hallam (1777–1859)** was a member of the Middle Temple, but he practised very little. He wrote on both literary and historical subjects, and contributed to *The Edinburgh Review*. His historical works include *The Constitutional History of England from the Accession of Henry VII to the Death of George II* (1827) and his *Introduction to the Literature of Europe in the Fifteenth, Sixteenth and Seventeenth Centuries* (1837–39). Hallam acquired a great and deserved reputation for solid scholarship. Like Gibbon, he tried to attune his style to his subject, and wrote in a grave and impressive manner, but, lacking the genius of Gibbon, he succeeded only in making his style lifeless and frigid.

THE DEVELOPMENT OF LITERARY FORMS

The amount of actual development during this period was not so great as the immense output. Authors were content with the standard literary forms, and it was upon these as models that the development took place.

1. Poetry. (*a*) This was indeed the golden age of the *lyric*, which reflected the Romantic spirit of the time in liberal and varied measure. It comprised the exalted passion of Shelley, the meditative simplicity of Wordsworth, the sumptuous descriptions of Keats, and the golden notes of Coleridge. It is to be noted that in form the lyric employed the ancient externals of the stereotyped metres and rhymes. There was some attempt at rhymeless poems in the work of Southey and the early poems of Shelley, but this practice was never general.

(*b*) With *descriptive and narrative poems* the age was richly endowed. One has only to recall Byron's early work, Keats's tales, Coleridge's supernatural stories, and Scott's martial and historical romances to perceive how rich was the harvest. Once more the poets work upon older methods. The Spenserian stanza is the favourite model, but the ballad is nearly as popular. These older types suffered some change, as was almost inevitable with such inspired minds at work upon them. The Spenserian manner was loosened and strengthened; it was given richer and more varied beauties in *The Eve of St Agnes*, and a sharper and more personal note in the *Childe Harold* of Byron. In the case of Wordsworth we observe the frequent use of blank verse for meditative purposes, as in *The Prelude*.

(*c*) *Satirical poems* were numerous; and their tone was fierce, for the success of the French Revolution led to the expression of new hopes and desires. Outstanding examples were Byron's *Don Juan* and *The Vision of Judgment* and Shelley's *Masque of Anarchy*.

2. Drama. Drama was written as freely as ever, but rather as a form of literary exercise than as a serious attempt at creating a new dramatic standard. Tragedy almost monopolized the activities of the major poets. Of all the tragedies Shelley's *The Cenci* came first in power and simplicity. Byron's tragedies had little merit as dramas; and Wordsworth's *The Borderers* and Coleridge's *Remorse* added little to the fame of their authors.

The comic spirit in drama was in abeyance. Shelley's *Œdipus Tyrannus, or Swellfoot the Tyrant*, is almost the only instance of it worth mention, and this was a poor specimen of that writer's creative power.

3. Prose. (*a*) *The Novel.* Of the different kinds of prose composition, the novel showed in this period the most marked development. This was largely due to the work of Scott and Jane Austen, who respectively established the historical and domestic types of novel.

With regard to the work of Scott, we can here only briefly summarize what has already been said. He raised the historical novel to the rank of one of the major kinds of literature; he brought to it knowledge, and through the divine gift of knowledge made it true to life; he fired historical characters with living energy; he set on foot the device of the unhistorical hero—that is, he made the chief character purely fictitious, and caused the historical persons to rotate about it; he established a style that suited many periods of history; and pervading all these advances was a great and genial personality that transformed what might have been mere lumber into an artistic product of truth and beauty.

Miss Austen's achievement was of a different kind. She revealed the beauty and interest that underlie ordinary affairs; she displayed the infinite variety of common life, and so she opened an inexhaustible vein that her successors were assiduously to develop.

(*b*) *Literary Criticism.* No previous period had seen literary criticism of such bulk or such generally high standard as that produced in the age under review. In addition to the work of the professional critics, such as Hazlitt (see p. 354) and the reviewers, many of the poets and imaginative prose-writers have left us critical works of great and enduring value. Mention may be made of Wordsworth's preface to the *Lyrical Ballads*; Coleridge's *Biographia Literaria* and lectures on Shakespeare and the other poets; Shelley's *The Defence of Poetry*, in reply to the provocative *The Four Ages of Poetry* of Peacock; and Lamb's *Specimens of English Dramatic Poets, who lived about the Time of Shakespeare.*

(*c*) *Periodical Literature.* At the beginning of this chapter we noted the chief members of a great new community of literary journals. These periodicals were of a new type. Previous literary journals, like *The Gentleman's Magazine* (1731), had been feeble productions, the work of elegant amateurs or underpaid hack-writers. Such papers had little weight. The new journals were supreme in the literary world; they attracted the best talent; they inspired fear and respect; and in spite of many defects their literary product was worthy of their reputation.

(*d*) *The Essay.* Finding a fresh outlet in the new type of periodical, the essay acquired additional importance. The purely literary essay, exemplified in the works of Southey, Hazlitt, and Lockhart, increased in length and solidity. It now became a review—that is, a commentary on a book or books under immediate inspection, but in addition expounding the wider theories and opinions of the reviewer. This new species of essay was to be developed still further in the works of Carlyle and Macaulay.

The miscellaneous essay, represented in the works of Lamb, acquired an increased dignity. It was growing beyond the limits set by Addison and Johnson. It was more intimate and aspiring, and contained many more mannerisms of the author. This kind also was to develop in the hands of the succeeding generation.

(*e*) Other prose works must receive scanty notice. The art of letter-writing still flourished, as can be seen in the works of Byron, Shelley, Keats, and Lamb. Lamb in particular has a charm that reminds the reader of that of Cowper. Byron's letters, though egotistical enough, are breezy and humorous.

Biographical work is adequately represented in *The Life of Byron*, by Moore, and *The Life of Scott*, by Lockhart. These books in their general outlines follow the model of Boswell, though they do not possess the artless self-revelation of their great predecessor. There is an advance shown by their division into chapters and other convenient stages, a useful arrangement that Boswell did not adopt.

The amount of historical research was very great, and the historians ranged abroad and tilled many fields; but in their general methods there was little advance on the work of their predecessors.

THE DEVELOPMENT OF LITERARY STYLE

1. Poetry. This period being instinct with the spirit of revolt, it may be taken for granted that in poetic style there is a great range of effort and experiment. The general tendency is toward simplicity of diction and away from the mannerisms of the eighteenth century. In the case of the major poets, the one who comes nearest in style to the eighteenth century is Byron; next to him, in spite of his theories of simplicity, comes Wordsworth, who often has a curious inflation of style that is kept within bounds only by his intense imaginative power. The best work of Coleridge and Shelley is marked by the greatest simplicity; but, on the other hand, Keats is too fond of golden diction to resist the temptation to be ornate.

2. Prose. In this period we behold the dissolution of the more formal prose style of the previous century. With this process the journalists and miscellaneous prose-writers have much to do. In the place of the older type we see a general tendency toward a useful middle style, as in the books of Southey and Hazlitt. Outside this mass of middle prose we have a range from the greatest simplicity to the highest efforts of poetic prose. At one end of the scale we have the perfectly plain style of Cobbett. The passage we give (from the *Rural Rides*) could not be simpler, but it is energetic and expressive:

> When I returned to England in 1800, after an absence from the country parts of it for sixteen years, the trees, the hedges, even the parks and woods, seemed so small! It made me laugh to hear little gutters, that I could jump over, called rivers. The Thames was but a 'creek!' But when in about a month after my arrival in London, I went to Farnham, the place of my birth, what was my surprise! Every thing was become so pitifully small! I had to cross in my postchaise the long and dreary heath of Bagshot. Then at the end of it, to mount a hill called Hungry Hill: and from that hill I knew that I should look down into the beautiful and fertile vale of Farnham. My heart fluttered with impatience, mixed with a sort of fear, to see all the scenes of my childhood; for I had learned before the death of my father and mother.

From Cobbett we range through a large number of writers, like Lockhart and Miss Austen, who write in the usual middle style to the more laboured manner of Scott, who in his descriptive passages adopts a kind of Johnsonese. When he writes in the Scots dialect he writes simply and clearly, but in his heavier moods we have a style like that which follows. Note the long and complicated sentences, and the laboured diction.

> The brow of the hill, on which the Royal Life-Guards were now drawn up, sloped downwards (on the side opposite to that which they had ascended) with a gentle declivity for more than a quarter of a mile, and presented ground, which, though unequal in some places, was not altogether unfavourable for the manœuvres of cavalry, until near the bottom, when the slope terminated in a marshy level, traversed through its whole length by what seemed either a natural gully or a deep artificial drain, the sides of which were broken by springs, trenches filled with water, out of which peats and turf had been dug, and here and there by some straggling thickets of alders, which loved the moistness so well that they continued to live as bushes, although too much dwarfed by the sour soil and the stagnant bog-water to ascend into trees. Beyond this ditch or gully the ground arose into a second heathy swell, or rather hill, near to the foot of which, and as if with the object of defend-

TABLE TO ILLUSTRATE THE DEVELOPMENT OF LITERARY FORMS

DATE	POETRY			DRAMA		PROSE		
	Lyric	Narrative-Descriptive	Satirical and Didactic	Comedy	Tragedy	Novel	Essay	Miscellaneous
1800	Wordsworth[1] Coleridge[1]	Wordsworth Southey Landor				J. Austen[14]		Coleridge[3]
1810	Byron Moore Campbell Hogg	Scott[12]				M. Edgeworth	Cobbett Jeffrey S. Smith	Southey[4]
1820	Shelley Keats	Byron[5] Hogg Shelley[8] Moore Keats[10]	J. and H. Smith Moore Shelley Byron[7]		Byron[6] Shelley[9]	Scott[13] W. Irving	Lockhart Hazlitt	W. Irving
1830	Elliott		Hood Elliott			Galt Cooper James Marryat	De Quincey[16] Lamb[15]	Wilson
1840					Wordsworth[2]	Ainsworth Lever		Moore[11] Lockhart[17]

[1] *Lyrical Ballads* (1798).
[3] *The Watchman* (1796).
[5] *Childe Harold's Pilgrimage* (1812).
[7] *Don Juan* (1819–24).
[9] *The Cenci* (1819).
[11] *The Life of Byron* (1830).
[13] *Waverley* (1814).
[15] *The Essays of Elia* (1823).
[17] *The Life of Scott* (1837–38).

[2] *The Borderers* (1842).
[4] *The History of Brazil* (1810–19).
[6] *Manfred* (1817).
[8] *Queen Mab* (1813).
[10] *Endymion* (1818).
[12] *The Lay of the Last Minstrel* (1805).
[14] *Northanger Abbey* (1798).
[16] *Confessions of an English Opium Eater* (1821).

ing the broken ground and ditch that covered their front, the body of insurgents appeared to be drawn up with the purpose of abiding battle.

Old Mortality

From Scott the evolution of style can be traced through the mannered, half-humorous ornateness of Lamb to the florid poetic prose of Wilson and the dithyrambic periods of De Quincey. As a final specimen we give an extract from the *Noctes Ambrosianæ*. The style is fervidly exclamatory, but it lacks the depth of De Quincey's at its best.

Shepherd. Oh that I had been a sailor! To hae circumnavigated the warld! To hae pitched our tents, or built our bowers, on the shores o' bays sae glittering wi' league-lang wreaths o' shells, that the billows blushed crimson as they murmured! To hae seen our flags burning meteor-like, high up amang the primeval woods, while birds, bright as ony buntin, sat trimmin their plumage amang the cordage, sae tame in that island where ship had haply never touched afore, nor ever might touch again, lying in a latitude by itsel' and far out o' the breath o' the tredd wunds! Or to hae landed with a' the crew, marines and a'—excep a guard on shipboard to keep aff the crowd o' canoes—on some warlike isle, tossing wi' the plumes on chieftains' heads, and soun'—soun'—soundin wi' gongs! What's a man-o'-war's barge, Mr Tickler, beautiful sicht tho' it be, to the hundred-oared canoe o' some savage Island-king!

CHAPTER XI

THE VICTORIAN AGE

TIME-CHART OF THE CHIEF AUTHORS

The thick line represents the period of important literary work.

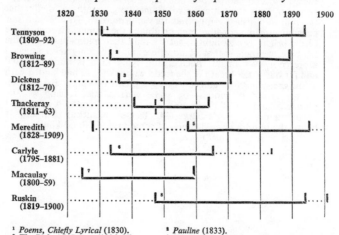

¹ *Poems, Chiefly Lyrical* (1830). ² *Pauline* (1833).
³ *The Pickwick Papers* (1836–37). ⁴ *Vanity Fair* (1847).
⁵ *The Ordeal of Richard Feverel* (1859). ⁶ *Sartor Resartus* (1833–34).
⁷ *Essay on Milton* (1825). ⁸ *The Seven Lamps of Architecture* (1849).

THE HISTORICAL BACKGROUND (1830–90)

1. An Era of Peace. The few colonial wars that broke out during the Victorian epoch did not seriously disturb the national life. There was one Continental war that directly affected Britain—the Crimean War—and one that affected her indirectly though strongly —the Franco-German struggle; yet neither of these caused any profound changes. In America the great civil struggle left scars that were soon to be obliterated by the wise statesmanship of her rulers.

The whole age may be not unfairly described as one of peaceful activity. In the earlier stages the lessening surges of the French Revolution were still felt; but by the middle of the century they had almost completely died down, and other hopes and ideals, largely pacific, were gradually taking their place.

2. Material Developments. It was an age alive with new activities. There was a revolution in commercial enterprise, due to the great increase of available markets, and, as a result of this, an immense advance in the use of mechanical devices. The new commercial energy was reflected in the Great Exhibition of 1851, which was greeted as the inauguration of a new era of prosperity. On the other side of this picture of commercial expansion we see the appalling social conditions of the new industrial cities, the squalid slums, and the exploitation of cheap labour (often of children), the painful fight by the enlightened few to introduce social legislation and the slow extension of the franchise. The evils of the Industrial Revolution were vividly painted by such writers as Dickens and Mrs Gaskell, and they called forth the missionary efforts of men like Kingsley.

3. Intellectual Developments. There can be little doubt that in many cases material wealth produced a hardness of temper and an impatience of projects and ideas that brought no return in hard cash; yet it is to the credit of this age that intellectual activities were so numerous. There was quite a revolution in scientific thought following upon the works of Darwin and his school, and an immense outburst of social and political theorizing which was represented in this country by the writings of men like Herbert Spencer and John Stuart Mill. In addition, popular education became a practical thing. This in its turn produced a new hunger for intellectual food, and resulted in a great increase in the productions of the Press and of other more durable species of literature.

LITERARY FEATURES OF THE AGE

The sixty years (1830–90) commonly included under the name of the Victorian age present many dissimilar features; yet in several respects we can safely generalize.

1. Its Morality. Nearly all observers of the Victorian age are struck by its extreme deference to the conventions. To a later age these seem ludicrous. It was thought indecorous for a man to smoke in public and (much later in the century) for a lady to ride a bicycle. To a great extent the new morality was a natural revolt against the grossness of the earlier Regency, and the influence of the Victorian Court was all in its favour. In literature it is amply reflected. Tennyson is the most conspicuous example in poetry, creating the priggishly complacent Sir Galahad and King Arthur, Dickens, perhaps the most representative of the Victorian novelists. took for his model the old picaresque novel; but it is almost laughable to observe his anxiety to be 'moral.' This type of writing is quite blameless, but it produced the kind of public that denounced the innocuous *Jane Eyre* as wicked because it dealt with the harmless affection of a girl for a married man.

2. The Revolt. Many writers protested against the deadening effects of the conventions. Carlyle and Matthew Arnold, in their different accents, were loud in their denunciations; Thackeray never tired of satirizing the snobbishness of the age; and Browning's cobbly mannerisms were an indirect challenge to the velvety diction and the smooth self-satisfaction of the Tennysonian school. As the age proceeded the reaction strengthened. In poetry the Pre-Raphaelites, led by Swinburne and William Morris, proclaimed no morality but that of the artist's regard for his art. By the vigour of his methods Swinburne horrified the timorous, and made himself rather ridiculous in the eyes of sensible people. It remained for Thomas Hardy (whom we reserve for the next chapter) to pull aside the Victorian veils and shutters and with the large tolerance of the master to regard men's actions with open gaze.

3. Intellectual Developments. The literary product was inevitably affected by the new ideas in science, religion, and politics. *On the Origin of Species* (1859) of Darwin shook to its foundations scientific thought. We can perceive the influence of such a work in Tennyson's *In Memoriam*, in Matthew Arnold's meditative poetry, and in the works of Carlyle. In religious and ethical thought the 'Oxford Movement,' as it was called, was the most noteworthy advance. This movement had its source among the young and eager thinkers of the old university, and was headed by the great Newman, who ultimately (1845) joined the Church of Rome. As a religious portent it marked the widespread discontent with the existing beliefs of the Church of England; as a literary influence it affected many writers of note, including Newman himself, Froude, Maurice, Kingsley, and Gladstone.

4. The New Education. The Education Acts, making a certain measure of education compulsory, rapidly produced an enormous reading public. The cheapening of printing and paper increased the demand for books, so that the production was multiplied. The most popular form of literature was the novel, and the novelists responded with a will. Much of their work was of a high standard, so much so that it has been asserted by competent critics that the middle years of the nineteenth century were the richest in the whole history of the novel.

5. International Influences. During the nineteenth century the interaction among American and European writers was remarkably fresh and strong. In Britain the influence of the great German writers was continuous, and it was championed by Carlyle and Matthew Arnold. Subject nations, in particular the Italians, were a sympathetic theme for prose and verse. The Brownings, Swinburne, Morris, and Meredith were deeply absorbed in the long struggle of the followers of Garibaldi and Cavour; and when Italian freedom was gained the rejoicings were genuine.

6. The Achievement of the Age. With all its immense production, the age produced no supreme writer. It revealed no Shakespeare, no Shelley, nor (in the international sense) a Byron or a Scott. The general literary level was, however, very high; and it was an age, moreover, of spacious intellectual horizons, noble endeavour, and bright aspirations.

POETS

I. ALFRED, LORD TENNYSON (1809–92)

1. His Life. Alfred Tennyson, the son of a clergyman, was born at his father's living at Somersby in Lincolnshire. After some schooling at Louth, which was not agreeable to him, he proceeded to Cambridge (1828). At the university he was a wholly conventional person, and the only mark he made was to win the Chancellor's Medal for a poem on Timbuctoo. He left Cambridge without taking a degree; but before doing so he published a small volume of mediocre verse. During the next twenty years he passed a tranquil existence, living chiefly with his parents, and writing much poetry. Pleasant jaunts—to the Lake District, to Stratford-on-Avon, and other places—varied his peaceful life, and all the while his fame as a poet was making headway. In 1844 he lost most of his small means in an unlucky speculation, but in the nick of time (1845) he received a Government pension. He was appointed Poet Laureate (1850) in succession to Wordsworth, married, and removed (1853) to Freshwater, in the Isle of Wight, which was his home for the next twenty years. In his later years recognition and applause came increasingly upon him, and he was regarded as the greatest poet of his day. In 1884 he was created a baron, sat in the House of Lords, and for a time took himself rather seriously as a politician, falling out with Gladstone over the Irish question. He died at Aldworth, near Haslemere, in Surrey, and was buried in Westminster Abbey.

2. His Poetry. When he was seventeen years old Tennyson collaborated with his elder brother Charles in *Poems by Two Brothers* (1827). The volume is a slight one, but in the light of his later work we can already discern a little of the Tennysonian metrical aptitude and descriptive power. His prize poem of *Timbuctoo* (1829) is not much better than the usual prize poem. His *Poems, Chiefly Lyrical* (1830), published while he was an undergraduate, are yet immature, but in pieces like *Isabel* and *Madeline* the pictorial effect and the sumptuous imagery of his maturer style are already conspicuous.

His volume of *Poems* (1833), which is often referred to as *Poems* (1832), because, in spite of its official title, it appeared in December of the earlier year, is of a different quality, and marks a decided advance. It contains such notable poems as *The Lady of Shalott*, *Œnone, The Lotos-Eaters*, and *The Palace of Art*, in which we see the Tennysonian technique approaching perfection. Then in 1842 he produced two volumes of poetry that set him once and for all among the greater poets of his day. The first volume consists mainly of revised forms of some of the numbers published previously, the second is entirely new. It opens with *Morte d'Arthur*, and contains *Ulysses, Locksley Hall*, and several other poems that stand at the summit of his achievement.

The later stages of his career are marked chiefly by much longer poems. *The Princess* (1847) is a serio-comic attempt to handle the theme that was then known as 'the new woman.' For the sake of his story Tennyson imagines a ladies' academy with a mutinously intellectual princess at the head of it. For a space a tragedy seems imminent, but in the end all is well, for the Princess is married to the blameless hero. The poem is in blank verse, but interspersed are several singularly beautiful lyrics. The humour is heavy, but many of the descriptions are as rich and wonderful as any Tennyson ever attempted.

In Memoriam (1850) caused a great stir when it first appeared. It is a very long series of meditations upon the death of Arthur Henry Hallam, Tennyson's college friend, who died at Vienna in 1833. Tennyson brooded over the subject for years; and upon this elegiac theme he imposed numerous meditations on life and death, showing how these subjects were affected by the new theories of the day. For the first, and probably the only, time, Tennyson's feelings were stirred and troubled. The result was the most deeply emotional, and probably the greatest, poetry he ever produced. The poem is adorned with many beautiful sketches of English scenery; and the metre—now called the *In Memoriam* metre—which is quite rare, is deftly managed.

Maud and Other Poems (1855) was received with amazement by the public. The chief poem is called a 'monodrama'; it consists of a series of lyrics which reflect the love and hatred, the hope and despair, of a lover who slays his mistress's brother, and then flies broken to France. The whole tone of the work is forced and fevered, and it ends in a glorification of war and bloodshed. It does not add to Tennyson's fame.

In 1859, 1869, and 1889 Tennyson issued a series of *Idylls of the King*, which had considered and attempted a great theme that Milton abandoned—that of King Arthur and the Round Table. Many doting admirers saw in the *Idylls* an allegory of the soul of man; but in effect Tennyson drew largely upon the simple tales of Malory, stripping them of their "bold bawdry" to please his public, and covering them with a thick coating of his delicate and detailed ornamentation. It is doubtful if this unnatural compound of Malory-Tennyson is quite a happy one, but we do obtain much blank verse of noble and sustained power.

The only other poem of any length is *Enoch Arden* (1864), which became the most popular of all, and found its way in translation into foreign languages. The plot is cheap enough, dealing with a seaman, supposedly drowned, who returns and, finding his wife happily married to another man, regretfully retires without making himself known. The tale, as ever, is rich with Tennysonian adornment. In particular there is a description of the tropical island where Enoch is wrecked that is among the highest flights of the poet:

> The mountain wooded to the peak, the lawns
> And winding glades high up like ways to Heaven,
> The slender coco's drooping crown of plumes,
> The lightning flash of insect and of bird,
> The lustre of the long convolvuluses
> That coiled around the stately stems, and ran
> Even to the limit of the land, the glows
> And glories of the broad belt of the world,
> All these he saw; but what he fain had seen

He could not see, the kindly human face,
Nor ever hear a kindly voice, but heard
The myriad shriek of wheeling ocean-fowl,
The league-long roller thundering on the reef.

His last poems contain a harsher note, as if old age had brought disillusion and a peevish discontent with the pleasant artifices that had graced his prime. Even the later instalments of the *Idylls of the King* contain jarring notes, and are often fretful and unhappy in tone. Among the shorter poems, *Locksley Hall Sixty Years After* (1886) and *The Death of Œnone* (1892) are sad echoes of the sumptuous imaginings of the years preceding 1842.

3. His Plays. Tennyson's dramas occupied his later years. He wrote three historical plays—*Queen Mary* (1875), *Harold* (1876), and *Becket* (1884). The last, owing chiefly to the exertions of Sir Henry Irving, the actor-manager, was quite a stage success. None, however, rank high as real dramatic efforts, though they show much care and skill. *The Falcon* (1879) is a comedy based on a story from Boccaccio; *The Cup* (1881) is based on a story from Plutarch, and scored a success, also through the skill of Irving. *The Foresters* (1892), dealing with the familiar Robin Hood theme, was produced in America.

4. His Poetical Characteristics. (*a*) *His Choice of Subject*. Tennyson's earliest instincts, as seen in the volumes of 1830, 1833, and 1842, led him to the lyric and legendary narrative as his principal themes, and these he handled with a skill and artistry which he rarely surpassed. Already, however, in the 1842 volume, there are signs of the ethical interest which was to be the mainspring of his later work. As a thinker, Tennyson lacked depth and originality. He was content to mirror the feelings and aspirations of his time, and his didactic work lacks the burning fire which alone can transform the didactic into truly great art. The requirements of his office as Poet Laureate led to the production of a number of occasional poems which have caused him to be described, contemptuously, as the newspaper of his age. Of them, all that need be said here is that it is surprising that they are as good as they are. For the rest, with notable exceptions such as *Ulysses* and *In Memoriam*, Tennyson's poems are best when he reverts to the lyric or narrative themes which were his original inspiration.

(*b*) *His Craftsmanship*. No one can deny the great care and skill shown in Tennyson's work. His method of producing poetry was slowly to evolve the lines in his mind, commit them to paper, and to revise them till they were as near perfection as he could make them. Consequently we have a high level of poetical artistry. No one excels Tennyson in the deft application of sound to sense and in the subtle and pervading employment of alliteration and vowel-music. Such passages as this abound in his work:

> Myriads of rivulets hurrying thro' the lawn,
> The moan of doves in immemorial elms,
> And murmuring of innumerable bees.
>
> *The Princess*

This is perhaps not the highest poetry, but shows only a kind of manual, or rather aural, dexterity; yet as Tennyson employs it it is effective to a degree.

His excellent craftsmanship is also apparent in his handling of English metres, in which he is a tireless experimenter. In blank verse he is not so varied and powerful as Shakespeare, nor so majestical as Milton, but in the skill of his workmanship and in his wealth of diction he falls but little short of these great masters.

(c) *His Pictorial Quality*. In this respect Tennyson follows the example of Keats. Nearly all Tennyson's poems, even the simplest, abound in ornate description of natural and other scenes. His method is to seize upon appropriate details, dress them in expressive and musical phrases, and thus throw a glistening image before the reader's eye:

> The silk star-broider'd coverlid
>   Unto her limbs itself doth mould
> Languidly ever; and, amid
>   Her full black ringlets downward rolled,
> Glows forth each softly-shadowed arm
>   With bracelets of the diamond bright:
> Her constant beauty doth inform
>   Stillness with love, and day with light.
>
> *The Day-Dream*

> Till now the doubtful dusk reveal'd
>   The knolls once more where, couched at ease,
>   The white kine glimmered, and the trees
> Laid their dark arms about the field:
>
> And sucked from out the distant gloom
>   A breeze began to tremble o'er
>   The large leaves of the sycamore,
> And fluctuate all the still perfume.
>
> *In Memoriam*

Such passages as these reveal Tennyson at his best; but once again the doubt arises as to whether they represent the highest poetry. They show care of observation and a studious loveliness of epithet; but they lack the intense insight, the ringing and romantic note, of the best efforts of Keats.

(*d*) Tennyson's *lyrical quality* is somewhat uneven. The slightest of his pieces, like *The Splendour Falls*, are musical and attractive; but on the whole his nature was too self-conscious and perhaps his life too regular and prosperous, to provide a background for the true lyrical intensity of emotion. Once or twice, as in the wonderful *Break, break, break* and *Crossing the Bar*, he touches real greatness:

> Break, break, break,
>   On thy cold gray stones, O Sea!
> And I would that my tongue could utter
>   The thoughts that arise in me.
>
> O well for the fisherman's boy,
>   That he shouts with his sister at play!
> O well for the sailor lad,
>   That he sings in his boat on the bay!
>
> And the stately ships go on
>   To their haven under the hill;
> But O for the touch of a vanished hand,
>   And the sound of a voice that is still!
>
> Break, break, break,
>   At the foot of thy crags, O Sea!
> But the tender grace of a day that is dead
>   Will never come back to me.

This lyric has a brevity, unity, and simple earnestness of emotion that make it truly great.

(*e*) The extracts already given have sufficiently revealed the qualities of his *style*. It can be quite simple, as in *The Brook* and *Will Waterproof's Lyrical Monologue*; but his typical style shows a slow and somewhat sententious progress, heavy with imagery and all the other devices of the poetical artist. In particular he is an adept at coining phrases—"jewels five words long," as he himself aptly expressed it; and he is almost invariably happy in his choice of epithet.

(*f*) His *reputation* has already declined from the idolatry in which he was held when he was alive. He himself foresaw "the clamour and the cry" that was bound to arise after his death. To his contemporaries he was a demigod; but younger men strongly assailed his patent literary mannerisms, his complacent acceptance of the evils of his time, his flattery of the great, and his somewhat arrogant assumption of the airs of immortality. Consequently for twenty years after his death his reputation suffered considerably. Once more reaction has set in, and his detractors have modified their attitude. He is not a supreme poet; and whether he will maintain the primacy among the singers of his own generation, as he undoubtedly did during his lifetime, remains to be seen; but, after all deductions are made, his high place in the Temple of Fame is assured.

II. ROBERT BROWNING (1812-89)

1. His Life. Browning was born at Camberwell, his father being connected with the Bank of England. The future poet was educated semi-privately, and from an early age he was free to follow his inclination toward studying unusual subjects. As a child he was precocious, and began to write poetry at the age of twelve. Of his predecessors Shelley in particular influenced his mind, which was unformed and turbulent at this time with the growing power within. After a brief course at University College Browning for a short period travelled in Russia (1833); then he lived in London, where he became acquainted with some of the leaders of the literary and theatrical worlds. In 1834 he paid his first visit to Italy, a country which was for him a fitful kind of home. In 1845 he visited Elizabeth Barrett, the poetess, whose works had strongly attracted him. A mutual liking ensured, and then, after a private marriage, a sort of elopement followed, to escape the anger of the wife's stern parent. The remainder of Browning's life was occupied with journeys between England and France and Italy, and with much poetical activity. His wife died at Florence in 1861, leaving one son. Browning thereupon left the city for good and returned to England, though in 1878 he went back once more to Italy. His works, after suffering much neglect, were now being appreciated, and in 1882 Oxford conferred upon him the degree of D.C.L. He died in Italy, and was buried in Westminster Abbey.

2. His Poems and Plays. His first work of any importance is *Pauline* (1833), an introspective poem, which shows very strongly the influence of Shelley, whom, at this period, Browning held in great reverence. *Paracelsus* (1835), the story of the hero's unquenchable thirst for that breadth of knowledge which is beyond the grasp of one man, brings to the fore Browning's predominant ideas—that a life without love must be a failure, and that God is working all things to an end beyond human divining. The style of the poem is diffuse, but the blank verse contains many passages of great beauty and is interspersed with one or two charming lyrics:

> Thus the Mayne glideth
> Where my love abideth.
> Sleep's no softer: it proceeds
> On through lawns, on through meads
> On and on, whate'er befall,
> Meandering and musical,
> Though the niggard pasturage
> Bears not on its shaven ledge
> Aught but weeds and waving grasses
> To view the river as it passes,
> Save here and there a scanty patch
> Of primroses too faint to catch
> A weary bee.

His next work was the play *Strafford* (1837), which was produced by the actor Macready, and which achieves real pathos toward the close. *Sordello* (1840), an attempt to decide the relationship between art and life, is Browning's most obscure work. The story of the hero, a Mantuan troubadour, is cumbered with a mass of detailed historical allusion, and the style, in spite of occasional passages of descriptive beauty, is too compressed.

It is convenient next to deal with the entire group of eight volumes, which, published separately from 1841 onward, were collected in one volume as *Bells and Pomegranates* in 1846. In addition to two collections of lyrical and narrative poems, this series included six plays, *Pippa Passes* (1841), *King Victor and King Charles* (1842), *The Return of the Druses* (1843), *A Blot on the 'Scutcheon* (1843), *Colombe's Birthday* (1844), *Luria; and a Soul's Tragedy* (1846). None of these is without its moments of drama, and they all show considerable spirit in their style. *Pippa Passes*, which was not intended for the stage, has an idyllic charm, and it contains fine songs. But Browning lacks the fundamental qualities of the dramatist. His amazingly subtle analysis of character and motive is not adequate for true drama because he cannot reveal character in action. His method is to take a character at a moment of crisis and, by allowing him to talk, to reveal not only his present thoughts and feelings but his past history. *Dramatic Lyrics* (1842) and

Dramatic Romances and Lyrics (1845) show this faculty being directed into the channel in which it was to achieve perfection—that of the dramatic monologue. In the latter volume appeared *The Italian in England*, *The Bishop orders his Tomb at Saint Praxed's*, and *Pictor Ignotus* among many others.[1] *Dramatic Lyrics* consists mainly of lyrics, such as *Cavalier Tunes*, and, most striking of all, those love lyrics which, though impersonal, were really the fruit of his happy marriage with Elizabeth Barrett. Of the love lyrics of this period *Meeting at Night* is typical:

> The grey sea and the long black land;
> And the yellow half-moon large and low;
> And the startled little waves that leap
> In fiery ringlets from their sleep,
> As I gain the cove with pushing prow,
> And quench its speed in the slushy sand.
>
> Then a mile of warm sea-scented beach;
> Three fields to cross till a farm appears;
> A tap at the pane, the quick sharp scratch
> And blue spurt of a lighted match,
> And a voice less loud, thro' its joys and fears,
> Than the two hearts beating each to each!

Now at the height of his powers, Browning produced some of his best work in *Men and Women* (1855), which, with the exception of the dedicatory *One Word More*, addressed to his wife, consists entirely of dramatic monologues. Here are to be found the famous *Fra Lippo Lippi*, *An Epistle containing the strange Medical Experience of Karshish, the Arab Physician*, *Andrea del Sarto*, *Cleon*. Most of them are written in blank verse. The year 1864 saw the publication of his last really great volume, *Dramatis Personæ*, again a collection of dramatic monologues. To illustrate their quality mention need be made of only such works as *Caliban upon Setebos*, *A Death in the Desert*, *Rabbi Ben Ezra*, and *Abt Vogler*. In style the poems have much of the rugged, elliptical quality which was on occasion the poet's downfall, but here it is used with a skill and a power which show him at the very pinnacle of his achievement.

The Ring and the Book (1868–69) is the story of the murder of a young wife, Pompilia, by her worthless husband, in the year 1698,

---

[1] Note: In the case of this, and the next two volumes, the poems mentioned originally appeared in the collections indicated. In some cases they were transferred to other volumes when Browning redistributed his poems in 1868.

and the same story is told by nine different people, and continues for twelve books. The result is a monument of masterly discursiveness.

The remaining years of Browning's long life saw the production of numerous further volumes of verse, few of which add greatly to his fame. To-day they are read by none but his most confirmed admirers. *Balaustion's Adventure* (1871), *Prince Hohenstiel-Schwangau, Saviour of Society* (1871), *Fifine at the Fair* (1872), *Red Cotton Night-Cap Country* (1873), *The Inn Album* (1875), *La Saisiaz, The Two Poets of Croisic* (1878), *Jocoseria* (1883), *Ferishtah's Fancies* (1884), and *Parleyings with Certain People of Importance in their Day* (1887), all suffer from the writer's obsession with thought content, and the psychologizing of his characters at the expense of the poetry. In too many of them the style betrays a wilful exaggeration of the eccentricities which he had once turned to such great account, but always the reader is liable to stumble across passages which, in striking landscape or lovely lyric, show that the true poetic gift is not completely absent.

His long life's work has a powerful close in *Asolando* (1889), which, along with much of the tired disillusion of the old man, has, in places, the firmness and enthusiasm of his prime. The last verses he ever wrote describe himself in the character he most loved to adopt:

> One who never turned his back but marched breast forward,
>   Never doubted clouds would break,
> Never dreamed, though right were worsted, wrong would triumph,
>   Held we fall to rise, are baffled to fight better,
>   Sleep to wake.
>
> No, at noonday in the bustle of man's worktime
>   Greet the unseen with a cheer!
> Bid him forward, breast and back as either should be,
>   "Strive and thrive!" cry, "Speed,—fight on, fare ever
>   There as here!"

3. Features of his Work. (*a*) *His Choice of Subject*. Browning's themes divide themselves broadly into three groups, philosophical or religious, love, and lighter themes as in *The Pied Piper of Hamelin*. His philosophical poems, on which his reputation rested in his own day, all bear on his central beliefs that life must ever be a striving for something beyond our reach, and that it is "God's task to make the heavenly period perfect the earthen." The obvious optimism of

> What I aspired to be,
> And was not, comforts me.

has been resented by more modern critics as a facile shirking of life's complexities. His love poems are, perhaps, his greatest achievement. They have a calm authenticity of tone.

Always, his first concern was with the human soul. He was particularly interested in abnormal people, and was able to project himself into their minds and to lay bare their feelings and motives. Yet his characters are not often completely objective, because so many of them are mouthpieces for his own philosophy.

He shows a fondness, too, for out-of-the-way historical settings and for foreign scenes, which, at his best, as in *The Bishop orders his Tomb at Saint Praxed's* and *Karshish*, are recreated with a vivid accuracy. Along with this interest in the unusual goes an obvious relish for the grotesque and macabre, which is seen at its most striking in *Childe Roland to the Dark Tower came*:

> Which, while I forded—good saints, how I feared
> To set my foot upon a dead man's cheek,
> Each step, or feel the spear I thrust to seek
> For hollows, tangled in his hair or beard!
> —It may have been a water-rat I speared,
> But, ugh! it sounded like a baby's shriek.

(b) *His Style.* Browning's style has been the subject of endless discussion, for it presents a fascinating problem. Attempts to elucidate his more obscure passages have sometimes led to a neglect of his very real poetic qualities. At his worst, his poems are a series of bewildering mental acrobatics, expressed in a wilfully harsh rhythm and vocabulary. At his best he can achieve a noble dignity, and a verbal music as good as anything produced by that master of melody, Tennyson. Above all, his verse reflects the abundant vitality of his character. He is master of a surprising variety of metrical forms and excels in the manipulation of rhythmic effects. In his greatest work even the notorious rugged angularity of his phrasing and vocabulary is turned to account, and produces a beauty peculiarly its own. The following extracts will suffice to show, in the first instance, his rhythmic and melodic skill, in the second, the fine effect which can be achieved by the rugged style which only too often could deteriorate into mere eccentricity.

> And one would bury his brow with a blind plunge down to hell,
> Burrow awhile and build, broad on the roots of things,
> Then up again swim into sight, having based me my palace well,
> Founded it, fearless of flame, flat on the nether springs.

And another would mount and march, like the excellent minion he
    was,
  Ay, another and yet another, one crowd but with many a crest,
Raising my rampired walls of gold as transparent as glass.
  Eager to do and die, yield each his place to the rest:
For higher still and higher (as a runner tips with fire,
    When a great illumination surprises a festal night—
Outlining round and round Rome's dome from space to spire)
  Up, the pinnacled glory reached, and the pride of my soul was in
    sight.

Abt Vogler

       Let us begin and carry up this corpse,
         Singing together.
       Leave we the common crofts, the vulgar thorpes,
         Each in its tether
       Sleeping safe on the bosom of the plain,
         Cared-for till cock-crow:
       Look out if yonder be not day again
         Rimming the rock-row!
       That's the appropriate country; there, man's thought,
         Rarer, intenser,
       Self-gathered for an outbreak, as it ought,
         Chafes in the censer!

A Grammarian's Funeral

(c) *His Descriptive Power.* In this respect Browning differs widely
from Tennyson, who slowly creates a lovely image by careful mass-
ing of detail. Browning cares less for beauty of description for its
own sake. In most of his work it is found only in flashes, where he
paints the background of his story in a few dashing strokes, or
crystallizes his meaning in an image whose beauty staggers us. He
is fond of striking primary colours which startle by their very vividness, and as a painter of movement he has few equals. The passages
which follow show two very different examples of his descriptive
skill:

       Yon otter, sleek-wet, black, lithe as a leech;
       Yon auk, one fire-eye in a ball of foam,
       That floats and feeds; a certain badger brown
       He hath watched hunt with that slant white-wedge eye
       By moonlight; and the pie with the long tongue
       That pricks deep into oakwarts for a worm,
       And says a plain word when she finds her prize.

Caliban upon Setebos

       Cleon the poet, (from the sprinkled isles,
       Lily on lily, that o'erlace the sea,
       And laugh their pride when the light wave lisps 'Greece')—
       To Protos in his Tyranny: much health!

They give thy letter to me, even now:
I read and seem as if I heard thee speak.
The master of thy galley still unlades
Gift after gift; they block my court at last
And pile themselves along its portico
Royal with sunset, like a thought of thee:
And one white she-slave from the group dispersed
Of black and white slaves, (like the chequer-work
Pavement, at once my nation's work and gift,
Now covered with this settle-down of doves)
One lyric woman, in her crocus vest
Woven of sea-wools, with her two white hands
Commends to me the strainer and the cup
Thy lip hath bettered ere it blesses mine.

Cleon

(d) *His Reputation.* Recognition was slow in coming, but, like Wordsworth, he lived to see his name established high among his fellows. He wrote too freely, and often too carelessly and perversely, and much of his work will pass into oblivion. His fame now rests on those four volumes, published between 1842 and 1864, which contain his love lyrics and dramatic monologues. No more is needed to place him among the truly great.

OTHER POETS

1. **Elizabeth Barrett Browning (1806–61)**, whose maiden name was Elizabeth Barrett, was the daughter of a West India planter, and was born at Durham. She began to write poems at the age of eight; her first published work worth mentioning was *An Essay on Mind; with Other Poems* (1826), which is of slight importance. When she was about thirty years old delicate health prostrated her, and for the rest of her life she was almost an invalid. In 1846, when she was forty, she and Robert Browning were married, and stole off to Italy, where they made Florence their headquarters. She was a woman of acute sensibilities, and was fervid in the support of many good causes, one of which was the attainment of Italian independence. On the death of Wordsworth in 1850 it was suggested that the Laureateship should be conferred upon her, but the project fell through. After a very happy married life she died at Florence.

Only the chief of her numerous poetical works can be mentioned here. After her first work noted above there was a pause of nine years; then appeared *Prometheus Bound* (1833). Other works are *The Seraphim and Other Poems* (1838), *Sonnets from the Portuguese*

(1847), *Casa Guidi Windows* (1851), *Aurora Leigh* (1857), an immense poem in blank verse, and *Last Poems* (1862). She wrote many of her shorter pieces for magazines, the most important contributions being *The Cry of the Children* (1841) for *Blackwood's* and *A Musical Instrument* (1860) for the *Cornhill*. As a narrative poet Mrs Browning is a comparative failure, for in method she is discursive and confused, but she has command of a sweet, clear, and often passionate style. She has many slips of taste, and her desire for elevation sometimes leads her into what Rossetti called "falsetto masculinity," a kind of hysterical bravado. Metrical faults and bad rhymes mar much of her verse, but in the intimate and ardent *Sonnets from the Portuguese*, on which her fame now rests, the form necessarily restricts her discursiveness, and her love for Robert Browning shines clear.

2. **Matthew Arnold (1822–88)** was a writer of many activities, but it is chiefly as a poet and critic that he now holds his place in literature. He was the son of the famous headmaster of Rugby, and was educated at Winchester, Rugby, and at Balliol College, Oxford, where he gained the Newdigate Prize for poetry. Subsequently he became a Fellow of Oriel College (1845). In 1851 he was appointed an inspector of schools, and proved to be a capable official. His life was busily uneventful, and in 1883 he resigned, receiving a pension from the Government. Less than five years afterwards he died suddenly of heart disease.

His poetical works are not very bulky. *The Strayed Reveller, and Other Poems* (1849) appeared under the *nom de plume* of 'A,' as did *Empedocles on Etna, and Other Poems* (1852). Then followed *Poems* (1853), with its famous critical preface, and *New Poems* (1867). None of these volumes is of large size, though much of the content is of a high quality. For subject Arnold is fond of classical themes, to which he gives a meditative and even melancholy cast common in modern compositions. In some of the poems—as, for example, in the nobly pessimistic *The Scholar-Gipsy*—he excels in the description of typical English scenery. In style he has much of the classical stateliness and more formal type of beauty, but he can be graceful and charming, with sometimes the note of real passion. His meditative poetry, like *Dover Beach* and *A Summer Night*, resembles that of Gray in its subdued melancholy resignation, but all his work is careful, scholarly, and workmanlike.

His prose works are large in bulk and wide in range. Of them all his critical essays are probably of the highest value. *Essays in*

Criticism (1865 and 1889) contains the best of his critical work, which is marked by wide reading and careful thought. His judgment, usually admirably sane and measured, is sometimes distorted a little by his views on life and politics. Nevertheless he ranks as one of the great English literary critics. As in his poetry, he shows himself to be the apostle of sanity and culture. He advocates a broad, cosmopolitan view of European literature as a basis for comparative judgments, and attacks 'provincialism' and lack of real knowledge. His style is perfectly lucid, easy and rhythmical, and not without a certain elegance and distinction. Arnold also wrote freely upon theological and political themes, but these were largely topics of the day, and his works on such subjects have no great permanent value. His best books of this class are *Culture and Anarchy* (1869) and *Literature and Dogma* (1873).

3. **Edward Fitzgerald (1809–83).** Born near Woodbridge, in Suffolk, Edward Fitzgerald was educated at the Grammar School, Bury St Edmunds, and at Trinity College, Cambridge, where he graduated in 1830. After this time he spent most of his life in Suffolk and was something of a recluse. However, he had many friends among the literary figures of his day, including Tennyson, Thackeray, and Carlyle.

Like Thomas Gray, he lives in general literature by one poem. This, after long neglect, came to be regarded as one of the great things in English literature. In 1859 he issued the *Rubáiyát* of the early Persian poet Omar Khayyám. His version is a very free translation, cast into curious four-lined stanzas, which have an extraordinary cadence, rugged yet melodious, strong yet sweet. The feeling expressed in the verses, with much energy and picturesque effect, is stoical resignation. Fitzgerald also wrote a prose dialogue of much beauty called *Euphranor: a Dialogue on Youth* (1851); and his surviving letters testify to his quiet and caustic humour.

4. **Arthur Hugh Clough (1819–61)** was born at Liverpool, and educated at Rugby, where Dr Arnold made a deep impression upon his mind. He proceeded to Oxford, where, like his friend Matthew Arnold, he later became a Fellow of Oriel College. He travelled much, and then became Warden of University Hall, London. This post he soon resigned, and some public appointments followed. He died at Florence, after a long pilgrimage to restore his failing health. His death was bewailed by Arnold in his beautiful elegy *Thyrsis*.

Clough's first long poem was *The Bothie of Tober-na-Vuolich* (1848), which is written in rough classical hexameters and contains some fine descriptions of the Scottish Highlands. He wrote little else of much value. His *Amours de Voyage* (1849) is also in hexameters; *Dipsychus* (1850) is a meditative poem. His poetry is charged with much of the deep-seated unrest and despondency that mark the work of Arnold. His lyrical gift is not great, but once at least, in the powerful *Say not the Struggle Naught Availeth*, he soared into greatness.

5. Henry Wadsworth Longfellow (1807–82) was born at Portland, Maine, and came of Yorkshire stock. He began to publish poetry when he was thirteen years old. After studying at Bowdoin College he travelled abroad to equip himself for the work of professor of modern languages at his college, a post which he accepted in 1829. In 1836 he was appointed to a similar position at Harvard, and more travelling followed. He resigned this professorship in 1854 in order to devote himself entirely to poetry, of which he had already produced a large amount.

In this place we have space to mention only the most important of his works. Such are *Outre-Mer: A Pilgrimage beyond the Sea* (1834–35), based upon his earliest travels; *Voices of the Night* (1839), a collection that includes some of his best shorter poems; *Evangeline* (1847), a tragical story of the early colonial days, written in smooth and melodious hexameters; *The Song of Hiawatha* (1855), a collection of Indian folk-tales, written in unrhymed octosyllabic verse; *The Courtship of Miles Standish* (1858); and *Tales of a Wayside Inn* (1863).

Longfellow was always a careful and assiduous poet, ranging over a great variety of subjects, but in his anxiety to excel in all branches of poetry he wrote too much, and thereby the general level of his poetry was lowered. His narrative power is quite considerable, and his descriptions, especially those of his native country, have grace and fidelity. He lacks, however, the fine fury and the high energy of style that distinguish the great poet. His lyrics are numerous, melodious, and often marked by true feeling, but they have not the demonic qualities that are necessary to place them in the front rank.

6. Dante Gabriel Rossetti (1828–82) was born in London, the son of an Italian refugee who was professor of Italian at King's College, where Rossetti received his early education. He began to compose poetry by the time he was six, and later studied drawing at the Royal Academy School (1846). Shortly after this (1848) he met Holman Hunt, Ford Madox Brown, and the painter Millais, with whom he formed the Pre-Raphaelite brotherhood. Ruskin, Swinburne, and William Morris were among his later friends, and Ruskin was of considerable financial assistance to him. Toward the close of his life he became a chloral addict, and, though he eventually broke himself of the habit, its effect upon his health was such that in 1872 his sanity was in question. He died near Margate.

The eldest of the Pre-Raphaelite school of artists and poets, Rossetti was himself both painter and poet. In art, as in poetry, he broke away from convention when he saw fit. His poetical works are small in bulk, consisting of two slight volumes, *Poems* (1870) and *Ballads and Sonnets* (1881).

Of the high quality of these poems there can be little question. With a little more breadth of view, and with perhaps more of the humane element in him, he might have found a place among the very highest. For he had real genius, and in *The Blessed Damozel* his gifts are fully displayed: a gift for description of almost uncanny splendour, a brooding and passionate introspection, often of a religious nature, and a verbal beauty as studied and melodious as that of Tennyson—less certain and decisive perhaps, but surpassing that of the older poet in unearthly suggestiveness. In his ballads, like *Rose Mary* and *Troy Town*, the same powers are apparent, though that is only a very little short of the greatest.

7. **Christina Georgina Rossetti (1830–94)** was a younger sister of the poet last named, and survived him by some years. Her life was uneventful, like her brother's, and was passed chiefly in London.

Her bent was almost entirely lyrical, and was shown in *Goblin Market and other poems* (1864), *The Prince's Progress and other poems* (1866), *A Pageant and other poems* (1881), and *Verses* (1893). Another volume, called *New Poems* (1896), was published after her death, and contains much excellent early work. Her poetry, perhaps less impressive than that of her brother in its descriptive passages, has a purer lyrical note of deep and sustained passion, with a somewhat larger command of humour. The mainspring of her inspiration was religion. On religious themes she writes with a transparent simplicity of tone and language and a great variety of metrical and melodic effects.

8. **William Morris (1834–96)** produced a great amount of poetry, and was one of the most conspicuous figures in mid-Victorian literature. He was born near London, the son of a wealthy merchant, and was educated at Marlborough and Oxford. His wealth, freeing him from the drudgery of a profession, permitted him to take a lively

and practical interest in the questions of his day. Upon art, education, politics, and social problems his great energy and powerful mind led him to take very decided views, sometimes of an original nature. Here we are concerned only with his achievement in literature.

The bulk of Morris's poetry was written during the first forty-five years of his life. *The Defence of Guenevere and Other Poems* (1858) shows his love of beauty of colour, sound, and scenery, and his passion for the medieval. In construction the poems of this volume are often faulty, and in style they have an abrupt roughness which is not seen in his later work. *The Life and Death of Jason* (1867), a heroic poem on a familiar theme, is told in smooth, easy couplets, and has the melancholy tone so common in Morris. *The Earthly Paradise* (1868–70) is a collection of tales, some classical, some medieval. In language and the predominance of the couplet they show the influence of Chaucer, though the languid harmony of Morris contrasts strongly with the racy vitality of his model. The best poetry in this work is to be found in the interspersed lyrics. His finest long narrative poem, *The Story of Sigurd the Volsung and the Fall of the Niblungs* (1877), is based on the Norse sagas, and has great vigour of language and rhythm, combined with fine descriptive passages. *Poems by the Way* (1891) contains some good miscellaneous pieces.

The literary production of the second part of Morris's life consisted mainly of prose romances, lectures, and articles. The best of his lectures are to be found in *Hopes and Fears for Art* (1882) and *Signs of Change* (1888), and his socialist political hopes for the regeneration of English life find their fullest expression in *A Dream of John Ball* (1888) and *News from Nowhere* (1891). These same aspirations are always felt in the prose romances to which he devoted the last years of his life. Among them are *A Tale of the House of the Wolfings* (1889), *The Roots of the Mountains* (1890), *The Story of the Glittering Plain* (1891), and *The Sundering Flood* (1898).

Morris's work reflects several strong influences: the interest in the medieval which drew him into the Pre-Raphaelite brotherhood; his reverence for Chaucer; his love of Icelandic saga, which combined with Chaucer to give his style an archaic flavour; and his socialist idealism. Like Rossetti, he had the artist's passion for beauty, which finds its best expression in his fine English landscapes and the rich, tapestried descriptions of his narrative poems. In style he was smoothly melodious, often to the point of monotony, and the dominant mood of his work is a dreamy melancholy.

9. **Algernon Charles Swinburne (1837–1909)** had a long life, and his poetical work was in proportion to it. Born in London, of aristocratic lineage, he was educated at Eton and Oxford. He left Oxford (1860) without taking a degree, and for the rest of his life wrote voluminously, if not always judiciously. He was a man of quick attachments and violent antagonisms, and these features of his character did much to vitiate some of his prose criticisms, of which he wrote a large number. A life of dissipation impaired his health, and in his later years, from 1879 onward, he lived in the care of his friend Theodore Watts-Dunton at Putney Hill, where he died.

Atalanta in Calydon (1865), an attempt at an English version of an ancient Greek tragedy, was his first considerable effort in poetic form, and it attracted notice at once. At a bound the young poet had attained to a style of his own: tuneful and impetuous movement, a cunning metrical craftsmanship, and a mastery of melodious diction. The excess of these virtues was also its bane, leading to diffuseness, breathlessness, and incoherence. *Poems and Ballads* (1866), a second extraordinary book, was, owing to its choice of unconventional subjects, criticized as being wicked. In it the Swinburnian features already mentioned are revealed in a stronger fashion. Only a few of his later poetical works can be mentioned here: *Songs before Sunrise* (1871), a collection of poems chiefly in praise of Italian liberty, some of them of great beauty; *Erechtheus* (1876), a further and less successful effort at Greek tragedy; and *Tristram and Other Poems* (1882), a narrative of much passion and force, composed in the heroic couplet. Some of his shorter poems were reproduced in two further series of *Poems and Ballads* in 1878 and 1889, but they are inferior to those of his prime.

Swinburne wrote a large number of plays, of which the most noteworthy are *The Queen Mother and Rosamond* (1860), with which he began his career as an author; three plays on the subject of Mary Queen of Scots, called *Chastelard* (1865), *Bothwell* (1874), and *Mary Stuart* (1881); *Locrine* (1887); and *The Sisters* (1892). The gifts of Swinburne are lyrical rather than dramatic, and his tragedies, like those of most of his contemporaries, are only of literary importance. His blank verse is strongly phrased, and in drama his diffuseness—that desire for mere sound and speed which was his greatest weakness—has little scope.

Throughout his life Swinburne produced a steady stream of critical works, which range over a wide field of literature. In not a few his evaluation of a writer was distorted by violent personal prejudice or approval, as in the cases of Landor and Hazlitt. But for the most part he shows a keen discrimination and a sureness of taste, which combine with his gift for impassioned, almost lyrical, elucidation of the beauties of great works to give the best of his utterances a permanent value. He is probably most successful in his studies of the Elizabethan or Jacobean dramatists or the English lyric poets. Among his most famous books are *William Blake* (1868), *A Study of Shakespeare* (1880), and *A Study of Ben Jonson* (1889).

10. **Arthur Edgar O'Shaughnessy (1844–81)** was born in London, of Irish descent. In 1861 he joined the staff of the British Museum Library, where a promising career was cut short by his early death. He wrote little, and his books came close upon each other: *An Epic of Women, and Other Poems* (1870), *Lays of France* (1872), *Music and Moonlight* (1874), and *Songs of a Worker* (1881), the last appearing after his death. His longer poems have a certain haziness and incoherence, but the shorter pieces have a musical and attractive style and a certain half-mystical wistfulness. His ode beginning "We are the music-makers" is often quoted, and other poems quite as good are *A Neglected Heart* and *Exile*.

11. **Walt Whitman (1819–92)** is perhaps the most individual literary figure that America has yet produced. He was born on Long Island, New York, but when quite young removed to Brooklyn, where in turn he was printer, school-teacher, journalist, and publisher. He was a middle-aged man when the publication of his poems drew the attention of the public to him. In 1862 he served as a voluntary worker in a soldiers' hospital, and shortly afterward a public appointment followed, but it was soon relinquished. He died at Camden, New Jersey.

His first important work was *Leaves of Grass* (1855), and a startling work it was. In its first edition it was a collection of twelve poems, treating of large and elemental subjects, and expressed with a megaphonic energy and unblenching audacity that quite shocked the sensitive minds of the time. The poems, of which the chief aim was to preach the glory of the common man, were written in *vers libre* of much force and confidence. Stripped bare of all the conventional ornaments of poetry, they make use of the idioms and rhythms of everyday speech. His other work, *Drum Taps* (1866), was inspired by his hospital experience. In spite of his lapses of taste and strenuous egotism, Whitman was a great and original poet, whose technique was to exert considerable influence upon the poetry of the coming age.

NOVELISTS

I. CHARLES DICKENS (1812–70)

1. His Life. Dickens was born near Portsea, where his father was a clerk in the Navy Pay Office. Charles, the second of eight children, was a delicate child, and much of his boyhood was spent at home, where he read the novels of Smollett, Fielding, and Le Sage. The works of these writers were to influence his own novels very deeply. At an early age also he became very fond of the theatre, a fondness that remained with him all his life, and affected his novels to a great extent. In 1823 the Dickens family removed to London, where the father, an improvident man of the Micawber type, soon drew them into money difficulties. The schooling of Charles, which had all along been desultory enough, was temporarily suspended. The boy for a time worked in a blacking factory while his father was an inmate of the debtors' prison of the Marshalsea. After a year or so financial matters improved; the education of Charles was resumed; then in 1827 he entered the office of an attorney, and in time became an expert shorthand-writer. This proficiency led (1832) to an appointment as reporter on the evening paper the *True Sun*, and later (1834) on *The Morning Chronicle*. In this capacity he did much travelling by stage-coach, during which a keen eye and a retentive memory stored material to exploit a greatness yet undreamed of. Previously, in 1833, some articles which he called *Sketches by Boz* had appeared in *The Monthly Magazine*. They were brightly written, and attracted some notice. In 1836 they were collected and published in two volumes.

In 1836 Messrs Chapman and Hall, a firm of publishers, had agreed to produce in periodical form a series of sketches by Seymour, a popular black-and-white artist. The subjects were of a sporting and convivial kind, and to give them more general interest some story was needed to accompany them. Dickens was requested to supply the 'book,' and thus originated *The Posthumous Papers of the Pickwick Club* (1836–37). Before the issue of the second number of the prints Seymour committed suicide, and Hablot K. Browne, who adopted the name of 'Phiz,' carried on the work. His illustrations are still commonly adopted for Dickens's books.

The Pickwick Papers was a great success; Dickens's fame was secure, and the rest of his life was that of a busy and successful novelist. He lived to enjoy a reputation that was unexampled, surpassing even that of Scott; for the appeal of Dickens was wider and more searching than that of the Scottish novelist. He varied his work with much travelling—among other places to America (1842), to Italy (1844), to Switzerland (1846), and again to America (1867). His popularity was exploited in journalism, for he edited *The Daily News* (1846), and founded *Household Words* (1849) and *All the Year Round* (1859). In 1858 Dickens commenced his famous series of public readings. These were actings rather than readings, for he chose some of the most violent or affecting scenes from his novels and presented them with full-blown histrionic effect. The readings brought him much money, but they wore him down physically. They were also given in America, with the greatest success. He died in his favourite house, Gad's Hill Place, near Rochester, and was buried in Westminster Abbey.

2. His Novels.[1] *Sketches by Boz* (1836), a series dealing with London life in the manner of Leigh Hunt, is interesting, but trifling when compared with *The Pickwick Papers* (1836), its successor. The plot of the latter book is rudimentary. In order to provide an occasion for Seymour's sketches Dickens hit upon the idea of a sporting club, to be called the Pickwick Club. As the book proceeds this idea is soon dropped, and the story becomes a kind of large and genial picaresque novel. The incidents are loosely connected and the chronology will not bear close inspection, but in abundance of detail of a high quality, in vivacity of humour, in acute and accurate observation, the book is of the first rank. It is doubtful if Dickens ever improved upon it. Then, before *Pickwick* was finished, *Oliver Twist* (1837) appeared piecemeal in *Bentley's Miscellany*; and *Nicholas Nickleby* (1838) was begun before the second novel had ceased to appear. The demand for Dickens's novels was now enormous, and he was assiduous in catering for his public. For his next novels he constructed a somewhat elaborate framework, calling the work *Master Humphrey's Clock*; but he sensibly abandoned the notion, and the books appeared separately as *The Old Curiosity Shop* (1840), which was an immense success, and *Barnaby Rudge* (1841), a historical novel. In 1842 he sailed to America, where his

[1] Note: With the exception of those for *Sketches by Boz*, *A Christmas Carol*, and *American Notes*, all the dates in this section are those on which serial publication of the works began.

experiences bore fruit in *American Notes* (1842) and *Martin Chuzzle-wit* (1843). These works were not complimentary to the Americans, and they brought him much unpopularity in the United States. *A Christmas Carol* (1843) and *Dombey and Son* (1846) appeared next, the latter being written partly at Lausanne. Then in 1849 he started *David Copperfield*, which contains many of his personal experiences and is often considered to be his masterpiece, though for many critics *The Pickwick Papers* retains its primacy.

From this point onward a certain decline is manifest. Most of his stories drag; his mannerisms become more apparent, and his splendid buoyancy is less visible. *Bleak House* (1852) and *Hard Times* (1854) were written for his *Household Words*; *Little Dorrit* (1855) appeared in monthly parts; *A Tale of Two Cities* (1859) and *Great Expectations* (1860) were for *All the Year Round*. After producing *Our Mutual Friend* (1864) he paid his second visit to America, and was received very cordially. He returned to England, but did not live to finish *The Mystery of Edwin Drood*, which was appearing in monthly parts when he died.

3. Features of his Novels. (*a*) *Their Popularity*. At the age of twenty-six Dickens was a popular author. This was a happy state of affairs for him, and to his books it served as an ardent stimulus. But there were attendant disadvantages. The demand for his novels was so enormous that it often led to hasty and ill-considered work: to crudity of plot, to unreality of characters, and to looseness of style. It led also to the pernicious habit of issuing the stories in parts. This in turn resulted in much padding and in lopsidedness of construction. The marvellous thing is that with so strong a temptation to slop-work he created books that were so rich and enduring.

(*b*) *His Interest in Social Reform*. Though Dickens's works embody no systematic social or political theory, from the first he took himself very seriously as a social reformer. His novels aroused public interest in many of the evils of his day, among them boarding schools, in *Nicholas Nickleby*, the workhouses, in *Oliver Twist*, the new manufacturing system, in *Hard Times*, and the Court of Chancery, in *Bleak House*. Deference to the fastidiousness of his public excluded the crudest realism from his pictures of poverty, and he seems to have built his hopes for improvement on the spread of the spirit of benevolence rather than upon political upheaval or formal legislation. In more ways than one his work suffered from his preoccupation with social problems. To it can largely be attributed the poetic justice of the conclusions of many of his novels, the exaggeration of such characters as the Gradgrinds, and the sentimental pictures of the poorer classes.

(c) *His Imagination.* No English novelist excels Dickens in the multiplicity of his characters and situations. *Pickwick Papers,* the first of the novels, teems with characters, some of them finely portrayed, and in mere numbers the supply is maintained to the very end of his life. He creates for us a whole world of people. In this world he is most at home with persons of the lower and middle ranks of life, especially those who frequent the neighbourhood of London.

(d) *His Humour and Pathos.* It is very likely that the reputation of Dickens will be maintained chiefly as a humorist. His humour is broad, humane, and creative. It gives us such real immortals as Mr Pickwick, Mrs Gamp, Mr Micawber, and Sam Weller—typical inhabitants of the Dickensian sphere, and worthy of a place in any literary brotherhood. Dickens's humour is not very subtle, but it goes deep, and in expression it is free and vivacious. His satire is apt to develop into mere burlesque, as it does when he deals with Mr Stiggins and Bumble. As for his pathos, in its day it had an appeal that appears amazing to a later generation, whom it strikes as cheap and maudlin. His devices are often third-rate, as when they depend upon such themes as the deaths of little children, which he describes in detail. His genius had little tragic force. He could describe the horrible, as in the death of Bill Sikes; he could be painfully melodramatic, as in characters like Rosa Dartle and Madame Defarge; but he seems to have been unable to command the simplicity of real tragic greatness.

(e) His *mannerisms* are many, and they do not make for good in his novels. It has often been pointed out that his characters are created not 'in the round,' but 'in the flat.' Each represents one mood, one turn of phrase. Uriah Heep is " 'umble," Barkis is "willin'." In this fashion his characters become associated with catch-phrases, like the personages in inferior drama. Dickens's partiality for the drama is also seen in the staginess of his scenes and plots.

(f) In time his *style* became mannered also. At its best it is neither polished nor scholarly, but it is clear, rapid, and workmanlike, the style of the working journalist. In the early books it is sometimes trivial with puns, Cockneyisms, and tiresome circumlocutions. This heavy-handedness of phrase remained with him all his life. In his more aspiring flights, in particular in his deeply pathetic passages, he adopted a lyrical style, a kind of verse-in-prose, that is blank verse slightly disguised. We add a passage of this last type. It can be scanned in places like pure blank verse:

> For she was dead. There, upon her little bed, she lay at rest. The solemn stillness was no marvel now.
>
> She was dead. No sleep so beautiful and calm, so free from trace of pain, so fair to look upon. She seemed a creature fresh from the hand of God, and waiting for the breath of life; not one who had lived and suffered death.
>
> Her couch was dressed with here and there some winter berries and green leaves, gathered in a spot she had been used to favour. "When I die, put near me something that has loved the light, and had the sky above it always." Those were her words.
>
> *The Old Curiosity Shop*

We give also a specimen of the typical Dickensian style. The reader should observe in it the qualities of ease, perspicuity, and humour:

> The particular picture on which Sam Weller's eyes were fixed, as he said this, was a highly coloured representation of a couple of human hearts skewered together with an arrow, cooking before a cheerful fire, while a male and female cannibal in modern attire: the gentleman being clad in a blue coat and white trousers, and the lady in a deep red pelisse with a parasol of the same: were approaching the meal with hungry eyes, up a serpentine gravel path leading thereunto. A decidedly indelicate young gentleman, in a pair of wings and nothing else, was depicted as superintending the cooking; a representation of the spire of the church in Langham Place, London, appeared in the distance; and the whole formed a "valentine," of which, as a written inscription in the window testified, there was a large assortment within, which the shopkeeper pledged himself to dispose of, to his countrymen generally, at the reduced rate of one and sixpence each.
>
> *The Pickwick Papers*

II. WILLIAM MAKEPEACE THACKERAY (1811–63)

1. His Life. Thackeray was born at Calcutta, and was descended from an ancient Yorkshire family. His father having died in 1816, the boy was sent to England for his education, and on the voyage home he had a glimpse of Napoleon, then a prisoner on St Helena. His school was the Charterhouse, and his college was Trinity College, Cambridge, which he entered in 1829. Both at school and college he struck his contemporaries as an idle and rather cynical youth, whose main diversions were sketching and lampooning his friends and enemies. The loss of his fortune drove him to seek some means of earning a living. For a time he had some intention of becoming an artist and studied art in Paris, but soon he turned to journalism. He contributed both prose and light verse to several periodicals, including *Punch* and *Fraser's Magazine*, winning his way slowly and with much difficulty, for his were gifts that do not gain ready recognition. It was not till nearly the middle of the century that *Vanity Fair* (1847–48) brought him some credit, though at first the book was grudgingly received. Thenceforward he wrote steadily and with increasing favour until his death, which occurred with great suddenness. Before his death he had enjoined his executors not to publish any biography, so that of all the major Victorian writers we have of him the scantiest biographical materials.

2. His Novels. For a considerable number of years Thackeray was groping for a means of expression, and wavered between verse, prose, and sketching. His earliest literary work consisted of light and popular contributions to periodicals. The most considerable of these are *The Yellowplush Correspondence* (1837–38), contributed to *Fraser's Magazine* and dealing with the philosophy and experiences of Jeames, an imaginary footman, and *The Book of Snobs* (1849), which originally appeared in *Punch* as *The Snobs of England*. Snobs, who continued to be Thackeray's pet abhorrence, are defined by him as those "who meanly admire mean things," and in this early book their widespread activities are closely pursued and harried. *The History of Samuel Titmarsh and the Great Hoggarty Diamond* (1841), and *The Fitzboodle Papers* (1842–43) appeared first in *Fraser's Magazine*. They are deeply marked with his biting humour and merciless observation of human weaknesses, but they found little acceptance. *The Memoirs of Barry Lyndon* (1844) is a distinct advance. It is a species of picaresque novel, telling of the adventures of a gambling rascal, an amiable scapegrace who prowls over Europe. In range the book is wider, and the grasp of incident and character is more sure. In *Vanity Fair* (1847–48) the genius of Thackeray reaches high-water mark. In theme it is concerned chiefly with the fortunes of Becky Sharp, an adventuress. In dexterity of treatment, in an imaginative power that both reveals and transforms, and in a clear and mournful vision of the vanities of mankind the novel is among the greatest in the language. *The History of Pendennis* (1848–50) continues the method of *Vanity Fair*. Partly autobiographical, it portrays life as it appears to the author. Thackeray refuses to bow to convention and precedent, except when these conform to his ideals of literature. In this book Thackeray openly avows his debt to Fielding, the master whom he equals and in places excels. *The History of Henry Esmond* (1852) is a historical novel of great length and complexity, showing the previous excellences of Thackeray in almost undiminished force, as well as immense care and forethought, a minute and accurate knowledge of the times of Queen Anne, and an extraordinary faculty for reproducing both the style and the atmosphere of the period. By some judges this book is considered to be his best. His novel *The Newcomes* (1853–55) is supposed to be edited by Pendennis. In tone it is more genial than its predecessors, but it ends tragically with the death of the aged Colonel Newcome. With *The Virginians* (1857–59) the list of the great novels is closed. This book, a sequel to *Henry Esmond*, is a record of the experiences of two lads called Warrington, the grandsons of Henry Esmond himself. In the story, a pale shadow of her former self, appears Beatrix Esmond, the fickle heroine of the earlier book.

In 1860 Thackeray was appointed first editor of *The Cornhill Magazine*, and for this he wrote *Lovel the Widower* (1860), *The Adventures of Philip* (1861–62), and a series of essays, charming and witty trifles, *The Roundabout Papers* (1860–63). Both in size and in merit these last novels are inferior to their predecessors. At his death he left an unfinished novel, *Denis Duval*.

Like Dickens, Thackeray had much success as a lecturer on both sides of the Atlantic, though in his methods he did not follow his fellow-novelist. Two courses of lectures were published as *The English Humourists of the Eighteenth Century* (1853) and *The Four Georges* (1860). All his life he delighted in writing burlesques, the best of which are *Rebecca and Rowena* (1850), a comic continuation of *Ivanhoe*, *The Legend of the Rhine* (1845), a burlesque tale of medieval chivalry, and *The Rose and the Ring* (1855), an excellent example of his love of parody.

3. His Poetry. On the surface Thackeray's verse appears to be frivolous stuff, but behind the frivolity there is always sense, often a barb of reproof, and sometimes a note of sorrow. *The Ballads of Policeman X* is an early work contributed in numbers to *Punch*. Others, such as *The White Squall* and *The Ballad of Bouillabaisse*, have more claim to rank as poetry, for they show much metrical dexterity and in places a touch of real pathos.

4. Features of his Works. (a) *Their Reputation.* While Dickens was in the full tide of his success Thackeray was struggling through neglect and contempt to recognition. Thackeray's genius blossomed slowly, just as Fielding's did; for that reason the fruit is more mellow

and matured. Once he had gained the favour of the public he held it, and among outstanding English novelists there is none whose claim is so little subject to challenge.

(b) *His Method*. "Since the author of *Tom Jones* was buried," says Thackeray in his preface to *Pendennis*, "no writer of fiction among us has been permitted to depict to his utmost power a MAN. We must drape him and give him a certain conventional simper." Thackeray's novels are a protest against this convention. Reacting against the popular novel of his day, and particularly against its romanticizing of rogues, he returns to the Fielding method: to view his characters steadily and fearlessly, and to set on record their failings as well as their merits and capacities. In his hands the results are not flattering to human nature, for most of his clever people are rogues and most of his virtuous folk are fools. But whether they are rogues, or fools, or merely blundering incompetents, his creations are rounded, entire, and quite alive and convincing.

(c) *His Humour and Pathos*. Much has been made of the sneering cynicism of Thackeray's humour, and a good deal of the criticism is true. It was his desire to reveal the truth, and satire is one of his most potent methods of revelation. His sarcasm, a deadly species, is husbanded for deserving objects, such as Lord Steyne and (to a lesser degree) Barnes Newcome. In the case of people who are only stupid, like Rawdon Crawley, mercy tempers justice; and when Thackeray chooses to do so he can handle a character with loving tenderness, as can be seen in the case of Lady Castlewood and of Colonel Newcome. In pathos he is seldom sentimental, being usually quiet and effective. But at the thought of the vain, the arrogant, and the mean people of the world Thackeray barbs his pen, with destructive results.

(d) His *style* is very near to the ideal for a novelist. It is effortless, and is therefore unobtrusive, detracting in no wise from the interest in the story. It is also flexible to an extraordinary degree. We have seen how in *Esmond* he recaptured the Addisonian style; this is only one aspect of his mimetic faculty, which in his burlesque finds ample scope. We add a typical specimen of his style:

> As they came up to the house at Walcote, the windows from within were lighted up with friendly welcome; the supper-table was spread in the oak-parlour; it seemed as if forgiveness and love were awaiting the returning prodigal. Two or three familiar faces of domestics were on the look-out at the porch—the old housekeeper was there, and young Lockwood from Castlewood in my lord's livery of tawny and blue. His dear mistress pressed his arm as

they passed into the hall. Her eyes beamed out on him with affection indescribable. "Welcome," was all she said: as she looked up, putting back her fair curls and black hood. A sweet rosy smile blushed on her face: Harry thought he had never seen her look so charming. Her face was lighted with a joy that was brighter than beauty—she took a hand of her son who was in the hall waiting his mother—she did not quit Esmond's arm.

Henry Esmond

III. THE BRONTËS

1. Their Lives. Charlotte (1816–55), Emily (1818–48), and Anne (1820–49) were the daughters of an Irish clergyman, Patrick Brontë, who held a living in Yorkshire. Financial difficulties compelled Charlotte to become a school-teacher (1835–38) and then a governess. Along with Emily she visited Brussels in 1842, and then returned home, where family cares kept her closely tied. Later her books had much success, and she was released from many of her financial worries. She was married in 1854, but died in the next year. Her two younger sisters had predeceased her.

2. Their Works. (*a*) **Charlotte Brontë.** Charlotte's first novel, *The Professor*, failed to find a publisher and only appeared in 1857 after her death. Following the experiences of her own life in an uninspired manner, the story lacks interest, and the characters are not created with the passionate insight which distinguishes her later portraits. *Jane Eyre* (1847) is her greatest novel. The love story of the plain, but very vital, heroine is unfolded with a frank truthfulness and a depth of understanding that are new in English fiction. The plot is weak, full of improbability, and often melodramatic, but the main protagonists are deeply conceived, and the novel rises to moments of sheer terror. In her next novel, *Shirley* (1849), Charlotte Brontë reverts to a more normal and less impassioned portrayal of life. Again the theme is the love story of a young girl, here delicately told, though the plot construction is weak. *Villette* (1853) is written in a reminiscent vein, and the character of Lucy Snowe is based on the author herself.

The truth and intensity of Charlotte's work are unquestioned; she can see and judge with the eye of a genius. But these merits have their disadvantages. In the plots of her novels she is largely restricted to her own experiences; her high seriousness is unrelieved by any humour; and her passion is at times over-charged to the point of frenzy. But to the novel she brought an energy and passion that gave to commonplace people the wonder and beauty of the romantic world.

(b) **Emily Brontë.** Though she wrote less than Charlotte, Emily Brontë is in some ways the greatest of the three sisters. Her one novel, *Wuthering Heights* (1847), is unique in English literature. It breathes the very spirit of the wild, desolate moors. Its chief characters are conceived in gigantic proportions, and their passions have an elemental force which carries them into the realms of poetry. In a series of climaxes the sustained intensity of the novel is carried to almost unbelievable peaks of passion, described with a stark, unflinching realism.

A few of her poems reach the very highest levels, though the majority lack distinction. They reveal the great courage and strength of her passionate nature, and, at her best, she uses simple verse forms with great intensity and a certain grandeur. Her finest poems are probably "No Coward Soul is Mine" and "Cold in the earth, and the deep snow piled above thee."

(c) **Anne Brontë** is by far the least important figure of the three. Her two novels, *Agnes Grey* (1847) and *The Tenant of Wildfell Hall* (1848), are much inferior to those of her sisters, for she lacks nearly all their power and intensity.

3. Their Importance in the History of the Novel. With the Brontës the forces which had transformed English poetry at the beginning of the century were first felt in the novel. They were the pioneers in fiction of that aspect of the romantic movement which concerned itself with the baring of the human soul. In place of the detached observation of a society or group of people, such as we find in Jane Austen and the earlier novelists, the Brontës painted the sufferings of an individual personality, and presented a new conception of the heroine as a woman of vital strength and passionate feelings. Their works are as much the products of the imagination and emotions as of the intellect, and in their more powerful passages they border on poetry. In their concern with the human soul they were to be followed by George Eliot and Meredith.

The following extract is taken from *Wuthering Heights*. In the heroine's declaration of the intensity of her passion for Heathcliff we see the heart of a woman laid bare with a startling frankness and depth of understanding. The lyrical tone, bordering on poetry, is new in the English novel.

> My great miseries in this world have been Heathcliff's miseries, and I watched and felt each from the beginning: my great thought in living is himself. If all else perished, and *he* remained, I should still continue to be; and if all else remained, and he were anni-

hilated, the universe would turn to a mighty stranger: I should not seem a part of it. My love for Linton is like the foliage in the woods: time will change it, I'm well aware, as winter changes the trees. My love for Heathcliff resembles the eternal rocks beneath: a source of little visible delight, but necessary. Nelly, I *am* Heathcliff! He's always, always in my mind: not as a pleasure, any more than I am always a pleasure to myself, but as my own being.

IV. GEORGE ELIOT (1819–80)

1. Her Life. Mary Ann Evans, who wrote under the pen-name of George Eliot, was the daughter of a Warwickshire land-agent. She was born near Nuneaton, and after being educated at Nuneaton and Coventry lived much at home. Her mind was well above the ordinary in its bent for religious and philosophical speculation. In 1846 she translated Strauss's *Life of Jesus*, and on the death of her father in 1849 she took entirely to literary work. She was appointed assistant editor of *The Westminster Review* (1851), and became a member of a literary circle. In later life she travelled extensively, and married (1880) J. W. Cross. She died at Chelsea in the same year.

2. Her Works. George Eliot only discovered her bent for fiction when well into the middle years of her life. Her first works consisted of three short stories, published in *Blackwood's Magazine* during 1857, and reissued under the title of *Scenes of Clerical Life* in the following year. Like her later novels they deal with the tragedy of ordinary lives, unfolded with an intense sympathy and deep insight into the truth of character. *Adam Bede* (1859) was a full-length novel, which announced the arrival of a new writer of the highest calibre. It gives an excellent picture of English country life among the humbler classes. The story of Hetty and the murder of her child is movingly told, and the book is notable for its fine characters, outstanding among whom are Mrs Poyser, Hetty, and Adam Bede himself. Her next work, considered by many her best, was *The Mill on the Floss* (1860). The partly autobiographical story of Maggie and Tom Tulliver is a moving tragedy set in an authentic rural background, and the character of Maggie is probably her most profound study of the inner recesses of human personality. As yet her novel is not overloaded by the ethical interests which direct the course of her later works. In style it is simple, often almost poetical. *Silas Marner: the Weaver of Raveloe* (1861) is a shorter novel, which again gives excellent pictures of village life; it is less earnest in tone, and has scenes of a rich humour, which are skilfully blended with the tragedy. Like *The Mill on the Floss*, it is somewhat marred by its melodramatic ending. With the publication of *Romola* (1863) begins a new phase of George Eliot's writing. The ethical interests which had underlain all her previous works now become more and more the dominating factor in her novels. The story of *Romola* is set in medieval Florence, but, in spite of the thorough research which lay behind it, the historical setting never really lives. Indeed, the note of spontaneity is lacking in this novel, which is most memorable for its study of degeneracy in the character of Tito Melema. *Felix Holt the Radical* (1866), probably the least important of her novels, is set in the period of the Reform Bill. Next came *Middlemarch, a Study of Provincial Life* (1871–72), in which George Eliot built up, from the lives of a great number of deeply studied characters, the complex picture of the life of a small town. Her characters suffer through their own blindness and folly, and the theme is treated with a powerful and inexorable realism. Her last novel, *Daniel Deronda* (1876), is still more strongly coloured by her preoccupation with moral problems: it is more of a dissertation than a novel. It is grimly earnest in tone and almost completely lacking in the lighter touches of her earlier work, though it has some fine scenes. In 1879 she published a collection of miscellaneous essays under the title of *Impressions of Theophrastus Such*.

3. Features of her Novels. (*a*) *Her Choice of Subject.* George Eliot carries still further that preoccupation with the individual personality which we have seen to be the prime concern of the Brontës. For her the development of the human soul, or the study of its relationship to the greater things beyond itself, is the all-important theme. There is relatively little striking incident in her novels, but her plots are skilfully managed. Behind all her writing there lies a sense of the tragedy of life, in which sin or folly brings its own retribution. Her preoccupation with this theme gives to her later work some of the features of the moral treatise.

(*b*) *Her characters* are usually drawn from the lower classes of society, and her studies of the English countryman show great understanding and insight. An adept at the development of character, she excels in the deep and minute analysis of the motives and reactions of ordinary folk. She brings to bear upon her study of the soul the knowledge of the student of psychology, and her characterization makes no concessions to sentiment. Her sinners, and she is particularly interested in self-deceivers and stupid people, are portrayed with an unswerving truthfulness.

(c) The tone of her novels is one of moral earnestness, and at times in her later work of an austere grimness. But almost always it is lightened by her *humour*. In the earlier novels this is rich and genial, though even there it has some of the irony which appears more frequently and more caustically in the later books.

(d) George Eliot's *style* is lucid, and, to begin with, simple, but later, in reflective passages, it is often overweighted with abstractions. Her dialogue is excellent for the revelation of character, and her command of the idioms of ordinary speech enables her to achieve a fine naturalness. Only rarely does she rise to the impassioned poetical heights of the Brontës, but her earlier novels, particularly *The Mill on the Floss*, are full of fine descriptions of the English countryside, and her faculty for natural description she never lost entirely.

4. Her Place in the History of the English Novel. She is of great importance in the history of fiction. Her serious concern with the problems of the human personality and its relationship with forces outside itself, her interest in detailed psychological analysis of the realms of the inner consciousness, did much to determine the future course of the English novel. The twentieth century has seen the rapid development of these interests, and it is significant that the reputation of George Eliot, which suffered a temporary eclipse after her death, has recovered during the last ten or twenty years to a surprising degree.

V. GEORGE MEREDITH (1828–1909)

Of the later Victorian novelists Meredith takes rank as the most noteworthy.

1. His Life. The known details of Meredith's earlier life are still rather scanty, and he himself gives us little enlightenment. He was born at Portsmouth, and for two years (1843–44) he was educated in Germany. At first (1845) he studied law, but, rebelling against his legal studies, took to literature as a profession, contributing to magazines and newspapers. Like so many of the eager spirits of his day, he was deeply interested in the struggles of Italy and Germany to be free. For some considerable time he was reader to a London publishing house; then, as his own books slowly won their way, he was enabled to give more time to their composition. For a time in 1867 he was temporary editor of *The Fortnightly Review*. He died at his home at Box Hill, Surrey.

2. His Poetry. Throughout his long life Meredith produced much poetry which, in style and subject-matter, can be regarded as the complement to his novels. Among his volumes were: *Poems* (1851), *Modern Love, and Poems of the English Roadside, with Poems and Ballads* (1862), *Poems and Lyrics of the Joy of Earth* (1883), *Ballads and Poems of Tragic Life* (1887), *A Reading of Earth* (1888), *Poems* (1892), and *A Reading of Life, with Other Poems* (1901).

In all his poetry thought is more important to Meredith than form. Accepting the contemporary theories of evolution and natural selection, he sees life as a long struggle to raise man from the near animal to a more spiritual being, a struggle in which much is to be gained by a "healthy exercise of the senses." His thoughts on this subject, his philosophy of love, and his mystical worship of nature are the main subjects of his verse. The obscurity of his work is increased by an over-compressed style, which endeavours to be striking by its conciseness and the vividness of its imagery. Bold metrical experiments, and an unconcern with mere verbal melody add still further to the unusual effect, which has limited admiration of his work to a relatively small circle of readers.

3. His Novels. Meredith's first novel of importance is *The Ordeal of Richard Feverel* (1859). Almost at one stride he attains to his full strength, for this novel is typical of much of his later work. In plot it is rather weak, and almost incredible toward the end. It deals with a young aristocrat educated on a system laboriously virtuous; but youthful nature breaks the bonds, and complications follow. Most of the characters are of the higher ranks of society, and they are subtly analysed and elaborately featured. They move languidly across the story, speaking in a language as extraordinary, in its chiselled epigrammatic precision, as that of the creatures of Congreve or Oscar Wilde. The general style of the language is mannered in the extreme; it is a kind of elaborate literary confectionery—it almost seems a pity on the part of the hasty novel-reader to swallow it in rude mouthfuls. Nevertheless, behind this appearance of artificiality there range a mind both subtle and sure, and an elfish, satiric spirit. Such a novel could hardly hope for a ready recognition; but its ultimate fame was assured.

The next novel was *Evan Harrington* (1861), which contains some details of Meredith's own family life; then followed *Emilia in England* (1864), the name of which was afterward altered to *Sandra Belloni*, in which the scene is laid partly in Italy. In *Rhoda Fleming* (1865) Meredith tried to deal with plebeian folk, but with indifferent success. The heroines of his later novels—Meredith was always careful to make his female characters at least as important as his male ones—are aristocratic in rank and inclinations. *Vittoria* (1867) is a sequel to *Sandra Belloni*, and contains much spirited handling of the Italian insurrectionary movement. Then came *The Adventures of Harry Richmond* (1871), in which the scene is laid in England, and *Beauchamp's Career* (1876), in which Meredith's style is seen in its most exaggerated form. In *The Egoist* (1879), his next novel, Meredith may be said to reach the climax of his art. The style is fully matured, with much less surface glitter and more depth and solidity; the treatment of the characters is close, accurate, and amazingly detailed; and the Egoist himself, Sir Willoughby Patterne —Meredith hunted the egoist as remorselessly as Thackeray pursued the snob—is a triumph of comic artistry. The later novels are of less merit. *The Tragic Comedians* (1880) is chaotic in plot and over-developed in style; and the same faults may be urged against *Diana of the Crossways* (1885), though it contains many beautiful passages; *One of our Conquerors* (1891) is nearly impossible in plot and style, and *The Amazing Marriage* (1895) is not much better.

We add a short typical specimen of Meredith's style. Observe the studied precision of phrase and epithet, the elaboration of detail, and the imaginative power.

She had the mouth that smiles in repose. The lips met full on the centre of the bow and thinned along to a lifting dimple; the eyelids also lifted slightly at the outer corners and seemed, like the lip into the limpid cheek, quickening up the temples, as with a run of light, or the ascension indicated off a shoot of colour. Her features were playfellows of one another, none of them pretending to rigid correctness, nor the nose to the ordinary dignity of gover-ness among merry girls, despite which the nose was of a fair design, not acutely interrogative or inviting to gambols. Aspens imaged in water, waiting for the breeze, would offer a susceptible lover some suggestion of her face; a pure smooth-white face, tenderly flushed in the cheeks, where the gentle dints were faintly intermelt-ing even during quietness. Her eyes were brown, set well between mild lids, often shadowed, not unwakeful. Her hair of lighter brown, swelling above her temples on the sweep to the knot, imposed the triangle of the fabulous wild woodland visage from brow to mouth and chin, evidently in agreement with her taste; and the triangle suited her; but her face was not significant of a tameless wildness or of weakness; her equable shut mouth threw its long curve to guard the small round chin from that effect; her eyes wavered only in humour, they were steady when thoughtfulness was awakened; and at such seasons the build of her winter-beech wood hair lost the touch of nymph-like and whimsical, and strangely, by mere outline, added to her appearance of studious concentration. Observe the hawk on stretched wings over the prey he spies, for an idea of this change in the look of a young lady whom Vernon Whitford could liken to the Mountain Echo, and Mrs Mountstuart Jenkinson pronounced to be "a dainty rogue in porcelain."

The Egoist

OTHER NOVELISTS

1. Benjamin Disraeli (1804–81) was born in London of a Jewish family. He studied law at Lincoln's Inn but early showed his interest in literature. After the success of his first novel he spent three years making the Grand Tour of Europe, returning to England in 1831. In 1837, at the fifth attempt, he succeeded in gaining a seat in Parliament—as member for Maidstone. Ten years later he was leader of the Tories in the Commons, and he became Prime Minister in 1868 and again in 1870. He was raised to the peerage in 1876 and died in 1881 after a short illness.

He began his literary career as a novelist. *Vivian Grey* (1826–27) soon set the fashionable world talking of its author. It dealt with fashionable society, it was brilliant and witty, and it had an easy arrogance that amused, incensed, and attracted at the same time. The general effect of cutting sarcasm was varied, but not improved, by passages of florid description and sentimental moralizing. His next effort was *The Voyage of Captain Popanilla* (1828), a modern *Gulliver's Travels*. The wit is very incisive, and the satire, though it lacks the solid weight of Swift's, is sure and keen. Disraeli wrote a good number of other novels, the most notable of which were *Contarini Fleming. A Psychological Autobiography* (1832), *Henrietta Temple* (1837), *Coningsby: or the New Generation* (1844), *Sybil: or The Two Nations* (1845), and *Tancred: or the New Crusade* (1847). These last books, written when experience of public affairs had added depth to his vision and edge to his satire, are polished and powerful novels dealing with the politics of his day. At times they are too brilliant, for the continual crackle of epigram dazzles and wearies, and his tawdry taste leads him to overload his ornamental passages. Disraeli also carried further the idea of *Captain Popanilla* by writing *Ixion in Heaven* and *The Infernal Marriage* (both published in *The New Monthly* 1829–30, and in book form in 1853), and *The Wondrous Tale of Alroy and the Rise of Iskander* (1833). These are half allegorical, half supernatural, but wholly satirical romances. In style the prose is inflated, but the later novels sometimes have flashes of real passion and insight.

2. Edward Bulwer-Lytton (1803–73) was the son of General

Bulwer. On the death of his mother he succeeded to her estate and took the name of Lytton, later becoming Lord Lytton. He was at first educated privately, and then at Cambridge, where he won a prize for English verse. He had a long and successful career both as a literary man and as a politician. He entered Parliament, was created in turn a baronet and a peer, and for a time held Cabinet rank.

His earliest efforts in literature were rather feeble imitations of the Byronic manner. His first novel was *Falkland* (1827), and then came *Pelham, or the Adventures of a Gentleman* (1828). These are pictures of current society, and are immature in their affectation of wit and cynicism. They contain some clever things, but they lack the real merit of the early novels of Disraeli. *Paul Clifford* (1830) changed the scene to the haunts of vice and crime, but was not at all convincing. Lytton now took to writing historical novels, the best of which were *The Last Days of Pompeii* (1834), *Rienzi, the Last of the Roman Tribunes* (1835), and *Harold, the Last of the Saxons* (1848). They are rather garish, but clever and attractive, and they had great popularity. He did not neglect the domestic novel, writing *The Caxtons. A Family Picture* (1849) and *My Novel* (1853); and the terror and supernatural species were ably represented by *A Strange Story* (1862) and *The Coming Race* (1871). Lytton is never first-rate, but he is astonishingly versatile. His plays, such as *Richelieu, or the Conspiracy* (1839) and *Money* (1840), had great success.

3. Charles Reade (1814–84) was born in Oxfordshire, being the youngest son of a squire. He was educated at Iffley and Oxford, and then, entering Lincoln's Inn, was called to the Bar. He was only slightly interested in the legal profession, but very fond of the theatre and travelling. After 1852 he settled down to the career of the successful man of letters. He died at Shepherd's Bush.

He began authorship with the writing of plays. As a playwright he had a fair amount of success, his most fortunate production being *Masks and Faces* (1852), written in collaboration with Tom Taylor. *Peg Woffington* (1853) was his first novel, and was followed by *Christie Johnstone* (1853), which deals with Scottish fisherfolk. *It is Never too Late to Mend* (1856) treats of prisons and of life in the colonies. *The Cloister and the Hearth* (1861), one of his best novels, is a story of the later Middle Ages, and shows the author's immense care and knowledge; *Hard Cash* (1863) is an attack upon private lunatic asylums; and *Griffith Gaunt, Or Jealousy* (1866), *Foul Play* (1868), and some other inferior books are in the nature of propaganda against abuses of the time.

When at his best Reade tells a fine tale, for he can move with speed and describe incident with considerable power. He has the dramatist's sense of situation, and his gift is for striking scenes rather than the careful integration of plot. Often he is melodramatic, and his characters lack subtlety and depth. His style is, for the most part, virile and concentrated, and his dialogue shows the influence of his theatrical experience. On occasion he tends to overload his story with historical detail, of which he accumulated great masses, or mar his style by overemphasis.

4. **Anthony Trollope (1815–82)** is another Victorian novelist who just missed greatness. The son of a barrister, he was born in London, educated at Harrow and Winchester, and obtained an appointment in the Post Office. After an unpromising start he rapidly improved, and rose high in the service.

A prolific novelist, Trollope began his career with Irish tales such as *The Kellys and the O'Kellys* (1848), which had little success, and then produced the Barsetshire novels on which his fame rests. This series, in which many of the same characters appear in several novels, deals with life in the imaginary county of Barsetshire and particularly in its ecclesiastical centre, Barchester. It began with *The Warden* (1855); then came *Barchester Towers* (1857), *Doctor Thorne* (1858), *Framley Parsonage* (1861), *The Small House at Allington* (1864), and finally *The Last Chronicle of Barset* (1866–67). Later Trollope turned to the political novel in the manner of Disraeli, but without the latter's political insight. Among his works in this kind were *Phineas Finn* (1869) and *Phineas Redux* (1874). One of his most interesting books is *An Autobiography* (1883).

Trollope is the novelist of the middle and upper-middle classes. With urbane familiarity and shrewd observation he presents an accurate, detailed picture of their quiet, uneventful lives in a matter-of-fact way which gives his works the appearance of chronicles of real life. His main concern is with character rather than plot, but his characters, though clearly visualized and described in great detail, lack depth, and Trollope never handles the profounder passions. The framework of his novel is a series of parallel stories moving with the leisureliness of everyday life. His style, efficiently direct, simple, and lucid, is seen to particular advantage in his dialogue. A vein of easy satire runs through many of his novels, and he makes skilful use of pathos. Within his limited scope he is a careful craftsman whose works retain their popularity.

5. Wilkie Collins (1824–89) is considered to be the most successful of the followers of Dickens. At one time, about 1860, his vogue was nearly as great as that of Dickens himself. Collins was born in London, and was a son of a famous painter. After a few years spent in business he took to the study of the law, but very soon abandoned that for literature. He was a versatile man, dabbling much in journalism and play-writing.

Collins specialized in the mystery novel, to which he sometimes added a spice of the supernatural. In many of his books the story, which is often ingeniously complicated, is unfolded by letters or the narratives of persons actually engaged in the events. To a certain extent this method is cumbrous, but it allowed Collins to draw his characters with much wealth of detail. His characters are often described in the Dickensian manner of emphasizing some humour or peculiarity. He wrote more than twenty-five novels, the most popular being *The Dead Secret* (1857), *The Woman in White* (1860) —the most successful of them all—*No Name* (1862), and *The Moonstone* (1868). *The Moonstone* is one of the earliest and the best of the great multitude of detective stories that now crowd the popular press. Collins was in addition one of the first authors to devote himself to the short magazine story; *After Dark* is a collection of some of his best pieces, linked together by a slight thread of connecting narrative.

6. Charles Kingsley (1819–75) was a Devonshire man, being born at Holne and brought up at Clovelly. He completed his education at Cambridge (1842), where he was very successful as a student, and took orders. During his early manhood he was a strenuous Christian Socialist, and for the first few years of his curacy he devoted himself to the cause of the poor. All his life was spent, first as curate and then as rector, at Eversley, in Hampshire. In the course of time his books brought him honours, including the professorship of history at Cambridge and a chaplaincy to the Queen.

His first novels, *Alton Locke, Tailor and Poet* (1850), and *Yeast, a Problem* (first published in *Fraser's Magazine* in 1848), deal in a robust fashion with the social questions of his day. They are crude in their methods, but they were effective both as fiction and social propaganda. *Hypatia, or New Foes with an Old Face* (1853), has for its theme the struggle between early Christianity and intellectual paganism; in workmanship it is less immature, but the cruelly tragic conclusion made it less popular than the others. *Westward Ho!* (1855), a tale of the good old days of Queen Elizabeth, marks the climax of his career as a novelist. At first the book strikes the reader as being wordy and diffuse, and all through it is marred with much tedious abuse of Roman Catholics; but once the tale roams abroad into exciting scenes it moves with a buoyant zest, and reflects with romantic exuberance the spirit of the early sea-rovers. *Two Years Ago* (1857) and *Hereward the Wake*, 'Last of the English' (1866) did not recapture the note of their great predecessor.

Kingsley excels as the manly and straightforward story-teller. His characters, though they are clearly stamped and visualized, lack delicacy of finish, yet they suit his purpose excellently. In treatment he revels in a kind of florid description which is not always successful.

As a poet Kingsley achieved some remarkable results, especially in his short poems. Of these a few, including the familiar *Sands of Dee*, *The Three Fishers*, and *Airly Beacon*, are of the truly lyrical cast: short, profoundly passionate, and perfectly phrased. In his longer works, such as his poetical drama, *The Saint's Tragedy* (1848), his hand is not nearly so sure. Kingsley could write also a rhythmic semi-poetical prose, as is seen in his book of stories from the Greek myths called *The Heroes* (1856) and to a less degree in his delightful fantasy *The Water Babies* (1863).

7. **Walter Besant (1836–1901)** is a good example of the class of light novelist that flourished in the later Victorian epoch. He was born at Portsmouth, educated at London and Cambridge, held a professorship in Mauritius, and then, returning to England (1867), settled down to the life of a novelist. Along with **James Rice (1844–82)** he wrote many novels, including *Ready-Money Mortiboy* (1872) and *The Golden Butterfly* (1876). These books do not aspire to be great literature, but they are healthy and amusing productions.

8. **George Borrow (1803–81)** had a curious career which did not lose its interest from his method of telling its story. He was born in Norfolk, and was the son of a soldier. From his earliest manhood he led a wandering life, and consorted with queer people, of whose languages and customs he was a quick observer. At one stage of his career he was a colporteur for the Bible Society, visiting Spain and Morocco (1835–39). Then he married a lady with a considerable income, and died a landed proprietor in comfortable circumstances.

His principal books were *The Bible in Spain* (1843), telling of his adventures as an agent of the Bible Society; *Lavengro* (1851) and

The Romany Rye (1857), dealing with his life among the gipsies; and *Wild Wales* (1862). His books are remarkable in that they seriously pretend to tell the actual facts of the author's life, but how much is fact and how much is fiction will never be accurately known, so great is his power of imagination. Taken as mere fiction, the books exert a strong and strange fascination on many readers. They have a naïve simplicity resembling that of Goldsmith, a wry humour, and a quick and natural shrewdness. As a blend of fact and fiction, of hard detail and misty imagination, of sly humour and stockish solemnity, the books stand apart in our literature.

9. **Nathaniel Hawthorne (1804–64)** is among the most famous of American novelists. He was born at Salem, near Boston, and was among the earliest students at Bowdoin College, in Brunswick, Maine. From an early age he devoted himself to literature, reading much in private. He wrote for magazines and did literary hack-work, for which he received little reward. After serving in the Boston Customs House, he took to farming, with no success. Subsequently the favourable reception of his later novels set him firmly in the career he had always preferred. In 1853 he received the appointment of consul at Liverpool, returning to America in 1860.

Hawthorne's earliest work was in the form of short stories, which appeared in book-form with the title of *Twice Told Tales* (1837); then came a second series of *Twice Told Tales* (1842), *Mosses from an Old Manse* (1846), *The Scarlet Letter* (1850), which brought him fame, and *The House of the Seven Gables* (1851). The novels are not very cheerful reading, being overshadowed with crime, shame, and sorrow, but they show power and sympathy, an intense (though slightly dis-eased) imagination, and a style marked by great care and clearness. In several respects he resembles George Eliot, though he lacks her humour, and in others he resembles Thomas Hardy, though his fiction lacks the elevation of the English writer.

10. **Richard D. Blackmore (1825–1900)** was born in Berkshire, and educated at Tiverton and Oxford. He was called to the Bar, but forsook the law for the occupation of a farmer, which suited him much better. He died at Teddington.

He began authorship by writing verse of little value; then turned to writing novels, which are much worthier as literature. The best of these are *Lorna Doone* (1869), an excellent historical romance of Exmoor, *The Maid of Sker* (1872), and *Cripps the Carrier* (1876). Blackmore had little skill in contriving plots, and many of his characters, especially his wicked characters, carry little conviction.

Yet he has a rare capacity for tale-telling and a real enthusiasm for nature. His style, though often eloquent, is too overloaded and effusive, yet *Lorna Doone* stands high among the novels based on local history.

11. Robert Louis Stevenson (1850–94) was born at Edinburgh, and was called to the Scottish Bar. He had little taste for the legal profession, and a constitutional tendency to consumption made an outdoor life necessary. He travelled much in an erratic manner, and wrote for periodicals. Then, when his malady became acute, he migrated to Samoa (1888), where the mildness of the climate only delayed a death which came all too prematurely. He lies buried in Samoa.

His first published works were of the essay nature, and included *An Inland Voyage* (1878), *Travels with a Donkey in the Cevennes* (1879), and *Virginibus Puerisque* (1881). His next step was into romance, in which he began with *The New Arabian Nights* (1882), and then had real success with *Treasure Island* (1883), a stirring yarn of pirates and perilous seas. Then came *The Strange Case of Dr Jekyll and Mr Hyde* (1886), a fine example of the terror-mystery novel, and several historical novels: *Kidnapped* (1886), *The Black Arrow* (1888), *The Master of Ballantrae* (1889), and *Catriona* (1893), which was a sequel to *Kidnapped*. With the exception of *The Black Arrow*, the historical novels deal with Scotland in the eighteenth century. At his death he left a powerful fragment, *Weir of Hermiston*.

In the essay Stevenson shows himself to be the master of an easy, graceful style, the result of much care and a close attention to artistic finish, though, on occasion, he is in danger of becoming over-solemn. It is, however, as a romancer that he now lives. A follower of the Scott tradition, he has a power of rapid narrative, which gains because it avoids the verbiage and digressions to which Scott himself was so prone. Such books as *Treasure Island* reflect the adventurous spirit which, in spite of his illness, he never lost, and in most of them the story moves well. Generally plot seems to have been of more importance to Stevenson than character, though, even so, some of his stories, such as *Kidnapped*, are rather episodic, while others, notably *The Master of Ballantrae*, fall away in a manner which suggests some lack of staying power. *Catriona* is a not very successful attempt to emulate Meredith's detailed character analysis, and it may be said that, with the exception of his unfinished masterpiece, *Weir of Hermiston*, which approaches more closely to the novel (as distinct from the romance) than any other of his works, few of Stevenson's books have deeply studied characters. In many ways he is at his best in his short stories, where there is not the same need for a long-sustained effort. Here his artistry, working in a limited scope, produced such masterpieces as *The Bottle Imp*. His wide knowledge of, and deep regard for, his native land find their expression in the racy, Lowland Scots vernacular which was his natural idiom, and which he uses to such effect in *Kidnapped* and *The Master of Ballantrae*.

Stevenson's true merits have long been obscured by the glamourizing and sentimentalizing of his illness and life in Samoa. As we move further away from his own time and see him in a truer perspective, we are able to recognize in him the conscious and expert craftsman, deeply anxious to study and formulate the technicalities of his craft. The importance to him of this study can be well estimated from his numerous letters on the subject to his friend and fellow-writer Henry James.

Stevenson's poetry is charming and dexterous. His best volumes are *A Child's Garden of Verses* (1885), *Underwoods* (1887) and *Ballads* (1890).

12. Francis Bret Harte (1839–1902) was born at Albany, New York, and was in succession a schoolmaster, a miner, a compositor, and a journalist. In 1868 he became editor of the newly founded *The Overland Monthly*, and later in life did much touring and lecturing. He was appointed consul at Glasgow (1880), then went to London, where he died.

His first noteworthy work consisted of short stories, which he contributed to magazines, including his own. These tales reflect much of his own earlier life, especially that spent in the Wild West. They are told with much humour and with no lack of sentiment. The best of them are *The Luck of Roaring Camp*, *The Outcasts of Poker Flat*, *Miggles*, and *Tennessee's Partner*. He had a broad simplicity of manner that gave his works a wide appeal, and he may be said to have founded the popular novel of the backwoods. His verse has much vivacity and humour. The most popular piece is called *Plain Language from Truthful James*, but its better-known title is *The Heathen Chinee*.

13. Mark Twain was the pen-name of **Samuel L. Clemens (1835–1910)**, who, like his fellow-humorist Bret Harte, had an early career not devoid of picturesque incident. Born in Florida, Missouri, he was in turn a pilot on the Mississippi, a silver-miner in Nevada, a journalist, and an editor. A pleasure-trip to Europe provided him with material for *The Innocents Abroad* (1869), which established his reputation as an American humorist of the first rank. He wrote much after this, and with much applause, but his run of prosperity was interrupted by the bankruptcy of a firm with which he was connected. This was the cause of his undertaking a lecturing tour round the world. In 1907, after the conclusion of his tour, he visited England, where he was warmly received, Oxford conferring upon him the degree of D.Litt.

Twain's work falls into three main classes, travel books, novels of the Mississippi, and romances. In the first group we have, in addition to *The Innocents Abroad*, *Roughing It* (1872), an account of his own experiences in the West, *A Tramp Abroad* (1880), which tells of further travels in Europe, and *Following the Equator* (1897), in which he writes of the world-wide lecture tour made toward the end of his life. In the best of them, *The Innocents Abroad*, we see a typical American turning on the Old World the sceptical eye of the New. And the result is a series of philistine, but vivid and amusing, pictures of Europe.

His best work is to be found in the novels of the Mississippi. *The Adventures of Tom Sawyer* (1876) and *The Adventures of Huckleberry Finn* (1885) break away from the cultured gentility of New England literature to give vivid, realistic, and racy pictures of life in the southern states. Of the two, *Huckleberry Finn* is generally adjudged the greater, in that it plumbs deeper levels of human experience than the more romantic *Tom Sawyer*. *Life on the Mississippi* (1883), though a travel book, belongs to this group, for its first half also deals with the great waterway, as Twain remembered it from his youth.

The romances, which include *The Prince and the Pauper* (1881), *A Connecticut Yankee in King Arthur's Court* (1889), and *Joan of Arc* (1896), are of a poorer quality. In these Twain lacked the stimulus of personal experience.

Like Whitman, Twain is important in American literature in that he broke away from the strong influence of European models, and helped to lay the foundations of a distinctively American tradition. A humorist, aiming to please the masses, his strokes are bold and broad, and the humour ranges from farce to bitter satire. Always he writes with his eye on the object, and his best works are firmly grounded in reality. His plots are rather episodic, but the episodes are well handled; his characters are drawn with a warm humanity, and his style has the spontaneous ease which gives his writings an enduring charm.

14. Mrs Elizabeth Cleghorn Gaskell (1810–65), was the daughter of William Stevenson, who was, at one time, a Unitarian minister. She was born in London, but, her mother dying a month after her birth, she was adopted by an aunt who lived at Knutsford, near Manchester. In 1832 she married William Gaskell, a distinguished Unitarian minister working in Manchester. Her death took place in Hampshire.

It is convenient to consider Mrs Gaskell's writings in two groups rather than in the chronological order of their appearance. Her first novel was a sociological study based on her experience of the conditions of the labouring classes in the new cities of the industrial North. *Mary Barton, A Tale of Manchester Life* (1848) gives a realistic view of the hardships caused by the Industrial Revolution as seen from the workers' point of view. It is weak in plot, but nevertheless has some fine scenes, and it is carried forward by the strength of its passionate sympathy with the downtrodden. *North and South* (1855) is on a similar theme and its plot is better managed. Like its predecessor it has some fine dramatic incidents. *Sylvia's Lovers* (1863) is a moralistic love story in a domestic setting, with which scenes of wilder beauty and human violence are well blended, but the novel is spoilt by its unsatisfactory and rather melodramatic ending. Her last, and unfinished, novel, *Wives and Daughters* (1866), is by many considered her best. It is an ironical study of snobbishness, which is remarkable for its fine female characters such as Mrs Gibson, Molly Gibson, and Cynthia Kirkpatrick.

Mrs Gaskell is, however, at her best in a different sphere—that of simple domesticity and everyday folk. *Cranford* (1853), her most celebrated work, is less a novel than a series of papers in the manner of *The Spectator*. Light, gently humorous in tone, the papers deal with life as the author had known it in Knutsford, and the characters, among them the celebrated Miss Matty, are unforgettable. In a similar vein are her shorter stories, *My Lady Ludlow* (1858) and *Cousin Phillis* (1863–64). Her other work consisted largely of short stories and the well-known biography of her friend, Charlotte Brontë, which appeared in 1857.

The writings of Mrs Gaskell combine something of the delicate humour of Jane Austen with a moralistic intention not unlike that of George Eliot, but she is far less in stature than either. Her workmanship is too often uncertain, and her plots are generally weak and not infrequently melodramatic. Often the pathos, which she can handle with great effect, deteriorates into sentimentality, while her aims as a moralist lead her into preaching. Her style is simple, lucid, and unaffected, and at her best she has a delicate grace and charm.

WRITERS OF MISCELLANEOUS PROSE

I. THOMAS CARLYLE (1795–1881)

1. His Life. Carlyle, who was born at Ecclefechan, in Dumfries-shire, was the son of a stonemason. He was educated at Annan and at Edinburgh University, and, giving up his intention of entering the Church, became for a time a school-teacher in Kirkcaldy. After a few years' teaching, during which he saved a little money, he abandoned the profession and removed to Edinburgh, where he did literary hack-work for a living. At this time (1818) he was poor in means and wretched in health, and his spiritual and bodily torments are revealed in *Sartor Resartus*. In 1826 he married Jane Welsh, an able woman who possessed a little property of her own; and after a brief spell of married life in Edinburgh they removed to Craigen-puttock, a small estate in the wilds of Dumfriesshire owned by Mrs Carlyle. Here they lived unhappily enough, but here Carlyle wrote some of his best-known books. In 1834 they removed to London, and settled permanently in Chelsea. Carlyle's poverty was still acute, and as a means of alleviating it he took to lecturing. He was moderately successful in the effort. Then his books, at first received with complete indifference or positive amazement and disgust, began to find favour, and for the last twenty years of his life he was prominent among the intellectual leaders of the time. His wife died in 1866, and in his latter years he was much afflicted with illness and by his deep concern for the state of public affairs. He died at Chelsea, and was buried among his own people at Ecclefechan.

2. His Works. Carlyle's earliest work consisted of translations, essays, and biographies. Of these the best are his translation of Goethe's *Wilhelm Meister's Apprenticeship* (1824), his *The Life of Schiller* (1825), and his essays on Burns and Scott. Then *Sartor Resartus. The Life and Opinions of Herr Teufelsdrockh* (1833–34) appeared piecemeal in *Fraser's Magazine*. It is an extraordinary book, pretending to contain the opinions of a German professor; but under a thin veil of fiction Carlyle discloses his own spiritual struggles during his early troubled years. The style is violent and exclamatory, and the meaning is frequently obscured in a torrent of words, but it has an energy and a rapturous ecstasy of revolt that quite take the breath away. Carlyle then turned to historical writing, which he handled in his own unconventional fashion. His major historical works are *The French Revolution* (1837), a series of vivid word-pictures rather than sober history, but full of audacity and colour; *Oliver Cromwell's Letters and Speeches* (1845), a huge effort relieved from tedium only by Carlyle's volcanic methods; the *Life of John Sterling* (1851), a slight work, but more genial and humane than his writing usually is; and *The History of Frederich II of Prussia, called Frederik the Great* (1858–65), enormous in scale and heavy with detail. His works dealing with contemporary events are numerous, and include *Chartism* (1840), *Past and Present* (1843), and *Latter-day Pamphlets* (1850). The series of lectures he delivered in 1837 was published as *On Heroes, Hero-Worship and the Heroic in History* (1841).

3. Features of his Works. (*a*) *His Teaching.* It is now a little difficult to understand why Carlyle was valued so highly as a sage in moral and political affairs. Throughout his works there is much froth and thunder, but little of anything that (to a later age) is solid and capable of analysis. Carlyle, however, was a man of sterling honesty, of sagacious and powerful mind, which he applied without hesitation to the troubles of his time. His influence, therefore, was rather personal, like that of Dr Johnson, and cannot be accurately gauged from his written works. His opinions were widely discussed and widely accepted, and his books had the force of *ex cathedra* pronouncements. In them he sometimes contradicted himself, but he did great service in his denunciation of shams and tyrannies, and in his tempestuous advocacy of hard work and clear thinking.

(*b*) *His Historical Method.* Carlyle's method was essentially biographical—he sought out the 'hero,' the superman who could benevolently dominate his fellows, and compel them to do better. Such were his Cromwell and his Frederick. His other aim was to make history alive. He denounced the 'Dryasdust' who killed the living force in history. To achieve his purpose he sought out and recorded infinite detail of life and opinion, and by means of his own masculine imagination and pithy style he brought the subject vividly before his reader's eye.

(*c*) His *style* is entirely his own. At the first glance a typical passage seems rude and uncouth: with many capital letters in the

German fashion, with broken phrases and ejaculations, he proceeds amid a torrent of whirling words. Yet he is flexible to a wonderful degree; he can command a beauty of expression that wrings the very heart: a sweet and piercing melody, with a suggestion, always present, yet always remote, of infinite regret and longing. In such divine moments his style has the lyrical note that requires only the lyrical metre to become great poetry.

The following are three specimens of his style. The first, based on German models, is in his cruder early manner; the second is more matured and restrained, and we note in this the quizzical humour; the third shows Carlyle in his most lyrical mood.

(1) "*Es leuchtet mir ein*, I see a glimpse of it!" cries he elsewhere: "there is in man a HIGHER than Love of Happiness: he can do without Happiness, and instead thereof find Blessedness! Was it not to preach-forth this same HIGHER that sages and martyrs, the Poet and the Priest, in all times, have spoken and suffered; bearing testimony, through life and through death, of the Godlike that is in Man, and how in the Godlike only has he Strength and Freedom? Which God-inspired Doctrine art thou also honoured to be taught; O Heavens! and broken with manifold merciful Afflictions, even till thou become contrite, and learn it! O, thank thy Destiny for these; thankfully bear what yet remain: thou hadst need of them; the Self in thee needed to be annihilated. By benignant fever-paroxysms is Life rooting out the deep-seated chronic Disease, and triumphs over Death. On the roaring billows of Time, thou art not engulfed, but borne aloft into the azure of Eternity. Love not Pleasure; love God. This is the EVERLASTING YEA, wherein all contradiction is solved: wherein whoso walks and works, it is well with him."

Sartor Resartus

(2) The good man,[1] he was now getting old, towards sixty perhaps; and gave you the idea of a life that had been full of sufferings; a life heavy-laden, half-vanquished, still swimming painfully in seas of manifold physical and other bewilderment. Brow and head were round, and of massive weight, but the face was flabby and irresolute. The deep eyes, of a light hazel, were as full of sorrow as of inspiration; confused pain looked mildly from them, as in a kind of mild astonishment. The whole figure and air, good and amiable otherwise, might be called flabby and irresolute; expressive of weakness under possibility of strength. He hung loosely on his limbs, with knees bent, and stooping attitude; in walking, he rather shuffled than decisively stept; and a lady once remarked, he never could fix which side of the garden walk would suit him best, but continually shifted, in cork-screw fashion, and kept trying both. A heavy-laden, high-aspiring, and surely much-suffering man. His

[1] Coleridge.

voice, naturally soft and good, had contracted itself into a plaintive snuffle and sing-song; he spoke as if preaching,—you would have said, preaching earnestly and also hopelessly the weightiest things. I still recollect his "object" and "subject," terms of continual recurrence in the Kantean province, and how he sang and snuffled them into "om-m-mject," "sum-m-mject." with a kind of solemn shake or quaver, as he rolled along. No talk, in his century or in any other, could be more surprising.

The Life of John Sterling

(3) In this manner, however, has the day bent downwards. Wearied mortals are creeping home from their field-labour; the village artisan eats with relish his supper of herbs, or has strolled forth to the village street for a sweet mouthful of air and human news. Still summer-eventide everywhere! The great sun hangs flaming on the utmost North-west; for it is his longest day this year. The hill-tops rejoicing will ere long be at their ruddiest, and blush Good-night. The thrush, in green dells, on long-shadowed leafy spray, pours gushing his glad serenade, to the babble of brooks grown audibler; silence is stealing over the Earth.

The French Revolution

II. THOMAS BABINGTON MACAULAY (1800–59)

1. His Life. Macaulay was born in Leicestershire, his father being Zachary Macaulay, the earnest upholder of negro emancipation. Macaulay was educated privately, and then at Cambridge. From his infancy he was remarkable for his precocity and his prodigious memory. At Cambridge he twice won the Chancellor's Medal for English verse, and in 1824 he was made a Fellow of Trinity College. The collapse of his father's business led him to study law, and he was called to the Bar in 1826. At first he contributed to *Knight's Quarterly Magazine*, but later he began writing his famous essays for *The Edinburgh Review*. Having entered Parliament as a Whig (1830), a very promising political career seemed to be opening before him when he accepted a lucrative legal post in India. He was in India for four years; then, returning to England, he re-entered political life, and became in turn Secretary of State for War and Paymaster-General of the Forces. In 1857 he was raised to the peerage, and died when he was still busy with his *History*.

2. His poetry was nearly all written early in his career, and most of it is included in his *Lays of Ancient Rome* (1842). In style the poems resemble the narrative poems of Scott, and in subject they are based upon the legends of early Rome, the best-known dealing with the story of Horatius. His verse is virile stuff, moving with vigour and assurance, and is full of action and colour. Like his prose, however, it is hard and brassy, and quite lacking in the softer qualities of melody and sweetness and in the rich suggestiveness of the early ballad. It is not great poetry, but it will always be popular with those who like plenty of action and little contemplation.

3. His Prose Works. Before he left for India Macaulay had written twenty-two essays for *The Edinburgh Review*; he added three during his stay in India, and finished eleven others after he returned to England. With the five biographies that he contributed to *The Encyclopædia Britannica*, these include all his shorter prose works. The essays are of two kinds—those dealing with literary subjects, such as those on Milton, Byron, and Bunyan, and the historical studies, including the famous compositions on Warren Hastings and Lord Clive. His method of essay-writing was as follows: he brought under review a set of volumes that had already been published on the subject, then, after a survey, long or short as the case might be, of these volumes, gave his own views at great length. His opinions were often one-sided, and his great parade of knowledge was often flawed with actual error or distorted by his craving for antithesis and epigram; but the essays are clearly and ably written, and they disclose an eye for picturesque effect that in places is almost barbaric.

His *History of England*, the first two volumes of which were published in 1849, was unfinished at his death. After two preliminary volumes, it began with the Whig revolution of 1688, and Macaulay intended to carry the story down to his own time. But he managed to compass within the four completed volumes only the events of a few years. His historical treatment is marked by the following features: (a) There are numerous and picturesque details, which retard his narrative while they add to the general interest. (b) The desire for brilliant effect resulted in a hard, self-confident manner, and in a lack of broader outlines and deeper views. These defects have deprived his *History* of much of its permanent value. (c) To this he added such a partiality for the Whig point of view that his statements, though they are always interesting and illuminating, are generally distrusted as statements of fact. To sum up, he said, "I shall not be satisfied unless I produce something which shall for a few days supersede the last fashionable novel on the tables of young ladies." He had full reason to be satisfied; his book had an instant and enormous success, which, however, has been followed by distrust and neglect.

The extract given below gives some idea of his style. It is entirely direct and clear, and free from any shade of doubt and hesitancy. Observe the use of the short detached sentence, and the copious and expressive vocabulary:

> Then was committed that great crime, memorable for its singular atrocity, memorable for the tremendous retribution by which it was followed. The English captives were left to the mercy of the guards, and the guards determined to secure them for the night in the prison of the garrison, a chamber known by the fearful name of the Black Hole. Even for a single European malefactor, that dungeon would, in such a climate, have been too close and narrow. The space was only twenty feet square. The air-holes were small and obstructed. It was the summer solstice, the season when the fierce heat of Bengal can scarcely be rendered tolerable to natives of England by lofty halls and by the constant waving of fans. The number of the prisoners was one hundred and forty-six. When they were ordered to enter the cell, they imagined that the soldiers were joking; and, being in high spirits on account of the promise of the Nabob to spare their lives, they laughed and jested at the absurdity of the notion. They soon discovered their mistake. They expostulated; they entreated; but in vain. The guards threatened to cut down all who hesitated. The captives were driven into the cell at the point of the sword, and the door was instantly shut and locked upon them.
>
> *Essay on Clive*

III. JOHN RUSKIN (1819–1900)

1. His Life. Ruskin was born in London, of Scottish parentage, and was educated privately before he went to Oxford. During his boyhood he often travelled with his father, whose business activities involved journeys both in England and abroad. After leaving the university Ruskin, who did not need to earn a living, settled down to a literary career. He was not long in developing advanced notions on art, politics, economics, and other subjects. In art he was in particular devoted to the cause of the landscape-painter Turner, and in social and economic theories he was an advocate of an advanced form of socialism. To the present generation his ideas appear innocuous, or even inevitable, but by the public of his own day they were received with shocked dismay. At first the only notice he received was in the jeers of his adversaries; but gradually his fame spread as he freely expounded his opinions in lectures and pamphlets, as well as in his longer books. In 1869 he was appointed Slade Professor of Fine Art at Oxford. Illness, however, which was aggravated by hard work and mental worries, led him to resign (1879) after a few years; and though shortly afterward (1883) he resumed the post, it had at last to be abandoned. He retired to Brantwood, on Coniston Water, in the Lake District, where he lived till his death, his later years being clouded by disease and despair.

2. His Works. Ruskin's works are of immense volume and complexity. For a start he plunged into what turned out to be the longest of his books, *Modern Painters*, the first volume of which was issued in 1843 and the fifth and last in 1860. This work, beginning as a thesis in defence of the painting of Turner, develops Ruskin's opinions on many other subjects. The first volume was not long in attracting notice, chiefly owing to its sumptuous style, which was of a kind unknown in English for centuries. *The Seven Lamps of Architecture* (1849) is a shorter and more popular work, which once again expounds his views on artistic matters. *The Stones of Venice* (1851–53), in three volumes, is considered to be his masterpiece both in thought and style. It is less diffuse than *Modern Painters*; there is a little more plan in the immense array of discursive matter; and the luxuriance of the style is somewhat curtailed. His other writings are of a miscellaneous kind, and comprise *The Two Paths* (1859), a course of lectures; *Unto this Last* (1860), a series of articles on political economy which began to appear in *The Cornhill Magazine*, but were stopped owing to their hostile reception; *Munera Pulveris* (1862–63), also an unfinished series of articles on political economy, published in *Fraser's Magazine*, and also withdrawn owing to their advanced views; *Sesame and Lilies* (1865), a course of two lectures, to which a third was added when the work was revised in 1871, and which is now the most popular of his shorter works; *The Crown of Wild Olive* (1866), a series of addresses; and *Præterita*, which was begun in 1885, and which is a kind of autobiography.

3. His Style. Ruskin himself often deplored the fact that people read him more for his style than for his creed. Many of his views, which he argued with power and sincerity, are now self-evident, so rapid sometimes is the progress of human ideas; but his prose style, an art as delicate and beautiful as any of those he spent his life in supporting, will long remain a delectable study. For its like we must return to the prose of Milton and Clarendon, and refine and sweeten the manner of these early masters to reproduce the effect that Ruskin achieves. In its less ornate passages Ruskin's diction is marked by a sweet and unforced simplicity; but his pages abound in purple passages, which are marked by sentences of immense length, carefully punctuated, by a gorgeous march of image and epithet, and by a sumptuous rhythm that sometimes grows into actual blank verse capable of scansion. In his later books Ruskin to a certain extent eschewed his grandiose manner, and wrote the language of the Bible, modernized and made supple; but to the very end he was always able to rise to the lyrical mood and fill a page with a strong and sonorous sentence.

The paragraph given below, it will be noticed, is one sentence. Observe the minute care given to the punctuation, the aptness of epithet, and the rhythm, which in several places is so regular that the matter can be scanned like poetry.

Then let us pass farther towards the north, until we see the orient colours change gradually into a vast belt of rainy green, where the pastures of Switzerland, and poplar valleys of France, and dark forests of the Danube and Carpathians stretch from the mouths of the Loire to those of the Volga, seen through clefts in gray swirls of rain-cloud and flaky veils of the mist of the brooks, spreading low along the pasture lands: and then, farther north still, to see the earth heave into mighty masses of leaden rock and heathy moor, bordering with a broad waste of gloomy purple that belt of field and wood, and splintering into irregular and grisly islands amidst the northern seas, beaten by storm, and chilled by ice-drift, and tormented by furious pulses of contending tide, until the roots of the last forests fall from among the hill ravines, and the hunger of the north wind bites their peaks into barrenness; and, at last, the wall of ice, durable like iron, sets, deathlike, its white teeth against us out of the polar twilight.

The Stones of Venice

OTHER WRITERS OF MISCELLANEOUS PROSE

1. Ralph Waldo Emerson (1803–82) was among the most important of the men of letters that America produced during this epoch. He was a notable disciple of Carlyle. He was born at Boston, of a distinguished clerical family, and educated at Harvard College. The death of his father had left the family in straitened circumstances, and Emerson took to school-teaching. From this he turned to the Church, and became a Unitarian minister. Religious doubts, however, drove him from the ministry, and feeble health sent him on a long sea-voyage (1832). Returning to America, he became a travelling lecturer, expounding his views on religion and philosophy. These opinions were further developed in several volumes of essays, whose clearness and attractiveness brought him much applause. Henceforth his life was uneventfully prosperous.

In 1847 he visited Europe, spending a week with Carlyle, and delivering lectures in England and Scotland. He died in his quiet home at Concord.

Emerson's works comprise eleven volumes of lectures and essays, which cover a wide choice of subjects, but deal chiefly with the conduct of life. In religion, like Carlyle, he was of no particular sect; but, again like Carlyle, he had high ideals, enthusiasm, and an honest desire for truth and justice. His style is remarkably uniform; it is sweet and limpid, and enlightened with apt illustrations. He is fond of using a series of short sentences in the manner of Macaulay. It is the ideal expository style, with the addition of sufficient literary grace to give it permanent value.

2. John Addington Symonds (1840–93) was among the foremost of the literary critics who flourished after the middle of the century. He was the son of a Bristol physician, and was educated at Harrow and Oxford. A tendency to consumption checked whatever desire he had to study the law, and much of his life was spent abroad.

A large proportion of his work was contributed to periodicals, and was collected and issued in volume form. The best collections are his two series of *Studies of the Greek Poets* (1873–76). His longest work is *The Renaissance in Italy* (1875–86), in which he contests Ruskin's views on art. In style he is often ornate and even florid, and in treatment he can be diffuse to tediousness; but as a critic he is shrewd and well informed.

3. Walter Horatio Pater (1839–94) was, both as a stylist and as a literary critic, superior to Symonds. Born in London, he was educated at Canterbury and Oxford, becoming finally a Fellow of Brasenose. He devoted himself to art and literature, producing some remarkable volumes on these subjects.

His first essays appeared in book-form as *Studies in the History of the Renaissance* (1873), and were concerned chiefly with art; *Marius the Epicurean* (1885) is a remarkable philosophical novel, and is the best example of his distinguished style; *Imaginary Portraits* (1887) deals with artists; and *Appreciations* (1889) is on literary themes, and is prefaced by an important essay on style.

Pater was the spokesman of the school of æsthetic criticism. His attention was always focused on form rather than on subject matter, and he saw criticism as the critic's attempt to put himself into sympathetic relationship with the artist in such a way as to derive the maximum of personal pleasure from the work of art.

As can be seen from his appreciation of Wordsworth, his unending quest for beauty and æsthetic pleasure could, on occasion, distort his judgment.

Pater's individual style is among the most notable of the latter part of the century. It is the creation of immense application and forethought; every word is conned, every sentence proved, and every rhythm appraised, until we have the perfection of finished workmanship. It is never cheap, but firm and equable, with the strength and massiveness of bronze. Its very perfections are a burden, especially in his novel; it tends to become frigid and lifeless, and the subtle dallyings with refinements of meaning thin it down to mere euphuism. In the novel the action is chilled, and the characters frozen until they resemble rather a group of statuary than a collection of human beings.

4. James Anthony Froude (1818–94) was born near Totnes, where his father was archdeacon. After three years at Westminster School he proceeded to Oxford, where he was not long in feeling the effects of the High Church movement led by Newman. From this he afterward broke away, and was elected to a fellowship at Exeter College, which he soon abandoned. He toiled ardently at literary work, contributing freely to *The Westminster Review* and other magazines. In 1860 he became editor of *Fraser's Magazine*.

Froude was a man of strong opinions, to which he gave free expression both by voice and pen, and his career was often marked with controversy. His handling of the life of Carlyle provoked much angry comment. In the course of time his true merits came to be valued adequately, and after being appointed to several Government commissions he was elected (1892) Regius Professor of Modern History at Oxford.

Froude's miscellaneous work was published in four volumes called *Short Studies on Great Subjects* (1867–83). His *History of England from the Fall of Wolsey to the Death of Elizabeth* (1856–70) was issued in twelve volumes. In period it covers the time of the Reformation, and in method it follows the lead of Carlyle in its great detail and picturesque description. In its general attitude it is an indirect, and therefore an unfair, attack upon the High Church views of Newman. Marred, as it undoubtedly is, by partisan bias, the work, nevertheless, is composed with much vigour, and is in the main accurate, though lax in detail. Other books are *The English in Ireland in the Eighteenth Century* (1872–74), *Cæsar* (1879), *Oceana, or England and her Colonies* (1886), and an Irish novel,

The Two Chiefs of Dunboy (1889). His biography of Carlyle was issued during the period 1882–84.

His style is free from the rhetorical flamboyance of Macaulay, and has a persuasive ease and charm.

5. Oliver Wendell Holmes (1809–94) was one of the most versatile of American writers. He was born at Cambridge, Massachusetts, and entered Harvard, where he made himself known as a writer of poems of the lighter kind. Abandoning the study of the law, he graduated in medicine, finishing his course with two years' study in Paris. He returned (1835) to practise medicine in Boston, and afterward (1847) was appointed professor of anatomy at Harvard Medical School. His work there was varied with some public lecturing on literary subjects.

As a poet Holmes wrote a great deal, and sometimes not very judiciously. Much the best of his poetry is of a humorous cast, like *The Deacon's Masterpiece: or The Wonderful One-Hoss Shay*. In the sentimental vein his methods are more heavy and less agreeable. As a poet, however, Holmes was always competent, and an adept at turning out graceful occasional verse.

His best literary efforts were three companion volumes, *The Autocrat of the Breakfast Table* (1857–58), contributed as a series of articles to *The Atlantic Monthly*, *The Professor at the Breakfast Table* (1860), and *The Poet at the Breakfast Table* (1872). The three, of which the first is by far the best, are a series of descriptive sketches, interspersed with verse, and each is held together by some kind of a plot. They are excellent examples of easy, witty conversation in the gracious, urbane manner of the eighteenth-century essayists, Addison and Steele, whom Holmes took as his models. There is much excellent humour, and some rather tedious moralizing and sentiment. Holmes also wrote several novels, the best of which is *Elsie Venner* (1861). In spite of the author's great tendency to diffuseness, the story is freshly told, and it became very popular.

6. The Historians. The nineteenth century produced many historical writers, of whom only a very few can find a place here.

(*a*) **Alexander William Kinglake (1809–91)** was born near Taunton, and educated at Eton and Cambridge. He was called to the Bar, and practised with some success, but in 1856 he retired to devote himself to literature. He saw much of the world, and watched the progress of the war in the Crimea. In 1857 he became Member of Parliament for Bridgwater.

His *The Invasion of the Crimea* (1863–87) is enormously bulky and full of detail. In attitude it is too favourable to the British commander, Lord Raglan, and in style it is tawdry; at its best, however, it is a picturesque narrative. His other work of note is *Eothen* (1844), an engaging and witty account of Eastern travel.

(*b*) **John Richard Green (1837–83)** was born and educated at Oxford, and became a curate in the East End of London. He was delicate in health, and was compelled to retire from his charge in 1869. His last years were spent in writing his historical works.

Of these works the best is *A Short History of the English People* (1874), which at once took rank as one of the few popular text-books which are also literature. It is devoted to the history of the *people* and not to wars and high politics. It is told with a terse simplicity that is quite admirable. *The Making of England* (1881) and *The Conquest of England* (1883) are the only two other full-length works he lived to finish.

(*c*) **Edward Augustus Freeman (1823–92)** was celebrated as the chief opponent of Froude. He was educated privately, and then at Oxford, where, much later, he became an honorary Fellow of Trinity College and Regius Professor of Modern History (1884). He wrote many historical works, the most valuable of which are *The History of the Norman Conquest of England* (1867–79) and *The Reign of William Rufus and the Accession of Henry the First* (1882). Freeman specialized in certain periods of English history, which he treated laboriously and at great length. This, as well as his arid style, makes his history unattractive to read, but he did much solid and enthusiastic work for the benefit of his students and successors.

(*d*) **William Hickling Prescott (1796–1859)** came earlier than the other historians we have mentioned in this section, and his methods were of an older type. He read very widely, but was content with a plain narrative, which his popular style made very attractive. He was intended for the law, but a serious eye-trouble, which afflicted him for most of his life, made such a profession impossible. His best works are *The History of Ferdinand and Isabella* (1836), *The History of the Conquest of Mexico* (1843), and *The History of the Conquest of Peru* (1847).

7. The Scientists. The nineteenth century beheld the exposition of scientific themes raised to the level of a literary art.

(*a*) **Charles Robert Darwin (1809–82)** is one of the greatest names in modern science. He was born at Shrewsbury, where he received his early education, passing later to Edinburgh and Cambridge. In

1831 he became naturalist in *The Beagle*, a man-of-war that went round the world on a scientific mission. This lucky chance determined his career as a scientist. The remainder of his life was laboriously uneventful, being devoted almost wholly to biological and allied studies.

His chief works are *The Voyage of the Beagle* (1839), a mine of accurate and interesting facts; *On the Origin of Species* (1859), which is to modern science what *The Wealth of Nations* is to modern economics—the foundation of belief; and *The Descent of Man* (1871). We cannot discuss his theories of evolution, but as general literature his books possess a living interest owing to their rich array of garnered evidence and their masterly gifts of exposition and argument.

(*b*) **Thomas Henry Huxley (1825–95)** was one of the ablest and most energetic of Darwin's supporters. He was born at Ealing, educated at London University, and became a surgeon in the Navy. His first post was on Nelson's *Victory*. Like Darwin, he travelled abroad on a warship, H.M.S. *Rattlesnake*, and during these four years (1846–50) he saw and learned much. Retiring from the Navy, he took enthusiastically to scientific research, and became President of the Royal Society and a prominent public figure in the heated discussions concerning the theories that were then so new and disturbing.

Huxley produced no work in the same class as *The Origin of Species*. His work consisted of lectures and addresses, which were issued in volume form as *Man's Place in Nature* (1863), *Lay Sermons, Addresses and Reviews* (1870), and *American Addresses* (1877).

THE DEVELOPMENT OF LITERARY FORMS

The Victorian epoch was exceedingly productive of literary work of a high quality, but, except in the novel, the amount of actual innovation is by no means great. Writers were as a rule content to work upon former models, and the improvements they did achieve were often dubious and unimportant.

1. Poetry. (*a*) The *lyrical* output is very large and varied, as a glance through the works of the poets already mentioned will show. In form there is little of fresh interest. Tennyson was content to follow the methods of Keats, though Browning's complicated forms and Swinburne's long musical lines were more freely used by them than by any previous writers.

(*b*) In *descriptive and narrative poetry* there is a greater advance to chronicle. In subject—for example, in the poems of Browning and Morris—there is great variety, embracing many climes and periods; in method there is much diversity, ranging from the cultured elegance of Tennyson's English landscapes to the bold impressionism of the poems of Whitman. The Pre-Raphaelite school, also, united several features which had not been seen before in combination. These were a fondness for medieval themes treated in an unconventional manner, a richly coloured pictorial effect, and a studied and melodious simplicity. The works of Rossetti, Morris, and Swinburne provide many examples of this development of poetry. On the whole we can say that the Victorians were strongest on the descriptive side of poetry, which agreed with the more meditative habits of the period, as contrasted with the warmer and more lyrical emotions of the previous age.

There were many attempts at purely narrative poetry, with interesting results. Tennyson thought of reviving the epic, but in him the epical impulse was not sufficiently strong, and his great narrative poem was produced as smaller fragments which he called idylls. Browning's *Ring and the Book* is curious, for it can be called a psychological epic—a narrative in which emotion removes action from the chief place. In this class of poetry *The Earthly Paradise* of William Morris is a return to the old romantic tale as we find it in the works of Chaucer.

2. Drama. Several of the major poets of the period wrote tragedy on the lines of the accepted models. Few of these attained to real distinction; they were rather the conscientious efforts of men who were striving to succeed in the impossible task of really reviving the poetical drama. Of them all, Swinburne's tragedies, especially those concerned with Mary Queen of Scots, possess the greatest warmth and energy; and Browning's earlier plays, before he overdeveloped his style, have sincerity and sometimes real dramatic power. As for comedy, it was almost wholly neglected as a purely literary form.

A development to be noticed is the popularity of the *dramatic monologue*. In *Ulysses*, *Tithonus*, and other pieces Tennyson achieved some of his most successful results; and Browning's host of monologues, wide in range and striking in detail, are perhaps his greatest contribution to literature. The method common to this kind of monologue was to take some character and make him reveal his inmost self in his own words.

3. Prose. (*a*) By the middle of the nineteenth century the *novel*, as a species of literature, had thrust itself into the first rank. We shall therefore consider it first.

In the novels of Thackeray and Dickens the various qualities of the domestic novel are gathered together and carried a stage forward. Dickens was a social reformer, and yet did much to idealize the England of his day, and to depict the life of the lower and middle classes with imagination and humour. As a satirist and an observer of manners Thackeray easily excels his contemporaries. With the Brontë sisters the romantic impulse was fully felt in the novel, to which they gave new intensity of passion, greater depth of intuitive sympathy, and a profound interest in the struggles of the individual soul. In this they were followed by George Eliot, who showed a closeness of application to the mental processes of her characters that was carried further in the work of Meredith, and has led to the 'psychological' novels of the present day.

In *Esmond* the historical novel made an advance. Here Thackeray was not content to master the history of the period he described; he sought to reproduce also the language and atmosphere. This is an extremely difficult thing to achieve, and is possible only in novels dealing with a limited period of time, but Thackeray scored a remarkable success.

(b) The development of the *short story*, as a separate species of literature, will be touched upon in the next chapter.

(c) In the case of the *essay* we have to note the expansion of the literary type into the treatise-in-little. This method was made popular by Macaulay, and continued by Carlyle, Symonds, Pater, and many others. Of the miscellaneous essayists, both Dickens, in some parts of *The Uncommercial Traveller*, and Thackeray, in *The Roundabout Papers*, successfully practised the shorter Addisonian type; and this again was enlarged and made more pretentious by Ruskin, Pater, and Stevenson.

(d) The *lecture* becomes a prominent literary species for a time. Carlyle, Thackeray, Dickens, and many others both in England and America published lectures in book-form. Earlier critics like Hazlitt and Coleridge had done so; but, almost for the first time, Ruskin gave a distinct style and manner to the lecture.

(e) The *historians* are strongly represented. Carlyle and Macaulay, in spite of their great industry and real care for history, have now fallen behind in the race as historians, and survive chiefly as stylists. The new method that arose was typified in the solid and valuable work of William Stubbs (1825–1901), Edward A. Freeman (1823–92), and **Samuel R. Gardiner (1829–1902).** These historians avoided the charms of literary style, concentrated upon some aspect of history, and, basing their results upon patient research into original authorities, produced valuable additions to human knowledge.

(*f*) We have already noticed that in this period the *scientific treatise* attained to literary rank. We may mention as early examples of this type Sir Thomas Browne's curious treatise on *Urne Buriall*, Burton's *The Anatomy of Melancholy*, and the graceful essays of Berkeley.

THE DEVELOPMENT OF LITERARY STYLE

With such an amount of writing as characterizes this age it is quite certain that both in prose and poetry a wide range of style will be observable.

1. Poetry. In the case of poetry the more ornate style was represented in Tennyson, who developed artistic schemes of vowel-music, alliteration, and other devices in a manner quite unprecedented. The Pre-Raphaelites carried the method still further. In diction they were simpler than Tennyson, but their vocabulary was more archaic and their mass of detail more highly coloured. The style of Browning was to a certain extent a protest against this aureate diction. He substituted for it simplicity and a heady speed, especially in his earlier lyrics; his more mature obscurity was merely an effect of his eager imagination and reckless impetuosity. Matthew Arnold, in addition, was too classical in style to care for over-developed picturesqueness, and wrote with a studied simplicity. On the whole, however, we can say that the average poetical style of this period, as a natural reaction against the simpler methods of the period immediately preceding, was ornate rather than simple.

2. Prose. With regard to prose, the greater proportion by far is written in the middle style, the established medium in journalism, in all manner of miscellaneous work, and in the majority of the novels. Outside this mass of middle prose, the style of Ruskin stands highest in the scale of ornateness; of a like kind are the scholarly elegance of Pater and the mannered dictions of Meredith and Stevenson. The style of Carlyle and that of Macaulay are both peculiar brands of the middle style, Macaulay's being hard, clear, and racy, and Carlyle's gruff and tempestuous, with an occasional passage of soothing beauty.

Of the simpler writers there is a large number, among whom many novelists find a place. We have space here to refer only to

TABLE TO ILLUSTRATE THE DEVELOPMENT OF LITERARY FORMS

Date	POETRY		DRAMA		PROSE		
	Lyrical	Narrative-Descriptive	Tragedy	Comedy	Novel	Essay	Miscellaneous
1840	Tennyson[1] E. B. Browning	Tennyson[2] Browning[4] Longfellow E. B. Browning			Dickens[8] Hawthorne	Carlyle Macaulay	Macaulay Carlyle[11]
1850	Browning[5] M. Arnold	Clough M. Arnold	Browning[6]		Thackeray[9] C. Brontë Kingsley		Ruskin[12] Borrow
1860	W. Morris	W. Morris Fitzgerald		C. Reade	Borrow C. Reade Trollope Collins G. Eliot Meredith[10]		Holmes
1870	C. G. Rossetti	Swinburne	Swinburne[7]		Bret Harte Besant	Thackeray Froude	Froude
1880	D. G. Rossetti	D. G. Rossetti	Tennyson[3]		Butler	Symonds Stevenson	Symonds
1890					Stevenson		

[1] *Poems* (1833).   [2] *Poems* (1833).
[3] *Queen Mary* (1875).   [4] *Pauline* (1833).
[5] *Dramatic Lyrics* (1842).   [6] *The Return of the Druses* (1843).
[7] *Chastelard* (1865).   [8] *The Pickwick Papers* (1836).
[9] *The Memoirs of Barry Lyndon* (1844).   [10] *The Ordeal of Richard Feverel* (1859).
[11] *Sartor Resartus* (1833–1834).   [12] *Modern Painters* (1843).

the easy-going journalistic manner of Dickens and to the subacid flavour of the prose of Thackeray.

We add a specimen of Stevenson's prose style. This style, which in its mannered precision is typical of many modern prose styles, is noteworthy on account of its careful selection of epithet, its clear-cut expressiveness, and its delicate rhythm.

But Hermiston was not all of one piece. He was, besides, a mighty toper; he could sit at wine until the day dawned, and pass directly from the table to the Bench with a steady hand and a clear head. Beyond the third bottle, he showed the plebeian in a larger print; the low, gross accent, the low, foul mirth, grew broader and commoner; he became less formidable, and infinitely more disgusting. Now, the boy had inherited from Jean Rutherford a shivering delicacy, unequally mated with potential violence. In the playing-fields, and amongst his own companions, he repaid a coarse expression with a blow; at his father's table (when the time came for him to join these revels) he turned pale and sickened in silence. Of all the guests whom he there encountered, he had toleration for only one: David Keith Carnegie, Lord Glenalmond. Lord Glenalmond was tall and emaciated, with long features and long delicate hands. He was often compared with the statue of Forbes of Culloden in the Parliament House; and his blue eye, at more than sixty, preserved some of the fire of youth. His exquisite disparity with any of his fellow-guests, his appearance, as of an artist and an aristocrat stranded in rude company, rivetted the boy's attention; and as curiosity and interest are the things in the world that are the most immediately and certainly rewarded, Lord Glenalmond was attracted by the boy.

Weir of Hermiston

CHAPTER XII

THE BIRTH OF MODERN LITERATURE

TIME-CHART OF THE CHIEF AUTHORS

The thick line indicates the period of important literary production.

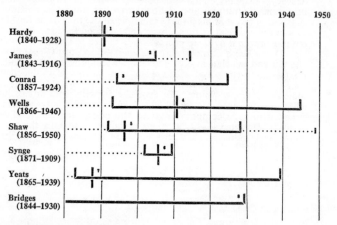

[1] *Tess of the D'Urbervilles* (1891).
[3] *Almayer's Folly* (1895).
[5] *Plays: Pleasant and Unpleasant* (1898).
[7] *The Wanderings of Oisin* (1889).

[2] *The Golden Bowl* (1904).
[4] *The History of Mr Polly* (1910).
[6] *The Playboy of the Western World* (1907).
[8] *The Testament of Beauty* (1929).

THE HISTORICAL BACKGROUND (1890–1918)

This period sees the end of the long reign of Queen Victoria (1901) and of the stability which the country had so long enjoyed. The shock administered by the Boer War (1899–1902) to the violent imperialism of the later years of the reign helped to divert attention from the cruder conceptions of imperial expansion to social problems at home. There ensued a period of sweeping social reform and unprecedented progress. The reawakening of a social conscience found its expression in the development of local government and the rapid extension of its influence upon the health, education, and happiness of the citizen. More than ever before political issues were fought on the basis of class loyalties, and this period sees the emergence and rapid growth of the Labour Party. Political passions ran high, and the years before the War saw serious labour troubles, many of them connected with the growth of Trades Unionism. Home Rule for Ireland, Free Trade or Protection, Votes for Women, the decline of agriculture and the growing urbanization of the country were major problems of the day. After the Boer War the aloofness which Britain had so long and prosperously maintained from European conflicts was abandoned in face of growing German strength, and national rivalries finally came to a head in the appalling struggle of 1914–18.

LITERARY FEATURES OF THE AGE

1. The Spread of Education. The full effect of the Education Act of 1870, strengthened by the Act of 1902, began to make itself felt in the pre-War years. The ladder of educational opportunity, from elementary school to university, was now available to the poorest boy who had the ability to take advantage of it, and literacy became the normal rather than the unusual thing. On literature the effect was profound. Not only was there a larger market than ever before for the 'classics' and for all types of fiction, but there arose an entirely new demand for works in 'educational' fields—science, history, and travel. As a profession and as a business, literature offered better financial prospects.

2. Enormous Output of Books. Authors and publishers were not slow to supply the public with what it wanted, and books poured from the presses with astonishing rapidity. Among them were numerous 'pot-boilers' by inferior writers intent only on financial gain. Even some great artists failed to resist the temptation of over-rapid and over-frequent production, and of too many of them it may be said that they wrote too much. The sacrifice of art to business was not new—it had affected adversely some of the work of Dickens—but in our period the commercialization of literature was carried to unprecedented limits, and the problem has continued to grow.

3. The Literature of Social Purpose. The spread of literacy was accompanied by the awakening of the national conscience to the evils resulting from the Industrial Revolution. More than ever before would-be reformers pinned their faith on the printed word and on the serious theatre as media for social propaganda, and the problem or discussion play and the novel of social purpose may be described as two of the typical literary products of the period.

4. The Dominance of the Novel. In view of the developments outlined above, it is not surprising that for the first time in its history the novel now became the dominant literary form in English. To a semi-educated modern taste prose fiction was (and still is) more palatable than poetry, which is a more sophisticated taste, while, by its nature, it is more accessible to the masses than drama. In addition, the novel is admirably suited as a vehicle for the sociological studies which attracted most of the great artists of the period.

5. The Rebirth of Drama. After a hundred years of insignificance drama again appears as an important literary form, and the thirty years under review see men of genius, who are also practical, experienced men of the theatre, creating a live and significant drama out of the problems of their age. Like the novelists, most of the important dramatists were chiefly concerned with the contemporary social scene, and though, toward the end of the period, there are signs of a revival of poetic drama, prose is the normal medium.

6. Experiments in Literary Form. Long before 1918 it had become obvious that in poetry, in the novel, and in drama the old traditional forms were outworn. Experimenters in all three fields were evolving new forms to sustain the new demands being made upon them. Progress is most rapid in the drama, but the novel too, in the hands of great masters, undergoes revolutionary changes, the importance of which is sometimes underestimated because they are overshadowed by more startling experiments of the inter-War period. In poetry experiments are less sensational, and the bulk of the poetry published is in the traditional manner. For the first time for many years poetry is the least significant of the important literary forms.

THE NOVELISTS

I. THOMAS HARDY (1840–1928)

1. His Life. Hardy was born at Upper Bockhampton, in the county of Dorset. He was descended from Nelson's Captain Hardy, and was the son of a builder. He was educated at a local school and later in Dorchester, and his youth was spent in the countryside around that town, where shortly afterward he began to study with an architect. In 1862 he moved to London as a pupil of the architect Sir Arthur Blomfield. His first published work was the rather sensational *Desperate Remedies*, which appeared anonymously in 1871. In the following year the success of *Under the Greenwood Tree* established him as a writer, and soon afterward he abandoned architecture for literature as a profession. Most of his writing life was spent in his native 'Wessex,' where his heart lies buried, though his ashes have a place among the great in Westminster Abbey. In 1910 he was awarded the Order of Merit.

2. His Novels. The involved construction of *Desperate Remedies* (1871) gave place to the charming idyll *Under the Greenwood Tree* (1872), one of the lightest and most appealing of his novels. It was set in the rural area he was soon to make famous as Wessex. The success of this book, though great, was eclipsed by that of the ironical *A Pair of Blue Eyes*, which appeared in *Tinsley's Magazine* in 1873; and the following year (1874) saw the first of the great novels which have made him famous, *Far from the Madding Crowd*, a tragi-comedy set in Wessex. The rural background to the story is an integral part of the novel, which reveals the emotional depths which underlie rustic life. *The Hand of Ethelberta* (1876), an unsuccessful excursion into comedy, was followed by the deeply moving *The Return of the Native* (1878), a study of man's helplessness before the malignancy of an all-powerful Fate. The victims, Clym Yeobright and Eustacia Vye, are typical of Hardy's best characters, and the book is memorable for its fine descriptions of Egdon Heath, which plays an important part in the action. Then, in quick succession, came *The Trumpet Major* (1880), *A Laodicean* (1881), and *Two on a Tower* (1882) before Hardy produced his next masterpiece, *The Mayor of Casterbridge* (1886), another study of the inexorable destiny which hounds man to his downfall. The chief character, Michael Henchard, is clearly conceived and powerfully drawn, the rustic setting of Casterbridge is skilfully portrayed, and the book contains some memorable scenes, including the opening one of the wife-auction at the fair. The rural setting is even more strikingly used in *The Woodlanders* (1887), the tragic story of Giles Winterbourne and Marty South, two of Hardy's most noble figures. Then, separated by *The Well-Beloved* (1892, reissued 1897), came Hardy's last and greatest novels, *Tess of the D'Urbervilles* (1891) and *Jude the Obscure* (1895), both of which, by their frank handling of sex and religion, aroused the hostility of conventional readers. They seem modest enough by the standards of to-day, but *Tess of the D'Urbervilles* was rejected by two publishers and originally appeared in a somewhat expurgated version, and the outcry which followed the appearance of *Jude the Obscure* led Hardy in disgust to abandon novel-writing, though at the height of his powers. In these two books we have the most moving of Hardy's indictments of the human situation; both contain unforgettable scenes; the studies of Tess and Sue are two of his finest portrayals of women, and the character of Jude surpasses in depth of insight anything Hardy had previously achieved.

In addition to his full-length novels Hardy published the following series of short stories—*Wessex Tales* (1888), *A Group of Noble Dames* (1891), *Life's Little Ironies* (1894), and *A Changed Man, The Waiting Supper and other Tales* (1913). He is not so much at home in the short story, and these collections live for the occasional powerful tale rather than as a whole.

3. His Poetry. Hardy began as a poet, and, though for a long time he was unable to find a publisher for his verse, he continued to write poetry. After the public outcry against his two greatest novels, he wrote only verse. *Wessex Poems* (written between 1865 and 1870) appeared in 1898, and there followed, in a steady stream, *Poems of the Past and Present* (1901), *The Dynasts* (Part I, 1903; II, 1906; III, 1908), *Time's Laughingstocks* (1909), *Satires of Circumstance* (1914), *Moments of Vision and Miscellaneous Verses* (1917), *Late Lyrics and Earlier* (1922), *Human Shows, Far Fantasies, Songs and Trifles* (1925), *Winter Words* (1928), *Collected Poems* (1932). If we except *The Dynasts*, his epic drama of the Napoleonic wars, cast in a gigantic mould, the bulk of Hardy's verse consists of short lyrics, pithily condensed in expression, often intentionally angular in rhythm, but always showing great technical care and a love of experimentation. As some of the titles suggest, they, like the novels, reveal concern with man's unequal struggle against an overwhelming fate, and, if they seldom echo the bitter accusations of his novels, many of them are deeply felt. *The Dynasts* is a great achievement with its 130 scenes and enormous gallery of portraits. In places it seems unduly long, but it has fine dramatic scenes and many warmly human moments. It is the final expression of Hardy's philosophy (see below). His other drama was *The Famous Tragedy of the Queen of Cornwall* (1923).

4. Features of his Novels. (*a*) *His Subjects.* Hardy's subject is the same in most of his novels. In all his greatest works he depicts human beings facing up to the onslaughts of a malign power. Accepting, as he did, the theory of evolution, Hardy saw little hope for man as an individual, and though his greatest figures have a marked individuality, Hardy's aim was to present Man or Woman rather than a particular man or a particular woman. He was a serious novelist attempting to present through fiction a view of life, and one entirely different from that of his great contemporaries Tennyson and Browning. Most frequently his mood was one of disillusioned pessimism, excellently summed up at the end of *The Mayor of Casterbridge* by Elizabeth Jane, "whose youth had seemed to teach that happiness was but the occasional episode in a general drama of pain." And yet Hardy was never quite certain of his philosophy: he hovered between the view of man as a mere plaything of an impersonal and malign Fate and man as a being possessing free will, in whom character is fate, until, in *The Dynasts*, he evolved the conception of the Immanent Will.

(b) *His Treatment of his Themes.* Hardy's preoccupation with his 'philosophy of life' is seen in the way in which he intrudes himself into his novels to point an accusing finger at destiny or to take the side of his protagonists, and in the over-frequent use of coincidence, through which he seeks to prove his case. Too often his plots hinge upon a sequence of accidents which have the most dire consequences, and, therefore, while he seldom fails to inspire in his readers his own deep pity for the sufferings of his characters, he frequently fails to attain the highest tragic levels. Allied with this use of coincidence are a fondness for the grotesque or unusual and a weakness for the melodramatic. Yet he handles striking situations with great firmness of touch and a telling realism, and all his best novels contain individual scenes which are unforgettable.

(c) *His characters* are mostly ordinary men and women living close to the soil. The individuality of some is sacrificed to Hardy's view of life, but while he is, by more modern standards, not really deep in his psychological analysis, characters like Jude and Sue, Tess, Henchard, and Eustacia Vye show considerable subtlety of interpretation. Such figures as Gabriel Oak (*Far from the Madding Crowd*) and Diggory Venn (*The Return of the Native*) are finely realized, country types blending with the countryside to which they belong, while the minor rustics, who are briefly sketched but readily visualized, are a frequent source of pithy humour, and act as a chorus commenting on the actions of the chief protagonists.

(d) *His Knowledge of the Countryside.* In this Hardy stands supreme. His boyhood was spent mainly in the country, and he had an acute and sensitive observation of natural phenomena. As a unifying influence in his novels, the Wessex scene which he immortalized is second only to his philosophy. But nature provides more than a mere background: often it is a protagonist in the story, an unfeeling, impersonal force exerting its influence upon the lives of the characters. Probably the finest examples of Hardy's use of nature are in *The Woodlanders* and in *The Return of the Native*.

II. HENRY JAMES (1843–1916)

1. His Life. Henry James came of a wealthy and cultured American family, was born in New York, and was educated in America and Europe before going to Harvard to read law (1862). He was a friend of the New England group of writers—among them James Russell Lowell, H. W. Longfellow, and William Dean Howells. It was as a contributor to Howells' *Atlantic Monthly* and other American magazines that James began his career as a writer. By the late 1860's the fascination of the older European civilization was making itself felt, and after spending much time in Europe he settled there in 1875, adopting London as his new home. There he lived until 1897, when he moved to Rye, where he spent the rest of his life. In 1915 he became a naturalized British subject.

2. His Works. James was a prolific writer. Novels, short stories, travel sketches, literary criticism, autobiography flowed from his pen with a regularity that is surprising in one who was, above all things, a consummate artist. His chief novels fall broadly into three groups. Beginning with *Roderick Hudson* (1875) we have four novels, all of them simpler and more straightforward in technique than his mature work, and these deal with the contrast between the young American civilization and the older European culture. The other three of this group are *The American* (1876–77), *The Europeans* (1878), and *The Portrait of a Lady* (1881). This last is much the best of his early novels, and in its subtle character analysis and careful craftsmanship it looks forward to the James of the later periods. Then come three novels mainly devoted to the study of the English character, *The Tragic Muse* (1890), *The Spoils of Poynton* (1897), and *The Awkward Age* (1899), of which *The Spoils of Poynton*, a relatively short novel, shows most clearly the development of his methods. The highwater mark of his career was reached in the three novels, *The Wings of the Dove* (1902), *The Ambassadors* (1903), and *The Golden Bowl* (1904), in which, turning again to the theme of the contrast between European and American cultures, he achieves a subtlety of character-study, a delicacy of perception, and an elaboration of artistic presentation which rank them high among modern novels. They do, however, make very heavy demands upon the concentration, alertness, and sensibility of the reader and have, therefore, never been generally popular. James also wrote some excellent studies of American life in *Washington Square* (1881), and *The Bostonians* (1886); a beautifully told and deeply moving study of a child's mind in *What Maisie Knew* (1897); and two works which he left unfinished at his death, *The Sense of the Past* and *The Ivory Tower*, both of which were published posthumously in 1917.

Of the short story James was an acknowledged master. To his credit he has almost a hundred tales, which began with his earliest contributions to American magazines and continued well into the middle of his writing life. Of them all *The Turn of the Screw* (1898) is probably the best known, but his interest in the occult is seen to be strong in *The Altar of the Dead, The Beast in the Jungle, The Birthplace, and other Tales* (1909). Other stories appeared in *The Madonna of the Future and other Tales* (1879), *The Aspern Papers and other Stories* (1888), *Terminations* (1895), and *The Two Magics* (1898).

His autobiographical writings were *A Small Boy and Others* (1913), *Notes of a Son and Brother* (1914), and the posthumous fragment, *Terminations* (1917)—not to be confused with the short story of that name. His letters, published in 1920, his *Notes on Novelists* (1914), and the essay, *The Art of Fiction* (1884), are of the utmost importance to the student of James, and further light is thrown upon his work by *The Notebooks of Henry James* (1947).

3. **Features of his Novels.** (a) *His Theory of the Novel.* An understanding of this is of vital importance, not only to the student of James's work, but to the reader of Virginia Woolf and Katherine Mansfield, as well as Conrad and the early George Moore, to name some of the more important of his followers. A study of James is essential to the study of the modern novel because he was one of the first to view it as an artistic form. To him the novel was primarily an art form to be judged solely by artistic canons, concerned, not with moral purpose, but with the objective and impartial presentation of the reality of life. In this picture there was no place for the extravagance of romance or the distortions of sentimentality. He was little concerned with external events and almost entirely with the detailed and elaborate study of the subtlest shades of human

reactions to the situations which he conceived. For such a study the traditional biographical technique of presentation was inadequate; for James's high conception of artistic pattern and finish it was altogether too loose; and his work shows the steady evolution of a technique to replace the outworn convention. For the novelist he saw unlimited possibilities of artistic achievement:

"The advantage, the luxury, as well as the torment and responsibility of the novelist, is that there is no limit to what he may attempt as an executant—no limit to his possible experiments, efforts, discoveries, successes."

(b) *His Technique*. James's preoccupation with technique, so clearly evident in the prefaces to the rewritten versions of his earlier novels, which he prepared for the definitive edition of 1907, became all-absorbing as he developed. By comparison with *The Golden Bowl*, the technique of *Roderick Hudson* seems almost elementary, though in this first novel he had already evolved the idea of presenting his story through the consciousness of a single character, discarding the ubiquity and omniscience of the traditional novelist. This character, often standing outside the main drama of the novel, acts as commentator and guide to the reader in many of James's books. In his earliest books, and in some of the works of his middle years, there was enough incident to create interest in the action as such; by the time he reached his three great novels the action had become almost entirely an internal one, and *The Golden Bowl* is more bare of incident than any of his works. As he matured his study of the subtleties of motive and the delicacies of emotional reaction grew more and more minute, and his attention to detail became more exacting. In a novel conceived on a large scale this could only lead to great length, in spite of the exclusion of all irrelevance. Add to this length a devious method of exposition, which consists of hints, allusions, and fastidious qualifications, and it is easy to see why James, superb artist that he is, has never achieved popularity with the reading public, by many of whom he has been dismissed as long-winded or affected.

(c) *His Subjects*. The key to James's choice of subject is to be found in his own life. An American fascinated by the charm of an older civilization, he finds a great many of his themes in the impact of one type of society upon the product of another, in the study of the processes of adjustment and their effect upon the development of the individual character. An intellectual and a member of an intellectual family, James throughout his novels portrays the lives of people such as himself. He is concerned with man as a social being, not with the deeper relations of man and his God. Because his chosen field is a sophisticated, intellectual society there is little of the elemental passions in his novels, except in so far as they are shown under the control of the mind. In spite of his deprecation of the moral-purpose novel, it is possible to deduce from the works which began with *The Spoils of Poynton* a definite ethical position, though implied rather than stated by the novelist. Identifying the good with the beautiful, he sees taste, artistic sensibility, and individual integrity as the prime virtues, ugliness and meanness of spirit as the great evils. Of the presence of evil in this life he seems to have been acutely aware.

(d) *His Characters*. James is primarily interested in a character developing as part of a social group. He has no interest in the poor or in the unintelligent. His figures are usually intellectuals like himself, sensitive, refined, sophisticated, controlling impulse by reason, and endowed with a faculty for acute self-analysis. They view their own motives and reactions with a remarkable detachment and an equal degree of subtlety.

(e) *His Style*. It goes without saying that one of James's artistic standards and preoccupation with technique is a superb stylist. The revelation of such delicate shades of feeling as he handles in his later novels must call for a mastery of language. His earlier style, like his earlier technique, seems loose by comparison with his later work. At his most mature he is tireless in his quest for the exact word, the perfect image, and the delicately suggestive rhythm. His dialogue is excellent, and almost the whole of *The Awkward Age* is cast in dialogue form, while his descriptive powers, even as early as *The Portrait of a Lady*, are of the highest order.

III. JOSEPH CONRAD (1857–1924)

1. His Life. Conrad, whose name was Józef Teodor Konrad Nałęcz Korzeniowski, was the son of an exiled Polish patriot and was born at Berdiczew, in the Ukraine, where he spent the first thirteen years of his life. He was educated at Cracow, and was intended for the university, but, as he was determined to go to sea, he went to Marseilles in 1874 and there joined the French Mercantile Marine. Four years later he landed at Lowestoft and joined the British merchant service. By 1885 he had his master mariner's certificate, and, before ill-health caused him to leave the sea in 1894, he had spent twenty years roaming the world in sail and steam ships.

gaining experience which was to prove invaluable. The year after his retirement saw the publication of his first novel, *Almayer's Folly* (1895), and from that time he lived in the South of England and devoted himself to his writing.

2. His Novels. Conrad's first two works were based on his experiences of Malaya. *Almayer's Folly* and *An Outcast of the Islands* (1896), if not among his best, give a foretaste of his later work in their use of a vivid tropical background, and in their study of a white man whose moral stamina was sapped by the insidious influence of the tropics. Then came one of his best novels, *The Nigger of the "Narcissus"* (1897), a moving story of life on board ship, remarkable for its powerful atmosphere, its sea description, and its character study—Donkin is one of the best of his many vividly drawn villains. After the five stories collected as *Tales of Unrest* (1898) appeared *Lord Jim: a Tale* (1900), the greatest of his early works. It is one of the best of Conrad's studies of men whose strength fails them in a moment of crisis, and is again a story of the sea. In it Conrad introduces for the first time his technique of oblique narrative, the story being told through the ironical Marlow, who reappears so frequently in later novels. *Youth—A Narrative; and two other Stories* (1902) and *Typhoon, and other Stories* (1903) contain seven tales which include some of Conrad's most powerful work. "Heart of Darkness" in the former collection is remarkable for an overwhelming sense of evil and corruption and for its excellent tropical backgrounds; "The End of the Tether" in the same volume has very vivid descriptions of Far-Eastern sea-scapes. *Typhoon* is unsurpassed as a book about the sea even by this supreme master of sea description. The stories in both collections were based on his own experiences. *Nostromo—A Tale of the Seaboard* (1904) shifts the scene to the coastline of Central America. Its story of revolution is grippingly told, and the book is full of vivid descriptions and has many well-drawn portraits. Some critics believe it to be his finest work, and certainly nothing after *Nostromo* seems as good. *The Mirror of the Sea—Memoirs and Impressions* (1906) is a series of essays based on his experiences in the oceans of the world, and, as always in Conrad, it contains excellent pictures. It was followed by the popular detective story *The Secret Agent—A Simple Tale* (1907), which, though it contains some one or two well-drawn figures and suggests quite powerfully the atmosphere of the Underworld, is not one of his best. The same may be said of the stories in *A Set of Six* (1908) and his tale of Russian revolutionaries, *Under*

Western Eyes (1911), of which the best features are the character of Razumov and, as so often, the atmosphere, in this case of fear. *'Twixt Land and Sea—Tales* (1912) contains three more short stories, and then came *Chance—A Tale in Two Parts* (1914), Conrad's most ambitious venture in the oblique method of story-telling. Here Marlow appears again as narrator, but the story is also told from several other points of view, and this technique, combined with an involved time sequence, makes the novel structurally one of his most confusing. After *Victory—An Island Tale* (1915) and a further collection of four short stories, *Within the Tides—Tales* (1915), which add little to his stature, Conrad wrote *The Shadow Line—A Confession* (1917), a short novel in which the suggestion of the supernatural is masterly. Of his other novels *The Rescue—A Romance of the Shallows* (1920) is long drawn out, but has moments of high excitement, and is an excellent study of primitive men; *The Arrow of Gold—A Story between Two Notes* (1919) and *The Rover* (1923) are both set in a background of European history—not very successfully; while *Suspense—A Napoleonic Novel* (1925), also a historical novel, was unfinished at his death. Mention should also be made of the autobiographical *A Personal Record* (1912) and *Notes on Life and Letters* (1921), important for Conrad's views on his own art, and of two novels, *The Inheritors—An Extravagant Story* (1901) and *Romance—A Novel* (1903), in which he collaborated with Ford Maddox Hueffer (later Ford Maddox Ford). Posthumously collected were *Tales of Hearsay* (1925), four stories, and *Last Essays* (1926).

3. **Features of his Novels.** (*a*) *His Subjects.* Conrad, the greatest modern romantic, sought his subjects wherever he could expect to find adventure in an unusual or exotic setting. His own experience of the sea and, in particular, of Malayan waters, was of immense value to him as a writer, and most of his best work is in one or both of these settings. While he is an excellent story-teller who gives deep thought to his technique of presentation, his prime interest is in character, in the tracing of the life of a man in such a way as to illuminate the inmost recesses of his soul. This preoccupation with character grew as time went on.

(*b*) *His Characters.* Instead of a straightforward analysis of character, Conrad preserves an objective detachment and presents his people in a series of brief, illuminating flashes which, by the end of his novel, have cohered into subtly studied and vital individuals. His insight into motive and impulse is deep, and never keener than when he is dealing with savages or whites demoralized by their environment. His characters, both men and women, are drawn from a wide range. They are rarely commonplace, and some of his best are dyed-in-the-wool villains like Kurtz in *The Heart of Darkness* and Donkin in *The Nigger of the " Narcissus."*

(*c*) *His View of Life.* Like Hardy, Conrad had a profound sense of the tragedy of life, but it did not lead him to a spirit of resentment or accusation. In man's struggle against hostile forces, in his display of loyalty, courage, and endurance in the face of heavy odds, he saw the finest thing in human life. He was a profound thinker, but would have nothing to do with sociological or problem novels. His aim was to present life as the senses perceived it, and his novels are free from didacticism. Yet, from the frequency with which he portrays men of faith and courage determined to abide by their duty to their fellows, it is easy to see that for Conrad these were the prime virtues.

(*d*) *His Technique.* A student of such masters of the novel as Henry James and the French writers Flaubert and Maupassant, Conrad was a conscious artist deeply concerned with the nature and method of his art, as his letters and prefaces show. *The Shadow Line* reveals him to be a master of the traditional direct narrative method, but much of his best work is in the oblique method first used in *Lord Jim.* Presenting his material in an easy, conversational manner through the medium of a spectator such as Marlow, he gradually builds up a picture through a series of brief sense impressions, which only reveal their full significance when they finally come together into a complete whole. Such a method makes greater demands upon the reader than the simple direct narrative, but is ideal for the kind of psychological investigation in which Conrad was interested, as well as for the creation of a subtle all-pervading atmosphere which gives the story its own unity. His evocation of atmosphere is tremendously powerful.

(*e*) *His Style.* Conrad's prose style is one of the most individual and readily recognizable in English, not, as might be expected in a Pole, for its eccentricities, but for its full use of the musical potentialities of the language. His careful attention to grouping and rhythm and to such technical devices as alliteration enables him, at his best, to achieve a prose that is akin to poetry. When he writes below his best he can become over-ornamental, self-conscious, and artificially stylized. His own views on style he makes abundantly clear in this passage from the preface to *The Nigger of the " Narcissus":*

All art . . . appeals primarily to the senses, and the artistic aim when expressing itself in written words must also make its appeal through the senses, if its high desire is to reach the secret spring of responsive emotions. It must strenuously aspire to the plasticity of sculpture, to the colour of painting, and to the magic suggestiveness of music —which is the art of arts. And it is only through complete unswerving devotion to the perfect blending of form and substance; it is only through an unremitting, never-discharged care for the shape and ring of sentences that an approach can be made to plasticity, to colour; and the light of magic suggestiveness may be brought to play for an evanescent instant over the commonplace surface of words; of the old, old words, worn thin; defaced by ages of careless usage.

IV. HERBERT GEORGE WELLS (1866–1946)

1. His Life. H. G. Wells was born and educated at Bromley in Kent. His father was an unsuccessful shop-keeper and professional cricketer, and already at thirteen Wells was earning a living as an apprentice, first to a chemist, then to a draper. Subsequently he became a teacher, and in 1884 entered the Normal School of Science, South Kensington, where he spent three years and gained much of the scientific knowledge which he was to turn to such good use. On leaving the College he again took up teaching, but in 1893 ill-health compelled him to leave the profession and turn to literature for a livelihood. He began as a journalist and contributed to such periodicals as *The Fortnightly Review, Pall Mall Gazette,* and *Saturday Review.* The year 1895 saw the publication of *The Time Machine,* first of the scientific romances which established him as a popular writer by 1900. In 1903 he joined the Fabian Society, only to leave it some six years later, though his interest in socialist political ideals remained strong for the rest of his life and he was later a keen supporter of the Labour Party. He put up as Labour candidate for London University, but he was not successful.

2. His Works. The most prolific of major modern writers, Wells poured out scientific romances, novels, pamphlets, popular educational works, with incredible speed and regularity. In his writing life of some fifty years, he produced just under a hundred works. The first ten years after *The Time Machine* (1895) were primarily concerned with the scientific romances on which much of his popularity still rests. Among them we may mention *The Stolen Bacillus and Other Stories* (1895), *The Wonderful Visit* (1895), *The Island of Dr Moreau* (1896), *The Invisible Man* (1897), *The War of the Worlds* (1898), *When the Sleeper Wakes* (1899)—revised as *The Sleeper*

Awakes (1911), *The First Men in the Moon* (1901), *The Food of the Gods* (1904). In these stories, full of romantic incident and ready invention, Wells exploited the contemporary interest in science, packing them with a wealth of accurate scientific detail which gave them a strong appearance of actuality. Their appeal was immediate and enormous.

Kipps (1905) marks the next turning-point in his career and was to be followed by the sociological novels in which his true greatness is seen. They include *Tono-Bungay* (1909), *Ann Veronica* (1909), *The History of Mr Polly* (1910), *The New Machiavelli* (1911), *Mr Britling sees it through* (1916), and, after a lapse of ten years, *The World of William Clissold* (1926). The forerunner of this phase had been the early *Love and Mr Lewisham* (1900). These novels, like his romances, are full of interesting incidents and dramatic scenes, and the good-humoured naturalness of their style makes them easy and attractive reading. They present a vivid picture of the contemporary social scene among the lower middle classes, which Wells had studied at first hand with close and detailed observation. In them his interest in problems of social adjustment and distinctions between classes is always apparent, but, kept within bounds, it does not overburden the story.

Marriage (1912) and *The Passionate Friends* (1913) begin a series of novels in which Wells's interest in social problems outweighs considerations of story and character. The novels which immediately follow these two, *The World Set Free* (1914), *The Wife of Sir Isaac Harman* (1914), *The Research Magnificent* (1915), *Joan and Peter, The Story of an Education* (1918), *The Undying Fire* (1919), *The Secret Places of the Heart* (1922), are all much inferior to the works of his great period.

The 1914–18 war stimulated much thought on the problems of world organization and reconstruction, and Wells now chose more regularly the prose treatise as his chief literary form. As early as 1901 *Anticipations of the Reaction of Mechanical and Scientific Progress upon Human Life and Thought* had introduced Wells to the public as a popular writer of social treatises, and it had been followed by *Mankind in the Making* (1903), *Socialism and the Family* (1906), *New Worlds for Old* (1908). Then with the War came *An Englishman Looks at the World* (1914), *The War that will End War* (1914), *The Elements of Reconstruction* (1916), *Russia in the Shadows* (1920), *The Salvaging of Civilization* (1921), and *Washington and the Hope of Peace* (1922). Throughout the thirties Wells steadily produced pamphlets, among them *The Work, Wealth and Happiness of Mankind* (1931), *After Democracy* (1932), *The Anatomy of Frustration* (1936)—and then the 1939–45 War brought a final burst of activity in this field which had absorbed so much of his attention. Among the many treatises of this period mention should be made of *The Fate of Homo Sapiens* (1939), *The New World Order* (1940), *The Rights of Man* (1940), *The Common Sense of War and Peace* (1940), *Science and the World-Mind* (1942).

This period of almost thirty years was not, however, devoted entirely to pamphleteering, and, in addition to his popular educational works, *The Outline of History* (1920) and *A Short History of the World* (1922), novels continued to flow from his pen. Many of the novels written during the thirties approached the manner of his maturity, and include *The Autocracy of Mr Parham* (1930), *The Bulpington of Blup* (1933), *Brynhild* (1937), *Apropos of Dolores* (1938), and *The Holy Terror* (1939).

Many of the works of H. G. Wells must go unmentioned, but we must not omit his *Experiment in Autobiography* (1934).

3. Features of his Novels. (*a*) *His Ideas.* Wells was concerned above all things with contemporary social problems, and he ranks with Shaw as a leader of advanced political thought of his day. As a socialist he was concerned first with the reconstruction of modern society on a more equitable basis, and this he felt to be attainable only through the spread of education. This belief led him to produce not only his many treatises but also the popular educational works on science. Educational opportunities and political equality for women were among the causes he supported, and, though his plans for a world order involved a large degree of socialization and the subordination of the individual will to the communal good, he was a strong advocate of the importance of developing the capacity of each individual to its utmost limits. In pursuit of this ideal of self-development he opposed many of the conventional restrictions of his day. He was very interested in sex relationships and marriage, and his advocacy of free love placed him among advanced thinkers. The problem of the adjustment of the individual to his social environment was his chief interest, and if he was the opponent of class privilege, for the proletariat *en masse* he had little respect, and he had the strongest suspicions of the methods of contemporary democracy. His sympathy lay with the individual, for whom he had the warmest affection. These views, which gave him such immense influence in his day, are most fully expounded in his eminently readable prose treatises; they also underlie, not only the poorer, over-didactic novels of the 1912–20 period, but also those mature works in which he shows himself a novelist of very considerable standing.

(b) *His Technique as a Novelist.* Like Conrad and Hardy, he was a novelist presenting a serious view of life. Unlike his great contemporaries, he often used the novel for didactic purposes, and his stature as a novelist is correspondingly less than theirs. His view of the function of the novel is admirably summed up in the following extract from his article, *The Contemporary Novel* (1911):

> It is to be the social mediator, the vehicle of understanding, the instrument of self-examination, the parade of morals and the exchange of manners, the factory of customs, the criticism of laws and institutions and of social dogmas and ideas. It is to be the home confessional, the initiator of knowledge, the seed of fruitful self-questioning. . . . The novelist is going to be the most potent of artists, because he is going to present conduct, devise beautiful conduct, discuss conduct, analyse conduct, suggest conduct, illuminate it through and through. . . . We are going to deal with political questions and religious questions, and social questions. . . . Before we have done we will have all life within the scope of the novel.

At his best Wells succeeds in reconciling these aims with the demands of art, and the great novels have a spontaneous vitality and unfailing good humour, a warmth of human understanding and a naturalness of style which entitle them to a high place in twentieth-century fiction. They present real life with great accuracy and breadth, and Wells shows himself a master of technique. But his technique is that of an older generation, of the traditional English novel. By the modern theories of the 'art' of the novel he was untouched, and his narrative method is always direct and uncomplicated. The air of reality which appears even in his scientific romances is most striking in the mature novels.

(c) *His Characters.* In his major novels Wells presents a large gallery of portraits, of which the best are studies of simple, lovable souls like Mr Polly or Kipps, ordinary men of no particular importance who are pitiful in their attempts to order their lives. For the most part his finest characters are drawn from the lower middle class, which he studied with sympathy and humour.

(d) *His humour* is one of the most appealing features of his best novels, and of none more than *Kipps* and *The History of Mr Polly.* Quietly and unobtrusively it plays round its subjects, sometimes providing whole scenes or incidents of fun, sometimes resting on a single word, inserted with apparent casualness. Many of his best characters are, indeed, humorous figures.

OTHER NOVELISTS

1. Samuel Butler (1835–1902) was the grandson of the Dr Samuel Butler, who was, in turn, Headmaster of Shrewsbury School and Bishop of Lichfield. Some idea of his childhood and his relations with his father, who was also in the church, can be gained from *The Way of All Flesh*, in which the figure of Theobald Pontifex is modelled on Canon Butler. He was educated at Shrewsbury and St John's College, Cambridge, where he won distinction in the Classical Tripos, and, after refusing to take orders, he unsuccessfully tried teaching. In 1859 he emigrated to New Zealand, and, after five years of successful sheep-farming, the first year of which he described in *A First Year in Canterbury Settlement* (1863), he returned to England to lead a life of leisured ease. Painting was his first hobby, and he was sufficiently successful for his work to be hung in the Royal Academy. But at the same time he pursued his interests in science, music, and literature.

Butler's versatility and breadth of interest are reflected in his pamphlets and prose treatises. Those inspired by the Darwinian theory of evolution (a doctrine which, with certain reservations, he whole-heartedly embraced) include *Life and Habit* (1877); *Evolution Old and New* (1879); *Unconscious Memory* (1880); *Luck or Cunning as the means of Organic Modification?* (1887). His classical interests are reflected in *The Trapanese Origin of the Odyssey* (1893), his prose translations, in 1898 and 1900, of the *Iliad* and *Odyssey*, and the amazing *The Authoress of the Odyssey* (1897). Among his other miscellaneous publications were the charming travel book *Alps and Sanctuaries of Piedmont and the Canton Ticino* (1881); *Shakespeare's Sonnets Reconsidered* (1899); *The Life and Letters of Dr Samuel Butler* (1896); *Ex Voto* (1888); and *Essays on Life, Art and Science* (1904). *The Notebooks of Samuel Butler* were posthumously published in 1912.

His reputation rests, however, not on these (though his studies in evolution throw a valuable light on passages in his fiction), but on his three novels, *Erewhon* (published anonymously 1872), its sequel, *Erewhon Revisited*, which appeared, with a revision of the earlier book, as *Erewhon and Erewhon Revisited* (1901), and *The Way of All Flesh* (1903). The first, a collection of a number of articles previously written, one as long ago as 1863, is the best of the many Utopias which appeared toward the end of the century. Church institutions, parental authority, the worship of machinery, and the treatment of crime were aspects of contemporary society which it satirized with a shrewd and penetrating irony. Its cloak of romantic narrative, its characterization, and the authenticity of its New Zealand setting gave it considerable popularity. Its sequel, *Erewhon Revisited*, is a more unified work, which is based largely on Butler's disbelief in the doctrine of the Ascension, here represented by Sunchildism, and the hypocrisy it entails. Again the sustained irony is most effective, and the work is full of mordant wit. *The Way of All Flesh*, published posthumously, is an important modern novel. Into its story of the house of Pontifex went much autobiographical reminiscence and most of Butler's chief ideas on life. It is a vindication of free will against Darwinian determinism, and an unflinching attack on the shams and hypocrisy of Victorian family life. It is remarkable for its frankness, its subtle study of the unconscious which gives depth to its psychological analysis, and the typical Butlerian wit and irony which are found throughout.

An acute and original thinker upon social problems, Butler ranks as the greatest prose satirist since Swift. Shams and hypocrisies of all kinds, whether religious, social, or political, he exposed with a fearless honesty and a humour which often turns into the most biting satire. As an indication of his influence on others it is sufficient to list among his disciples Shaw, D. H. Lawrence, Somerset Maugham, and Wells. He considered himself to be primarily a thinker, but the artistic qualities of *The Way of All Flesh* are sufficient to assure him of fame when the views he expounded have all been abandoned or disproved, or absorbed as everyday commonplaces.

2. George Moore (1852–1933) was born in Ireland of a family of country gentry. He was educated at Oscott and, after a brief experience of the Army, went to Paris at the age of eighteen to study painting. There he came under those artistic influences which were to have such a lasting effect upon his literary work—the painters Degas, Renoir, Gauguin, Cézanne, and Van Gogh, the contemporary novelists Zola, Flaubert, and Goncourt, and the recently dead Balzac. After some years as an artistic dilettante in Paris he was forced by financial difficulties to return to England, where for some years he earned a precarious living as an art critic. In 1901, his reputation as a novelist now established, he returned to Ireland, where, with his friends Yeats and A. E. (George Russell), he assisted in the renaissance of Irish literature, and especially in the birth of the Irish National Theatre. Ten years later he returned finally to England.

Moore began his career as a detached, impartial realist on the French model, seeking his subjects in the lower and more sordid sides of life, which he studied with remarkable photographic detail. *A Modern Lover* (1883), *A Mummer's Wife* (1885), *A Drama in Muslin* (1886), and *Spring Days* (1888) were followed by the greater and deeply moving study of the misfortunes of a poor servant girl, *Esther Waters* (1894), a realistic yet sympathetic picture of life among the lowest classes. His next two novels, *Evelyn Innes* (1898) and its sequel *Sister Teresa* (1901), are really two parts of one work, a long and elaborate character-study on a religious theme, which, though it has the same detailed background as his earlier novels, marks the beginning of the movement away from naturalism toward a more mystical type of writing. Under the stimulus of the Irish literary revival this departure was carried still further, and *The Untilled Field* (1903), a collection of thirteen short stories of Irish life, and *The Lake* (1905), a novel also set in Ireland, both show Moore making considerable use of Irish folk-lore rather in the manner advocated by Yeats. After his return to England he produced two of his most finished novels in *The Brook Kerith, A Syrian Story* (1916), a boldly conceived and exquisitely told story of the origins of the Christian faith, and *Héloïse and Abélard* (1921), his own version of the famous medieval story. Of his other novels only *Aphrodite in Aulis* (1930) merits mention here.

Moore was first and foremost an artist. From the French masters he adopted the conception of the novel as an accurate, impartial, and detached study of life as it really is, a study to be judged only by the artistic skill of its presentation, while from Pater he first gained insight into the artistic potentialities of English prose. An acute and critical mind, a keen observation of life, an urbane detachment, with its attendant incapacity to experience the deeper levels of emotion, a sharp and often malicious wit, and a delicate ear for the rhythms of language equipped him admirably for the exploitation of his chosen form. As a realist he excels Gissing by virtue of his complete detachment, his total lack of sentimentality, and his respect for formal qualities. Throughout his career his style develops steadily, until in *The Brook Kerith* and *Héloïse and Abélard* it achieves a formal perfection, an exquisite simplicity and lucidity which are the supreme achievement of the conscious artist.

His interest in human nature and his psychological insight into the inner processes of the mind (not least into his own) lead him to devote much space in his novels to the analysis of mental states, and his studies of women are particularly good. It is this combination of insight with an easy natural style, often almost colloquial, which gives enduring appeal to those autobiographical works on which many critics feel that his fame will ultimately rest. These are *Confessions of a Young Man* (1888), dealing with his early life; *Memoirs of My Dead Life* (1906); his picture of the Irish literary world in *Hail and Farewell!—Ave* (1911), *Salve* (1912), *Vale* (1914); and the later *Avowals* (1919), and *Conversations in Ebury Street* (1924).

3. **George Robert Gissing (1857–1903)**, the son of a Wakefield chemist, entered Owens College, Manchester, as an exhibitioner and distinguished himself as a prize-man in classics and English literature. A career of exceptional promise was wrecked when he was imprisoned for stealing from other students, and from that time for many years his life was one of extreme hardship and unrelieved misery. He made two disastrous marriages, and subsisted in the London slums on the meagre earnings of a literary hack. In 1888–89 he visited Italy and Greece, and a second trip to the same area was undertaken in 1897–98. Toward the end of his career growing recognition brought financial relief, but popularity came only after his death.

As chronicles of the life of the slums, Gissing's earlier novels are unequalled in English. His backgrounds are filled in with unflinching realism, with an eye for concrete detail, and often with great power. But he is no social reformer; for the squalid and savage people he describes he sees no hope, and he has little sympathy with them, yet he is unable to achieve the detachment of the photographic realist. Gissing's novels reveal an inability to get away successfully from his own experiences. They burn with a fierce resentment, which springs from his sense of the injustice of a world where outward circumstance can be such a decisive factor in human life. His own personality is deeply impressed on most of his novels and the autobiographical element in them is strong. His most frequent theme is the tragic plight of a sensitive soul doomed by fate to a sordid existence, and many of these studies are marred by Gissing's self-pity. His best work is deeply moving, yet as an artist his shortcomings are many. His sense of proportion is often faulty, his plots awkwardly constructed or spun out to an unreasonable length, his themes and characters are frequently repeated with but slight variations, his dialogue is poor, and his work is almost completely lacking in the poise which comes from a sense of humour. His claims as a novelist rest on the value of his work as a social document and, more important, on the depth of his insight into the minds of his characters. His studies of almost morbid states of mind and his method of psychological analysis show the influence of the Russian Dostoevski, and to a considerable degree anticipate the line of development of the English novel since his own day.

The novels which seem likely to live are *Demos, a Story of English Socialism* (1886), *Thyrza* (1887), *The Nether World* (1889), *New Grub Street* (1891), and the unexpectedly mellow *The Private Papers of Henry Ryecroft* (1903), while the best of his other work is found in *Charles Dickens, a Critical Study* (1898) and the travel book based on his Mediterranean tours, *By the Ionian Sea* (1901).

Among his lesser novels we may mention *The Unclassed* (1884), *The Emancipated* (1890), *Born in Exile* (1892), *The Odd Women* (1893), *In the Year of Jubilee* (1894), *Eve's Ransom* (1895), *The Whirlpool* (1897), *The House of Cobwebs and Other Stories* (1906), and his unfinished romance *Veranilda* (1904).

4. Enoch Arnold Bennett (1867–1931) was born at Hanley in the Potteries and was the son of a local solicitor. He was educated at Newcastle-under-Lyme, studied law, and worked for some time as a clerk in his father's office before going to a similar job in London in 1893. He began to contribute articles to periodicals and became sub-editor, then editor, of the magazine *Woman*. This post he left in 1900 in order to devote all his energies to writing, and three years later he settled in France, where he married a Frenchwoman in 1907. Returning to this country in 1911, he eventually settled in Essex, and during the 1914–18 War he was for a time Director of British Propaganda in France.

He was the author of some eighty volumes of novels, short stories, essays, articles, and plays. In many ways he is the victim of his own literary facility, and his reputation as a novelist rests on some half-dozen of his many works. He is to the Black Country what Hardy is to Wessex, and his masterpiece *The Old Wives' Tale* (1908), *Clayhanger* (1910), *Hilda Lessways* (1911), and *These Twain* (1916) are all set in this district. These four novels, and the later *Riceyman*

Steps (1923), which is set in the sordid areas of Clerkenwell, are his best. *The Old Wives' Tale* is a long, realistic novel, which traces the steady evolution of the Potteries from the age of Victoria toward modern times. As a detailed social document it is of the greatest interest; as a novel it is full of human warmth and sympathy, is enlivened by Bennett's humour, which is sometimes kindly, often caustic or ironical. *The Old Wives' Tale* ranks with the greatest novels of modern English literature. Of the three novels published as *The Clayhanger Family* (1925), *Clayhanger* is the best. Its biting exposure of the religious bigotry of the five towns has certain resemblances to the work of Samuel Butler. All three, *Clayhanger*, *Hilda Lessways*, and *These Twain*, are notable for the vividness of their setting and the depth of insight with which the chief figures are studied. *Riceyman Steps* is a typically realistic revelation of lower-class London life as it revolves round the central figure of a miserly shopkeeper, but it contains also a portrait of a charwoman, Elsie, whose self-sacrifice and devotion bring beauty to an otherwise sordid tale. *Riceyman Steps* is the only one of his later works that approaches his best achievements.

Arnold Bennett is interested, not in propaganda or philosophy, but in giving a realistic account of the lives of ordinary people. He has an eye for detail, an unfailing interest in human life, intuitive understanding of character, and a freedom from any ideological aims or bias which place him high as a realist. Warm as is his sympathy for the poor, and strong as is his dislike for the narrowness of English provincial life, Bennett can present life without any of the distortion which is the besetting danger of the reformer. For the grim industrialism of the Potteries he has a real affection, and, though he is aware of its shortcomings, he has a rare faculty for describing its beauties. It is this same faculty for evoking the beauty and romance of the ordinary lives of ordinary folk which is one of the most attractive features of his best novels. His dialogue is usually excellent, but he appears to be insensitive to the finer graces of the English language, and his prose compares unfavourably with that of Galsworthy.

Unfortunately, in his quest for success, Bennett determined to give the reading public exactly what it wanted. He made a great deal of money, but wrote a great many novels unworthy of his talents. Among his lesser novels mention may be made of *A Man from the North* (1898), *Anna of the Five Towns* (1902), *The Grand Babylon Hotel* (1902), *A Great Man* (1904), *Sacred and Profane Love*

(1905), *Buried Alive* (1908), *The Card* (1911), *The Pretty Lady* (1918), *Mr Prohack* (1922), and *Lord Raingo* (1926).

To list the almost innumerable minor works of Bennett is impossible here. They comprise short stories and essays such as *Tales of the Five Towns* (1905), *The Grim Smile of the Five Towns* (1907), *The Matador of the Five Towns* (1912), *Books and Persons* (1917), *Things that have interested me* (1921–26); plays such as *Milestones* (1912), *The Honeymoon* (1912), *The Great Adventure* (1913), *The Love Match* (1922); and such books as *The Truth about an Author* (1903) and *The Author's Craft* (1914).

5. Rudyard Kipling (1865–1936) was born in Bombay but soon moved to Lahore, when his father, a professor of archæological sculpture, was appointed curator of the Government Museum there. At the age of six he was sent to England to school, and two years later he entered United Services College, Devon, the life of which he was to immortalize in *Stalky & Co.* (1899). On his return to India he was a reporter for the Lahore *Civil and Military Gazette* and the Allahabad *Pioneer* (1882–87), before beginning a two years' voyage to England which took him through China, Japan, and the United States, and led to the articles which were collected as *From Sea to Sea* (1900). Subsequently he travelled widely in many parts of the world, lived for four years in the U.S.A. (1892–96), and finally settled at Rottingdean, on the Sussex coast. His literary fame brought him many honours, including the Nobel Prize for Literature (1907) and the Rectorship of St Andrews University (1922–25).

Kipling was a prolific, very versatile writer, and had from the outset all the qualities necessary for popularity. His journalistic experience served him in good stead throughout his career, and his prose works, which include stories of Indian life, of children, and of animals, are told with great vitality. He has an inventive faculty, a romantic taste for the adventurous and the supernatural, and an apparently careless, very colloquial style, which ensured for his work a popular reception. His insistent proclamation of the superiority of the white races, of Britain's undoubted mission to extend through her imperial policy the benefits of civilization to the rest of the world, his belief in progress and the value of the machine, found an echo in the hearts of many of his readers. Into the period of the decadent writers he swept like a gale of invigorating salt air, glorifying the values of action, manliness, loyalty, and self-sacrifice, and, if his work betrayed occasional lapses of taste or excursions into the melodramatic or sentimental, they were not faults of such a kind as to affect the popularity he had enjoyed from the moment of his first English publications. But there was more in Kipling than a mere popular writer. His achievement in revitalizing literature in the 1890's is not to be underestimated. His painting of Anglo-Indian and of native life is extremely good: his portraits of soldiers, natives, and of children are also vividly drawn, though the characterization is not deep: his background is clearly visualized and realistically presented, and he has a great ability to create an atmosphere of mystery. The apparent carelessness of style is an effect deliberately and skilfully cultivated, and his stories are expertly constructed.

His best-known prose works include *Plain Tales from the Hills* (1888); *Soldiers Three* (1888); *The Phantom Rickshaw* (1888); *Wee Willie Winkie* (1888); *Life's Handicap* (1891); *Many Inventions* (1893); *The Jungle Book* (1894); *The Second Jungle Book* (1895); *Captains Courageous* (1897); *The Day's Work* (1898); *Kim* (1901); *Just-so Stories for Little Children* (1902); *Puck of Pook's Hill* (1906); *Rewards and Fairies* (1910); *Debits and Credits* (1926); and *Limits and Renewals* (1932).

As a poet Kipling claims credit for reintroducing realism and a racy vigour into the verse of the nineties. At his best he achieves genuine poetry; at his worst he can be mechanically and stridently crude. He lacks delicacy of touch. He is a ceaseless experimenter in verse forms and rhythms, and his main themes are those of his prose works. His verse is to be found in *Departmental Ditties* (1886); *Barrack-room Ballads* (1892); *The Seven Seas* (1896); *The Five Nations* (1903); *Inclusive Verse, 1885–1918* (1919) and *Poems, 1886–1929* (1930).

GENERAL SURVEY OF THE NOVEL (1890–1918)

1. The Dominance of the Novel. One of the most striking features of the history of the novel is the speed with which it has developed. Not before the eighteenth century did it appear as a serious rival to poetry and drama; throughout the nineteenth its status grew rapidly in the hands of the Brontës, Dickens, Thackeray, George Eliot, and Meredith. In the period now under review the novel for the first time gains an undoubted ascendancy over all other literary forms, an ascendancy it has maintained until very recent years. Its growing importance has been accompanied by serious study of the art of the novelist, and, from a technical point of view, the progress of the last sixty years is unequalled in all its previous history.

2. The Conception of the Novel as an Art Form. The problem of the aim and scope of the novelist is now seriously posed in England for the first time. Hardy, Wells, Conrad, James, Galsworthy, and Moore devoted themselves to this question. All would have endorsed the statement of Wells: "Before we have done we will have all life within the scope of the novel." From the definition of ends to means was a short step, and James and Conrad evolved techniques which revolutionized the novel. They abandoned the direct loose biographical method in favour of an indirect or oblique narrative, with great concern for pattern and composition, and characterization built on the study of the inner consciousness. It is in this manner that much modern fiction has been written.

3. The Novel of Ideas and Social Purpose. To Hardy the aim of the novel was to interpret life through a picture of human existence so presented as to express the author's philosophy. He overweights his case, whereas Conrad interprets life without sacrifice of art. Allied to this view of the novel is that of Butler, Wells, and Galsworthy, who saw it as a means of social propaganda, a medium for disseminating their ideas on religion, shifting social values, and family life. Others holding this view included **Mark Rutherford (1831–1913)**, whose real name was William Hale White, and whose chief novels were *The Autobiography of Mark Rutherford* (1881), *Mark Rutherford's Deliverance* (1885), and *The Revolution in Tanner's Lane* (1887); **J. D. Beresford (1873–1947)**, who wrote *The Early History of Jacob Stahl* (1911), *A Candidate for Truth* (1912), *The House in Demetrius Road* (1914), and *The Invisible Event* (1915); **Gilbert Cannan (1884–1955)**, author of *Peter Homunculus* (1909), *Round the Corner* (1913), *Little Brother* (1912), *Old Mole* (1914), *Mendel* (1916), *The Stucco House* (1918), and *Pugs and Peacocks* (1921); **Olive Schreiner (1855–1920)**, who wrote *The Story of an African Farm* (1883); and **Grant Allen (1848–99)**, author of *The Woman Who Did* (1895).

4. Realism. Another view was that of Moore, who aimed to present life with detached, photographic accuracy, regardless of moral or ideological considerations, judging his work by æsthetic canons alone. This was also Gissing's aim, though his concern with the artistic considerations was in reality slight. In this tradition were the works of **Rhoda Broughton (1840–1920)**—*Not Wisely, but Too Well* (1867), *Red as a Rose is She* (1870), *Belinda* (1883), and *Dr Cupid* (1886); of **Oliver Onions (1873–1961)**, who wrote *Little Devil Doubt* (1909), *Good Boy Seldom* (1911), *In Accordance with the*

Evidence (1912), *The Debit Account* (1913), and *The Story of Louie* (1913); of Israel Zangwill (1864–1926), who wrote *The Children of the Ghetto* (1892), *Ghetto Tragedies* (1893), "*They that Walk in Darkness*" (1899), and *Dreamers of the Ghetto* (1898); of Arthur Morrison (1863–1945), *Tales of Mean Streets* (1894) and *A Child of the Jago* (1896); and of John Davidson (1857–1909), *Perfervid, the Career of Ninian Jamieson* (1890), *Baptist Lake* (1894), and *The Wonderful Mission of Earl Lavender* (1895). Many short-story writers were influenced by the realist conception of fiction, which also makes itself felt in the works of the novelists of social purpose.

5. **French and Russian Influences.** From Flaubert (1821–80), the brothers de Goncourt (Jules 1830–70, Edmond 1822–96), Zola (1840–1902), Maupassant (1850–93), and Balzac (1799–1850), English writers learned the minutely accurate portrayal of everyday life, and the new conception of the novel as an art form, in which structure, pattern, style, and finish were of fundamental importance. In Dostoevsky (1821–81), Turgenev (1818–83), and Tolstoy (1828–1910), they found a new interest in the darker, hidden sides of human nature, and a different form and structure.

6. **The Growing Popularity of the Short Story.** Foreign influences were equally strong in the short story, which became widely practised. Hardy, Bennett, Conrad, Gissing, Kipling, Wells, and Moore all used this medium with success, and Henry James is perhaps the greatest short-story writer in English. Other writers in this field include Mark Rutherford (1831–1913), Hubert Crackanthorpe (1865–97), Frederick Wedmore (1844–1921), William Pett Ridge (1860 (?)–1930), A. St John Adcock (1864–1930), Barry Pain (1864–1928), W. W. Jacobs (1863–1943), Oliver Onions (1873–1961), James Stephens (1882–1950), R. B. Cunninghame Graham (1852–1936), and Marmaduke Pickthall (1875–1936).

A writer who greatly influenced future generations was 'Saki' (Hector Hugh Munro) (1870–1916), whose brief narratives in epigrammatic style aimed to humiliate the elderly upper-middle classes of the Edwardian era, cruelly enjoying to the point of sadism the revelation of their pretentious authoritarianism. Saki's witticism and sense of humour have something in common with present-day black comedy. His best work is found in *Reginald* (1904), *The Chronicles of Clovis* (1911), and *Beasts and Super-Beasts* (1914).

The short story was found to be particularly suited to tales of detection and the supernatural. Once Conan Doyle (see below) had established the character of his private detective, vast numbers of writers hastened to produce bizarre mysteries and even more bizarre sleuths. As for the supernatural, no-one bettered the work of **Montague Rhodes James (1862–1936)**, Provost of Eton and Vice-Chancellor of Cambridge University, whose very small output was contained in two volumes of *Ghost Stories of an Antiquary* (1904, 1911). More prolific and almost as successful was **Algernon Blackwood (1869–1951)**, whose interest in the occult and the uncanny influenced his career from *John Silence* (1908) to *Tales of the Uncanny and Supernatural* (1949).

7. The Survival of Romance. In the novel, as in drama, romance survived in this age of realism. Resurrected by Stevenson (see p. 410), it inspired Kipling and was carried to unprecedented heights by Conrad. Enormous numbers of romances were penned by other writers to satisfy the demand for the exciting, the unusual, the exotic, and the remote. Some of these writers achieved a popularity and financial success denied to their greater contemporaries. **Sir Arthur Conan Doyle (1859–1930)**, author of the world-famous Sherlock Holmes stories and of *Micah Clarke* (1889), *The White Company* (1891), *The Exploits of Brigadier Gerard* (1896), and *Rodney Stone* (1896); **Sir H. Rider Haggard (1856–1925)**, who wrote *King Solomon's Mines* (1886), *She* (1887), *Allan Quatermain* (1887), and *Ayesha, or The Return of She* (1905); **Stanley J. Weyman (1855–1925)**, author of *A Gentleman of France* (1893), *Under the Red Robe* (1894), and *Ovington's Bank* (1922); **H. Seton Merriman (1862–1903)**, whose real name was Hugh Stowell Scot, author of *The Slave of the Lamp* (1892), *With Edged Tools* (1894), and *In Kedar's Tents* (1897); and **Anthony Hope (Hawkins) (1863–1933)**, author of *The Prisoner of Zenda* (1894) and *Rupert of Hentzau* (1898); all became household names. Less well known, though possibly superior to all of these, was **Maurice Hewlett (1861–1923)**, author of *The Forest Lovers* (1898), *New Canterbury Tales* (1901), *The Life and Death of Richard Yea-and-Nay* (1900), and *The Queen's Quair* (1904). The best-known works of **Kenneth Grahame (1859–1932)** were *The Golden Age* (1895), *Dream Days* (1898), and the famous *The Wind in the Willows* (1908).

Moonfleet (1898) was a West Country adventure story with ghostly undertones, but the author, **J. Meade Falkner (1858–1932)**, used the supernatural as the basis of his only other novels, *The Lost Stradivarius* (1895) and *The Nebuly Coat* (1903).

8. The Growth of Regional Fiction. The success of Hardy as a novelist of Wessex stimulated fiction set in particular regions, such as the novels of the "Five Towns," which are Bennett's best work.

Westmorland was the setting of the novels of **Constance Holme**, who gained little recognition until long after the publication of *Crump Folk going Home* (1913), *The Lonely Plough* (1914), *The Splendid Fairing* (1920), and *The Trumpet in the Dust* (1921). **Eden Phillpotts (1862–1960)** is the novelist of Devonshire in *Children of the Mist* (1898), *The Human Boy* (1899), and *The Secret Woman* (1905). It was in the fiction of Scotland and Ireland that regionalism flourished most strongly. **The Kailyard School** in Scotland, including Barrie, produced novels of the Scottish countryside, in which accuracy of background was sacrificed for popular success. Among these novelists were **Ian Maclaren (1850–1907)**, whose real name was John Watson, and who wrote *Beside the Bonnie Brier Bush* (1894), *A Doctor of the Old School* (1896), and *Kate Carnegie* (1896); **S. R. Crockett (1860–1914)**, author of *Mad Sir Uchtred of the Hills* (1894), *The Black Douglas* (1899), *The Stickit Minister and Some Common Men* (1893), and *The Lilac Sunbonnet* (1894); and **Gabriel Setoun (1861–1930)**, whose real name was Thomas Nicoll Hepburn, author of *Robert Urquhart* (1896) and *The Skipper of Barncraig* (1901). A realist who wrote in a Scottish setting was **G. D. Brown (1869–1902)** with his fine novel *The House with the Green Shutters* (1901). In Ireland the growth of regionalism in the novel was but one aspect of that revival of Irish literature which found its greatest manifestation in the poetry of Yeats and the drama of Synge. Besides Moore we should mention **Standish O'Grady (1846–1928)**—*Red Hugh's Captivity* (1889), *The Flight of the Eagle* (1897), and *The Bog of Stars* (1893); **Emily Lawless (1845–1913)**, author of *Hurrish* (1886) and *With Essex in Ireland* (1890); and the partnership between **Edith Œnone Somerville** and **Violet Martin** (Martin Ross) which produced *Some Experiences of an Irish R.M.* (1899).

DRAMATISTS

I. GEORGE BERNARD SHAW (1856–1950)

1. His Life. George Bernard Shaw was born in Dublin of Irish Protestant stock, and there received a somewhat scanty education at a number of local schools, including the Wesleyan Connexional School. Most of his cultural background he owed to his mother, a talented woman with whom, in 1876, he came to London. Here he became an active member of the Fabian Society soon after it was founded in 1884, and he not only wrote pamphlets on politics and economics but did much platform speaking as his part in the campaign to disseminate the ideals of Fabian socialism. From

1885 to 1908 he won fame as a journalist—with the *Pall Mall Gazette* (1885); *The World*, as an art critic; *The Star* (1888), as a music critic; *The World* again (1890–94), this time as a music critic; and, most important of all, as dramatic critic for the *Saturday Review* (1895–98). It was for this paper that he wrote the well-known articles attacking the sentimentality and insincerity of the theatre of the nineties. In the meantime, after an abortive attempt to become a novelist (he wrote four unsuccessful novels: *Immaturity*, *The Irrational Knot*, *Love among the Artists*, and *Cashel Byron's Profession*), Shaw commenced dramatist with *Widowers' Houses* (1892). But none of his ten plays of the nineties met with success on the stage. Indeed, recognition was delayed for over ten years, and then it came first from abroad—on the Continent and in America. Then in 1904–6 the Court Theatre, under the famous Vedrenne-Barker management, presented his plays consistently, and his reputation was assured. By the end of the First World War Shaw had become a cult. In 1925 he was awarded the Nobel Prize for Literature, and four years later Sir Barry Jackson founded the Shaw Festival at Malvern, for which Shaw wrote new plays until 1949, when his last full-length play, *Buoyant Billions*, was performed there. At the time of his death in 1950, such was the strength of the 'Shaw legend,' there were few who did not know him as a personality, though many may not have known his work.

2. His Plays. Shaw's plays are here considered in the order of their composition. His first works were received with hostility, and the need to create his own audience led him to publish some of them before they were produced. Where, in the following account, two dates are given for a play, they indicate the date of composition and the date of first production. A single date indicates that the play was produced almost as soon as completed. Of his later pieces, few, except those which he withheld from the stage, had difficulty in finding a producer, though his work was first seen in places as far apart as Newcastle, New York, Croydon, and Warsaw,

Plays: Pleasant and Unpleasant (1898) contained seven works, three "unpleasant," four "pleasant." The "unpleasant" were *Widowers' Houses* (1892), *Mrs Warren's Profession* (1894: banned by the censor, privately produced 1902: publicly produced 1925), and *The Philanderer* (1893: 1905). The first two are unflinching and deep examinations of slum landlordism and organized prostitution respectively. They are well constructed and contain flashes of Shavian wit, but their serious realism proved unpalatable for the times and merely brought their author notoriety. The same earnestness mars the more narrowly topical *The Philanderer*, a satire on the pseudo-Ibsenites and their attitude to woman. Having failed to put over his ideas directly and seriously, Shaw adopted a humorous, witty approach in the first of the "pleasant" plays—*Arms and the Man* (1894)—an excellent and amusing stage piece which pokes fun at the romantic conception of the soldier, and which has since achieved great popularity. It was the first of the truly Shavian plays. *Candida* (1895), which presents a parson, his wife, and a poet involved in 'the eternal triangle,' has more human warmth than many of his works, and the main interest is focused on the characters rather than on any thesis. This interest in character is seen in the study of Napoleon in the amusing but slight *The Man of Destiny* (1895: 1897), and in the witty and spirited *You Never Can Tell* (1897: 1899). In both, Shaw's views are less stridently proclaimed, though in the former his attempts to show the 'ordinariness' of Napoleon lead him to produce a rather unsatisfactory character.

The Devil's Disciple (1897), *Cæsar and Cleopatra* (1898: 1899), and *Captain Brassbound's Conversion* (1899: 1900) were collected in *Three Plays for Puritans* (1901). The first satirizes the melodrama by using all its ingredients with a typically Shavian difference. It also shows the humanity of a supposed villain and pokes fun at the rigid narrowness of the people who scorned him. It is full of fun, excellently constructed, and has been very popular. *Cæsar and Cleopatra*, though on a more lavish scale, does for its two main characters what *The Man of Destiny* did for Napoleon, studies great historical personages as ordinary human beings. The character of Cæsar is interesting as an embodiment of Shaw's idea of a leader of men—energetic, courageous, and controlling his passions by his reason. *Captain Brassbound's Conversion* treats of the stupidity of revenge as a guiding force in life. The theme is well handled, and the moral is veiled by thoroughly amusing comedy.

Man and Superman (1903: 1905), one of Shaw's most important plays, deals half seriously, half comically, with woman's pursuit of her mate. The play is Shaw's first statement of his idea of the Life Force working through human beings toward perfection, and this, he feels here, can be reached only by the selective breeding which will eventually produce the superman. The play is unconventional in its construction, especially in the third act, entitled "Don Juan in Hell," but it is a fine drama and contains three notable characters in Ann Whitefield, John Tanner, and 'Enery Straker.

John Bull's Other Island (1904) is a good-humoured satire on English and Irish prejudices as seen chiefly in the characters of Tom Broadbent and Larry Doyle, about whom the play revolves. It was originally written for the Irish National Theatre, but was not well received there.

Religion and social problems are again the main topics in *Major Barbara* (1905), which deals with the paradoxical situation where the attempts of the Salvation Army to remedy social evils can only be continued through the charity of those whose money-getting has caused those evils. The same critical alertness and depth of insight are brought to bear on the medical profession in his amusing satire *The Doctor's Dilemma* (1906), and on the marriage conventions in *Getting Married* (1908).

The Shewing Up of Blanco Posnet (1909) is a melodramatic piece about religious conversion against a background of horse-stealing and lynch-law in the West. Banned as blasphemous by the censor, it was first produced at the Abbey Theatre, Dublin. Next came one of his least satisfactory works, *Misalliance* (1910), which contains little beyond a rather inconclusive discussion of the parent-child relationship, and then the slight but witty *The Dark Lady of the Sonnets* (1910).

In *Fanny's First Play* (1911) and *Androcles and the Lion* (1912) Shaw once again took religion as his main theme. In the former, which gave Shaw his first long run in London, the religious theme is combined with an attack on the critics and a further study of the relations between parents and children. The latter is an examination of the nature of early Christian religious experience, conducted with genuine honesty and considerable insight, in a vein partly serious, partly comic. Indeed, the comedy is so amusing that the underlying seriousness is all too easily missed.

Social conventions and social weaknesses were treated again in *Pygmalion* (1912: 1913), a witty and highly entertaining study of class distinction, and in *Heartbreak House* (1913: 1921), which, though set in the War period, really treats of upper-class disillusionment during the pre-War years. This over-lengthy conversation piece is modelled on the drama of Chekhov, and its loose construction reflects Shaw's absorption in his theme at the expense of his form, but as social criticism it goes deep, and it contains a number of well-drawn characters, chief among them Captain Shotover.

Back to Methuselah (1921) and *St Joan* (1923: 1924) are further studies of religion. The first is a cycle of five plays concerned with the conception of the evolutionary force which will bring man to perfection. Selective breeding now gives way to the idea of an indefinitely long life which will allow man to outgrow his limiting passions and achieve a state of pure contemplation and eventual happiness. The cycle is an immense effort of the imagination, but as a practical theatrical proposition has little to recommend it. *St Joan* is probably Shaw's finest play. In it the independence of the true Protestant is seen in opposition to the forces of organized society. Joan herself is a finely drawn character, and, in spite of its length and the great quantity of discussion it contains, the play is most effective on the stage.

None of the plays written after *St Joan* is comparable in quality with his best work. Here it must suffice to mention them. They were *The Apple Cart* (1929); *Too True to be Good* (1932); *On the Rocks* (1933); *The Six of Calais* (1934); *The Simpleton of the Unexpected Isles* (1934); *The Millionairess* (1936); *Geneva* (1938); *In Good King Charles's Golden Days* (1939); *Buoyant Billions* (1949).

3. Features of his Plays. (*a*) *His Ideas.* Shaw believed that the ideas of his plays were their most important feature. He saw the stage as a platform for his views and reluctantly adopted the rôle of 'entertainer' only when his three "unpleasant" plays failed. When his fame was assured he again gave more prominence to his themes, and, though his theatrical art was never forgotten, it was very often subordinated to his concern with a thesis. Yet Shaw will be remembered not as a prophet, but as a dramatist, an artist in the theatre. Already many of the ideas with which he inspired or horrified his generation are accepted as commonplace. Shaw's fundamental aim in his drama was the bettering of the lot of humanity. Scoffing at the romantic view of life, he examined man and his social institutions with intellectual courage and shrewd, irreverent insight. Slum landlords, prostitution, marriage conventions, social prejudices, the romanticized soldier, the glamorous historical figure, the medical profession, the critics, religion—these are but some of the people and things which came under the microscope of his rationalism. His earliest work was emphatically socialist, and socialism, later in a more moderate form, remained his hope for humanity. *Man and Superman* and then *Back to Methuselah* proclaimed the creed of Creative Evolution which would eventually bring about perfection, in the first play through selective breeding, in the second through an incredible longevity. Religion was the main theme of his later plays. It was Shaw's delight always to turn the social scene inside out, to show the other side of the accepted picture, a process which he undertook with a roguish humour, a delight in shocking the conventions, and a provocative mixture of serious argument and more or less fantastic fooling. Not infrequently his sense of fun ran away with him and his serious meaning was overshadowed.

(b) *His Prefaces* are very striking. In them he expounds views more or less closely connected with those which underlie the plays which follow. They were first used in his earliest works, when his only method of reaching a public was through the printed copy, but he continued to use them throughout his career. It seems probable that the prefaces, rather than the plays themselves, will ultimately be accepted as the definitive statement of his ideas. Emphatic and authoritarian in tone, yet touched with an attractive geniality, they are closely argued and in a most incisive style. Often they reveal truly deep thought; sometimes they are spoilt by an obvious desire to be clever which carries the author further than he would otherwise have gone. In some of them there is also the tendency of the zealous reformer to write down to his reader, and this can be irritating, though it must be recognized that this seems more obvious now that the ideas he expounds are generally accepted than it may have done at the time of their penning.

(c) *His Wit.* From the days of *Widowers' Houses* Shaw's wit sparkles through his plays: with *Arms and the Man* it began to have great prominence. Wit is the very essence of Shavian comedy, in which the dramatist, standing outside the world he creates, sees it with an impish detachment. His sense of fun is undying, and there is in his drama an endless stream of exuberant vitality and gaiety of spirit. Sometimes his sense of humour is uncontrolled and the result is disturbing, but generally it can be said that there is a serious purpose underlying his fun. In a dramatist so intellectual, so persistently witty, so detached from his subjects, it is not surprising to find that there is relatively little emotion. Shaw rarely touches the depths of true tragedy, even in *St Joan*, and in his work as a whole the emotional passages are brief. Indeed, Shaw seems to distrust the emotions, as we can gather from his attitude toward love and his ideal of the pure intelligence, which is the ultimate perfection envisaged in *Back to Methuselah*.

(d) *His Characters.* After Shakespeare no English dramatist equals Shaw in the variety and vividness of his characters, though he lacks almost entirely that interest in the individual *per se* which is one of Shakespeare's qualities. The characters of Shaw are largely seen as the products, good or bad, of social forces, or as the representatives of ideas. Some are mere mouthpieces for his theories, while others are really projections of his own personality. None the less he has contributed many memorable characters to the national heritage; among them Alfred Doolittle (*Pygmalion*), 'Enery Straker (*Man and Superman*), Larry Doyle (*John Bull's Other Island*), Sir Ralph Bloomfield Bonnington (*The Doctor's Dilemma*). Many of his characters are built with Dickensian skill around one idiosyncrasy, and Shaw is an apt caricaturist. He is particularly successful in the creation of women characters, and it is interesting to note that he has no real heroes and no villains.

(*e*) *His dialogue* was from the beginning of the highest order. Throughout his life Shaw was a brilliant talker, and he used this gift to great advantage in his plays. He excels in brief, witty exchanges and, above all, in the handling of extremely long speeches when his characters put forward their carefully reasoned arguments. He had the art of making the long discourse as interesting and dramatic as action, and this was something new to the stage. His brilliance in this has never been surpassed.

(*f*) *His Dramatic Technique.* In spite of the emphasis which he placed on his ideas, Shaw rarely neglected the art of the theatre, and his best plays are excellent on the boards. His sense of the stage was clearly illustrated in the skill with which he supervised rehearsals of his own plays. He made full use of the tricks of the trade and was a master of the art of surprise. His plays often contain an almost bewildering variety of mood, which demands great flexibility of response from his audience. To begin with he followed the conventional dramatic patterns of his age, and it was only when his reputation was established that he began such experiments as the epilogue to *Man and Superman* and the gigantic cycle of *Back to Methuselah*. One of his most interesting innovations is the use of the long stage direction, written with all the care and artistry of his dialogues and prefaces.

4. His Prose Works. In addition to his plays and novels Shaw published a number of political and critical prose works, among them *The Quintessence of Ibsenism* (1891), *Dramatic Opinions and Essays* (1907), *The Intelligent Woman's Guide to Socialism* (1928), and *Everybody's Political What's What* (1944).

II. JOHN MILLINGTON SYNGE (1871–1909)

1. His Life. Synge was born at Rathfarnham, County Dublin and took a degree at Trinity College, Dublin. Some years of wandering on the Continent, chiefly in Paris, came to an end when he met W. B. Yeats in 1899. Yeats persuaded him to abandon his Bohemian life and return to Ireland and the Isles of Aran. Here Synge was inspired by the beauty of his surroundings, the humour, tragedy, and poetry of the life of the simple fisher-folk, and the loveliness of the native dialect. His first play, *The Shadow of the Glen*, was produced at the Abbey Theatre, Dublin, in 1903, and soon afterwards he joined Lady Gregory and W. B. Yeats as a director of the theatre, for which he wrote his six plays. He died of cancer at the age of thirty-eight before his last play, *Deirdre of the Sorrows*, was finished. His non-dramatic works include *The Aran Islands* (1907), the vigorous and colloquial *Poems and Translations* (1909), and *In Wicklow, West Kerry and Connemara*, published in 1911.

2. **His Plays.** Synge was the greatest dramatist in the rebirth of the Irish Theatre. His plays are few in number but they are of a stature to place him among the greatest playwrights in the language. *The Shadow of the Glen* (1903) is a comedy based on an old folk-tale, which gives a good if somewhat romantic picture of Irish peasant life. At its first performance the character of Nora was taken to be an unfavourable reflection on Irish womanhood, and the play was badly received. It was followed by *Riders to the Sea* (1904), a powerful, deeply moving tragedy in one act, which deals with the toll taken by the sea in the lives of the fisher-folk of the West Coast of Ireland. The play has a grand, stark simplicity, and a controlled intensity of feeling, which is most impressive. *The Well of the Saints* (1905) is a rather fantastic comedy based on a legend, part French, part Irish in origin. Then, though it was not staged until three years later, came *The Tinker's Wedding* (1907), a folk-play in two acts, usually considered the least good of his works. Production of the play was originally held up by doubts about the reception which would be given to its satire on the Roman clergy and the marriage sacrament. It was with *The Playboy of the Western World* (1907) that Synge reached the pinnacle of his achievement. Again the play is based on an old legend, but it is altogether broader in scope than his other work, and the subtle study of the development of the central character, Christy Mahon, is the theme around which Synge builds a riotously funny comedy, full of spontaneous vitality, which gives an excellent, if satirical, picture of the Irish character. It was this satirical vein which led to the play's hostile reception in Ireland, though in England its greatness was at once

recognized. Synge's last play, *Deirdre of the Sorrows* (1910), was still in its unrevised form at his death. It takes up an old Irish legend in which the themes of love and death are tragically yet gloriously interwoven. The play is simple in theme and in structure, but the sustained beauty of its prose, the depth of the experiences which it handles, and the unity of its tragic effect give to its simplicity a tremendous majesty.

3. Features of his Plays. (*a*) *His Choice of Subject.* The decisive event in Synge's life was his going, at the suggestion of Yeats, to the Isle of Aran. His experiences there, and later in Ireland, gave him the theme and style of his drama. He saw and felt deeply the life of the peasants wringing a hard living from sea and soil; its tragedy, its comedy, its poetry and dignity are all captured in his work. Synge reacted strongly against the almost photographic reporting of the plays of the realistic movement, which, he felt, missed the essential poetry and joy of life, that "rich joy found only in what is superb and wild in reality." Ibsen and his influence he felt to be pernicious, and, like Yeats, he sought inspiration in the legends and myths of earlier days. But where Yeats sought in the myth the elements of a philosophy, Synge used it merely as the core around which were built his studies of Irish life and character. His keen insight into human nature and his skill in the delineation of character are best seen in Nora (*The Shadow of the Glen*), Christy Mahon (*The Playboy of the Western World*), and Deirdre. Often his view of the Irish character is an ironical one, and we have seen the result of this in the reception of his plays.

In Aran, too, Synge appreciated, probably for the first time, the fundamental importance in the life of man of the forces of nature. The presence of nature is felt in every one of his plays. Sometimes as a fearsome relentless enemy (*Riders to the Sea*), sometimes as a kind comforter (*The Well of the Saints*), but always as a chief actor in the drama or as a source of imagery, nature is present. Synge views nature with something of the mysticism, and much of the same careful sensitive observation, that we find in Wordsworth, but he shows no tendency to build up a philosophy of nature. He is not didactic or moralistic; his approach to nature has in it something pagan.

(*b*) *His Treatment of his Themes.* Synge's genius is seen in both comedy and tragedy, though the latter is, perhaps, his more natural element. Tragedy is always close at hand in his comedies, but his tragedies are unrelieved by any comedy. *Riders to the Sea* and

Deirdre of the Sorrows are completely tragic in tone. What relief there is in *Deirdre* comes only from the poetry. His attempt to capture for the theatre what he feels to be the reality of life is Synge's chief preoccupation. For the most part he shows little concern with the tricks of the theatre, the complexities of plot development, the startling dénouement, and all the stock-in-trade of the stage. Simplicity is the keynote of his plays—simplicity of theme, simplicity of construction; in some the end is obvious before the play has well begun. Yet Synge's plays are immensely powerful on the stage, a quality which they draw from the intensity of the emotional experiences which underlie them, and the enchantment of Synge's inimitable style.

(c) *His Style.* Synge's style is unique. His plays are written in prose, but they have the rhythms and cadences of poetry, a poetry springing from the natural idiom of the peasant. This speech, rich in natural music and full of vivid imagery, is increased in power by its compression, and by the simplicity which is only achieved by much revision. Synge's style has the vitality of the great genius.

The following speeches, taken from the end of *Riders to the Sea*, where the mother mourns the loss of the sixth and last of her sea-faring sons, are typical of the simple, moving style.

> MAURYA [*puts the empty cup mouth downwards on the table, and lays her hands together on Bartley's feet*]. They're all together this time, and the end is come. May the Almighty God have mercy on Bartley's soul, and on Michael's soul, and on the souls of Sheamus and Patch, and Stephen and Shawn [*bending her head*]; and may He have mercy on my soul, Nora, and on the soul of every one is left living in the world.
> *She pauses, and the keen rises a little more loudly from the women, then sinks away.*
> MAURYA [*continuing*]. Michael has a clean burial in the far north, by the grace of the Almighty God. Bartley will have a fine coffin out of the white boards, and a deep grave surely. What more can we want than that? No man at all can be living for ever, and we must be satisfied.
> *She kneels down again, and the curtain falls slowly.*

At other times Synge achieves richness of description and a warm beauty. This is particularly seen in *Deirdre of the Sorrows* and the last part of *The Well of the Saints*. These speeches by Mary and Martin Doul, when they have again lost their sight, after having had it miraculously restored, show Synge in this vein:

> MARY DOUL. There's the sound of one of them twittering yellow birds do be coming in the spring-time from beyond the sea, and

there'll be a fine warmth now in the sun, and a sweetness in the air the way it'll be a grand thing to be sitting here quiet and easy smelling the things growing up, and budding from the earth.

MARTIN DOUL. I'm smelling the furze a while back sprouting on the hill, and if you'd hold your tongue you'd hear the lambs of Grianan, though it's near drowned their crying is with the full river making noises in the glen.

OTHER DRAMATISTS

1. Henry Arthur Jones (1851–1929), the son of a farmer, was born at Grandborough, in Buckinghamshire, and received a rather brief grammar-school education before becoming a shop assistant. For some years he was a commercial traveller, until the success of *The Silver King* (1882) enabled him to take up the drama as a career.

Under the influence of T. W. Robertson (see p. 479), Jones did much to prepare the ground for the new drama of ideas and social purpose. His work widened considerably the field from which the dramatist could select his theme. Though he could on occasion write comedies, he was essentially serious in outlook and felt that the drama should present, not romance or spectacle, but real life. His views are stated in the Preface to *Saints and Sinners* (1884). The search for a deeper drama led to his verse experiment, *The Tempter* (1893), and in the field of comedy his witty *The Liars* (1897) was a forerunner of the new comedy of manners to be perfected by Wilde. Jones was a skilled workman with a real sense of the theatre and the ability to create effective scenes, but, in every branch of drama he attempted, his limitations prevented him from bringing to fruition his advanced ideas. In his serious plays he lacked breadth of outlook and depth of thought, while his effectiveness was greatly diminished by his weakness for melodrama and sentimentality, by a certain artificiality in his characters, and frequently by his over-earnestness. Lack of the true fire spoiled his attempts at poetic drama, and in comedy he was often heavy-handed. Jones's true value is as an innovator who pointed the way for others greater than himself.

Of his sixty or so plays mention may also be made of *Judah* (1890), *Michael and his Lost Angel* (1896), and *Mrs Dane's Defence* (1900).

2. Sir Arthur Wing Pinero (1855–1934) was born in London. He was the son of a solicitor and was intended to follow that profession. At the age of nineteen he became an actor, and his stage experiences in many parts of the country included some years at the Lyceum with Sir Henry Irving. In 1882, five years after his first play, £200 *a Year* (1877), he abandoned acting for a career as a playwright.

Like Henry Arthur Jones, Pinero is an early practitioner of the realistic drama, but he lacks Jones's extreme earnestness, and his lighter touch, combined with his deference to the tastes of his audience, made him more popular. He began his career with lively light comedies in which he achieved considerable success. Then followed a series of social satires, of which a typical example is *The Weaker Sex* (1888), and plays like *Sweet Lavender* (1888) in the sentimental manner of the day. But Pinero's quality was only fully revealed in his four social problem plays, of which the two best-known are *The Second Mrs Tanqueray* (1893) and *The Notorious Mrs Ebbsmith* (1895). These plays are more serious in tone and better in character-study than most of Pinero's, but, though tragic in theme, they seldom touch the deeper springs of tragic emotion. Pinero's theatrical technique is good; his plots, if sometimes improbable, are generally well handled; his dialogue is lively, and there is no lack of interest. But his work lacks depth. His picture of life is limited to the upper classes, while his character-drawing is rarely deep and not always consistent. Sentimentality mars some of his plays, and his anxiety to give his audience what it wanted results sometimes in theatricality.

Apart from those already mentioned, the following plays may be listed: *The Magistrate* (1885), *Dandy Dick* (1887), *Trelawney of the "Wells"* (1898), *The Princess and the Butterfly; or the Fantastics* (1897), *The Gay Lord Quex* (1899), *Iris* (1901), and *Mid-Channel* (1909).

3. John Galsworthy (1867–1933), the son of a wealthy lawyer, was born in Surrey and was educated at Harrow and Oxford. He travelled abroad for a year before being called to the Bar in 1890. He was, however, far from happy in his profession, though he had a great interest in the law and had all the lawyer's impartiality and fairness. Always, though living in cultured ease, he was troubled by the social problems of the day, the inequalities and injustices of the social system, which became the main theme of his writing.

In 1919 he refused the offer of a knighthood, but his work was ultimately recognized by the award of the Order of Merit in 1929 and the Nobel Prize for Literature four years later.

Galsworthy began his literary career as a novelist, and, after publishing some half-dozen works of little note, including the novelette *Jocelyn* (1898) and *The Island Pharisees* (1904), he wrote his first great successful novel, *The Man of Property* (1906), which was to become the first part of the immense family novel, *The Forsyte Saga* (published in an omnibus volume 1922). The other books which complete the work are *In Chancery* (1920), *To Let* (1921), and the interludes which link the three major sections, *Indian Summer of a Forsyte* (1917) and *Awakening* (1920). These last four are not as good as the first part, but nevertheless *The Forsyte Saga* as a whole is one of the striking achievements in modern fiction. It is a cool, controlled, ironical dissection of the Forsytes, a typical City family, and this series of stories handles a vast canvas of figures with firmness and skill. The family chronicle covers thirty-four years to the death of Queen Victoria, and gives an admirable picture of the upper-middle classes in the changing society of the end of the nineteenth century. Behind their common love of property the members of the Forsyte family are cleverly differentiated, and Soames Forsyte, his wife Irene, and old Jolyon are masterpieces of characterization. The fortunes of the family, as seen in its post-1918 generation, are described in *The White Monkey* (1924), *The Silver Spoon* (1926), and *Swan Song* (1928), which, with two more interludes, *A Silent Wooing* (1927) and *Passers By* (1927), were collected together as *A Modern Comedy* (1929). This series is conceived on a smaller scale, and has not the high quality of its predecessor, but, none the less, is a work of considerable merit. While the novels of these two series were being written, Galsworthy produced a number of works which add little to his stature. Nearly all show the same interest in sociological problems which underlies *The Forsyte Saga* and *A Modern Comedy*. They include *The Country House* (1907), *Fraternity* (1909), *The Patrician* (1911), *The Dark Flower* (1913), *The Freelands* (1915), *Beyond* (1917), *Saint's Progress* (1919), and then, later, come *Maid in Waiting* (1931) and *Flowering Wilderness* (1932).

As a novelist Galsworthy reflects the contemporary interest in sociological problems. His most important works give an objective, ironical portrait of the upper-middle class to which he himself belonged. They are earnest and sincere analyses of its weakness and inadequacies, and, like his plays, show him to be primarily a social critic. Class rather than character is his concern, and even his best characters are to a considerable extent types: motive and impulse are of secondary importance to him. He is a realist with a keen and accurate observation, and handles his material with a restraint, delicacy, and impartiality which at once prompt the description 'gentlemanly.' His chief weapon is irony, and his satire is kept well in hand. His dialogue has the naturalness that we expect of the author of the plays, and his style has the polished ease and urbanity which are ideal for his type of fiction, but it can, and does, reflect deep feelings.

As a dramatist Galsworthy belongs to the realist tradition of Jones and Pinero. He says himself in a magazine article "Some Platitudes concerning Drama" (*Fortnightly Review*, December 1909): "Every grouping of life and character has its inherent moral; and the business of the dramatist is so to pose the group as to bring that moral poignantly to the light of day," and his plays are all didactic in purpose. Galsworthy was a social reformer, objectively and impartially posing a problem, showing always both sides of the question, and leaving his audience to think out the answer. His chief protagonists are usually social forces in conflict with each other, and the human figures in his drama, though real enough and very true to ordinary life, are studied more as products of these forces than as individuals who are of interest for their own sake. To this extent they are types. But, in spite of his apparent detachment, Galsworthy obviously feels a warm sympathy for the victims of social injustice, and especially for the poor and downtrodden, and the underlying warmth of his drama is one of the qualities which distinguishes him most clearly from Granville-Barker. Where the latter is almost exclusively intellectual in appeal, Galsworthy calls into play the feelings as well as the mind of his audience. His characters are well studied and his psychological insight is particularly well seen in his studies of internal conflict. In the construction of his plays he shows a fine sense of form, and the best of them are excellent stage pieces. His dialogue and situations are natural, and he never lapses into sentimentality or melodramatic distortion. His legal training shows itself in his frequent studies of social problems arising from the injustices of the law, in the excellent trial scenes found in his plays, and, perhaps above all, in the clarity of vision with which he followed his deliberately chosen path in the drama. His ideas on the drama are to be found in his collection of essays *The Inn of Tranquillity* (1912).

Of his best-known plays *The Silver Box* (1906) deals with the inequality of justice; *Strife* (1909) with the struggle between Capital and Labour; *Justice* (1910) with the cruelty of solitary confinement; *The Skin Game* (1920) with the different values of the old aristocracy and the newly rich businessman; *Loyalties* (1922) with class loyalties and prejudices; and *Escape* (1926) with the inadequacy of the administration of justice and the attitude of different types of people toward an escaped prisoner.

In addition to his novels and plays, Galsworthy published some verse in *Moods, Songs, and Doggerels* (1912), *The Bells of Peace* (1921), *Verses New and Old* (1926), and several collections of essays and stories, among them *A Commentary* (1908), *A Motley* (1910), *The Inn of Tranquillity* (1912), *A Sheaf* (1916), *Five Tales* (1918), *Another Sheaf* (1919), *Caravan* (1925), *Castles in Spain* (1927), *On Forsyte 'Change* (1930).

4. Harley Granville-Barker (1877–1946) was born in London and was on the stage by the age of thirteen. He was associated with the Stage Society (founded 1898) as actor, producer, and manager, and was responsible for introducing to the public the work of Shaw and Galsworthy. He was involved in other theatrical ventures at the Royal Court Theatre (1904–7) and at the Savoy Theatre (1912–14). In spite of the high quality of his productions, both ventures failed. About the time of the First World War he was working in England and America, and he established himself as one of the great producers of his age. He was also a Shakespearian critic of considerable standing. By virtue of his professional experience he was able to view the plays in a light totally different from that of the academic critics, and his Prefaces, which bring the discussion of Shakespeare out of the study and back to the boards, are major landmarks in the history of twentieth-century Shakespeare criticism. They are as follows: *Series I* (1927); *Series II* (1930); *Series III—Hamlet* (1936); *Series IV—Othello* (1945); *Series V—Coriolanus* (1949).

Granville-Barker's few plays are of considerable significance in the theatrical history of our period. He carried the pursuit of realism and naturalism further than any of his predecessors, and his plays come closer to ordinary day-to-day existence, with the futility of which he is much concerned. His plays are discussions of contemporary problems, and his themes include the marriage conventions, the inheritance of tainted money, sex, and the position of women. Hating sentimentality in any form, he is essentially intellectual in his treatment and lacks the sympathetic warmth of the more popular Galsworthy. His tone is generally serious and often heavy, and some of his plays proved to be beyond the understanding of the most penetrating readers and were never produced. His concern with his theme, and his fearless attempts to pose his problem fairly and squarely before the minds of his audience without prejudging the issue, often lead to a lack of incident and a surprising neglect of theatrical considerations. His greatest merits as a dramatist are found in his character studies and extremely natural dialogue.

His most important plays are *The Marrying of Ann Leete* (1899), *The Voysey Inheritance* (1905), *Waste* (1907), *The Madras House* (1910), *The Secret Life* (1923).

5. Sir William Schwenk Gilbert (1836–1911) was born in London and educated at London University. He served as an officer in the Militia (1868) and worked for a time as a clerk in the Privy Council Office. He first established his reputation as a writer of comic verse for magazines, and his work was collected in *Bab Ballads* (1869) and *More Bab Ballads* (1873). In 1871, with his libretto for the comic opera *Thespis*, for which Sir Arthur Sullivan (1842–1900) composed the music, began the partnership which, between 1875 and 1896, produced the famous Savoy Operas for Richard D'Oyley Carte (1844–1901). Before and after this period, Gilbert produced both comic and serious plays in prose and verse. He was knighted in 1907.

Though Gilbert is unlike any other dramatist of our period, his influence on later writers has been considerable, and his work leads directly to the comedy of manners and Oscar Wilde (*q.v.*). Ignoring the contemporary trend toward realism, he moves in the world of burlesque extravaganza, though his delicately ironical wit veils a seriousness which periodically comes to the surface even in his most humorous pieces. Early plays, like *Pygmalion and Galatea* (1871) and *Randall's Thumb* (1871), show his serious vein in full possession. The irony and wit of his fantasies and of the Savoy Operas to some extent conceal the shrewdness of his satirical thrusts at the institutions of his day, thrusts which are delivered with a fine precision of phrase and all the dexterity of an accomplished verse artist.

Among his plays are *Dulcamara* (1866), *The Palace of Truth* (1870), *The Wicked World* (1873), *The Happy Land* (1873) (with G. A. à Beckett), *Broken Hearts* (1875), *Engaged* (1877).

The Savoy Operas, for which he wrote the librettos, were *Trial by Jury* (1875), *The Sorcerer* (1877), *H.M.S. Pinafore* (1878), *The Pirates of Penzance* (1879), *Patience* (1881), *Iolanthe* (1882), *Princess Ida* (1884), *The Mikado* (1885), *Ruddigore* (1887), *The Yeomen of the Guard* (1888), *The Gondoliers* (1889), *Utopia, Limited* (1893), and *The Grand Duke* (1896).

6. Oscar Wilde (1856–1900), the son of a famous Irish surgeon, was born in Dublin. In his youth he showed brilliant promise, though his genius was perverse and wayward. He was Queen's Scholar of Trinity College, Dublin, and Berkeley Gold Medallist for Greek studies. In 1874 he became a scholar of Magdalen College, Oxford, where he became an apostle of the æsthetic cult of Pater. He took a First-class in Classical Moderations and Litterae Humaniores, and his poem *Ravenna* won the Newdigate Prize in 1878. From Oxford he went to London where he was the centre of an artificial, decadent society, famous for his wit and brilliant conversation. He made an American tour in 1882 and was well received. After that he rose quickly to literary fame, but, when at the height of his powers, he was sentenced at the Old Bailey to two years' imprisonment (1895). At the age of forty-four he died in Paris.

In poetry, prose, and drama, Wilde embodies the spirit of the decadent school of the nineties. His literary descent from Pater and the Pre-Raphaelites is clearly seen in his early poetry. It is far removed in subject from the realities of ordinary life; it lacks emotional depth and is artistic and ornately decorative in style. But his earlier works, *Poems* (1881) and *The Sphinx* (1894), are overshadowed by the simpler and more powerful *The Ballad of Reading Gaol* (1898), which was written during his imprisonment.

Wilde's prose has the qualities of his early verse. His stories and one novel are typical products of the æstheticism of his group— ingenious, witty, polished, and ornamental in style, but lacking in human warmth. Their main appeal is intellectual. Apart from *Lord Arthur Savile's Crime* (1887); *The Canterville Ghost* (1887); *The Happy Prince and Other Tales* (1888); and his novel, the well-known *The Picture of Dorian Gray* (1890); Wilde also wrote *De Profundis* (1897). This long introspective work, written while he was in prison, was published in part in 1905, but the whole was not published until 1949.

It is, however, as a dramatist that Wilde survives to-day. He began with two serious pieces of little worth, *Vera, or the Nihilists* (printed 1880) and *The Duchess of Padua* (printed 1883), and they were followed by *Salomé* (1892), which was used by Richard Strauss as the libretto for his opera of that name. Then came the four comedies on which his reputation rests: *Lady Windermere's Fan* (1892), *A Woman of No Importance* (1893), *An Ideal Husband* (1895), and, best of them all, *The Importance of Being Earnest* (1895). They are comedies of manners in the Sheridan tradition, aristocratic in tone and outlook, and with all the conscious artistic grace and refinement of his other work. He paints a picture of the elegance and ease of the upper classes of his day, but, unlike some of his contemporaries, he has no interest in its moral implications. Again his appeal is largely intellectual; his characters are mere caricatures, often so alike as to be difficult to distinguish, and they have little human warmth. The continued popularity of his plays depends on the dialogue, with its hard glitter, its polish and scintillating wit. His cynicism finds an outlet in the profusion of neat paradoxes, and the tone suggests a rather insolent condescension toward his audience. To Wilde's concern with dialogue, plot and character are both subordinate. His plays are carelessly constructed, and the plots smothered by the flow of wit, flaws which, together with the insincere sentimentalism of his first three comedies, were quickly seized upon by the critics. Only in *The Importance of Being Earnest* did Wilde achieve real artistic harmony.

7. **Sir James Barrie (1860–1937)**, the Scottish novelist and playwright, was born in Kirriemuir and educated at Dumfries Academy and Edinburgh University. After some experience as a journalist in Nottingham, he came to London and wrote for the *St James's Gazette* and several periodicals. He was famous as a novelist before he was known as a dramatist, and, apart from his early experiments, and *My Lady Nicotine* and later Peter Pan fairy books, wrote mainly about the Scottish country people, whom he studied with great sympathy and understanding.

Barrie was the chief member of the Kailyard School of novelists (see p. 460). His first novels *Better Dead* (1887), *When a Man's Single* (1888), and *My Lady Nicotine* (1890), all suffer from that excess of sentimentality which is his chief weakness. The short dialect stories, collected in *Auld Licht Idylls* (1888) and *A Window in Thrums* (1889), are kindly sketches of the simple village life of his native district, and contain several good portraits. Of his other novels we should mention the over-romantic, sentimental, but immensely popular *The Little Minister* (1891) and his two studies of sentimentalism, *Sentimental Tommy* (1896) and *Tommy and Grizel* (1900).

From 1900 onward the stage claimed most of his attention. Among the dramatists of the period Barrie is unique in that his work belongs to no school, nor did it establish a school of its own. In many plays he turns his back on the realities of life and seeks refuge in a world of make-believe and charming fantasy, created by his own peculiar mixture of whimsicality, quaintness, sentimentality, pathos, and humour. The best of his fantasies and romances had a delicacy of touch which delighted audiences who were very ready to be moved by his simple grace and charm. The worst of them were mawkish and exaggerated and are best forgotten. Sentimental romances like *The Professor's Love Story* (1894), the dramatized version of *The Little Minister* (1897), *Quality Street* (1902), and *Mary Rose* (1920) usually capture a certain public, while, of his fantasies, *Peter Pan* (1904) and *A Kiss for Cinderella* (1916) have always been popular. In other plays Barrie shows an ability to blend fantasy and reality, and beneath the surface of fantastic humour is a core of serious thought and a satirical, often cynical, view of the society of his day. Often the serious aspect is almost hidden by the surface fantasy, and many charmed audiences failed to realize the depth of the play. *The Admirable Crichton* (1902), *What Every Woman Knows* (1908), *The Twelve-pound Look* (1910), *The Will* (1913), and *Dear Brutus* (1917) are probably the best known of these.

Barrie's drama as a whole shows him to be a fine technician with a strong sense of the demands of the theatre. His characters are usually slight but charming, and he shows a tender affection for the day-dreamers and failures of the world. His dialogue is good and is handled with the sensitivity of one who had a real feeling for words.

GENERAL SURVEY OF THE DRAMA (1890–1918)

1. The Drama in Mid-Victorian England. From the dramatic point of view the first half of the nineteenth century was almost completely barren. As we have seen, many of the major poets had tried drama, but none of them had achieved any success. The greater part of their work never saw the stage. The professional theatre of the period was in a low state. Among the respectable middle classes it was despised as a place of vice. Audiences did nothing to raise the standard, which remained deplorably low. The popular pieces of the day were melodrama, farces, and sentimental comedies, which had no literary qualities whatever, were poor in dialogue and negligible in characterization, and relied for their success upon sensation, rapid action, and spectacle. Prominent among the writers of melodrama in the period was **Dion Boucicault** **(1822–90).**

But this was also the age of the great actor—the age of Edmund Kean (1789–1833), William Charles Macready (1793–1873), and Sir

Henry Irving (1838–1905), when a successful play was one which offered a 'meaty' part to the star. Not unnaturally it was a period of Shakespearian revivals, staged on a lavish scale, and it was in 1879 that the Shakespeare Memorial Theatre was built at Stratford-on-Avon.

2. The Growth of Realism: the Problem Play. Within the melodrama itself there can be traced a significant development from romantic and historical themes to more domestic themes, and this movement toward realism received considerable impetus from the work of **T. W. Robertson (1829–71)**, a writer of comedies, who introduced the idea of a serious theme underlying the humour, and characters and dialogue of a more natural kind. Robertson, however, did little more than point the way, and he never entirely freed himself from the melodrama and sentimentalism around him. His chief plays were *Society* (1865), *Caste* (1867), *Play* (1868), and *School* (1869). The same limitations affected the more serious work of **Henry Arthur Jones** (see p. 470) and, to a less extent, the plays of **Sir A. W. Pinero** (see p. 470). It was not until the nineties, when the influence of Ibsen (see p. 482) was making itself strongly felt, and Shaw produced his first plays, that the necessary impetus was there to carry the serious drama over into the field of social, domestic, or personal problems. A period so keenly aware of social problems was an admirable breeding-ground for the drama of ideas, and the themes of drama became the problems of religion, of youth and age, of labour and capital, and above all, now that Ibsen had torn down the veil which had kept the subject in safe obscurity, of sex. In widening the scope of the drama Ibsen and then Shaw, Galsworthy, and Granville-Barker were of paramount importance, and they did much to create a tradition of natural dialogue. New psychological investigations reinforced the interest in character as distinct from plot, and the realistic drama of our period aimed at the impartial presentation of real life, contemporary rather than historical. To begin with, its concern was primarily with the upper classes; and its problems, except in Shaw, were handled discreetly, but gradually it turned to other social levels and became more daring in its themes. The weakness of the new, realistic, intellectual drama was its lack of anything to fire the imagination, its lack of poetry in the widest sense, and its greatest danger was that it might lapse into mere social photography. The greatest dramatists, like Shaw and Galsworthy, rose above these limitations. The dramatists of the new order were, however, a small minority, and while they struggled for recognition, melodrama and musical comedy continued to flourish. But such was the force of the work of this minority that it established the drama of ideas as the drama of the early twentieth century.

3. The Growth of Repertory in England and Ireland. The arduous struggle to create an audience for the new drama led its champions to seek additional support in the provinces, and thus came into being the repertory movement. A season of Shaw repertory was given in 1904 at the Court Theatre under the Vedrenne-Barker management, and in 1907 **Miss A. E. F. Horniman (1860–1937)** abandoned her active interest in the Abbey Theatre, Dublin (see below) to found "Miss Horniman's Company," which, at the Gaiety Theatre, Manchester, developed into the Manchester Repertory Company. Its chief aim was to encourage the writing of realistic problem plays in the new tradition, and among the dramatists who there came to the fore were: **St John Ervine (1883–1971)**—*Mixed Marriage* (1911), *Jane Clegg* (1913), *John Ferguson* (1915), *The First Mrs Fraser* (1929), and *Robert's Wife* (1937); **W. Stanley Houghton (1881–1913)** —*The Dear Departed* (1908), *The Master of the House* (1910), *The Younger Generation* (1910), *Fancy-free* (1911), and *Hindle Wakes* (1912); **Allan Monkhouse (1858–1936)**—*Mary Broome* (1911), *The Education of Mr Surrage* (1912), *The Grand Cham's Diamond* (1924), and *First Blood* (1926).

Other repertory companies of distinction were founded in Liverpool (1911) and Birmingham (1913).

But most important of the theatrical developments outside London was the creation of the Irish National Theatre in Dublin. The idea of a national drama was born in the minds of Yeats and some of his contemporaries. In 1904 the generosity of Miss Horniman gave them the Abbey Theatre, of which Yeats, Synge, and Lady Gregory were directors. Of the dramatists who wrote for this theatre, Yeats and Synge (see pp. 484 and 466) looked on the drama as a thing of the emotions, and, reacting against realism, sought their themes among the legends, folklore, and peasantry of Ireland. In their drama we have poetry in the truest sense, though Yeats's dramatic gifts were limited. In the hands of Synge and **Lady Gregory (1859–1932)** there developed a new comedy. Lady Gregory's plays were published as *Seven Short Plays* (1909), *Irish Folk History Plays* (1912), *New Comedies* (1913), *Three Wonder Plays* (1922), and *Three Last Plays* (1928). A third stream in the new Irish drama is represented in the work of **Lennox Robinson**

(1886–1958) who, following the more realistic trend of the day, wrote *The Clancy Name* (1908), *The Crossroads* (1909), *Harvest* (1910), *Patriots* (1912), *The Dreamers* (1915), *The Lost Leader* (1918), *The Whiteheaded Boy* (1916), *The Round Table* (1924), and *Crabbed Youth and Age* (1924).

4. The Growth of Comedy. Since the days of Sheridan and Goldsmith there had been no worthwhile comedy until Robertson attempted to present a gently ironical view of life as it really existed. His lead was followed in plays like *The Deacon* (1890) and *The Liars* (1897), by H. A. Jones, and by Oscar Wilde, in whose hands the comedy of manners attained heights untouched since the eighteenth century. In the same tradition, if with a difference, was the work of W. S. Gilbert.

5. The Beginnings of the Poetic Drama. Despite the efforts of the major Victorian poets, there was no tradition of poetic drama at the beginning of our period. By 1920 there were signs of a rebirth, but the atmosphere in which realistic, naturalistic drama throve was uncongenial to poetic drama. At the Abbey Theatre Yeats attempted to revive poetry on the stage, but he lacked the essential qualities of the dramatist. **Stephen Phillips (1864–1915)** wrote a number of blank-verse plays, including *Paolo and Francesca* (1900), *Herod* (1901), *Ulysses* (1902), *The Son of David* (1904), and *Nero* (1906), but he had little popular appeal. **Masefield**, too, experimented in poetic drama (see p. 491) with but limited success, while **Gordon Bottomley (1874–1948)**, who wrote a number of quite powerful poetical dramas, saw hope for this form only in the amateur theatre. Among his plays were *The Crier by Night* (1902), *Midsummer Eve* (1905), *King Lear's Wife* (1915), *Gruach* (1921), and *Culbin Sands* (1932). It was also during this period that **John Drinkwater (1882–1937)** began his career with poetic dramas—*Rebellion* (1914), *The Storm* (1915), *The God of Quiet* (1916), and *X = O: A Night of the Trojan War* (1917). But the true poetic drama was that of Synge which, though not in verse, had all the qualities which these lesser dramatists in varying degrees lacked. At this point it may be convenient to mention the work of **Lord Dunsany (1878–1957)**, whose career as a dramatist began in 1909 with *The Glittering Gate*. One of the best exponents of the one-acter, he merits inclusion in our consideration of poetic drama (although he writes in prose) by virtue of the romance on which his plays are built and his ability to conjure up a most powerful atmosphere, often of the Orient. Among his dramas the best-known are *The Gods of the Mountain* (1911), *A Night at an*

Inn (1916), *The Queen's Enemies* (1916), *The Laughter of the Gods* (1919), and *If* (1921).

6. Foreign Influences on the Drama. Lack of space forbids more than the briefest mention of foreign influences on the drama of the period. Most important was that of the Norwegian, **Henrik Ibsen (1828–1906)**, whose work became known in England about 1890 and gave an enormous impetus to the realist movement, to the deeper study of character, and to a far subtler conception of plot and character presentation. More than any other, Ibsen may claim credit for extending the scope of the modern dramatist. Other foreign influences of less importance were the works of the Norwegian, **Björnstjerne Björnson (1832–1910)**, the Swede, **August Strindberg (1849–1912)**, and the Russians, **Anton Chekhov (1860–1904)**, **Count Leo Tolstoy (1828–1910)**, and **Maxim Gorky (1868–1936)**.

7. The growing importance of the dramatist and critic is a notable feature of the period. By 1920 the dominance of the actor-manager has given way to the conception of team-acting. By this time it is also the author who draws the audience. With this change goes the development of a more critical attitude in the audience itself, which is due, in no small measure, to the growth of scientific criticism. In this field **William Archer (1856–1924)** did great service, while, both as critic and playwright, Shaw did much to change the attitude of his public.

POETS

I. WILLIAM BUTLER YEATS (1865–1939)

1. His Life. Born near Dublin of a cultured Irish family, Yeats was educated in London but returned to Ireland in 1880 and soon afterwards embarked on a literary career. Recognition came quickly, and in 1891 he became a member of the Rhymers' Club, of which **Ernest Dowson (1867–1900)** and **Lionel Johnson (1867–1902)** were also members. Soon after 1890 Yeats began writing plays, and, as a strong adherent of the Irish Nationalist Movement, he did much to assist in the creation of a national theatre. The efforts of Yeats and his friends finally bore fruit when, in 1902, the Abbey Theatre, Dublin, came under the management of the Irish National Theatre Company. Of this theatre, which was to play so great a part in the revival of Irish drama, Yeats was made a director, along with J. M. Synge and Lady Gregory. In later years his interest in the cause of Irish freedom led him first to an active participation in the disturbances of 1916 and then to a public career which culminated in his election to the Senate of the Irish Free State (1922-28). In 1923 he was awarded the Nobel Prize for Literature. He died in the South of France (1939) and his body was reinterred in Ireland in 1948.

2. His Poetry. Like so many of his contemporaries, Yeats was acutely conscious of the spiritual barrenness of his age, and his whole artistic career is best seen as an attempt, at first to escape from the sordid materialism which he found on every hand, and later to formulate a new positive ideal which would supply his spiritual needs. In the easy charm and delicate, smooth grace of his early work, the influence of the Pre-Raphaelites is clearly seen. It has something of the melancholy picturesqueness of that school, but with a mystical, dream-like quality peculiarly its own. A believer in magic and kindred arts, Yeats sought to escape into the land of 'faery,' and looked for his themes in Irish legend and the simple, elemental impulses of man's primitive nature. The best remedy for the emptiness of the present seemed to lie in a return to the simplicity of the past. To this period belong his narrative poem *The Wanderings of Oisin* (1889), which first established his reputation, *Poems* (1895), *The Wind among the Reeds* (1899), and *The Shadowy Waters* (1900); and it was in these early days that he wrote many of the lyrics, whose simplicity of style and melodic beauty have found them a place in numerous collections of modern verse. Probably the best-known of them is *The Lake Isle of Innisfree* (written in 1893):

> I will arise and go now, and go to Innisfree,
>   And a small cabin build there, of clay and wattles made;
> Nine bean rows will I have there, a hive for the honey bee,
>   And live alone in the bee-loud glade.
>
> And I shall have some peace there, for peace comes dropping slow,
>   Dropping from the veils of the morning to where the cricket sings;
> There midnight's all a glimmer, and noon a purple glow,
>   And evening full of the linnet's wings.
>
> I will arise and go now, for always, night and day,
>   I hear lake-water lapping with low sounds by the shore;
> While I stand on the roadway, or on the pavements grey
>   I hear it in the deep heart's core.

Between 1900 and 1910 much of Yeats's time was devoted to the drama and philosophical and literary essays, but such poetry as was produced during this period shows a gradual movement away from the escapism of his early work, and a steadily growing courage in grasping the nettle of contemporary reality. The increasing realism of this period is clearly seen in *The Green Helmet and Other Poems* (1910) and *Responsibilities* (1914), which strike a more personal note. It was, however, the impact of the 1914–18 war, and even more of the Irish troubles of 1916, which brought him face to face with the need to grapple with the realities of life. His mystical and philosophical studies and his excursions into spiritualism led to the promulgation of a new philosophical system, and much of the poetry of this period was devoted to the expounding of his theories, which are most fully stated in his prose work *A Vision* (1925). In 1919 he published *The Wild Swans at Coole*, a collection of poems similar to those in *Responsibilities*, but with the added force of a new maturity which is most clearly to be seen in the poems dealing with his own experiences. The peak of his achievement is reached in *The Tower* (1928) and *The Winding Stair and other Poems* (1933), in which he handles philosophical themes with a compact precision of style and a great mastery of rhythm and language. He continued to write with undiminished vigour until his death, and to his last period belong the Crazy Jane poems, some of which had appeared in *The Tower* and *The Winding Stair*. In them his philosophy, hidden beneath a mask of childlike simplicity, is put into the mouths of such characters as The Fool. They appeared in *New Poems* (1938) and *Last Poems* (1939).

3. **His Drama.** Though Yeats wrote some twenty plays, and was so intimately concerned with the foundation of the Irish National Theatre, it is clear that, like many great lyric poets, he lacked the essential qualifications of the dramatist. The virtues of his plays are in their poetry. For him his themes were always of primary importance, and there is a close parallel between the subjects of his lyrics and those of his plays. His characters, too, were drawn from Irish legend (*e.g.*, Cuchulain) and from among those simple types to be found in so many of his poems. There is little or no attempt at character study, and his figures are mere mouthpieces for his ideas, which find expression in fine poetic speeches. Between 1917 and 1926 he produced a number of plays on the Japanese No model, and these highly stylized pieces are completely lacking in actuality and make no use of the normal machinery of the theatre. His plays include *The Countess Cathleen* (1892), *The Land of Heart's Desire* (1894), *The Shadowy Waters* (1900), *Cathleen ni Houlihan* (1902), *On Baile's Strand* (1904), *The King's Threshold* (1904), *The*

Hour-glass (1904), *Deirdre* (1907), *The Resurrection* (1913), *At the Hawk's Well* (1917), *The Only Jealousy of Emer* (1919), *Calvary* (1921), and *The Cat and the Moon* (1926).

4. His Prose. Yeats's most important prose work is to be found in the essays which set forth his artistic and philosophical ideas— *Ideas of Good and Evil* (1903), *Discoveries* (1907), *The Cutting of an Agate* (1912), and *Per Amica Silentia Lunæ* (1918). But most important of all was *A Vision* (1925), a very difficult work; it was partly dictated to his wife by spirits, and in it we have the fullest exposition of his philosophy. A study of this work is essential to the full understanding of his later poetry. Yeats's prose has many of the qualities of his poetry. It is simple and lucid, and is enriched with pungent phrases and rich pictures. All the poet's flair for *le mot juste* is used to give his writing an appealing persuasiveness which is enhanced by its rhythmical charm.

5. Qualities of his Poetry. (*a*) *His Philosophy.* It is no exaggeration to describe Yeats as one of the most difficult of modern poets. His preoccupation with the attempt to formulate a philosophical system which could replace the scientific materialism of his age underlies most of his later verse. It is doubtful whether he ever succeeded in crystallizing a completely systematized philosophy, and his most comprehensive exposition of his ideas, *A Vision* (1925), is in many places very obscure.

After his brief period of Pre-Raphaelite escapism he gradually evolved his own positive faith. His trust was in the imagination and intuition of man rather than in scientific reasoning, and his attempt was to reach back, through the study of Irish folklore and legend, to the primitive impulses of human life. The natural man (the peasant or the fool) he felt to be more in contact with these primary forces than the intellectual man of the world, and this idea, and his great belief in passion or frenzy, led in his later work to a constant assertion of the importance of the human individuality. An ideal type of being was the 'solitary soul,' above the crude world of politics and action. Yeats believed in fairies, magic, and other forms of superstition, and his later thought was much influenced by his study of Indian and other mystical philosophies and the excursions into spiritualism, which became more frequent after his marriage, in 1916, to a medium. Convinced of the immortality of the soul, he saw in man a dual personality, made up of 'Self,' which is the product of man's social training, and 'Anti-Self,' which is constantly struggling against self to find freedom in the world of the spirit. Between this world of spirit and the world of reality he found a bridge in poetry.

(b) *His Use of Symbols.* Yeats's philosophy is often expressed through a carefully devised system of symbols, some purely private, others drawn from his study of philosophy or his reading in the works of the French *symbolistes*, or of earlier symbolical poets, particularly Blake and Shelley. By means of them he succeeds in expressing those deep emotional experiences which he felt to be otherwise incapable of poetical communication, but sometimes they serve only to accentuate the obscurity of his poems. The reader's difficulties arise mainly from Yeats's use of the same symbol to represent a variety of things; thus the Tower may represent, among other things, an intellectual refuge, or the soul's yearning for the world of the spirit. Others of his well-known symbols are the moon, the swan, and Byzantium.

(c) *His Artistry.* From the first Yeats was an accomplished poetic artist, though his mastery of language and rhythm grew steadily throughout his career. From the Pre-Raphaelite æstheticism of his early verse, with its quest for beauty, its conscious, often senti-mental, simplicity, and its languid, melodic grace, he developed a more direct and virile expression. There is the same delicacy of workmanship, and the gorgeous phrase still flashes among the everyday language and personal direct expression of his maturity. Always he uses the traditional verse forms, modified sometimes to suit his own needs, but now his rhythms approach more closely to those of ordinary speech; yet the subtlety of his patterns is such that the music of his verse is of the highest quality. His compact, closely woven style, each word used with calculated effect, lends itself readily to a wide variety of subjects. The deceptive simplicity that is Yeats's at his most subtle is to be seen in the strikingly effective Crazy Jane poems.

II. ROBERT BRIDGES (1844–1930)

1. His Life. The wish of Bridges that no biography of him should be published has left us with only the major facts of his life. He was born at Walmer, in Kent, of a well-to-do country family, and both the county of his birth and the good fortune which made it unnecessary for him to earn a living have left indelible marks on his work. In 1854 he went to Eton, and from there to Oxford in 1863. At both places he showed considerable academic prowess. He began as a medical student at St Bartholomew's Hospital, London, in 1869, proceeded to his M.B. in 1874, and was for three years (1878-81) a practising physician in London hospitals. An attack of pneumonia then brought his medical career to a close, and he retired to Yattendon, in Berkshire. He was an unsuccessful candidate for the Oxford chair of poetry in 1895, and twelve years later he moved to Chilswell, on the outskirts of Oxford, where he lived until his death, enjoying the friendship of many of the finest minds of his generation in an atmosphere of peace and prosperous, cultured leisure. He was made Poet Laureate in 1913, and in the same year helped to found the Society for Pure English.

2. His Poetry. Though Bridges was writing poetry while still at Eton, little of his earliest work survives. His first volume, *Shorter Poems*, appeared anonymously in 1873, and further volumes under the same title were added in 1879, 1880, 1890, and 1894. They contained many of his best-known lyrics—*A Passer-by*, *London Snow*, *I will not let thee go*, and *The Downs*. His subjects, mainly love and nature, are handled with flawless taste and restraint, and with the delicate artistry of an accomplished technician. His is the art which conceals art, and his mastery of rhythms, sure ear for verbal music, and lightness of touch give to these lyrics something of the quality of the best Elizabethan songs.

His sonnet sequence, *The Growth of Love*, privately printed in 1876, was published in 1889 after many alterations. The seventy-nine sonnets, a mixture of Petrarchan and Shakespearian forms, have all the technical excellence which we expect of Bridges, but they lack depth of feeling.

Prometheus the Firegiver (1883) and *Eros and Psyche* (1885) are elaborate but over-lengthy poems. Fine pictures of the Italian countryside and an occasional pleasing lyric cannot compensate for the tedium of the earlier work, while the success of the elaborately constructed *Eros and Psyche* is largely one of metrical technique.

A long period, mainly devoted to poetic drama and literary criticism, intervened before *New Poems* (1899), a volume, which, though it contains some good landscapes and wonderfully clear recollections of his youth, is below the usual standard of Bridges. In *Poems in Classical Prosody* (1903) and *Later Poems* (1914) the poet enters the fields of politics and war, subjects which, as Bridges handles them, are unworthy of the technical skill lavished upon them. These volumes contain much of his poorest work.

October and Other Poems (1920) and *New Verse* (1925) again show Bridges as a great lyric poet. Memories of his childhood and

experiences of his later years are all handled with the artistry of
Bridges at his best. Of the skill of this last period *Cheddar Pinks*,
from *New Verse*, is a fair illustration:

> Mid the squander'd colour
>   idling as I lay
> Reading the Odyssey
>   in my rock-garden
> I espied the cluster'd
>   tufts of Cheddar pink
> Burgeoning with promise
>   of their scented bloom
> All the modish motley
>   of their bloom to-be
> Thrust up in narrow buds
>   on the slender stalks
> Thronging springing urgent
>   hasting (so I thought)
> As if they fear'd to be
>   too late for summer—
> Like schoolgirls overslept
>   waken'd by the bell
> Leaping from bed to don
>   their muslin dresses
>   on a May morning:
>
> Then felt I like to one
>   indulging in sin
> (Whereto Nature is oft
>   a blind accomplice)
> Because my aged bones
>   so enjoy'd the sun
> There as I lay along
>   idling with my thoughts
> Reading an old poet
>   while the busy world
> Toil'd moil'd fuss'd and scurried
>   worried bought and sold
> Plotted stole and quarrel'd
>   fought and God knows what.
> I had forgotten Homer
>   dallying with my thoughts
> Till I fell to making
>   these little verses
> Communing with the flowers
>   in my rock-garden
>   on a May morning.

In 1929 Bridges published his long philosophical poem *The Testament of Beauty*, an attempt to show beauty as the supreme force in

life, and to trace man's growth to perfect wisdom. He draws upon almost every field of knowledge, and the poem, over-lengthy and digressive, suffers from its unorthodox spellings and an unusual laxity in matters of technique. However, it contains many fine passages, and, in spite of its weaknesses, stands high among English philosophical poems on the grand scale. The following extract will give some idea of its style:

> Consider a plant—its life—how a seed faln to ground
> sucketh in moisture for its germinating cells,
> and as it sucketh swelleth, til it burst its case
> and thrusting its roots downward and spreading them wide
> taketh tenure of the soil, and from ev'ry raindrop
> on its dribbling passage to replenish the springs
> plundereth the freighted salt, while it pricketh upright
> with its flagstaff o'erhead for a place in the sun,
> anon to disengage buds that in tender leaves
> unfolding may inhale provender of the ambient air:
> and, tentacles or tendrils, they search not blindly
> but each one headeth straightly for its readiest prey;
> and haply, if the seed be faln in a place of darkness
> roof'd in by men—if ther should be any ray or gleam
> how faint soe'er, 'twil crane and reach its pallid stalk
> pushing at the crevice even to disrupt the stones.

3. His Drama. Like most nineteenth-century poets, Bridges tried his hand at drama and with the same results. *The Feast of Bacchus* (1889), *Palicio* (1890), *The Christian Captives* (1890), *The Return of Ulysses* (1890), *Achilles in Scyros* (1890), *The Humours of the Court* (1893), *Nero Part I* (1885), and *Nero Part II* (1894) are merely literary exercises in drama in the Elizabethan or classical traditions. They reveal an almost complete ignorance of the craft of the theatre, and a complete inability to create characters, while they are devoid of real passion. His masque, *Demeter*, written in 1904 for the opening of Somerville College, Oxford, is equally academic. The gift of Bridges was for lyric, not dramatic poetry.

4. His Prose. From 1887 to 1907 Bridges concentrated his attention on literary criticism. Apart from his regular leaders in *The Times Literary Supplement* and other occasional articles, he published *On the Elements of Milton's Blank Verse in "Paradise Lost"* (1887), *On the Prosody of "Paradise Regained" and "Samson Agonistes"* (1889), his essay on *John Keats* (1895), and *The Influence of the Audience on Shakespearean Drama* (1926). To the essays on Milton he brought all his own experience of metrical experiment, and his work on *Samson Agonistes* has ensured a truer appreciation of the qualities of its verse. Equally valuable was his examination of the revised version of *Hyperion* as compared with the original one, which appeared in his essay on Keats. His study of Shakespeare's audience consists mainly of a strongly biased attempt to blame the groundlings for anything in the plays which he felt to be coarse or in any way undesirable, and it is typical of the capricious unreliability of many of his opinions on literature. Thus, where Bunyan, Dryden, Pope, Browning, were concerned, he could see little that was good, and he maintained his opinions, some of them formed on a relatively slight acquaintance with the author, with a stubborn aggressiveness. His prose style is simple, lucid, unaffected, and workmanlike, and the essays are admirable in their use of copious quotations to illustrate his arguments.

5. Miscellaneous Publications. Brief mention should be made of his fine anthology of prose and verse, *The Spirit of Man* (1916), and of his publication in 1918 of *Poems of Gerard Manley Hopkins*. Of the importance to English poetry of this volume, which, but for Bridges, had remained for ever unknown, we shall have more to say later (see pp. 529–33).

6. Features of his Poetry. (*a*) *His Choice of Subject.* Saved by his wealth from the economic struggles of the workaday world, aristocratic and conservative by inheritance, Bridges passed his life almost undisturbed by the ferment of ideas around him. His poetry is seldom concerned with the sterner issues of life, and then not usually with success. The beauties of nature, the charm of landscape in particular, the joy and romance of love, memories of an almost idyllic childhood, these are the themes which he treated with the good breeding and absence of passion demanded of a gentleman.

(*b*) *His Artistry.* Bridges lived for poetry alone. To the study and practice of his art he devoted his whole life. Every effect, every word almost, at any rate in his lyrics, is the result of careful consideration. The result is a limpid clarity of style, a delicacy of touch, a perfection of musical appeal, and a subtlety of rhythmic pattern which give his work an easy 'rightness.' Yet this art, so wonderfully concealed, gives to his most personal poems a remoteness of feeling which betrays the careful craftsman lying behind them.

(*c*) *His Metrical Experiments.* The use of metre was, for Bridges, the most important aspect of poetic technique. From his earliest publications he experimented ceaselessly in an attempt to throw off what he felt to be the shackles of conventional patterns and approach more closely to the rhythms of cultured speech. The attempt, so successfully made in his best lyrics, is seen in its latest and most extreme form in the "loose alexandrines" of *The Testament of Beauty*.

OTHER POETS

1. John Masefield (1878–1967). Born at Ledbury, in Herefordshire, Masefield embarked early on a wandering life which was to give him first-hand experience of life before the mast and as a menial worker in America. In 1897 he returned to England and joined the staff of the *Manchester Guardian*. He settled in London and in 1902 began the long stream of publications which brought him fame, and with it the two greatest distinctions open to an English poet; in 1930 he became Poet Laureate, and in 1934 he received the Order of Merit.

Masefield's first poetry was in the vein of Kipling (then at the height of his popularity)—the poetry of action and adventure, but with a Chaucerian breadth of humanity. *Salt-water Ballads* (1902) began the long line of sea-poems on which much of his popularity still rests. Written from first-hand experience, they blend a sense of the romance and beauty of the sea with a thorough knowledge of seamen. *Ballads and Poems* (1910) shows developing technical skill, but *The Everlasting Mercy* (1911) marks a new epoch in his writing. The violent, often crude, realism of this poem in octosyllabic couplets, which deals with the affairs of the drink-sodden Saul Kane and the life of country taverns, is a deliberately shocking protest against the anæmia which afflicted contemporary poetry. It was followed in similar vein by *The Widow in the Bye Street* (1912), *The Daffodil Fields* (1913), and *Lollingdon Downs* (1917). *Dauber* (1913), written under the same impulse, combines with its realism many fine passages which catch the wonder and magic of the sea, while his best narrative poems, *Reynard the Fox* (1919) and *Right Royal* (1920), though vigorously realistic, are more natural in tone and show his love for country life, which appears later in the warm beauty of *The Land Workers* (1943), which gives excellent pictures of the rural England of his youth. Of his other collections of verse mention may be made of *Midsummer Night* (1928), *Collected Poems* (1932), *End and Beginning* (1934), and *Wonderings* (1943).

A born story-teller, Masefield had a tremendous zest for life and a broad humanity, and he did much to restore realism to contemporary English poetry. In both narrative and lyric poems his vitality and simple style have a definite appeal, but he rarely touches the deeper levels of human experience, and his verse technique is too often faulty.

In addition to his poetry, Masefield wrote novels, among them *Sard Harker* (1924), *Odtaa* (1926), *The Bird of Dawning* (1933); some dozen dramas; and a quantity of miscellaneous prose, including *Shakespeare* (1911), *Gallipoli* (1916), and *The Battle of the Somme* (1919).

Of his drama it is enough to say that, apart from *The Tragedy of Nan* (1909), it is of little importance. He has touched on historical and domestic themes, and between 1915 and 1928 he wrote a number of plays, mainly on religious themes, which show clearly the influence of his study of the Japanese No drama. Mention may be made of the following: *The Campden Wonder* (1907); *The Tragedy of Pompey the Great* (1910); *Good Friday* (1917); *Melloney Holtspur* (1922); *The Trial of Jesus* (1925); *The Coming of Christ* (1928).

2. Walter de la Mare (1873–1956) was born in Kent of Huguenot stock and educated at St Paul's Cathedral Choir School before going into business in a London office. After some years of contributing to magazines he published his first book, *Songs of Childhood* (1902), under the pseudonym of Walter Ramal, and in 1908 he took to literature as a career when he was granted a civil list pension for his literary work. He was a prominent member of the Georgian group of poets (see p. 500), and, to the present day, has remained a major figure in the world of English poetry. He received honorary degrees from the universities of Cambridge, St Andrews, Bristol, and London, and was an Honorary Fellow of Keble College, Oxford.

De la Mare began as a writer for children, and a certain naïve, childlike simplicity which appeared in his early work has established itself as one of his most distinctive qualities. A true Georgian, he rarely found his inspiration in the burning problems of modern life, preferring from the beginning to concentrate on romance and nature as his main themes. These he has handled with an artistry which has woven from moonlight, quietness, and mystery a magic peculiarly his own. Many of his poems have an elfish humour which is quite unmistakable. *The Listeners and other Poems* (1912) and *Peacock Pie* (1913) have this translucent quality, but show the poet, as he matures, occasionally sounding a more profound note. But even during the two great wars of this century he has remained for the most part aloof from the politico-social problems which have vexed the souls of his younger contemporaries. *The Fleeting and other Poems* (1933), *Bells and Grass* (1941), *Collected Poems* (1942), *The Burning Glass and other Poems* (1945), and *The Traveller* (1946), to mention some of the most notable of his volumes, embody the same love of nature; the elusive, dream-like quality; the simplicity which is the product of consummate artistry; and the technical ability which has enabled him to turn to the use of the modern writer the traditional forms of English poetry.

A novelist and gifted short-story writer who has the ability to create and sustain a powerful atmosphere, he has produced, since *Henry Brocken* (1904), several collections of short stories. Among them mention may be made of *The Riddle and other Stories* (1923) and *The Lord Fish and other Stories* (1933). His best-known prose work and his longest novel, *The Memoirs of a Midget*, appeared in 1921, while his discriminating and stimulating anthologies are well represented by *Early One Morning* (1935) and *Love* (1943).

3. **Edmund Charles Blunden (1896–1974)**, who was educated at Christ's Hospital and Oxford, saw service with the Royal Sussex Regiment in the 1914–18 War and was decorated for gallantry. In 1922 he won the Hawthornden Prize for *The Shepherd*, and from 1924 to 1927 was Professor of English Literature at Tokyo University. He returned to Oxford as a Fellow of Merton College (1931–43), and, after the Second World War, he was appointed (1948) a member of the British Liaison Mission in Japan, where he did much lecturing.

Few modern poets have been more deeply rooted in the central tradition of English poetry than Edmund Blunden. He is primarily a pastoral poet, seeking inspiration in the sights, sounds, and smells of the English countryside, subjects which he has handled with a Shelleyan lucidity and a technical subtlety which has yet allowed the authentic rural spirit to shine through his verse. A prolific writer, he first came to notice as a contributor to the later volumes of *Georgian Poetry* (see p. 500), and his popularity has remained unimpaired, even though later opinion has reacted against the Georgian school as a whole. As can be seen in some of his more horrific war poems, his experience in the First World War was not without its effect on his verse, but the impact was not sufficient to make any radical change in the nature of his art. His interest in the peace and beauty of nature, the accuracy of his observation, his delight in delicate rhythms, and that fondness for archaisms which aroused the interest of Robert Bridges in Blunden's earliest work, all are still to be found in *Shells by a Stream* (1944), which contains many of his finest lyrics.

In prose, too, Blunden shows his delight in the musical subtleties of our language and a remarkable felicity of phrase, and he has produced work of lasting merit not only in literary biography but also in his books on rural England.

Of his collections of poems we may mention *Pastorals* (1916), *The Waggoner and other Poems* (1920), *English Poems* (1925), *Choice or Chance* (1934), *Poems 1930–40* (1941), *Shells by a Stream* (1944), and *After the Bombing* (1948). His painting of the English scene is to be found in *The Face of England* (1932), *English Villages* (1941), and *Cricket Country* (1944), while among his biographies are *Leigh Hunt* (1930), *Thomas Hardy* (1942), and *Shelley* (1946).

4. A. E. Housman (1859–1936) was born at Bromsgrove and educated at Bromsgrove School and Oxford. After ten years in the Patent Office he became (1892) Professor of Latin at University College, London, a post which he held until offered the chair of Latin at Cambridge in 1911, which he held until his death.

The poetry of A. E. Housman has close affinities of mood with that of the poets of the end of the nineteenth century, and even more markedly with the writings of Hardy. His poetical output was small, consisting entirely of three slender volumes, *A Shropshire Lad* (1896), on which his reputation mainly rests, *Last Poems* (1922), and the posthumously published *More Poems* (1936). Yet his popularity and influence have been out of all proportion to the slender bulk of his verse. *A Shropshire Lad* is a series of sixty-three poems set for the most part in the country of the Welsh border, of which Housman is the prophet, as Hardy is of Wessex. The predominant mood is one of cultured, ironical disillusionment with life, though the poet's appreciation of natural beauty is everywhere to be felt. Tragic in tone, often to the point of morbidity, the poems have the polished ease and restraint which might be expected of so fine a classical scholar. They are concise, sometimes epigrammatic, in expression, yet always perfectly easy to understand, and the emotion is handled with a sureness of touch which never mars an effect by over-emphasis. His two later volumes are written in the same mood and reveal the same high qualities of craftsmanship. *The Name and Nature of Poetry* (1933), his one critical work on English literature, is a brief exposition of his own views upon his art.

5. W. H. Davies (1871–1940) was born at Newport, in Monmouthshire. He left school at an early age and was apprenticed to a maker of picture frames, but he took to a tramping life in America and England. An account of his adventures is to be found in *The Autobiography of a Super-Tramp* (1908), of which the best-known section is probably that which tells of his loss of a leg while attempting to board a moving freight train. It was followed by more autobiography in *A Poet's Pilgrimage* (1918) and *Later Days* (1925).

Davies's first-hand experience of tramps and doss-houses is turned to account in his poetry, but on these subjects his work lacks the fibre of the truly great and is often marred by flaws of taste. His reputation rests mainly on those short pieces in which, with something of the simplicity of Wordsworth's lyrics, he expresses his obvious enjoyment of natural beauty. Unlike Wordsworth, however, he rarely goes below surface impressions in search of a deeper significance. His is mainly a pictorial art, modestly content to try to capture the fleeting impressions of the senses in a direct, simple, unpretentious style. The result is occasionally banal, but often charming, and the reader is constantly surprised by a striking felicity of image. His love poems have the same qualities as his nature lyrics.

Among his volumes of verse are *The Soul's Destroyer and other Poems* (1905), *New Poems* (1907), *Collected Poems* (1916, 1928, 1934), and *Love Poems* (1935).

6. **Lascelles Abercrombie (1881–1938)** was born in Cheshire and educated at Malvern and Manchester University, where he studied science. After experience as a journalist in Liverpool he became a lecturer in poetry at the University of that city (1922–29) before going as Professor of English Literature to Bedford College, London (1929).

Abercrombie was one of the original contributors to *Georgian Poetry*, and, though his work reflected at various times his interest in nearly all the major writers from Tennyson to Bridges, his greatest enthusiasm was for the blend of the emotional and intellectual which he found in the poets of the metaphysical school. He searched many out-of-the-way fields for subjects suitable for treatment in the metaphysical manner, and, as a result, his studies of spiritual conflict are often unconvincing. But he was a considerable metrical artist with a fine rhythmic sense, and he frequently surprises the reader with a striking image and the splendour and vigour of his writing. He is most at home in a compressed and somewhat angular blank verse, and has a particular fondness for the dramatic monologue. He had not the qualities to make him either truly great or widely popular, and it is, perhaps, significant that we find him devoting most of the last twenty years of his life mainly to literary criticism.

His main publications were: *Interludes and Poems* (1908); *Emblems of Love Designed in Several Discourses* (1912); *Thomas Hardy* (1912); *An Essay Towards a Theory of Art* (1922); *The Idea of Great Poetry* (1925); *Romanticism* (1926); *Collected Poems* (1930); *Poetry: Its Music and its Meaning* (1932).

Abercrombie was also a considerable experimenter in poetic drama during the 1920's. Recognizing the need for a new medium if poetic drama were to be revived, he attempted to adapt the rhythms of blank verse to modern needs. But, though they contain fine poetry, his plays lack the dramatic interest which springs from action and character-study. They include *Deborah* (1913), *The Adder* (1913), *The End of the World* (1914), *The Staircase* (1922), *The Deserter* (1922), *Phoenix* (1923), and *The Sale of St Thomas* (first part 1911, completed 1930).

THE POETS OF THE 1914–18 WAR

The First World War brought to public notice many poets, particularly among the young men in the armed forces, while it provided a new source of inspiration for writers of established reputation. Not a few of the younger poets were killed or died in the struggle, and it is impossible to estimate the loss sustained by English poetry in their deaths. Three of the most significant of the new poets are dealt with in some detail: among the others mention must be made of **Julian Grenfell (1888–1915), C. H. Sorley (1892–1915), Robert Nichols (1893–1944), Robert Graves (1895–), Edmund Blunden (1896–1974)**, and **Laurence Binyon (1869–1943)**. A representative selection of the work of poets of this War will be found in *Anthology of War Poetry*, edited by Robert Nichols and published in 1943.

There can be no clearer reflection of the changing national attitude toward the conflict as the weary years brought disillusionment than that found in the poetry of these men. Broadly two phases may be distinguished. The first was one of patriotic fervour, almost of rejoicing in the opportunity of self-sacrifice in the cause of human freedom, and a revival of the romantic conception of the knight-at-arms. Many writers, indeed, lived and served throughout the War and preserved unblemished this fervour of the early years. But, as the carnage grew more appalling and the end seemed as distant as ever, other poets arose with the declared intention of shattering this illusion of the splendour of war by a frankly realistic picture of the suffering, brutality, squalor, and futility of the struggle. The work of this last group, though at first greeted with derision or angry protest, has probably withstood the passage of time better than that of the earlier. Perhaps something of its realism and its depth of understanding has found an echo in the experience of disillusioned post-War generations.

1. Rupert Brooke (1887–1915). Though his war poetry is small in bulk, Brooke is usually considered typical of the early group of war poets, perhaps because his sonnet, "If I should die, think only this of me," has appeared in so many anthologies of twentieth-century verse. Educated at Rugby and Cambridge, Brooke began to write poetry while still at the University. In 1911 he settled at Grantchester, the village near Cambridge which he was to immortalize in "The Old Vicarage, Grantchester," and then during 1913–14 he travelled in America and the South Seas. He joined the Army in 1914, and in the following year died on active service at Scyros, in the Mediterranean.

Brooke's poetry is essentially that of a young, cultured man of leisure. His earliest work betrays something of the affected cynicism of the decadents (see p. 499), but, after a brief and not very successful excursion into the fields of cruder realism, he turned to nature and simple pleasures as his chief inspirations. On these and themes of similar simplicity, Brooke wrote with a youthful, healthy joy in life, a subtlety of observation, and an appreciation of natural beauty, which found for his work a ready place in *Georgian Poetry* (see p. 500). Like Davies, however, he seldom delved below external appearances, and the thought underlying his work usually lacks depth and originality. The ease and limpid simplicity of his verse, partly the result of considerable metrical skill, are eminently suited to his subjects. A reputation (partly deserved, but probably exaggerated) for sentimentality, and the reaction against his attitude to war have resulted in a sharp decline in his once great popularity; but his faults were largely those of youth, and his qualities suggest that he had considerable potentialities.

His poetry was published in *Poems* (1911); *1914 and other Poems* (1915); and *Collected Poems* (1918). His one critical work, *John Webster and the Elizabethan Drama* (1916), indicates a real appreciation of the dramatist and his period. *Letters from America* (1916) is his other prose work.

2. Siegfried Sassoon (1886–1967) based nearly all his most worth-while work on his experiences in the War. Educated at Marlborough and Cambridge, he saw infantry service in Western Europe and Palestine and was decorated for gallantry. First-hand knowledge of the conditions of trench warfare produced in him a bitter disillusion-ment, a brief period as a conscientious objector, and, above all, a determination to shock the people at home into a realization of the ghastly truth. *Counter-attack* (1918), a collection of violent, em-bittered poems, confirmed the notoriety which had rapidly grown out of his occasional writings for periodicals, and it is still the best known of his collections of poetry. With a studied bluntness and often a provocative coarseness of language, Sassoon painted the horrors of life and death in the trenches, dug-outs, and hospitals, and a merciless and calculated realism gave to his work a vitality not previously found in our war poetry. Some critics have found his horrors mechanical or exaggerated, but he still maintains his reputa-tion among readers of poetry. Should that eventually decline, to his credit will always remain the fact that his was the work to inspire the greatest of all the war poets, Wilfred Owen. In a similar vein to *Counter-attack*, though less successful, were *War Poems* (1919) and *Satirical Poems* (1926), but his more recent volumes, *The Heart's Journey* (1928) and *Vigils* (1935), were more concerned with attempts to capture for his reader momentary impressions of beauty. *Collected Poems* was published in 1947.

Sassoon also achieved eminence as a writer of prose. *Memoirs of a Fox-hunting Man*, which won the Hawthornden Prize in 1929, *Memoirs of an Infantry Officer* (1930), and *Sherston's Progress* (1936), collected in 1937 as *The Complete Memoirs of George Sherston*, are thinly disguised autobiographies, the last two volumes of which deal mainly with Sassoon's war-time experiences, and this perennial theme is taken up again in *Siegfried's Journey* (1945). *The Old Century* (1938), *The Weald of Youth* (1942), and a biography of George Meredith published in 1948 are his other recent books. His style is simple, lucid, and most appealing, and his handling of lan-guage betrays the poet's great sensitivity. A lover of the countryside, of rural sports, of music and painting, Sassoon represented a class which is now fast disappearing, and his work gives an admirable picture of a life of cultured leisure.

3. Wilfred Owen (1893–1918) was the greatest of the war poets. He was born at Oswestry and educated at Birkenhead and London University, and, after spending some time as a tutor in France, he served as an infantry officer from 1915 until his death. He was awarded the Military Cross.

As early as 1910 Owen was writing verse in the romantic tradition of Keats and Tennyson, and the influence of French poetry, the product of his stay in France, was never completely shaken off. But the work by which he lives was all produced after his meeting in 1917 with Sassoon. His experience of the trenches had brought him rapidly to maturity, and Sassoon set his feet on the path which he himself had already taken. With a frank realism, free from the violent bitterness of so much of Sassoon's poetry, Owen set out to present the whole reality of war—the boredom, the hopelessness, the futility, the horror, occasionally the courage and self-sacrifice, but, above all, the pity of it. He himself wrote: "I am not concerned with Poetry. My subject is War, and the pity of War. The Poetry is in the pity." And never has the pity of war been more deeply felt or more powerfully shown. Though his satire is often sharp, he never loses his artistic poise, and his most bitter work has a dignity which is truly great.

A gifted artist with a fine feeling for words and a subtle rhythmic sense, Owen was a ceaseless experimenter in verse techniques. Probably the most influential part of his technique was the pararhyme, which was so enthusiastically adopted by later poets. Indeed, Owen's influence on these writers was very great in spite of the slimness of the volume of his poems, which were collected and published by Siegfried Sassoon in 1920. In both technique and mood the post-War generation found in him a congenial spirit, and it is tempting, though profitless, to speculate on what he might have become had he not, by a cruel blow of fate, been killed in action just seven days before the Armistice.

The Poems of Wilfred Owen (1931) is a much more complete collection of his works and contains an excellent memoir by Edmund Blunden.

GENERAL SURVEY OF POETRY (1890–1918)

1. The Decadents. The poetry of the Pre-Raphaelites, Swinburne, Morris, and the Rossettis (see p. 384–388) leads, by a natural progression, to *the decadents* of the 1890's, who, adopting Pater as their prophet and "art for art's sake" as their slogan, put behind them the grim realities of their age. **Ernest Dowson (1867–1900)** and **Lionel Johnson (1867–1902)**, with a number of other poets, formed The Rhymers' Club of which Yeats was, for a time a member. This group had little to say that was worthwhile, and concentrated on ornamenting the triviality of their subject with a carefully sought, other-worldly beauty of sound. A more vital and positive outlook appeared in the work of the maturing Yeats and of Bridges, while Kipling (who was to be followed by the Masefield of such works as *The Everlasting Mercy*) was already introducing a new and racy vigour into English poetry.

2. The Georgians. The decadent conception of poetry, so unhealthy and devitalized, had little hope of long survival, and by 1900 the search for a more natural type of verse had already begun. It resulted in the poetry of the Georgian School, much of which appeared in the five volumes of *Georgian Poetry*, published between 1912 and 1922 from The Poetry Bookshop of **Harold Monro**. In addition to the work of **Rupert Brooke, Edmund Blunden, W. H. Davies, Walter de la Mare**, and **Lascelles Abercrombie**, these collections included poems by **Gordon Bottomley (1874–1948), John Drinkwater (1882–1937), James Elroy Flecker (1884–1915), John Freeman (1880–1929), W. W. Gibson (1878–1963), Ralph Hodgson (1871–1962), Edward Shanks (1892–1953)**, and **Sir John (J. C.) Squire (1884–1958)**. These poets had, of course, their clearly recognizable individual qualities, but were alike in their rejection of the ideas of the decadents, their quest for simplicity and reality, their love of natural beauty, especially as found in the English landscape, and their adherence to the forms and techniques of the main traditions of English poetry. In their own way they, too, were escapist; for the most part, their work shows little awareness of the industrial world around them, and often it has an all too obvious facility of technique and shallowness of feeling. But, though later writers like the Sitwells and Roy Campbell have attacked these weaknesses, it must be allowed that the Georgian poets have contributed something to our poetic heritage, and their regular appearance in anthologies suggests that the best of them may have established for themselves a permanent place in the English poetic tradition. Akin to the Georgians in his natural simplicity and his love for the countryside is **Edward Thomas (1878–1917)**.

3. Reaction against the Georgians: Imagism. Before the first volume of *Georgian Poetry* appeared the seeds of revolt against its ideals were being sown in the lectures of **T. E. Hulme (1883–1917)**, who, though he wrote only five short poems himself, has exercised a profound influence on English poetry. Reacting against the facility and looseness of texture of much Georgian poetry, Hulme insisted that poetry should restrict itself to the world perceived by the senses, and to the presentation of its themes in a succession of concise, clearly visualized, concrete images, accurate in detail and precise in significance. He also advocated the use of *vers libre*, with its unlimited freedom, and its rhythms approaching more closely to those of everyday speech than to those of conventional verse patterns. Hulme's ideas were quickly taken up, particularly by the expatriate Americans, **H.D.** (Hilda Doolittle) **(1886–1961)** and **Ezra Pound** (see p. 544), who coined the name Imagism for this movement. Its organ, *The Egoist*, appeared in 1914 and in the same year Pound edited *Des Imagistes*, an anthology of poetry by followers of the school. Later appeared three collections under the title *Some Imagist Poets* (1915–17), and in 1930 the final *Imagist Anthology*. The pursuit of the sequence of very concise images and the use of *vers libre* often led to obscurity and licence, and the movement was strongly criticized and quickly died out. Yet Hulme's conception of the clearly visualized, concrete image is one of the most distinctive underlying ideas of later poetry, and its effect is seen particularly clearly in the work of T. S. Eliot and the poets of the thirties. A prominent English member of the Imagist school was **Richard Aldington (1892–1962)**.

4. The Limited Influence of War Poetry. Apart from the work of Owen, the War of 1914–18 produced little to influence the general development of English poetry. Owen's grim realism, his consciousness of the pity and waste of war, struck a responsive chord in the post-War writers, who were also much influenced by his rhythmic patterns and his discovery of the potentialities of para-rhyme.

5. The Search for a New Tradition. The general picture of our period is, then, one of uncertainty and experiment, of a desire for the establishment of a tradition but of doubt about where it is to be found. The decadents quickly give way to the Georgians, who are, in turn, attacked by the Imagists, and the latter, after a brief existence, disappear as a school. In this quest for a new tradition, Yeats is evolving a positive philosophy, and, within the limits of the conventional poetic forms, both he and Bridges are experimenting with new rhythmic patterns. The position of contemporary poetry was clearly stated by Bridges in a review in *The Times Literary Supplement* in 1912. He wrote, "There are abundant signs that English syllabic verse has long been in the stage of artistic exhaustion of form which follows great artistic effort." It remained for the post-War poets, with the work of Yeats, Hopkins, Owen, and the

Imagists before them, to carry further this struggle to create a new poetic tradition.

WRITERS OF MISCELLANEOUS PROSE

1. Gilbert Keith Chesterton (1874–1936) was born in London and educated at St Paul's and the Slade School of Art. He began as a writer with reviews of books on art for *The Bookman*, and in 1900 Chesterton was writing for the *Daily News*. His contributions to this paper established him as a popular figure. His book *Orthodoxy* (1908) makes it clear that he had already accepted the tenets of the Roman Catholic Church, and in 1922 he became a member of that communion, to the defence of which much of his writing was directed.

Essayist, novelist, critic, biographer, poet, and even dramatist, Chesterton was a writer of undeniable versatility, yet all his work was characterized by quizzical humour, scintillating wit, and a delight in mental gymnastics, paradox, and epigram. He was fundamentally a serious writer, the advocate of medievalism, Roman Catholicism, and a romantic, mystical view of life, though his jesting concealed the philosophical import which underlay even his most extravagant novels. Of his fiction we may mention *The Napoleon of Notting Hill* (1904), *The Club of Queer Trades* (1905); *The Man who was Thursday* (1908); *Manalive* (1912); and the Father Brown detective stories beginning with *The Innocence of Father Brown* (1911). These short stories were a landmark in the history of detective fiction, which illustrated not only his fondness for the unexpected but his ability to find magic in the most unlikely places.

As a critic, Chesterton showed particular interest in the Victorian period, e.g. *The Victorian Age in Literature* (1913) and *Charles Dickens* (1906). It was, however, in his occasional pieces that he was seen at his best. There the journalist in him was more a help than a hindrance, and he ranks high among twentieth-century essayists. All his typical qualities are seen at their best in *Heretics* (1905); *All Things Considered* (1908); and *Tremendous Trifles* (1909).

Of the several volumes of verse which he published, it suffices to say that they had verve but little else, and his technique was obvious and mechanical.

2. Joseph Hilaire Pierre René Belloc (1870–1953) was born near Paris, the son of a French lawyer and his English wife. He was educated at the Roman Catholic Oratory School, Birmingham, and at Balliol College, Oxford, of which he was a Scholar. In 1902 he became a naturalized British subject, and from 1906 to 1910 was a Liberal M.P.

Beginning with *Verses and Sonnets* (1896), Belloc wrote poetry, fiction, history, travel books, and numerous essays; in all fields he achieved some measure of popular success. As a historian he showed particular interest in his native France, especially at the time of the Revolution, and the bulk of his work takes the form of historical biography—*Danton* (1899); *Robespierre* (1901); *Marie Antoinette* (1909); *Richelieu* (1930). Like *A History of England* (1925–31), these works show Belloc to be a propagandist whose views were influenced by his Roman Catholicism and an attachment to the romantic view of history. This last is a weakness he shared with Chesterton, with whom he had much in common.

His excellent essays owe their attractiveness to the graceful ease and simplicity of his style, and the imagination and insight of the poet which often underlay them. The same charm and lightness are to be found in his travel books, of which by far the best is *The Path to Rome* (1902).

Belloc's love of the English countryside, particularly of Sussex, and his light satirical wit were the chief inspirations of his verse which, if rarely deep, has a lyric simplicity and careful artistry. Some of his most popular writings were his children's verses—*The Bad Child's Book of Beasts* (1896), *Cautionary Tales for Children* (1908), etc.

3. **William Henry Hudson (1841–1922)** was the son of an American sheep-farmer living in Argentina, where Hudson was born, near Buenos Aires. An early illness left him a semi-invalid for life, and in 1868 he settled in England, where he married some eight years later. A period of poverty, during which he eked out a living as a contributor to magazines, was brought to an end by the grant of a Civil List Pension in 1901, the year after he became a naturalized Englishman, and by the success of his novel *Green Mansions* (1904). He did much valuable work for the protection of British bird life and the creation of bird sanctuaries.

After two unsuccessful excursions into the field of romance with his novels *The Purple Land that England Lost* (1885) and *A Crystal Age* (1887) Hudson turned to the type of work in which he was to establish his reputation. *The Naturalist in La Plata* (1892) and *Idle Days in Patagonia* (1893), two collections of essays, have all the spontaneous authenticity which distinguishes his writings upon places and experiences he has known personally. This is one of the qualities that gives distinction to his *Far Away and Long Ago: A*

History of My Early Life (1918), to his collection of short stories, *El Ombú* (1902), and to his most popular work, *Green Mansions: A Romance of the Tropical Forest* (1904), all of which are set in South America. His great love for birds is clearly seen in *Birds in a Village* (1893), *British Birds* (1895), *Birds in London* (1898), *Birds and Man* (1901), *Birds in Town and Village* (1919), and *Birds of La Plata* (1920); his affection for the English countryside is the starting point for *Nature in Downland* (1900), *Hampshire Days* (1903), *Afoot in England* (1909), and *A Shepherd's Life* (1910).

Hudson lacks the inventive faculty and the human sympathy which alone can create living characters. He is, therefore, a naturalist rather than a novelist. His meticulous observation of natural phenomena is, however, accompanied by an intuitive perception of the spiritual forces of nature and a feeling almost of kinship with animals. It is these qualities, and his ability to recapture the very spirit of the place he describes, which lift his writings far above naturalist reporting. The simplicity and directness of his charming style are the result of careful artistry, and he ranks as a modern master of English prose.

4. Naturalists and Travellers. In addition to W. H. Hudson, we may include in our period the naturalist **John Richard Jefferies (1848–87)**, a close observer of men and animals in the countryside. These subjects he presents in a colourful, often over-elaborate prose, but with genuine sympathy and insight. Among his best-known works are *The Gamekeeper at Home* (1878), *Wild Life in a Southern County* (1879), *The Amateur Poacher* (1879), *Wood Magic, a Fable* (1881), *Bevis, the Story of a Boy* (1882), *The Life of the Fields* (1884), and *The Toilers of the Field* (1892).

George Bourne (George Sturt) **(1863–1927)** also wrote of village life in the days before mass production and easy communications. Most evocative of his books are *Change in the Village* (1912) and *The Wheelwright's Shop* (1923). His *Journals* were definitively edited in 1967.

The period is particularly rich in the literature of travel and exploration. Greatest of the travel books was probably *Travels in Arabia Deserta* (1888) by **C. M. Doughty (1843–1926)**. The works of **R. B. Cunninghame Graham (1852–1936)** show the extent of his travels, which embraced South America, the Near and Far East, and Mexico. His best-known works include *Mogreb-el-Acksa* (1898) and *The Ipané* (1899). Also set in the East are *Saïd the Fisherman* (1903) and *Oriental Encounters, Palestine and Syria*

(1918), the one a biography and the other a collection of stories by **M. W. Pickthall (1875–1936)**. **Norman Douglas (1868–1953)**, the author of a number of books on the Mediterranean lands, is most remembered for *Siren Land* (1911), *Fountain in the Sand* (1912), and *Old Calabria* (1915), while of the works of **H. M. Tomlinson (1873–1958)** the best known are *The Sea and the Jungle* (1912) and *Old Junk* (1918). Mountaineering is the subject of the writings of **Edward Whymper (1840–1911)**, whose *Scrambles among the Alps* (1870) was followed by *Travels among the Great Andes of the Equator* (1892).

5. **Essayists.** The revival of the short periodical essay is one of the features of this period. With the possible exception of Chesterton, the most outstanding exponent of this form was the witty, urbane, polished **Sir Max Beerbohm (1872–1956)**, who couches his satirical thrusts in faultless, graceful prose. His essays appear in *The Works of Max Beerbohm* (1896), *More* (1899), *Yet Again* (1909), *And Even Now* (1920), and his broadcast talks, published as *Mainly On the Air* (1946). Others who made their mark in this field were **E. V. Lucas (1868–1938)**, traveller, biographer of Charles Lamb, and author of an immense number of essays notable for their lightness of touch, their ease and naturalness. Some of them are found in *Character and Comedy* (1907), *Old Lamps for New* (1911), *Loiterer's Harvest* (1913), and *Cloud and Silver* (1916). Not unlike Lucas in his appeal was 'Alpha of the Plough', the pseudonym of the journalist **A. G. Gardiner (1865–1946)**, whose two best-known collections are *Pebbles on the Shore* (1917) and *Leaves in the Wind* (1920). Of the essays of Belloc, Chesterton, and Galsworthy mention has been made elsewhere.

6. **Philosophers.** Science and philosophy for the common man had, in 1918, only begun to make their appearance, but at least two thinkers of importance had already established their reputations. The influence of the thought of **Henry Havelock Ellis (1859–1939)** upon the work of post-War novelists can scarcely be overestimated. His *Studies in the Psychology of Sex* (1897–1910) appeared in America, owing to official opposition in this country. Among his other works were *The New Spirit* (1890), *Man and Woman* (1894), *The Task of Social Hygiene* (1912). **Bertrand Russell (1872–1970)**, brilliant mathematician, and one of the outstanding thinkers of his age, was chiefly concerned with philosophy in his earlier books— *The Philosophy of Leibnitz* (1900), *Principles of Social Reconstruction* (1917), *Mysticism and Logic* (1918), *The Analysis of Mind* (1921),

and *An Outline of Philosophy* (1927). After these many educational and social studies appeared regularly from his pen, as well as mathematical and philosophical works. His later books included *The Analysis of Matter* (1927), *Marriage and Morals* (1929), *The Conquest of Happiness* (1930), *The Scientific Outlook* (1931), *History of Western Philosophy* (1946), *Human Knowledge, Its Scope and Limits* (1948), and *Authority and the Individual* (1949).

7. Literary Critics. The growing status of English literature as a subject worthy of serious study is reflected in the foundation of chairs of English Literature at Oxford (1904) and Cambridge (1911), and in the rapid increase in the number of critical works appearing from the presses. From Oxford came the work of three of the best-known critics of our period: **A. C. Bradley (1851–1935)**, author of the famous *Shakespearean Tragedy* (1904) and *Oxford Lectures on Poetry* (1909); **Sir Walter Raleigh (1861–1922)**, whose best work is in *Milton* (1900), *Wordsworth* (1903), *Shakespeare* (1907), and *Six Essays on Johnson* (1910); and **W. P. Ker (1855–1923)**, who wrote *Epic and Romance* (1897), *The Dark Ages* (1904), *Essays on Medieval Literature* (1905), *The Art of Poetry* (1923), and *Form and Style in Poetry* (1928). The prolific **George Saintsbury (1845–1933)**, writing in Edinburgh, is perhaps best remembered for his *Elizabethan Literature* (1887), *A History of Criticism* (1900–4), *A History of English Prosody* (1906), and *The Peace of the Augustans* (1916). **Sir Edmund Gosse (1849–1928)** greatly helped to revive interest in the Metaphysical Poets and to explain Ibsen's plays. His *Father and Son* (1907) presented the moral crisis of the mid-nineteenth century when his father's scientific career and religion came into conflict with the new Darwinism.

This age sees, in particular, a growing interest in Shakespearian studies. In addition to H. Granville Barker (see p. 474), other writers who contributed to modern knowledge and appreciation of the dramatist included **Edward Dowden (1843–1913), John Addington Symonds (1840–93), Sir Arthur Quiller-Couch (1863–1944), and John Dover Wilson (1881–1969)**.

CHAPTER XIII

THE INTER-WAR YEARS

TIME-CHART OF THE CHIEF AUTHORS

The thick line indicates the period of important literary production.

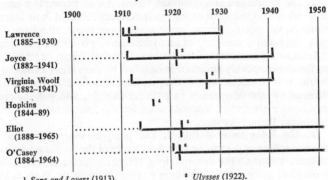

¹ *Sons and Lovers* (1913).   ² *Ulysses* (1922).
³ *To the Lighthouse* (1927).
⁴ *Poems of Gerard Manley Hopkins* (published by Bridges, 1918).
⁵ *The Waste Land* (1922).   ⁶ *Juno and the Paycock* (1924).

THE HISTORICAL BACKGROUND (1918–39)

This period was almost completely overshadowed by the two World Wars—the after-effects of the first and the forebodings of the second. After the Treaty of Versailles attention in England was still mainly concentrated on foreign affairs—the growing pains of the new League of Nations, uncertainty in the Middle East, and troubles in India and Ireland. The Treaties of Locarno (1925) diminished, at least temporarily, anxieties in Europe, and home affairs began again to dominate English political thought. The General Strike of 1926 was a major manifestation of the post-War slump, which culminated in the 'depression' and its problems of want and unemployment, which made the early thirties a period of great distress, particularly for the industrial areas. Foreign problems again came to the fore with the rise to power of the Nazis in Germany, and from 1934 until 1939 there was mounting tension abroad, and at home a gradual return to prosperity as industry was geared to rearmament. Spiritually the period saw the immediate post-War mood of desperate gaiety and determined frivolity give way to doubt, uncertainty of aim, and a deeper self-questioning on ethical, social, and political problems, until the outbreak of hostilities in 1939, followed by the critical situation after the evacuation of Dunkirk, enabled the nation to achieve a new unanimity of purpose.

LITERARY FEATURES OF THE AGE

1. The Breakdown of Established Values. Of no period is it more true to say that the spirit of the age is perfectly reflected in its literature. Novel, poetry, drama, and miscellaneous prose, all mirror the perplexity and uncertainty of aim which sprang from the post-War breakdown of accepted spiritual values. The multiplicity of reactions to the contemporary situation is equalled by the variety of literary work. It is significant that in the literature of our period there is an attempt to find new values in political thought, and politics and psychology are indeed essential clues for the interpretation of the inter-War literary scene.

2. The Resurgence of Poetry. The pre-War years had seen a relative eclipse of poetry, and the dominance of the novel and drama as literary forms. The demand, long before expressed by Yeats, for a new and living poetical tradition was met between the Wars in his own work and in that of the new poets—T. S. Eliot, W. H. Auden, Cecil Day Lewis, and Louis MacNeice. Poetry again became a vital literary form closely in touch with life, and if it did not oust the novel from its primacy it certainly outstripped the drama.

3. Variety of Technical Experiment. It is doubtful whether any period of English literature saw experiments so bold and various as those of the inter-War years. A natural corollary of the quest for new values and for a new vital tradition was the desire for new forms and methods of presentation, and in all the major literary genres the age produced revolutionary developments.

4. The Influence of Radio and Cinema. Though it is impossible to assess with any accuracy the effect on literature of these two inventions, there can be no doubt that the rapid development of two such important media had an enormous impact. In so far as the radio brought literature into the home, in the form of broadcast stories, plays, and literary discussion, and opened up an entirely new field for authors, its influence was for the good. On the other hand, the great quantity and variety of poorer radio entertainment readily accessible for more than two-thirds of each day almost certainly reduced the time devoted to reading. The same may be said of the cinema, which, for many people, became the main form of leisure activity, while, in spite of the numerous screen adaptions of novels, it can scarcely be claimed that the cinema has done as much as the radio to stimulate literary interest. At the same time it must be remembered that film techniques were the basis of a number of experiments in the novel.

5. The Speed of Life. In the inter-War years life generally was lived in an atmosphere of hustle and restlessness never before known. At work and at play the demand was for more and faster action, stronger and more violent stimulus, and the general atmosphere thus created was by its very nature inimical to the cultivation of literary pursuits, which necessarily demand a degree of calmness of spirit and leisure of mind.

THE NOVELISTS

I. DAVID HERBERT LAWRENCE (1885–1930)

1. His Life. D. H. Lawrence was the most striking figure in the literary world between the Wars. He was born at Eastwood, in Nottinghamshire, the son of a miner, and was educated at Nottingham High School. On leaving school he had a brief experience of business life, and then became a pupil teacher in his native village. He trained for the teachers' certificate at University College, Nottingham, and then was for some time a teacher in Croydon, but, on the publication of *The White Peacock* (1911), he abandoned teaching for literature. He married Frieda Weekley, a German, and previously wife of a Nottingham Professor. Because of his attitude toward the War and his wife's nationality, he was cruelly persecuted, and this, with the suppression of *The Rainbow* (1915) as obscene, and the banning of an exhibition of his paintings by the police, made Lawrence try to leave England. His passport was withheld, however, and it was 1919 before he got away. From then on his life was a continuous search, in many parts of the world, for a society more suited to one of his ideals—Italy, Malta, Ceylon, Australia, California, and New Mexico were among the places where he lived. In

1929 he returned finally to Europe, and in the following year died of tuberculosis at Vence in France.

2. His Prose. Lawrence is another example of the prolific modern writer. In the nineteen years between his first published novel and his death he produced over forty volumes of fiction (novels and short stories), poetry, plays, treatises, and essays, and not a year passed without the publication of something from his pen. It is, however, as a novelist that he is chiefly remembered. *The White Peacock* (1911) is a story of unhappy human relationships set in the area he knew so well, and, if the book lacks the depth and seriousness of his later work, it already reveals his concern with one of his chief themes, the conflict between man and woman, and much of his remarkable gift for fine description and lyric emotion. A slighter work, *The Trespasser* (1912), was followed by the largely autobiographical *Sons and Lovers* (1913), an extremely powerful novel of deep sincerity, which studies with great insight the relationship between son and mother. By many it is considered the best of all his work. Then came *The Rainbow* (1915), suppressed as obscene, which treats again the conflict between man and woman. Not until 1921 was he able to find a publisher for its sequel, *Women in Love*, an important novel for the student of Lawrence's views upon human life. Equally significant is *Aaron's Rod* (1922), a more mature work of greater stylistic quality. From his experiences during the War and his later visit to Australia sprang *Kangaroo* (1923), which he called a "thought adventure." The discussion of the world situation at times overweights the novel, but, both in this and in *The Boy in the Bush* (1924), Lawrence depicts the Australian background with striking vividness. This same faculty for capturing the spirit of a country is one of the better features of *The Plumed Serpent* (1926), an over-lengthy work which deals with Mexican life, and which is typical of Lawrence in its stress on the values of the primitive as opposed to the civilized. Two years later appeared in Florence *Lady Chatterley's Lover* (1928), a novel in which sexual experience is handled with a wealth of physical detail and uninhibited language which until 1960 caused its suppression in this country. It is Lawrence's last embittered fling at what he felt to be the prurience of mind which sheltered behind conventional notions of sex, and he claimed that it was "very truly moral."

Lawrence was also a short story writer of considerable power, and he published many collections, among which are *The Prussian Officer* (1914); *England, my England* (1922); *The Ladybird, The Fox,*

The Captain's Doll (1923); *St Mawr, together with The Princess* (1925); *The Woman who Rode Away, and other Stories* (1928); *The Virgin and the Gipsy* (1930); and *The Lovely Lady* (1933). Of his essays and travel books mention may be made of *Twilight in Italy* (1916); *Sea and Sardinia* (1921); *Reflections on the Death of a Porcupine* (1925); and *Mornings in Mexico* (1927).

3. His Poetry. It was as a poet that Lawrence first appeared in print with magazine contributions in 1910, and he continued to write poetry throughout his life. Its most striking feature is its fundamental similarity to his prose. We may see a parallel to the strong autobiographical element of *Sons and Lovers* in the intensely personal poems of his early collections, and, if the urgency of personal problems is no longer so great in the later volumes, all his poetry has that vital surge and that dynamic power which are typical of his novels. So, too, the themes of his novels, his hatred of "what man has made of man," his passionate belief in the primitive and elemental impulses, are the major themes of his verse, while the acute sensitivity to natural beauty, which studs the novels with striking descriptive passages, is found in his poems on animals and flowers. The impatience with careful craftsmanship which underlies his reaction against the 'well-made' novel finds expression in the *vers libre* of his poetry, and in an overwhelming spontaneity and direct simplicity of utterance. His collections include: *Love Poems and Others* (1913), *Amores* (1916), *Look! We have come through* (1917), *New Poems* (1918), *Tortoises* (1921), *Birds, Beasts and Flowers* (1923), *Collected Poems* (1928), *Pansies* (1929), *Last Poems* (1933).

4. Features of his Novels. (*a*) *His Themes.* Like Hardy, Lawrence used the novel to present to his reader his own interpretation of life; both writers were concerned with the basic problems of human existence, man's relationships with his fellows and with the universe beyond himself. He combined a violent hatred of the values of modern mechanized civilization with a love of the primitive and natural, and a passionate belief in the importance of the development of each unique individuality—"the slow building up of an integral personality through the years." Scorning the merely intellectual faculties, he placed his trust in the experiences of the senses, which for him seem to gain in value as they become more violent. Man's primitive instincts and the impulses which spring from his unconscious mind are his safest guides in life—"All I want is to answer to my blood, direct, without fribbling intervention of mind, or moral, or what-not." His portrayals of these vital experiences, of which the most important appears to be the sexual relationship, indicate that he is deeply conscious of their religious nature; so that, though sex is frequently his theme, it is handled as a sacred thing, spiritual not animal, and this, as he himself claims, remains true even of *Lady Chatterley's Lover*. Lawrence is, then, the prophet of the primitive instincts and passions; his own appeal is to the heart rather than the head. He seeks to persuade, not by the reasoning faculty, but by the emotional impact of his writing. Many of his fundamental ideas are set out in his three treatises, *Fantasia of the Unconscious* (1922), *Psycho-analysis and the Unconscious* (1923), and *Apocalypse* (1931).

(*b*) *His Treatment of his Themes*. Lawrence shows little concern with the novel as an art form, and the reader is less impressed by his technical skills than by the verve and passionate intensity of his writing. It is this impassioned presentation of his themes which accounts for his poorest as well as his finest qualities. At one time it leads him into the extravagances of violent over-earnestness; at another it raises him to the heights of poetical utterance. At his best he is content to allow his ideas to emanate naturally from his characters, and his philosophy is assimilated to his art, but as he progresses his didactic fervour leads him more and more frequently to direct statement. Because he is so deeply involved in his themes and pays so little attention to artistic qualities, there is a sameness about many of his novels. He has little sense of humour, and the feelings he expresses most frequently and strongly are those of hatred and contempt. But, in spite of his many failings, Lawrence is undoubtedly a writer of great imaginative force, whose best work has a spontaneous vitality seldom equalled in the novel.

(*c*) *His Style*. If we judge Lawrence's style by the standards of the meticulous artist, with finely attuned ear and an eye for accuracy of detail of grammar, we shall often find him lacking. But for careless-ness in these ways he more than atones by the spontaneity and vivid-ness of his writing when his feelings are deeply engaged. In his use of symbol and the magnificent descriptive powers, which are never better seen than in his painting of natural scenery, he approaches closely to poetry. He often achieves a perfect naturalness of dia-logue, which is seen particularly in his masterly handling of the coarse dialects of Australia (*The Boy in the Bush*) and of the Not-tinghamshire mining villages (*Sons and Lovers* and *Lady Chatterley's Lover*). In the last-named work we have, too, the extreme example of his hatred of the conventions which place taboos on certain words. In all matters, and particularly when dealing with sex, he speaks with the utmost frankness and fearlessness.

(*d*) *His Characters.* The most striking feature of Lawrence's characters is the resemblance that so many of them bear to their creator. Paul Morel in *Sons and Lovers*, R. L. Somers in *Kangaroo*, and Birkin in *Women in Love* are clearly projections of himself. In his other characters there are many similarities. They share his bitterness and darkness of spirit, and like him they live passionately and fully. They are creatures of strong impulse and primitive emotions, and they are studied with a remarkable depth of understanding and keenness of insight. Lawrence is particularly successful in his analysis of the unconscious.

II. JAMES JOYCE (1882–1941)

1. His Life. James Joyce, the son of middle-class Irish parents, was born in Dublin, where, in preparation for a career in the Roman Catholic church, he was educated in Jesuit colleges and at the Royal University. He abandoned the idea of taking orders, however, and shortly after the turn of the century he left Ireland for France. In Paris he studied medicine and thought of becoming a professional singer. During the 1914–18 War he taught languages in Switzerland (he was medically unfit for service), and afterward returned to Paris, where he settled down to a literary life, struggling continually against ill-health and public opposition to his work.

2. His Novels. Of the later Joyce there are already signs in his first work, *Dubliners* (begun 1900, published 1914). The narrative technique is straightforward, but these objective, short-story studies of the sordid Dublin slums are powerfully written, and their prose style, though simple, has a distinct individual flavour. Set in the same city is *A Portrait of the Artist as a Young Man* (1916), an intense account of a developing writer torn between the standards of an ascetic, religious upbringing and his desire for sensuousness. Though the work is largely autobiographical (Stephen Dedalus is Joyce), the writer preserves a cool detachment in the precise analysis of his hero's spiritual life. His handling of the sexual problems involved is particularly forthright. An earlier version, much more conventional in style, was *Stephen Hero*, which was not published until 1944. The artistic dilemma of Stephen–Joyce was re-expressed in his unsuccessful play *Exiles* (1918). Stephen Dedalus appears again in *Ulysses* (1922), a study of the life and mind of Leopold and Mrs Bloom during a single day. It is modelled on the *Odyssey* of Homer, but it is set in the squalor of Dublin's slums. There are parallel characters in the two works, and the structure is in each case the same; these likenesses are deliberately invoked to stress the sordid meanness of modern life as contrasted with life in the heroic age. The 'stream of consciousness' technique and the internal monologue are used with great power, and Bloom has been described as "the most complete character in fiction." The material is handled objectively and with a frankness that caused the book to be banned as obscene: the style shows clearly Joyce's mastery of language, his ingenuity, brilliance, and power. Published in the same year as *The Waste Land*, it presents a similar view of the hopeless dilemma of man in the post-War world. It appeared in *The Little Review* in America, but was banned after the fifth instalment, and this ban was not lifted in England until 1933. Joyce's only other novel was *Finnegan's Wake* (1939), parts of which had appeared as early as 1927 and 1928 as *Work in Progress* and *Anna Livia Plurabelle*. In it he has developed his technique to a point where subtlety and complexity produce incomprehensibility. It is a study of the history of the human race from its earliest beginnings, as seen in the incoherent dreams of a certain Mr Earwicker. The use of an inconsecutive narrative and of a private vocabulary adds to the confusion, but it cannot conceal the poetic furor, the power, and brilliant verbal skill of the work.

3. Features of his Novels. (*a*) *His Subjects*. Joyce is a serious novelist, whose concern is chiefly with human relationships—man in relation to himself, to society, and to the whole race. This is true also of his latest work, though his interest in linguistic experiments makes it difficult to understand his meaning. Acutely aware of the pettiness and meanness of modern society, and of the evils which spring from it, he is unsurpassed in his knowledge of the seamy side of life, which he presents with startling frankness. He is a keen and subtle analyst of man's inner consciousness, and, in common with the psycho-analysts of his day, he is much preoccupied with sex.

(*b*) *His Technique*. In the quest of the twentieth-century novelists for a new technique by which to present the contemporary human dilemma, Joyce is a pioneer, and his lead has been followed by many major writers. He was a ceaseless experimenter, ever anxious to explore the potentialities of a method once it was evolved, and in his use of the 'stream of consciousness' technique, and in his handling of the internal monologue, he went further and deeper than any other. His sensitiveness, his depth of penetration into the human consciousness, give to his character-study a subtlety unparalleled in his day, and if, in his attempts to catch delicate and elusive shades of feeling and fix them in words, he has frequently become incomprehensible, the fact remains that a character like Leopold Bloom is a unique and fascinating creation.

(c) *His Style.* Joyce's style develops from the straightforward, simple writing of *Dubliners* to the complex allusiveness and the bewildering originality of *Finnegan's Wake.* In the latter, a broken narrative, with abrupt transitions, and logical sentence links omitted, together with a new vocabulary, produces writing which is often purely 'private' in its significance; for words are coined by the breaking up of one word and the joining of its parts to parts of other words similarly split, and roots of words from many languages are employed. Joyce's interest in language and his eager experimentation are unequalled in any period of our literature. He has a sensitive ear for verbal rhythms and cadences, and uses language in his books as part of an elaborately conceived artistic pattern, in which much of the unity of his work lies. With the beauty of language for its own sake only he is usually little concerned, yet his writing is often of great imaginative power and has a musical quality which enables even his incomprehensible passages to be read aloud with considerable pleasure. His genius is for the comic rather than the tragic view of life, and his work is full of wit, puns (often in several languages), and startling conceits. The humour varies from broad comedy to intellectual wit, but is mainly sardonic in tone.

III. VIRGINIA WOOLF (1882–1941)

1. Her Life. The daughter of the eminent Victorian critic and scholar, Sir Leslie Stephen, Virginia Woolf was born into a circle where standards of culture, taste, and intelligence were of the highest. From the reading and conversations of her formative years she acquired an unusually wide literary background and a cosmopolitan culture. She began her writing career as a contributor to literary journals, and, after her marriage (1912) to Leonard Woolf, she shared in the activities of the Hogarth Press, which published the work of many rising men and advanced thinkers. Though her first novel appeared in 1915, her reputation was originally made as a critic of penetration and independent judgment. In fact, it was only with

Orlando: a Biography (1928) that she scored anything like a popular success, and she is likely to remain a novelist for the few.

2. Her Works. *The Voyage Out* (1915), her first novel, is told in the conventional narrative manner, but with a concentration of interest upon character and a delicacy of touch typical of all her work. The same emphasis on character-analysis and the same lack of incident characterize *Night and Day* (1919), another study of personal adjustment and development. Then came her first really mature work, *Jacob's Room* (1922), in which her distinctive technique is fully used for the first time. By a series of disconnected impressions, revealed mainly through the consciousness of people with whom he came into contact, we are made aware of the personality of Jacob. These momentary impressions, which shift and dissolve with the bewildering inconsequence of real mental processes, are revealed by the use of the internal monologue, and from them we are intended to build up gradually a complete conception of the young man. This same method, handled with greater firmness, is again used in *Mrs Dalloway* (1925). Though what little 'event' there is occupies only one day, Virginia Woolf is enabled to create not only the lives of her chief characters, which are studied with a penetrating subtlety, but even the London background. *To the Lighthouse* (1927) shows a still firmer mastery of the 'stream of consciousness' technique, and is by many accounted her finest work. Its study of the relationships of the members of the Romney family achieves a greater artistic unity than is found in her previous novels, and yet preserves all her usual subtlety of analysis. The ultimate development of her method appears in *The Waves* (1931), from which plot, in the normally accepted sense, is almost entirely lacking. It is a symbolic work of great poetic beauty, in which the consciousness of the six characters is studied in a series of internal monologues. An ambitious, and clearly an experimental, work, it is remarkable for its sensitive perception of changing moods, and the skill with which the six characters are distinguished. It has been well described as a prose-poem. *Flush* (1933), *The Years* (1937), in which she again deals with family relationships, and the unfinished *Between the Acts* (1941) show her usual delicacy of touch and brilliant technical mastery, but the first two fall below the level of her major works, while of the last it is difficult to attempt an assessment. Standing alone among her novels, and therefore last to be considered here, is the fantasy, *Orlando, a Biography* (1928), which may be said to have established her reputation with the wider reading public. With a verve and spirit utterly different from the movement of her other novels, it traces from Elizabethan to modern times the life of Orlando, who not only appears as a number of different people, but even changes sex in the middle of the story. It is full of vivid colour and striking evocations of historical periods and settings.

In addition to her novels, Virginia Woolf wrote a number of essays on cultural subjects, which appear in *Mr Bennett and Mrs Brown* (1924); *The Common Reader* (1925); *A Room of One's Own* (1929); *The Second Common Reader* (1932); *Roger Fry* (1940); *The Death of the Moth* (1942); and *The Moment* (1947). They reveal her as a critic of penetrating insight and superb stylistic gifts.

3. Features of her Novels. (*a*) *Her Themes.* Although, as her essay *Mr Bennett and Mrs Brown* makes clear, Virginia Woolf reacted against the novel of social manners as produced by writers like Arnold Bennett, she was none the less concerned with the realities of life. But for her the realities were inward and spiritual rather than outward and material; of the life depicted by Bennett and Wells she knew nothing. The elusiveness of these inner realities is the recurrent theme of her novels. Her characters are seen in search of them, and the search is followed with profound insight, but it would seem that she never solved the problem of the ultimate meaning of life, for her novels, unlike those of Lawrence, give no solution.

(*b*) *Her Technique.* It is in this field that Virginia Woolf makes her most important contribution to the novel. Conventional conceptions of the novel she entirely rejected, replacing emphasis on incident, external description, and straightforward narrative by an overriding concern with character presentation by the 'stream of consciousness' method. This technique was not a new one. Dorothy Richardson had used it—*Pointed Roofs* (1915), *Backwater* (1916), *Honeycomb* (1917), etc. So had James Joyce, a greater exponent of this method than either. Its great advantages are that it offers previously undreamed-of possibilities for the analysis of mental states; its disadvantages, the great demands it makes on the reader, and the dangers of incoherence and mere virtuosity, which beset the author because of the lack of a logical time sequence and the temptation to go into the most minute detail. Virginia Woolf uses this technique with ever-growing sureness of purpose; her keen mind and magnificent artistic sense enable her to weld the parts into a unified artistic whole of sensitive, subtle portraiture. Her studies of mood and impulse are handled with an almost scientific precision and detachment, and yet she has a great gift for lyrical exposition.

(c) *Her Characters.* "I believe that all novels deal with character, and that it is to express character—not to preach doctrines, sing songs, or celebrate the glories of the British Empire—that the form of the novel, so clumsy, verbose and undramatic, so very elastic and alive, has been evolved." Thus did she express her concern with character, and of her method she wrote: "Let us record the atoms as they fall upon the mind in the order in which they fall, let us trace the pattern, however disconnected and incoherent in appearance, which each sight or incident scores upon the consciousness." For this probing of the inner workings of the mind Virginia Woolf's penetrating insight equipped her admirably. Her range of characters is small: it has been said that she was unable to portray anyone who did not share her own unusual qualities, and it is certainly true that some of her figures, though studied with amazing subtlety, fail to come alive for the reader. Even so, in the delicate analysis of motive, impulse, and reaction to situation, she sets a standard which very few have been able to attain, and of the three chief characters in *Mrs Dalloway*, at least, we may claim that we know them from the inside as we know few other characters.

(d) *Her Style.* As might be expected of one of her background and artistic gifts, Virginia Woolf is a prose-writer of genius. It is in her prose style that her poetic qualities are most clearly seen. It has all the poise and charm of the cultured woman and conscious artist. She uses words with a keen sense of their rhythmic and musical potentialities; her style is richly figurative (*The Waves* is the best example of this), and the precision of her images is in keeping with the accuracy and delicacy of her character analysis.

OTHER NOVELISTS

1. Edward Morgan Forster (1879–1970), the son of a cultured family, was educated at Tonbridge and had travelled widely. An intellectual and Fellow of King's College, Cambridge, he ranked among the most cosmopolitan men of his day.

His novels are only five in number. After the early *Where Angels Fear to Tread* (1905), with its well-drawn characters, its comedy, and the typical concern with the conflict between two different cultures, comes *The Longest Journey* (1907), a less attractive work, which does, however, show the same skill in characterization. *A Room with a View* (1908), like his first novel, is set in Italy, and contains excellent comedy very delicately handled. Then come his two masterpieces, *Howards End* (1910), and, much later, *A Passage to India* (1924), both of which deal with the misunderstandings which arise in relationships, between individuals in the one case, and between races in the other. *A Passage to India* was the latest of his novels, and is unrivalled in English fiction in its presentation of the complex problems which were to be found in the relationships between English and native people in India, and in its portrayal of the Indian scene in all its magic and all its wretchedness.

But though his output was small, the quality of his work was such as to place him among the foremost writers of the period. As well as his novels he published three collections of short stories, *The Celestial Omnibus* (1911), *The Story of the Siren* (1920), and *The Eternal Moment* (1928), and two critical works, *Aspects of the Novel* (1927) and *Abinger Harvest* (1936). A collection of miscellaneous essays, lectures, and talks, some on political and others on artistic themes, appeared in 1951 under the title, *Two Cheers for Democracy*. He is a writer for the discerning rather than a best-seller. Basically a moralist, concerned with the importance of the individual personality, the adjustments it must make and the problems it must solve when it comes into contact with a set of values different from its own, he is the advocate of culture, tolerance, and civilization against barbarity and provincialism. He studies the complexities of character with a subtlety of insight and an appreciation of the significance of the unconscious which mark him as a modern. His characters are rounded and vital. He has great gifts for telling a story, but he disregards conventional plot construction and frequently introduces startling, unexpected incidents. His craftsmanship is of the highest order. With a cool, often ironic, detachment, he presents the problems arising from his imagined situation with fairness and breadth of outlook, though he is to some extent lacking in emotional fire and human warmth. He has an excellent faculty for capturing the very feel and tone of his background—*A Passage to India* offers a good example of this. Though his best novels often touch tragedy, his true field is comedy, whimsical, delicate, and biting, which is never long absent from his work. He combines a style as easy and cool as his general attitude toward his problems and characters, with a gift for good dialogue, marked descriptive powers, lightness of touch and precision, and conciseness of presentation.

   2. Aldous Leonard Huxley (1894–1963), descendant of the famous scientist, T. H. Huxley, was educated at Eton and Balliol College, Oxford, where he began his literary career as a poet. In 1917 he was editor of *Oxford Poetry*, and he was a contributor to the Sitwell anthology, *Wheels*. Under the pseudonym Autolycus, he wrote for *The Athenæum* when he left the University. He was a man of the widest culture, with an insatiable thirst for knowledge, and he travelled widely. In 1939 he settled in California, where he stayed for the rest of his life.

To trace the development of Huxley's writing from the romantic tone and artistic finish of *The Burning Wheel* (1916) and *The Defeat of Youth* (1918), or the blasé cynicism and sensuality of *Leda* (1920) —the three volumes which contain his youthful verse—to the point where he writes *Eyeless in Gaza* (1936) is to watch a steadily growing seriousness of manner, and a deeper concern with the attempt to show the barrenness of contemporary values, and to present a positive ideal which will serve a disenchanted and hopeless world. The lighthearted satire on contemporary society found in *Crome Yellow* (1921) gives way to the equally lively, but more sensational and more daring, study of post-War disillusionment and immorality in *Antic Hay* (1923). In *Those Barren Leaves* (1925) a more earnest note enters in the discussions of moral problems. It was followed by his most successful piece of fiction, *Point Counter Point* (1928), which is technically of interest as Huxley's attempt "to musicalize fiction," and is even more striking as a mordant, unflinching picture of a disillusioned, frustrated society, in which the healthy life of the senses has been paralysed by the bonds of an inhibiting ethical code. *Brave New World* (1932) gives a satirical picture of what he imagines the world would be under the rule of science—no disease, no pain, but no emotion, and, worse, no spiritual life. Technically this novel leaves much to be desired, but it provokes much frightening thought. In *Eyeless in Gaza* (1936) Huxley's faith in the life of the spirit, which first became evident in *Those Barren Leaves*, again finds expression. Whole portions of the book, particularly toward the end, consist of little more than dissertations on moral themes. After settling in America, he produced two satirical novels in the witty, daring manner of his early works, though both have obvious links with his more philosophical books. These two, *After Many a Summer* (1939) and *Time must have a Stop* (1944), were followed by *The Perennial Philosophy* (1946), which stated his views on the importance of spiritual integrity directly and seriously.

Huxley's prime importance is as a reflector of the feelings of his age. As a novelist he has limitations; he has no deep characterization, and his novels are slight in plot, but, like those of T. L. Peacock, they provide plenty of opportunity for conversation and discussion. The subjects discussed reveal him to be a man of great knowledge and wide culture. He is, above all things, a satirist, whose tone can vary from jovial irony to biting malice, and the striking incisiveness of his satire springs from an easy, polished style, a great gift for epigram, a ready wit, and an alert mind.

In addition to his novels, books of philosophy, and verse, Huxley wrote a number of books of essays and short stories, among them *Limbo* (1920); *Mortal Coils* (1922); *On the Margin* (1923); *Jesting Pilate* (1926); *Essays New and Old* (1926); *The Olive Tree, and other Essays* (1936); and the striking *The Devils of Loudun* (1952), a reconstruction of a famous seventeenth-century witch-hunt.

GENERAL SURVEY OF THE NOVEL (1918–39)

1. The Novel as an Interpreter of Life. The disillusionment, cynicism, despair, and bewilderment in face of the crumbling of established moral values which characterize the post-War world are nowhere more clearly seen than in the novel, which still maintained its supremacy among literary forms. This very supremacy, combined with the elasticity of its form and content, inclined the inter-War generation to look to the novel for an interpretation of the contemporary scene. Of the serious novelists, some attempted to establish new values to replace the old; others were content to portray the complexities of inter-War life with no attempt at deeper purpose. A third group, which includes some of the most important writers of the period, found itself driven by this lack of generally accepted values to focus attention on the impact of life on the individual consciousness. Character, rather than action, is the interest of this group, character which it aims to present rather than analyse or explain. In the work of this group an interpretation of life is often implicit, rarely directly stated.

2. Experiments in the Evolution of a New Technique. The master of the pre-War novelists was Henry James; of the inter-War years the most significant writer was James Joyce. A comparison of their works will make clear most of the changes which came over the novel during our period. Basically the movement was away from the controlled, finished, artistic form advocated by James to a novel altogether more loose, more fluid, and less coherent, though none the less aware of its artistic methods and purpose. Impressionism gave place to an expressionistic technique, by which the novelist sought to present, not the outward appearance, but what he conceived to be the inner realities of life. In the attempt to approximate more closely to the underlying incoherence of life, the new 'formlessness' was deliberately exploited. The presentation of the 'stream of consciousness' (see p. 517), the use of the interior monologue, the detailed tracing of the freakish associations of ideas, and an allusive style were the chief weapons of the novelist attempting to write from within the mind of his character. From the exploitation of these techniques there developed a subjective novel of a type previously unknown. Discontinuity of time, and a complex and elusive progression based on the inter-weaving of recurrent motifs, replaced the simple, chronological development of plot, which, in its traditional sense, disappears almost entirely. The effect of the whole is closely akin to that achieved by the post-Impressionist painters. Apart from James Joyce, Virginia Woolf, and Aldous Huxley, others who experimented in this way included **Dorothy Miller Richardson (1873–1957)**, who devoted her whole career to a series of novels under the collective title of *Pilgrimage*. These describe by nebulous impressions the heroine's 'adventure of personality.' The author was one of the first to employ the 'stream of consciousness' technique; another was **May Sinclair (1865–1946)**, a prolific novelist in many different modes, whose novels included *The Life and Death of Harriet Frean* (1922) and *The Allinghams* (1927).

3. The Influence of Psychology. Before the War the rapid development of the science of psychology had already done much to deepen and enrich the study of human character in the novel, but its full impact was not felt until the inter-War period, when the works of **Sigmund Freud (1856–1939)** became a handbook for all interested in the study of personality. *Interpretation of Dreams* (translated 1913), *Wit and its Relation to the Unconscious* (translated 1916) and *Psychopathology of Everyday Life* (translated 1914) opened the way to the exploration of the vast fields of the subconscious and the unconscious, and thus encouraged the novelist's tendency to dwell more and more within the mind of his character. To the influence of Freud, as well as to the general breakdown of Victorian moral attitudes, must be ascribed the preoccupation with sex, which is one of the dominant features of the inter-War novel, while the psychoanalysts and Dostoevsky probably share the responsibility for the contemporary interest in morbid mental states. D. H. Lawrence,

James Joyce, and Virginia Woolf were among major writers whose work reflects strongly the influence of modern psychology. Others worthy of note who reacted to the stimulus of Freud and his followers included **Rebecca West (1892–)**, who wrote *The Return of the Soldier* (1918) and *The Judge* (1922); **Theodore Francis Powys (1875–1953)**, whose symbolic pictures of evil include *Mr. Tasker's Gods* (1925) and *Mr Weston's Good Wine* (1927); his brother **John Cowper Powys (1872–1963)**, author of *Wolf Solent* (1929) and *A Glastonbury Romance* (1932) and May Sinclair (see p. 522); **Wyndham Lewis (1884–1957)** was originally an artist. In *Blast* (1914–15) and *Time and Western Man* (1927) he violently attacked contemporary literature and writers, believing that the intellect was of greater importance than emotion or imagination. This attitude was the basis of his novels *Tarr* (1912), *The Childermass* (1928), and *The Apes of God* (1930). **Elizabeth Bowen (1899–1973)** combined a sensitivity for atmosphere and personality with skill in social satire; her work was largely devoted to the subtle emotions of love affairs in conventional middle-class society. Her best novels were *The Hotel* (1927), *The House in Paris* (1935), and *The Death of the Heart* (1938). Deep Freudian undertones are always apparent in the novels of **Dame Ivy Compton-Burnett (1892–1969)**, a supreme exponent of passionate crime set in a domestic background. Her plots are excellently constructed, though the action is very limited. She is a mistress of revealing dialogue, which constitutes her chief method of exposition, and her delineation of warped characters is of a high order. Her novels include *Brothers and Sisters* (1929), *Men and Wives* (1931), *A House and its Head* (1935), *Daughters and Sons* (1937), *Parents and Children* (1941), and *Elders and Betters* (1944). A writer whose complex study of uncertainty and inadequacy brought acclaim was the Australian **Ethel F. Robertson** (Henry Handel Richardson) **(1870–1946)**, author of the trilogy *The Fortunes of Richard Mahony* (1917–29).

Although a short-story writer, **Katherine Mansfield** (Katherine Beauchamp) **(1888–1923)** may be considered at this stage. She wrote of loneliness and insecurity, the idealization of a love usually unattainable, and the bitterness of reality. Because of the economy of her narrative and her use of selective, significant dialogue, she was one of the most important influences on short-story writers of the 1930's. Most of her small output was contained in *Bliss and Other Stories* (1920) and *The Garden Party and Other Stories* (1922).

4. The Lack of Popularity of the 'New' Novelists is not surprising:

their concern with the subtlest shades of motive and inner impulse called for readers as delicately sensitive as themselves, while the preoccupation of some with the morbid inevitably provoked distaste. Their techniques were not only revolutionary but complex, and made enormous demands upon the reader. Yet these writers have revolutionized the craft of fiction to an extent which suggests that the impression of their work is indelibly fixed upon all future writing of genuine significance.

5. Writers in the Established Tradition were inevitably more popular. While Galsworthy, Wells, and Bennett steadily produced new work, reputations were being made by novelists writing after the manner of an earlier generation, though they were all, in varying degrees, influenced by new developments. Among these 'traditional' writers were **Sir Hugh Walpole (1884–1941)**, whose numerous books include *Mr. Perrin and Mr. Traill* (1911), *The Green Mirror* (1918), *Portrait of a Man with Red Hair* (1925), *The Cathedral* (1922), and four lengthy novels of the Herries series, beginning with *Rogue Herries* (1930).

William Somerset Maugham (1874–1965) was born in Paris. At the age of ten he came to England; he was educated at King's School, Canterbury, and Heidelberg University, and worked as a doctor at St Thomas's Hospital, London. He began his literary career as a novelist and then turned to the drama, from which he made enough money to allow him to devote himself entirely to literature (see p. 550). During the 1914–18 War he served first with the Red Cross and then in the Intelligence Service. He travelled widely in Europe and the Far East, and at the outbreak of the Second World War was living in France. The story of his life there and eventual escape to England was told in *Strictly Personal* (1942).

Maugham's novels reveal him as a cynical cosmopolitan presenting life in an ironically detached manner which does not flinch in the face of the mean or sordid. A realist, with an intense interest in human nature, keenly aware of the contradictions and frustrations of life, he was a poised, finished artist, who wrote in a prose that was clear, precise, and simple. His experiences in hospitals provided him with the knowledge of London's poorer quarters, in which were set such early works as *Liza of Lambeth* (1897) and *Mrs Craddock* (1902). From his travels he drew the background of *The Moon and Sixpence* (1919) and *The Painted Veil* (1925). His best novel was undoubtedly *Of Human Bondage* (1915), a study in frustration, which had a strong autobiographical element. Among his other fiction, mention must be made of *Cakes and Ale* (1930), which dealt with genius involved with vulgarity that was full of happy life, and with deadly pseudo-intellectual society; and *The Razor's Edge* (1944), concerning the moral and spiritual emptiness of affluent America. He was a prolific writer of short stories, many of them set in the Far East and the Pacific; with highly professional skill, Maugham depicted relationships between the sexes and the unhappiness, even cruelty, resulting from them.

John Boynton Priestley (1894–), the son of a schoolmaster, was born in Bradford and educated at Trinity Hall, Cambridge. He is a novelist, critic, dramatist, and essayist, and during the Second World War he became well known as a broadcaster. Priestley's fame as a novelist was established by the popular *The Good Companions* (1929), a long story of the adventures of a touring concert-party. It showed all the friendly ease and ordinariness of Priestley at his best. It is, indeed, as a portrayer of the everyday life of the everyday person that he excels. His figures are clearly if rather shallowly drawn, and his style has an appealing ease and naturalness, though nothing of distinction. Among his other novels are *Angel Pavement* (1930), *Let the People Sing* (1939), *Daylight on Saturday* (1943), *Bright Day* (1946), and *Festival at Farbridge* (1951). Priestley is a talented essayist (see p. 561), while his literary criticism is to be found in *George Meredith* (1926), *The English Comic Characters* (1926), *Thomas Love Peacock* (1927), *The English Novel* (1927), and *Literature and Western Man* (1960).

Equally prolific and successful was **Sir Compton Mackenzie (1883–1972)**, who achieved fame with *Carnival* (1912) and *Sinister Street* (1913–14). From the last-named was developed the Sylvia Scarlett trilogy (1918–19). After the success of three novels on the Church—*The Altar Steps* (1922), *The Parson's Progress* (1923), and *The Heavenly Ladder* (1924)—there came a period of only partial success, despite the care he lavished on "Four Winds of Love" (1937–45). Late in life, while retired in the Hebrides, he began a new career as a humorist, with such pleasantly light novels as *The Monarch of the Glen* (1941), *Whisky Galore* (1947), and *Rockets Galore* (1957).

Others whose reputation requires that they be mentioned here are **Francis Brett Young (1884–1954)**, whose popularity rests on *The Black Diamond* (1921), *Portrait of Clare* (1927), and *My Brother Jonathan* (1928) and **Charles Morgan (1894–1958)**, author of *The Fountain* (1932), *Sparkenbroke* (1936), *The Voyage* (1940), and *The Empty Room* (1941). **Henry Williamson (1895–1977)**, shattered by his war experiences, wrote of youth and the countryside, e.g. in *Dan-*

delion Days (1922), and then produced fifteen novels, largely autobio-graphical—*A Chronicle of Ancient Sunlight* (1951–69)—illustrating the history of his time. His fame rests chiefly on *Tarka the Otter* (1927), an unsentimental account of an animal from its own point of view.

One should note those who wrote regional fiction, which, as has been stated earlier, proved so popular before the War. Among them were **Lewis Grassic Gibson** (James Leslie Mitchell) **(1901–35)**, whose novels of Aberdeen, collected under the title *A Scots Quair*, were published between 1932 and 1934; **Mary Webb (1881–1927)**, author of novels set in Shropshire, such as *The Golden Arrow* (1916), *Gone to Earth* (1917), *Seven for a Secret* (1922), and her best, *Precious Bane* (1924); and **Sheila Kaye-Smith (1884–1956)**, who wrote about Sussex in, for example, *Joanna Godden* (1921) and *The End of the House of Alard* (1923). In this context one must mention a hilariously effective parody of the worst aspects of the regional novel; this is *Cold Comfort Farm* (1932) by **Stella Gibbons. Walter Greenwood (1903–74)** depicted in *Love on the Dole* (1933) the miseries of Salford in the Great Depression; a picture of Yorkshire at the same time was found in *A Modern Tragedy* (1934) by **Phyllis Eleanor Bentley (1894–)**, but more popular was the romanticized country-town life in *South Riding* (1936) by **Winifred Holtby (1898–1935)**. The short stories of **Caradoc Evans (1883–1945)** attempted to use Welsh idiom as the basis of English prose-poetry; *My People* (1915) and *Capel Sion* (1916) vehemently attacked the bigotry and hypocrisy of his fellow-countrymen. More generous towards the people of Wales, but critical of their conditions of work, was *How Green Was My Valley* (1939) by **Richard Llewellyn Lloyd (1907–)**.

A historical novelist whose works have a striking authenticity —partly because he can write convincingly in the style of the period portrayed—is **Robert Graves (1895–)**, author of *I, Claudius* (1934), *Claudius the God* (1934), *Count Belisarius* (1938), *Sergeant Lamb of the Ninth* (1940), *Wife to Mr. Milton* (1943), and *The Golden Fleece* (1944). He raised considerable controversy by the views he expressed in two scholarly works on mythology, *The White Goddess* and *The Greek Myths*.

6. War Books. Another reflection of the disillusionment of the post-War generation is to be found in literature on the War itself, which began to appear once the catastrophe was sufficiently remote. *Undertones of War* (1928), by the poet **Edmund Blunden (1896–1974)**, was a magnificently underwritten exposure of ugliness and futility; more savage in his condemnation was **Robert Graves**, whose *Goodbye* *to All That* appeared in 1929. **Siegfried Sassoon** gave the disguise of fiction to his experiences (see p. 498), as did **Ford Madox Ford (1873–1939)**, but whereas the former gained instant success, the latter gained little credit for *Some Do Not* (1924), *No More Parades* (1925), *A Man Could Stand Up* (1926), and *Last Post* (1928). He was more influential as the founder of *The English Review* (1908–9), and the friend of many great contemporary artists. By contrast, *Death of a Hero* (1929) gave a most effective start to the career of **Richard Aldington (1892–1962)**. Other writers who found in their war experiences the subject-matter of literature were **C. E. Montague (1867–1928)**—*Disenchantment* (1922), *Fiery Particles* (1923), and *Rough Justice* (1926); **R. H. Mottram (1883–1971)**, whose fame derived from *The Spanish Farm* (1924), which was expanded into a trilogy during the next three years; and **Henry Williamson** (see p. 525) whose experiences were crystallized in *The Wet Flanders Plain* (1929) and *The Patriot's Progress* (1930).

7. **Satire**, which is found in the plays of Sir Noël Coward and Somerset Maugham, appears frequently in the novel. The fiction of Maugham is in the same spirit as his plays (see p. 550), with its irony and scathing wit. Two other satirists of the period must be mentioned. One is **Rose Macaulay (1881–1958)**, whose works include *Potterism* (1920), *Dangerous Ages* (1921), *Told by an Idiot* (1923), *Orphan Island* (1924) and *Keeping Up Appearances* (1928); the other is **Ronald Firbank (1886–1926)**. Aesthete, recluse, eccentric, he wrote brief novels consisting largely of fragmentary conversations among wealthy people and their parasites. Action is inconsequential, conversation is wittily spectacular, and everyone is highly unconventional. The best of his few novels are *Valmouth* (1919), *Prancing Nigger*—formerly called *Sorrow in Sunlight*—(1929), and *Concerning the Eccentricities of Cardinal Pirelli* (1926). *The Rock Pool* (1935) caused a furore because of its lightly disguised account of his friends in their futile search for trivial excitement, but its author, **Cyril Connolly (1903–74)**, will be remembered chiefly as co-editor with Stephen Spender of the literary periodical *Horizon* (1939–50).

8. **Escapist Novels.** As in all periods of great emotional and moral tension, there was in the twenties a demand for escapist literature, which was partly met by such light though imaginative works as *South Wind* (1917) by **Norman Douglas**; *Mr. Fortune's Maggot* (1927) and *The True Heart* (1929) by **Sylvia Townsend Warner**; *Memoirs of a Midget* (1921) by **Walter de la Mare**; and the two fantasies entitled *Lady into Fox* (1922) and *A Man in the Zoo* (1924) by **David Garnett**.

9. It is extremely difficult to categorize the autobiographical-novel-sketch comedies with tragic implications that are *Mr. Norris Changes Trains* (1935) and *Goodbye to Berlin* (1939), glimpses of the nightmare world of Germany in the thirties. These are by the poet-playwright **Christopher Isherwood** (see p. 557). There seems no connection between him and **Richard Hughes (1900–76)**, who has an international reputation on the strength of his three well-spaced novels. *A High Wind in Jamaica* (1929) is escapist, but it also contains one of his best portayals of children; then came *In Hazard* (1938), a sea story; and in 1961 *The Fox in the Attic*, which like Isherwood's books, deals with Germany, but during the political chaos following the First World War; it was planned as the first of a series but only *The Wooden Shepherdess* (1973) was added. **Leopold Hamilton Myers (1881–1944)** wrote of a semi-imaginary sixteenth-century India where events were both romantic and sordidly real, fantastic and horrifying, exciting and comic, all overlaid with the belief that evil was less corrupting than insincerity and lack of faith. Four related novels (1929–40) were republished in 1943 as *The Near and the Far*.

10. The growth of the American novel is one of the striking features of the period. Lack of space forbids a detailed survey, but one may say that, since the turn of the century, not only has the U.S.A. given encouragement and shelter to artists whose work met with opposition in this country, but Americans have been among the boldest so far as experiments in technique are concerned, and this is a period famous for technical experiment. The basis of most of their work was realism, the depiction of the contemporary scene no matter how unlovely, the exposure of corruption and lack of moral values in organizations and in people, the consideration of emotional crises and moral dilemmas at all levels of society, and the portrayal of the individual and the depths or heights with which he can be faced.

The most famous writer is **Ernest Hemingway (1898–1962)**, who published between the Wars *The Sun Also Rises* (1926), *Men without Women* (1927), *A Farewell to Arms* (1929), *To Have and Have Not* (1937) and *For Whom the Bell Tolls* (1940). For him violent action brings out the essentials of manliness, especially comradeship, endurance and the acceptance of danger as a way of life; in the world of Hemingway women are of little importance. Yet for all his concern with the harshness of reality, he was extremely sensitive to beauty. His stark, emphatic, often almost curt language influenced a whole generation of writers. **William Faulkner (1897–1962)**, author of *Soldier's Pay* (1926), *The Sound and the Fury* (1929),

Sanctuary (1931), *Light in August* (1932) and *Absalom! Absalom!* (1936) often deals with the poor and the deprived of the South; everywhere is depravity and the sense of doom. Each novel is an experiment in construction, and the language can become extremely complex. **F. Scott Fitzgerald (1896–1940)** is chiefly remembered for *The Great Gatsby* (1925), *Tender is the Night* (1934) and *The Last Tycoon* (1941). Like the characters of his novels, he frenetically sought after social and financial success, for ever hounded by the fear of being a failure or, worse, an outsider. He is considered to be the spokesman of The Jazz Age. However, it was **Sinclair Lewis (1885–1951)** who had the most immediate impact on the public. He showed the smug complacency, philistinism and corruption of the commercial middle-classes in *Main Street* (1920), *Babbitt* (1923) and *Arrowsmith* (1925); yet he was always inclined to exaggerate situations, and his satire was weakened by an affection for the very sort of people whom he exposed. *Dodsworth* (1929) even verged on the sentimental.

Others who greatly influenced the style and attitudes of English writers were **John Dos Passos (1896–1970)**, who in this period produced *Manhattan Transfer* (1925), *The 42nd Parallel* (1930) and *1919* (1932); **Theodore Dreiser (1871–1945)**—*Sister Carrie* (1910) and *An American Tragedy* (1925); **Erskine Caldwell (1903–)**—*Tobacco Road* (1932), *God's Little Acre* (1933); **James M. Cain (1892–)**—*The Postman Always Rings Twice* (1934); and **James T. Farrell (1904–)**—*Young Lonigan* (1932), *The Young Manhood of Studs Lonigan* (1934), *Judgment Day* (1935).

POETS

I. Gerard Manley Hopkins (1844–89)

Hopkins is a unique figure in the history of English poetry. His work was not generally available until 1918, when his friend Bridges published a slim volume of poems culled from his letters and manuscripts. But for Bridges, it is likely that this fine poetry, which has exercised a great influence on later poets, would never have been known. Hopkins, a convert in his twenty-second year to Catholicism, is not only the first really great religious poet in English since Milton, but he was the creator of an original poetic medium, so much his own that a major modern critic has doubted whether it can ever be used by another writer. No modern poet has been the the centre of more controversy or the cause of more misunderstanding.

1. His Life. The son of a cultured and deeply artistic family, Hopkins was educated at Highgate (1854) and Balliol College, Oxford, which he entered as an Exhibitioner in 1863. Both at school and University he gained the highest academic distinctions. In 1866 after severe mental conflict, and in the face of strong family opposition, he entered the Roman Catholic Church, and in 1867 was an assistant at the Oratory School, Birmingham, then in charge of John Henry (later Cardinal) Newman. A year later he had decided to join the Jesuit novitiate, and, after a long and exhaustive training, he was ordained in 1877. Four years of preaching in various parts of the country were followed (1882–84) by a period in which he taught Latin and Greek at Stonyhurst. In 1884 he received the Chair of Greek at the Royal University of Ireland, Dublin, a post he held until his death.

About the effect on his poetry of his entry into the Jesuit Order, controversy has raged. Some have maintained that it led to the stunting of his poetic development, almost to sterility, others that the Jesuit discipline resolved his earlier inner conflicts, and deepened and intensified his emotional experiences. But it is indisputable that the decision of 1868 was the most vital of his artistic life, and an understanding of the religious discipline to which he submitted himself is essential to a full appreciation of his poetry. Unfortunately, his poetic technique has caused as much controversy as his life, with the result that he has been seen either as a priest-philosopher or as a technical innovator. A true appreciation of his work must be based on a recognition of the fundamental wholeness of his life and writings.

2. His Poetry. While still at school Hopkins was already writing poetry expressing his intense appreciation of natural beauty in a sensuous, Keatsian manner which has something of the rich vividness of his later work. At Oxford, where he was thrown into the midst of the religious conflicts of the 1860's, an ascetic streak in his make-up became more apparent, and the fragments of his Oxford verse which remain show a considerable chastening of his enthusiasm for the riches of nature. The controversies with which he was surrounded brought to a head his own inner conflict; the result was his conversion. In 1868, before joining the Jesuits, he burnt all the poems on which he could lay hands, feeling the sensuous writings of his youth and the very profession of poet to be incompatible with the new disciplines he was about to accept. Such early poetry as we possess survived accidentally in manuscripts and diaries.

In 1875, when his long training as a Jesuit was reaching its end, he broke his self-imposed silence with *The Wreck of the "Deutsch-land,"* a great ode occasioned by the sinking in a storm of the *Deutschland,* which had on board five nuns, refugees from religious persecution. The poem is wider in scope than the title suggests. It contains the crystallized religious experience of his seven years' poetic silence, and has considerable autobiographical significance. In its eight-line stanzas the typical Hopkins technique is seen for the first time. Sprung-rhythm, counterpoint rhythm, alliteration, assonance, internal rhyme, coinages, and unorthodox syntax give to the poem a revolutionary appearance which led the editor of the Jesuit organ *Month* to refuse to print it after originally accepting it. But, if it is difficult in thought and unconventional in technique, it is full of brilliant passages, and has an artistic and emotional unity of the highest order.

Hopkins continued to write poetry until the end of his life, though his output was very small. From 1875 onward his writing was exclusively religious, and the ecstatic enjoyment of nature found in the sonnets of his early maturity is a sacramental experience. Nature is a manifestation of the beauty of God, a call to praise. Through his period of priesthood, in, among other places, Manchester and Liverpool, a growing concern with man is perceptible. The evils of the industrial system he saw as man's falling-off from God, his rejection of the grace won for him by Christ. *Felix Randal* is typical of his warm sympathy with men and his concern with their souls. But the deepest and most intensely personal of his poems belong to his Dublin period (1884–89). Whatever the cause, Hopkins then passed through a period of intense depression, which is movingly revealed in the sonnets of 1884–85. In their passionate, direct simplicity they stand apart from most of Hopkins's work, and they have been described as his greatest poems. His defiant refusal to capitulate to this despair is to be seen in *Carrion Comfort*:

> Not, I'll not, carrion comfort, Despair, not feast on thee;
> Not untwist—slack they may be—these last strands of man
> In me or, most weary, cry *I can no more.* I can;
> Can something, hope, wish day come, not choose not to be.
> But ah, but O thou terrible, why wouldst thou rude on me
> Thy wring-world right foot rock? lay a lionlimb against me? scan
> With darksome devouring eyes my bruisèd bones? and fan,
> O in turns of tempest, me heaped there; me frantic to avoid thee
>   and flee?
>   Why? That my chaff might fly; my grain lie, sheer and clear.

Nay in all that toil, that coil, since (seems) I kissed the rod,
Hand rather, my heart lo! lapped strength, stole joy, would laugh,
    chéer.
Cheer whom though? the hero whose heaven-handling flung me,
    fóot tród
Me? or me that fought him? O which one? is it each one? That
    night, that year
Of now done darkness I wretch lay wrestling with (my God!) my
    God.

3. Features of his Poetry. (*a*) *His Love of Nature.* A sensuous
love of nature, based on a minute observation, is found in most of
Hopkins's poetry, especially before about 1878. His early struggle
to reconcile his obvious enjoyment of natural beauty with the
ascetic life, the Jesuit resolved in his sacramental view of natural
beauty. His great delight lay in the discovery of the *inscape*, or
inner pattern, which gave to each thing its distinctive beauty. His
feelings at the perception of this inscape he described by the term
instress.

(*b*) *His Use of Language.* One of Hopkins's most obvious idiosyncrasies is in his choice and use of language. He believed that
poetry called for a language distinct from that of prose, a language
rich in suggestion both to the senses and the intellect. His vocabulary is drawn from many sources, archaic, colloquial, and dialect
words all being used. He had a particular fondness for compound
epithets, such as "drop-of-blood-and-foam-dapple cherry," and for
evocative coinages. A full appreciation of a word may well demand
of the reader a knowledge of its derivation. At times the result is
obscurity, and this is increased by his deliberate distortion of normal
syntax, either to compel the reader's attention, or to give to key
words the stress they deserve. But, whatever the difficulties arising
from vocabulary, syntax, or compression of thought, Hopkins
is always precise in his use of words, and his poetry has the muscular
vitality of expression of the true Shakespearian tradition.

(*c*) *His Rhythmic Patterns.* Hopkins's most important experiment is with *sprung rhythm*, which appeared first in *The Wreck of
the* "*Deutschland*," and is based on the irregular verse of *Samson
Agonistes.* The basic principle of this attempt to break away from
strictly conventional patterns is that each foot contains one stress,
possibly, but not necessarily, followed by any number of unstressed
syllables. Hopkins felt it to be "the least forced, the most rhetorical
and emphatic of all possible rhythms." *Counterpoint rhythm* is the
use in two consecutive feet of a reversal of the predominant rhythm

of a line. Every rhythmic effect in Hopkins is the result of careful and deliberate workmanship, and so important did he consider a true understanding of his intentions that his manuscripts make use of some twenty symbols, rather like those of a musical score. Thus we have ″ or ‵ or ‵ to indicate heavy stresses, ◡ to indicate reversed feet, as in counterpoint, and so on. Unfortunately, he was not consistent in the use of these symbols, and, to avoid confusion, Bridges omitted from the 1918 edition all but the most vital. After *The Wreck of the "Deutschland"* he devoted much time to typically individual modifications of the sonnet form, which he used with the greatest freedom. A brief summary can do no more than indicate the nature of Hopkins's experiments, but it is important to add that the full import of rhythm in his poetry can only be gathered if it is read aloud after close and delicately sensitive study of its orchestration.

(*d*) *His imagery* is remarkable for its richness. His appreciation of nature, his reading of the great English poets, particularly Shakespeare, and of the Bible, are all evident. Often he shows that blend of the emotional and intellectual which distinguishes the poetry of the seventeenth-century metaphysicals (see p. 139). But, whatever their sources or affinities, the images of Hopkins's poetry are distinctively his own—always precise and vitally illuminating, usually briefly expressed, and often suggesting more than one possible interpretation.

II. T. S. ELIOT (1888–1965)

With the possible exception of Yeats, no twentieth-century poet has been held in such esteem by his fellow-poets as Eliot. During the 1930's his influence was enormous, and, if his pre-eminence is no longer so stridently proclaimed, he seems assured of his place among the great English poets who have directed poetic impulses into new channels.

1. His Life. Though he became a naturalized British subject in 1927, Eliot was born in St Louis, Missouri (U.S.A.). His family was of Devonshire origin, and its traditions were in commerce and academic studies. He entered Harvard in 1906, and, after one year (1910–11) at the Sorbonne in Paris, he spent a year at Oxford reading Greek philosophy. After a brief experience of teaching at Highgate School, he entered business (1916), and spent eight years in Lloyd's Bank in the City. At this time he was assistant editor of *The Egoist* (1917–19), and in 1923 began his career as editor of *The*

Criterion. Later he became a director of Faber and Faber, the publishers. Among the many literary honours bestowed upon him mention may be made of: Charles Eliot Norton Professor of Poetry at Harvard (1932–33), President, Classical Association (1944), Nobel Prize for Literature (1948), and Order of Merit (1948). At various times he received honorary degrees from twelve universities in Europe and America.

2. His Poetry. Eliot's first volume of verse, *Prufrock and Other Observations* (1917), portrays in contemptuous, and often wittily ironical, satire, the boredom, emptiness, and pessimism of its own day. The poet tries to plumb the less savoury depths of contemporary life in a series of sordid episodes. The irregularities of rhyme scheme and line length in his verse form, the pressure of his condensed and often vividly contrasted images, the skilful use of rhythmic variations, and the restrained power of his style distinguished Eliot as a gifted, original artist. *Poems* (1920) is in much the same mood, but, as often happens in Eliot, the verse form is completely changed, the irregular verse paragraph giving place to a four-line stanza rhyming *abcb*. The difficult monologue *Gerontion* in this volume shows Eliot's free adaptation of the blank verse of the later Elizabethan dramatists.

His much-discussed poem *The Waste Land* (1922) made a tremendous impact on the post-War generation, and is considered one of the most important documents of its age. The poem is difficult to understand in detail, but its general aim is clear. Based on the legend of the Fisher King in the Arthurian cycle, it presents modern London as an arid, waste land. The poem is built round the symbols of drought and flood, representing death and rebirth, and this fundamental idea is referred to throughout. Other symbols in the poem are, however, not capable of precise explanation. In a series of disconcertingly vivid impressions, the poem progresses by rather abrupt transitions through five movements—"The Burial of the Dead," "The Game of Chess," "The Fire Sermon," "Death by Water," and "What the Thunder Said." Throughout appears the figure of Tiresias, whose presence helps to give the work unity. Its real unity, however, is one of emotional atmosphere. The boredom of his earlier poetry gives way to a mood of terror in face of an outworn and disintegrating civilization, a terror deeply felt, even when hidden beneath the surface irony of some parts of the poem. The style shows a typical compression of clearly visualized, often metaphysical imagery, a vocabulary essentially modern, and a subtly suggestive use of the rhythms of ordinary speech. One of its greatest difficulties lies in the numerous allusions to out-of-the-way writers, and the notes which Eliot himself provided are often inadequate. But, in spite of its complexities and apparent ambiguities, the poem is a powerfully moving presentation of sterility and disruption. The following extract from "The Game of Chess" (though here the allusion is to *Antony and Cleopatra*) will give an idea of its modernity, its allusiveness, and its variety of style.

> The chair she sat in, like a burnished throne,
> Glowed on the marble, where the glass
> Held up by standards wrought with fruited vines
> From which a golden Cupidon peeped out
> (Another hid his eyes behind his wing)
> Doubled the flames of sevenbranched candelabra
> Reflecting light upon the table as
> The glitter of her jewels rose to meet it,
> From satin cases poured in rich profusion;
> In vials of ivory and coloured glass
> Unstoppered, lurked her strange synthetic perfumes,
> Unguent, powdered, or liquid—troubled, confused
> And drowned the sense in odours; stirred by the air
> That freshened from the window, these ascended
> In fattening the prolonged candle-flames,
> Flung their smoke into the laquearia,
> Stirring the pattern on the coffered ceiling.
>   .   .   .   .   .
> "My nerves are bad to-night. Yes, bad. Stay with me.
> "Speak to me. Why do you never speak. Speak.
>   "What are you thinking of? What thinking?
>   What?
>   "I never know what you are thinking. Think."

Poems 1909–1925 adds only "The Hollow Men" to his earlier work. The five movements of this short poem again treat of the hopelessness and emptiness of modern life. The level regularity of its short two-stress line, so different from the metrical variety of *The Waste Land*, is eminently fitted to its mood.

His next major work, *Ash Wednesday* (1930), is probably his most difficult. It marks the beginning of a new phase in the poet's development, in which he finds hope in the discipline of the Christian religion, though, as yet, the old outlook persists in his mind and constantly comes to the fore. Consonant with this new attitude are his use of medieval mysticism and allegory, his imagery from the Old Testament prophets, and the allusions to the offices of the Church. Obscure images and symbols and the lack of a clear, logical structure make the poem difficult. Its six parts are six impressions of a mental and emotional state. With less concentrated vigour than his earlier poems, *Ash Wednesday* is more lyrical in spirit, and its use of repetition, assonance, and internal rhyme gives it a musical suggestiveness which conveys much of its meaning long before its intellectual content can be fully mastered.

The thirties were devoted mainly to poetical drama and literary criticism, and *Four Quartets* (1944) contains his next and most recent non-dramatic poetry. The four poems in this work appeared separately: *Burnt Norton* (1936), *East Coker* (1940), *The Dry Salvages* (1941), and *Little Gidding* (1942). In them we become aware of the intensity of Eliot's search for religious truth, which leads finally to a new hope in the Christian idea of rebirth and renewal. The poems are again difficult, but this is now owing to subject matter rather than technique. The underlying emotional experiences are not only complex but difficult to communicate, and it is better to try to grasp the general sense of the whole before attempting a detailed analysis of thought content. The main theme of this deeply serious meditation is the consideration of Time and Eternity; other themes are Eliot's exploration of the artistic consciousness, and of the potentialities and significance of words. There is no clearly traceable central thought sequence, but, as one poem follows another, we see the poet groping his way toward truth, and it is significant that each poem in turn is easier of comprehension. The mood of the poems is one of restrained but deeply emotional contemplation. Their general tone is mellower and the underlying experiences more varied. The thought is closely woven, but the style is less involved. There is the same precision of language, but less allusiveness than in *The Waste Land*, though again the precise significance of his symbols is difficult to determine. As the title *Four Quartets* suggests, each poem is built on a musical pattern; it has five movements, in which the themes stated in the first are developed through variations to a resolution in the last, and the inner structure of all four poems is very similar. The accentual verse, which he began to use in *The Hollow Men*, is now seen in its most flexible form.

3. His Drama. He wrote seven dramas, the fragment, *Sweeney Agonistes* (1926–27), *The Rock* (1934), *Murder in the Cathedral* (1935), *The Family Reunion* (1939), *The Cocktail Party* (1949), *The Confidential Clerk* (1953), *The Elder Statesman* (1958). They contain some of the best dramatic poetry since the Elizabethans, and mark definite stages in Eliot's emotional growth, yet mostly lack the essential qualities of drama. *Sweeney Agonistes*, in the mood of his earlier poetry, has little dramatic conflict or character development, and is mainly of interest for its development of the accentual verse of his later works. The main interest of his pageant play, *The Rock*, lies in the fine choruses and Eliot's concern with religious matters. In *Murder in the Cathedral* some drama is to be found in the moving speeches of the Chorus of the women of Canterbury, in whom a profoundly felt change does take place, but there is also the inner conflict in Becket, and the confrontation of Church and State. In *The Family Reunion* and in *The Cocktail Party* the characters are modern. These plays offer an interesting parallel with *Four Quartets*, in that all three works are concerned with the theme of rebirth and regeneration. *The Confidential Clerk* (1953) is a thought-provoking play which contains, under its surface wit and comedy, serious consideration of such questions as the nature of identity and the effects of heredity, and which underlines the importance of coming to grips with one's true self.

4. His Prose. Eliot's first collection of essays, *The Sacred Wood*, appeared in 1920, but the greater part of his prose work belongs to the 1930's. His main concern is literary criticism, though *The Idea of a Christian Society* (1939) is a significant indication of the direction of his development. The greatest critic since Matthew Arnold, Eliot may claim to rank among the greatest in English. Among the more frequently stated of his fundamental ideas are: the essential oneness of the Western literary tradition and its influence on the modern writer; the importance of poetic form and its ability to convey meaning through the feelings as much as through the mind; the need for the poet to reduce to universal significance his individual experiences. Eliot's prose style is remarkable for its compact lucidity and precision. Among his prose works mention may be made of the following: *For Lancelot Andrewes* (1928), *Selected Essays 1917–1932* (1932), *The Use of Poetry and the Use of Criticism* (1933), *Elizabethan Essays* (1934), *After Strange Gods* (1934), *Points of View* (1941), and *What is a Classic?* (1945).

5. Features of his Poetry. (*a*) The most immediate impression made by Eliot's verse is its *difficulty*. The nature and cause of this difficulty have changed during his career. In his earlier poetry the obscurity seemed to result from a technique deliberately cultivated. A condensed and often oblique expression, in which necessary links were frequently omitted, Eliot acquired from the French Symbolistes, and his admiration of Pound and the Imagist theories strengthened this. Demanding a great deal of his reader, the early Eliot was extremely allusive, and deliberately vague or ambiguous in his use of symbols. The resulting difficulty was by many of his admirers exalted into a merit. The difficulty of the later poetry springs from the nature of his subjects—states of mind and experiences incapable of precise formulation and therefore difficult to communicate. A deliberate loosening of his style, and a reduction in the number of out-of-the-way allusions, have made him easier to follow, but in *Four Quartets* there is still much difficulty, and his meaning is often sensed through the rhythms and music of his verse before it is mastered by the mind.

(b) *His Imagery.* A close study of Eliot's imagery is essential to any comprehension of his work. Like the Imagists, he is always concrete, and his pictures are clearly realized and based on close and accurate observation. Many images, such as those of the sea, appear time and again with different effects, and in *Four Quartets* the development of the poem can best be traced in the changing significance of recurrent images. Eliot shows a particular fondness for the metaphysical conceit with its subtle blend of emotion and intellect.

OTHER POETS

1. Wystan Hugh Auden (1907–1973), the son of a York doctor, was educated at Gresham's School, Holt, and Oxford. On leaving the university he spent some time in Germany. During the Spanish Civil War he served with the Republican forces in non-combatant capacities, and his interest in Spanish politics was reflected in one of his finest poems, *Spain*. He left England for the U.S.A. in 1939, became a citizen of that country, and lived there until 1972, save for the period when he was Professor of Poetry at Oxford.

Though still a young man, he was accepted as a leading poet, and one whose influence was felt in much contemporary verse. It has been said that he merely followed the fashion; rather, in his day he set the fashion. He came under the influence of Hopkins and Eliot, and, like the latter, he was deeply aware of the hollowness of a disintegrating civilization during 'A time of crisis and dismay', to quote his own words. But, unlike Eliot, Auden found his solution to the world's problems in left-wing political ideologies. A spokesman of the masses (whom he contemplated with warm understanding, compassion, and deep insight), Auden showed clearly in his early poetry a faith in violent social upheaval as a means to a better order. Yet he was outspokingly anti-Romantic, and, like others in his group of writer-friends, stressed the importance of 'clinical' and 'objective' attitudes. At times he over-simplified issues for the sake of emphasizing his radical views, often he swept on in generalizations; but he had the ability to experience and express the spirit of the age, the questionings and hopes and dreads of a generation about to confront fascism. However, the frequent image of a lone wanderer in an empty landscape makes one consider whether Auden himself had any sure faith in the creeds which were supposedly his guides. His later poems revealed a new note of mysticism in his approach to human problems. The change resulted partly from his living in the U.S.A. away from the European war and partly from a new stirring towards Christianity; this concern with religion and the effect it had on his poetry may be compared with T. S. Eliot. The best poetry in this later style is to be found in *Nones* (1951).

He attempted, with considerable success, to prevent poetry from becoming exclusively 'highbrow', and found subjects among the everyday, often sordid, realities of a diseased social order. Modern influences strongly felt in his work were those of the psychologists, particularly of Freud; and Auden was profoundly conscious of sex and its importance in human relationships. His approach to everything around him was that of the intelligent intellectual, and he followed Eliot in his partiality for the poetry of the Metaphysicals, especially in their use of allegory and of detailed images unified into a pattern. It is therefore not unexpectedly that one finds much of his best work in exquisite and often movingly tender lyrics, songs and sonnets, where he is least concerned with sociological theories. Nor should one forget that he was a poet of landscape—sometimes the wild, empty hills and barren places, sometimes the industrial scene with its crowded figures; this latter, perhaps, offered him the greater attraction, for it showed Man at his finest as the inventor and the reshaper of Nature.

Technically, Auden was an artist of great virtuosity, a ceaseless experimenter in verse form, with a fine ear for the rhythm and music of words. Stephen Spender, himself no mean practitioner, described him as the most accomplished technician then writing poetry in English. Essentially modern in tone, Auden had a wide variety of styles—often he wrote with a noisy jazziness and gaiety, often in a cynically satirical vein, and on occasions he could be slangily 'tough.' But usually he showed a delight in elliptical thought and closely packed imagery, and, if his proletarianism sometimes led him into flaws of taste, it also led him to exploit more fully than any of his predecessors the riches and vigour of everyday idiom and vocabulary.

His best poetry is to be found in *Poems* (1930), *The Orators* (1932), *Look, Stranger* (1936), *New Year Letter* (1941), *The Age of Anxiety* (1948), *Collected Shorter Poems 1930–1944* (1950). His two anthologies—*The Poet's Tongue* (1935) with John Garrett, and *The Oxford Book of Light Verse* (1938)—greatly stimulated interest in popular literature which is a sincere expression of emotion even though it cannot be dignified by the name of poetry.

2. Stephen Spender (1909–77) was educated at University College School, Hampstead, and at Oxford. After leaving the university he spent two years in Germany and then moved to Vienna. A Liberal by family tradition, Spender joined the Communist Party and, like Auden, served as a non-combatant with the Republican armies during the Spanish Civil War.

A member of the Auden group, Spender was deeply aware of the sufferings and unhappiness of the inter-war period, and pinned his hopes for the future on left-wing theories. But his political faith was always involved in a struggle with his concern for the individual. The most introspective of the poets connected with Auden, he showed a tendency to look more and more within himself for his subject-matter. Most of his poems were short lyrics, and he was at his best when, shaking off his political ideas, he gave rein to his considerable lyrical gifts. He wrote most movingly of the pity of war and the emotions of a lover. Spender combined a subtlety of insight with an artistic sensitivity far greater than that of Auden, and had none of the latter's stridency. In his early poetry he showed awareness of the modern technological age and its machinery, but his was a sensuous imagination, and his appeal was more often to the feelings than the intellect. His best poetry is found in *Poems* (1933), *Vienna* (1934), *The Still Centre* (1939), *Ruins and Visions* (1942); *Collected Poems 1928–53* appeared in 1955. Spender's critical works include *The Destructive Element* (1935) and *Poetry Since 1939* (1947), but most interesting was his autobiography, *World Within World* (1951), which gave a fascinating picture of his generation and its attitudes.

3. C. Day Lewis (1904–72), a descendant on his mother's side from Oliver Goldsmith, was born in Eire, but while still in his infancy he came to England on the appointment of his father as vicar of Edwinstowe, in Nottinghamshire. He was a scholar of Sherborne

School and an exhibitioner of Wadham College, Oxford, and while at the university edited *Oxford Poetry* (1927) with his contemporary W. H. Auden. Until 1935 Day Lewis was a schoolmaster in Scotland and at Cheltenham College, but in that year he abandoned teaching for a full-time career in literature. After that he produced not only poetry but novels, detective stories, children's tales, literary criticism, and broadcasting material. In 1951 he received the Chair of Poetry at Oxford, to be succeeded in 1956 by his friend W. H. Auden.

Though he is usually associated with the school of Auden, Day Lewis wore his colours with a difference. He, too, found hope for a distracted world in left-wing ideals (see *The Magnetic Mountain*), but he is more balanced and common-sensical than many of the political poets of the thirties. In matters of technique he owes much to the poetry of Eliot and Hopkins, though he reacted strongly against the despair so powerfully voiced in *The Waste Land*. His early *Transitional Poem* (1929) is metaphysical in manner, closely packed and concise in idea and imagery, but structurally rather confused. *From Feathers to Iron* (1931), one of his best collections, is more personal than much of the writing which immediately follows it, and less obscure than some parts of *Transitional Poem*. It reveals a considerable lyric gift and that great love of nature which constantly appears in his writing. The best of his political verse appeared in *The Magnetic Mountain* (1933), where, more strongly under the influence of Auden, he adopts much of the latter's colloquialism and freedom of manner, and elevates the normal vigour of his verse to the point of stridency. In this volume we can see clearly his fondness for imagery drawn from machinery and similar aspects of modern life. In *A Time to Dance* (1935) Day Lewis shows narrative powers of a high order, while his sea narrative. 'The Loss of the Nabara', a story of the Spanish Civil War, in *Overtures to Death and Other Poems* (1938), has been hailed as one of the best sea poems for many years. Since the beginning of the 1939–45 War the mood of Day Lewis sobered considerably. He devoted much time to the perfecting of his technique, and he produced excellent work in *Word over All* (1943) and *Poems* (*1943–47*), published in 1948. These volumes consist largely of personal lyrics. The technical excellence of his latest poetry may owe not a little to the disciplines to which he inevitably submitted himself in his excellent verse translation, *The Georgics of Virgil* (1940).

We can do no more than list some of his prose works: *A Hope for Poetry* (1934), *Poetry for You* (1945), and *The Poetic Image* (1947) in the field of criticism; and the novels, *The Friendly Tree* (1936), *Starting Point* (1937), and *Child of Misfortune* (1939).

4. Louis MacNeice (1907–63), the son of an Irish bishop, was born in Belfast and educated at Marlborough and Oxford, where he distinguished himself as a classical scholar. In 1930 he was appointed classics lecturer at Birmingham University, and six years later he became lecturer in Greek at Bedford College, London. He travelled in Europe and America, and for a while in 1940 he lectured on poetry at Cornell University. In 1941 he joined the B.B.C.

Like Day Lewis, MacNeice was a member of the Auden group, but, unlike the others, he never embraced wholeheartedly any political creed, though he was as acutely aware as any of them of the failings of the inter-War years. He combines a keen, analytical observation of contemporary life with a strong common sense, and a very definite sense of humour, while his classical training has impressed itself upon the form and style of his work. A purer artist than Auden, MacNeice is acutely aware of the musical and rhythmical potentialities of language, and he writes with a control, finish, lightness of touch, and a structural sense which are often lacking among the members of his group, though, on occasion, he will, for effect, fall into a looser manner. His poetry is in the main didactic or lyrical, and it is in the short lyric that he has done his best work. Perhaps the unwillingness to adopt a positive attitude toward the problems of modern life, which has, in other ways, been an asset, deprives his work of that driving force which is essential in good didactic poetry. Even in his lyrics a veneer of casualness too often conceals the underlying emotions. In another medium MacNeice did valuable work as a pioneer in the use of poetic drama for broadcasting (see *The Dark Tower* (1946)). His critical study, *The Poetry of W. B. Yeats* (1941), is one of the best books on the subject.

MacNeice's poetry has appeared in the following collections: *Poems* (1935); *The Earth Compels* (1938); *Autumn Journal* (1939); *Plant and Phantom* (1941); *Springboard* (1944); *Holes in the Sky* (1948); and *Collected Poems* (1949).

Mention should also be made of his prose books, *Modern Poetry: A Personal Estimate* (1938) and *Letters from Iceland* (1937)—written with W. H. Auden; and of his drama in the Auden-Isherwood tradition, *Out of the Picture* (1937).

5. Dame Edith Sitwell (1887–1964), the eldest of the celebrated children of Sir George Sitwell, of Renishaw Hall, in Derbyshire, was born at Scarborough and educated privately. With her brothers, **Osbert (1892–1969)** (see p. 598) and **Sir Sacheverell (1897–)**, she edited *Wheels: an Annual Anthology of Modern Verse*, which appeared between 1916 and 1921 and revolted strongly against the popular Georgian poetry.

Like all the poets who achieved prominence in our period, Edith Sitwell was deeply conscious of the unhappiness and spiritual emptiness of the inter-War years, but, where the Auden school found its hope in politics, she sought to escape into the world of childhood and art. She shares with her brothers a nostalgic regret for the culture whose disappearance she was called upon to witness, and all her writing reflects her aristocratic background and outlook. With great verbal dexterity, much wit, and a jewelled brilliance of effect, her early poetry, as seen in *Clowns' Houses* (1918), *The Wooden Pegasus* (1920), and *Bucolic Comedies* (1923), creates a wholly artificial world from the dreams of childhood. She is essentially an artist, exploiting to the full the magic of language, ceaselessly experimenting with verse forms and patterns, and her technical virtuosity is most strikingly seen in *Façade* (1922). In a single word or brief phrase she can achieve a striking effect, and the vividness of her imagery and her love of rich colour contribute much to the charm of her work. She is particularly fond of describing the perceptions of one sense in terms of another (*e.g.*, a "pig-snouted breeze"). Often, however, her poetry seems to be made up of a series of more or less connected sense impressions, which, though striking in themselves, seem to lead the reader nowhere. During more recent years her verse lost much of its earlier brittleness, and the humanity which underlies all her writing became more apparent.

As a critic, Edith Sitwell tends, as her own poetry might lead us to suppose, to lay overmuch stress upon the patterns and technical skills of poetry, as though verbal artistry were all in all. None the less her sensitive analysis of the poetry of Pope in *Alexander Pope* (1930) did much to provoke a revaluation of the work of that unjustly neglected artist.

In addition to those works already mentioned, her publications include *The Sleeping Beauty* (1924); *Troy Park* (1925); *Collected Poems* (1930); *The Pleasures of Poetry* (1931–34); *Bath* (1932); *The English Eccentrics* (1933); *Aspects of Modern Poetry* (1934); *Street Songs* (1942); and *The Song of the Cold* (1945).

6. Ezra Pound (1885–1972). Of the Imagist poets (see p. 500) only Pound gained lasting fame, not only as a poet but as one who helped many other writers to achieve their best work. Born in the U.S.A., he lived in London from 1908 to 1920, then in Paris, and from 1924 to 1945 in Italy. His admiration of Mussolini resulted in his being charged with treason at the end of the War. Considered unfit to plead, he was held prisoner in hospital until 1958, a forlorn scapegoat for the sins of fascism.

He was always a centre of controversy because of his iconoclastic views on everything from poetry to economics (often founded on half-knowledge or a perverse determination to be different), but his influence on contemporary literature was exemplified by the homage paid to him by T. S. Eliot. Pound's translations from Italian, Provençal, Latin, etc., were far from accurate, but they recreated the spirit of the originals; he re-established the epigram as a verse form, strengthened by the influence of Japanese. To him poetry was the embodiment of melody, images, and provocative thought—basics of most good poetry—but they produced an 'originality' in Pound's verse which Eliot considered lacking in most poetry of the past century. *Hugh Selwyn Mobberly* (1920) was an arraignment of 'culture' (a word that Pound abhorred), the urge by writers "to maintain 'the sublime' in the old sense", and in retrospect can be considered as significant as—though less famous than—*The Waste Land*.

Pound's life in Italy was largely devoted to writing *The Cantos* which appeared part by part and were always in the process of being revised; eventually they remained unfinished. They were a vast survey of history from his own very limited and biased point of view; they were extremely erudite, highly allusive, and expressive of personal, often fragmented, experiences, in a compaction of images made all the more bewildering because of their references to foreign languages and literatures. When he was in prison awaiting trial, he was deprived of books; thus he was forced to rely on his own mind and personality for emotional sustenance. *The Pisan Cantos* (1948) which resulted may be considered his best; certainly they are the most attractive, because of their sympathy for humanity and the sheer beauty of their words. Pound's survey of contemporary society and its problems was published between 1925 and 1969; a very necessary *Annotated Index* came out in 1958 before the appearance of the last twenty-one *Cantos*. No matter how confused were Pound's political ideas, and despite the increasingly personal and elliptical language he employed, he was a poet till the very end.

GENERAL SURVEY OF POETRY (1918–39)

1. Poetry in the Post-War World. The hopes for a brave new world, so quickly dissipated in 1918, gave way to the disillusionment and despair which found their supreme expression in *The Waste Land* (1922) and *The Hollow Men* (1925). A new awareness of sociological factors enabled the writers of this period to perceive a disintegrating culture with no positive values to replace it. There was need for a new world, for a new outlook on life. As yet a political answer to this problem had not penetrated into poetry to any extent; it did not do so until the appearance of the Auden school.

2. Developments in Poetic Technique. The modern tension, so different from the complacency of the mid-Victorian period or of the Georgians, so much more realistic in its facing-up to life than the escapism of the decadents, clearly demanded a new poetic technique. As Bridges saw, the old poetic forms were outworn, and, partly influenced by Whitman, the new poets turned to free verse. The development of a new medium also owed much to the poetry of Hopkins (published 1918), with its sprung rhythms, complex verbal patterns, and disregard for normal syntax.

3. The 'Difficulty' of Modern Poetry. Such an emphasis on the evolution of new forms had obvious dangers, chief among them a lack of proportion which elevated form above substance, and a glorification of eccentricity for its own sake. The freedom of *vers libre* encouraged licence, and the pursuit of novelty increased the obscurity which came from the attempt to communicate complex states of mind. Much of the poetry of the period is admittedly difficult, and poetry was in danger of becoming an art for the initiated few. This trend was emphasized by the popularity of the metaphysical conceit, which accompanied the rebirth of interest in Donne and his fellows, the growing use of symbolism under the influence of Yeats and the French Symbolistes, and the imitation of the allusiveness of the early Eliot. On the question of difficulty Eliot himself wrote: "We can only say that it appears likely that poets in our civilisation, as it exists at present, must be difficult. Our civilisation comprehends great variety and complexity, and this variety and complexity, playing upon a refined sensibility, must produce various and complex results. The poet must become more and more comprehensive, more allusive, more indirect, in order to force, to dislocate if necessary, language into his meaning."

As examples of the more difficult poets of our period, we mention **Wyndham Lewis (1884–1957)** and **William Empson (1906–)**.

4. Psychology and Politics. Already in the twenties the new interest in psychological research had turned poets to a deeper investigation of the hidden impulses of man. In the early Eliot, for instance, we have that rather inconsequential revelation of the most secret thoughts of the character, which became known as the internal monologue. It was, in fact, in psychology and politics that the poets of the thirties, led by **W. H. Auden**, sought a solution to the world problems. **Karl Marx (1818–83)** and **Sigmund Freud (1856–1939)** inspired much of the underlying thought of the poetry of this decade. Auden and his followers, basing their thought on left-wing political ideals, took up the cause of the masses, whose lives they studied with genuine sympathy and often with striking realism. Some of them actively supported the Republican side in the Spanish Civil War, and their proletarian sympathies led to some rather cheap satire on contemporary England. In the poorer poets political writing deteriorated into mere pamphleteering; in the best we have a serious attempt to produce something positive and constructive.

Though Eliot and Hopkins were among their acknowledged masters in matters of technique, the poets of the thirties were strongly critical of the conception of poetry for the few. In an attempt to make contact with a wider audience, they abandoned the academic style for a more colloquial expression, and used the vocabulary, idiom, and rhythms of everyday speech with considerable force and vigour. They found much to admire, not only in the simple diction and rhythmical subtleties of Yeats, but also in the variety of his themes, and the fresh constructive outlook which lay behind them.

The impact of psychology on the poets of this decade is seen in the importance attached to sex in such writers as **Auden** and **Dylan Thomas** (see p. 583), and in the interest in the individual personality seen in such poets as **Spender**. Freud's revelation of the importance of the subconscious and his development of psycho-analysis lent greater depth to this study.

The work of the Auden school first gained notice in the anthology *New Signatures*, published in 1932 by **Michael Roberts (1902–48)**, a keen supporter of the new poetry. From 1933 onward it continued to appear in *New Verse*, edited by **Geoffrey Grigson**, a magazine which also published the work of such widely differing poets as **Dylan Thomas, George Barker,** and **David Gascoyne.**

5. Surrealism. Such a straightforward development as is here outlined is, of course, an over-simplification of a complex and constantly shifting situation, and it is now time to glance at some of the other movements and schools which arose in our period. About 1930 surrealism, which had been so strong on the Continent in literature as well as in art, was felt in this country. Its influence was limited and brief, and its only real advocate among established writers was **Sir Herbert Read (1893–1968).** But the escape from the complex problems of contemporary life which surrealism offered had its appeal for a number of young English poets.

6. The New Traditionalism. Many poets would have nothing to do with surrealism or experiment beyond certain limits; they were concerned with the expression of their individual emotional development and their reactions to their environment. Thus, with a basis of tradition, they concerned themselves with new attitudes, and with the place of old values in a new society. **Roy Campbell (1901–57),** a South African dedicated to movement, colour, adventure, vigour, published *Adamastor* (1930) and *Flowering Rifle* (1939). **Edwin Muir (1887–1959)** illustrated the rugged dignity and calm beauty of the Orkneys in *Variations on a Time Theme* (1934), *Journeys and Places* (1937), *The Labyrinth* (1949), and *One Foot in Eden* (1956). The gentle Scots cleric **Andrew Young (1885–1971)** wrote with an intimate knowledge of the creatures and plants of the countryside. Detailed observation and lucid phraseology were the hallmark of his poems collected in 1936 and 1948. The poetry of **Robert Graves** (see p. 526), like his prose, was only recognized as some of the finest of the period long after it had been published. He wrote in traditional forms, but his wide knowledge of the Classics brought about a conciseness of expression, a simple strength of construction, and a restraint that added power to emotion. All was tinged with irony. His concern was people, particularly those stirred by love or sex, and their sufferings as heart and mind sought to destroy each other. Collections of his poems appeared in 1927, 1938, 1946, 1959, and 1968. **Robert Frost (1874–1963)** was born in the U.S.A. and lived much of his life in New Hampshire. Not only was he the most popular poet in America but he became famous in England too, where his first two books had been published. Frost refused to have anything to do with verse experiment. He wrote in traditional styles about real situations, the countryside and landscape, people who had found contentment despite privation; he was particularly concerned with isolation and the failure to communicate. Though he often employed the dramatic monologue, usually in blank verse, he showed his true mastery in the lyric. Frost's moralizing could become prosy and sentimental, but at best he achieved what he considered to be the only aim of poetry—"It begins in delight and ends in wisdom." He believed in old-fashioned virtues and made them seem important; above all, he could sum up a situation, person, or mood in a phrase which held one's attention and yet by its simplicity could be understood by readers of all ages. From his books one may select *North of Boston* (1914), *New Hampshire* (1923), *West-Running Brook* (1928), *A Further Range* (1936), *Complete Poems* (1951).

7. The Georgian Survivors. Many poets of the Georgian tradition continued to write apparently unaffected by the new spirit of the age as they had been by the War. Among these poets were John Masefield, Alfred Noyes, Walter de la Mare, W. H. Davies, Gordon Bottomley, W. W. Gibson, and Herbert Palmer, to mention only a few. As they became increasingly isolated from contemporary interests, so their influence waned.

8. The Quest for Stability. The picture of the inter-War years is, then, one of continued uncertainty and experiment in an age well described in the title of Auden's collection, *The Age of Anxiety*, which was not, however, published until 1948. There was still no strongly established poetic tradition to compare in stability with that of the Victorian age, but at least the inter-War poets had passed through the despair of the middle twenties and had produced something like a constructive approach to life. In such an age it is natural to find a great proportion of didactic verse, but even in the work of those poets who devoted themselves most whole-heartedly to finding a solution to the problems of a perplexed generation, we find lyric poetry of great intrinsic value.

DRAMATISTS

1. Sean O'Casey (1884–1964) was born in Dublin, and worked as a labourer, living in the crowded tenements of Dublin's slums, which he describes so vividly in his early plays. After his early stage successes he made literature his career, and in 1926 received the Hawthornden Prize.

O'Casey's first play, *The Shadow of a Gunman*, was produced at the Abbey Theatre in 1923. Its setting is the slum tenements of Dublin, in their crowded squalor, and it is an unflinching study of the Anglo-Irish War of 1920, capturing well all the bloodiness and violence of the struggle and the dangerous intensity of the lives of the participants, his characters. O'Casey, as later, uses the device of a mouthpiece character, who here gives an ironical commentary on the events. The chief heroic character is a woman, as in *Juno and the Paycock* (1924), an infinitely more mature play, and his masterpiece. Again the setting is the Dublin slums: the time now the civil disturbances of 1922. It is a vivid and intensely powerful play, in which rich, almost grotesque humour covers yet emphasizes the underlying bitter tragedy. Three of O'Casey's finest creations figure here—the deeply pitying Juno, her worthless husband, the 'Paycock,' and his boon companion, Joxer Daly. *The Plough and the Stars* (1926), a tragic chronicle play dealing with the Easter rising of 1916, is equally realistic in its exposure of the futility and horror of war. There is the same blend of grotesque humour and deep tragedy, and once again O'Casey makes use of the mouthpiece character.

His next play, *The Silver Tassie* (1929), was refused by the Abbey Theatre and failed on the boards, though some have described it as the most powerful tragedy of our day. War is still the theme, now the 1914–18 War. O'Casey gives an impassioned and bitter picture of the footballer hero returning paralysed from the trenches. It is unflinching in its truthfulness, and the suffering in the play is intense —perhaps there is too much suffering and too little action. It is of particular interest because here O'Casey experiments with the mingling of the realistic and expressionistic types of drama. His introduction of a symbolic technique is seen in the blending of prose and rhythmic chanted verse, which gives tremendous power to the second act in particular. How far his experiments have, as has been thought, subdued his great gifts it is difficult to say, but his later plays *Within the Gates* (1933), *The Star Turns Red* (1940), *Purple Dust* (1940), *Red Roses for Me* (1946), *Oak Leaves and Lavender* (1946), and *Cockadoodle Dandy* (1949), do not have the intense life of his best three, though the magic of his language remains.

Juno and the Paycock, The Plough and the Stars, and *The Silver Tassie* marked O'Casey out as the greatest new figure in the inter-War theatre. His own experience enabled him to study the life of the Dublin slums with the warm understanding with which Synge studied the life of the Irish peasantry, and, like Synge, he could draw magic from the language of the ordinary folk he portrayed. His dialogue is vivid, racy, and packed with metaphor, and his prose is rhythmical and imaginative. He had, too, Synge's gift of mingling comedy with the tragedy that is his main theme. In O'Casey the mood changes rapidly. Comedy is seldom long absent, yet one can never forget the grim, underlying sadness. He draws what he sees with a ruthless objectivity and an impressionistic vividness of detail.

2. **Sir Noël Coward (1899–1973)** was a prolific writer whose versatility proved his bane. The failure to realize the promise shown in some of his early work must be partly attributed to the ease with which he could produce a commercial success. As a dramatist he began with light comedy—*I'll Leave It to You* (1920) and *The Young Idea* (1923). Then followed *The Rat Trap* (1924) and a group of plays which exposed the emptiness and triviality of the smart set, and satirized county society, the new rich, and conventional morality. *The Vortex* (1924), *Fallen Angels* (1925), and *Easy Virtue* (1926) made Coward notorious. He then turned to the more easily acceptable vein of the frivolous-cum-sentimental with *Bitter Sweet* (1929), *Private Lives* (1930), *Cavalcade* (1931), *Conversation Piece* (1934), *Blithe Spirit* (1941), *Present Laughter* (1943), and *This Happy Breed* (1943). His popularity rested on the brilliance of a sophisticated but rather shallow wit, blasé and cynical, which produced a dialogue of scintillating epigrams; the appeal to sentiment popular at the moment; the effervescent excitement which was the dominant mood of many of his later plays; and above all his superb theatrical technique. He made the most of all the possibilities of stage and actors, and the handling of some of his plays by such an expert man of the theatre as C. B. Cochran increased the popular appeal still further.

3. **William Somerset Maugham (1874–1965).** Between 1904 and 1933, when he finally abandoned the stage, because of failure of his bitter comedy *Sheppey*, Maugham wrote some thirty plays, often at the rate of two or three a year. Though by 1914 he had written more than ten plays, his most memorable, though not his most profitable, work belonged to the inter-War period. After the realistic tragedy of *A Man of Honour* (1903) he made his name and fortune with gay, light-hearted comedies, full of wit and epigram. Among them were *Lady Frederick* (1907), *Mrs Dot* (1908), and *Jack Straw* (1908). The last of these purely commercial plays was *Home and Beauty* (1919). Two years later appeared *The Circle* (1921), a true comedy of manners and his best play. *Our Betters*, which though produced in New York in 1917 was not seen in England until 1923, and *The Constant Wife* (1927) are in the same tradition. Maugham's temperament was ideal for comedy of this kind. A shrewd observer of life and a keen student of human nature, he was a highly intelligent man of the world, cherishing few illusions, and rarely admitting any trace

of sentimentality into his drama. His best plays are the ironical comment of a cynically humorous observer, aiming to present life as it really is. In many ways he reminds us of the Restoration dramatists. With the broadening of the themes goes the maturing of his dialogue, which gradually shakes off its early tinsel brilliance for a pithy, economical style, to which his verbal skill gives a consummate ease. His plays are expertly constructed; his early successes depended largely on the theatrical quality of his work. Maugham is an uneven dramatist, whose work shows considerable diversity of tone and mood. He offered realistic tragedy in *A Man of Honour* and the much better *For Services Rendered* (1932); the glitter of the early comedies; the true comedy of manners; and occasionally the stronger and more serious situations of *Cæsar's Wife* (1919), *The Letter* (1927), and *The Sacred Flame* (1928).

4. **J. B. Priestley (1894–).** Priestley has written more than thirty plays since he began with *Dangerous Corner* (1932). He has a wide range—comedy, farce, morality, social comment—and he has achieved great popularity; his interest in the time theories of J. W. Dunne (see p. 559) has led him to numerous experiments in construction, the best of which are *Time and the Conways* (1937), *I Have Been Here Before* (1937), and *An Inspector Calls* (1946). The last named is possibly his most interesting, for the unexpected time-shift is used to illustrate his humanitarianism and his disgust at social pretence. In 1939 he produced the stimulating but commercially unsuccessful *Johnson Over Jordan*, a modern morality play in which he uses the techniques of expressionism.

Priestley the ardent reformer, and Priestley the commonsensical, plain man, both appear in his dramas. His typically Yorkshire humour is part of the almost aggressive 'bonhomie' of much of his work. His characters are soundly drawn, the dialogue is pungent, and his plays are always good theatre. His chief lack is of poetic insight, which alone can make the greatest drama out of the metaphysical problems that engaged his mind in his experimental work. Among his more conventional comedies, each a well-made theatrical piece, are *Laburnum Grove* (1933), *Eden End* (1934), and *When We Are Married* (1938). In the 1940's he became heavily allegorical and symbolic, with a loss of dramatic interest, in *They Came to a City* (1943), *Desert Highway* (1943), and *The Linden Tree* (1948). This style of writing has been eminently suitable for his adaptation of Iris Murdoch's novel *A Severed Head* (1964), one of Priestley's few ventures into drama in the last two decades.

5. James Bridie (1888–1951), which is the pen-name of Henry Mavor, was born in Glasgow, where he was educated at the University and practised as a doctor until 1938. His interest in drama led him, at the age of forty, to begin his career as a successful and prolific dramatist.

Bridie's plays are a peculiar mixture of argument, philosophy, violent incident, wit, and whimsical fancy. The youthfulness of his spirit is revealed in his delight in romance, in a good yarn packed with incident, but his drama rarely lacks argumentative passages, the product of an irrepressible side of his personality. Character-study is probably his chief interest, and he is particularly successful when dealing with the Scottish types with which he was so familiar. He is a prolific writer—there are some thirty plays on a wide range of subjects—and his handling of his material has shown considerable versatility, while his typically individual methods of construction are illustrated in his use of such devices as the prologue, or the long-outmoded soliloquy. Sometimes a certain lack of inventiveness makes itself felt in the middle and end of plays which have good first acts, and he is not always a good craftsman. His dialogue, however, is apt, and is enlivened by a ready wit. Among his best-known plays are *The Anatomist* (1931), *Tobias and the Angel* (1932), *Jonah and the Whale* (1932), *A Sleeping Clergyman* (1933), *Susannah and the Elders* (1938), *Mr Bolfry* (1943), *It Depends What You Mean* (1944), *Dr Angelus* (1947), and *Daphne Laureola* (1949).

6. Eugene O'Neill (1888–1953) is the first American dramatist of international significance. The son of an actor, he spent his early years in a great variety of occupations. Journalism, gold-prospecting, acting, office work, and experience as a merchant seaman were among the many jobs which gave him that experience of real life which has proved so valuable in his plays. He studied drama at Princeton University, and was for a time at Harvard. He wrote his first play in 1913, and his earliest work was produced by the Provincetown Players. Recognition came quickly, however, and in 1920 he was awarded the Pulitzer Prize.

O'Neill began in the realist tradition, but abandoned it after *Anna Christie* (1922), a strongly realistic work dealing with the redemption of a prostitute. Since then he has experimented unceasingly with new techniques of presentation, new dramatic forms, and original dialogue. He is, indeed, a versatile dramatist of great originality. *Strange Interlude* (1931) illustrates his use of aside and soliloquy, by means of which the action of the play is carried on at two levels.

Other experiments are his revival of the chorus, his use of a highly stylized speech and of rather confusing masks. On occasion his originality leads to obscurity, and his audience cannot always be certain of his meaning, but he is a dramatist of immense force and powerful imagination, and his best plays show a real sense of theatre.

He is a serious dramatist, concerning himself with major issues of his time—religion, philosophy, psycho-analysis, and scientific thought are the basis of many of his works, such as *Dynamo* (1929), *Mourning Becomes Electra* (1931), and *Days Without End* (1934). Not infrequently he runs to great length—*Days Without End* is at least twice the length of the normal play, while his latest play, *The Iceman Cometh* (1946), contains ten acts.

O'Neill is by far the greatest exponent in English of the 'expressionist' drama, of whose aims and techniques more is to be said (see p. 557). Among his plays are *The Emperor Jones* (1920), *Beyond the Horizon* (1920), *The Hairy Ape* (1922), *Desire under the Elms* (1924), *All God's Chillun got Wings* (1924), *The Great God Brown* (1926), *Lazarus Laughed* (1927), *Ah! Wilderness* (1933), and a *Long Day's Journey into Night* (1956).

GENERAL SURVEY OF THE DRAMA (1918–39)

1. Conditions in the Theatre. In 1920 the English theatre was in poor condition. Of the serious dramatists of established reputation, Shaw had produced nothing since *Pygmalion* (1913), unless we include *Heartbreak House*, which was withheld from the stage until 1921; Granville Barker had written no original play for ten years, and not until *The Skin Game* appeared in 1920 did Galsworthy write anything of merit comparable with *Justice* (1910) and the plays which immediately preceded it. The demand for light, escapist entertainment for troops on leave had made farce, spectacle, and musical comedy supreme on the London stage, and their popularity was to dwindle but slowly while there was a Ben Travers (1886–) writing farces for such an accomplished team as the Tom Walls, Ralph Lynn, Robertson Hare combination, a Noël Coward able to produce work like *Private Lives* (1930) and *Cavalcade* (1931), and a C. B. Cochran (1872–1951) to stage spectacle as it had never been staged before. In the early part of this period the cause of serious drama in England depended almost entirely on a few enlightened individuals who were prepared to place their art before their pocket. Chief among them were Lilian Baylis (1874–1937) at the Old Vic Theatre, Sir Barry Jackson (1879–1961), working both in Birmingham and London, and Sir Nigel Playfair (1874–1934) at the Lyric Theatre, Hammersmith.

The arrival of the cinema constituted a new threat to the theatre. Its precise effect on the older form is difficult to determine. Certainly it has become the entertainment of the masses, though how far they would have patronized the theatre had the cinema never existed cannot be determined. Certain it is that the theatre considered, and still considers, the cinema as an immensely powerful competitor, and it is perhaps significant that to-day Entertainments Tax gives preferential treatment to the theatre. However that may be, the ability of the cinema to offer sensation, spectacle on a scale impossible in the theatre, and the thrill of the gangster film undoubtedly had a deleterious effect on a number of lesser dramatists, who, failing to recognize in the cinema a new art form, attempted to vie with it on its own ground. The result was the production of more lavish spectacles and of a whole stream of thriller plays. The best of these latter rose above the merely imitative, and one thinks of *The Ringer* (1926), by the prolific Edgar Wallace (1875–1932); *Rope* (1929) and *Gas Light* (1939), by Patrick Hamilton (1904–62); *The Fourth Wall* (1928), by A. A. Milne (1882–1956); and *Murder on the Second Floor* (1929), by Frank Vosper (1899–1937).

It is equally difficult to evaluate the effect on the commercial theatre of the development of broadcasting. On the one hand, potential audiences were undoubtedly remaining at home to enjoy drama with the least trouble and at the lowest possible expense. On the other hand, radio drama did much to interest a wider public in drama, and thus helped the professional stage, and at the same time it offered dramatists new opportunities.

More hopeful aspects of dramatic activity during the period under review are the growth of the amateur dramatic movement, under the guidance of the British Drama League (founded 1919) and the Scottish Community Drama Association, which has done much to stimulate interest in drama in all ranks of society, and the success of the Malvern Festival (begun in 1929).

2. The Decline of Realism. From 1890 to 1920 the pursuit of realism and naturalism had dominated the work of most of the important English dramatists, though for Synge and Shaw 'mere' realism had always been inadequate. By 1920 Yeats's dissatisfaction with that drama which was an objectively accurate portrayal of the surface of life was felt by the theatre-going public as a whole. It had had more than enough of realism, and the time was ripe for

change. Of the older dramatists, Shaw and Galsworthy continued in the realistic tradition; indeed, each wrote his best play in the immediate post-War years. But Shaw had always been a realist with a difference, and Galsworthy too was of a calibre to rise above the level of mere social photography. Nor were there wanting newer writers in this well-established tradition. We had **Clemence Dane** (Winifred Ashton) **(1887–1965)** writing *A Bill of Divorcement* (1921) and *Mariners* (1926), before she turned to light comedy; there was also **Allan Monkhouse (1858–1936)**, whose work has already been mentioned in connexion with the Manchester school (see p. 480); **John Van Druten (1901–59)**, who achieved fame with *Young Woodley* (1928), and further successes with *There's Always Juliet* (1931) and *The Voice of the Turtle* (1943); **Patrick Hamilton** (see p. 554); and **Walter Greenwood (1903–74)** and **Ronald Gow (1897–)**, collaborating with a dramatization of *Love on the Dole* (1934).

Even so, the movement from realism is the keynote of our period. The greatest new inter-War dramatist, **O'Casey** (see p. 548), though he bases his plays on an unflinchingly truthful picture of Dublin slum life, transforms his work into what is really poetry even before *The Silver Tassie*. Writers such as **J. M. Barrie** and **A. A. Milne** cater for the renewed demand for sentimentalism, from which not even the more realistic *Journey's End* (1929), by **R. C. Sherriff (1896–1975)**, is entirely free. Another interesting symptom of the movement away from everyday existence is the concern with the after-life manifested in such plays as *Outward Bound* (1923), by **Sutton Vane (1888–1963)**. But more significant than these are the main trends which we now go on to consider.

3. The Development of Comedy. In the twenty years under review comedy was undoubtedly the most popular dramatic form. The satirical, cynical work of Somerset Maugham, and the blasé sophistication of Noël Coward, caught exactly the atmosphere of the later twenties. Other comic dramatists of the period were **Frederick Lonsdale (1881–1954)**, whose *Aren't We All?* (1924), *The Last of Mrs Cheyney* (1925), *On Approval* (1927), and *The High Road* (1927) have not retained the popularity gained for them by their epigrammatic glitter; **Sir A. P. Herbert (1890–1971)**, who wrote two delightful comic operas in *Tantivy Towers* (1931) and *Derby Day* (1932); and **A. A. Milne (1882–1956)**, who shows some of the gentle humour, whimsical fancy, and sentimentality of Barrie. His best-known plays include *Mr Pim Passes By* (1919) and *The Dover Road* (1922). But, in spite of the popularity of comedy, there was not among the comedy writers of this period a dramatist of major stature. Of the two best, Maugham would seem to have had his heart in the novel rather than in drama, while Coward failed to make the best of the talent which he undoubtedly possessed.

4. **The popularity of the history play** was second only to that of comedy. Though Shaw had used historical themes since *The Man of Destiny* (1895), it may be claimed that the vogue of this genre in modern times began with the work of **John Drinkwater (1882–1937)**. He was educated at Oxford High School and Birmingham University, after which he spent twelve years in business. He was one of the founders of the Birmingham Repertory Company, by which his earliest plays were produced. His four short plays in verse were followed by *Abraham Lincoln* (1918), which, appearing at exactly the right time for the sentiments it expressed, enjoyed enormous popular success. The study of Lincoln, at once the statesman of vision and ideals and the homely family man, was interspersed with poetical choruses to produce an overall sense of dignity. Drinkwater tried but failed to copy this success with *Oliver Cromwell* (1921) and *Robert E. Lee* (1923).

There followed numerous history plays which achieved success on the West End stage: *The Man with a Load of Mischief* (1924) by **Ashley Dukes**; *The Lady with the Lamp* (1929) by **Reginald Berkeley**; *The Barretts of Wimpole Street* (1930) by **Rudolf Besier**; *The Venetian* and *The Rose without a Thorn* (1932) by **Clifford Bax**; *Richard of Bordeaux* (1932) by '**Gordon Daviot**' (Elizabeth Mackintosh); *The Brontës* (1933) by **Alfred Sangster**; *Viceroy Sarah* (1934) and *The First Gentleman* (1940) by **Norman Ginsbury**; and the delightful short plays by **Laurence Housman** on the life of Queen Victoria.

5. **The revival of poetic drama** is another development of the inter-War period which illustrates the dissatisfaction with realism and the tradition of naturalistic prose dialogue. Experiments in verse drama were made by a number of eminent poets, but their success on the commercial stage was very limited, though the plays of **T. S. Eliot** (see p. 536) have attracted considerable attention. Almost the only other success was that of **James Elroy Flecker's (1884–1915)** *Hassan* (1922), a highly coloured, Oriental play, lacking in characterization and dramatic appeal, but rich in imagery, which achieved a temporary popularity, perhaps due in part to the use it made of ballet and the music of Delius. The later plays of **John Masefield** (see p. 491) failed to achieve the level of the earlier *The Tragedy of Nan* (1909) and are almost unknown in the theatre,

and the same may be said of that work of **Lascelles Abercrombie** (see p. 495) which falls into our period. In his later drama **Gordon Bottomley (1874–1948)** frankly abandoned hope for poetry in the professional theatre, and designed his work for amateurs. In the thirties the verse plays of W. H. Auden (see p. 538) and **Christopher Isherwood (1904–)** achieved a certain *succès d'estime*, chiefly among those who sympathized with the sociological aims and political tenets of *The Dog Beneath the Skin* (1935), *The Ascent of F.6* (1936), and *On the Frontier* (1938). T. S. Eliot's *Murder in the Cathedral*, written for performance in Canterbury Cathedral (see p. 536), was followed in 1936 by *Thomas Cranmer of Canterbury* by **Charles Williams (1886–1945)**. But, as in the pre-War period, the real spirit of poetic drama was caught by one whose normal medium was prose. Even apart from his 'expressionist' experiments, we may say that **O'Casey's** work shows more of the genuine poetic fire than that of any of the dramatists here mentioned except T. S. Eliot, and over the latter he scores by virtue of his infinitely greater dramatic gifts.

In spite of the considerable experiments, however, it seems certain that the inter-War period was an age inimical to poetic drama. There was, however, an apparent need for something new in the way of form and medium, and the attempts to satisfy that need are our next concern.

6. Experiments Abroad and at Home. The reaction against realism was felt on the Continent before it was felt in England. By 1920 there was experimental drama being written in Russia, Germany, Czechoslovakia, Italy, and France. Important dramatists contributing to the new movement were **Luigi Pirandello (1867–1936)**—*Six Characters in Search of an Author* (seen in England 1922); and **Karel Capek (1890–1938)**—*R.U.R.* (seen in England 1923), Jean Cocteau, Georg Kaiser, and Ernst Toller.

Of the experiments, by far the most influential was 'expressionism.' 'Expressionist' drama was concerned not with society but with man. It aimed to offer a deep, subjective, psychological analysis, not so much of an individual as of a type, and it made much of the subconscious. For such a study established dramatic forms and methods of expression were inadequate, and the expressionists threw overboard the conventional structure in favour of an unrestricted freedom. Their dialogue was often cryptic and patterned, now verse, now prose, and was in every way as far removed from the naturalistic prose of the realist school as can well be imagined. Symbolic figures, embodiments of inner, secret impulses, were introduced on the stage in the attempt to make clear the psycho-logical complexities of character. Such a drama was, of its very nature, 'difficult,' and could hardly be expected to hold the popular stage in England for very long. Indeed, in this country the most extreme forms of expressionism were rarely practised. Dramatists as a whole responded very little to the new Continental ideas, and 'expressionism' may now be said to be largely a thing of the past. Of expressionist dramatists writing in English the most important was undoubtedly the American, **Eugene O'Neill** (see p. 552), while his fellow-countryman, **Elmer Rice (1892–1967)**, did write one play in this kind, *The Adding Machine* (seen here 1924), before turning over to realism. In England the influence of expressionism is to be seen in **O'Casey's** *The Silver Tassie* and **Priestley's** *Johnson over Jordan*.

A less sensational form of experiment is to be seen in the work of **James Bridie** (see p. 552).

WRITERS OF MISCELLANEOUS PROSE

1. Giles Lytton Strachey (1880–1932) was born in London and educated at Trinity College, Cambridge. He was a member of the 'Bloomsbury Group' and, as critic and writer, dominated the liter-ary world of the twenties. His reputation was made by *Eminent Victorians* (1918), a number of short portraits in which, with telling irony, an irreverent and malicious insight, and a keen eye for human failings, he established the style of modern biography and of 'de-bunking' the Victorians. It was therefore somewhat surprising to find him neglecting the opportunities offered by his subject in *Queen Victoria* (1921) and presenting a portrait in the main sympathetic; while *Elizabeth and Essex* (1928), by far his most popular though not his best work, revealed an unexpected weakness for romance. *Portraits in Miniature* (1931) found him back in the realm of the short character sketch in the style he had made his own.

Strachey combined a genuine sense of the past with a shrewd eye, a keen and ready wit; he strove to attain the elegance and precision of expression inspired by his admiration for French literature. He could allow his irony to spoil his judgment, but, if he sometimes presented a distorted figure, there was no disputing the fine sense of character which enabled him to create real human beings where had formerly been idealized models of all the virtues.

2. Scientists and Philosophers. The impact on inter-War literature of the work of **Sigmund Freud (1856–1939)** has been discussed in our survey of the novel. The period was also one of unprecedented popular interest in many branches of pure and applied science, a phenomenon undoubtedly connected with the rapid increase in educational facilities. Several names, other than those of H. G. Wells and Bertrand Russell, stand out among the writers of popular scientific works—A. N. Whitehead (1861–1947), mathematician and philosopher, and author of *Science and the Modern World* (1926), *Religion in the Making* (1926), *Process and Reality* (1929), *Nature and Life* (1934); Sir James Jeans (1877–1946), the astronomer, whose most popular works were *The Universe Around Us* (1929), *The Mysterious Universe* (1930), and *The Stars in their Courses* (1931); Sir Julian Huxley (1887–1975), who wrote *Scientific Research and Social Needs* (1934), *Evolutionary Ethics* (1943), and *Man in the Modern World* (1947); Sir James George Frazer (1854–1941), whose vast survey of primitive religious beliefs, *The Golden Bough* (abridged version 1922), influenced numerous writers; Sir Arthur Eddington (1882–1944), with *The Nature of the Physical Universe* (1928); J. B. S. Haldane (1892–1964), author of *Possible Worlds* (1927), *The Causes of Evolution* (1933), *Science and Everyday Life* (1939), and *Science Advances* (1947); Lancelot Hogben (1895–1972), who achieved fame with *Mathematics for the Million* (1936) and *Science for the Citizen* (1938); and J. W. Dunne (1875–1949) whose works, *The Serial Universe* (1934) and *An Experiment with Time* (1927), fascinated many writers.

3. **Critics and Scholars.** The spread of interest in literature, and the consequent increase in the numbers of literary works published, we have noted in the preceding chapters. Between the Wars this increase continued. In addition to the critical work of such practising artists as T. S. Eliot, two Cambridge scholars came to the fore in this period. The first, I. A. Richards (1893–), wrote *Principles of Literary Criticism* (1924), *Science and Poetry* (1925), *Practical Criticism* (1929); the second, F. R. Leavis (1895–1978), produced *New Bearings in English Poetry* (1932), *Revaluation* (1936), *The Great Tradition* (1948). Of the other critics who established or confirmed their reputations during the period, mention should be made of Sir H. J. C. Grierson (1866–1960), authority on the metaphysical poets, and author of *The Background of English Literature* (1925), *Cross-Currents in the Literature of the Seventeenth Century* (1929), *A Critical History of English Poetry* (1945), and a remarkably fine edition of the works of Donne; of Sir E. K. Chambers (1866–1954), who followed his *The Mediæval Stage* (1903) with the brilliant *The Elizabethan*

Stage (1923), *Shakespeare, a Survey* (1925), and *English Literature at the Close of the Middle Ages* (1945).

The rapid growth of Shakespeare studies continued unabated, and new names which became familiar in this field included those of **G. B. Harrison, John Palmer, Wilson Knight,** and **H. B. Charlton.**

4. **Translators.** Popular interest in English literature was accompanied by a growing desire to know something of the literature of other countries. Three names stand out among the many translators who tried to satisfy this demand. **Sir Gilbert Murray (1866–1957),** authority on the Greek drama, translated into prose and verse many of the plays of Ancient Greece, and his translations have been presented on the stage with striking success. Most of his work appeared before our period begins, but its popularity continues to grow. The translations from the Russian of **Constance Garnett** established the works of Turgeniev, Tolstoy, Dostoevsky, and Chekhov as part of the literary background of Englishmen of culture. It is convenient to include at this point our third name—**Arthur Waley (1889–1966),** who produced numerous excellent verse translations from the Chinese.

5. **Travellers.** The taste for travel literature did not abate in the slightest during the inter-War years. Among numerous ephemeral 'pot-boilers' appeared work of greater merit and interest from the pen of the almost legendary **T. E. Lawrence (1888–1935)** in *The Seven Pillars of Wisdom* (1926); from **H. V. Morton,** author of *In the Steps of the Master* (1934), *In the Steps of St Paul* (1936), and the books *In Search of* England, Scotland, Wales, etc.; from **Freya Stark,** who wrote the popular *The Valleys of the Assassins* (1934), *A Winter in Arabia* (1940), *East is West* (1945), *Perseus in the Wind* (1948), and *Traveller's Prelude* (1950). Two other travel books deserve mention: *Brazilian Adventure* (1933) by Peter Fleming, and *South Latitude* (1938) by F. O. Ommanney.

6. **Biographers.** The work of Lytton Strachey undoubtedly gave an impetus to the writing of historical biography in the period under review. Second in stature to Strachey was probably **Philip Guedalla (1889–1944),** whose *Palmerston* (1926), *The Duke* (1931), and *The Two Marshals* (1943) achieved considerable popular success. **Sir Winston Churchill** (see p. 598) used the period when he was in the political shadows to write *The World Crisis 1911–1918* (1923–31), *My Early Life* (1930), and *Marlborough* (1933–38), all of which exhibited his flair for dramatizing history to make it as readable as fiction. To select among the other biographers is a thankless task,

but names which at once leap to mind are those of **Sir Arthur Bryant, John Buchan, A. F. Pollard, J. E. Neale**, and **Peter Quennell**, a brief list which omits the names of the authors of many fine 'lives.' In fact, if we include in this section autobiography, it is probably true to say that between the Wars no other form of non-fiction was more popular than this. It is also significant that the biographies and autobiographies which achieved success were not only those of national and international figures. Typical of the times were *Testament of Youth* (1933) by **Vera Brittain (1896–1970)**, a tribute to her friend Winifred Holtby; *The Journal of a Disappointed Man* (1919) by **W. N. P. Barbellion** (Bruce Frederick Cummings) **(1889– 1919)**; *Confessions and Impressions* (1930) by **Ethel Mannin (1900–)**; and *Twenty-Five* (1926) by **Beverley Nichols (1899–)**. One cannot, however, omit the picture of eighteenth-century England provided by James Woodforde in his newly discovered *The Diary of a Country Parson* (1924–31), and of nineteenth-century rural life in another discovery, *Kilvert's Diary* (1938).

7. Historians. Of the growth of historical biography we have treated briefly above. It was but one aspect of a remarkable interest in history which distinguishes this age. Among historians whose work has had a success other than with specialist students the greatest is probably **G. M. Trevelyan (1876–1962)**, author of *England under the Stuarts* (1904), *A History of England* (1926), *Blenheim* (1930), and *English Social History* (1944). *A History of Europe* (1935), by **H. A. L. Fisher (1865–1940)**, and *Religion and the Rise of Capitalism* (1926), by **R. H. Tawney (1880–1962)** were two single works of stature sufficient on their own to place their authors among the great modern historians. A more prolific author was **G. G. Coulton (1858– 1947)**, whose many works on the Middle Ages include *Five Centuries of Religion* (1923–28) and *Medieval Panorama* (1938). *A History of Everyday Things in England* (1933) by **Marjorie** and **C. H. B. Quennell** was a landmark in social history, and in economic history the most influential work was probably *The Economic Consequences of the Peace* (1919) by **Lord Keynes.**

8. Essayists. The popularity of the essay continued undiminished. All the essayists mentioned in the preceding chapter continued to publish during the inter-War years, and, of the writers who achieved fame mainly in other media, the following wrote essays: **A. A. Milne** —*Not that it Matters* (1919), *If I May* (1920); **J. B. Priestley**— *I for One* (1923), *Open House* (1927), *Apes and Angels* (1928), *The Balconinny and other Essays* (1929), and *Self-selected Essays* (1932);

Virginia Woolf—*The Death of the Moth* (1942), and *The Moment* (1947); **Aldous Huxley**—*Along the Road* (1925), *Essays New and Old* (1926), *Do What You Will* (1929), *Holy Face and Other Essays* (1929), and *Music at Night* (1931). A new name which came to the fore after 1918 was that of **Robert Lynd (1879–1949)**, journalist, and author of easy, witty essays which gained enormous popularity. Among his collections are *The Pleasures of Ignorance* (1921), *Selected Essays* (1923), *The Little Angel* (1926), and *It's a Fine World* (1930).

9. Pioneer Magazines. The importance of artistic and literary magazines in the evolution of new artistic ideals and standards is particularly great during this period. Among the more influential were *The English Review, The Egoist, The Criterion, The Athenæum, Scrutiny,* and *Rhythm.* None of them can be said to have found 'popular' approval, but their influence was out of all proportion to their limited circulation. Unfortunately, few of them survived for long, and of the few some were forced to close down owing to material difficulties arising from the shortages of the Second World War.

CHAPTER XIV

THE MID-TWENTIETH CENTURY

1. THE NOVEL

The uncertainty of the War- and post-War years is reflected in the concern of many novelists about the disintegration of society, and their lack of positive optimism, while the frequency with which violence and sadism appear as themes is not surprising in a world grown accustomed to the thought of genocide, global conflict, and nuclear destruction.

However, many of the younger generation of writers are involved in the new psychological problems arising from the bizarre and contradictory nature of an affluent society which is discontented with itself, and yet is interested chiefly in retaining or acquiring material comforts. A mixture of realism, cynicism, dark comedy, shrewd comment, and satire is used to express their search for stability and basic values. Stark individualism is often the essence of characterization; novelists are not infrequently interested in the individual's flight from an environment with which he cannot cope, or his attempts to find satisfaction by abandoning selfishness for love, service, and even sacrifice. The future is rarely clear; happiness is often the discovery of some small assurance amid an uncertain and even incomprehensible environment.

Because of technological advances, space exploration, and the threat of nuclear and germ warfare, there has been a tremendous increase in science fiction—novels about the future on other planets, or on an earth catastrophically altered. The public has preferred *The Day of the Triffids*, *The Kraken Wakes*, *The Midwich Cuckoos*, and *The Outward Urge*, by **John Wyndham** (J. B. Harris) **(1903–69)**, but S–F devotees think highly of Brian W. Aldiss, Fred Hoyle, Ray Bradbury, J. G. Ballard, Arthur C. Clarke, and Isaac Asimov.

The contemporary English novel has been affected to an inestimable extent by three entirely new influences.

Never before have novels from the U.S.A. been so widely read. Many of these have been characterized by detailed realism, lack of reticence, brutality, disillusion, and criticism of the national and international scene; they have dealt in a penetrating manner with the frustrations and emotional storms largely caused by urban-commercial life.

Outstanding writers much admired in England include **Henry Miller (1891–)**, whose *Tropic of Cancer* (1931) has only recently become available to the general public, and whose latest claim to fame rests on *The Rosy Crucifixion* trilogy (1949–60); **John Steinbeck (1902–68)**, *The Grapes of Wrath* (1939), *Cannery Row* (1945), *East of Eden* (1952); **Nelson Algren (1909–)**, *The Man with the Golden Arm* (1949) and *A Walk on the Wild Side* (1956); **Bernard Malamud (1914–)**, *The Natural* (1952), *The Assistant* (1957), *The Fixer* (1966); **Saul Bellow,** born in Canada **(1915–)**, *The Adventures of Augie March* (1953), *Henderson the Rain King* (1959), *Herzog* (1964); **Carson McCullers (1917–67)**, *The Heart is a Lonely Hunter* (1940), *The Member of the Wedding* (1946), *Clock without Hands* (1961); **Jerome David Salinger (1919–)**, *The Catcher in the Rye* (1951), *Raise High the Roofbeam, Carpenter* (1963); **James Jones (1921–)**, *From Here to Eternity* (1951); **Jack Kerouac (1922–69)**, *On the Road* (1957), and *The Dharma Bums* (1959); **Norman Mailer (1923–)**, *The Naked and the Dead* (1948), *The Deer Park* (1955); **James Baldwin (1924–)**, *Go Tell It on the Mountain* (1953), *Another Country* (1962), *No Name in the Streets* (1971); **Truman Capote (1924–)**, *Other Voices, Other Rooms* (1948), *The Grass Harp* (1951), *Breakfast at Tiffany's* (1958); **John Barth (1930–)**, *The Sot-Weed Factor* (1960), *Giles Goat-Boy* (1966); **John Updike (1932–)**, *Rabbit, Run* (1960), *Couples* (1968); and **V. S. Naipaul** from Trinidad **(1932–)**, *The Mystic Masseur* (1957), *A House for Mr Biswas* (1961), and *The Mimic Man* (1967). Nor can one ignore the impact of particular novels which not only were best-sellers but literary achievements of note—for example, *Invisible Man* (1952) by Ralph Ellison; *Lolita* (1955) by the naturalized Russian Vladimir Nabokov; *To Kill a Mockingbird* (1960) by Harper Lee; *Catch-22* (1961) by Joseph Heller; and *The Pawnbroker* (1962) by Edward Lewis Wallant.

In addition to the flood of American fiction, novels translated from foreign languages are available in large numbers, and have therefore influenced contemporary writers. The effect of Kafka, Mann, and Gide has continued over many years, but a later generation of writers is making itself felt—men like Günter Grass, Heinrich Böll, Alberto Moravia, the Russians Pasternak and Solzhenitsyn, Jean Genet, and the all-important existentialists from France—Jean-Paul Sartre, Albert Camus, and Simone de Beauvoir.

This treasury of novels has been made available chiefly because of the revolution in publishing. Writers today enjoy a larger public and wield a vaster power because of the new-style paperback volume. This dates from the issue of ten sixpenny books by Penguin in 1935. Aided by the insatiable wartime demand, paperbacks have become an essential part of most people's leisure. Bookshops are no longer the only means of distribution; the books themselves are not necessarily reprinted works. About 100 million copies are sold each year, and one can expect about 25,000 titles to be available at any time. A best-seller has enormous sales.

The preoccupation with the sexual origin of action (see p. 522) has developed into an overriding interest in sexuality, and the use of language which once would have been considered too offensive to print. The permissive attitude to novel-writing has been challenged on a number of occasions, but it has been largely accepted since the failure, in 1960, of a prosecution against the issuer of an unexpurgated edition of *Lady Chatterley's Lover*, by D. H. Lawrence.

The advent of television has not caused a reduction in the amount of reading; rather, it has stimulated interest. The non-stop demand for TV material has resulted in dramatized versions of novels and short stories, and the resurgence or even creation of interest in the original books. Prestige serials too have brought to the general public many novels of which they would otherwise never have heard. The reverse process is also true. Series and serials written for television have become so popular that they have been rewritten as novels; though usually of ephemeral interest and showing few signs of literary merit, they have provided entertainment for millions.

Probably the best-known novelist of the period under consideration is **Graham Greene (1904–)** who, like so many of his fellow-writers, came from the professional classes and after public school went up to Oxford University. He has written a considerable number of novels which, while popular, have none the less pleased the critics because of the tautness of their construction and their imaginative exploration of character. Whatever he writes seems to be topical, not just in subject-matter and location but in the emotions stimulated, for Greene has the gift of evoking the atmosphere of a period as well as giving an accurate depiction of the surroundings. The world is brutal and humourless; in it his characters pursue or are pursued. Usually they are insignificant people with a little authority who are forced to make a choice and to suffer the pangs of indecision and conscience. Greene's Roman Catholicism has encouraged him to see action as a series of moral dilemmas; he depicts not right and wrong but fundamental good and fundamental evil; his characters seek after evil sometimes on principle and sometimes from lack of initiative to do otherwise, and in doing so they acknowledge the reverse of evil. By accepting the Devil they believe in God. The settings of his novels range from West Africa to Cuba, England to Viet Nam; by selecting significant details he sketches in a background that looks authentic and then, by symbolic touches, draws one's attention to matters of special importance. The most noteworthy of Greene's novels are *It's a Battlefield* (1934), *England Made Me* (1935), *Brighton Rock* (1938), *The Power and the Glory* (1940), *The Heart of the Matter* (1948), *The End of the Affair* (1951), *The Quiet American* (1955), *A Burnt-Out Case* (1961), *The Comedians* (1966), and *Travels with My Aunt* (1969). Graham Greene's short stories have become increasingly popular; recent collections are *May We Borrow Your Husband?* (1967) and *Shades of Greene* (1976). He has also written what he calls 'entertainments.' These are stories of crime and retribution, but they too are concerned with moral difficulties bedevilling people in a confused and violent world. The best of these books are *A Gun for Sale* (1936), *The Ministry of Fear* (1943), *The Third Man* (1950), and a satire on contemporary spy novels, *Our Man in Havana* (1958).

Whereas Graham Greene ranges the world for his material, an essentially English novelist is **Charles Percy Snow** (Lord Snow) **(1905–)**, whose career as a novelist developed from a lifetime spent in the higher reaches of the Civil Service. He gives an insight into English society from the 1920's onward while describing the moral development of his hero, Lewis Eliot, the narrator of a whole series of novels. From Eliot's rise to the upper ranks of the Civil Service, one realizes that he and many of his associates are concerned only with the attainment of power over others and control of their own weaknesses. Moral, social, intellectual, and political power are illustrated, and their achievement by personal contacts, hidden influence, clever scheming, shrewd guesses, and the ability to be on the right side at a crucial moment. It is inevitable that the central figure, with every self-justification one would expect, changes from a young man of liberal ideas to a trusted official with 'acceptable' views and 'sound' principles. The story and the characters apart from the hero have less interest than the survey of English society and the forces acting within it; Snow's evaluation of his times is in terms of policy-making, governmental decisions, middle-class attitudes, and the needs of the Establishment. A dignified aloofness, a lack of emotion, and a sameness of style and approach mark Snow's analysis of the power-motive in life; for all that, there has been a large and influential body of readers for *Strangers and Brothers* (1940), *Time of Hope* (1949), *The Masters* (1951), *The New Men* (1954), *The Conscience of the Rich* (1958), and *Corridors of Power* (1964). Lord Snow's scientific studies and his career in science and technology led to his extolling their virtues and deploring the lack of contact between the arts and the modern technological age. He gave his views in the 1959 Rede Lecture, *The Two Cultures and the Scientific Revolution*, which provoked F. R. Leavis to deliver a counterblast in the Richmond Lecture of 1962.

Evelyn Waugh (1903–66) became the outstanding satirist of the thirties. Educated at Lancing and Oxford, he was very much a man of intellect who could stand aside and castigate a world which had no values except the need to make money and have fun; his main characters were snobs, and one of the cardinal sins was vulgarity. His heroes were virtuous but naïve young men who suffered embarrassment and hardship because they failed to understand or defeat the many exponents of vice. Quite impersonally, Waugh treated everything with a lack of seriousness; he did not even show any indignation at the unfairness which beset his characters. The novels were strings of hilarious incidents and effervescent dialogue by which he poked fun even at the class to which he belonged. Examples are *Decline and Fall* (1928), *Vile Bodies* (1930), *Black Mischief* (1932), *Scoop* (1938), and *Put Out More Flags* (1942). A sign of his growing seriousness and disillusion was *The Loved One* (1948), a savage satire on American funeral customs and the two-faced affluent society of that country. Partly as a result of his Army experiences and partly because of his conversion to Roman Catholicism, Waugh's later novels, beginning with *Brideshead Revisited* (1945), had a new feeling of concern, though still illuminated by wit and sardonic comment; in them was a nostalgic sympathy with a world that had ended, and which, for all its foolishness, had been more joyous and less harmful than the present. The characters were drawn with warm understanding and developed in depth; the structure too showed careful planning and far greater complexity. The later style was seen at its best in the *Sword of Honour* trilogy—*Men at Arms* (1952), *Officers and Gentlemen* (1955), and *Unconditional Surrender* (1961)—which treated of the loss of ideals as men faced war with its savagery, muddle, cynicism, inefficiency, and incongruousness. He gradually ceased to believe in all that the central figure stood for, as if he no longer believed in himself or his class in post-War society. The mood became sombre and resigned, but to the end there was a vein of rich comedy which lit up the enveloping darkness.

Another of the older generation was **Lionel Poles Hartley (1895–1972)**, who wrote of 'denaturized humanity' characterized by a sense of loneliness; this was usually produced by the denial or frustration of love because of an urge to dominate the loved one. This is the theme of the *Eustace and Hilda* trilogy (1944–47); the two children go about their mutually destructive ways. L. P. Hartley was particularly vivid in describing without sentimentality the relationships of children and their attitudes to adults. The best example of this was *The Go-Between* (1953); as so often happened in his novels, the person who most needed human sympathy was the one victimized by those who seemed to offer affection. He returned to this theme in *The Hireling* (1957), *The Betrayed* (1966), and *The Harness Room* (1971). The world he dealt with was an outdoor one, with people who had leisure to enjoy, and money to obtain their ends. When he produced his vision of the future, *Facial Justice* (1960), he saw it as a horror from which all beauty had been removed, where a drab mediocrity prevailed, and the element of competition had been removed. His style of writing was painstakingly lucid; imagery and symbolism were of the utmost importance; and his somewhat melodramatic plots were most carefully constructed. Hartley was, above all, a fine craftsman with a rare sense of word values.

Anthony Dymoke Powell (1905–), a product of Eton and Oxford, observes in detail the peculiarities of the upper middle-classes; they are all snobs with no deep-rooted virtues, and yet they succeed in their blandly assumed role of governing and leading their 'inferiors,' about which he knows very little. Powell's series of novels is to provide a large-scale view of the times and numerous varieties of 'the best people'; *Music of Time*, as it is called, includes *A Question of Upbringing* (1951), *A Buyer's Market* (1952), *The Acceptance World* (1955), *Casanova's Chinese Restaurant* (1960), and *The Kindly Ones* (1962). There are many comical moments in his novels, and the satire is the more telling by reason of the wit and epigrammatic comment which come naturally to an author so selective of words and a former literary editor of *Punch*. Unfortunately, there is little variety in the events, and his world is a very limited one; the characters, despite their eccentricities, are not attractive, and they all tend to speak in the unnatural language of a writer bent on being witty.

Henry Green (Henry Yorke) **(1905-69)** had a gift for capturing authentic speech rhythms in a language rich with imagery; with considerable artistry, he viewed situations from the point of view of one who seemed quite unsophisticated. He reduced narrative to the barest framework of events, and developed his themes almost entirely by the conversation of his characters. Though he was writing in the 1920's, his reputation was largely post-War. His novels include *Living* (1929), *Loving* (1945), *Concluding* (1948), *Nothing* (1950), and *Doting* (1952).

Very different in his technique was **Herbert Ernest Bates (1905-74)**, who also remained in comparative obscurity until the War despite *The Poacher* (1935), a highly sensitive evocation of country places and people. Then his short stories of the R.A.F. brought him fame; these were *The Greatest People in the World* (1941) and *How Sleep the Brave* (1941). After these Bates wrote a great number of short stories and novels—perhaps he made writing seem too easy—among the best of which were *The Wedding Party* (1965) and *The Four Beauties* (1968). He became probably the best known of contemporary short-story writers, dealing with the subtlety of relations between people leading restricted lives, often centred on a young woman in some amorous situation beyond her full comprehension; he wrote of country-folk in a setting which was not only authentic but was closely integrated with the characters and the mood of the situation. Something of his feeling for place and its effect on people was shown in his adventure story *Fair Stood the Wind for France* (1944) and in four novels about the newly rich city intruders, the hilariously vulgar and dishonest Larkin family of *The Darling Buds of May* (1958), *When the Green Woods Laugh* (1960), etc. As if to give further proof of his versatility, Bates wrote of Burma and India, his most noteworthy novel being *The Jacaranda Tree* (1949).

John Masters (1914-) belongs to the class of Empire rulers who found there was no Empire to rule, and whose entire way of life had become outdated in a decade. He came of a family that had always served in India with the Army. After a distinguished military career, he wrote a series of novels dealing with different moments in Indian history and their connection with some member of the Savage family. Not only was the detail historically accurate and the sense of a real India omnipresent, but an aura of mysticism increasingly influenced the characters. The land, its people, and its beliefs absorb European invaders; the Savage men, ostensibly the rulers, are the servants of India, obedient to its mesmeric powers. Most famous of these novels are *Nightrunners of Bengal* (1951) and *Bhowani Junction* (1954). Many of his other books have a military setting—for instance, *Fandango Rock* (1959)—and, as one might expect, he has a sympathetic understanding of the professional soldier, as in *The Field Marshal's Memoirs* (1975).

Considerable praise has been given to **Lawrence George Durrell (1912–)** for his four novels known collectively as *The Alexandria Quartet*. There are in them scenes of great beauty and imagination; the language is rich, sensuous, and evocative; the author has skill in describing subtle shifts of emotion; and yet there is a certain lack of humanity about the characters and an unreality about the places. The expatriate Englishman has succumbed to the magic and the languor of the Eastern Mediterranean. Perhaps the most interesting aspect of the novels is that each explains and amplifies situations already described from a different point of view, what Durrell calls the 'relativity proposition.' Not unexpectedly, he seems now to devote his mind to the writing of poetry.

In a world of increasing sameness, the individual who is different has attracted many writers. The most outstanding of such was **Joyce Cary (1888–1957)**. Himself a vigorous extrovert, he delighted in portraying exuberant, bizarre figures who existed according to a code of their own. He had the rare gift of combining comedy, even farce, with the pathetic and the movingly beautiful. His portrayal of character was objective; he detested nothing but what was dull, and he appreciated eccentricity when it arose to imaginative heights. The best of Cary was seen in *Mister Johnson* (1939), inspired by his own career with the Nigerian political service, and *The Horse's Mouth* (1944), the third book of a trilogy concerning a genuinely creative artist and his boisterous, amoral, unorganized life. A later trilogy— *Prisoner of Grace* (1952), *Except the Lord* (1953), and *Not Honour More* (1955)—lacked the early flamboyance; the novels were slower-moving and saddening, but they gave a convincing picture of sixty changing years by closely relating the social and political background to the development of the characters. Cary's personal convictions were perhaps best expressed in *The Captive and the Free* (1959).

In some ways comparable is **James Patrick Donleavy (1926–)**, an expatriate American who has established himself in Ireland. He made his name with *The Ginger Man* (1955), a formless but violent picture of a man without scruples, inhibitions, aims, or satisfactions who blasts his way through the debaucheries of Dublin and leaves a trail of emotional wreckage. Equally lonely and without purpose except the urge to live the day are the heroes of *A Singular Man* (1963) and *The Onion Eaters* (1971). Sheer vigour and rapid-fire, sometimes telegraphese, language carry the reader along even if he does not always know where.

Colin Henry Wilson (1931–). *The Outsider* (1956) brought his name to the fore and announced the theme that was to be peculiarly his: the individualist who can become the enemy of society and of himself. Wilson finds 'complete intensity' in beatniks, rebels, and criminals; he concerns himself with mysticism and metaphysics because "darkness is man's natural element." *The World of Violence* (1963) and *Man Without a Shadow* (1963) also illustrate the individual's refusal to be the victim of either God or Chance in a world of violence, sex, and crime.

Very different indeed is the work of **Angus Frank Johnstone Wilson (1913–),** a product of Westminster School and Oxford University and a scholar whose career has been largely spent in the British Museum. His satire is outstandingly effective because it is derived from the meticulous observation of details and a firm belief in certain moral values. In his novels and collections of short stories, such as *The Wrong Set* (1949) and *Such Darling Dodos* (1950), he deals with the misfits and neurotics of the middle classes with their shrinking incomes, their ideas grown outmoded in the harsh materialism of post-War Britain, their declining confidence in themselves. Sometimes evil is very real, as in *Hemlock and After* (1952), but people are usually a mixture of physical defects, intellectual weaknesses, and fears of inadequacy; he hates stupidity, silliness, and pseudo-intellectualism, and can be extremely cruel in exposing the foibles of his society. Somewhat different are *The Old Men at the Zoo* (1961), a nightmare of the political future, and *Late Call* (1964), which shows the present nightmare of a new town and its new but useless values. Most satisfying is *The Middle Age of Mrs Eliot* (1958) which concentrates on a central figure, and in showing her enforced reappraisal of herself gives a picture of warmth and sympathy not usually found in a Wilson novel.

Failure is also the main interest of **Keith Spencer Waterhouse (1929–),** though *There Is a Happy Land* (1957) is a recreation of childhood in Yorkshire through the unsentimental eyes of a child. *Billy Liar* (1959) showed a young man combating the ugliness and tedium of a provincial town, and the severe limits of his own abilities, by retreating into a fantasy world; he had either to ignore reality or integrate it into his dreams. *Jubb* (1963) took escapism a step further into impotent middle age where satisfaction was sought in futile 'good works,' pornography, and the lonely life of the peeping-tom. People with no talents and fast-departing youth are seen in *The Bucket Shop* (1969) as they desperately and angrily try to survive when they have no reason to deserve success. Waterhouse has extended his interests by writing plays (*Billy Liar, All Things Bright and Beautiful, Say Who You Are*), film scenarios, and television scripts.

The search for compassion and security in a world without foundations is described in the work of another Yorkshireman, **David Storey (1933–)**, who trained as an artist at the Slade School and then, after a variety of dead-end but unusual jobs, turned to writing. *This Sporting Life* (1960), influenced by his career as a professional rugby player, brought him to prominence, to be followed by *Flight into Camden* (1960). The daily round is drab and unrewarding, and one is dogged by a sense of failure; therefore one must seek strength from someone else and flee from reality. But Storey shows that one must identify oneself with a group having unity of emotion. and that one can gain the fullest satisfaction only from being absorbed. His most ambitious book is *Radcliffe* (1963), which deals with the love-hate relationship of two men, the developing schizophrenia of one of them, and the destruction of all that seemed stable. Ironically, only violence and unhappiness result from the enforcement of what Radcliffe believes to be moral authority.

Frederick Raphael (1931–) was born in the U.S.A. but educated at Charterhouse and Cambridge, and made his career in this country as a writer for radio, films, and television, and as a novelist. In books such as *The Earlsdon Way* (1958), *The Limits of Love* (1960), *Darling* (1965), *Like Men Betrayed* (1970), and *The Glittering Prizes* (1976) he shows that life is merely a fraud and one survives by condoning it; the generations belong to separate worlds, love is an uneasy compromise between selfish personalities, daily life is a rat-race from which at heart one is loth to escape, and the 'accepted' scheme of things proves in the long run to be the only one worth accepting.

Pamela Hansford Johnson (Lady Snow) **(1912–78)** was a writer of wit and comedy, though basically concerned with moral issues, especially those which deserve to be regarded as special cases. Convention offers an answer, but one is led to realize that the answer would be unfair; on the other hand, the solution offered by the characters is not necessarily acceptable, for she insists on certain concepts of good and evil. One sometimes feels that she presents a set of situations and leaves one to understand the hopelessness of

THE MID-TWENTIETH CENTURY 573

trying either to resolve the dilemma or pass a judgment. This impasse of morality is illustrated by *The Last Resort* (1956), *The Humbler Creation* (1959), *The Honours Board* (1970), and *The Good Listener* (1975). Possibly her best work is *The Unspeakable Skipton* (1958), with its portrayal of a mad, self-centred novelist working on an endless book. *Catherine Carter* (1952) had as its setting the theatrical world of the nineteenth century, and this interest in stage-life was also evinced, though here it was that of modern times, in *Cork Street, Next to Hatters* (1965).

William Cooper (Harry Summerfield Hoff) (**1910–**) joined the Civil Service after taking a degree at Cambridge University. Strangely, perhaps, he may be considered as the originator of the Angry Young Man who revolts against the system which has nurtured him. *Scenes from Provincial Life* (1950) and *Scenes from Married Life* (1961) were accounts of rebellion against dull and conventional provincial society, but the 'rebel' was himself so lacking in initiative that his demand for freedom was little more than a search for a different job where he could follow the conventions but make more money. Amusing and naughty, the former novel paved the way for later writers with more violent and shocking ideas of rebellion. Progress and tradition in the bourgeois world were the theme of *The Ever-Interesting Topic* (1953), and Cooper explored variations on it in *Memoirs of a New Man* (1966), *Love on the Coast* (1973), and *You're Not Alone* (1976).

A little later **John Barrington Wain** (**1925–**), eventually to be Professor of Poetry at Oxford University, published *Hurry On Down* (1953), a more carefully considered portrait of the Angry Young Man. In this it is even clearer that the anti-hero wants to opt out of a society he despises and yet stay in it without any responsibilities. The novel is a whirl of almost farcical action, expressed in the clichés and imaginative turns of phrase that constitute mid-century conversational wit. Wain objected to being termed an A.Y.M., and his later novels—for instance *The Contenders* (1958), *A Travelling Woman* (1959), *Strike the Father Dead* (1962)—and his short stories *Nuncle* (1960) were amusing but carefully considered delineations of young people frantically, sometimes desperately, trying to discover foundations of some sort.

Kingsley Amis (**1922–**) is another university don who began his literary career by depicting an anti-hero who, having found a means of abandoning his lowly origins, is disillusioned by the society into which he infiltrates. *Lucky Jim* (1954) is about a man who claims that he wants little from life but a few simple pleasures, but has no dislike for the material benefits to be culled from rising above himself. He unconsciously recognizes that, despite his sneers, he has much in common with the Establishment; his embarrassment is that he is unable to cope with the new environment. The anti-hero realizes that the accepted political and aesthetic values are a sham, but he has nothing to put in their place; although he can expose and destroy, he cannot create. In the end he achieves a measure of success and therefore self-satisfaction, conditioned by his knowing that it is based on compromise with the system he claims to despise. In different spheres of life this attitude is shown in *That Uncertain Feeling* (1955), *I Like It Here* (1958), *Take a Girl Like You* (1960), *One Fat Englishman* (1963), and *Girl, 20* (1971). Amis's novels are characterized by fast movement, wit, and some extremely funny incidents. These qualities are much to the fore, but without the backbiting and pseudo-culture one expects in an Amis novel, in *The Egyptologists* (1965), written in collaboration with Robert Conquest. Uncharacteristic is *The Anti-Death League* (1966), which tells of spies and nuclear warfare but is essentially an onslaught against God because He is death, and human beings are powerless against His wanton cruelty. One wonders sometimes whether Amis himself despises the culture with which his entire life has been associated, and that something of his own rebellion is shown by his expert interest in jazz, James Bond, and science fiction.

A feature of recent writing has been the number of writers from the North who kept something of their attitude and accent, and used their home territory as a setting for novels much concerned with social conditions and the troubles of young people in an affluent society. Waterhouse and Storey have already been mentioned, and it was **John Braine (1922–)** who seemed to announce most clearly the philosophy of the times.

Room at the Top (1957) and *Life at the Top* (1962) are set in the West Riding. They show that nothing is barred in the rat-race for material comfort and social status. Yet when one has reached the top one has nothing but the trappings of wealth, and these lose their attraction when one is always conscious of the contempt of the society into which one has forced an entrance. He elaborated the theme in *Stay With Me Till Morning* (1970)—prosperous families in Yorkshire, the need for excitement to offset approaching middle age, the search for that excitement in business deals, social gatherings, and a variety of sexual adventures. The need to pretend eternal youth and to reassure oneself by promiscuity is at the heart of *The Crying Game* (1968), *The Queen of a Distant Country* (1972), and *Waiting for Sheila* (1976). When Braine deals with more spiritual problems in *The Vodi* (1959) and *The Jealous God* (1964) he is less successful and less popular.

Yorkshire is also the setting used by **Stan Barstow (1928-)** in *A Kind of Loving* (1960) and *The Watchers on the Shore* (1966), novels which dealt with a lower level of the struggle to 'the top.' In addition to his description of the determination to move up and outward, Barstow deals with the clash of values—the material and ephemeral against the cultural and permanent. In these novels, and in *Ask Me Tomorrow* (1962) and *Joby* (1964), the hero is a lonely young man incapable of establishing lasting relationships with other people, aware of his own inexperience and inadequacy, and seeking for some sort of assurance. A later work of Barstow's is *A Season with Eros* (1971).

Alan Sillitoe (1928-) sets his stories chiefly around Nottingham. He deals with working people who, still aware of the Great Depression though living in comparative affluence, insist that they are the victims of a repressive system and see life as a means of retaliation against authority and an imagined conspiracy of bureaucrats and capitalists. Their world is a chaos of violence, undeserved suffering, selfishness, and crude humour. In every way it is insecure; the hero of *Saturday Night and Sunday Morning* (1958) welcomes insecurity, for it provides the excitement which contemporary society otherwise lacks; when there is a 'danger' of order coming into his life he must create new elements of insecurity. *The Loneliness of the Long-Distance Runner* (1959) also blames society for the shortcomings of its members, and looks on anti-social conduct as a justifiable means of reprisal. There is a sameness about Sillitoe's books—*The Death of William Posters* (1966), *A Start in Life* (1970), *The Widower's Son* (1976): the working class is always victimized, 'those with the money' are always tyrants, the Great Depression never ended, and enjoyment often consists of making a nuisance of oneself.

Far more effectively realistic although a humorist at heart is **Colin MacInnes (1914-)**, an Australian by birth. He deals with the shabby sub-worlds of modern society where there is restless activity, colour, money, and surface enjoyment, all providing an unsettled cover to the sordid loneliness of the big city where life is one of uncertainty, fear, and lack of purpose. He writes of young people and their ephemeral careers, prostitutes and policemen, and above all of coloured people, whether native to this country or immigrants. His novels proceed at a tremendous pace, enlivened by a pop-language based on the street slang of the day, and imbued with sincere regard for the inhabitants of the coloured ghettos and an equal hatred of racial warfare and those who encourage it. *City of Spades* (1957) first attracted attention, and then came *Absolute Beginners* (1959) and *Mr Love and Justice* (1960).

At this juncture it is appropriate to mention the South African **Alan Stewart Paton (1903–)**. *Cry, the Beloved Country* (1948) and *Too Late the Phalarope* (1953) made their mark in this country, and most effectively brought attention to the plight of Negroes in the white man's dehumanizing cities, the collapse of stabilizing values, and the real effects of apartheid. *Hofmeyr* (1964) was less important because of its sheer length.

William Gerald Golding (1911–) deals with man's instinct to destroy what is good, whether it is material or spiritual. Treating of cruelty, selfishness, and the yearning after power, he puts his viewpoint very clearly—evil is apparent everywhere, and is with difficulty held at bay, and good is almost impossible to achieve. Each of his novels is a unique fable for the times in which symbolism plays an overridingly important part. Nevertheless, they are convincingly realistic, and his characters are feasible, even though they are forced by unnatural circumstances into unnatural situations. His best-known novel is *Lord of the Flies* (1954), in which civilization is shown to be a mere veneer that cracks and splinters under the slightest pressure, but *The Inheritors* (1955) most effectively illustrates his view that innocence, good, happiness were instinctive before Homo sapiens developed, and with him an all-destructive urge to evil. *Pincher Martin* (1956) with its brilliantly conceived plot, *Free Fall* (1959), and *The Scorpion God* (1971) are studies of individuals who deliberately reject heaven and, as all humans must, sink satisfied into hell. *The Spire* (1964), however, shows man apparently achieving something that is good; yet everything connected with it is evil. The reader is left to wonder whether mankind can ever attain or create anything that is wholly good.

Anthony Burgess (John Burgess Wilson) **(1917–)** spent a number of years in Malaysia, from which he derived inspiration for his *Malayan Trilogy* (1956–59), a picture of that country at the end of imperial rule and a study of the relationships between races. However, it was *A Clockwork Orange* (1962)—and later *The Wanting Seed* (1962) and *The Clockwork Testament* (1974)—that showed the real Burgess.

The humour becomes almost madly farcical, and one is faced with horror, satire, pessimism, wondering how one can accept the author's "need to laugh in the face of a desperate future." Teenage violence and teenage lack of concern are expressed in 'nadsat,' the teenage language of the future; the world is evil where 'reclamation treatment' by violence and horror is considered acceptable.

Malcolm Lowry (1907–57) was an alcoholic who saw life as a phantasmagoria of hallucinations. *Under the Volcano* (1947) was to have been part of a larger work, but it remained the sole product of his tortured brain. The hero has lived through the downfall of Western society and, suffering his private hell, drives himself still further into the sufferings of the damned. He knows what the end must be, but he persists on his course, denying anything that may alleviate his agonies because he represents mankind, who cannot or will not resist the drift towards doom. Some critics consider this novel to be one of the greatest of the century, but it has never been fully appreciated.

George Orwell (Eric Hugh Blair) **(1903–50)** was a typical product of the inter-War years. His proletarian sympathies and his contempt for the upper-middle-class society from which he sprang were shown in the sardonic *Keep the Aspidistra Flying* (1936). Yet there was a love-hate attitude towards the idea of Empire and the White Man's Burden in *Burmese Days* (1934); and in *The Road to Wigan Pier* (1937), a picture of squalor and hopelessness during the Great Depression, he seemed to despise the very type he represented, the left-wing intellectual striving to identify himself with the victims. It was only after the Second World War that Orwell became a figure of outstanding importance, and then it was because of *Animal Farm* (1945), an expression of his own disillusion. This was a closely knit allegory on the degeneration of communist ideals into dictatorship, expressed in an incisive, witty, deceptively simple style reminiscent of Voltaire. Utterly different was *Nineteen Eighty-Four* (1949), a terrifying prognostication of the hatred, cruelty, fear, loss of individuality, and lack of human love that the future would bring. The common man whom Orwell admired was reduced to a political and social nonentity; human dignity and decency were dead because of mass apathy and tolerance of evil.

Arthur Koestler (1905–). Hungarian by birth, he became a journalist for German papers, was captured by Franco's forces in the Spanish Civil War and sentenced to death; after a spell in French internment camps he joined the Foreign Legion. His personal experience of prison-camps and man's inhumanity are the inspiration of *Scum of the Earth* (1941), and the basis of his fearsome picture of corruption and the corrupt use of power in *Darkness at Noon* (1941), a vision of the future where Stalinist repression rules. The sufferings of the common man are also seen among Jews trying to create a new way of life in *Thieves in the Night* (1946).

Patrick Victor Martindale White (1912–), the best-known Australian novelist of today, also sees with disillusioned eyes. *Riders in the Chariot* (1961) is set in Sydney, but the city represents the world and the various forms that goodness can take in people; but against these the reality of evil strives and succeeds. White's reputation, however, largely rests on *Voss* (1957), a story of Australian exploration based on fact; he makes the great wastes of the continent an overwhelming presence, their mystery enhanced by the supernatural rapport between two lovers.

Percy Howard Newby (1918–) is best known for his two comedies dealing with the clash between European and Arabic cultures, *The Picnic at Sakkara* (1955) and *A Guest and his Going* (1959). More significant are *A Step to Silence* (1952), *The Barbary Light* (1962), *A Lot to Ask* (1973), and *Kith* (1977), which are presentations in various forms of the moral dilemma facing Newby's generation, and the personal difficulties of living amid the collapse of a culture. Each person is lost in the storm, and must rely on himself alone to survive spiritually as well as physically.

When so many writers find almost nothing to commend the present and the near future, it is not surprising that some have retreated from actuality and created their own worlds. The best known of these was **John Ronald Reuel Tolkien (1892–1973)**, Professor of Anglo-Saxon and then of Language and Literature at Oxford from 1925 to 1959, whose novels became something of a cult, especially among intellectuals. *The Hobbit* (1937), ostensibly a children's book, and *The Lord of the Rings* (1954–55) present a world that is an amalgam of fairy lore, Norse mythology, epic, and Arthurian legends. Tolkien himself claimed no seriousness for this work, but one finds it difficult to believe him when one considers its length, and the care bestowed on interweaving its complex stories. The language too was specially created to suit the characters, very much the brain-child of an expert philologist.

Mervyn Peake (1911–68) produced three long books, *Titus Groan* (1946), *Gormenghast* (1950), and *Titus Alone* (1959). These weird fantasies, mixing farce with grandeur, evil with innocence, cannot be categorized, and are still attractive only to the few. Tradition rules the Gothic enormity of a castle and all who dedicate their lives to its service. Each book is an epic, a romance, a comedy, a Gothic fairy-tale, a horror story, an allegory made all the more effective by inspired irony. It becomes all the more a nightmare when Titus realizes that the world outside the castle is more terrifying than Gormenghast itself.

Finally, one must consider some of the many outstanding novelists who are women and seem proud to assert themselves as such. Very much the intellectual is **Muriel Sarah Spark (1918–)**. She is the creator of bizarre situations illustrating contemporary life, and revealing its not too discreditable foolishnesses. She does so with a wit, elegance, and sense of mature fun that is unique today in *The Comforters* (1957), *Robinson* (1958), *The Ballad of Peckham Rye* (1960), *The Girls of Slender Means* (1963), and *The Abbess of Crewe* (1974). As a Roman Catholic, she accepts the supernatural and understands the power of the spirit to influence the course of events. Violence is part of her world, and yet she views it with detachment, even impassivity; the world is mad, and therefore anything can happen. More serious and perhaps less successful (for she does not care to probe too deeply into strong emotions or to involve herself in complex situations), are *The Prime of Miss Jean Brodie* (1961) and *The Mandelbaum Gate* (1965).

Jean Iris Murdoch (1919–), after being educated at Oxford University, held a post with UNRRA before becoming a don. *Under the Net* (1954) was typical of its time in giving a richly amusing view of the Angry Young Man rushing after affluence, and seeking truth where no truth exists. But *The Flight from the Enchanter* (1956) was a study in cruelty and power, the sufferings of a man who allows others to cause the suffering which he himself cannot bear to inflict. As one might expect of a student of philosophy who began her writing career with an evaluation of Jean-Paul Sartre, she found her métier in tightly constructed studies of human relations under stress, as in *The Sandcastle* (1957) and *The Bell* (1958). The approach is intellectual rather than passionate, with considerable dependence on the symbolism of actions and situations. Iris Murdoch has become increasingly concerned with the juxtaposition of the sombre and the comic to form a macabre story about unbalanced characters incapable of dealing with normality. *A Severed Head* (1961) is the triumph of militant women, highly intelligent and cruel. The characters move and interchange relationships in a way unrelated to human emotions.

Sex and sexual symbolism, even horror, become more apparent in further convolutions of love and desire in *An Unofficial Rose* (1962), *The Unicorn* (1963), *An Accidental Man* (1971), and *The Sacred and Profane Love Machine* (1974).

Like Muriel Spark, **Doris May Lessing (1919–)** spent part of her life in Africa. She utilized her experiences there, as in *African Stories* (1964), to picture the situation of black people subjected to the authority of whites, and to air her view that the solution to the problem would come from the application of Marxist doctrines. Usually her theme is the dilemma of the New Woman who, despite her emancipation, is still expected to conform with conventional ideas of a woman's life. Yet her characters are disillusioned with this life; love generates a loneliness and impermanence. Four novels under the overall title of *Children of Violence* (1952–65) have as their heroine a woman with the significant name of Martha Quest. *The Golden Notebook* (1962) is extremely long, and not very well organized; despite its being considered a novel, it is a compendium of Doris Lessing's views on all those issues which have occupied her. More in the usual Lessing style are *The Story of a Non-Marrying Man* (1972) and *The Memoirs of a Survivor* (1975).

Brigid Antonia Brophy (1929–) began her career with witty comments on the foibles of modern society, such as *Hackenfeller's Ape*, (1953) and *The King of a Rainy Country* (1956), and rapidly became one of the most vociferous champions of Women's Lib. *The Snow Ball* (1964) is a strident manifesto of female rights rather than a novel, and her rights are to possess every man, to gain revenge on Don Juan by demanding sexual satisfaction from all she encounters. Other novels pursuing the Brophy-line are *The Adventures of God in his Search for the Black Girl* (1973) and *Pussy Owl* (1976), but *In Transit* (1969) can be recommended as an exercise in neo-James Joyce prose.

Edna O'Brien (1936–) is another disciple of Women's Lib. *The Country Girls* (1960), *The Lonely Girl* (1962), and *Girls in their Married Bliss* (1964) tell of the adventures of two amorous Irishwomen in a world where men are vain creatures, assertive but usually feeble in performance. In *August is a Wicked Month* (1965) woman neither gives nor receives pleasure; she is insatiable in her demands, making sex the instrument of her power. The belief that marriage is a succession of frustrations and limitations is also expressed in *The Pumpkin Eater* (1962) by **Penelope Ruth Mortimer (1918–)**.

To end on a happier note, one may instance **Lynne Reid Banks**

(1929–), whose shabby world of the bed-sitter is a retreat from bigotry and artificiality. The people she meets when living in *The L-Shaped Room* (1960) are eccentric, often immoral, always barely surviving, but she obtains from them love and understanding. One may well compare this story of the unmarried mother with *The Millstone* (1965) by **Margaret Drabble (1939–)**. The struggle to survive amid physical and spiritual difficulties is also the theme of *An End to the Running* (1962) by Lynne Reid Banks; it is a novel of Israel and again the story of a woman who succeeds because of her determination and sense of purpose.

Lack of space prevents one from doing more than mention a very restricted number of novels which increased the reputation of their writers and will long be worth serious reading: *The Aerodrome* (1941) by Rex Warner; *Odd Man Out* (1945) by Frederick Lawrence Green; *The Cruel Sea* (1951) by Nicholas Monsarrat; *The Breaking of Bumbo* (1959) by Andrew Sinclair; *When the Kissing Had to Stop* (1960) by Constantine FitzGibbon; *Jason* (1961) by Henry Treece; *The Bull from the Sea* (1965) by Mary Renault; *Travelling People* (1963) by B. S. Johnson; and *Cards of Identity* (1965) by Nigel Dennis.

One cannot make a survey of the modern novel without reference to **Cecil Scott Forester (1899–1966)**, who wrote probably more best-sellers than any other writer in English of the century, and who created the character of Captain Horatio Hornblower. Almost as important as a popular writer was **Ian Fleming (1908–64)** whose James Bond stories satisfied contemporary interest in the sophisticated brutality of spying. Later that interest shifted to the even more callous world created by **John Le Carré (D. J. M. Cornwell)**.

2. POETRY

The period of the War produced much poetry; moreover, it sold well to a wide public, often in anthologies of which the best known was *Poems from the Forces* (1942, 1943), edited by **Keidrych Rhys**. Some, of course, dealt with the War in the most obvious ways—the boredom and frustration of Service life, the waste, the appreciation of friendship, a deep understanding of the English landscape, and the possibility of violent death.

Greatest attention at the time was paid to **Sidney Keyes (1922–44)**, whose work was contained in *The Iron Laurel* (1942) and *Cruel Solstice* (1944). Most of the poems had been written while he was at Oxford University, the quality was uneven, the symbolism oppressive, but he seemed to express the attitudes of his generation.

Another poet of great promise was **Alun Lewis (1919–44)** who, like Keyes, published only one volume before he was killed; this was *Raiders' Dawn* (1942). He depicted the soldier as the exile, the solitary, the victim of futility, and his experience had been enriched by what he had seen in India. Some critics now consider that the best war poetry came from **Keith Douglas (1920–44)** whose *From Alamein to Zem-Zem* (1946) expressed the sense of futility in rigidly disciplined language that was coldly angry and bitingly ironical. **Alan William Rook (1909–)** made a considerable impression with *Soldiers, This Solitude* (1942) and *These Are My Comrades* (1943), but abandoned literature on leaving the Forces.

Other young men turned to writing poetry because of their experiences during the War, and went on to extend their interest. One such was **Roy Broadbent Fuller (1912–)** who began as a solicitor, turned poet because of his service with the Royal Navy in the Middle East, and eventually was elected Professor of Poetry at Oxford University. His war poetry was published in *The Middle of a War* (1942) and *A Lost Season* (1944). Later came *Epitaphs and Occasions* (1949) which by its disciplined forms, spare language, and analytical approach, was seen as a counterblast to the so-called 'romantic' poetry inspired by Dylan Thomas immediately after the War. Fuller went on to become more daring in his experiments in form, and to concern himself with the state of people in the contemporary politico-economic climate; yet some of his best poetry, because of his innate sympathies for others, deals with love. **Charles Stanley Causley (1917–)** was another writer from the Navy, as is suggested by the titles of his early volumes—*Hands to Dance* (1951) and *Farewell, Aggie Weston* (1951). What mattered to him was the lost innocence of youth, country life, social groups and their habits, though all was lightened by a streak of humour in him. His poetry is most attractive when he uses a springing ballad rhythm in a language, deceptively casual, that owes much to folk-song, as in *Johnny Alleluia* (1961). His interest in popular literature was further shown by his edition of *Modern Folk Ballads* (1966). **Alan Ross (1922–)** was educated at Haileybury and Oxford, and then served with the Navy. *The Derelict Day* (1947) is derived from the grimness of life around him, and yet he seemed able to brush it aside. His delight in gaiety and colour transcended the darkness he encountered. He has travelled in many parts of the world, and has been affected by the spirit of the places and their attractiveness. Later collections of merit are *Something of the Sea* (1952) and *African Negatives* (1961).

During the War the individual and not the community became the centre of interest for poets, even for Auden and Spender. This new attitude was evident in the Apocalyptic Movement, led by **J. F. Hendry (1912–)**, **Henry Treece (1912–66)**, and **G. S. Fraser (1915–)** whose poetry appeared in three anthologies they compiled—*The New Apocalypse* (1940), *The White Horseman* (1941), and *The Crown and the Sickle* (1945). The movement proclaimed its hatred of the Machine Age, its faith in the individual as the hope of humanity, and its belief in myth. The poet's aim was to express 'his own private perspective on the world,' though not in an immediately intelligible way. Before long the members of the group went their own ways, and its influence was lost.

Dylan Marlais Thomas (1914–53) may be described as the originator of neo-romantic poetry in the forties and the enemy of intellectualism in verse. He was a true Celt, deeply passionate, and with a wonderful if somewhat uncontrolled appreciation of the magic of language, especially in his earlier poems. He drew upon the human body, sex, and the Old Testament for much of his imagery and complex word-play, and his verse was splendidly colourful and musical. The depth and intensity of his passion, his verbal gifts, and the technical skill which underlay his metrical experiments, all suggested that Thomas had the makings of a great poet, especially when later he learnt to impose discipline on his writing and to make his imagery less a matter of his private understanding. Adulation of Thomas reached such a degree of fervour in the U.S.A. and Britain that his real virtues were often obscured and his faults ignored. Since his untimely death, a more balanced attitude to his work has been established, and more attention given to his prose works, which are in many ways an extension of his poetry. His work appeared in *18 Poems* (1934), *Twenty-five Poems* (1936), *The Map of Love* (1939), and *Deaths and Entrances* (1946), but he is best known for *Under Milk Wood* (1954), a verse 'play' written specially for radio and at times presented as a solo reading by the author himself.

The so-called neo-romanticism of the post-War years was influenced by Thomas rather than the Apocalyptics. In some ways there was a return to the spirit of the eighteenth century. Quietness, sadness, a small experience stimulating a stream of thought, sometimes with religious or mystical associations, and appreciation of landscape—these were the characteristics of many a writer.

Laurie Lee (1914–) is one who, firmly based on tradition, finds his material in the many countries where he has lived. There is nothing profound, no organized view of human experience or commentary on the world's affairs; he catches the moment and makes it worth considering. Some of his best work is in *The Sun My Monument* (1944), *The Bloom of Candles* (1947), and *My Many-Coated Man* (1955). **Norman Cornthwaite Nicholson (1914–)**, born in Millom, Cumberland, and forced by illness to lead an uneventful life there, came to love the town, its surroundings and inhabitants. In unpretentious, unambiguous language he expresses his feelings for the spirit of the place, and because he knows the people so well he finds himself personally concerned with all human situations. A strong religious faith is evident in his work, and, indeed, he has written religious plays. The reader becomes part of Cumbria when he studies *Rock Face* (1948), *The Pot Geranium* (1954), or *A Local Habitation* (1972). **Kathleen Jessie Raine (1908–)** has always been influenced by a childhood spent in Northumberland. She studied science, and so her observation is detailed and precise, and her language a model of clarity even when it is symbolic, as can be seen in *The Pythoness* (1949), *The Hollow Hill* (1964), and *On a Deserted Shore* (1973). She believes in the ideals of past generations, and her verse is founded on traditional culture. **Charles Tomlinson (1927–)** writes of the real world of landscape and uses it as a taking-off point for his philosophy; his attention is objectively focused on small things and their beauty with an intensity that is electric. A feeling of stillness pervades much of his work, perhaps encouraged by his delight in painting. The freedom with which his verse moves owes something to Hopkins; despite his use of abstractions and symbols, his musical language is as real as his subject-matter, witness *The Necklace* (1955), *Seeing is Believing* (1960), *The Way of the World* (1969), and *Written in Water* (1972). The poet most obviously influenced by Dylan Thomas was another Welshman, **Vernon Phillips Watkins (1906–67)**, whose *Lady with the Unicorn* (1948) and *Cypress and Acacia* (1959) show his reliance on Welsh legend and the verbal preciosity of his more famous countryman.

Another Romantic was **John Francis Heath-Stubbs (1918–)**, whose highly symbolic virtuosity in *Wounded Thammuz* (1942) and *The Charity of the Stars* (1949) showed how deeply and eruditely he involved himself with myth and the colourful past, chiefly because he saw only failure in the present, especially the failure of love. Later works include *The Triumph of the Muse* (1958) and *The Blue-Fly in his Head* (1962). **Lawrence George Durrell** (see p. 570) first published verse in 1931 and is still not fully recognized. He is essentially literary in his approach, yet he has surrendered himself to the magic of the Mediterranean and to Eastern mysticism. He aims at perfection of form and at evoking beauty from word sounds and rhythmic patterns. He writes of himself and places, and the moods they encourage, remote from contemporary conflicts. *Cities, Plains and People* (1946) is his best-known book of verse, but some of his finest poetry can be read in *The Tree of Idleness* (1955) and *Plant-Magic Man* (1973).

There was a time when **James Falconer Kirkup (1923–)** seemed to promise great things; *The Drowned Sailor* (1947) was typical of the times with its hatred of violence, but facility and his involvement in translation may have weakened his emotional intensity in *The Descent into the Cave* (1954) and *The Refusal to Conform* (1963). **Alexander Comfort (1920–)** has always been at his best in lyrics fashioned to suit his epigrammatic style. As he is a distinguished doctor and psychologist, he is much concerned with emotions arising from death and sexual love, from *A Wreath for the Living* (1943), through *Haste to the Wedding* (1962) right up to *Coming Together* (1975). **Elizabeth Joan Jennings (1926–)** is contemplative, almost withdrawn, a poet of place and its significant relationship with people. Her verse is elusive in quality, and extremely personal, for her natural reserve increased with illness. *A Way of Looking* (1955) is typical; other important volumes are *The Mind Has Mountains* (1966) and *Relationships* (1972).

Two poets who began writing in the inter-War years but established themselves afterwards are **George Barker (1913–)** and **David Gascoyne (1916–)**; both are antipathetic to the intellectual approach, both were originally surrealists. Barker, who has spent most of his later career in the U.S.A., is very conscious of the failure of the world; he has no solution to its problems, but he seeks to identify himself with those who suffer. *Eros in Dogma* (1944), *News of the World* (1950), *A Vision of Beasts and Gods* (1954), and *The Golden Chains* (1968) are characterized by stream-of-consciousness techniques which engender evocative but often over-complex imagery. Gascoyne has a high seriousness and a religious conviction which helps him to endure the world's agony; latterly he has become more descriptive and less effective, and involved in nightmare imagery, as in *Night Thoughts* (1956). His best poetry appeared in *Poems* (1948) and *A Vagrant, and Other Poems* (1950).

The outstanding event in English poetry since the last War has been the popular success of **Sir John Betjeman (1906–)**. He describes the middle class's habits, prejudices, fears, hopes, and idiosyncrasies; his themes are childhood, nostalgia for the past, Victorian architecture (especially churches), and places associated with boyhood memories, particularly East Anglia. Betjeman has a flair for selective and cogent detail; the skilled craftsmanship of the numerous verse forms is concealed under the garb of simplicity, and this keeps his ironical wit under restraint. In a language which is easily appreciated, he offers to the older generation the happiness of the past and an escape from the harsh present. This highly successful verse appeared in *Old Lights for New Chancels* (1940), *Selected Poems* (1948), *A Few Late Chrysanthemums* (1954), and *Collected Poems* (1958).

During the Festival of Britain, the Barrow Poets hoped to hawk their verse in the streets, but when a licence was refused they gave readings in pubs and public places, a venture which not only succeeded but encouraged the idea of bringing poetry to the masses. Very much different was what became known as The Movement resulting from *Poets of the 50's* (1950) edited by **Dennis Joseph Enright (1920–)** and another collection from largely the same poets, *New Lines* (1956, 1963) edited by **Robert Conquest (1917–)**. The Movement professed no interest in stylistic innovation, and in neoclassic mood concerned itself with reality. Most of the poets concerned were academics—Wain, Amis, Holloway, Davie, Enright himself; with them were Larkin, Gunn, and Jennings. Enright's own poems, such as *Laughing Hyena* (1953), *Some Men Are Brothers* (1960), *The Old Adam* (1965), deal with individual man in all his conditions, showing pity and indignation for his sufferings, and faith in his innate dignity. His language is based on colloquial speech stripped of elaborations, a style that well suits his ironical disgust of hypocrisy and cruelty. Robert Conquest's poetry is devoted more to a view of landscape with Man as an integral part. The approach is intellectual and the subject-matter is reality. Some of his best verse is in *Poems* (1955), but also worth reading are *Between Mars and Venus* (1962) and *Arias for a Love Opera* (1969). Of their university-based colleagues, suffice to say that **Donald Alfred Davie (1922–)** is primarily concerned with the use of language, which in his early poems was extremely difficult, and with style, which is characterized by gracefulness. His works include *A Winter Talent* (1957) and *Events and Wisdoms* (1964). **John Wain** (see p. 573) gives a moral dignity to his verse, as in *Mixed Feelings* (1951) and *Weep before God* (1961), but too often he is prosaic and unambitious, a charge which can also be laid against **John Holloway (1920–)** and *The Minute* (1956); his bent is for exposition and criticism rather than poetry. It is strange to see **Kingsley Amis** (see p. 573) in this company, but his early poems conformed with the beliefs of The Movement; more in keeping with the tone of his novels is *A Look Round the Estate* (1967). The other poets in this group will be considered later, for they soon developed in their own individual ways.

Some poets deal with the contemporary world by commenting on its violence in a language which is based on the colloquial and is abundant yet precise in its imagery. Conventional forms of verse are rarely used, for the writers insist on form being governed by its relevance to theme and mood. **Vernon Scannell (1922–)** is one who treats of insecurity and violence by selecting everyday incidents; his economical language and simple metres are enriched with metaphor from present-day life, and add power to the macabre and cruel situations which attract his attention and the expression of his belief in Man's goodness. *Mavericks* (1957) was an anthology designed as a counterblast to *New Lines*. Recent works include *A Sense of Danger* (1962), *Epithets of War* (1969), *Company of Women* (1971), and *The Apple Raid* (1974). **Jon Silkin (1930–)** also deals with human suffering, destruction, and the integration of humanity with its environment; his curt, elliptical language, rich in imagery, is governed by controlled rhythms, so that even when he is mordantly critical he produces a deep richness of expression. *The Re-Ordering of the Stones* (1961), *Nature with Man* (1963), and *Anana Grass* (1971) show him to be one of the most perceptive and compassionate writers of his generation. **Peter Neville Frederick Porter (1929–)**, an expatriate Australian, is scathingly antagonistic to many aspects of contemporary life, and yet he is very much a part of it. His sometimes formal, sometimes mockingly casual, phrases are carefully pointed to deal with urban life and the political scene, as in *Words without Music* (1968) and *The Last of England* (1970). **Thomas William (Thom) Gunn (1929–)** has now settled in the U.S.A. after years of travel. He writes of the multitudinous forms of energy which characterize our cities, and of self-destructive violence. He sees life to be tough, cynical, loveless, meaningless, but still finds some tenderness in the essentially animal nature of man. His later work evinces a more subdued attitude and a willingness to meditate rather than react with vigour. Because of his style, which is logical, economical, and startling in its imagery, he has been compared with John Donne. Gunn is best known for *Fighting Terms* (1954), *The Sense* *of Movement* (1957), *My Sad Captains* (1961), *Touch* (1967), and *Moly* (1971). Perhaps more influential is **Ted Hughes (1930-)**, especially because of *The Hawk in the Rain* (1957). His 'verbal belligerence,' partly influenced by his interest in the Yorkshire dialect and traditional oral literature, gives a positiveness to his views. He sees power and vitality as essential principles always contending against death, the failure of God to create a satisfactory universe, the ever-present strength of evil, and personal survival as the only goal to achieve. Yet under the harsh, pessimistic exterior and the gruesome humour there lies great tenderness. Hughes has a gift for describing the Yorkshire landscape, and for understanding animals in an unsentimental manner. In animals he sees the certainties, the pointlessness, and the violence that are part of man's life, and he uses them to clarify and intensify human experience. His important recent works are *Woodwo* (1967), *Crow* (1970), *Crow Wakes* (1971), and *Eat Crow* (1972). For a time he was married to **Sylvia Plath (1932-63)**, an American with a distinguished academic career who settled in England. Amid violence, she appreciated the richness of everyday life, especially the world of nature, yet all in a context of mental unbalance that eventually brought her to suicide. Terse, lyrical, witty, she expressed values that were worth suffering for in *The Colossus* (1960), *Ariel* (1965), and *Crossing the Water* (1971).

Very unlike the foregoing writers is **Thomas Blackburn (1916-)**. Despite his detached and even sardonic view of life, he sees the unifying power of love in the relationships of children, especially in childhood and during marriage. In *The Outer Darkness* (1953), *In the Fire* (1956), and *A Smell of Burning* (1961) one sees how Blackburn can use myth and classical allusion to illustrate modern situations, and achieve a dignity of language out of forceful colloquial English. Very much a loner is **Philip Larkin (1922-)**. He accepts defeatism and rootlessness as part of existence. There is in his work a sense of loss, of beauty departed, of the changing qualities of English life. He obtains his pleasures (though often melancholy ones) from his observation of little situations and places, and from dwelling on their associations, all very personal, and he expresses them in a clear, easily comprehended fashion. *The Less Deceived* (1955), *The Whitsun Weddings* (1964), and *High Windows* (1974) are representative works, but he also edited *The Oxford Book of Twentieth Century English Verse*.

One must refer to the revival of interest in regional poetry. **Patrick Kavanagh (1905-67)** dealt in a colloquial, deceptively naïve manner with rural scenes and conditions in Ireland. He lightly mocked pretentiousness, even his own. Two very different books are *The Great Hunger* (1942) and *Come Dance with Kitty Stobling* (1960). **Keidrych Rhys (1915–)** is typical of the Welsh national movement of the time, and founded and edited *Wales* (1937–60). But the work of **Ronald Stuart Thomas (1913–)** is known to far more people. The bleak, relentless landscape and the tough, uncompromising people with their austere traditionalism provide pictures of harshness and suffering in the minimum of words; they show the writer's compassion, his love-hate relationship, and his ability to give a universal application to a little episode. Some of his best verse is in *Song at the Year's Turning* (1955), *The Bread of Truth* (1963), and *Pietà* (1966). In Scotland the outstanding figure was **Hugh McDiarmid** (Christopher Murray Grieve) **(1892–1978)** who revived the Lowland Scots dialect, Lallans, as an instrument of literature. Although he was writing long before the War—*Sangschaw*'s date is 1925—his impact was not felt until much later. His use of scientific terms, neologisms, and foreign phrases made more difficult his vociferous insistence that science and Marxism would solve all economic ills, but his visionary fervour and sense of the comic could produce poetry even amid absurdities. *In Memoriam James Joyce* (1955) and *A Clyack-Sheaf* (1969) show him at his best; he also edited *Northern Numbers, The Voice of Scotland*, and *The Golden Treasury of Scottish Poetry*. The nationalist movement in verse was also encouraged by *Modern Scottish Poetry* (ed. Maurice Lindsay, 1946) and *Scottish Verse 1851–1951* (ed. Desmond Young, 1952). Two poets who write in English but whose subject-matter and approach are always Scottish are **Norman Alexander McCaig (1910–)** and **William Sydney Graham (1918–)**.

This rapid survey of modern poetry would not be complete without reference to two established writers of a somewhat younger generation. **Dominic Frank (Dom) Moraes (1938–)** attracted attention with *A Beginning* (1957), *Poems* (1960), and *John Nobody* (1965). His Indian origin may partly account for his concern with construction and metrical experiment; he is adept at using myth, allusion, and symbolism, though these not infrequently provide a luxurious cover for rather banal ideas. **George Mann MacBeth (1932–)** always has an intellectual approach and yet aims to make an immediate popular appeal. A careful craftsman, he can use any style he considers appropriate, from the most traditional to the almost shockingly outré, while his subject-matter ranges from the elegiac to the macabre. Like so many of his contemporaries, MacBeth deals with violence and cruelty, but he has the quality of pity, he interprets the past with sympathy, and reveals the essential qualities of other writers whom he subjects to analysis and evaluation. *A Form of Words* (1954), *The Broken Places* (1963), *The Colour of Blood* (1967), and *Shrapnel* (1973) place him in the forefront of modern poets.

And, finally, one should not fail to mention a number of American writers whose poetry is well known in this country and has influenced many admirers—Laura Riding, Adrienne Rich, W. S. Mervin, Anne Sexton, and Theodore Roethke.

3. DRAMA

The immediate result of the wartime black-out was the closing down of London theatres for some time; but not only did they soon reopen, but they were never completely dominated by the frivolous gaiety of 'leave entertainment,' as in the 1914–18 War. A great step forward was made in that companies sponsored by C.E.M.A. (Council for the Encouragement of Music and the Arts) and E.N.S.A. (Entertainments National Service Association) took drama into the provinces, to the smallest villages, and wherever Army camps and workers' hostels were situated. They created a vast new public, which was responsible for the boom which immediately followed the War.

C.E.M.A. was transformed into the Arts Council, which dispenses State patronage by way of grants, and is therefore the means by which some of the smaller experimental groups continue to exist. During the War and after it, the prestige of the Old Vic Theatre Company was enormous, though its training school and children's theatre soon fell victims of the economy drive; in 1963 the Old Vic became the temporary home of the National Theatre company. Another aspect of subsidized drama is the considerable number of annual festivals, aimed largely at tourists but offering splendid opportunities even to small enterprises 'on the fringe.' One must also stress the importance of the Royal Shakespeare Theatre at Stratford, and its sister-company based on London, as well as the steady increase in university theatres and theatres sponsored by local authorities, many of which seek to encourage future audiences by educating children to appreciate all forms of drama.

Drama in the forties was dominated by three men. **Christopher Fry (1907–)** illustrated the vitality of verse drama and caught the mood of the times in the witty pyrotechnics of *The Boy with a Cart* (1939), *A Phoenix Too Frequent* (1946), and *The Lady's Not for Burning* (1949). Sir Terence Rattigan (1911–77) achieved tremendous success with such professionally neatly constructed displays of human relationships as *Flare Path* (1942), *The Winslow Boy* (1946), *The Browning Version* (1948), *Separate Tables* (1954), *Ross* (1960), and *Cause Célèbre* (1977). Peter Ustinov (1921–) contributed to the success of his many plays by acting in them, though his highest achievement came later with *The Love of Four Colonels* (1951) and *Romanoff and Juliet* (1956).

However, for some time English dramatists seemed to have nothing in common with the leading foreign writers whose influence suddenly made itself felt in the early 1950's. First and foremost was Bertolt Brecht (1898–1956), with his uncompromising views on production, his use of songs and music, his humanitarian communism, and his insistence on the alienation of the audience and the actor from the character even as he projects the play into the midst of the onlookers. After Brecht, the most important influence was Samuel Beckett (1906–), formerly James Joyce's secretary, who wrote in French. *Waiting for Godot* (1952; Eng. trans. 1954) is a static representation without structure or development, using only meandering, seemingly incoherent dialogue to suggest despair of a society which is destroying itself and of mankind unsuspectingly surrendering its natural liberties. Other dramatic devices of Beckett are *Endgame* (1955) and *Krapp's Last Tape* (1958). Some foreign writers wielding great influence at present are, from the U.S.A., Arthur Miller, Tennessee Williams, and Edward Albee; from Germany, Weiss and Hochhuth; from Switzerland, Dürrenmatt; from Italy, Ugo Betti; from France, Cocteau, Genet, Ionesco, Anouilh, Sartre; and from Spain, Arrabal.

A revolution in playwriting came about when television appeared into everyone's home, but there is no space to consider it here, especially as one can rarely read the scripts. Suffice to say that a dramatist can now not only write for television, but write *only* for it, and a considerable number of authors, such as Alun Owen, Clive Exton, and John Mortimer, are associated with the small screen rather than the public stage.

A writer of the well-constructed play is Peter Levin Shaffer (1926–) whose *Five Finger Exercise* (1958) examined a broken family hiding beneath a façade of respectability. He became concerned with the conflict between idealism and evil, depicting it in the historical spectacle *The Royal Hunt of the Sun* (1964), two double-bills, *The Battle of the Shrivings* (1970), and *Equus* (1973).

Some of the new stage theories were utilized by **John Whiting (1915–63)**, even in his imaginatively farcical *A Penny for a Song* (1951). *Marching Song* (1954), dealing with self-destruction, explored the possibilities of mounting tension without action, but remained cold despite the truth of the emotions analysed. Far more successful was *The Devils* (1961), also on the theme of salvation and destruction, good and evil, and based on Aldous Huxley's *The Devils of Loudun*. More Brechtian in its construction was the very popular *A Man for All Seasons* (1960) by **Robert Oxton Bolt (1924–)**, which dealt not only with Thomas More's strivings against various antagonists but the conflict within himself to determine the principles for which he would die. Most of Bolt's career has been given to writing for films, but he returned to the theme of power politics and the clash of ambitions in *Vivat! Vivat, Regina* (1970). Very different had been his first success—*Flowering Cherry* (1957), set in the present and dealing with self-deception striving to disguise failure.

English drama took an entirely new turn with the establishment in 1956 of the English Stage Company at the Royal Court Theatre. It aimed to present the best foreign plays and to encourage new native writers; its private productions without decor gave inestimable help to young actors and writers, and helped to disseminate new ideas. Outstanding among its products was **John James Osborne (1929–)**, whose *Look Back in Anger* (1956) gave the strongest fillip to the concept of the Angry Young Man; the tragi-comic depiction of the failure, the liar, and the irresponsible showed him bolstered up with optimism and nostalgia for a past that always seemed better than the present. A better-constructed play on the same topic was *Epitaph for George Dillon* (1957), written in collaboration with Anthony Creighton, but when he reworked the theme in *The Entertainer* (1957) he merely provided a vehicle for a star actor. After some more unsuccessful productions, *Luther* (1961) regained some prestige for him, though the sixteenth-century man of religion is shown as an A.Y.M. of his time. *Inadmissible Evidence* (1964), in which self-indulgence and vanity underlies the anti-hero's disgust at hypocrisy and outdated laws, had considerable success, but in seeking to attack everything and to concern himself with abnormalities of sex, Osborne seemed to lose his way in *Plays for England* (1963), *A Patriot for Me* (1965), *West of Suez* (1971), and *Watch It Come Down* (1976).

John Arden (1930–) achieved success at the Royal Court with *Live Like Pigs* (1958), a Brechtian survey of behaviour by means of words, music, song, and symbolism. *The Happy Haven* (1960) was an expressionist farce with masks. When he dealt with very real people involved in a complex situation and seeking for principles to guide them, as in *Serjeant Musgrave's Dance* (1959), Arden produced his best work. He used historical events as settings for the evaluation of morality in *Armstrong's Last Goodnight* (1964) and *Left-Handed Liberty* (1965). With his wife, Arden has written many experimental pieces for amateurs, especially young people.

Ann Jellicoe (1927–) is best known for her plays about the violent, unorganized world of the teenager expressed in semi-articulate dialogue which illustrates the insecurity and meaninglessness of a frivolous world; these plays are *The Sport of My Mad Mother* (1956) and *The Knack* (1961). Not many English writers have attempted to follow Arrabal, Ionesco, and Albee into the theatre of the absurd, but one who retreats from reason and deals with the logic of the non-sequitur is **Norman Frederick Simpson (1919–)** author of *A Resounding Tinkle* (1957), *One-Way Pendulum* (1959), *The Cresta Run* (1965) and a number of one-act farces of words without action. Other Royal Court productions of note were *The Mulberry Bush* by Angus Wilson, *Love from Margaret* by Evelyn Ford, *The Long and the Short and the Tall* by Willis Hall (who then devoted most of his time to radio and television), and Nigel Dennis's *Cards of Identity*, a witty onslaught on the dogmatism which restricts modern man.

The Theatre Royal, Stratford (East London), was from 1953 to 1961 the Theatre Workshop of Joan Littlewood where producer, playwright, and actors worked in a dedicated fashion to alter a script into a stage-piece satisfactory to them all; indeed, so much was changed and added in rehearsal-discussions that one wonders how far the final version is a true representation of the author's original intentions.

The most notable products were **Brendan Behan (1923–64)** and **Shelagh Delaney (1939–)**. Behan's short but tumultuous life included spells in Borstal and prison for political offences, and his plays too are tumultuous. They have little plot, but numerous themes expressed with all the fervour, fluency and imaginative figuration of Irish rhetoric. His comedy *The Quare Fellow* (1954) was more successful than the melodrama of Irish troubles in *The Hostage* (1958). Shelagh Delaney became famous for her combination of sordid realism and romantic dream fantasy in *A Taste of Honey* (1958), in which she conjures up the innocence of young love and, by contrast, the conflicts of mother-daughter relationship and of homosexuality. Since this play she has achieved little. Theatre Workshop's other successes include Frank Norman's musical *Fings Ain't Wot They Used to Be* (1959) and the collectively composed *Oh! What a Lovely War*.

For a time the leading figure in post-War drama was **Arnold Wesker (1932–)** whose loosely related trilogy—*Chicken Soup with Barley* (1958), *Roots* (1959), *I'm Talking About Jerusalem* (1960)—dealt with East End Jews in search of security, principles, and happiness. Though he attempted to show the working-class over nearly thirty years, he had reluctantly to admit that there was a lack of progress; there was also a lack of purpose, for the Welfare State had brought comfort and destroyed causes. Wesker seemed unsure of what he was trying to prove, for at times he apparently sought after pseudo-culture or a return to nineteenth-century socialism. *Chips with Everything* (1962) was part comedy, part satire, part a tragic allegory heavily coloured with mysticism. *Their Very Own and Golden City* (1965) was a long, elaborate study of socialism and social progress, but Wesker again showed that his views on society were out of date, and he had given himself up to pessimism, as he also did in *The Friends* (1970). Wesker was responsible for founding Centre 42, which was to take the arts to neglected places.

Another dealing with the Jewish East End is **Bernard Kops (1928–)**, who wrote rather sentimentally of young people trying to establish contacts; his mixture of fantasy and social message, wit, song, dance, and diatribe is seen in *The Hamlet of Stepney Green* (1956) and *The Dream of Peter Mann* (1960); but there is a new toughness, even cynicism, in the outrageously comic *Enter Solly Gold* (1962).

Henry Livings (1929–) verges on the theatre of the absurd with his exposures of people and their needs in a dehumanized world, and the stupidity they display; his plays are strings of incidents, each relating to a character—his 'ten-minute takes'—and yet he has successfully employed a great variety of styles. The almost plotless *Big Soft Nellie* (1961) was followed by a Services comedy, *Nil Carborundum* (1962); *Kelly's Eye* (1963) was a sensational melodrama but *Eh?* (1964) a zany farce. After the play-revue *Little Mrs Foster* (1966), Livings settled for farce in a more conventional framework with *Honour and Offer* (1968) and *The Finest Family in the Land* (1970). But *Pongo Plays* (1971) are short Lancashire comedies set in the late nineteenth century.

David Mercer (1928–) is not unlike Livings in some ways. In short scenes, monologues, outpourings of wit, he gives pictures of people isolated in their environment and finding in madness or eccentricity the only relief from tension. Such is the impact of the modern world that one must rebel against it or hide away. His plays include *Ride a Cock Horse* (1965), *A Suitable Case for Treatment* (1966), *After Haggerty* (1970), and *Duck Song* (1974). David Storey (see p. 572) also sees madness or craziness as the only defence, but his comedies are expressed in a more conventional form, usually a central incident which involves a number of people given to expressing themselves about society, as in *The Restoration of Arnold Middleton* (1966), *The Contractor* (1969), *The Changing Room* (1971), and *Life Class* (1974). The influence of Beckett is immediately seen in the plays of Tom Stoppard (1937–), a Czech who eventually settled in this country. His characters are suspended in isolation; they do nothing but philosophize; they know less about themselves than the audience does; words, acts, ideas all seem part of a stream of irrelevancies. He made a name for himself with *Rosencrantz and Guildenstern Are Dead* (1966), followed by *The Real Inspector Hound* (1968), but more recent plays—*Jumpers* (1972), *Travesties* (1974), and *Dirty Linen* (1976)—have extended his reputation in the commercial theatre.

Harold Pinter (1930–) conveys the rambling ambiguities and silences of everyday conversation with an amazing authenticity that is obviously much influenced by Beckett, and uses them to build up the sense of menace and scarcely restrained violence which characterize *The Birthday Party* (1958), *The Dumb Waiter* (1960), and *The Caretaker* (1960). The plays are quite short and set in an enclosed, claustrophobic space; the characters are always in doubt about their function, and in fear of someone or something 'outside'. More recently Pinter has written on a larger scale and in a less restricted way, for instance in *A Night Out* (1961) and *The Homecoming* (1965), but he still prefers the shorter play, as in *Silence* (1969), and the drama of unidentified menace, such as *Old Times* (1971). Among Pinter's many achievements, he has demonstrated how plays for radio and television can be adapted to suit the stage, and that the so-called legitimate drama can gain much from the techniques necessitated by other media. John Clifford Mortimer (1923–) is another who made his name and learnt his methods from radio and television, *Dock Brief* (1957) being developed from a TV script. His aim is to write sympathetically about "the lonely, the neglected, and the unsuccessful" and to combat the established rules in whatever form they take, as in *The Wrong Side of the Park* (1960) and *Two Stars for Comfort* (1972), but when he writes full-length plays he tends to lose his incisiveness and his understanding of the nuances of character. More successful are the comedies *Collaboration* (1973) and *The Bells of Hell* (1977), and his tender, autobiographical review of an era in *A Voyage Round My Father* (1970).

Smaller theatres, acting in the round, audience involvement—these are typical of post-War conditions in drama. Now it is believed by some that the writer and the actor must make a direct attack on the audience by horrifying, shocking, even disgusting situations. **Edward Bond (1935–)** is one of these writers. Even his imagery is violent, and expressed in terse, unambiguous language; all authority is evil, man is in social, political, and mental chains, and the world is a place of despair. *Saved* (1965), *Narrow Road to the Deep North* (1968), *Lear* (1971), *Bingo* (1974), and *The Fool* (1975)—each is an imaginatively different expression of his basic philosophy, but *Early Morning* (1968) is an excellent example of 'black' farce. **Giles Cooper (1918–66)** wrote two comedies, *Everything in the Garden* (1962) and *Happy Family* (1966), which were more than satires on the middle classes; they were revelations of a cheerless society without hope of amelioration. This stripping bare of middle-class morality was the basis of *The Rattle of a Simple Man* (1963), *Staircase* (1966), and *Mother Adam* (1970) by **Charles Dyer (1928–)** but Dyer is also concerned with the sufferings that arise from a failure to establish contact. Fringe theatres have been particularly given to dealing with the least attractive forms of modern life in a way that aimed to shock, as with Snoo Wilson's *The Beast* (1974) and *I Was Hitler's Maid* by Chris Wilkinson. The best-known exponent of the style is **David Halliwell (1936–)**. His *Little Malcolm and his Struggle against the Eunuchs* (1965) shows the A.Y.M's revolutionary fervour inevitably turning into fascism, and *K. D. Dufford . . .* (1969) explores a horror situation from what the author terms a 'multi-viewpoint,' a technique he employs also in *Much from Three Angles* (1970) and *Bleats from a Brighouse Pleasureground* (1971).

What has been called the Theatre of Cruelty has also been exploited by **David Rudkin** (*Afore Night Come*, 1962) and **Johnny Speight** (*The Knacker's Yard*, 1962) but the outstanding writer of 'black' farce, where violence, death, cruelty, and callousness are accepted without comment as essential parts of humanity, was **Joe Orton (1933–67)**. His amoral insouciance and brilliant wit made up for much in *Entertaining Mr Sloane* (1964), *Loot* (1967), and *What the Butler Saw* (1969). Not at all comic are the plays of E. A. Whitehead (1933–); they are pessimistic depictions of lazy, unheroic lives and valueless day-dreams, but softened by their compassion towards the women victims of this sleazy world. His noteworthy plays are *The Foursome* (1971), *Alpha Beta* (1972), and *The Sea Anchor* (1974). Another writer who is able to write very convincingly as if from a woman's point of view is Frank Marcus (1928–), though the situations he presents are unusually complex. His best plays are *The Formation Dancers* (1964), *The Killing of Sister George* (1965), *Mrs Mouse, Are You Within?* (1968), and *Notes on a Love Affair* (1972).

Two writers have experimented in many different styles and yet remained basically traditional in their construction of plays: Alan Bennett (1934–) offers satire of genteel society and nostalgia for past ideals, all in an atmosphere that suggests a certain shabbiness and lack of real values (*Forty Years On* (1968), *Getting On* (1971), *Habeas Corpus* (1973)); and Christopher Hampton (1946–) ranges from clever middle-class comedy to historico-social document (*When Did You Last See My Mother?* (1967), *The Philanthropist* (1970), *Savages* (1973), *Treats* (1976). But more versatile than even the above, and far more imaginative in his handling of material, is Peter Nichols (1927–). *A Day in the Death of Joe Egg* (1967) is a most sensitive depiction of marriage and a spastic child; *Forget-Me-Not-Lane* (1971) recalls the War years through the eyes of young people, a comedy mélange of music, personal reminiscences, impersonations, and moments of history; *The National Health* (1969) and *Chez Nous* (1974) are mordant satires in a language that forces one to listen even when it hurts.

To conclude this brief consideration of some modern playwrights it is fitting to mention two highly skilled and very amusing writers of box-office successes. William Douglas Home (1912–) made his name with *The Chiltern Hundreds* (1947) and followed it with many others, including *The Reluctant Debutante* (1955), *The Secretary Bird* (1969), *Lloyd George Knew My Father* (1974), and *The Kingfisher* (1977). Alan Ayckbourn (1939–) has found the right style to assure himself of West End comedy 'runs' with *Relatively Speaking* (1967), *How the Other Half Loves* (1970), and the trilogy of *The Norman Conquests* (1974).

4. WRITERS OF MISCELLANEOUS PROSE

After the War came volumes of dispatches, correspondence, and dossiers, few of which now interest anyone but the historian; the same may be said of the memoirs of wartime leaders. One book, however, which is likely to keep its reputation is *The Last Days of Hitler* (1956) by H. R. Trevor-Roper. Vast numbers of escape stories and true adventures found millions of readers; *The Wooden Horse* (1949) by Eric Williams and *The Jungle Is Neutral* (1949) by F. Spencer Chapman are some of the few which remain popular. Perhaps the best personal statement from a combatant was *The Last Enemy* (1942) by Richard Hillary. Among writers on the War, **Sir Winston Churchill (1874-1965)** stands supreme. His speeches, beginning with *Into Battle* (1941) add further splendour to British oratory, and *The Second World War* (1948-54) combines the breadth and grasp of a great mind with literary gifts rare in a politician.

The most popular form of non-fiction is always biography and autobiography. An outstanding work in this category was the four-volume reminiscences of Sir Osbert Sitwell which were issued between 1945 and 1949. Others who published works largely relating to their early days were Sean O'Casey (*I Knock at the Door* and *Pictures in the Hallway*), Sir Charles Oman (*Memories of Victorian Oxford*), Richard Church (*Over the Bridge*), James Kirkup (*Sorrows, Passions and Alarms*), Laurie Lee (*Cider with Rosie*) and George Bernard Shaw (*Sixteen Self Sketches*). Equally fascinating are some books by people who became known to the public only after they had written of their memories. There are unique qualities of observation and the selection of the significant in *Portrait of Elmbury* by John Moore, the trilogy of *Lark Rise to Candleford* by Flora Thompson, and the veterinary tales of Yorkshire by 'James Herriot.'

Two travellers attained great success as writers: one was Gerald Durrell, whose experiences were recounted in *The Overloaded Ark*, *The Bafut Beagles*, and *A Zoo in my Luggage*, and whose account of childhood in *My Family and Other Animals* ranks with the best of its kind; the other was the South African Laurens van der Post, author of *The Lost World of the Kalahari* and *Venture to the Interior*. Sir Arthur Grimble delighted many with his stories of the Pacific in *A Pattern of Islands* and *Return to the Islands*; and Lawrence Durrell (see p. 570) recaptured the atmosphere and mood of the Eastern Mediterranean in *Prospero's Cell* and *Bitter Lemons*.

The post-War period has seen the publication of many excellent books by great historians; indeed, it is difficult to select from so many gifted scholars and incisive writers. Sir Arthur Bryant appealed to many people at a very difficult time with *English Saga 1840–1940* and *The Years of Endurance, 1793–1802*, and later with *The Age of Elegance, 1812–1822*. More specialized in their subject-matter are D. W. Brogan and A. L. Rowse, though, because of its sentimental appeal, the latter's *The Early Churchills* attracts the general reader. C. V. Wedgwood has made the seventeenth century her province with such works as *Montrose, The King's Peace*, and *The King's War*; while A. J. P. Taylor has offered expositions of power-politics in *The Habsburg Monarchy, Bismarck*, and *The Struggle for Mastery in Europe 1848–1918*. On a more limited scale, but with a wealth of illuminating detail, are *The Reason Why* and *The Great Hunger* by Cecil Woodham-Smith, which deal largely with nineteenth-century Ireland, and John Prebble's four books on the destruction of the Scottish clan system. Finally, one must mention what are perhaps the most outstanding works of post-War historians—*Europe in Decay* and *Avenues of History* by Sir Lewis Namier, and Sir Arnold Toynbee's *Civilisation on Trial, The World and the West*, and the colossal *Study of History* published between 1934 and 1959.

Works on religion and philosophy reflect a growing concern among serious thinkers about contemporary changes in moral standards, and the need of the general public for principles relevant to a time of insecurity and emotional upheaval. Two writers who have had more influence than most are C. S. Lewis, with *The Problem of Pain* and *The Screwtape Letters*, and Bertrand Russell (see p. 559). Two artists whose writings have attained more than a national reputation are Sir Kenneth Clark, whose books include *Landscape into Art* and *Civilisation: A Personal View*, the latter being developed from his highly praised television series; and Sir Nikolaus Pevsner, who wrote *An Outline of European Architecture* and edited the comprehensive *Buildings of England*.

Popular scientific literature has grown to amazing proportions, but here one can mention only a few of the more important writers who published books during the period. Sir Julian Huxley enhanced his reputation with *On Living in a Revolution* and *Man in the Modern World*, as did Sir James Jeans with *Physics and Philosophy*. Jacob Bronowski showed himself to be both a scientist and a literary critic, but reached his widest audience with *The Ascent of Man*, developed from a television series. Other scientists who commanded attention are C. H. Waddington, J. D. Bernal, W. W. Sawyer, Margaret Mead, and Sir Mortimer Wheeler; their main interests range from mathematics to archaeology, but all have gained applause for the style in which their books are written, quite apart from the attractions of the subject-matter.

Much of the best literary criticism will be mentioned in the Bibliography to this book and therefore need not be referred to in this chapter. However, this chapter is the proper place to draw attention to *The Heritage of Symbolism* by Sir Maurice Bowra, as well as his *Heroic Poetry* and *The Romantic Imagination*; *Style* by F. L. Lucas; *Explorations* by L. C. Knights; and William Empson's *Seven Types of Ambiguity* and *Some Versions of the Pastoral*. In conclusion one might notice three important side-issues of literature. Nevill Coghill popularized Chaucer by modernizing his language not only in books but on radio and television, and in a musical; Kingsley Amis made an appraisal of science-fiction in *New Maps of Hell*; and Peter and Iona Opie opened up entirely new territory with *The Oxford Dictionary of Nursery Rhymes*, *The Lore and Language of Schoolchildren*, and *Children's Games in Street and Playground*.

SUGGESTIONS FOR FURTHER READING

(*Works in the following list are in chronological order to enable the student to gain some impression of the changing trends of criticism.*)

GENERAL

ed. P. F. Wilson and B. Dobrée, *The Oxford History of English Literature* (1945–); D. Daiches, *A Critical History of English Literature* (1960); ed. B. Ford, *A Guide to English Literature* (rev. 1961); W. J. Entwistle and E. Gillett, *The Literature of England, A.D. 500–1960* (rev. 1962); ed. A. C. Baugh, *A Literary History of England* (rev. 1967); ed. G. Sampson, *The Concise Cambridge History of English Literature* (rev. 1970); E. Légouis and L. Cazamian, *A History of English Literature* (rev. 1971); ed. var., *History of Literature in the English Language* (1971).

E. A. Baker, *History of the English Novel* (1924–39); W. Allen, *The English Novel: A Short Critical History* (1954); T. O. Beechcroft, *The Modest Art: A Survey of the Short Story in English* (1968).

H. J. C. Grierson and J. C. Smith, *A Critical History of English Poetry* (1944); K. Hopkins, *English Poetry: A Short History* (1963).

A. Nicoll, *A History of English Drama 1660–1900* (rev. 1952).

The Cambridge History of American Literature (rev. 1969); M. Lindsay *History of Scottish Literature* (1977).

CHAPTER I: THE OLD ENGLISH PERIOD

(i) **General and Social Background:** D. Whitelock, *The Audience of 'Beowulf'* (1951); D. Whitelock, *The Beginnings of English Society* (1952); R. I. Page, *Life in Anglo-Saxon England* (1970); F. M. Stenton, *Anglo-Saxon England* (rev. 1971); D. J. V. Fisher, *The Anglo-Saxon Age* (1973).

(ii) **Literature:** C. W. Kennedy, *The Earliest English Poetry* (1943); S. B. Greenfield, *A Critical History of Old English Literature* (1966); ed. E. G. Stanley, *Continuations and Beginnings: Studies in Old English Literature* (1966); C. L. Wrenn, *A Study of Old English Literature* (1967); T. A. Shippey, *Old English Verse* (1972); D. Pearsall, *Old English and Middle English Literature* (1977).

(iii) **Translations:** R. K. Gordon, *Anglo-Saxon Poetry* (1926); C. W. Kennedy, *Early English Christian Poetry* (1952); ed. G. N. Garmonsway, *The Anglo-Saxon Chronicle* (1953); B. Mitchell, *'The Battle of Maldon' and other Old English Poems* (1965); M. Alexander, *The Earliest English Poems* (1966); M. Alexander, *Beowulf* (1973).

CHAPTER II: THE MIDDLE ENGLISH PERIOD

(i) **General and Social Background:** G. G. Coulton, *Medieval Panorama* (1938); J. R. H. Moorman, *Church Life in England in the Thirteenth Century* (1945); A. L. Poole, *From Domesday Book to Magna Carta* (1951);

D. M. Stenton, *English Society in the Early Middle Ages* (1952); J. J. Bagley, *Life in Medieval England* (1960); A. Bryant, *The Medieval Foundation* (1966).

(ii) **Literature:** W. P. Ker, *Epic and Romance* (1908); C. S. Lewis, *The Allegory of Love* (1936); B. Dickins and R. M. Wilson, *Early Middle English Texts* (1950); G. Kane, *Middle English Literature* (1951); R. S. Loomis, *The Development of Arthurian Romance* (1963); ed. J. A. W. Bennett and G. V. S. Smithers, *Early Middle English Verse and Prose* (1966); R. M. Wilson, *Early Middle English Literature* (rev. 1968); R. Woolf, *The English Religious Lyric in the Middle Ages* (1968); D. Mehl, *Middle English Romances of the Thirteenth and Fourteenth Centuries* (1969); ed. J. Burrow, *English Verse 1300–1500* (1977); D. Pearsall, *Old English and Middle English Poetry* (1977).

(iii) **Translations:** R. S. Loomis and R. Ward, *Medieval English Verse and Prose in Modernized Versions* (1948); J. J. R. Tolkien, *Sir Gawain, The Pearl, Sir Orpheo* (1975).

CHAPTER III: THE AGE OF CHAUCER, 1350–1450

(i) **General and Social Background:** E. Power, *Medieval People* (1924); G. R. Owst, *Literature and Pulpit in Mediaeval England* (1933); C. S. Lewis, *The Allegory of Love* (1936); G. M. Trevelyan, *Illustrated English Social History*, Vol. 1 (1944); H. S. Bennett, *Chaucer and the Fifteenth Century* (1947); G. Kane, *Middle English Literature* (1951); A. R. Myers, *England in the Late Middle Ages* (1952); A. Bryant, *The Age of Chivalry* (1963); ed. M. Hussey, *Chaucer's World* (1967); F. R. H. Du Boulay, *An Age of Ambition: English Society in the Late Middle Ages* (1970); ed. J. Burrow, *English Verse 1300–1500* (1977); D. Pearsall, *Old English and Middle English Poetry* (1977).

(ii) **Chaucer:** N. Coghill, *The Poet Chaucer* (1949); J. Speirs, *Chaucer the Maker* (1951); ed. W. H. Clemen, *Chaucer's Early Poetry* (1964); M. Bowden, *A Reader's Guide to Geoffrey Chaucer* (1965); ed. A. C. Cawley, *Chaucer's Mind and Art* (1969); D. S. Brewer, *Chaucer* (rev. 1973); J. Norton-Smith, *Geoffrey Chaucer* (1974); M. Chute, *Geoffrey Chaucer of England* (1977).

(iii) **Other Poets:** E. T. Donaldson, '*Piers Plowman*': *The C-Text and its Poet* (1949); E. Salter, '*Piers Plowman*': *an Introduction* (1962); H. Fisher, *John Gower: Moral Philosopher and Friend of Chaucer* (1965); M. J. C. Hodgart, *The Ballads* (rev. 1962).

CHAPTER IV: FROM CHAUCER TO SPENSER, 1450–1550

(i) **General and Social Background:** H. S. Bennett, *The Pastons and their England in an Age of Transition* (rev. 1931); M. P. Gilmore, *The World of Humanism 1453–1517* (1952); H. S. Bennett, *English Books and their Readers 1475–1557* (1952); R. Weiss, *Humanism in England during the Fifteenth Century* (rev. 1957); H. A. Mason, *Humanism and Poetry in the Early Tudor Period* (1959).

(ii) **Poetry:** I. A. Gordon, *John Skelton: Poet Laureate* (1943); A. R. Heiserman, *Skelton and Satire* (1961); T. Scott, *Dunbar: A Critical Exposition of the Poems* (1966); J. MacQueen, *Robert Henryson: A Study of the Major Narrative Poems* (1967); D. A. Pearsall, *John Lydgate* (1970).

(iii) **Drama:** E. K. Chambers, *The Medieval Stage* (1903); H. Craig, *English Religious Drama of the Middle Ages* (1955); A. P. Rossiter, *English Drama from Early Times to the Elizabethans* (1950); G. Wickham, *Early English Stages 1300–1600* (1959); ed. N. Denny, *Medieval Drama* (1973).

CHAPTER V: THE AGE OF ELIZABETH, 1550–1630

(i) **General and Social Background:** J. D. Wilson, *Life in Shakespeare's England* (1911); H. Craig, *The Enchanted Glass: The Elizabethan Mind in Literature* (1936); L. C. Knights, *Drama and Society in the Age of Jonson* (1937); E. M. W. Tillyard, *The Elizabethan World Picture* (1943); A. L. Rowse, *The England of Elizabeth* (1950); J. R. Hale, *England and the Italian Renaissance* (1954); F. E. Halliday, *Shakespeare in his Age* (1956); J. Simon, *Education and Society in Tudor England* (1966).

(ii) **Spenser:** P. Parker, *The Allegory of 'The Faerie Queen'* (1960); P. Bayley, *Edmund Spenser: Prince of Poets* (1971).

(iii) **Donne:** see p. 603.

(iv) **Other Poets:** J. Buxton, *Sir Philip Sidney and the English Renaissance* (1954); F. S. Boas, *Sir Philip Sidney: Representative Elizabethan* (1955); J. W. Lever, *The Elizabethan Love Sonnet* (1966).

(v) **Drama:** E. K. Chambers, *The Elizabethan Stage* (1923); M. C. Bradbrook, *Themes and Conventions of Elizabethan Tragedy* (1935); G. B. Harrison, *Elizabethan Plays and Players* (1940); F. T. Bowers, *The Elizabethan Revenge Tragedy, 1587–1642* (1940); M. C. Bradbrook, *The Growth and Structure of Elizabethan Comedy* (1955); T. B. Tomlinson, *A Study of Elizabethan and Jacobean Tragedy* (1964); A. Gurr, *The Shakespearean Stage, 1574–1642* (1970).

(vi) **Marlowe:** F. S. Boas, *Christopher Marlowe: A Biographical and Critical Study* (1940); H. Levin, *The Overreacher* (1954); J. B. Stearne, *Marlowe* (1964): A. L. Rowse, *Christopher Marlowe* (1964).

(vii) **Shakespeare:** A. C. Bradley, *Shakespearean Tragedy* (1904); H. Granville-Barker, *Prefaces to Shakespeare* (1927–47); G. W. Knight, *The Imperial Theme* (1931); E. M. W. Tillyard, *Shakespeare's History Plays* (1944); H. B. Charlton, *Shakespearian Tragedy* (1948); G. W. Knight, *The Wheel of Fire* (1949); E. M. W. Tillyard, *Shakespeare's Problem Plays* (1949); E. M. W. Tillyard, *Shakespeare's Last Plays* (rev. 1951); B. Evans, *Shakespeare's Comedies* (1960); M. M. Charney, *Shakespeare's Roman Plays* (1961); J. D. Wilson, *Shakespeare's Happy Comedies* (1962); C. J. Sisson, *Shakespeare's Tragic Justice* (1962); E. Schanzer, *The Problem Plays of Shakespeare* (1963); E. K. Chambers, *Shakespeare: A Survey* (rev. 1964); A. L. Rowse, *Shakespeare's Sonnets* (1964); L. B. Campbell, *Shakespeare's Histories* (rev. 1964); K. Muir, *Shakespeare: The Comedies* (1965); K. Muir and S. Schoenbaum, *A New Companion to Shakespeare Studies* (1971); ed. M. Bradbury and J. Palmer, *Shakespearian Comedy* (1972); A. L. Rowse, *Shakespeare the Man* (1973); R. Speaight, *Shakespeare: The Man and his Achievement* (1977).

(viii) **Jonson:** E. B. Partridge, *The Broken Compass: A Study of the Major Comedies* (1958); S. K. Orgel, *The Jonsonian Masque* (1965).

(ix) **Other Dramatists:** L. B. Wallis, *Fletcher, Beaumont and Company* (1947); C. Leech, *The John Fletcher Plays* (1962); C. Leech, *John Webster: A Critical Study* (1951); ed. B. Morris, *John Webster* (1970); T. A. Dunn,

Philip Massinger (1957); P. B. Murray, *A Study of Cyril Tourneur* (1965).

(x) **Prose:** F. H. Anderson, *The Philosophy of Francis Bacon* (1949); J. G. Crowther, *Francis Bacon* (1960); B. Vickers, *Francis Bacon and Renaissance Prose* (1968); C. S. Lewis, *The Literary Impact of the Authorised Version* (1950).

CHAPTER VI: THE AGE OF MILTON, 1630-60

(i) **General and Social Background:** H. J. C. Grierson, *Cross-Currents in English Literature of the Seventeenth Century* (1929); B. Willey, *The Seventeenth Century Background* (1934); S. L. Bethell, *The Cultural Revolution of the Seventeenth Century* (1951); C. V. Wedgwood, *Poetry and Politics under the Stuarts* (1960); D. Bush, *English Literature in the Earlier Seventeenth Century* (rev. 1962); M. Ashley, *England in the Seventeenth Century* (rev. 1967); M. Ashley, *Life in Stuart England* (rev. 1967).

(ii) **Milton:** E. M. W. Tillyard, *Studies in Milton* (1951); D. C. Allen, *The Harmonious Vision: Studies in Milton's Poetry* (1954); D. Daiches, *Milton* (rev. 1959); C. Ricks, *Milton's Grand Style* (1963); W. Empson, *Milton's God* (rev. 1965); E. M. W. Tillyard, *Milton* (rev. 1966); ed. C. A. Patrides, *Milton's Epic Poetry* (1967); P. Murray, *Milton: The Modern Phase* (1967); W. R. Parker, *Milton* (1968).

(iii) **Donne:** E. Hardy, *Donne: A Spirit in Conflict* (1943); J. B. Leishman, *The Monarch of Wit: An Analytical and Comparative Study of the Poetry of John Donne* (1951); R. E. Hughes, *The Progress of the Soul* (1969); R. C. Bald, *John Donne* (1970).

(iv) **Marvell:** M. C. Bradbrook and M. G. Lloyd Thomas, *Andrew Marvell* (1940); P. Légouis, *Andrew Marvell: Poet, Puritan, Patriot* (rev. 1965); J. B. Leishman, *The Art of Marvell's Poetry* (1966); J. M. Wallace, *Destiny his Choice: The Loyalism of Marvell* (1968).

(v) **Other Poets:** H. J. C. Grierson, *Metaphysical Lyrics and Poems of the Seventeenth Century* (1921); G. Williamson, *The Donne Tradition* (1930); J. B. Leishman, *The Metaphysical Poets* (1934); A. Alvarez, *The School of Donne* (1961); J. Bennett, *Five Metaphysical Poets* (1964); J. H. Summers, *George Herbert: His Religion and Art* (1954); M. G. Chute, *Two Gentle Men: The Lives of George Herbert and Robert Herrick* (1960); T. S. Eliot, *George Herbert* (1962); G. I. Wade, *Thomas Traherne* (1944); A. L. Clements, *The Mystical Poetry of Thomas Traherne* (1969); F. E. Hutchinson, *Henry Vaughan* (1947); R. A. Durr, *On the Mystical Poetry of Henry Vaughan* (1962).

(vi) **Drama:** F. S. Boas, *An Introduction to Stuart Drama* (1946); C. Leech, *John Ford and the Drama of his Time* (1957); ed. J. R. Brown and B. Harris, *Jacobean Theatre* (1960).

(vii) **Prose:** B. H. G. Wormald, *Clarendon: Politics, History and Religion 1640-1660* (1951); J. Bennett, *Sir Thomas Browne* (1962).

CHAPTER VII: THE AGE OF DRYDEN, 1660-1700

(i) **General and Social Background:** B. Willey, *The Seventeenth Century Background* (1934); C. V. Wedgwood, *Poetry and Politics under the Stuarts* (1960); G. N. Clark, *The Later Stuarts, 1660-1714* (1955); G. M. Trevelyan, *England under the Stuarts* (rev. 1960).

(ii) **Dryden:** D. Nichol Smith, *Dryden* (1950); A. Roper, *Dryden's Poetic*

Kingdoms (1965); B. A. King, *Dryden's Major Plays* (1966); W. Myers, *Dryden* (1973).

(iii) **Other Poets:** J. H. Wilson, *The Court Wits of the Restoration* (1948); G. Walton, *Metaphysical to Augustan: Studies in Tone and Sensibility of the Seventeenth Century* (1955).

(iv) **Drama:** B. Dobrée, *Restoration Tragedy 1660–1720* (1929); W. Connely, *Young George Farquhar* (1949); D. Underwood, *Etherege and the Seventeenth Century Comedy of Manners* (1958); ed. J. R. Brown and B. Harris, *Restoration Theatre* (1965); J. E. Cunningham, *Restoration Drama* (1966); W. H. Van Voris, *The Cultivated Stance: The Designs of Congreve's Plays* (1967); K. Muir, *The Comedy of Manners* (1970).

(v) **Prose:** A. Bryant, *Samuel Pepys* (1933–38); H. Talon, *John Bunyan* (1951); R. Sharrock, *John Bunyan* (1954); M. Furlong, *Puritan's Progress: a Study of John Bunyan* (1975); W. G. Hiscock, *John Evelyn and his Family Circle* (1955).

CHAPTER VIII: THE AGE OF POPE, 1700–50

(i) **General and Social Background:** L. Stephen, *English Literature and Society in the Eighteenth Century* (1904); B. Willey, *The Eighteenth Century Background* (1940); J. R. Sutherland, *A Preface to Eighteenth Century Poetry* (1948); I. Jack, *Augustan Satire* (1952); J. Butt, *The Augustan Age* (1956); G. Tillotson, *Augustan Studies* (1961); D. J. Milburn, *The Age of Wit 1650–1750* (1966); R. Trickett, *The Honest Muse: A Study in Augustan Verse* (1967).

(ii) **Swift:** K. Williams, *Jonathan Swift and the Age of Compromise* (1959); I. Ehrenpreis, *Swift: The Man, his Works and the Age* (1962); D. Donoghue, *Swift* (1969); W. A. Speck, *Swift* (1969); D. Ward, *Swift: An Introductory Essay* (1973); A. L. Rowse, *Jonathan Swift, Major Prophet* (1975).

(iii) **Defoe:** J. R. Sutherland, *Daniel Defoe* (1972); ed. P. Rogers, *Defoe: The Critical Heritage* (1972).

(iv) **Other Prose Writers:** W. Connely, *Sir Richard Steele* (1934); D. G. James, *The Life of Reason: Hobbes, Locke, Bolingbroke* (1949); P. Smithers, *The Life of Joseph Addison* (rev. 1968).

(v) **Pope:** E. Sitwell, *Alexander Pope* (1930); N. Ault, *New Light on Pope* (1949); G. Tillotson, *On the Poetry of Pope* (rev. 1950); R. A. Brower, *Alexander Pope: The Poetry of Allusion* (1959).

(vi) **Drama:** F. N. W. Bateson, *English Comic Drama 1700–1750* (1929); F. S. Boas, *An Introduction to Eighteenth Century Drama* (1953).

CHAPTER IX: THE AGE OF TRANSITION, 1740–1800

(i) **General and Social Background:** L. Stephen, *English Literature and Society in the Eighteenth Century* (1904); C. Hussey, *The Picturesque* (1927); O. Elton, *A Survey of English Literature 1730–1780* (1928); B. Willey, *The Eighteenth Century Background* (1940); R. Trickett, *The Honest Muse: A Study in Augustan Verse* (1962); K. Clark, *The Gothic Revival* (rev. 1962); R. Alter, *Rogue's Progress: Studies in the Picaresque Novel* (1964).

(ii) **The Johnson Circle:** J. Boswell, ed. G. B. Hill and L. F. Powell, *The Life of Samuel Johnson, LL.D.* (1934–50); W. K. Wimsatt, *The Prose Style* *of Samuel Johnson* (1941); M. Joyce, *Samuel Johnson* (1955); W. J. Bate, *The Achievement of Samuel Johnson* (1955); H. Pearson, *Johnson and Boswell* (1958); J. Wain, *Samuel Johnson* (1974).

R. M. Wardle, *Oliver Goldsmith* (1958).

ed. F. A. Pottle, *Boswell's London Journal* (1950); *Boswell on the Grand Tour* (1953–55); *Boswell: The Ominous Years* (1963); *James Boswell: The Earlier Years* (1966).

(iii) **Poetry:** W. C. Brown, *The Triumph of Form: A Study of the Late Masters of the Heroic Couplet* (1948).

D. Cecil, *The Poetry of Thomas Gray* (1945); D. Cecil, *Two Quiet Lives* (1948); R. W. Ketton-Cremer, *Thomas Gray* (1955); M. Golden, *Thomas Gray* (1964).

P. L. Carver, *The Life of a Poet: A Biography of William Collins* (1967).

D. Cecil, *The Stricken Deer: The Life of Cowper* (1929); M. J. Quinlan, *William Cowper: A Critical Life* (1953); M. Golden, *In Search of Stability: The Poetry of William Cowper* (1960).

D. Grant, *James Thomson: Poet of 'The Seasons'* (1951).

L. Haddakin, *The Poetry of Crabbe* (1955).

C. Devlin, *Poor Kit Smart* (1961); M. Dearnley, *The Poetry of Christopher Smart* (1969).

C. Keith, *The Russet Coat* (1956); T. Crawford, *Burns: A Study of the Poems and Songs* (1960); D. Daiches, *Robert Burns* (rev. 1966); H. Douglas, *Robert Burns* (1976).

J. M. Murry, *William Blake* (1936); N. Frye, *Fearful Symmetry: A Study of William Blake* (1947); G. W. Digby, *Symbol and Image in William Blake* (1957); M. Wilson, *The Life of William Blake* (rev. 1971).

(iv) **The Novel:** I. P. Watt, *The Rise of the Novel: Studies in Defoe, Richardson and Fielding* (1957); F. W. Bradbrook, *Jane Austen and her Predecessors* (1966).

T. C. D. Eaves and B. D. Kimpel, *Samuel Richardson* (1971); W. M. Sale, *Samuel Richardson: Master Printer* (1971).

E. Jenkins, *Henry Fielding* (1947); F. H. Dudden, *Henry Fielding: His Life, Works and Times* (1952); A. H. Wright, *Henry Fielding: Mask and Feast* (1965); R. Alter, *Fielding and the Nature of the Novel* (1968).

F. S. Boege, *Smollett's Reputation as a Novelist* (1947); L. M. Knapp, *Tobias Smollett: Doctor of Men and Manners* (1949); D. Bruce, *Radical Doctor Smollet* (1964).

W. B. Piper, *Laurence Sterne* (1965); D. Thomson, *Wild Excursions: The Life and Fiction of Laurence Sterne* (1972).

J. Hemlow, *The History of Fanny Burney* (1958); W. Gerin, *The Young Fanny Burney* (1961).

(v) **Other Prose:** P. Magnus, *Edmund Burke* (1939); ed. P. P. Stanlis, *The Relevance of Edmund Burke* (1964); M. Joyce, *Edward Gibbon* (1953); H. L. Bond, *The Literary Art of Edward Gibbon* (1960).

(vi) **Sheridan:** J. W. Cove, *Sheridan: His Life and his Theatre* (1947).

CHAPTER X: THE RETURN TO NATURE, 1790–1830

(i) **General and Social Background:** O. Elton, *A Survey of English Literature 1780–1830* (1912); A. Bryant, *Years of Victory* (1944); C. M. Bowra, *The Romantic Imagination* (1950); A. E. Rodway, *Godwin and the*

Age of Transition (1952); G. Hough, *The Romantic Poets* (1953); M. Peckham, *Beyond the Tragic Vision* (1962); A. E. Rodway, *The Romantic Conflict* (1963).

(ii) **Wordsworth**: H. l'A. Fausset, *The Lost Leader* (1933); J. C. Smith, *A Study of Wordsworth* (1944); H. Darbishire, *The Poet Wordsworth* (1950); M. Moorman, *William Wordsworth* (1957–65); C. Salvesen, *The Landscape of Memory: A Study of Wordsworth's Poetry* (1965); M. Drabble, *Wordsworth* (1966).

(iii) **Coleridge**: J. L. Lowes, *The Road to Xanadu: A Study in the Ways of the Imagination* (1927); ed. H. House, *Coleridge* (1953); R. H. Fogle, *The Idea of Coleridge's Criticism* (1962); J. Cornwell, *Coleridge, Poet and Revolutionary* (1973).

(iv) **Byron**: P. Quennell, *Byron: The Years of Fame* (1935); P. Quennell, *Byron in Italy* (1941); M. K. Joseph, *Byron the Poet* (1964); L. A. Marchand, *Byron's Poetry* (1966); J. D. Jump, *Byron* (1972).

(v) **Shelley**: E. Blunden, *Shelley* (1946); C. H. Baker, *Shelley's Major Poetry* (1948); K. N. Cameron, *The Young Shelley* (1951); D. King-Hele, *Shelley: His Thought and Work* (1960); K. N. Cameron, *Shelley and his Circle* (1961–70).

(vi) **Keats**: Lord Gorell, *John Keats: The Principle of Beauty* (1948); F. Inglis, *Keats* (1966); I. Jack, *Keats and the Mirror of Art* (1967): R. Gittings, *John Keats* (1968).

(vii) **Other Poets**: G. Carnall, *Robert Southey and his Age* (1960); J. W. and A. Tibble, *John Clare* (rev. 1972).

(viii) **Scott**: U. Pope-Hennessey, *Sir Walter Scott* (1948); D. Davie, *The Heyday of Sir Walter Scott* (1961); A. Welsh, *The Hero of the Waverley Novels* (1963); ed. A. N. Jeffares, *Scott's Mind and Art* (1969); E. Johnson, *Sir Walter Scott: The Great Unknown* (1970); C. Oman, *The Wizard of the North* (1973).

(ix) **Austen**: M. Lascelles, *Jane Austen and her Art* (1939); A. H. Wright, *Jane Austen's Novels* (1953); F. W. Bradbrook, *Jane Austen and her Predecessors* (1966); D. Mansell, *The Novels of Jane Austen* (1973); J. Rees, *Jane Austen: Woman and Writer* (1976).

(x) **Other Novelists**: C. Dawson, *His Fine Wit: A Study of Thomas Love Peacock* (1970); M. Butler, *Maria Edgeworth* (1972).

(xi) **Lamb**: E. Blunden, *Charles Lamb and his Contemporaries* (1933).

(xii) **De Quincey**: J. C. Metcalf, *De Quincey* (1940); J. E. Jordan, *Thomas De Quincey: Literary Critic* (1953); ed. B. Dobrée, *Thomas De Quincey* (1965).

(xiii) **Hazlitt**: C. M. Maclean, *Born under Saturn* (1943); P. P. Howe, *The Life of William Hazlitt* (rev. 1947); H. C. Baker, *William Hazlitt* (1962).

CHAPTER XI: THE VICTORIAN AGE, 1830–90

(i) **General and Social Background**: G. K. Chesterton, *The Victorian Age in Literature* (1913); O. Elton, *A Survey of English Literature 1830–1880* (1920); F. L. Lucas, *Ten Victorian Poets* (1940); G. M. Trevelyan, *Illustrated English Social History: The Nineteenth Century* (1944); G. Hough, *The Last Romantics* (1947); B. Willey, *Nineteenth Century Studies* (1949); J. H. Buckley, *The Victorian Temper: A Study in Literary Culture* (1952); W. Irvine, *Apes, Angels and Victorians* (1955); B. Willey, *More Nineteenth*

Century Studies (1956); R. Williams, *Culture and Society 1780–1950* (1958); C. Petrie, *The Victorians* (1960); R. Williams, *The Long Revolution* (1961); J. H. Miller, *The Disappearance of God: Five Nineteenth-Century Writers* (1964).

(ii) **Tennyson:** C. Tennyson, *Alfred Tennyson* (1949); J. B. Stearne, *Tennyson* (1966); C. Ricks, *Tennyson* (1972).

(iii) **Browning:** W. C. De Vane, *A Browning Handbook* (rev. 1956); T. Blackburn, *Robert Browning: A Study of his Poetry* (1967); P. Drew, *The Poetry of Browning* (1970).

(iv) **Other Poets:** C. B. Tinker and H. F. Lowry, *The Poetry of Matthew Arnold* (1941); D. G. James, *Matthew Arnold and the Decline of English Romanticism* (1961); D. Bush, *Matthew Arnold: A Survey of his Poetry and Prose* (1971).

W. Gaunt, *The Pre-Raphaelite Tragedy* (1942); O. Doughty, *A Victorian Romantic: Dante Gabriel Rossetti* (1949); D. S. R. Wellard, *The Pre-Raphaelites in Literature and Art* (1953); R. S. Grylls, *Portrait of Rossetti* (1964); J. D. Hunt, *The Pre-Raphaelite Imagination* (1968).

M. B. Grennan, *William Morris: Medievalist and Revolutionary* (1946); E. P. Thompson, *William Morris: Romantic to Revolutionary* (1955); R. P. Arnot, *William Morris: The Man and the Myth* (1964).

A. Hayter, *Mrs. Browning: A Poet's Work and its Setting* (1962).

(v) **Dickens:** R. J. Cruikshank, *Charles Dickens and Early Victorian England* (1949); K. J. Fielding, *Charles Dickens* (1958); R. Garis, *The Dickens Theatre: A Reassessment of the Novels* (1965); C. Hibbert, *The Making of Charles Dickens* (1967); F. R. and Q. D. Leavis, *Dickens the Novelist* (1970); J. Casey, *The Violent Effigy: A Study of Dickens' Imagination* (1973).

(vi) **Thackeray:** G. N. Ray, *The Buried Life* (1952); G. Tillotson, *Thackeray the Novelist* (1954); G. N. Ray, *Thackeray* (1955–58); I. M. Williams, *Thackeray* (1968).

(vii) **The Brontës:** F. E. Ratchford, *The Brontës' Web of Childhood* (1941); L. L. Hinkley, *The Brontës: Charlotte and Emily* (1948); I. S. Ewbank, *Their Proper Sphere: A Study of the Brontë Sisters as Early Victorian Female Novelists* (1966); N. Sherry, *Charlotte and Emily Brontë* (1969); J. Hewish, *Emily Brontë* (1969); M. Peters, *Unquiet Soul: Biography of Charlotte Brontë* (1975).

(viii) **Eliot:** J. Bennett, *George Eliot: Her Mind and Art* (1948); W. J. Harvey, *The Art of George Eliot* (1961); T. S. Pearce, *George Eliot* (1973); R. Liddell, *The Novels of George Eliot* (1977).

(ix) **Trollope:** M. Sadleir, *Trollope: A Commentary* (rev. 1945); A. O. J. Cockshut, *Anthony Trollope* (1955); R. ap Roberts, *Trollope, Artist and Moralist* (1971).

(x) **Other Novelists:** D. Cecil, *Early Victorian Novelists* (1934); K. Tillotson, *Novels of the Eighteen-Forties* (1954); L. Cazamian, *The Social Novel in England 1830–1850* (1973).

A. Pollard, *Mrs. Gaskell* (1965); W. A. Craik, *Elizabeth Gaskell and the English Provincial Novel* (1975).

K. Robinson, *Wilkie Collins* (1951).

R. B. Martin, *The Dust of Combat: A Life of Charles Kingsley* (1959); S. Chitty, *The Beast and the Monk: The Life of Charles Kingsley* (1974); B. Colloms, *Charles Kingsley* (1975).

L. Cooper, *Robert Louis Stevenson* (1947); D. Daiches, *Robert Louis Stevenson* (1947); J. C. Furnas, *Voyage to Windward* (1951).

(xii) **Carlyle:** F. A. Lea, *Carlyle: Prophet of Today* (1943); J. Symons, *Carlyle: The Life and Ideas of a Prophet* (1952).

(xiii) **Macaulay:** D. Knowles, *Lord Macaulay* (1960).

(xiv) **Ruskin:** P. Quennell, *John Ruskin: The Portrait of a Prophet* (1949); D. Leon, *Ruskin the Great Victorian* (1949); J. Evans, *John Ruskin* (1954); J. D. Rosenberg, *The Darkening Glass* (1963).

CHAPTER XII: THE BIRTH OF MODERN LITERATURE, 1890–1918

(i) **General and Social Background:** H. Jackson, *The Eighteen Nineties* (1913); D. Hoare, *Some Studies in the Modern Novel* (1938); H. V. Routh, *English Literature and Ideas in the Twentieth Century* (1946); V. de S. Pinto, *The Crisis in English Poetry 1880–1940* (1951); R. Williams, *Culture and Society 1780–1950* (1958); A. C. Ward, *Twentieth Century Literature 1901–1960* (1964); R. H. Ross, *The Georgian Revolt, 1910–1922* (1967); F. Swinnerton, *The Georgian Literary Scene* (rev. 1969); C. Gillie, *Movements in English Literature 1900–1940* (1975).

(ii) **Hardy:** E. Blunden, *Thomas Hardy* (1942); D. Cecil, *Hardy the Novelist* (1943); J. I. M. Stewart, *Thomas Hardy* (1971); M. Millgate, *Thomas Hardy: His Career as a Novelist* (1971); D. Hawkins, *Hardy: Novelist and Poet* (1976).

(iii) **James:** F. O. Matthiessen, *Henry James: The Major Phase* (1946); D. W. Jefferson, *Henry James and the Modern Reader* (1964); S. Chatman, *The Later Style of Henry James* (1972).

(iv) **Conrad:** J. D. Gordan, *Joseph Conrad: The Making of a Novelist* (1940); M. C. Bradbrook, *Joseph Conrad: England's Polish Genius* (1941); L. Gurko, *Joseph Conrad: Giant in Exile* (1965).

(v) **Wells:** N. Nicholson, *H. G. Wells* (1950); B. Bergonzi, *The Early H. G. Wells: A Study of the Scientific Romances* (1961); W. Bellamy, *The Novels of Wells, Bennett, Galsworthy 1890–1910* (1971); N. and J. Mackenzie, *The Time Traveller: The Life of H. G. Wells* (1973).

(vi) **Kipling:** R. Croft-Cooke, *Rudyard Kipling* (1948); B. Dobrée, *Rudyard Kipling: Realist and Fabulist* (1967); P. Mason, *Kipling: The Glass, the Shadow and the Fire* (1975).

(vii) **Other Novelists:** M. C. Donnelly, *George Gissing, Grave Comedian* (1954).

P. N. Furbank, *Samuel Butler* (1948); L. Holt, *Samuel Butler* (1964).

L. Stevenson, *The Ordeal of George Meredith* (1954).

D. Barker, *Writer by Trade: A View of Arnold Bennett* (1966); M. Drabble, *Arnold Bennett* (1974); J. Lucas, *Arnold Bennett: A Study of his Fiction* (1974).

(viii) **Shaw:** H. Pearson, *Bernard Shaw: His Life and Personality* (1942); D. MacCarthy, *Shaw: The Plays* (1951); J. B. Kaye, *Bernard Shaw and the Nineteenth Century Tradition* (1958); M. Meisel, *Shaw and the Nineteenth-Century Theater* (1963); L. Hugo, *Bernard Shaw: Playwright and Preacher* (1971).

(ix) **Synge:** ed. L. Robinson, *The Irish Theatre* (1940); L. A. G. Strong,

John Millington Synge (1941); A. Price, *Synge and the Anglo-Irish Drama* (1961); R. Skelton, *The Writings of J. M. Synge* (1971).

(x) **Other Dramatists:** A. Nicoll, *English Drama 1900–1930* (1973).

D. Barker, *The Man of Principle: A View of John Galsworthy* (1963).

W. D. Dunkel, *Sir Arthur Pinero: A Critical Biography with Letters* (1943).

G. Woodcock, *The Paradox of Oscar Wilde* (1949); St. J. Ervine, *Oscar Wilde: A Present Time Appraisal* (1951); H. M. Hyde, *Oscar Wilde: The Aftermath* (1963).

(xi) **Yeats:** V. K. N. Menon, *The Development of William Butler Yeats* (1942); A. N. Jeffares, *W. B. Yeats: Man and Poet* (1949); T. R. Henn, *The Lonely Tower: Studies in the Poetry of W. B. Yeats* (1950); A. G. Stock, *W. B. Yeats: His Poetry and Thought* (1961); R. Cowell, *W. B. Yeats* (1969); E. Malins, *A Preface to Yeats* (1974).

(xii) **Other Poets:** A. M. Hardie, *Edmund Blunden* (1958).

A. J. Guerard, *Robert Bridges* (1942); E. Thompson, *Robert Bridges 1844–1930* (1945).

G. Richards, *Housman: 1897–1936* (1942); N. Marlow, *A. E. Housman: Scholar and Poet* (1958).

M. Spark, *John Masefield* (1953).

J. E. Walsh, *Strange Harp, Strange Symphony: The Life of Francis Thompson* (1968).

H. Coombes, *Edward Thomas* (1956); E. Blunden, *War Poets, 1914–1918* (1958); H. Owen, *Journey from Obscurity: Wilfred Owen, 1893–1918* (1963–5); C. Hassall, *Rupert Brooke* (1964); B. Bergonzi, *Heroes' Twilight: A Study of the Literature of the Great War* (1965); M. Thorpe, *Siegfried Sassoon* (1966); J. Silkin, *Out of Battle: The Poetry of the Great War* (1972).

CHAPTER XIII: THE INTER-WAR YEARS, 1918–39

(i) **General and Social Background:** R. Graves and A. Hodge, *The Long Week-End* (1940); L. Hudson, *The Twentieth Century Drama* (1946); B. I. Evans, *English Literature between the Wars* (1948); A. Wilson and J. Philippe, *For Whom the Cloche Tolls* (1953); D. Daiches, *The Present Age: after 1920* (1958); G. S. Fraser, *Vision and Rhetoric: Studies in Modern Poetry* (1959); A. C. Ward, *Twentieth Century English Literature 1901–1960* (1964); C. K. Stead, *The New Poetic* (1964); A. Nicoll, *English Drama 1900–1930* (1973); C. Gillie, *Movements in English Literature 1900–1940* (1975).

(ii) **Lawrence:** R. Aldington, *Portrait of a Genius But . . .* (1950); F. R. Leavis, *D. H. Lawrence: Novelist* (1955); G. Hough, *The Dark Sun* (1956); K. M. Sagar, *The Art of D. H. Lawrence* (1966); ed. S. Spender, *D. H. Lawrence: Novelist, Poet, Prophet* (1973).

(iii) **Joyce:** J. Campbell and H. M. Robinson, *A Skeleton Key to 'Finnegans Wake'* (1947); L. A. G. Strong, *The Sacred River: An Approach to James Joyce* (1949); W. Y. Tindall, *A Reader's Guide to James Joyce* (1960); R. Ellmann, *The Consciousness of Joyce* (1977).

(iv) **Woolf:** E. M. Forster, *Virginia Woolf* (1942); J. K. Johnstone, *The Bloomsbury Group* (1954); D. Daiches, *Virginia Woolf* (rev. 1963); J. Bennett, *Virginia Woolf: Her Art as a Novelist* (rev. 1964); B. Blackstone, *Virginia Woolf: A Commentary* (1972).

(v) **Other Novelists:** L. Trilling, *E. M. Forster* (1944); W. H. Stone, *The Cave and the Mountain: A Study of E. M. Forster* (1966).

A. Alpers, *Katherine Mansfield* (1954).

J. A. Atkins, *Aldous Huxley* (rev. 1967); P. Bowering, *Aldous Huxley: A Study of the Major Novels* (1968); G. Woodcock, *Dawn and the Darkest Hour* (1972); S. Bedford, *Aldous Huxley* (1973–4).

(vi) **Hopkins:** J. Pick, *Gerard Manley Hopkins: Priest and Poet* (1942); W. H. Gardner, *Gerard Manley Hopkins* (1948–9); N. H. Mackenzie, *Hopkins* (1968); P. Milward, *Landscape and Inscape* (1975).

(vii) **Eliot:** H. Gardner, *The Art of T. S. Eliot* (1949); G. Williamson, *A Reader's Guide to T. S. Eliot* (1955); F. O. Matthiessen, *The Achievement of T. S. Eliot* (rev. 1958); D. E. Jones, *The Plays of T. S. Eliot* (1960); N. Fry, *T. S. Eliot* (1963).

(viii) **Other Poets:** F. Scarfe, *W. H. Auden* (1949); M. K. Spears, *The Poetry of W. H. Auden: The Disenchanted Island* (1963); J. Fuller, *A Reader's Guide to W. H. Auden* (1970).

G. S. Fraser, *Ezra Pound* (1960); D. Davie, *Ezra Pound: Poet as Sculptor* (1965).

C. M. Bowra, *Edith Sitwell* (1948); J. Lehmann, *Edith Sitwell* (1952).

(ix) **O'Casey:** D. Krause, *Sean O'Casey: The Man and his Work* (1960); R. G. Hogan, *The Experiments of Sean O'Casey* (1960).

CHAPTER XIV: THE MID-TWENTIETH CENTURY, 1939–

(i) **General and Social Background:** F. Kermode, *Romantic Image* (1957); D. Daiches, *The Present Age: from 1920* (1958); A. Alvarez, *The Shaping Spirit* (1958); G. S. Fraser, *The Modern Writer and his World* (rev. 1964); K. Allsop, *The Angry Decade* (rev. 1964); A. C. Ward, *Twentieth Century English Literature 1901–1960* (1964); L. A. Fiedler, *Waiting for the End: The American Literary Scene from Hemingway to Baldwin* (1965); M. Geismar, *American Moderns: From Rebellion to Conformity* (1968); W. W. Robson, *Modern English Literature* (1970).

(ii) **The Novel:** P. H. Newby, *The Novel 1940–50* (1951); F. R. Karl, *A Reader's Guide to the Contemporary English Novel* (1963); A. Burgess, *The Novel Now* (1967).

A. H. Wright, *Joyce Cary: A Preface to his Novels* (1958); G. L. Larsen, *The Dark Descent: The Novels of Joyce Cary* (1965).

C. Burkhart, *I. Compton-Burnett* (1965).

M. Kinkead-Weekes and I. Gregor, *William Golding* (1967).

K. Allott and M. Farris, *The Art of Graham Greene* (1951); J. A. Atkins, *Graham Greene* (rev. 1966).

A. S. Byatt, *Degrees of Freedom: The Novels of Iris Murdoch* (1965).

C. Hollis, *A Study of George Orwell* (1956); R. Rees, *George Orwell: Fugitive from the Camp of Victory* (1961); J. Calder, *Chroniclers of Conscience: A Study of George Orwell and Arthur Koestler* (1968); W. Steinhoff, *The Road to 1984* (1975).

R. Greacen, *The World of C. P. Snow* (1962); J. Thale, *C. P. Snow* (1964).

D. Stanford, *Muriel Spark* (1963).

F. J. Stopp, *Evelyn Waugh: Portrait of an Artist* (1958); M. Bradbury, *Evelyn Waugh* (1964); ed. D. Pryce-Jones, *Evelyn Waugh and his World* (1973); C. Sykes, *Evelyn Waugh* (1975).

(iii) **Poetry:** A. Thwaite, *Contemporary English Poetry* (1959); R. N. Currey, *Poets of the 1939–1945 War* (1960); ed. M. Schmidt and G. Lindop, *British Poetry since 1960* (1972).

M. Kirkham, *The Poetry of Robert Graves* (1969).

ed. D. Glen, *Hugh MacDiarmid* (1972).

D. Holbrook, *Llareggub Revisited* (1962); C. FitzGibbon, *The Life of Dylan Thomas* (1965); W. T. Moynihan, *The Craft and Art of Dylan Thomas* (1966).

(iv) **Drama:** L. Kitchin, *Mid-Century Drama* (rev. 1962); J. R. Taylor, *Anger and After* (rev. 1969); J. R. Taylor, *The Second Wave: British Drama in the Seventies* (1971); F. Lumley, *New Trends in Twentieth Century Drama* (rev. 1972); J. W. Lambert, *Drama in Britain 1964–1973* (1974); A. Kennedy, *Six Dramatists in Search of a Language* (1975).

J. Fletcher, *Samuel Beckett's Art* (1967); F. Doherty, *Samuel Beckett* (1971); H. Kenner, *A Reader's Guide to Samuel Beckett* (1973).

A. Carter, *John Osborne* (1969); S. Trussler, *The Plays of John Osborne: An Assessment* (1969).

R. Hayman, *John Arden* (1968).

R. Hayman, *Arnold Wesker* (1970).

M. Esslin, *Pinter: A Study of his Plays* (rev. 1973).

INDEX

The pages on which authors are dealt with most fully are shown in black type.